AFRICA *100-101*

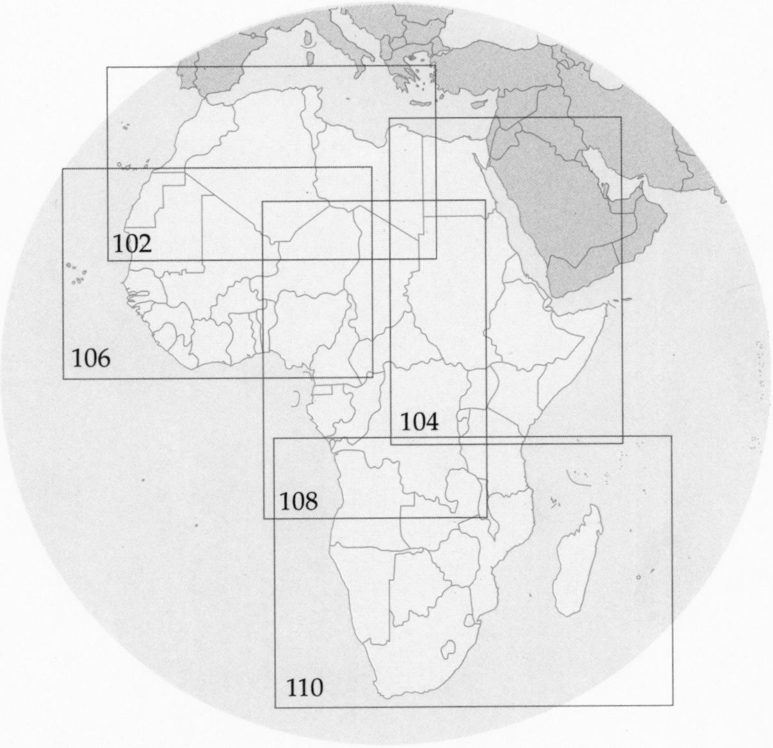
102
106
104
108
110

EUROPE *112-113*

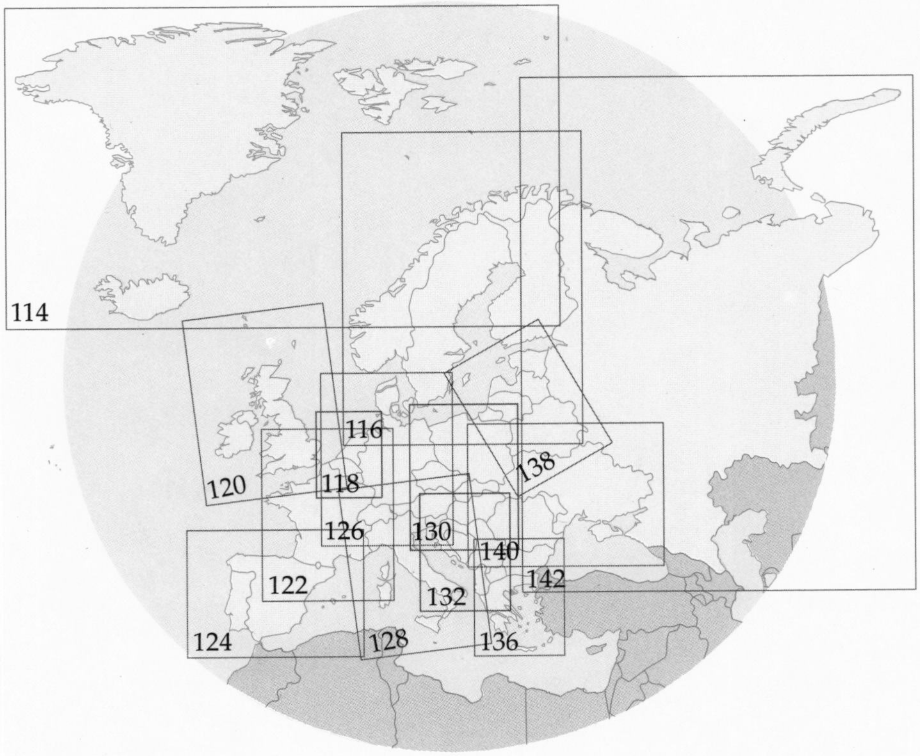
114
116
120
118
138
126
130
140
142
122
132
124
128
136

ATLAS OF THE WORLD

ATLAS OF THE WORLD

FAMILY LEARNING

THE COMPREHENSIVE ATLAS FOR THE WHOLE FAMILY

A Dorling Kindersley Book

Family Learning

Editorial Direction
Andrew Heritage

Cartographers
Pamela Alford, James Anderson, Sarah Baker-Ede, Dale Buckton, Roger Bullen, Jan Clark, Martin Darlison, Sally Gable, Jeremy Hepworth, Julia Lunn, Simon Mumford, John Plumer, David Roberts, Jane Voss

Digital Cartography Created in DK Cartopia by
Phil Rowles, Rob Stokes

Project Designers
Karen Gregory, Paul Williams

Design Assistance
Anthony Cutting, Nicola Liddiard

Project Editor
Debra Clapson

Editor (US)
Constance M. Robinson

Index-Gazetteer
Natalie Clarkson, Ruth Duxbury, Simon Lewis, Julia Lynch

DTP System Manager
Tokiko Morishima

Managing Editor
Lisa Thomas

Managing Art Editor
Philip Lord

Production
David Proffit

Picture Research
Andrea Sadler

First American Edition, 1998
Published in the United States by DK Publishing Inc.
95 Madison Avenue, New York, New York, 10016

Visit us on the World Wide Web at http://www.dk.com

A CIP catalog record for this book is available from the Library of Congress.

ISBN 0-7894-3617-5

Film output by The Printed Word, London, UK
Printed and bound by Oriental Press, Dubai

Picture Credits

Every effort has been made to trace the copyright holders and we apologize in advance for any unintentional omissions. We would be pleased to insert the appropriate acknowledgment in any subsequent edition of this publication.

t =top, b= bottom, a=above, c= center, l= left, r= right.

Adams Picture Library: 236cr; **G Andrews:** 239cl; **Aspect Picture Library:** K Naylor 206cr; F Nichols 236cl; B Seed 213cr; D Donne **Bryant Stock Picture Agency:** 202cl; **J Allan Cash:** 195cr, 210cl, 211cl, 228cr, 234cr; **Bruce Coleman Ltd:** 17bc, 198cr; M Berge 240cl; G Cubitt 204cr, 212cl; MP Kahl 202cr; G Langesbury 208cl; O Langrand 203cr; Luiz C Marigo 17cl (below); F Prenzel 238cr; **Colorific:** J Howard 238cl; Lehtikuva 18bc (above); Reza / Black Star 19tl; M Rogers 204cl; **Comstock:** 234cl; T Eigeland 207cl; **Compix:** 240cr; J Leach 239cr; B McGrath 214cr; **James Davis Travel Photography:** 197cr, 201cl, 216cr, 218cr, 220cl, 221cr, 228cl, 229cl, 241cr; Chris Fairclough **Colour Library:** 222cl; J Guest 235cr; **Finnish Tourist Board:** 217cl; **Robert Harding Picture Library:** 14c, 15tr, 17tr, 18cr (below), 19tc, 194cr, 198cl, 215cr, 222cr, 223cr, 226cr, 232cl; David Atchison-Jones 241cl; Robert Francis 17cl(above); G Hellier 223cl; **Photri:** 14br, 14cr (above), 14tr; R Rainford 219cr; C Rennie 231cl; J Ross 227cr; G Roli 216cl; A Woolfitt 230cl; **Hutchison Library:** 209cl, 213cl; Robert Francis 212cr; Christine Pemberton 196cr; Bernard Regent 211cr; **Image Bank:** 13ccl; Melchior Di Giacomo 19bl; G Jung 227cl; T Madison 237cr; ME Newman 221cl; **Images Colour Library:** 233cl; **Impact:** GJ Norman 230cr; C Penn 205cl; **Frank Lane Picture Agency:** D Hoadley 16tr; **Lorna Stanton:** 57tr; **N.A.S.A.:** 11tl; **Oxford Scientific Films:** Lon E Lauber 15br; **Panos Pictures:** N Cooper 195cl; R Giling 200cr; J Hartley 209cr; D Hulcher 235cl; S Sprague 201cr, 206cl; **Pictor International:** 16tr (below), 17tl, 17cr, 18c; **Planet Earth Pictures:** John Eastcott/Yva Momatiuk 17tc; **REX Features:** 232cr; **Science Photo Library:** Martin Bond 13ccr; Ray Ellis 17br; David Parker 13cr; **South American Pictures:** J Berrange 196cl; **Frank Spooner Pictures:** Iliona-Figaro Magazine 197cl; N Jallot 225cr; **Tony Stone Images:** 14cr (below), 16tc (below), 215cl; Doug Armand 194cl; Oliver Benn 199cl; Joe Cornish 219cl; Shaun Egan 220cr; Rosemary Evans 225cl; H Richard Johnston 15cr (above); Hideo Kirshara 218cl; Peter/Steph Lamberti 15cr (below); Angus M Makillop 19bc; Steven Rothfeld 18br, 207cr; Alan Smith 217cr; Dennis Stone 205cr; **J Tempest:** 229cr; **Topham Picturepoint:** 210cr; **Trip:** T Goodman 208cr; V Shuba 226cl; V Sidoropolev 231cr; **Tony Waltham:** 13cl; P Woods: 233cr; **World Pictures:** 202cl, 237cl; **ZEFA Picture Library:** 199cr, 224cr; Everts 224cl; F Lanting 214cl; Sunak 200cl, **Bruce Coleman Ltd**: B&C Colhoun 15cla; C Ott 2tr; **Robert Harding Picture Library**: 52tr; 57tr; T Gervis 57cr; 62bl; G Renner 58cla; **Image Bank**: S Proehl 54bl; **Images Colour Library**: 63cra; **Pictor International Ltd**: 53cr; 54ca; 56bl; 61tr; **Pictures Colour Library**: 54cra; 63crb; **Science Photo Library**: K Kent 51cr; P Menzell 63br; **Stockmarket**: 61cl; 61br; Brandenburg 59cb; Rosenbach 57br; **Tony Stone Images**: 53crb; 55cla; 57tc; 62tr; G Allison 59tc; 60cra; P Chesley 51c; A Sacks 51crb; L Ulrich 60bc; **Trip**: J Dennis 51br; **World Pictures**: 55cr.

Jacket
BACK COVER: **Bruce Coleman:** crb; **Colorific:** br; **James Davis Travel Photography:** tr and cra; **Getty Images:** clb; **Robert Harding Picture Library:** tl and cla; **Peter Woods:** bl.
FRONT COVER: **James Davis Travel Photography:** tl; **Robert Harding Picture Library:** cla/T Gervis clb; **Oxford Scientfic Films:** bl; **Pictor International:** tr; **Image Bank:** cra; **Trip:** crb; **Getty Images:** br; INSIDE FRONT COVER: **Science Photo Library**

KEY TO MAP SYMBOLS

BOUNDARIES

	Full international border
	Disputed *de facto* border
	Territorial claim border
x x x x	Cease-fire line
	Undefined boundary
	Internal administrative boundary

COMMUNICATION FEATURES

	Major road
	Minor road
	Railroad
✈	International airport

DRAINAGE FEATURES

	Major perennial river
	Minor perennial river
	Seasonal river
	Canal
	Waterfall
	Perennial lake
	Seasonal lake
	Wetland

ICE FEATURES

	Permanent ice cap/ice shelf
▲ ▲ ▲ ▲	Summer limit of pack ice
▲ ▲ ▲	Winter limit of pack ice

LANDSCAPE FEATURES

	Sandy desert
△	Mountain
▽	Depression depth
◭	Volcano
)(	Pass/tunnel
+	Site of interest

ADMINISTRATIVE CENTRES

●	Capital
●	Internal administrative capital

NAMES

TAIWAN	Country
JERSEY (to UK)	Dependent territory
PARIS	Capital
KANSAS	Administrative region
Dordogne	Cultural region
Sahara	Landscape feature
Mont Blanc 15,770ft	Mountain/pass
Blue Nile	Drainage feature
Sulu Sea	Ocean feature
Chile Rise	Underwater feature

INSET MAP SYMBOLS

	Urban area
	City
	Park
▪	Place of interest
▫	Suburb/district

Contents

HOW THE WORLD WORKS

pages 8–19

The Earth in Space *10–11*
The Earth's Structure *12–13*
Shaping the Landscape *14–15*
Climate and Vegetation *16–17*
People and Planet *18–19*

THE WORLD TODAY

pages 20–48

The Political World *22–23*
The Physical World *24–25*
Time Zones *26–27*
Geology & Structure *28–29*
World Climate *30–31*
Ocean Currents *32–33*
Life Zones *34–35*
Population *36–37*
Languages *38–39*
Religion *40–41*
The Global Economy *42–43*
Global Conflict *44–45*
Governments of the World *46–47*
World Tourism *48*

THE UNITED STATES OF AMERICA

pages 49–64

Physical US *50–51*
Political US *52–53*
Industry and Resources *54–55*
Agriculture and Land Use *56–57*
Population *58–59*
Environmental Issues *60–61*
National Parks *62–63*
State flags *64*

THE WORLD ATLAS

pages 8–19

North & Central America *66–67*

Western Canada & Alaska *68–69*
Eastern Canada *70–71*
Northeast US *72–73*
Southeast US *74–75*
Bermuda
Central US *76–77*
West US *78–79*
Los Angeles & Hawaii
Southwest US *80–81*
Mexico *82–83*
Central America *84–85*
The Caribbean *86–87*
Jamaica, Barbados, & St Lucia

South America *88–89*

Northern South America *90–91*
Western South America *92–93*
Galapagos Islands
Brazil *94–95*
Southern South America *96–97*
The Atlantic Ocean *98–99*

Africa *100–101*

Northwest Africa *102–103*
Northeast Africa *104–105*
West Africa *106–107*
Central Africa *108–109*
Sao Tome & Principe
Southern Africa *110–111*

HOW THE WORLD WORKS

THE WORLD WE INHABIT IS ANCIENT, yet dynamic, and is constantly being shaped and molded by natural forces. This section looks at the nature of these forces, and shows how humans have populated and organized its surface.

THE EARTH IN SPACE

THE EARTH IS ONE OF NINE PLANETS that orbit a large star – the Sun. Together they form the solar system. All life on Earth – plant, animal, and human – depends on the Sun. Its energy warms our planet's surface, powers the wind and waves, drives the ocean currents and weather systems, and recycles water. Sunlight also gives plants the power to photosynthesize – to make the foods and oxygen on which organisms rely. The fact that the Earth is habitable at all is due to its precise position in the solar system, its daily spin, and an annual journey around the Sun at a constant tilt. Without these, and the breathable atmosphere that cloaks and protects the Earth, it would be as barren as our near-neighbors Venus and Mars.

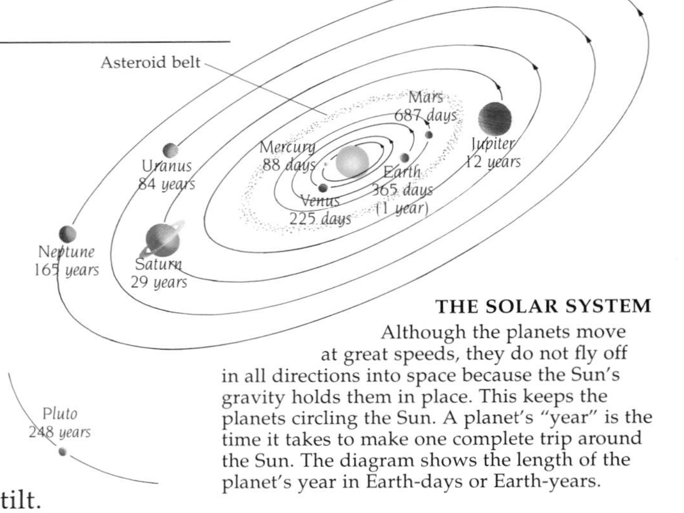

Asteroid belt
Mars 687 days
Jupiter 12 years
Mercury 88 days
Earth 365 days (1 year)
Venus 225 days
Uranus 84 years
Saturn 29 years
Neptune 165 years
Pluto 248 years

THE SOLAR SYSTEM
Although the planets move at great speeds, they do not fly off in all directions into space because the Sun's gravity holds them in place. This keeps the planets circling the Sun. A planet's "year" is the time it takes to make one complete trip around the Sun. The diagram shows the length of the planet's year in Earth-days or Earth-years.

THE SUN IS 865,000 MILES (1,392,000 KM) ACROSS. IT HAS A CORE TEMPERATURE OF 25 MILLION°F (14 MILLION°C)
Huge solar flares, up to 125,000 miles (200,000 km) long, lick out into space

The Relative Sizes of the Sun and Planets

WITH THEIR AVERAGE TEMPERATURE

The Life Zone
Mercury Day 806°F Night -292°F
Venus 870°F
Earth 60°F
Mars -9.5°F
Jupiter -238°F
Saturn -292°F
Uranus -346°F
Neptune -364°F
Pluto -382°F

The Earth seems to be the only habitable planet in our solar system. Mercury and Venus, which are closer to the Sun, are hotter than an oven. Mars, and planets still farther out, are colder than a deep freeze.

Many Very Eager Mountaineers Jog Swiftly Up New Peaks

You can use this sentence to remember the sequence of planets.

The Planets and their Distances from the Sun

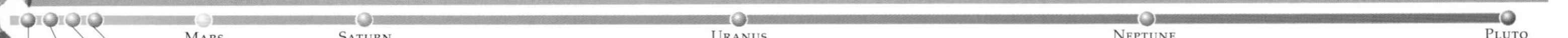

Mercury 36,000,000 miles (57,910,000 km)
Venus 67,200,000 miles (108,200,000 km)
Earth 92,900,000 miles (149,500,000 km)
Mars 141,600,000 miles (227,940,000 km)
Jupiter 483,000,000 miles (778,330,000 km)
Saturn 886,700,000 miles (1,426,980,000 km)
Uranus 1,783,000,000 miles (2,870,990,000 km)
Neptune 2,800,000,000 miles (4,497,070,000 km)
Pluto 3,670,000,000 miles (5,913,520,000 km)

The Four Seasons

The Earth always tilts in the same direction on its 590 million-mile (950 million-km) journey around the Sun. This means that each hemisphere in turn leans toward the Sun, then leans away from it. This is what causes summer and winter.

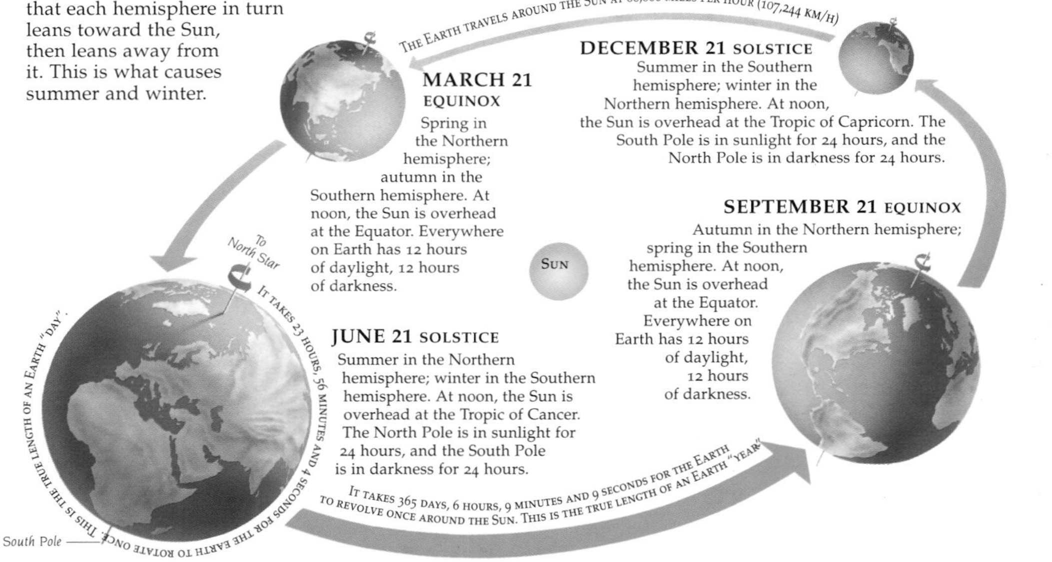

The Earth travels around the Sun at 66,000 miles per hour (107,244 km/h)
To North Star
Sun
It takes 23 hours, 56 minutes and 4 seconds for the Earth to rotate once. This is the true length of an Earth "day".
South Pole
It takes 365 days, 6 hours, 9 minutes and 9 seconds for the Earth to revolve once around the Sun. This is the true length of an Earth "year".

MARCH 21 EQUINOX
Spring in the Northern hemisphere; autumn in the Southern hemisphere. At noon, the Sun is overhead at the Equator. Everywhere on Earth has 12 hours of daylight, 12 hours of darkness.

DECEMBER 21 SOLSTICE
Summer in the Southern hemisphere; winter in the Northern hemisphere. At noon, the Sun is overhead at the Tropic of Capricorn. The South Pole is in sunlight for 24 hours, and the North Pole is in darkness for 24 hours.

SEPTEMBER 21 EQUINOX
Autumn in the Northern hemisphere; spring in the Southern hemisphere. At noon, the Sun is overhead at the Equator. Everywhere on Earth has 12 hours of daylight, 12 hours of darkness.

JUNE 21 SOLSTICE
Summer in the Northern hemisphere; winter in the Southern hemisphere. At noon, the Sun is overhead at the Tropic of Cancer. The North Pole is in sunlight for 24 hours, and the South Pole is in darkness for 24 hours.

24 Hours in the Life of Planet Earth

The Earth turns a complete circle (360°) in 24 hours, or 15° in one hour. Countries on a similar line of longitude (or "meridian") usually share the same time. They set their clocks in relation to Greenwich Mean Time (GMT). This is the time at Greenwich (London, England), on longitude 0°. Countries east of Greenwich are ahead of GMT. Countries to the west are behind GMT.

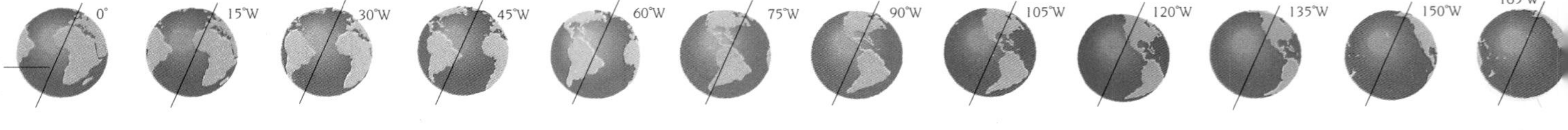

Noon at GMT
Greenwich 1200 hrs 0°
Dakar 1100 hrs 15°W
E. Greenland 1000 hrs 30°W
Rio de Janeiro 0900 hrs 45°W
Caracas 0800 hrs 60°W
New York 0700 hrs 75°W
Mexico City 0600 hrs 90°W
Calgary 0500 hrs 105°W
Los Angeles 0400 hrs 120°W
E. Alaska 0300 hrs 135°W
Honolulu 0200 hrs 150°W
Pacific Ocean 0100 hrs 165°W
Noon everywhere on this meridian

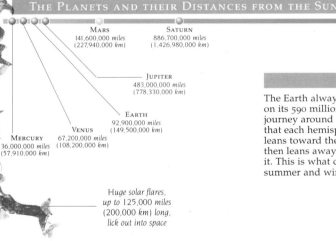

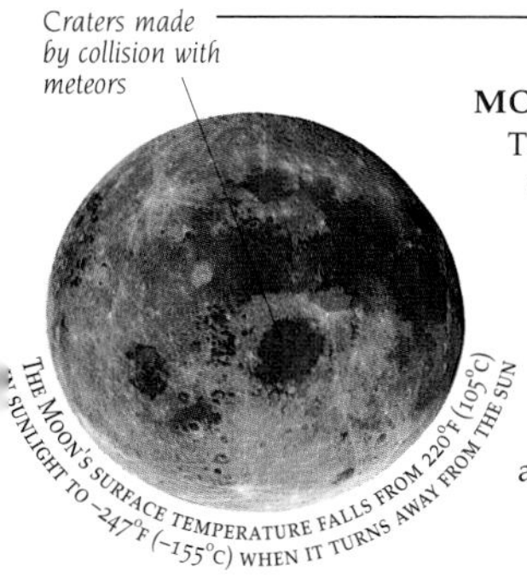
Craters made by collision with meteors
The Moon's surface temperature falls from 220°F (105°C) in sunlight to −247°F (−155°C) when it turns away from the Sun

MOON AND EARTH

The Moon is a ball of barren rock 2,156 miles (3,476 km) across. It orbits the Earth every 27.3 days at an average distance of 238,700 miles (384,400 km). The Moon's gravity is only one-sixth that of Earth – too small to keep an atmosphere around itself, but strong enough to exert a powerful pull on the Earth. The Moon and Sun together create tides in the Earth's oceans. The period between successive high tides is 12 hours 25 minutes. The highest (or "spring") tides occur twice a month, when the Moon, Sun, and Earth are in line.

MAGNET EARTH

The Earth acts like a gigantic bar magnet. As the Earth spins in space, swirling currents are set up within its molten core. These movements generate a powerful magnetic field.

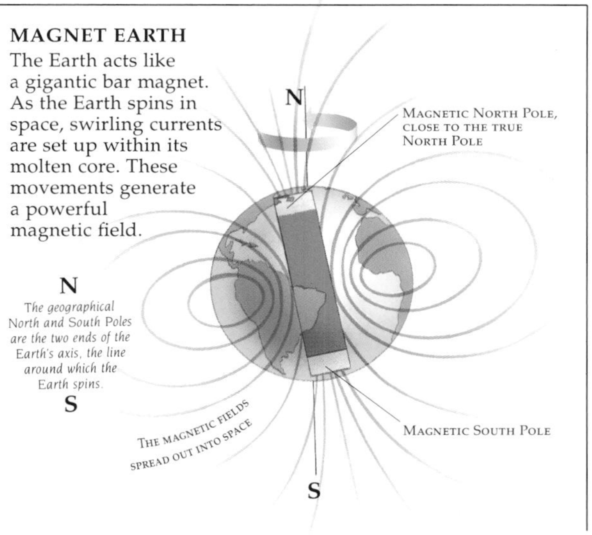
N
Magnetic North Pole, close to the true North Pole
N
The geographical North and South Poles are the two ends of the Earth's axis, the line around which the Earth spins.
S
The magnetic fields spread out into space
Magnetic South Pole
S

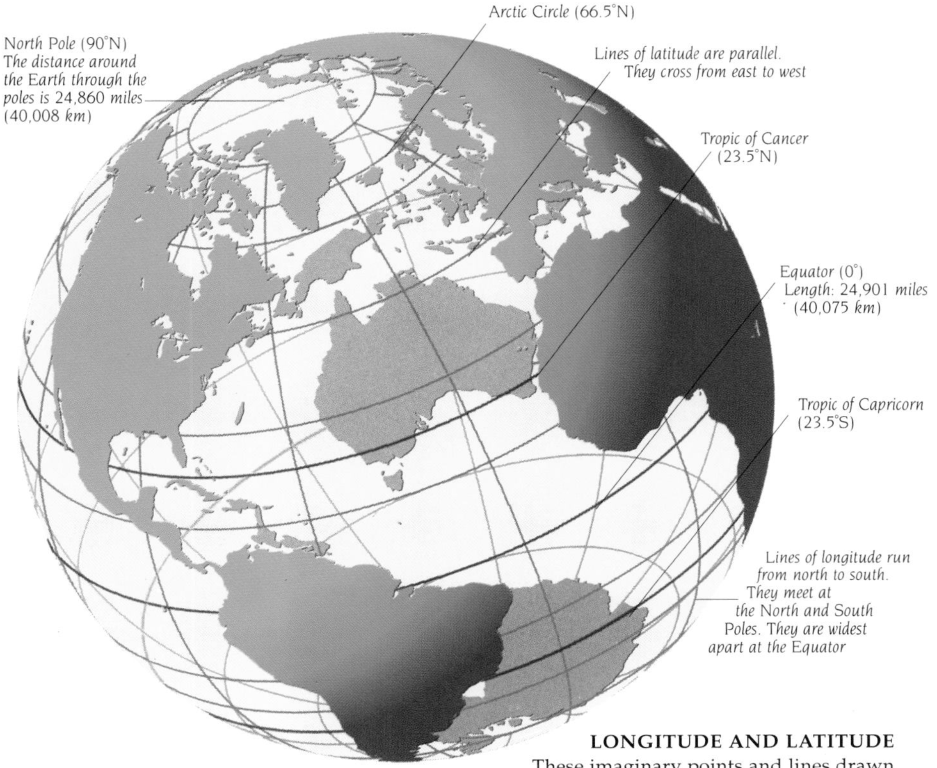
Arctic Circle (66.5°N)
North Pole (90°N)
The distance around the Earth through the poles is 24,860 miles (40,008 km)
Lines of latitude are parallel. They cross from east to west
Tropic of Cancer (23.5°N)
Equator (0°)
Length: 24,901 miles (40,075 km)
Tropic of Capricorn (23.5°S)
Lines of longitude run from north to south. They meet at the North and South Poles. They are widest apart at the Equator

LONGITUDE AND LATITUDE

These imaginary points and lines drawn on the Earth's surface help locate places on a map or globe. The Earth spins around an axis drawn between the North and South Poles through the center of the planet. Lines of longitude are vertical lines running through the Poles. Lines of latitude are horizontal lines drawn parallel to the Equator, the line around the middle of the Earth.

Diameter of Earth at equator
7,927 miles (12,756 km)

Diameter from pole to pole
7,900 miles (12,714 km)

Mass
5,988 million, million million tonnes (tons)

THE ATMOSPHERE

An envelope of gases such as nitrogen and oxygen surrounds our planet. It provides us with breathable air, filters the Sun's rays, and retains heat at night.

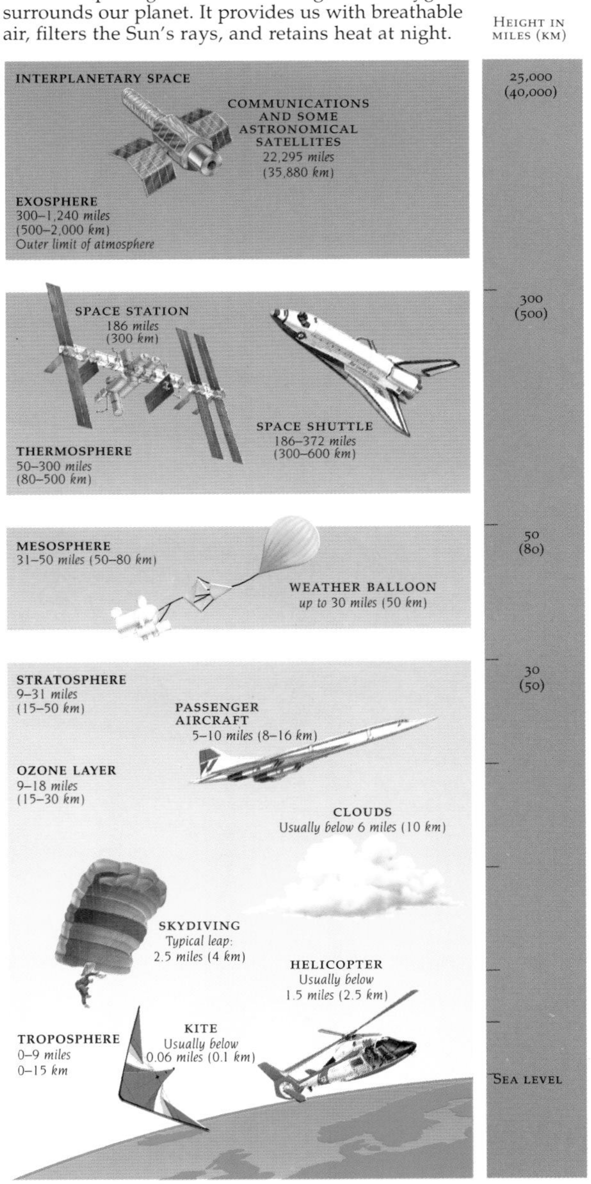
Height in miles (km)
Interplanetary space
Communications and some astronomical satellites
22,295 miles (35,880 km)
Exosphere
300–1,240 miles (500–2,000 km)
Outer limit of atmosphere
25,000 (40,000)
Space station
186 miles (300 km)
Space shuttle
186–372 miles (300–600 km)
Thermosphere
50–300 miles (80–500 km)
300 (500)
Mesosphere
31–50 miles (50–80 km)
Weather balloon
up to 30 miles (50 km)
50 (80)
Stratosphere
9–31 miles (15–50 km)
Passenger aircraft
5–10 miles (8–16 km)
30 (50)
Ozone layer
9–18 miles (15–30 km)
Clouds
Usually below 6 miles (10 km)
Skydiving
Typical leap: 2.5 miles (4 km)
Helicopter
Usually below 1.5 miles (2.5 km)
Troposphere
0–9 miles
0–15 km
Kite
Usually below 0.06 miles (0.1 km)
Sea level

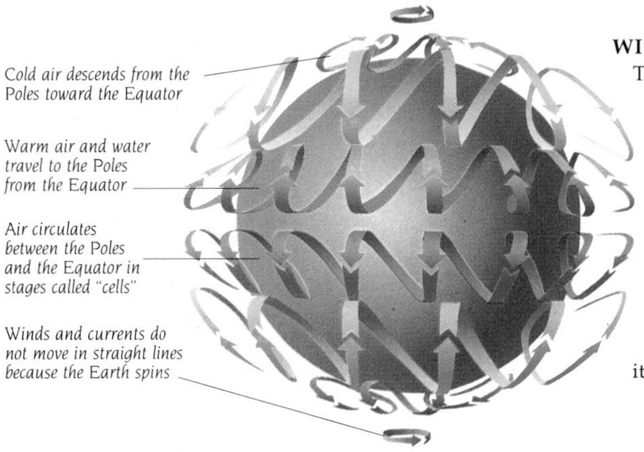
Cold air descends from the Poles toward the Equator
Warm air and water travel to the Poles from the Equator
Air circulates between the Poles and the Equator in stages called "cells"
Winds and currents do not move in straight lines because the Earth spins

WINDS AND CURRENTS

The world's winds and ocean currents are caused by the way the Sun heats the Earth's surface. More heat energy arrives at the Equator than at the Poles because the Earth is curved and tilted. Warm air and warm water carry much of this energy toward the Poles, heating up the higher latitudes. Meanwhile cool air and water move back toward the Equator, lowering its temperature.

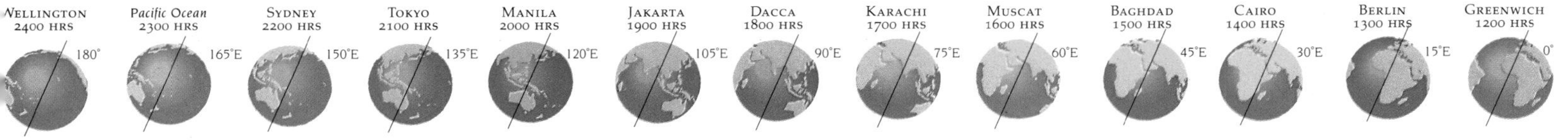
Wellington 2400 hrs
180°
Pacific Ocean 2300 hrs
165°E
Sydney 2200 hrs
150°E
Tokyo 2100 hrs
135°E
Manila 2000 hrs
120°E
Jakarta 1900 hrs
105°E
Dacca 1800 hrs
90°E
Karachi 1700 hrs
75°E
Muscat 1600 hrs
60°E
Baghdad 1500 hrs
45°E
Cairo 1400 hrs
30°E
Berlin 1300 hrs
15°E
Greenwich 1200 hrs
0°

THE EARTH'S STRUCTURE

THE EARTH IS IN SOME WAYS like an egg, with a thin shell around a soft interior. Its hard, rocky outer layer – the crust – is up to 45 miles (70 km) thick under the continents, but less than 5 miles (8 km) thick under the oceans. This crust is broken into gigantic slabs, called "plates," in which the continents are embedded. Below the hard crust is the mantle, a layer of rocks so hot that some melt and flow in huge swirling currents. The Earth's plates do not stay in the same place. Instead, they move, carried along like rafts on the currents in the mantle. This motion is very slow – usually less than 2 in (5 cm) a year – but enormously powerful. Plate movement makes the Earth quake and volcanoes erupt, causes immense mountain ranges such as the Himalayas to grow where plates collide, and explains how, over millions of years, whole continents have drifted across the face of the planet.

DRIFTING CONTINENTS

CURRENTS OF MOLTEN ROCK DEEP WITHIN THE MANTLE SLOWLY MOVE THE CONTINENTS. OVER TIME, THEY APPEAR TO "DRIFT" ACROSS THE EARTH'S SURFACE.

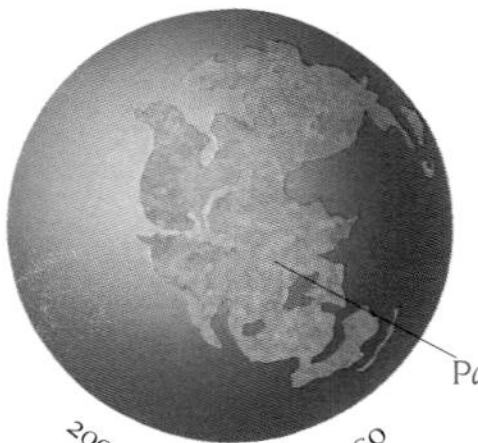
Pangaea
200 MILLION YEARS AGO
All of today's continents were joined in one supercontinent, called Pangaea. It began to break up about 180 million years ago.

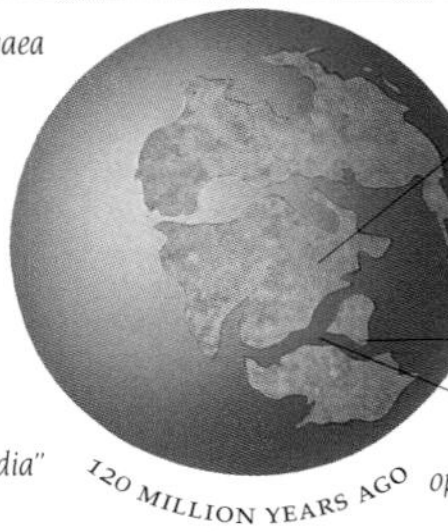
"Africa"
"India"
"Atlantic Ocean" opening up
120 MILLION YEARS AGO
The Atlantic Ocean splits Pangaea into two. India has broken away from Africa.

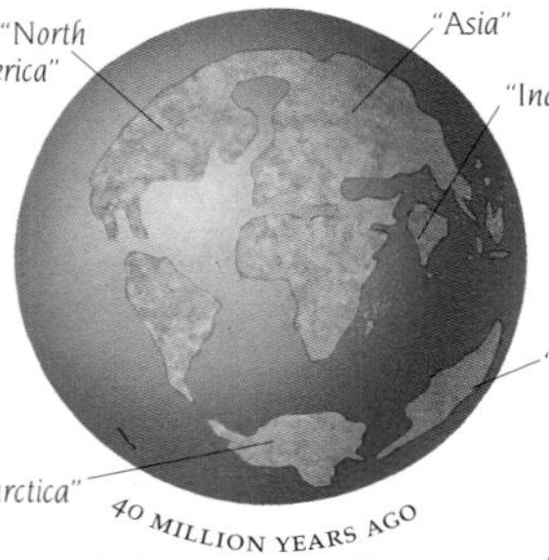
"North America"
"Asia"
"India"
"Australia"
"Antarctica"
40 MILLION YEARS AGO
India is moving closer to Asia. Australia and Antarctica have separated.

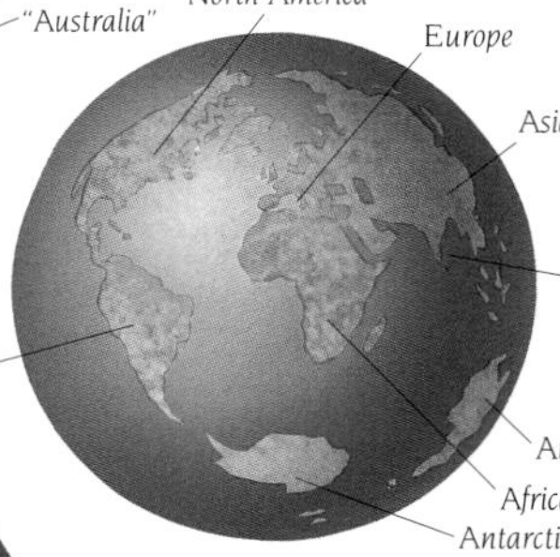
North America
Europe
Asia
South America
Africa
Antarctica
TODAY
India has collided with Asia, pushing up the Himalaya Mountains.

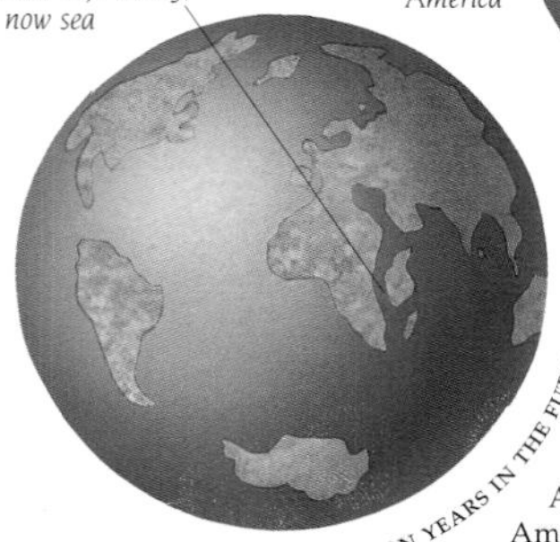
Great Rift Valley, now sea
50 MILLION YEARS IN THE FUTURE ?
If today's plate movements continue, the Atlantic Ocean will be 775 miles (1,250 km) wider. Africa and Europe will fuse, the Americas will separate again, and Africa east of the Great Rift Valley will be an island.

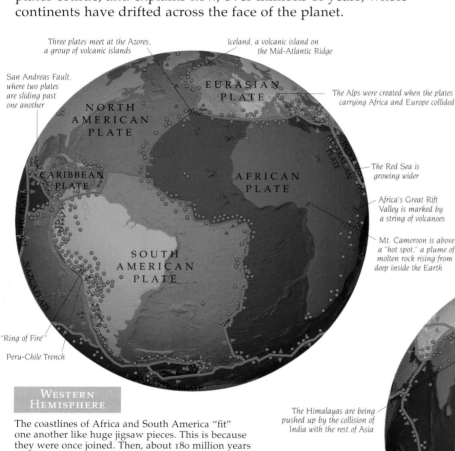

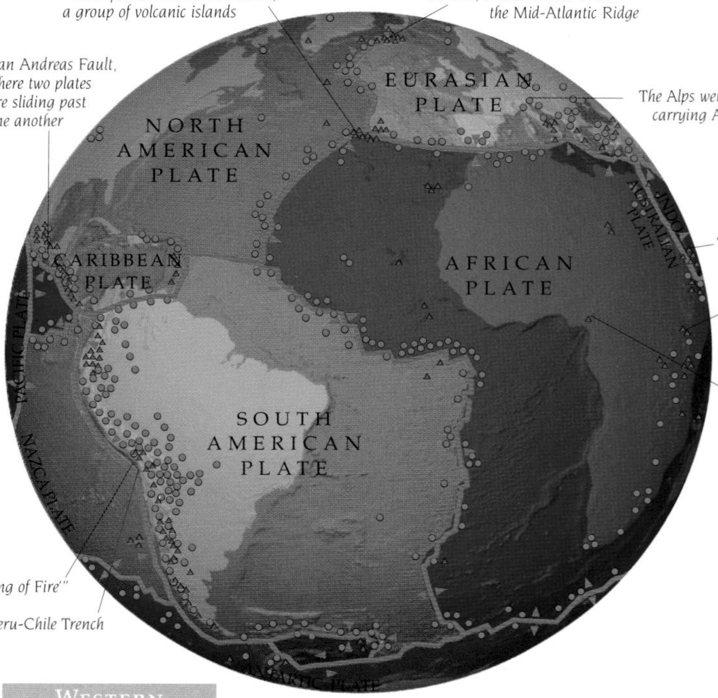
Three plates meet at the Azores, a group of volcanic islands
Iceland, a volcanic island on the Mid-Atlantic Ridge
San Andreas Fault, where two plates are sliding past one another
EURASIAN PLATE
The Alps were created when the plates carrying Africa and Europe collided
NORTH AMERICAN PLATE
INDO-AUSTRALIAN PLATE
The Red Sea is growing wider
CARIBBEAN PLATE
AFRICAN PLATE
PACIFIC PLATE
Africa's Great Rift Valley is marked by a string of volcanoes
Mt. Cameroon is above a "hot spot," a plume of molten rock rising from deep inside the Earth
SOUTH AMERICAN PLATE
NAZCA PLATE
"Ring of Fire"
Peru-Chile Trench
ANTARCTIC PLATE

WESTERN HEMISPHERE

The coastlines of Africa and South America "fit" one another like huge jigsaw pieces. This is because they were once joined. Then, about 180 million years ago, a crack appeared in the Earth's crust. Hot liquid rock (magma) rose through the crack and cooled, forming new oceanic crust on either side. As the ocean grew wider, the continents moved apart. The process continues today.

The "Ring of Fire" passes through Japan.
Mariana Trench, 6.8 miles (11,033 m) deep, where an ocean plate dives into the mantle
EURASIAN PLATE
The Hawaiian islands lie over a "hot spot"
PHILLIPINE PLATE
PACIFIC PLATE
The Himalayas are being pushed up by the collision of India with the rest of Asia
The Java Trench, 4.6 miles (7,450 m) deep, runs parallel to a long chain of active volcanoes in Southeast Asia
INDO-AUSTRALIAN PLATE
Highly volcanic New Zealand lies on the "Ring of Fire"

EASTERN HEMISPHERE

Most earthquakes and volcanoes occur around the edges of crustal plates (or plate margins). Australia, in the middle of the Indian-Australian plate, has no active volcanoes and is rarely troubled by earthquakes. Things are very different in neighboring New Zealand and New Guinea, which lie on the notorious Pacific "Ring of Fire." The Ring forms a line all the way round the Pacific rim, through the Philippines, Japan, and North America, and down the coast of South America to New Zealand.

KEYBOX

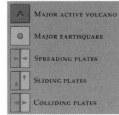

- △ MAJOR ACTIVE VOLCANO
- ● MAJOR EARTHQUAKE
- SPREADING PLATES
- SLIDING PLATES
- COLLIDING PLATES

THE ATLANTIC OCEAN IS GROWING WIDER BY 1 IN (2.5 CM) A YEAR – ABOUT THE SAME SPEED THAT FINGERNAILS GROW. THE NAZCA PLATE IS SLIDING THREE TIMES FASTER UNDER SOUTH AMERICA, PUSHING UP THE ANDES.

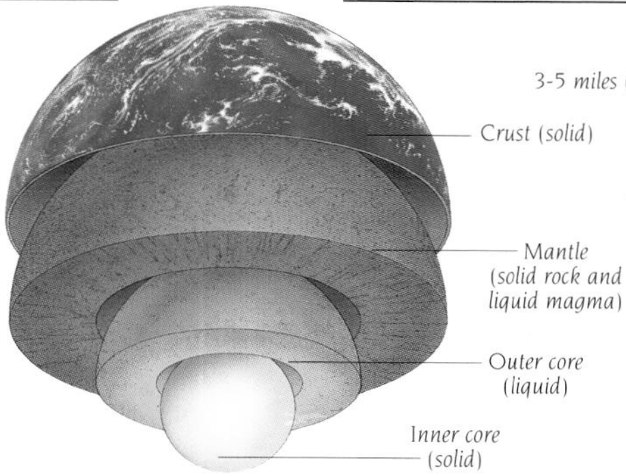
Crust (solid)
Mantle
(solid rock and liquid magma)
Outer core
(liquid)
Inner core
(solid)

THE LAYERED EARTH

The Earth has layers, like an egg. The core is made of metals such as iron and nickel. This is surrounded by a rocky mantle and a thin crust.

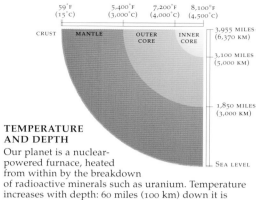

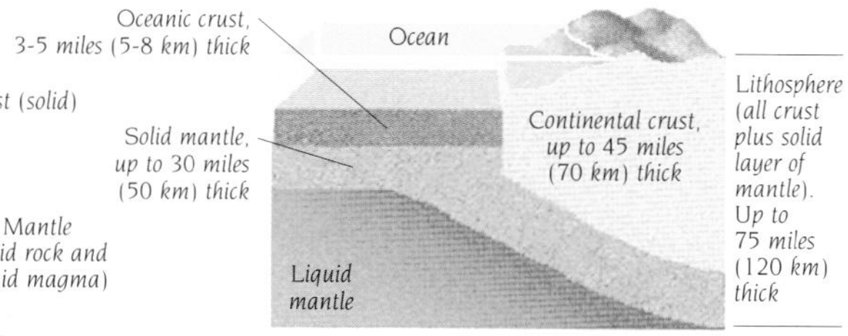
Oceanic crust, 3-5 miles (5-8 km) thick
Ocean
Solid mantle, up to 30 miles (50 km) thick
Continental crust, up to 45 miles (70 km) thick
Lithosphere (all crust plus solid layer of mantle). Up to 75 miles (120 km) thick
Liquid mantle

CRUST

Crust is of two kinds: continental and oceanic. Continental crust is older, thicker, and less dense. Beneath the crust is a solid layer of mantle. Together, these form the lithosphere, which is broken into several plates. These float on the liquid mantle layer.

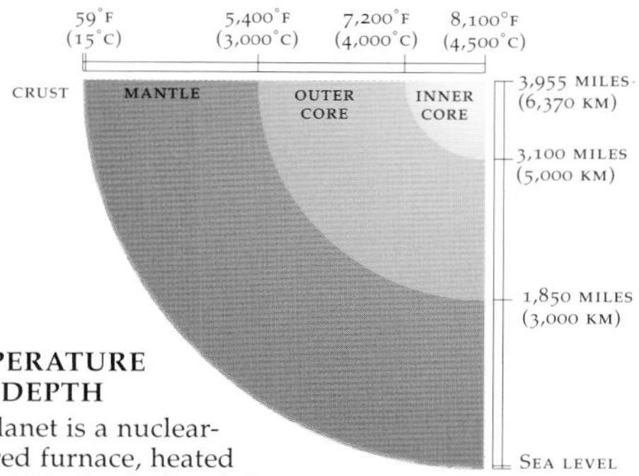
59°F (15°C)
5,400°F (3,000°C)
7,200°F (4,000°C)
8,100°F (4,500°C)
CRUST
MANTLE
OUTER CORE
INNER CORE
3,955 MILES (6,370 KM)
3,100 MILES (5,000 KM)
1,850 MILES (3,000 KM)
SEA LEVEL

TEMPERATURE AND DEPTH

Our planet is a nuclear-powered furnace, heated from within by the breakdown of radioactive minerals such as uranium. Temperature increases with depth: 60 miles (100 km) down it is 2,460°F (1,350°C), hot enough for rocks to melt.

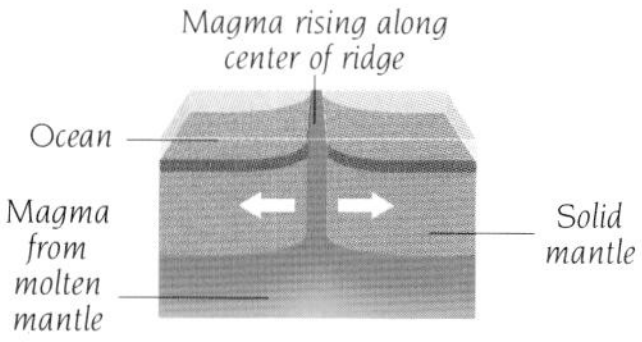
Magma rising along center of ridge
Ocean
Magma from molten mantle
Solid mantle

SPREADING PLATES

When two plates move apart, molten rock (magma) rises from the mantle and cools, forming new crust. This is called a constructive margin. Most are found in oceans.

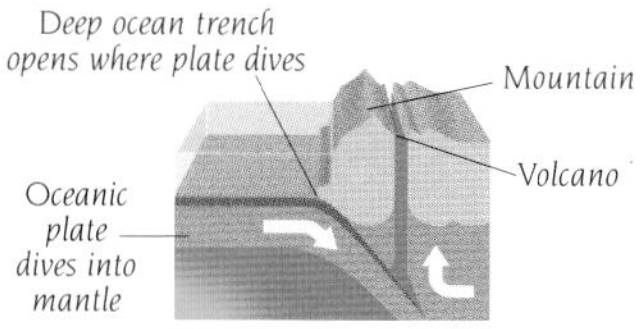
Deep ocean trench opens where plate dives
Mountain
Volcano
Oceanic plate dives into mantle

COLLIDING PLATES THAT DIVE

When two ocean plates or an ocean plate and a continent plate collide, the denser plate is forced under the other, diving down into the mantle. These are destructive margins.

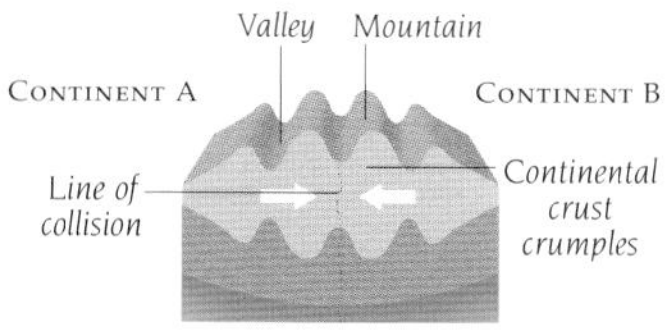
Valley
Mountain
Continent A
Continent B
Line of collision
Continental crust crumples

COLLIDING PLATES THAT BUCKLE

When two continents collide, their plates fuse, crumple, and push upward. Mountain ranges such as the Himalayas and the Urals have been formed in this way.

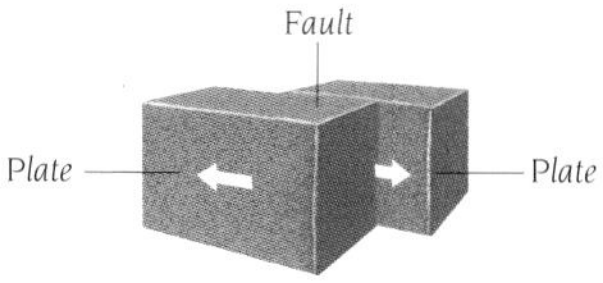
Fault
Plate
Plate

SLIDING PLATES

When two plates slide past one another, intense friction is created along the "fault line" between them, causing earthquakes. These are called conservative margins.

MID-ATLANTIC RIDGE ICELAND
Most constructive margins are found beneath oceans, but here in volcanic Iceland one comes to the surface.

VOLCANO JAVA
Diving plates often build volcanic islands and mountain chains. Deep ocean trenches form offshore.

FOLDING STRATA ENGLAND
The clash of continental plates may cause the Earth to buckle and twist far from the collision zone.

SAN ANDREAS FAULT
A huge earthquake may one day occur somewhere along California's San Andreas Fault, seen here.

EXPLOSIVE VOLCANO

About 50 of the world's 600 or so active volcanoes erupt each year. Explosive pressure is created by the buildup of magma, gases, or superheated steam.

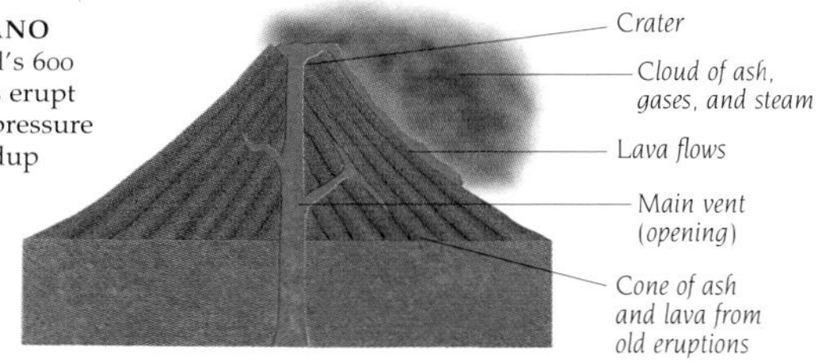
Crater
Cloud of ash, gases, and steam
Lava flows
Main vent (opening)
Cone of ash and lava from old eruptions

HOT SPOT HAWAII

Hawaii is on a "hot spot" in the Earth's crust. This is a plume of hot magma that rises from the mantle and breaks through the thin ocean crust to feed a volcano. As the crust moves, the volcano is carried away, but the hot spot stays, forming a new volcano.

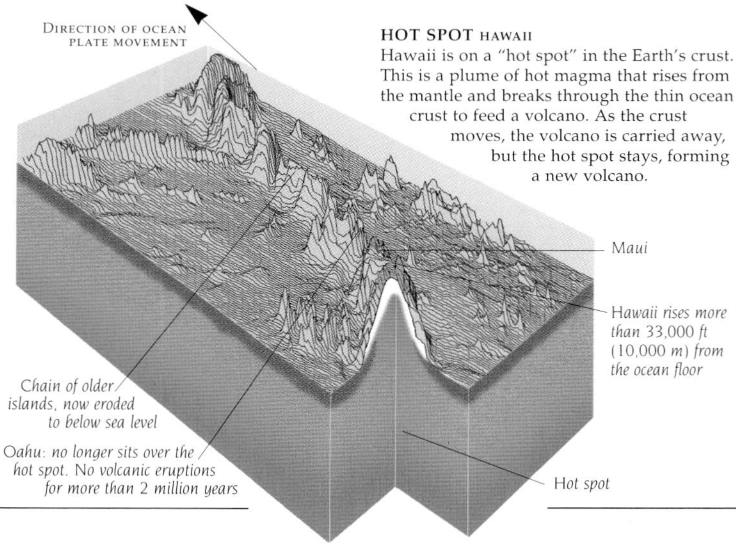
Direction of ocean plate movement
Maui
Hawaii rises more than 33,000 ft (10,000 m) from the ocean floor
Chain of older islands, now eroded to below sea level
Oahu: no longer sits over the hot spot. No volcanic eruptions for more than 2 million years
Hot spot

SOME MAJOR QUAKES AND ERUPTIONS

This map shows some of the worst natural disasters in recorded history. Over one million earthquakes and about 50 volcanic eruptions are detected every year. Most are minor or occur where there are few people, so there is no loss of human life or great damage to property. But crowded cities and poorly-constructed buildings are putting ever-greater numbers at risk.

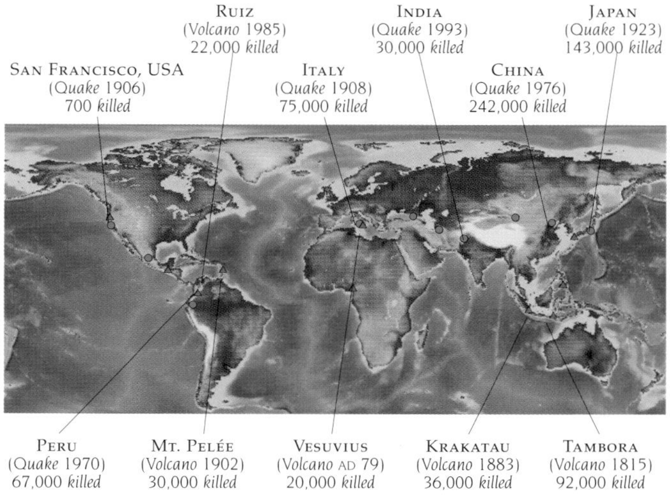
Ruiz (Volcano 1985) 22,000 killed
India (Quake 1993) 30,000 killed
Japan (Quake 1923) 143,000 killed
San Francisco, USA (Quake 1906) 700 killed
Italy (Quake 1908) 75,000 killed
China (Quake 1976) 242,000 killed
Peru (Quake 1970) 67,000 killed
Mt. Pelée (Volcano 1902) 30,000 killed
Vesuvius (Volcano AD 79) 20,000 killed
Krakatau (Volcano 1883) 36,000 killed
Tambora (Volcano 1815) 92,000 killed

Shaping the Landscape

LANDSCAPES ARE CREATED and changed – even destroyed – in a continuous cycle. Over millions of years, constant movements of the Earth's plates have built its continents, islands, and mountains. But as soon as new land is formed, it is shaped (or "eroded") by the forces of wind, water, ice, and heat. Sometimes change is quick, as when a river floods and cuts a new channel, or a landslide cascades down a mountain slope. But usually change is so slow that it is invisible to the human eye. Extremes of heat and cold crack open rocks and expose them to attack by wind and water. Rivers and glaciers scour out valleys, the wind piles up sand dunes, and the sea attacks shorelines and cliffs. Eroded materials are blown away or carried along by rivers, piling up as sediments on valley floors or the seabed. Over millions of years these may be compressed into rock and pushed up to form new land. As soon as the land is exposed to the elements, the cycle of erosion begins again.

Key to All Maps

Area covered in ice today	Area drained by major river
Ice and snow 18,000 years ago	Protected coastline
Desert	Coast affected by tidal swell
Wind direction (simplified)	Coast affected by storm waves

THE "ROOF OF NORTH AMERICA"
Steeply-sloping Denali (also called Mt. McKinley), Alaska, is North America's highest mountain at 20,320 ft (6,194 m). It is a fairly "young" mountain, less than 70 million years old. The gently sloping Appalachians in the east of the continent are very much older. Once, they were probably higher than Denali is today. But more than 300 million years of ice, rain, and wind have worn them down.

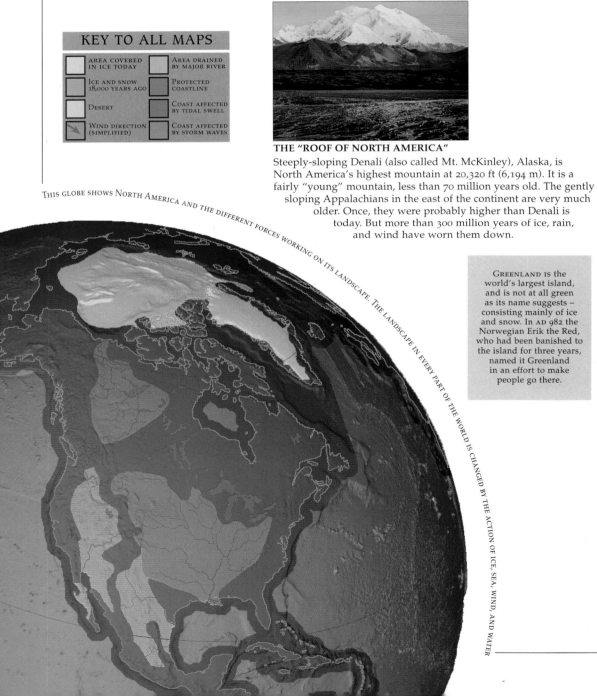

This globe shows North America and the different forces working on its landscape. The landscape in every part of the world is changed by the action of ice, sea, wind, and water

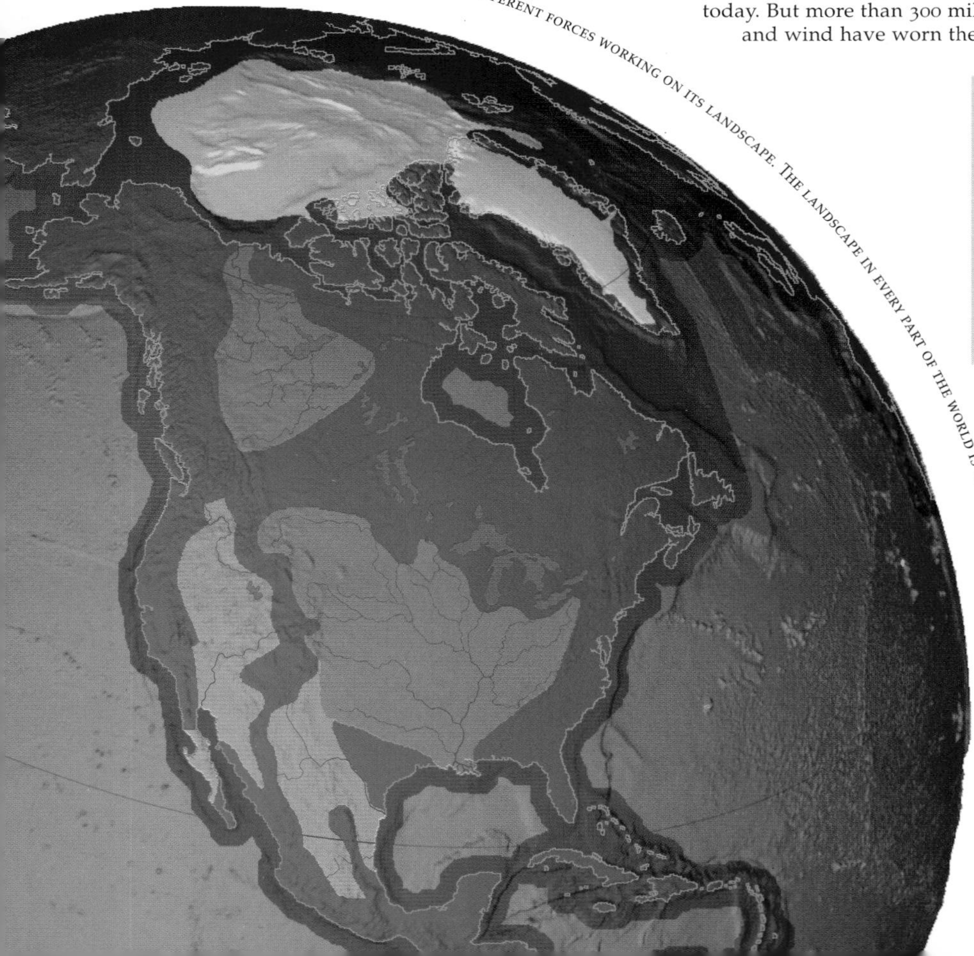

Greenland is the world's largest island, and is not at all green as its name suggests – consisting mainly of ice and snow. In AD 982 the Norwegian Erik the Red, who had been banished to the island for three years, named it Greenland in an effort to make people go there.

Ice Action

ALASKA

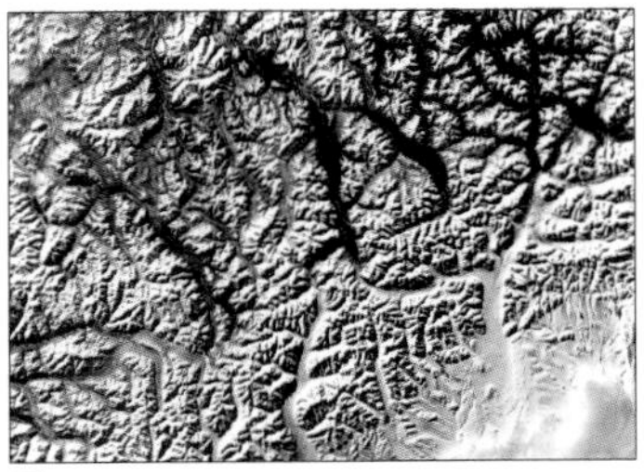

Areas close to the North Pole are permanently covered in snow and ice. Glaciers are rivers of ice that flow towards the sea. Some glaciers are more than 40 miles (60 km) long.

Sea Action

CAPE COD

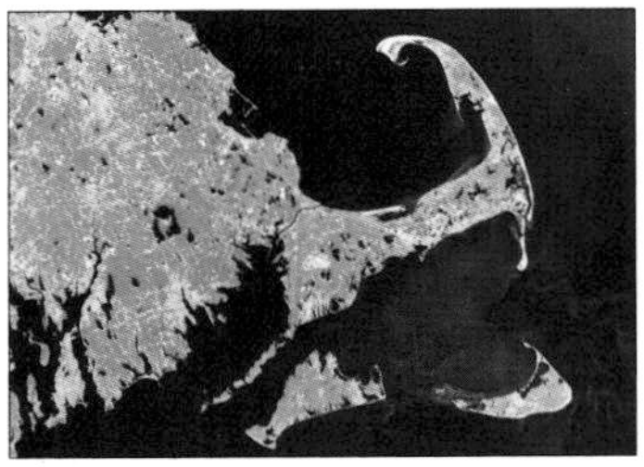

Cape Cod, a sandy peninsula 65 miles (105 km) long, juts out like a beckoning finger into the Atlantic Ocean. Its strangely-curved coastline has been shaped by wave action.

Wind Action

DEATH VALLEY

Death Valley is the hottest, driest place in North America. Its floor is covered in sand and salt. Winds sweeping across the valley endlessly reshape the loose surface.

Water Action

MISSISSIPPI RIVER

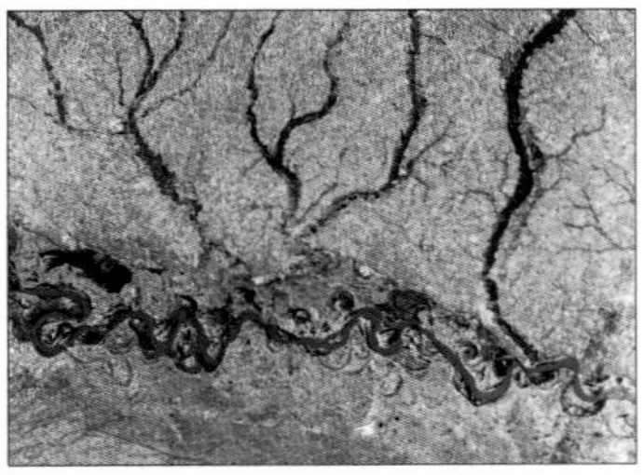

The Mississippi River and its many tributaries frequently change course. Where two loops are close together, the river may cut a new path between them, leaving an "oxbow lake."

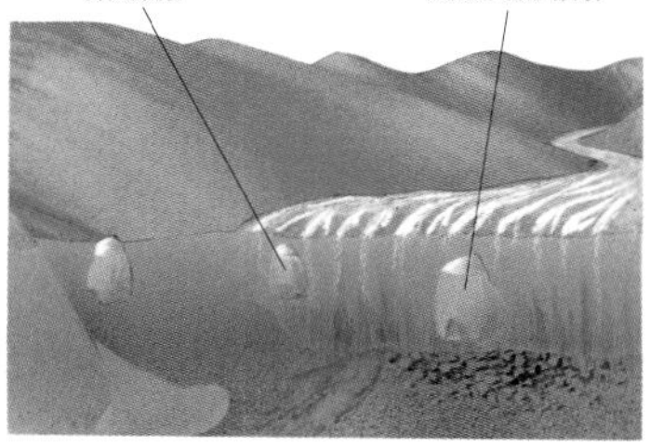
Ice floats because it is less dense than seawater
Only one-ninth of an iceberg shows above sea level

A GLACIER REACHES THE SEA

When a glacier enters the sea, its front edge or "snout" breaks up and forms icebergs – a process called calving. These "ice mountains" are then carried away by ocean currents.

ICE COVER

key on opposite page

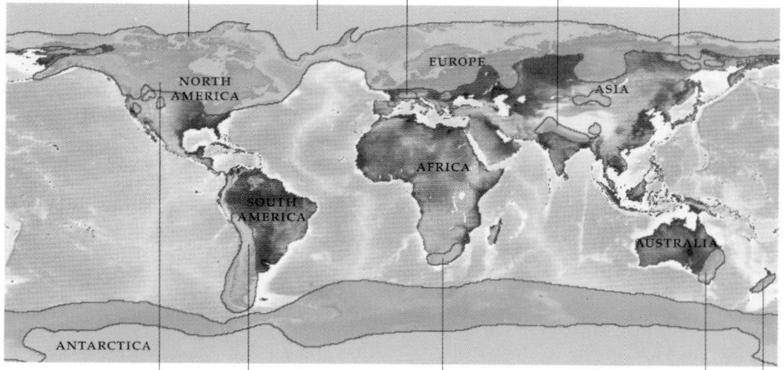
Area covered by ice today
Greenland's icecap
Alps
Himalayas
Area covered by ice 18,000 years ago
NORTH AMERICA
EUROPE
ASIA
AFRICA
SOUTH AMERICA
AUSTRALIA
ANTARCTICA
Ice once covered much more land than today
Andes
Drakensberg
Australian Alps
Southern Alps

NORDFJORD NORWAY

One sign of glacial action on the landscape is the fjord. These long, narrow, steep-sided inlets are found along the coasts of Norway, Alaska, Chile, and New Zealand. They mark the points where glaciers once entered the sea.

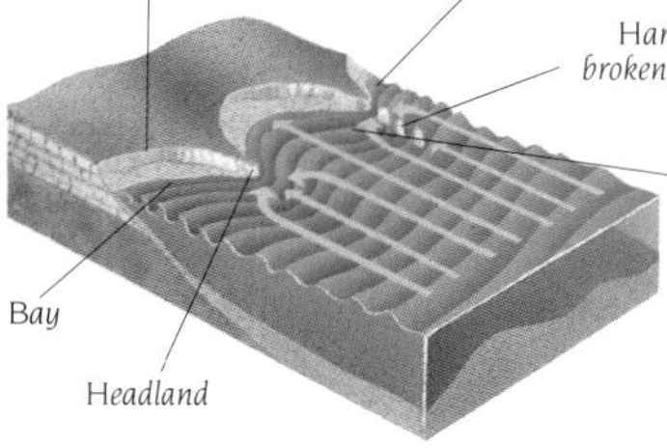
Rock eroded here
Rock fragments and sand deposited here
Hard rock headland broken into small sections
Advancing sea waves
Bay
Headland

COASTAL ATTACK

The ceaseless push and pull of waves on a shore can destroy even the hardest rocks. The softest rocks are eroded first, leaving headlands of hard rock that survive a little longer.

COASTAL EROSION

key on opposite page

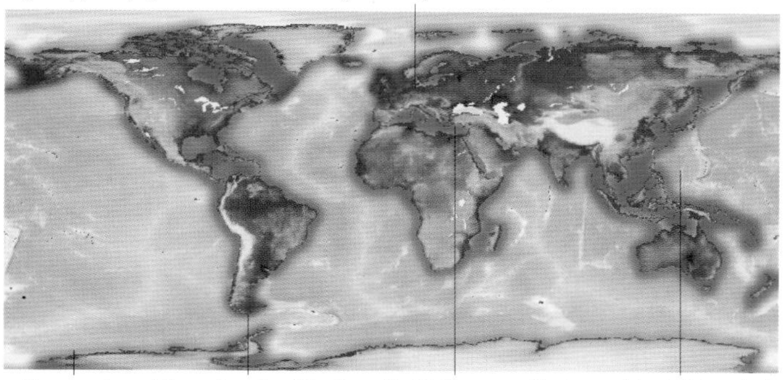
Northwest Europe's shorelines are heavily eroded by Atlantic storms
Permanent ice protects Antarctica's shores
The southern tip of South America is notorious for its devastating storms
The Mediterranean Sea is enclosed by land, so there is little coastal erosion
Islands help protect Asia's mainland from advancing waves

WAVE POWER

The powerful action of waves on an exposed coast can erode a coastline by several feet a year.

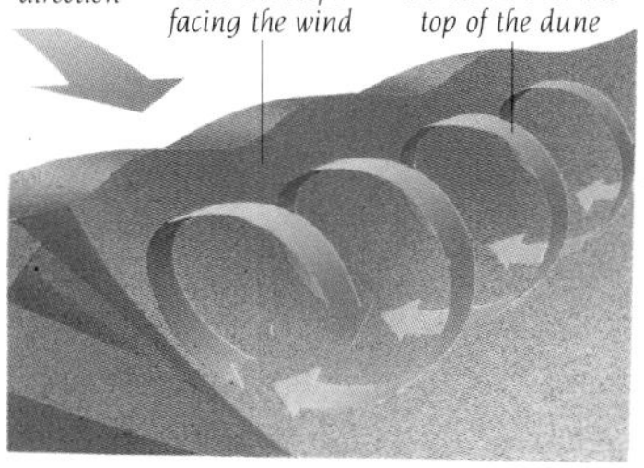
Wind direction
The sheltered slope is steeper than the slope facing the wind
Dunes advance when sand particles are blown over the top of the dune

DESERT DUNE

Dunes are slow-moving mounds or ridges of sand found in deserts and along some coastlines. They only form when the wind's direction and speed is fairly constant.

THE GREAT DESERTS

key on opposite page

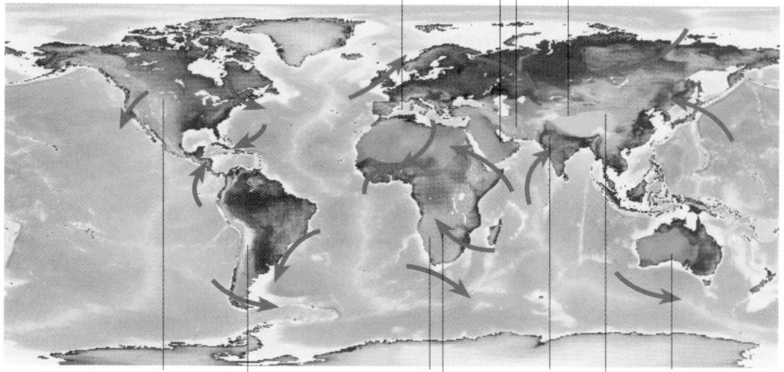
Sahara
Arabian
Kara Kum
Takla Makan
Great Basin
Atacama
Namib
Kalahari
Thar
Gobi
Great Victorian

NAMIB DESERT SOUTHERN AFRICA

The sand dunes seen in the center of the picture are about 160 feet (50 m) high. Winds are driving them slowly but relentlessly towards the right. Not all deserts are sandy. Wind may blow away all the loose sand and gravel, leaving bare rock.

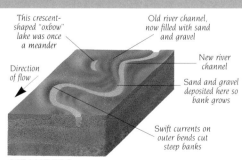

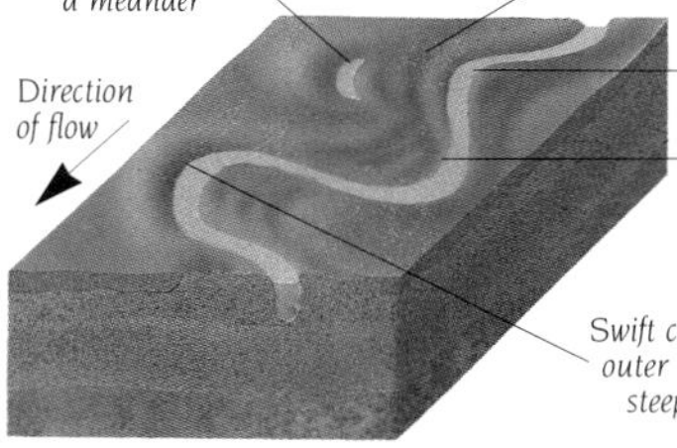
This crescent-shaped "oxbow" lake was once a meander
Old river channel, now filled with sand and gravel
New river channel
Direction of flow
Sand and gravel deposited here so bank grows
Swift currents on outer bends cut steep banks

MEANDERS

River banks are worn away most on the outside of bends, where water flows fastest. Eroded sand and gravel are built up into banks on the inside of bends, in slower-moving water.

THE LARGEST RIVER BASINS

key on opposite page

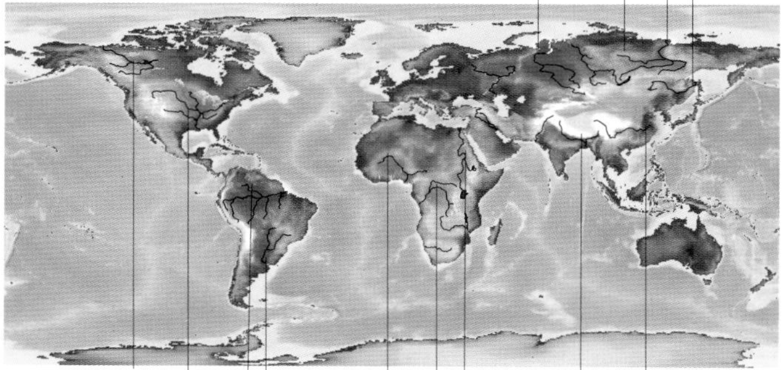
Ob'
Yenisey
Lena
Amur
Mackenzie
Mississippi
Amazon
Paraná
Niger
Congo
Nile
Ganges
Yangtse

WINDING RIVER ALASKA

The more a river winds across a plain, the longer it becomes and the more slowly it flows.

CLIMATE AND VEGETATION

THE EARTH IS the only planet in our solar system which supports life. Most of our planet has a breathable atmosphere, and sufficient light, heat, and water to support a wide range of plants and animals. The main influences on an area's climate are the amount of sunshine it receives (which varies with latitude and season), how close it is to the influence of ocean currents, and its height above sea level. Since there is more sunlight at the Equator than elsewhere, and rainfall is highest here too, this is where we find the habitats which have more species of plants and animals than anywhere else: rain forests, coral reefs, and mangrove swamps. Where rainfall is very low, and where it is either too hot, such as in deserts, or too cold, few plants and animals can survive. Only the icy North and South Poles, and the frozen tops of high mountains, are practically without life.

WEATHER EXTREMES
Weather is a powerful influence on how we feel, the clothes we wear, the buildings we live in, the color of our skin, the plants that grow around us, and what we eat and drink. Extreme weather events such as heat waves, hurricanes, blizzards, tornadoes, sandstorms, droughts, and floods, can be terrifyingly destructive.

TORNADO
Tornadoes are whirlwinds of cold air that develop when thunderclouds cross warm land. They are extremely violent and unpredictable. Windspeeds often exceed 180 miles (300 km) per hour.

TROPICAL STORMS
These devastating winds develop when air spirals upward above warm seas. More air is sucked in and the storm begins to move. They bring torrential rain, thunder and lightning, and destruction.

DROUGHT
Long periods without water kill plants. Stripped of its protective covering of vegetation, the soil is easily blown away.

OCEAN CURRENTS

Currents are a powerful influence on climates. They are like great rivers in the ocean that carry warm water (orange) away from the Equator and cold water (blue) toward the Equator.

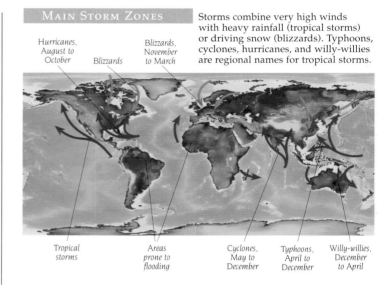

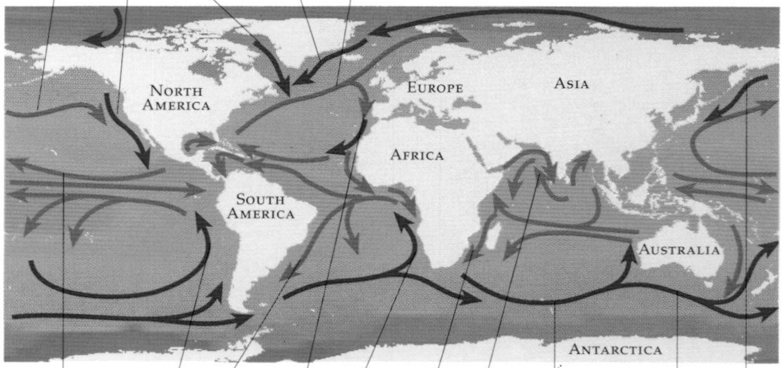
California current
E. Greenland current
North Pacific current
Labrador current
Gulf Stream
North America
Europe
Asia
Africa
South America
Australia
Antarctica
Equatorial currents
Brazil current
Peru current
Benguela current
Canaries current
Agulhas current
Monsoon Drift
Antarctic circumpolar current
W. Australia current
Kuro Shio current

MAIN STORM ZONES

Storms combine very high winds with heavy rainfall (tropical storms) or driving snow (blizzards). Typhoons, cyclones, hurricanes, and willy-willies are regional names for tropical storms.

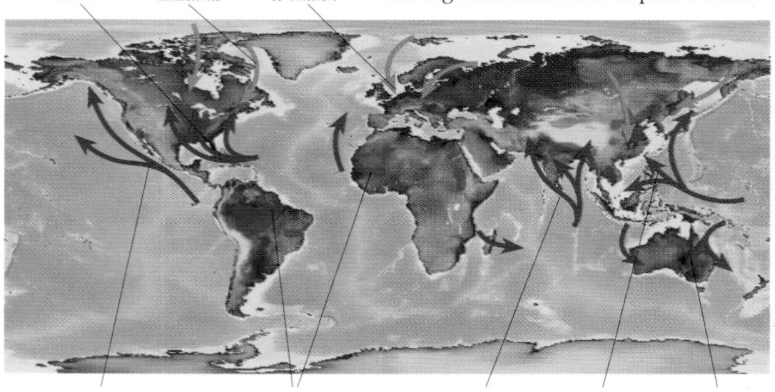
Hurricanes, August to October
Blizzards
Blizzards, November to March
Tropical storms
Areas prone to flooding
Cyclones, May to December
Typhoons, April to December
Willy-willies, December to April

TEMPERATURE

Average temperatures are very different around the world. Areas close to the Equator are usually hot (orange on the map); those close to the Poles usually cold (deep blue). The hottest areas move during the year from the Southern to the Northern hemispheres.

AVERAGE JANUARY TEMPERATURE

Arctic Circle
Tropic of Cancer
Equator
Tropic of Capricorn
Antarctic Circle

AVERAGE JULY TEMPERATURE

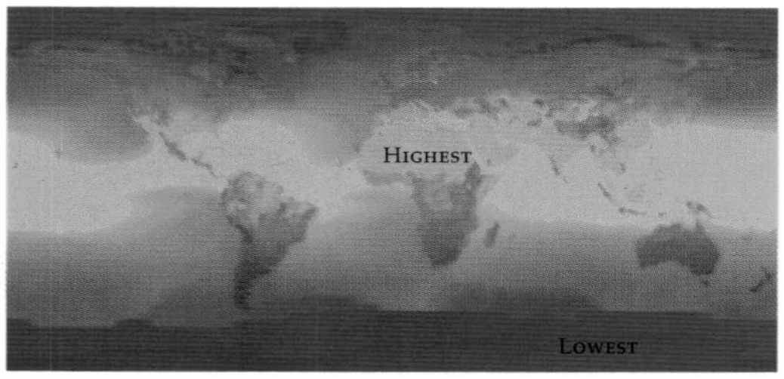
Highest
Lowest

HIGHEST: 136°F (58°C), Sahara

LOWEST: -129°F (-89°C), Antarctica

RAINFALL

The wettest areas (grey) lie near the Equator. The driest are found close to the tropics, in the center of continents, or at the Poles. Elsewhere, rainfall varies with the season, but it is usually highest in summer. Asia's wet season is known as the monsoon.

AVERAGE JANUARY RAINFALL

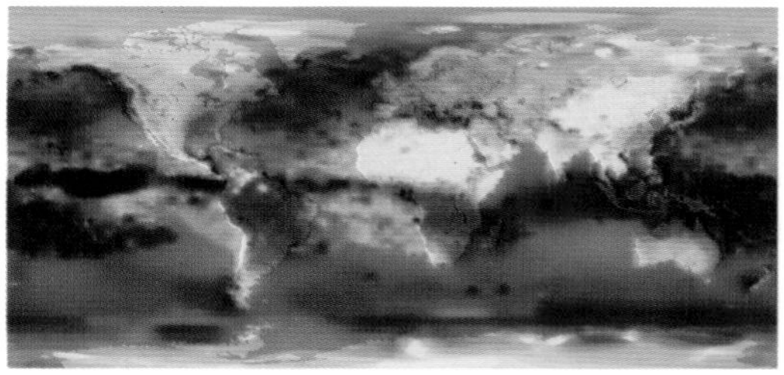
Arctic Circle
Tropic of Cancer
Equator
Tropic of Capricorn
Antarctic Circle

AVERAGE JULY RAINFALL

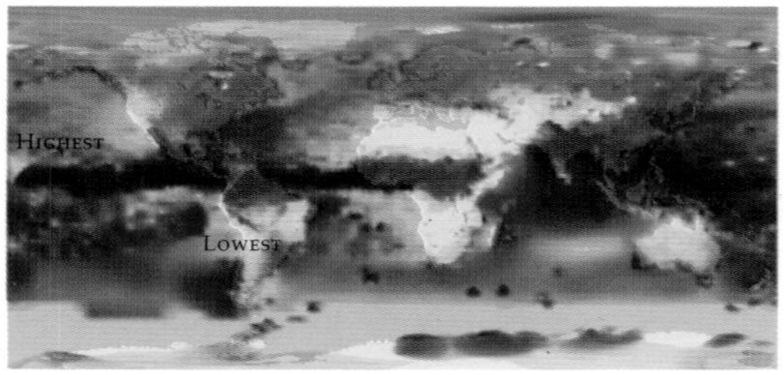
Highest
Lowest

HIGHEST IN 1 YEAR: 460 in (11.68 m), Hawaii

LOWEST: No rain in more than 14 years, Atacama Desert

BROADLEAF FOREST

Temperate climates have no great extremes of temperature, and plentiful rainfall. Drought is very unusual. Forests usually contain a wide variety of broad-leaved or deciduous trees, such as beech, oak, and maple, that shed their leaves in autumn.

TUNDRA

As long as frozen soil melts for at least two months of the year, mosses, lichens, and ground-hugging shrubs can survive. They are found around the Arctic Circle and on mountains.

NEEDLELEAF FOREST

Forests of cone-bearing, needleleaf trees such as pine and fir cover much of northern North America, Europe, and Asia. They are evergreen and can survive long frozen winters. Most have tall, straight trunks and down-pointing branches. This reduces the amount of snow that can settle on them. The forest floor is dark because leaves absorb most of the incoming sunlight.

MEDITERRANEAN

Hot dry summers and warm wet winters typical of this region are also found in small areas of Southern Africa, the Americas, and Australia. Mediterranean-type vegetation can vary from dense forest to thinly spread evergreen shrubs.

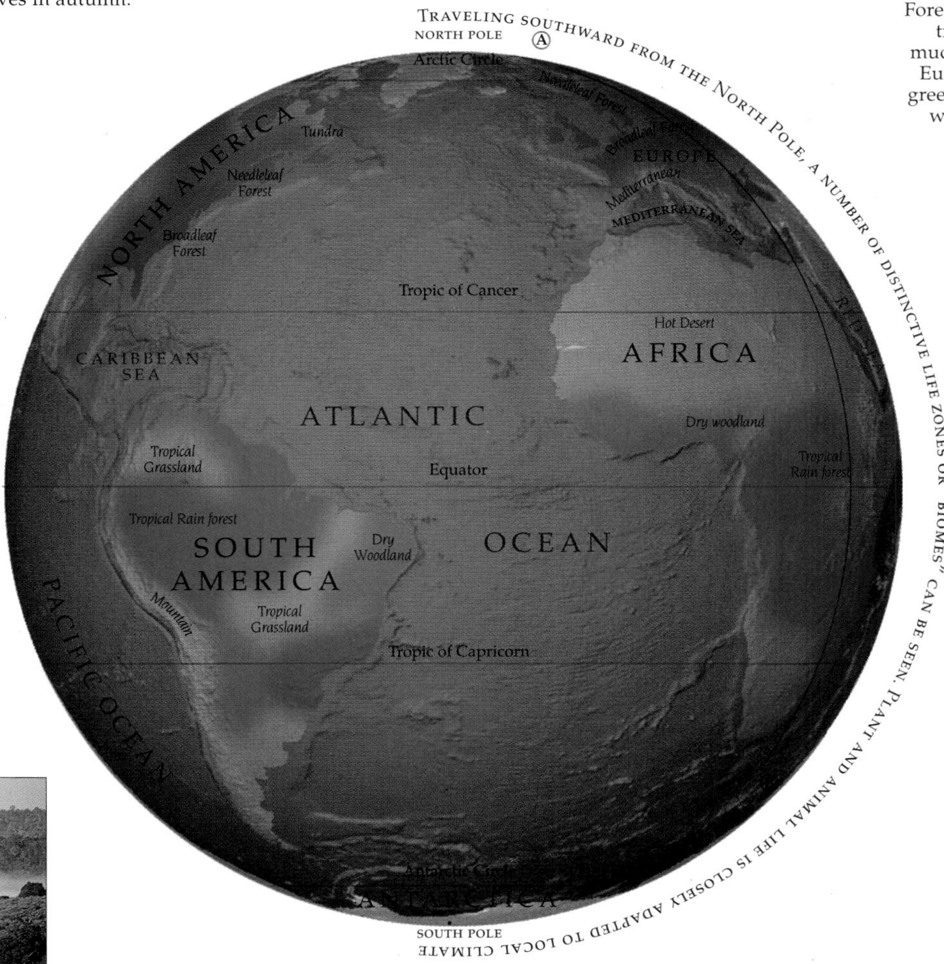

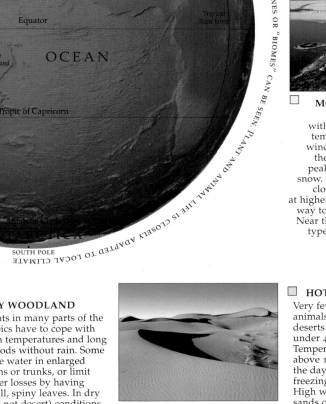

Traveling southward from the North Pole, a number of distinctive life zones or "biomes" can be seen. Plant and animal life is closely adapted to local climate
North Pole
A
Arctic Circle
Needleleaf Forest
Tundra
NORTH AMERICA
Needleleaf Forest
Broadleaf Forest
EUROPE
Mediterranean
MEDITERRANEAN SEA
Tropic of Cancer
Hot Desert
AFRICA
CARIBBEAN SEA
ATLANTIC
Dry woodland
Tropical Grassland
Equator
Tropical Rain forest
Tropical Rain forest
SOUTH AMERICA
Dry Woodland
OCEAN
Tropical Grassland
Mountain
PACIFIC OCEAN
Tropic of Capricorn
Antarctic Circle
ANTARCTICA
South Pole

MOUNTAIN

Vegetation changes with height because the temperature drops and wind increases. Even on the Equator, mountain peaks can be covered in snow. Although trees may cloak the lower slopes, at higher altitudes they give way to sparser vegetation. Near the top, only tundra-type plants can survive.

TROPICAL RAIN FOREST

The lush forests found near the Equator depend on year-round high temperatures and heavy rainfall. Worldwide, they may contain 50,000 different kinds of trees and support several million other plant and animal species. Trees are often festooned with climbing plants, or covered with ferns and orchids that have rooted in pockets of water and soil on trunks and branches.

DRY WOODLAND

Plants in many parts of the tropics have to cope with high temperatures and long periods without rain. Some store water in enlarged stems or trunks, or limit water losses by having small, spiny leaves. In dry (but not desert) conditions, trees are widely spaced, with expanses of grassland between, called savanna.

HOT DESERT

Very few plants and animals can survive in hot deserts. Rainfall is low – under 4 in (10 cm) a year. Temperatures often rise above 104°F (40°C) during the day, but drop to freezing point at night. High winds and shifting sands can be a further hazard to life. Only specially adapted plants, such as cacti, can survive.

NORTH-SOUTH CROSS-SECTION THROUGH EUROPE AND AFRICA

THE LINE RUNNING BETWEEN POINTS A AND B ON THE MAP IS THE LINE OF THE CROSS-SECTION

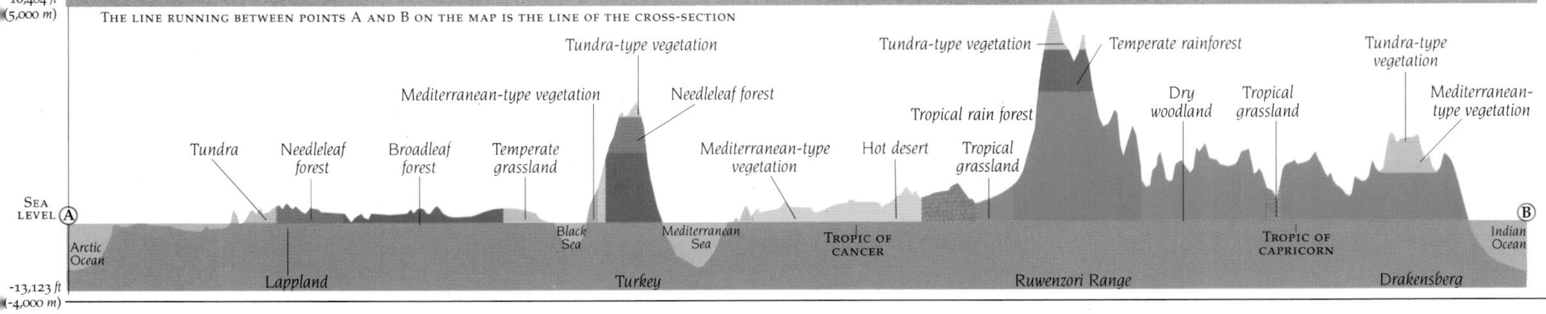

16,404 ft (5,000 m)
Sea level A
-13,123 ft (-4,000 m)
Tundra
Needleleaf forest
Broadleaf forest
Temperate grassland
Mediterranean-type vegetation
Tundra-type vegetation
Needleleaf forest
Mediterranean-type vegetation
Hot desert
Tropical grassland
Tropical rain forest
Tundra-type vegetation
Temperate rainforest
Dry woodland
Tropical grassland
Tundra-type vegetation
Mediterranean-type vegetation
B
Arctic Ocean
Black Sea
Mediterranean Sea
Tropic of Cancer
Tropic of Capricorn
Indian Ocean
Lappland
Turkey
Ruwenzori Range
Drakensberg

PEOPLE AND PLANET

SOON, THERE WILL BE 6 billion people on Earth, and numbers are rising at the rate of about one million every week. People are not distributed evenly. Some areas, such as parts of Europe, India, and China, are very densely populated. Other areas – particularly deserts, polar regions, and mountains – can support very few people. Almost half of the world's population now lives in towns or cities. This is quite a recent development. Until 1800, most people lived in small villages in the countryside, and worked on the land. But since then more and more people have lived and worked in much larger settlements. A century ago, most of the world's largest cities were in Europe and North America, where new industries and businesses were flourishing. Today, the most rapidly growing cities are in Asia, South America, and Africa. People who move to these cities are usually young adults, so the birthrate among these new populations is very high.

A CROWDED PLANET?

If the 5.5 billion people alive today stood close together, they could all fit into an area no larger than the small Caribbean island of Jamaica. Of course, so many people could not live in such a small place. Areas with few people are usually very cold, such as land near the Poles and in mountains, or very dry, such as deserts. Areas with large populations often have ferti[le] land and a good climate for crops. Cities support hug[e] populations because they are wealthy enough to buy in everything they need.

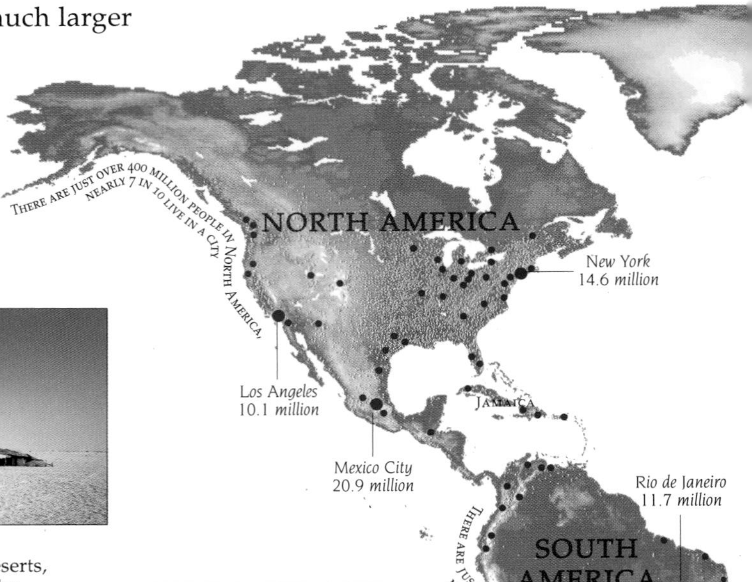
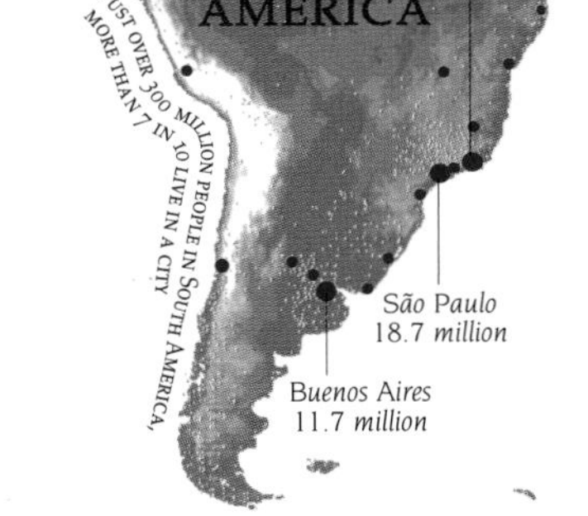

There are just over 400 million people in North America, nearly 7 in 10 live in a city
NORTH AMERICA
New York
14.6 million
Los Angeles
10.1 million
Jamaica
Mexico City
20.9 million
Rio de Janeiro
11.7 million
SOUTH AMERICA
There are just over 300 million people in South America, more than 7 in 10 live in a city
São Paulo
18.7 million
Buenos Aires
11.7 million

MAIN MAP KEY

- Orange represents towns and cities
- City with more than 1 million people.
- City with more than 10 million people

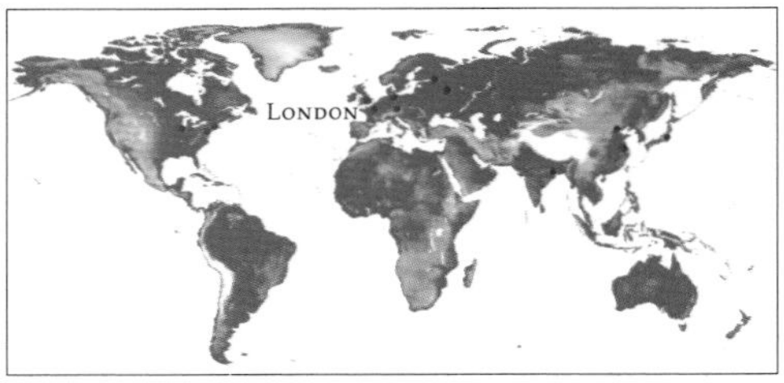

London

MILLIONAIRE CITIES 1900
Less than a century ago there were only 13 cities with more than one million people living in them. All the cities were in the northern hemisphere. The largest was London, with seven million people.

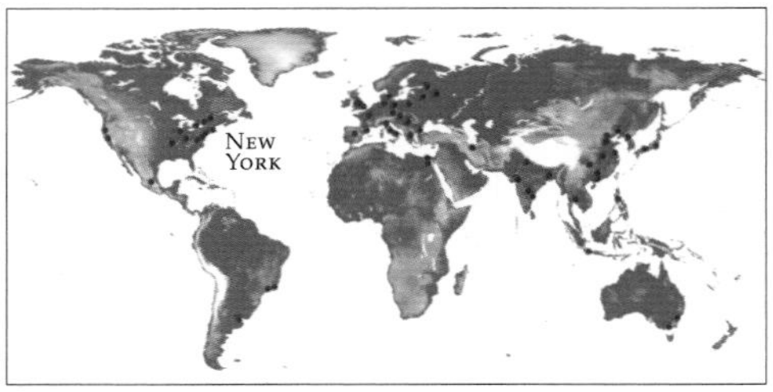

New York

MILLIONAIRE CITIES 1950
By 1950, there were nearly 70 cities with more than one million inhabitants. The largest was New York.

SAHARA AFRICA
The Sahara, like all deserts, is thinly populated. The Tuareg of the northern Sahara are nomads. They travel in small groups because food sources are scarce. Their homes have to be portable.

MONGOLIA ASIA
Traditionally, Mongolia's nomadic people lived by herding their animals across the steppe. Today, their felt tents, or *gers*, are often set up next to more permanent houses.

AMAZONIA SOUTH AMERICA
The Yanomami people gather plants in the rain forest and hunt game, but they also grow crops in small forest gardens. Several families live together in a "village" under one huge roof.

MALI AFRICA
The Dogon people of Mali use mud to construct their elaborate villages. Every family has its own huts and walled areas in which their animals are penned for the night.

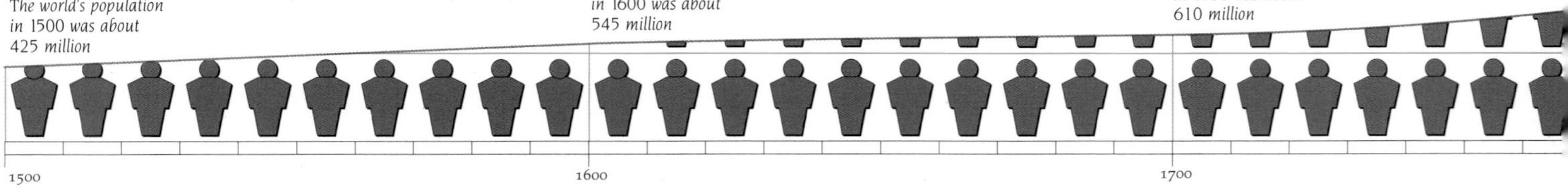

The world's population in 1500 was about 425 million
The world's population in 1600 was about 545 million
The world's population in 1700 was about 610 million
1500
1600
1700

EACH FIGURE ON THE GRAPH REPRESENTS 500 MILLION PEOPLE

POOR SUBURB
Densely-populated "shanty towns" have grown on the fringes of many cities in the developing world. Houses are usually built from discarded materials.

RICH SUBURB
Cities are often surrounded by areas where the richest people live. Population densities are low, and the houses may be luxurious, with large gardens or swimming pools. People in these suburbs rely on their cars for transportation. This allows them to live a great distance from places of work and leisure in the city center.

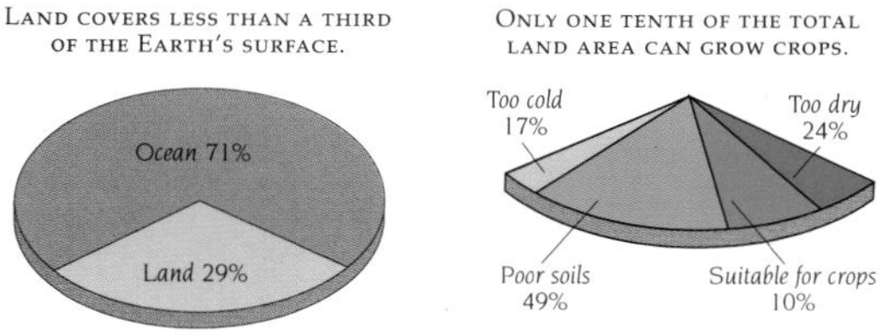
LAND COVERS LESS THAN A THIRD OF THE EARTH'S SURFACE.
Ocean 71%
Land 29%
ONLY ONE TENTH OF THE TOTAL LAND AREA CAN GROW CROPS.
Too cold 17%
Too dry 24%
Poor soils 49%
Suitable for crops 10%

CULTIVATION
Only a small proportion of the Earth's surface can grow crops. It may be possible to bring more land – such as deserts – into production, but yields may be low and costly.

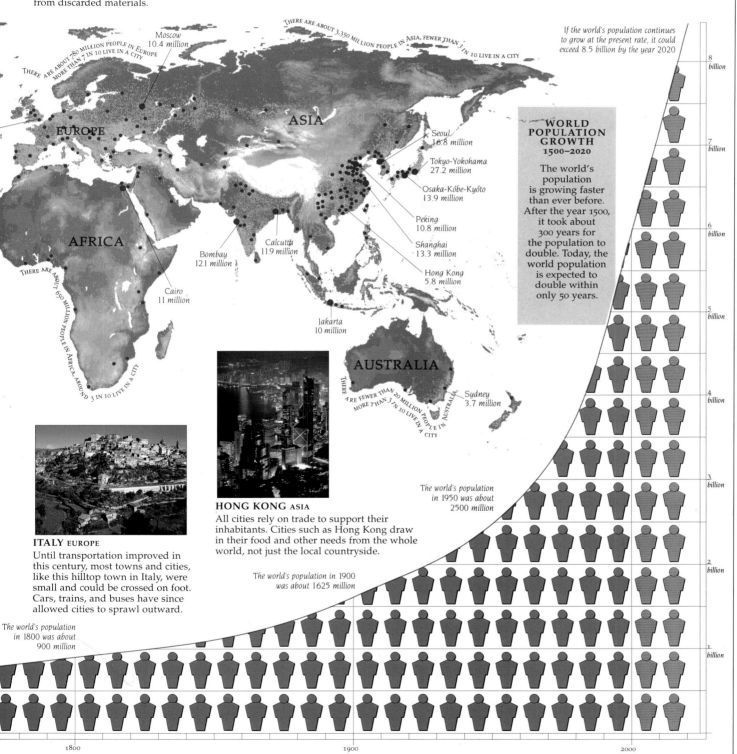

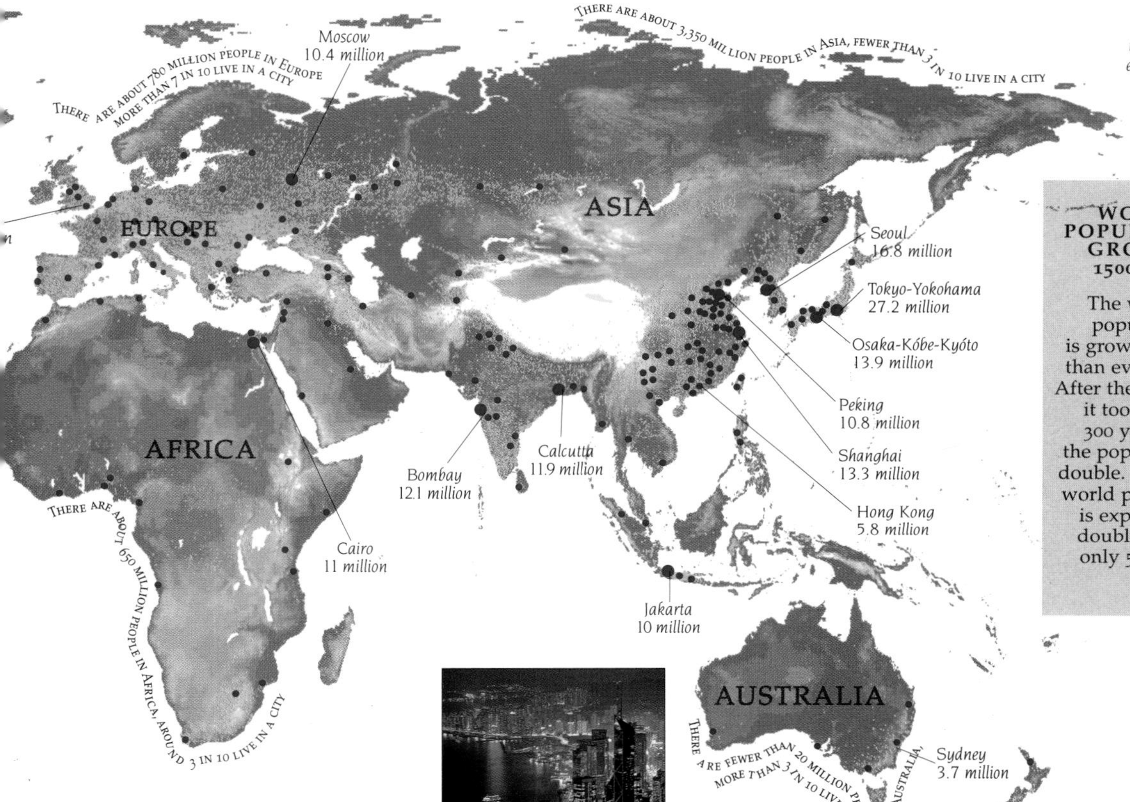
EUROPE
ASIA
AFRICA
AUSTRALIA
THERE ARE ABOUT 780 MILLION PEOPLE IN EUROPE MORE THAN 7 IN 10 LIVE IN A CITY
THERE ARE ABOUT 3,350 MILLION PEOPLE IN ASIA, FEWER THAN 3 IN 10 LIVE IN A CITY
THERE ARE ABOUT 650 MILLION PEOPLE IN AFRICA, AROUND 3 IN 10 LIVE IN A CITY
THERE ARE FEWER THAN 20 MILLION PEOPLE IN AUSTRALIA, MORE THAN 3 IN 10 LIVE IN A CITY
Moscow 10.4 million
Seoul 16.8 million
Tokyo-Yokohama 27.2 million
Osaka-Kóbe-Kyóto 13.9 million
Peking 10.8 million
Shanghai 13.3 million
Hong Kong 5.8 million
Calcutta 11.9 million
Bombay 12.1 million
Cairo 11 million
Jakarta 10 million
Sydney 3.7 million

HONG KONG ASIA
All cities rely on trade to support their inhabitants. Cities such as Hong Kong draw in their food and other needs from the whole world, not just the local countryside.

ITALY EUROPE
Until transportation improved in this century, most towns and cities, like this hilltop town in Italy, were small and could be crossed on foot. Cars, trains, and buses have since allowed cities to sprawl outward.

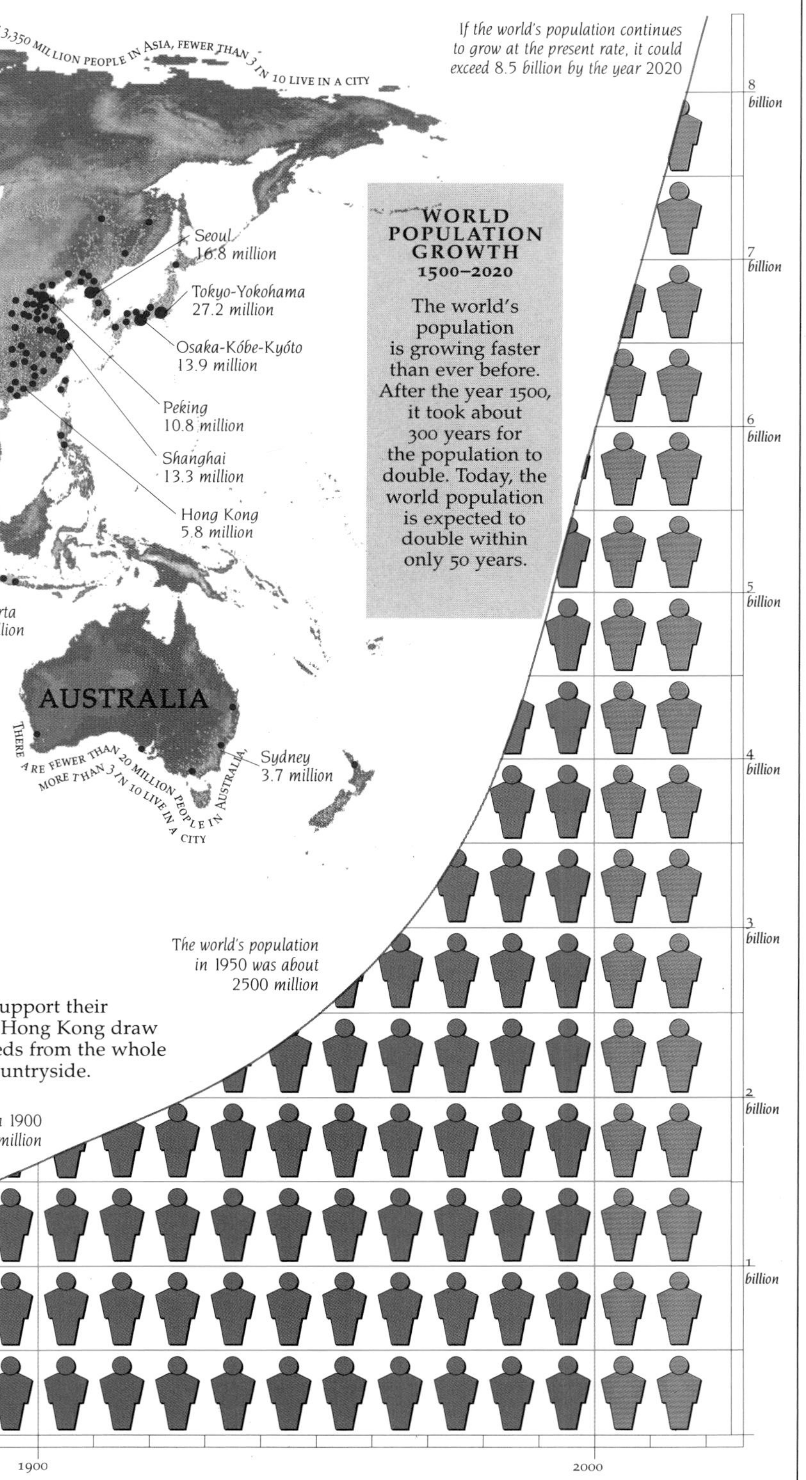
If the world's population continues to grow at the present rate, it could exceed 8.5 billion by the year 2020
The world's population in 1950 was about 2500 million
The world's population in 1900 was about 1625 million
The world's population in 1800 was about 900 million
1 billion
2 billion
3 billion
4 billion
5 billion
6 billion
7 billion
8 billion
1800
1900
2000

WORLD POPULATION GROWTH 1500–2020

The world's population is growing faster than ever before. After the year 1500, it took about 300 years for the population to double. Today, the world population is expected to double within only 50 years.

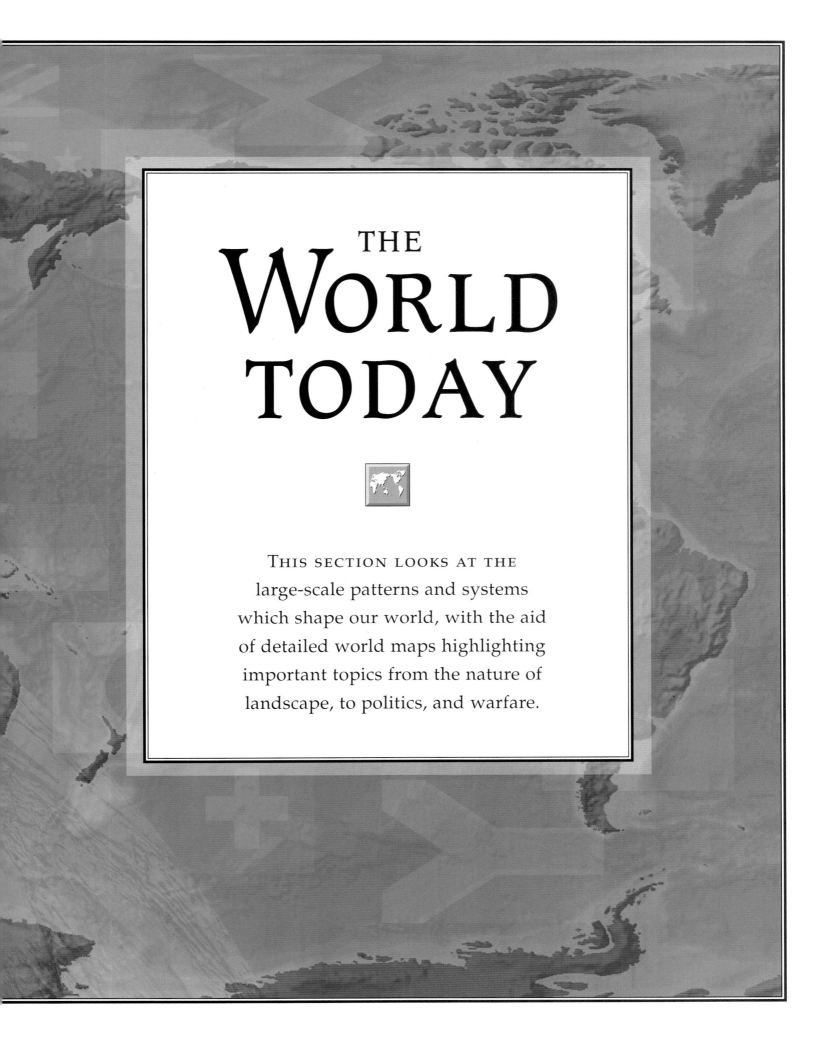

THE WORLD TODAY

THIS SECTION LOOKS AT THE large-scale patterns and systems which shape our world, with the aid of detailed world maps highlighting important topics from the nature of landscape, to politics, and warfare.

THE POLITICAL WORLD

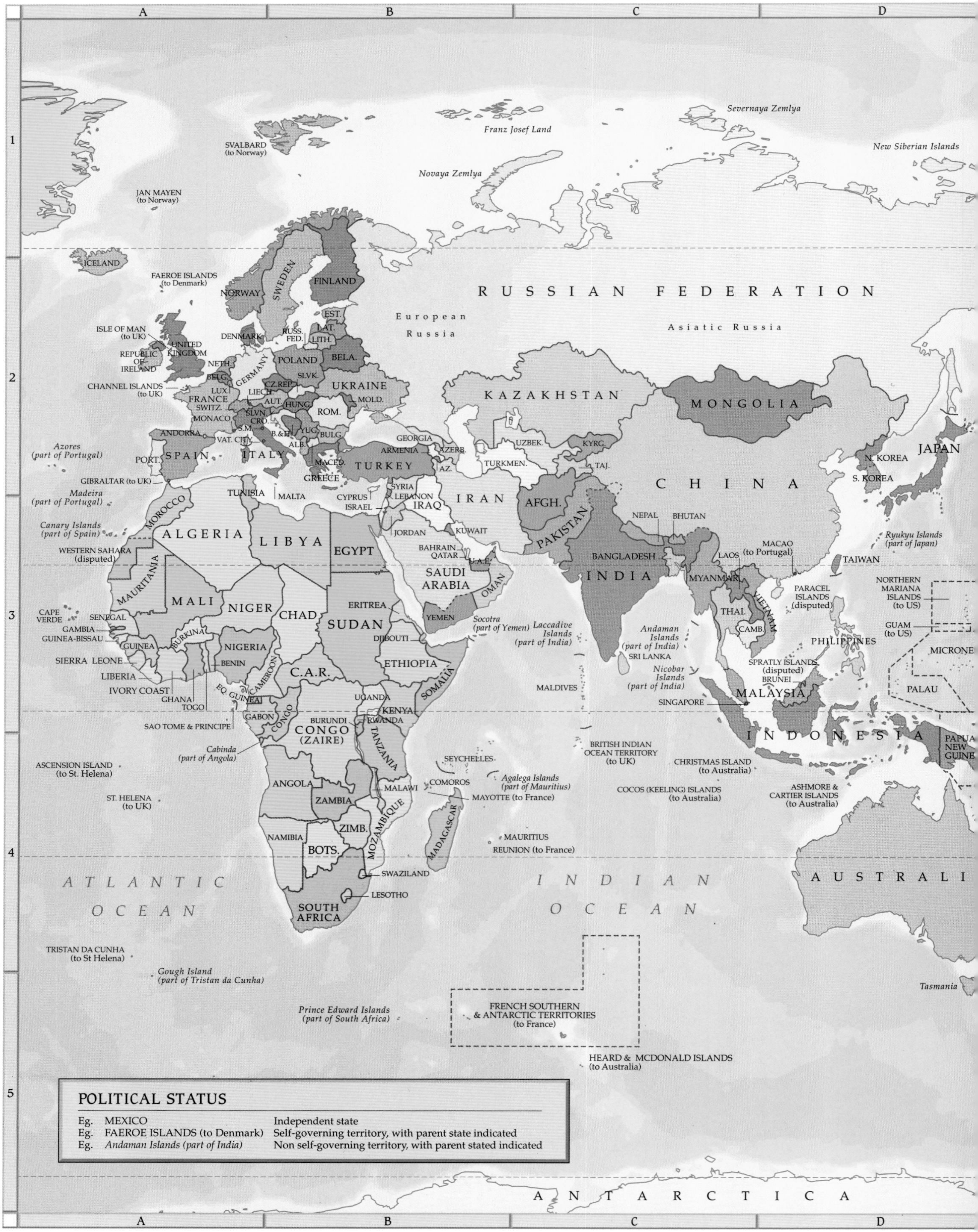
A
B
C
D
1
2
3
4
5
Severnaya Zemlya
Franz Josef Land
New Siberian Islands
SVALBARD
(to Norway)
Novaya Zemlya
JAN MAYEN
(to Norway)
ICELAND
FAEROE ISLANDS
(to Denmark)
NORWAY
SWEDEN
FINLAND
RUSSIAN FEDERATION
European Russia
Asiatic Russia
EST.
LAT.
LITH.
RUSS. FED.
DENMARK
ISLE OF MAN
(to UK)
UNITED KINGDOM
REPUBLIC OF IRELAND
NETH.
POLAND
BELA.
BELG.
GERMANY
SLVK.
UKRAINE
CHANNEL ISLANDS
(to UK)
LUX.
CZ.REP.
LIECH.
FRANCE
SWITZ.
AUT.
HUNG.
MOLD.
ROM.
SLVN.
MONACO
CRO.
S.M.
ANDORRA
VAT. CITY
B.&H.
YUG.
BULG.
ALB.
Azores
(part of Portugal)
PORT.
SPAIN
ITALY
MACED.
GREECE
GEORGIA
ARMENIA
AZERB.
AZ.
TURKEY
KAZAKHSTAN
UZBEK.
KYRG.
TURKMEN.
TAJ.
MONGOLIA
N. KOREA
JAPAN
S. KOREA
CHINA
GIBRALTAR (to UK)
Madeira
(part of Portugal)
TUNISIA
MALTA
CYPRUS
ISRAEL
SYRIA
LEBANON
IRAQ
IRAN
AFGH.
PAKISTAN
NEPAL
BHUTAN
Canary Islands
(part of Spain)
MOROCCO
ALGERIA
LIBYA
EGYPT
JORDAN
KUWAIT
BAHRAIN
QATAR
U.A.E.
BANGLADESH
INDIA
MACAO
(to Portugal)
LAOS
TAIWAN
Ryukyu Islands
(part of Japan)
WESTERN SAHARA
(disputed)
SAUDI ARABIA
OMAN
MYANMAR
VIETNAM
THAI.
CAMB.
PARACEL ISLANDS
(disputed)
NORTHERN MARIANA ISLANDS
(to US)
GUAM
(to US)
MAURITANIA
MALI
NIGER
CHAD
SUDAN
ERITREA
YEMEN
Socotra
(part of Yemen)
Laccadive Islands
(part of India)
Andaman Islands
(part of India)
SRI LANKA
PHILIPPINES
MICRONE
CAPE VERDE
SENEGAL
GAMBIA
GUINEA-BISSAU
GUINEA
BURKINA
NIGERIA
DJIBOUTI
ETHIOPIA
SIERRA LEONE
BENIN
LIBERIA
IVORY COAST
GHANA
TOGO
CAMEROON
C.A.R.
SOMALIA
EQ. GUINEA
UGANDA
KENYA
MALDIVES
Nicobar Islands
(part of India)
SPRATLY ISLANDS
(disputed)
BRUNEI
MALAYSIA
PALAU
SINGAPORE
SAO TOME & PRINCIPE
GABON
CONGO
BURUNDI
RWANDA
CONGO (ZAIRE)
TANZANIA
INDONESIA
PAPUA NEW GUINE
Cabinda
(part of Angola)
BRITISH INDIAN OCEAN TERRITORY
(to UK)
CHRISTMAS ISLAND
(to Australia)
ASCENSION ISLAND
(to St. Helena)
SEYCHELLES
Agalega Islands
(part of Mauritius)
COMOROS
MAYOTTE (to France)
ANGOLA
MALAWI
ZAMBIA
MOZAMBIQUE
MADAGASCAR
ST. HELENA
(to UK)
COCOS (KEELING) ISLANDS
(to Australia)
ASHMORE & CARTIER ISLANDS
(to Australia)
ZIMB.
NAMIBIA
BOTS.
MAURITIUS
REUNION (to France)
SWAZILAND
LESOTHO
SOUTH AFRICA
ATLANTIC OCEAN
INDIAN OCEAN
AUSTRALI
TRISTAN DA CUNHA
(to St Helena)
Gough Island
(part of Tristan da Cunha)
Tasmania
Prince Edward Islands
(part of South Africa)
FRENCH SOUTHERN & ANTARCTIC TERRITORIES
(to France)
HEARD & MCDONALD ISLANDS
(to Australia)
POLITICAL STATUS
Eg. MEXICO Independent state
Eg. FAEROE ISLANDS (to Denmark) Self-governing territory, with parent state indicated
Eg. Andaman Islands (part of India) Non self-governing territory, with parent stated indicated
ANTARCTICA

CONTINENTAL COLOURS

North & West Asia

South & East Asia

Australasia & Oceania

North & Central America

South America

Europe

Africa

Largest country
Russian Federation
6,592,863 sq miles
(17,075,400 sq km)

Smallest country
Vatican City
0.17 sq miles
(0.44 sq km)

Country with the most international borders
China
15

Total number of countries
192

E
F
G
H
ARCTIC OCEAN
Queen Elizabeth Islands
GREENLAND
(to Denmark)
Baffin Island
Arctic Circle
Alaska
(part of US)
CANADA
Aleutian Islands (part of US)
Kurile Islands
(part of Russ. Fed.)
ST. PIERRE
& MIQUELON
(to France)
PACIFIC OCEAN
UNITED STATES
ATLANTIC OCEAN
BERMUDA
(to UK)
PUERTO RICO (to US)
BRITISH VIRGIN ISLANDS (to UK)
VIRGIN ISLANDS (to US)
ANGUILLA (to UK)
ST. KITTS & NEVIS
Tropic of Cancer
ANTIGUA & BARBUDA
MONTSERRAT (to UK)
GUADELOUPE (to France)
DOMINICA
MARTINIQUE (to France)
ST. LUCIA
BARBADOS
ST. VINCENT & THE GRENADINES
GRENADA
TRINIDAD & TOBAGO
MIDWAY ISLANDS
(to US)
Guadelupe
(part of Mexico)
MEXICO
DOM. REP.
TURKS & CAICOS ISLANDS (to UK)
CAYMAN ISLANDS
(to UK)
BAHAMAS
HONDURAS
BELIZE
CUBA
JAMAICA
NAVASSA I.
(to US)
HAITI
NETH. ANT.
(to Neth.)
ARUBA
(to Neth.)
WAKE ISLAND
(to US)
Hawaii
(part of US)
Revillagigedo Islands
(part of Mexico)
MARSHALL ISLANDS
JOHNSTON ATOLL (to US)
GUATEMALA
EL SALVADOR
NICARAGUA
COSTA RICA
PANAMA
CLIPPERTON ISLAND
(to French Polynesia)
WALLIS & FUTUNA
(to France)
KINGMAN REEF (to US)
PALMYRA ATOLL (to US)
BAKER & HOWLAND ISLANDS
(to US)
JARVIS ISLAND
(to US)
Galapagos Islands
(part of Ecuador)
VENEZUELA
COLOMBIA
FRENCH GUIANA
(to France)
Equator
NAURU
KIRIBATI
ECUADOR
GUYANA
SURINAME
TUVALU
TOKELAU
(to NZ)
SOLOMON ISLANDS
PERU
BRAZIL
VANUATU
COOK ISLANDS
(to NZ)
BOLIVIA
NEW CALEDONIA
(to France)
FIJI
FRENCH POLYNESIA
(to France)
PARAGUAY
Tropic of Capricorn
CORAL SEA ISLANDS
(to Australia)
TONGA
SAMOA
NIUE (to NZ)
AMERICAN SAMOA
(to US)
San Felix Island
(part of Chile)
NORFOLK ISLAND
(to Australia)
Lord Howe Island
(part of Australia)
Kermadec Island
(part of NZ)
PITCAIRN ISLANDS
(to UK)
Easter Island
(part of Chile)
Sala y Gomez
(part of Chile)
San Ambrosia Island
(part of Chile)
CHILE
URUGUAY
ARGENTINA
Juan Fernandez Island
(part of Chile)
NEW ZEALAND
Chatham Island
(part of NZ)
PACIFIC OCEAN
Bounty Island
(part of NZ)
Campbell Island
(part of NZ)
Macquarie Island (part of Australia)
FALKLAND ISLANDS
(to UK)
CHILE
SOUTH GEORGIA & SOUTH SANDWICH ISLANDS
(to UK)
Antarctic Circle
ANTARCTICA
2
3
4
5

ABBREVIATIONS

AFGH. *Afghanistan*
ALB. *Albania*
AUT. *Austria*
AZ. or AZERB. *Azerbaijan*
B. & H. *Bosnia & Herzegovina*
BELG. *Belgium*
BULG. *Bulgaria*
BOTS. *Botswana*
CAMB. *Cambodia*
CRO. *Croatia*
CZ. REP. *Czech Republic*
DOM. REP. *Dominican Republic*
EST. *Estonia*
HUNG. *Hungary*
KYRG. *Kyrgyzstan*
LAT. *Latvia*
LIECH. *Liechtenstein*
LITH. *Lithuania*
LUX. *Luxembourg*
MACED. *Macedonia*
MOLD. *Moldova*
NETH. *Netherlands*
NETH. ANT. *Netherland Antilles*
PORT. *Portugal*
ROM. *Romania*
RUSS. FED. *Russian Federation*
SLVK. *Slovakia*
SLVN. *Slovenia*
S. M. *San Marino*
SWITZ. *Switzerland*
TAJ. *Tajikistan*
THAI. *Thailand*
TURKMEN. *Turkmenistan*
U. A. E. *United Arab Emirates*
UZBEK. *Uzbekistan*
VAT. CITY *Vatican City*
YUG. *Yugoslavia*
ZIMB. *Zimbabwe*

The Physical World

A B C D

1

Severnaya Zemlya

Spitsbergen

Franz Josef Land

New Siberian Islands

Greenland Sea

Novaya Zemlya

Laptev Sea

Barents Sea

Kara Sea

Denmark Strait

Norwegian Sea

Scandinavia

Yenisey

Central Siberian Plateau

Lena

Khrebet Cherskogo

Iceland

West Siberian Plain

Ob'

S i b e r i a

Baltic Sea

North European Plain

Volga

Ural Mountains

Sea of Okhotsk

British Isles

North Sea

Lake Baikal

Sakhalin

2

E U R O P E

A S I A

Lake Balkhash

Altai Mountains

Manchurian Plain

Amur

Bay of Biscay

Alps

Danube

Aral Sea

Gobi

Balkans Mts

Black Sea

Caucasus

Caspian Sea

Tien Shan

Plain

Hokkaido

Azores

Iberian Peninsula

Mediterranean Sea

Anatolia

Pamirs

Kunlun Mountains

Yellow River

Sea of Japan

Honshu

Hindu Kush

K2 8611m

Plateau of Tibet

Japan

Maderia

Atlas Mts

Iranian Plateau

Indus

Himalayas

Yellow Sea

Kyushu

Japan Trench

Zagros Mountains

Syrian Desert

Mount Everest 8848m

Yangtze

East China Sea

Canary Islands

S a h a r a

Libyan Desert

Ganges

Ryukyu Islands

Ahaggar

Persian Gulf

Thar Desert

Tibesti

Nile

Red Sea

Arabian Peninsula

Deccan

Taiwan

Philippine Sea

A F R I C A

Western Ghats

Eastern Ghats

Bay of Bengal

3

S a h e l

Arabian Sea

Mekong

South China Sea

Philippine Islands

Philippine Trench

Mariana Islands

Cape Verde Islands

Lake Chad

Gulf of Aden

Niger

Ethiopian Highlands

Horn of Africa

Arabian Basin

Andaman Islands

Sri Lanka

Adamawa Highlands

Great Rift Valley

Nicobar Islands

Caroline

Malay Peninsula

Maldive Islands

Gulf of Guinea

Congo Basin

Somali Basin

Sumatra

Borneo

Celebes

Lake Victoria

East Indies

Congo

Kilimanjaro 5895m

ATLANTIC

Lake Tanganyika

Seychelles

Java Sea

New Guinea

Ascension Island

Java Trench

Java

Arafura Sea

Great Rift Valley

Lake Nyasa

Great Barrier

OCEAN

Angola Basin

Timor Sea

St. Helena

I N D I A N

Zambezi

Mozambique Channel

Madagascar

Ninetyeast Ridge

Namib Desert

Great Sandy Desert

Mauritius

Mid-Atlantic Ridge

Kalahari Desert

R union

4

O C E A N

AUSTRALIA

Great Victoria Desert

Nullarbor Plain

Darling

Drakensberg

Cape Basin

Southwest Indian Ridge

Southeast Indian Ridge

Tristan da Cunha

Cape of Good Hope

Gough Island

Bass Strait

Tasmania

Kerguelen

5

Winter limit of pack ice

South Indian Basin

Summer limit of pack ice

ANTARCTICA

A B C D

Largest continent
ASIA
17,176,000 sq miles
(44,485,900 sq km)

Smallest continent
AUSTRALIA
3,445,600 sq miles
(8,924,100 sq km)

Tallest mountain
MT. EVEREST, CHINA/NEPAL
29,028 ft (8,848 m)

Largest lake
CASPIAN SEA, ASIA
143,236 sq miles
(370,980 sq km)

Longest river
NILE, AFRICA
4,160 miles
(6,695 km)

E
F
G
H
ARCTIC OCEAN
Ellesmere Island
Queen Elizabeth Islands
Greenland
Siberian Sea
Summer limit of pack ice
Beaufort Sea
Baffin Bay
Baffin Island
Chukchi Sea
Brooks Range
Bering Strait
Mackenzie
Great Bear Lake
Mount McKinley (Denali) 6194m
Winter limit of pack ice
Great Slave Lake
Hudson Bay
Péninsula d'Ungava
Labrador Sea
Bering Sea
Aleutian Basin
Aleutian Islands
Aleutian Trench
Gulf of Alaska
Coast Mountains
Rocky Mountains
Canadian Shield
Lake Winnipeg
Laurentian Highlands
NORTH AMERICA
Great Lakes
Vancouver Island
Grand Banks of Newfoundland
Emperor Seamounts
Coast Ranges
Great Plains
Appalachian Mts
Mississippi
Mendocino Fracture Zone
Mid Atlantic Ridge
North America Basin
Lower California
Sierra Madre Occidental
Sierra Madre Oriental
Gulf of Mexico
Tropic of Cancer
Hawaiian Islands
Hawaii
Yucatan Peninsula
West Indies
Greater Antilles
ATLANTIC OCEAN
Central Pacific Basin
Marshall Islands
Caribbean Sea
Lesser Antilles
Middle America Trench
PACIFIC OCEAN
Polynesia
Micronesia
Line Islands
Guiana Highlands
Equator
Galapagos Islands
Amazon
Amazon Basin
Phoenix Islands
SOUTH AMERICA
Marquesas Islands
Andes
Samoa
Brazil Basin
Brazilian Highlands
Cook Islands
Tuamotu Islands
Peru Basin
Planalto de Mato Grosso
Fiji
Vanuatu
Tonga
New Caledonia
Tropic of Capricorn
Kermadec Trench
East Pacific Rise
Easter Island
Gran Chaco
Paraná
Cerro Aconcagua 6959m
Tasman Sea
Southwest Pacific Basin
Juan Fernandez Islands
Pampas
North Island
New Zealand
South Island
Argentine Basin
Patagonia
Campbell Plateau
Falkland Islands
South Georgia
Tierra del Fuego
Cape Horn
South Sandwich Islands
Drake Passage
Antarctic Peninsula
Antarctic Circle
2
3
4
5
ELEVATION
4 000 m 13 124 ft
2 000 m 6 562 ft
1 000 m 3 281 ft
500 m 1 640 ft
250 m 820 ft
100 m 328 ft
Sea Level
-250 m -820 ft
-500 m -1 640 ft
-1 000 m -3 281 ft
-2 000 m -6 562 ft
-3 000 m -9 843 ft
-4 000 m -13 124 ft

Time Zones

A B C D

1
SVALBARD (to Norway) +1
Franz Josef Land
Severnaya Zemlya
A R
New Siberian Islands
Novaya Zemlya +5
JAN MAYEN (to Norway)
–1
+1
Arctic Circle
+2
ICELAND 0
FAEROE ISLANDS (to Denmark)
SWEDEN
NORWAY
FINLAND
RUSSIAN FEDERATION
+10
+3 European Russia
+4
+5
+7 Asiatic Russia +8
+9
ISLE OF MAN (to UK)
UNITED KINGDOM 0
DENMARK
RUSS. FED.
EST.
LAT.
LITH.
REPUBLIC OF IRELAND
NETH.
GERMANY
POLAND
BELA.
BELG.
LUX.
CZ.REP.
SLVK.
UKRAINE
+2
MOLD.
+4
KAZAKHSTAN
+4
MONGOLIA
+8
2
CHANNEL ISLANDS (to UK)
FRANCE
LIECH.
AUT.
HUNG.
SWITZ.
SLVN.
CRO.
ROM.
MONACO
ANDORRA
+1
S.M.
B.&H.
YUG.
BULG.
VAT. CITY
ALB.
GEORGIA
ARMENIA
AZERB.
UZBEK.
KYRG.
Azores (part of Portugal)
PORT. 0
SPAIN
ITALY
MACED.
TURKEY
+2
AZ.
+2
+5
TURKMEN.
TAJ.
N. KOREA
JAPAN
+8
CHINA
S. KOREA
+8
GIBRALTAR (to UK)
GREECE
Madeira (part of Portugal)
MOROCCO
TUNISIA
MALTA
CYPRUS
ISRAEL
SYRIA
LEBANON
IRAQ
IRAN +3½
AFGH. +4½
+5
PAKISTAN
Canary Islands (part of Spain)
ALGERIA
LIBYA
EGYPT
JORDAN
KUWAIT
NEPAL +5¾
BHUTAN +6
WESTERN SAHARA
Tropic of Cancer
BAHRAIN
QATAR
+3
U.A.E.
BANGLADESH
+6
LAOS
MACAO (to Portugal)
TAIWAN
MAURITANIA
0
MALI
+1
NIGER
CHAD
+2
SAUDI ARABIA
OMAN
INDIA +5½
+6½
MYANMAR
NORTHERN MARIANA ISLANDS (to US)
CAPE VERDE –1
SENEGAL
GAMBIA
GUINEA-BISSAU
ERITREA
SUDAN
YEMEN
Laccadive Islands (part of India)
Andaman Islands (part of India)
THAI.
VIETNAM
+7
CAMB.
PARACEL ISLANDS (disputed)
GUAM (to US)
3
BURKINA
GUINEA
NIGERIA
DJIBOUTI
PHILIPPINES
MICRONE
SIERRA LEONE
BENIN
CAMEROON
ETHIOPIA
+3
SOMALIA
SRI LANKA
SPRATLY ISLANDS (disputed)
BRUNEI
+8
+10
LIBERIA
C.A.R.
+9
PALAU
IVORY COAST
GHANA
TOGO
0
EQ. GUINEA
UGANDA
KENYA
MALDIVES
MALAYSIA
Equator
SINGAPORE
GABON
CONGO
RWANDA
BURUNDI
SAO TOME & PRINCIPE
CONGO (ZAIRE)
TANZANIA
+7
INDONESIA
+8
PAPUA NEW GUINE
Cabinda (part of Angola)
BRITISH INDIAN OCEAN TERRITORY (to UK)
ASCENSION ISLAND (to St. Helena)
SEYCHELLES
CHRISTMAS ISLAND (to Australia)
ANGOLA
COMOROS
+6½
MALAWI
MAYOTTE (to France)
COCOS (KEELING) ISLANDS (to Australia)
ASHMORE & CARTIER ISLANDS (to Australia)
ST. HELENA (to UK)
ZAMBIA
MOZAMBIQUE
ZIMB.
+3
MADAGASCAR
NAMIBIA
BOTS.
MAURITIUS
REUNION (to France)
+9½
Tropic of Capricorn
4
+1
SWAZILAND
+8
+10
ATLANTIC OCEAN
+2
INDIAN OCEAN
AUSTRALIA
LESOTHO
+10½
SOUTH AFRICA
TRISTAN DA CUNHA (to St. Helena)
+5
+11
Gough Island (part of Tristan da Cunha)
Greenwich Meridian
Tasmania
Prince Edward Islands (part of South Africa)
FRENCH SOUTHERN & ANTARCTIC TERRITORIES (to France)
+5
+5
HEARD & MCDONALD ISLANDS (to Australia)
5
–2 –1 0 +1 +2 +3 +4 +5 +6 +7 +8 +9 +1

11:00	12:00	13:00	14:00	15:00	16:00	17:00	18:00	19:00	20:00	21:00	22

Antarctic Circle
ANTARCTICA
(except for Graham Land, Antarctica is not subject to any time zo

A B C D

The numbers represented thus: +2/–2, indicate the number of hours ahead or behind GMT (Greenwich Mean Time) of each time zone.

Except for Graham Land, Antarctica is not subject to any time zone.

The Russian Federation spans the most time zones – nine in all. When it is midnight in Moscow it is 9am the following day in the far east of Siberia.

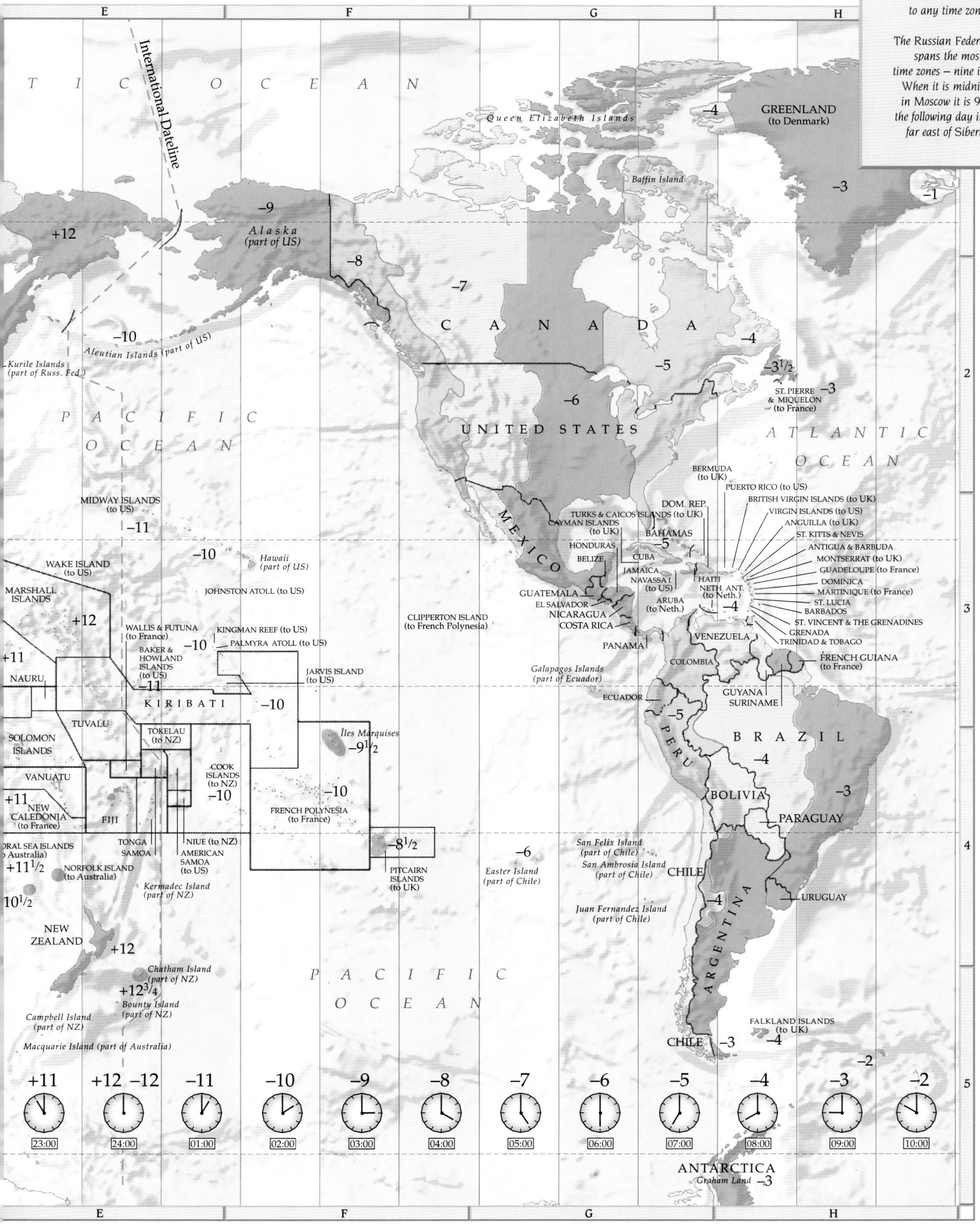
E
F
G
H
International Dateline
PACIFIC OCEAN
Queen Elizabeth Islands
GREENLAND (to Denmark)
–4
–3
–1
Baffin Island
–9
Alaska (part of US)
+12
–8
–7
CANADA
–10
Aleutian Islands (part of US)
Kurile Islands (part of Russ. Fed.)
–4
–5
–3½
ST. PIERRE & MIQUELON (to France)
–3
–6
UNITED STATES
ATLANTIC OCEAN
BERMUDA (to UK)
PUERTO RICO (to US)
BRITISH VIRGIN ISLANDS (to UK)
VIRGIN ISLANDS (to US)
ANGUILLA (to UK)
ST. KITTS & NEVIS
ANTIGUA & BARBUDA
MONTSERRAT (to UK)
GUADELOUPE (to France)
DOMINICA
MARTINIQUE (to France)
ST. LUCIA
BARBADOS
ST. VINCENT & THE GRENADINES
GRENADA
TRINIDAD & TOBAGO
DOM. REP.
TURKS & CAICOS ISLANDS (to UK)
CAYMAN ISLANDS (to UK)
BAHAMAS
–5
MEXICO
HONDURAS
BELIZE
CUBA
JAMAICA
NAVASSA I. (to US)
HAITI
NETH. ANT. (to Neth.)
ARUBA (to Neth.)
–4
GUATEMALA
EL SALVADOR
NICARAGUA
COSTA RICA
PANAMA
VENEZUELA
COLOMBIA
FRENCH GUIANA (to France)
GUYANA
SURINAME
ECUADOR
–5
PERU
BRAZIL
–4
–3
BOLIVIA
PARAGUAY
CHILE
–4
ARGENTINA
URUGUAY
MIDWAY ISLANDS (to US)
–11
–10
Hawaii (part of US)
WAKE ISLAND (to US)
JOHNSTON ATOLL (to US)
MARSHALL ISLANDS
+12
CLIPPERTON ISLAND (to French Polynesia)
WALLIS & FUTUNA (to France)
KINGMAN REEF (to US)
PALMYRA ATOLL (to US)
BAKER & HOWLAND ISLANDS (to US)
–10
+11
NAURU
–11
JARVIS ISLAND (to US)
Galapagos Islands (part of Ecuador)
KIRIBATI
–10
TUVALU
TOKELAU (to NZ)
Îles Marquises
–9½
SOLOMON ISLANDS
VANUATU
COOK ISLANDS (to NZ)
–10
–10
+11
NEW CALEDONIA (to France)
FIJI
FRENCH POLYNESIA (to France)
TONGA
SAMOA
NIUE (to NZ)
AMERICAN SAMOA (to US)
–8½
–6
San Felix Island (part of Chile)
San Ambrosia Island (part of Chile)
CORAL SEA ISLANDS (to Australia)
+11½
NORFOLK ISLAND (to Australia)
PITCAIRN ISLANDS (to UK)
Easter Island (part of Chile)
Kermadec Island (part of NZ)
Juan Fernandez Island (part of Chile)
10½
NEW ZEALAND
+12
Chatham Island (part of NZ)
+12¾
Bounty Island (part of NZ)
Campbell Island (part of NZ)
Macquarie Island (part of Australia)
PACIFIC OCEAN
FALKLAND ISLANDS (to UK)
–4
CHILE
–3
–2
+11
+12 –12
–11
–10
–9
–8
–7
–6
–5
–4
–3
–2
23:00
24:00
01:00
02:00
03:00
04:00
05:00
06:00
07:00
08:00
09:00
10:00
ANTARCTICA
Graham Land –3
2
3
4
5

Geology & Structure

A
B
C
D
1
2
3
4
5
Ural Mountains
EURASIAN PLATE
Alps
ANATOLIAN PLATE
IRANIAN PLATE
Himalayas
ARABIAN PLATE
PHILIPPINE PLATE
AFRICAN PLATE
INDO-AUSTRALIAN PLATE
ANTARCTIC PLATE

GEOLOGICAL REGIONS

Continental Shield

Sedimentary Rocks

Igneous Rock Types

Coral Formation

MOUNTAIN RANGES

Formation expressed as millions of years ago

Alpine (5 to 23 M)

Hercynian (290 to 362 M)

Caledonian (386 to 439 M)

Worst landslide
YUNGAY, PERU
31 May, 1970
17,500 killed

Worst volcanic eruption
MT. PELÉE, MARTINIQUE
8 May 1902
40,000 killed

Worst earthquake
TANGSHAN, CHINA
28 JULY 1976
242,419 killed

E
F
G
H
NORTH AMERICAN PLATE
Rocky Mountains
JUAN DE FUCA PLATE
Arctic Circle
Tropic of Cancer
CARIBBEAN PLATE
COCOS PLATE
AROLINE LATE
ISMARCK LATE
SOLOMON PLATE
FIJI PLATE
PACIFIC PLATE
Equator
Andes
NAZCA PLATE
SOUTH AMERICAN PLATE
Tropic of Capricorn
SCOTIA PLATE
ANTARCTIC PLATE
Antarctic Circle
2
3
4
5

TECTONIC FEATURES

Earthquake Zone

Hot Spot

Volcanic Zone

Rift Valleys

PLATE BOUNDARIES

Sliding Plates

Spreading Plates

Colliding Plates

Uncertain Plate Boundary

World Climate

A
B
C
D
1
2
3
4
5
POLAR EASTERLIES
Arctic Circle
WESTERLIES
Buran (Jan.)
Mistral
Föhn
Bora
Etesian (Jun.-Oct.)
Bora
ATLANTIC OCEAN
Sirocco
Khamsin
Southwest Monsoon(Apr.-Sept.)
Typhoon (Jul.-Oct.)
Tropic of Cancer
NORTH EAST TRADES
Harmattan
Haboob (Jan.)
Equator
SOUTH EAST TRADES
Northeast Monsoon(Oct.-Mar.)
SOUTH EAST TRADES
Willy Willies
Tropic of Capricorn
ATLANTIC OCEAN
INDIAN OCEAN
WESTERLIES
Antarctic Circle
POLAR EASTERLIES
Average January Temperature
Average July Temperature
TEMPERATURE
°C
°F
30
86
20
68
10
50
0
32
-10
14
-20
-4
-30
-22

CLIMATE TYPES

- Ice Cap
- Tundra
- Subarctic
- Cool Continental
- Warm Humid
- Mediterranean
- Semiarid
- Arid
- Tropical
- Humid Equatorial

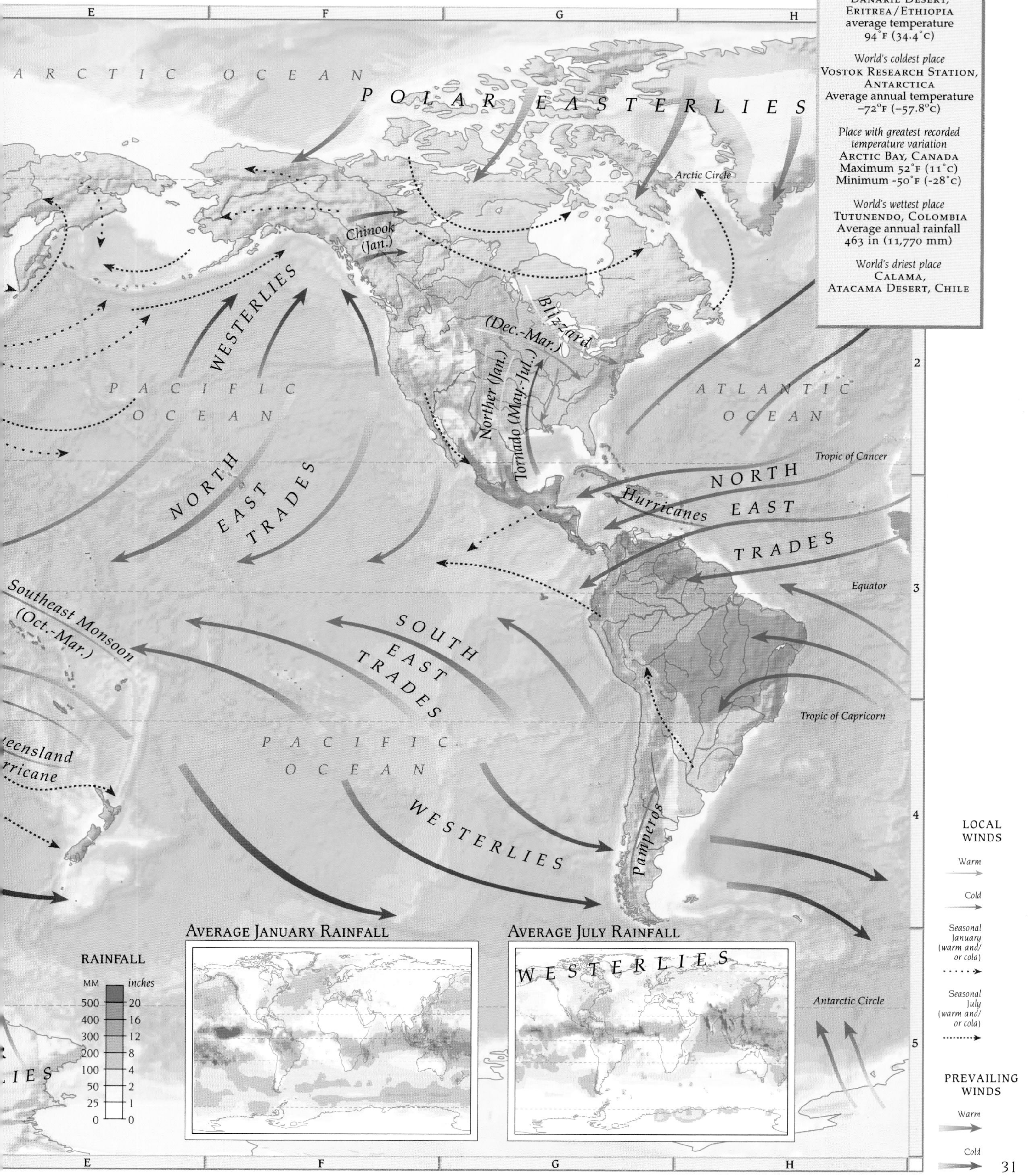
E
F
G
H
ARCTIC OCEAN
POLAR EASTERLIES
Arctic Circle
Chinook (Jan.)
Blizzard (Dec.-Mar.)
Norther (Jan.)
Tornado (May-Jul.)
WESTERLIES
PACIFIC OCEAN
ATLANTIC OCEAN
Tropic of Cancer
NORTH EAST TRADES
Hurricanes
NORTH EAST TRADES
Equator
Southeast Monsoon (Oct.-Mar.)
SOUTH EAST TRADES
Tropic of Capricorn
PACIFIC OCEAN
Queensland Hurricane
WESTERLIES
Pamperos
WESTERLIES
Antarctic Circle
2
3
4
5
AVERAGE JANUARY RAINFALL
AVERAGE JULY RAINFALL
RAINFALL
MM inches
500 20
400 16
300 12
200 8
100 4
50 2
25 1
0 0
LOCAL WINDS
Warm
Cold
Seasonal January (warm and/or cold)
Seasonal July (warm and/or cold)
PREVAILING WINDS
Warm
Cold

World's hottest place
DANAKIL DESERT, ERITREA/ETHIOPIA
average temperature
94°F (34.4°C)

World's coldest place
VOSTOK RESEARCH STATION, ANTARCTICA
Average annual temperature
−72°F (−57.8°C)

Place with greatest recorded temperature variation
ARCTIC BAY, CANADA
Maximum 52°F (11°C)
Minimum -50°F (-28°C)

World's wettest place
TUTUNENDO, COLOMBIA
Average annual rainfall
463 in (11,770 mm)

World's driest place
CALAMA, ATACAMA DESERT, CHILE

Ocean Currents

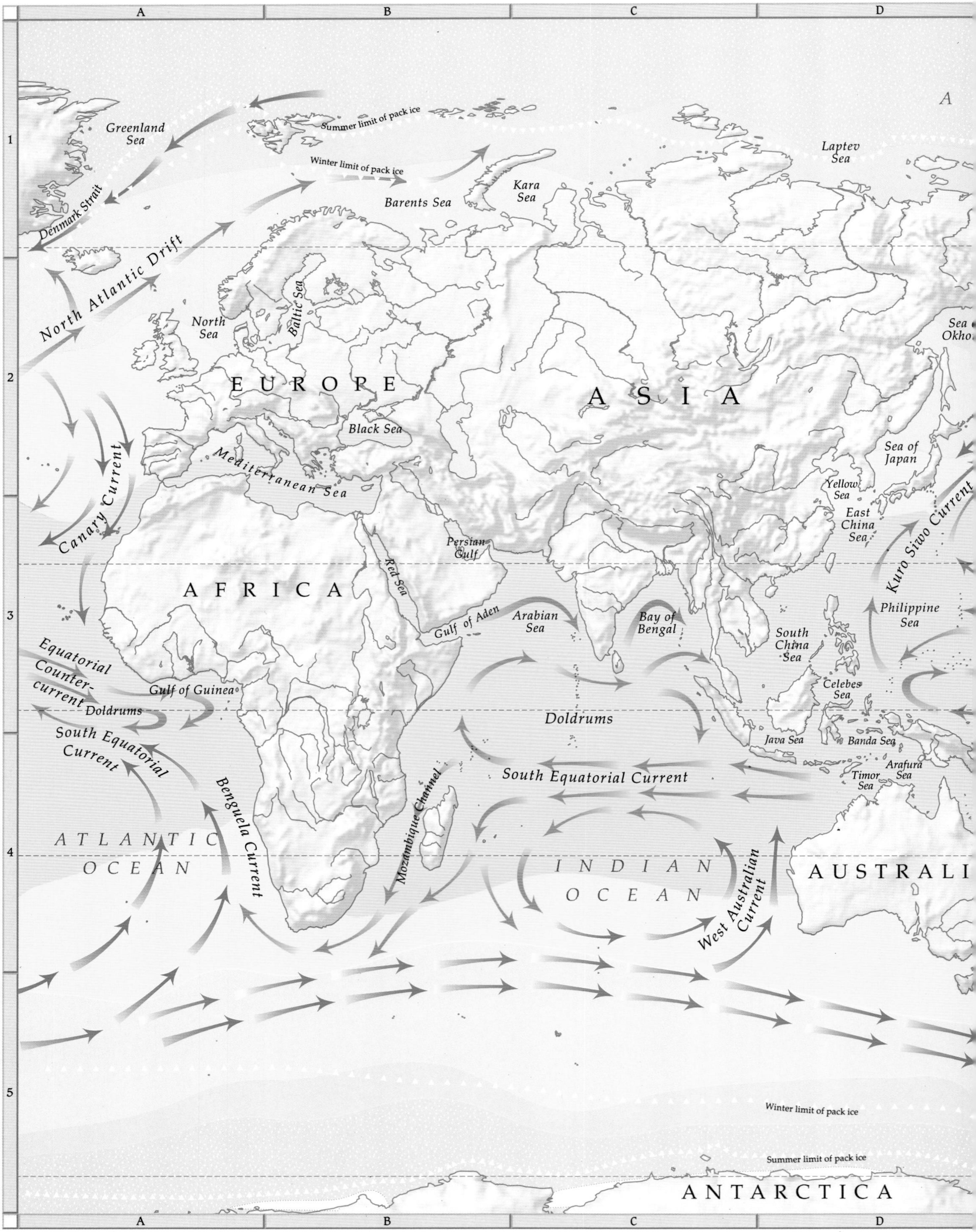

ANNUAL MEAN OCEAN TEMPERATURE

68° to 86°F
20 to 30°C

50° to 68°F
10 to 20°C

32° to 50°F
0 to 10°C

28° to 32°F
-2° to 0°C

Annual mean extent of sea ice below 28°F/-2°C

Permanent ice shelf

Prevailing warm Ocean current

Prevailing cold Ocean current

Largest ocean
Pacific Ocean
63,855,000 sq miles
(165,384,000 sq km)

Smallest ocean
Arctic Ocean
5,108,000 sq miles
(13,230,000 sq km)

Deepest known point
Mariana Trench
35,827 ft (10,920 m)
below sea level

Greatest ocean current
Antarctic Circumpolar Current
(West Wind Drift)
flows at 4.3 billion cu ft
(1.3 billion cu m) per second

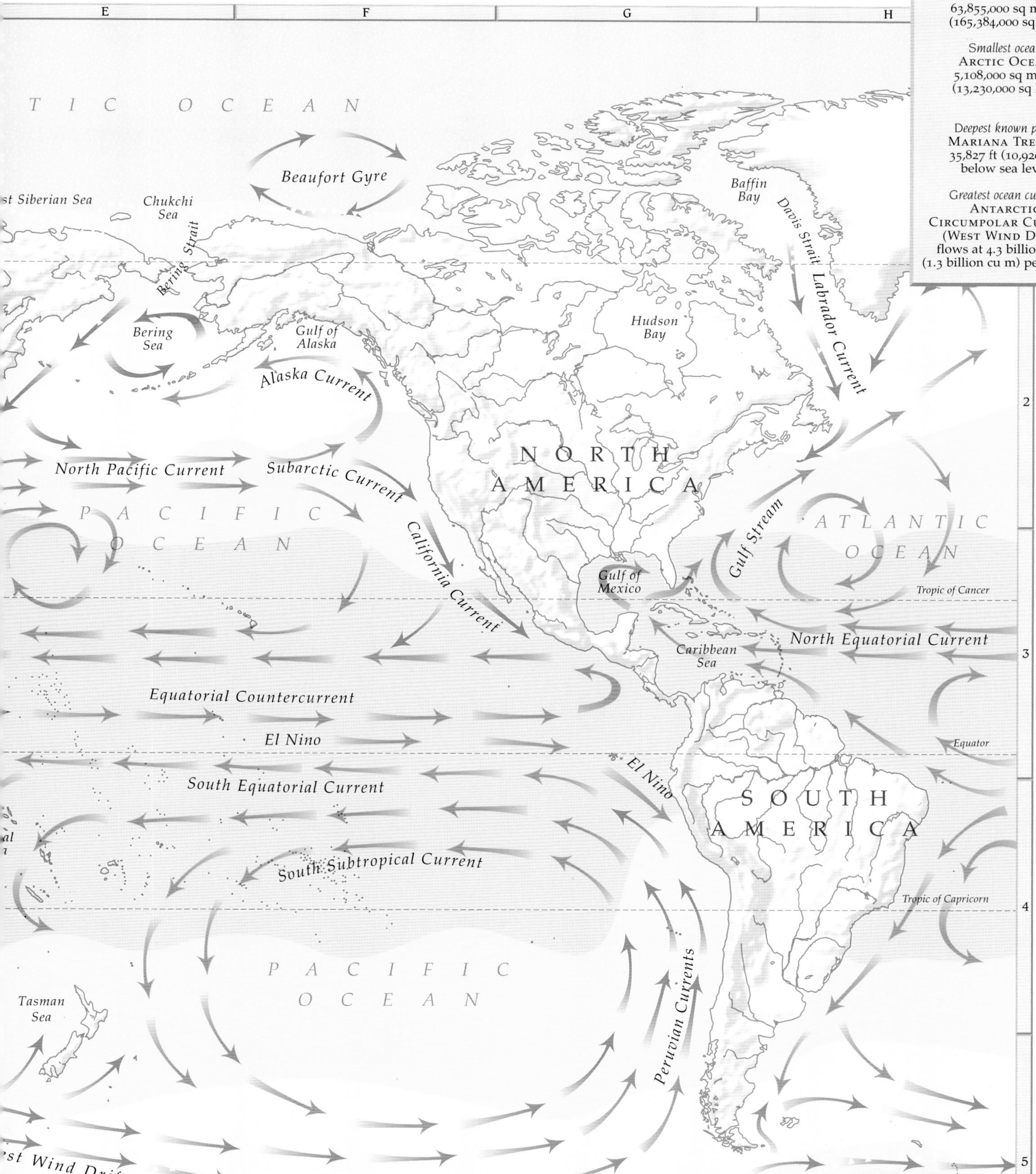
E
F
G
H
TIC OCEAN
Beaufort Gyre
st Siberian Sea
Chukchi Sea
Bering Strait
Bering Sea
Gulf of Alaska
Alaska Current
Baffin Bay
Davis Strait
Labrador Current
Hudson Bay
NORTH AMERICA
North Pacific Current
Subarctic Current
PACIFIC OCEAN
California Current
Gulf Stream
ATLANTIC OCEAN
Gulf of Mexico
Tropic of Cancer
North Equatorial Current
Caribbean Sea
Equatorial Countercurrent
El Nino
Equator
South Equatorial Current
El Nino
SOUTH AMERICA
South Subtropical Current
Tropic of Capricorn
PACIFIC OCEAN
Peruvian Currents
Tasman Sea
st Wind Drift
Antarctic Circle
ANTARCTICA
2
3
4
5

LIFE ZONES

A
B
C
D
1
2
3
4
5
ARCTIC
Severnaya Zemlya
Spitsbergen
Franz Josef Land
New Siberia Islands
Greenland Sea
Novaya Zemlya
Laptev Sea
Barents Sea
Kara Sea
Denmark Strait
Norwegian Sea
Scandinavia
Iceland
Yenisey
Central Siberian Plateau
Lena
Khrebet Cherskog
West Siberian Plain
Ob'
Ural Mountains
Siberia
North Sea
Baltic Sea
North European Plain
Volga
Sea of Okhotsk
British Isles
Lake Baikal
Sakha
EUROPE
ASIA
Alps
Altai Mountains
Manchurian Plain
Bay of Biscay
Aral Sea
Danube
Caucasus
Balkans Mts
Black Sea
Caspian Sea
Tien Shan
Gobi
Sea of Japan
Hokka
Iberian Peninsula
Anatolia
Pamirs
Kunlun Mountains
Yellow River
Japan
Honshū
Mediterranean Sea
Atlas Mts
Iranian Plateau
Plateau of Tibet
Yellow Sea
Zagros Mountains
Indus
Himalayas
Kyūshū
Yangtze
East China Sea
Sahara
Libyan Desert
Persian Gulf
Ganges
Ryukyu Islands
Ahaggar
Thar Desert
Tibesti
Nile
Red Sea
Arabian Peninsula
Deccan
Taiwan
AFRICA
Mekong
Sahel
Arabian Sea
Western Ghats
Eastern Ghats
Bay of Bengal
South China Sea
Mariana Islands
Lake Chad
Niger
Gulf of Aden
Ethiopian Highlands
Horn of Africa
Sri Lanka
Adamawa Highlands
Great Rift Valley
Malay Peninsula
Caroline
Gulf of Guinea
Congo Basin
Congo
Lake Victoria
Sumatra
Borneo
East Indies
Lake Tanganyika
Java Sea
Java
New Guinea
ATLANTIC OCEAN
INDIAN OCEAN
Great Rift Valley
Lake Nyasa
Arafura Sea
Timor Sea
Zambezi
Mozambique Channel
Madagascar
Great Barrier
Namib Desert
Kalahari Desert
Great Sandy Desert
AUSTRALIA
Great Victoria Desert
Drakensberg
Nullarbor Plain
Darling
Cape of Good Hope
Bass Strait
Tasmania
Kerguelen
ANTARCTICA

CLIMATE TYPES

- Polar
- Tundra
- Mountain
- Needleleaf Forest
- Broadleaf Forest
- Temperate Grassland
- Temperate Rain forest
- Mediterranean
- Dry Woodland
- Tropical Grassland
- Tropical Rain forest
- Hot Desert
- Cold Desert
- Wetland

Country with greatest biodiversity
BRAZIL

Country with greatest proportion of protected land
ECUADOR
(37.7%)

Most forested country in the world
SURINAME
91% covered by forest

E
F
G
H
OCEAN
st Siberian Sea
Beaufort Sea
Ellesmere Island
Queen Elizabeth Islands
Greenland
Baffin Bay
Baffin Island
Chukchi Sea
Brooks Range
Bering Strait
Mackenzie
Great Bear Lake
Great Slave Lake
Arctic Circle
Hudson Bay
Labrador Sea
Labrador
Canadian Shield
Bering Sea
Aleutian Islands
Gulf of Alaska
Coast Mountains
Rocky Mountains
Lake Winnipeg
NORTH AMERICA
Vancouver Island
Great Lakes
Coast Ranges
Great Plains
Appalachian Mts
Mississippi
ATLANTIC
OCEAN
Lower California
Sierra Madre Occidental
Sierra Madre Oriental
Gulf of Mexico
Tropic of Cancer
Hawaiian Islands
Hawaii
Polynesia
Yucatan Peninsula
Greater Antilles
West Indies
Caribbean Sea
Lesser Antilles
Micronesia
Marshall Islands
PACIFIC
Line Islands
Guiana Highlands
Equator
Galapagos Islands
Amazon
Amazon Basin
Phoenix Islands
Andes
SOUTH AMERICA
Marquesas Islands
Samoa
Cook Islands
Fiji
Tonga
Tuamotu Islands
Planalto de Mato Grosso
Brazilian Highlands
New Caledonia
Tropic of Capricorn
Gran Chaco
Paraná
OCEAN
Tasman Sea
North Island
South Island
New Zealand
Patagonia
Falkland Islands
Tierra del Fuego
Cape Horn
Drake Passage
Antarctic Peninsula
Antarctic Circle
2
3
4
5

POPULATION

A
B
C
D
1
2
3
4
5
SVALBARD (to Norway)
JAN MAYEN (to Norway)
ICELAND 78
FAEROE ISLANDS (to Denmark) 78
NORWAY 77
SWEDEN 78
FINLAND 76
EST. 70
LAT. 68
LITH. 70
DENMARK 75
UNITED KINGDOM 76
REPUBLIC OF IRELAND 75
NETH. 77
BELG. 77
GERMANY 76
POLAND 72
BELA. 69
UKRAINE 69
LUX. 76
FRANCE 78
SWITZ. 78
CZ. REP. 73
SLVK. 71
AUT. 77
HUNG. 69
ROM. 70
MOLD. 68
LIECH. 77
SLVN. 73
CRO. 71
MONACO 77
S.M. 81
ANDORRA 78
B.&H. 72
YUG. 72
BULG. 71
VAT. CITY
ALB. 72
MACED. 72
ITALY 77
PORT. 75
SPAIN 77
GREECE 77
GIBRALTAR (to UK) 76
MALTA 76
TUNISIA 68
CYPRUS 77
ISRAEL 77
LEBANON 75
SYRIA 66
TURKEY 67
GEORGIA 73
ARMENIA 71
AZERB. 71
AZ.
RUSSIAN FEDERATION 65
KAZAKHSTAN 69
UZBEK. 69
TURKMEN. 66
KYRG. 68
TAJ. 70
MONGOLIA 64
CHINA 69
N. KOREA 70
S. KOREA 72
JAPAN 79
IRAN 67
IRAQ 66
AFGH. 43
PAKISTAN 61
NEPAL 54
BHUTAN 51
BANGLADESH 58
INDIA 60
MYANMAR 60
MACAO (to Portugal) 79
TAIWAN 74
LAOS 52
THAI. 70
CAMB. 50
VIETNAM 65
PHILIPPINES 65
NORTHERN MARIANA ISLANDS (to US) 63
GUAM (to US)
MICRONESIA 68
PALAU 71
BRUNEI 74
MALAYSIA 71
SINGAPORE 74
INDONESIA
PAPUA NEW GUINEA
SRI LANKA 73
MALDIVES 63
JORDAN 72
KUWAIT 75
BAHRAIN 74
QATAR 72
U.A.E. 73
OMAN 71
SAUDI ARABIA 70
YEMEN 52
MOROCCO 69
WESTERN SAHARA (disputed)
ALGERIA 67
LIBYA 63
EGYPT 64
MAURITANIA 52
MALI 47
NIGER 47
CHAD 48
SUDAN 53
ERITREA
CAPE VERDE 65
SENEGAL 49
GAMBIA 45
GUINEA-BISSAU 44
GUINEA 44
BURKINA 45
NIGERIA 56
SIERRA LEONE 46
LIBERIA 55
IVORY COAST 51
GHANA 56
TOGO 58
BENIN 48
CAMEROON 58
EQ. GUINEA 54
SAO TOME & PRINCIPE 67
C.A.R. 41
DJIBOUTI 49
ETHIOPIA 48
SOMALIA 47
UGANDA 45
KENYA 56
RWANDA 47
BURUNDI 46
GABON 54
CONGO 53
CONGO (ZAIRE) 48
TANZANIA 49
SEYCHELLES 70
COMOROS 58
MAYOTTE (to France)
ANGOLA 46
ZAMBIA 48
MALAWI 44
MOZAMBIQUE 46
MADAGASCAR 57
MAURITIUS 69
REUNION (to France)
NAMIBIA 59
BOTS. 64
ZIMB. 53
SWAZILAND 57
LESOTHO 61
SOUTH AFRICA 66
ATLANTIC OCEAN
INDIAN OCEAN
AUSTRALIA 78
ANTARCTICA

POPULATION DENSITY PER SQUARE MILE

More than 195

115 – 195

77 – 115

38 – 77

11 – 38

Less than 11

Data not available

Most populated country
China
1,192 million people

Least populated country
Vatican City
738 people

Most densely populated country
Monaco
6,390 people per sq mile

Least densely populated country
Mongolia
0.3 people per sq mile

Highest fertility rate
Rwanda
average number of children per mother
8.5

Lowest fertility rate
Germany
average number of children per mother
1.5

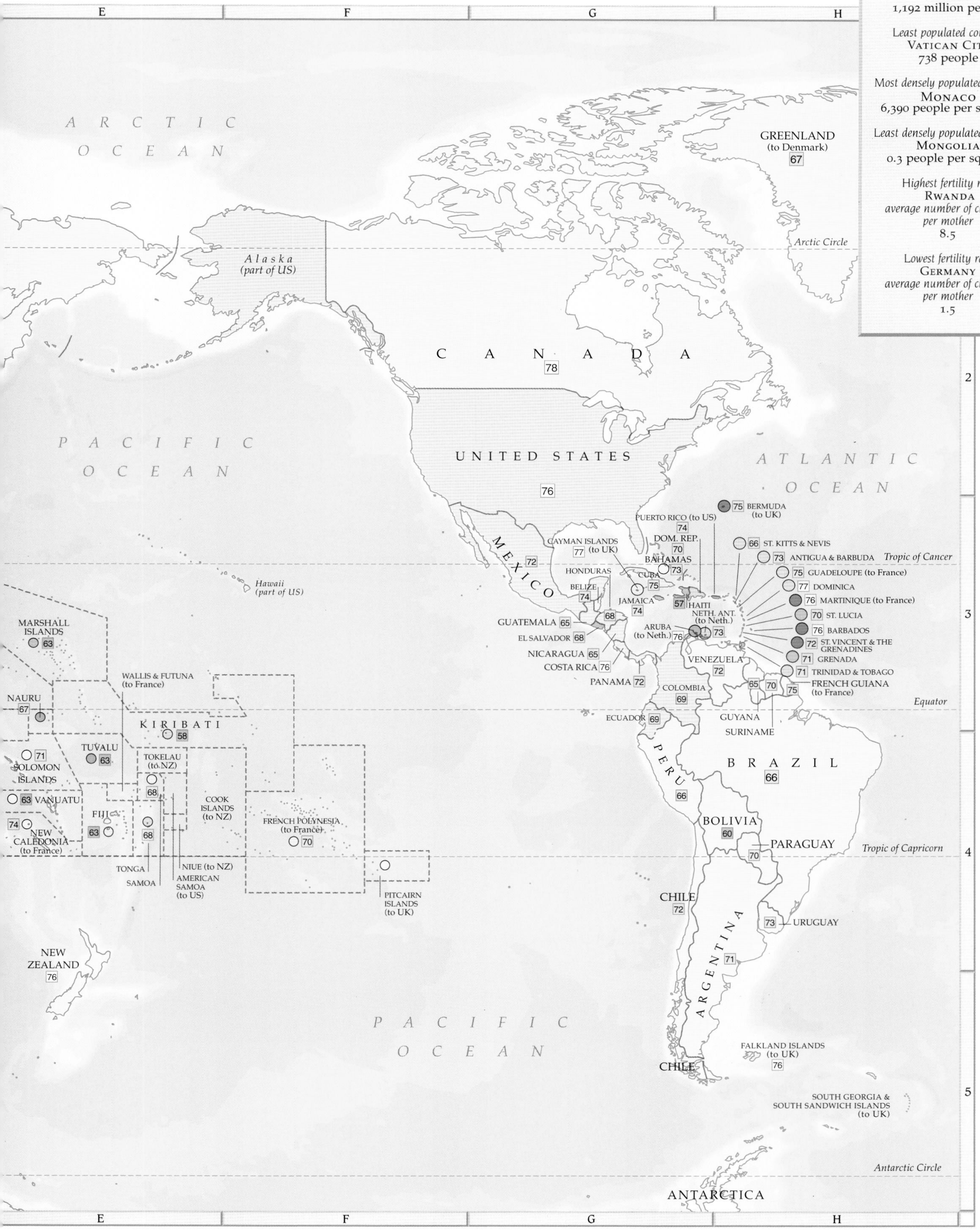
E
F
G
H
ARCTIC OCEAN
GREENLAND (to Denmark) 67
Arctic Circle
Alaska (part of US)
CANADA 78
2
PACIFIC OCEAN
UNITED STATES 76
ATLANTIC OCEAN
75 BERMUDA (to UK)
PUERTO RICO (to US) 74
DOM. REP. 70
CAYMAN ISLANDS (to UK) 77
MEXICO 72
BAHAMAS 73
66 ST. KITTS & NEVIS
73 ANTIGUA & BARBUDA
Tropic of Cancer
75 GUADELOUPE (to France)
77 DOMINICA
76 MARTINIQUE (to France)
70 ST. LUCIA
76 BARBADOS
72 ST. VINCENT & THE GRENADINES
71 GRENADA
71 TRINIDAD & TOBAGO
HONDURAS 68
CUBA 75
BELIZE 74
JAMAICA 74
57 HAITI
NETH. ANT. (to Neth.) 73
ARUBA (to Neth.) 76
Hawaii (part of US)
3
GUATEMALA 65
EL SALVADOR 68
NICARAGUA 65
COSTA RICA 76
PANAMA 72
VENEZUELA 72
COLOMBIA 69
65 70 75
FRENCH GUIANA (to France)
Equator
ECUADOR 69
GUYANA
SURINAME
MARSHALL ISLANDS 63
WALLIS & FUTUNA (to France)
NAURU 67
KIRIBATI 58
TUVALU 63
71 SOLOMON ISLANDS
TOKELAU (to NZ) 68
63 VANUATU
FIJI 63
74 NEW CALEDONIA (to France)
68
COOK ISLANDS (to NZ)
FRENCH POLYNESIA (to France) 70
TONGA
SAMOA
NIUE (to NZ)
AMERICAN SAMOA (to US)
PITCAIRN ISLANDS (to UK)
PERU 66
BRAZIL 66
BOLIVIA 60
PARAGUAY 70
Tropic of Capricorn
4
CHILE 72
73 URUGUAY
ARGENTINA 71
NEW ZEALAND 76
PACIFIC OCEAN
FALKLAND ISLANDS (to UK) 76
CHILE
5
SOUTH GEORGIA & SOUTH SANDWICH ISLANDS (to UK)
Antarctic Circle
ANTARCTICA
E
F
G
H

AVERAGE LIFE EXPECTANCY

More than 75
66 – 75
56 – 65
45 – 55
Less than 45

LANGUAGES

A
B
C
D
1
2
3
4
5
Icelandic
Lapp
Finnish
Germanic
Celtic
Slavic
Romance
Greek
Samoyed
Yakut
Mari
Tuvash
Mordvinian
Tungus-Manchu
Kazakh
Khalka Mongol
Oyrat
Turkic
Uighur
Mongol
Korean
Japanese
Mandarin
Pashto
Persian
Punjab
Hibu
Tibetan
Cantonese
Berber
Dravidian
Tamil
Austro-Asiatic
Filipino
Cebuano
Austronesian
Malay
Dayak
Bahasa Indonesia
Javanese
Papua
Fulani
Hausa
Bantu
Amharic
Somali
Swahili
Bantu
Bantu
Khoisan
Creoles
Malagasy
Afrikaans
Nguni
ATLANTIC OCEAN
INDIAN OCEAN

MAIN INTERNATIONAL LANGUAGES

- Chinese
- Spanish
- Arabic
- Hindi
- English
- French
- Russian
- Portuguese
- Arabic/French
- French/other
- English/other
- Arabic/other
- Hindi/English/Other
- Chinese/Other
- Russian/Other
- English/French
- English/Spanish
- Spanish/Other
- Portuguese/Other
- Other Language

Language Group *Bantu*

Other Language *Hausa*

Uninhabited Land

Languages spoken by greatest number of people

Mandarin Chinese
931,100,000 speakers

English
463,000,000 speakers

Hindi
400,000,000 speakers

Spanish
371,000,000 speakers

Russian
290,000,000 speakers

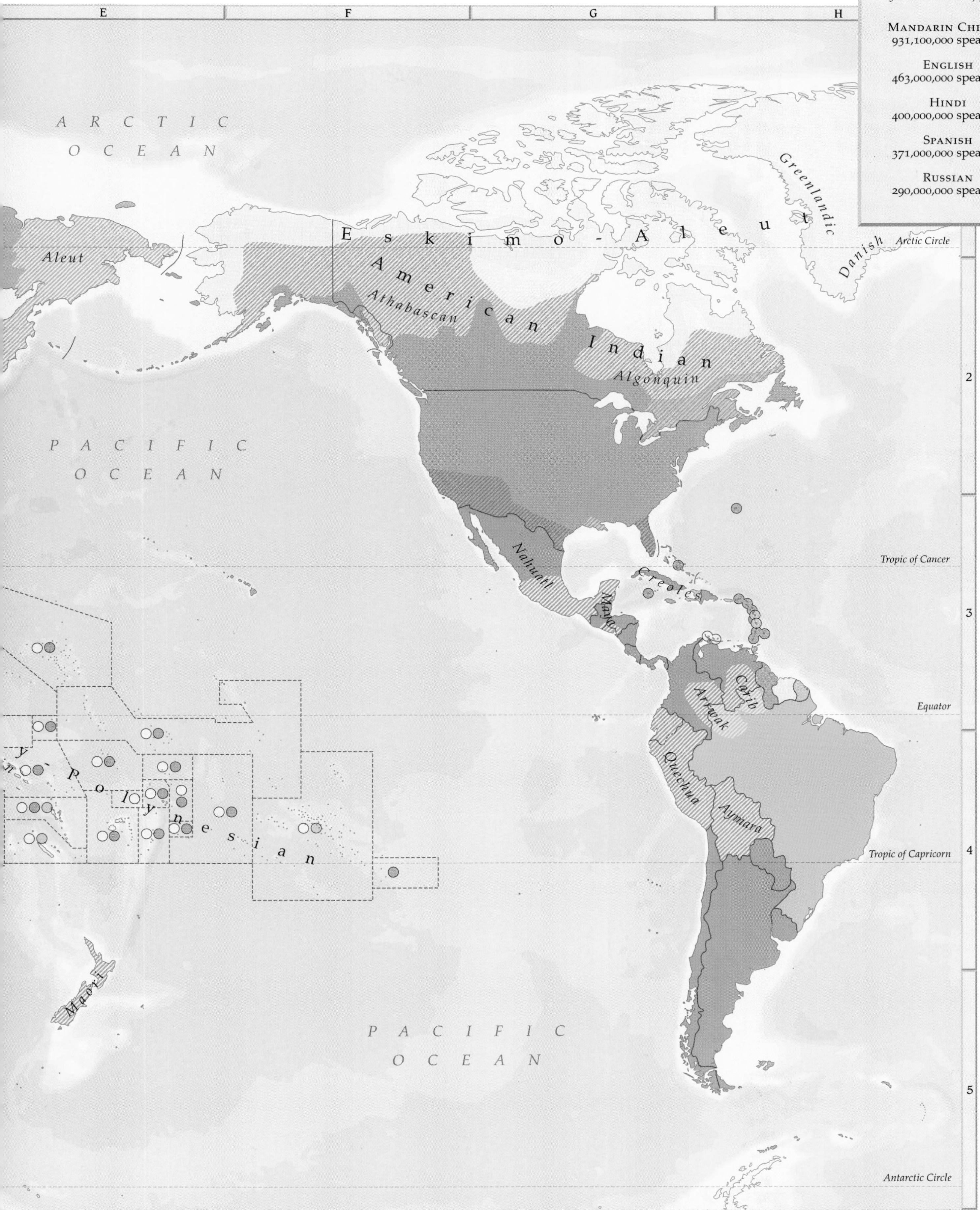
E
F
G
H
ARCTIC OCEAN
PACIFIC OCEAN
PACIFIC OCEAN
Aleut
Eskimo-Aleut
Greenlandic
Danish
Arctic Circle
American Indian
Athabascan
Algonquin
Tropic of Cancer
Nahuatl
Creoles
Maya
Carib
Arawak
Equator
Quechua
Aymara
Tropic of Capricorn
Polynesian
Maori
Antarctic Circle
2
3
4
5

Religion

MAJORITY RELIGIONS

- Chinese
- Protestant Christianity
- Catholic Christianity
- Orthodox Christianity
- Shi'a Islam
- Sunni Islam
- Hinduism
- Judaism
- Theravada Buddhism
- Mahayana Buddhism
- Tibetan Buddhism
- Other

Estimated number of adherents to each religion

CHRISTIANITY
1.6 billion

ISLAM
1.1 billion

HINDUISM
750 million

BUDDHISM
340 million

CHINESE RELIGIONS
260 million

E
F
G
H
ARCTIC OCEAN
GREENLAND
(to Denmark)
Arctic Circle
Alaska
(part of US)
CANADA
2
PACIFIC OCEAN
UNITED STATES
ATLANTIC OCEAN
BERMUDA
(to UK)
PUERTO RICO
(to US)
DOM. REP.
BRITISH VIRGIN ISLANDS (to UK)
VIRGIN ISLANDS (to US)
ANGUILLA (to UK)
ST. KITTS & NEVIS
ANTIGUA & BARBUDA
MONTSERRAT (to UK)
GUADELOUPE (to France)
DOMINICA
MARTINIQUE (to France)
ST. LUCIA
BARBADOS
ST. VINCENT & THE GRENADINES
GRENADA
TRINIDAD & TOBAGO
TURKS & CAICOS ISLANDS (to UK)
CAYMAN ISLANDS
(to UK)
BAHAMAS
Tropic of Cancer
MEXICO
HONDURAS
BELIZE
CUBA
Hawaii
(part of US)
JAMAICA
HAITI
NETH. ANT.
(to Neth.)
ARUBA
(to Neth.)
3
MARSHALL ISLANDS
GUATEMALA
EL SALVADOR
NICARAGUA
COSTA RICA
PANAMA
VENEZUELA
COLOMBIA
FRENCH GUIANA
(to France)
Equator
NAURU
KIRIBATI
ECUADOR
GUYANA
SURINAME
TUVALU
TOKELAU
(to NZ)
SOLOMON ISLANDS
BRAZIL
PERU
VANUATU
COOK ISLANDS
(to NZ)
NEW CALEDONIA
(to France)
FIJI
FRENCH POLYNESIA
(to France)
BOLIVIA
PARAGUAY
Tropic of Capricorn
4
TONGA
SAMOA
AMERICAN SAMOA
(to US)
PITCAIRN ISLANDS
(to UK)
CHILE
URUGUAY
ARGENTINA
NEW ZEALAND
PACIFIC OCEAN
FALKLAND ISLANDS
(to UK)
CHILE
5
Antarctic Circle
ANTARCTICA

STATE POLICY

Secular Ideologies Governing ▲

Marxist states during 20th Century ●

Non-pluralist states ■

The Global Economy

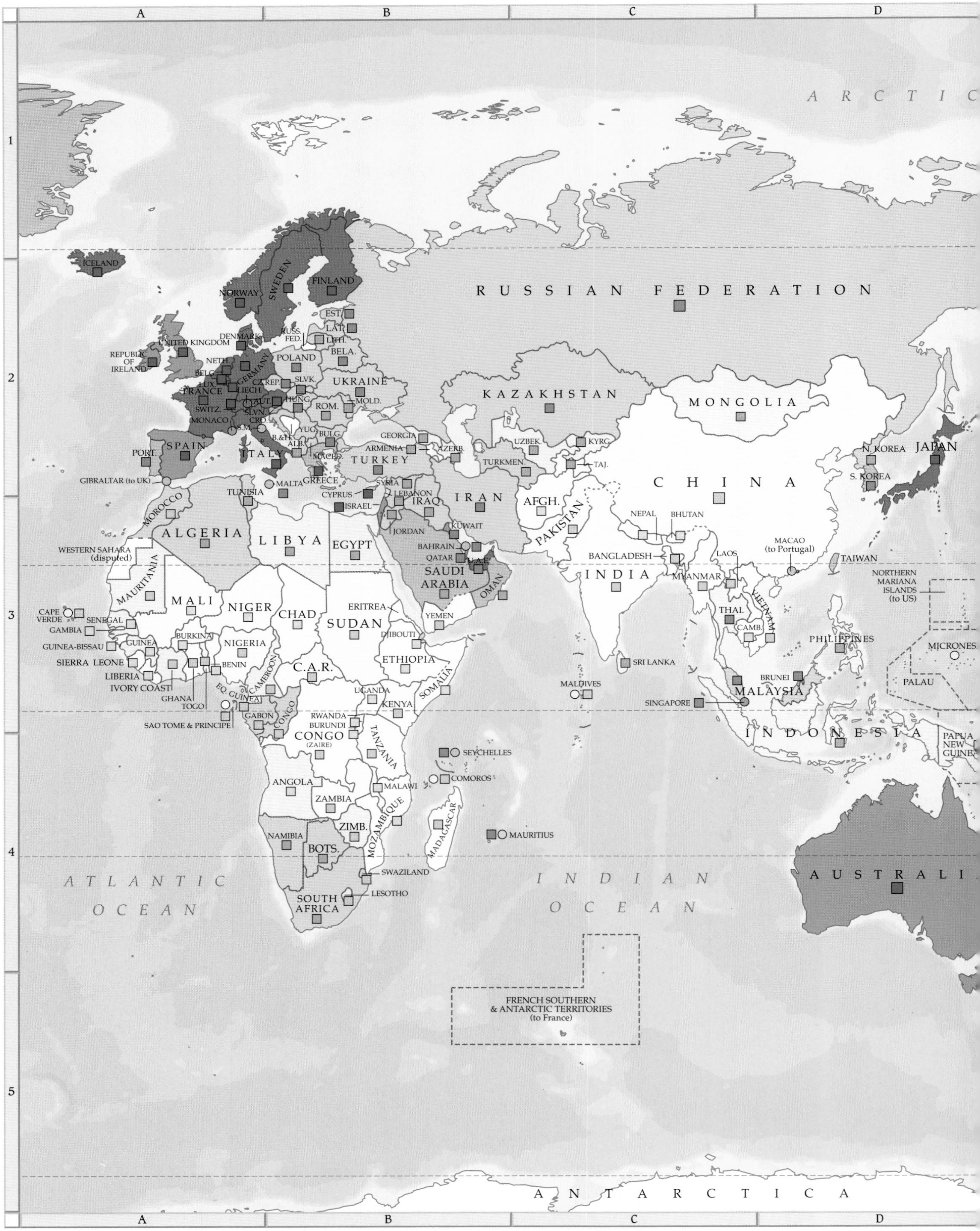
A
B
C
D
1
2
3
4
5
ARCTIC
ICELAND
NORWAY
SWEDEN
FINLAND
RUSSIAN FEDERATION
EST.
LAT.
LITH.
RUSS. FED.
DENMARK
UNITED KINGDOM
REPUBLIC OF IRELAND
NETH.
BELG.
LUX.
GERMANY
POLAND
BELA.
UKRAINE
CZ. REP.
SLVK.
LIECH.
FRANCE
SWITZ.
AUT.
HUNG.
MOLD.
ROM.
SLVN.
CRO.
MONACO
S.M.
B.&H.
YUG.
BULG.
ALB.
MACED.
GREECE
PORT.
SPAIN
ITALY
GIBRALTAR (to UK)
MALTA
TUNISIA
MOROCCO
ALGERIA
LIBYA
EGYPT
WESTERN SAHARA (disputed)
MAURITANIA
MALI
NIGER
CHAD
SUDAN
ERITREA
DJIBOUTI
ETHIOPIA
SOMALIA
CAPE VERDE
SENEGAL
GAMBIA
GUINEA-BISSAU
GUINEA
SIERRA LEONE
LIBERIA
IVORY COAST
BURKINA
GHANA
TOGO
BENIN
NIGERIA
CAMEROON
C.A.R.
EQ. GUINEA
SAO TOME & PRINCIPE
GABON
CONGO
CONGO (ZAIRE)
UGANDA
KENYA
RWANDA
BURUNDI
TANZANIA
ANGOLA
ZAMBIA
MALAWI
MOZAMBIQUE
ZIMB.
NAMIBIA
BOTS.
SWAZILAND
LESOTHO
SOUTH AFRICA
MADAGASCAR
SEYCHELLES
COMOROS
MAURITIUS
TURKEY
GEORGIA
ARMENIA
AZERB.
CYPRUS
SYRIA
LEBANON
ISRAEL
JORDAN
IRAQ
IRAN
KUWAIT
BAHRAIN
QATAR
U.A.E.
SAUDI ARABIA
OMAN
YEMEN
KAZAKHSTAN
UZBEK.
TURKMEN.
KYRG.
TAJ.
AFGH.
PAKISTAN
MONGOLIA
CHINA
NEPAL
BHUTAN
BANGLADESH
INDIA
SRI LANKA
MALDIVES
MYANMAR
LAOS
THAI.
VIETNAM
CAMB.
MACAO (to Portugal)
TAIWAN
N. KOREA
S. KOREA
JAPAN
PHILIPPINES
BRUNEI
MALAYSIA
SINGAPORE
INDONESIA
NORTHERN MARIANA ISLANDS (to US)
PALAU
PAPUA NEW GUINEA
AUSTRALIA
ATLANTIC OCEAN
INDIAN OCEAN
FRENCH SOUTHERN & ANTARCTIC TERRITORIES (to France)
ANTARCTICA

ECONOMIC PERFORMANCE
GNP *per capita* 1995 $US

- *More than* 20,000
- 10,000 *to* 20,000
- 5,000 *to* 10,000
- 1,000 *to* 5,000
- 500 *to* 1,000
- 250 *to* 500
- *Less than* 250
- *Data not available*

45% of world trade is accounted for by
FRANCE
GERMANY
JAPAN
UK
USA

Highest GNP per capita
SWITZERLAND
US$ 36,230

Lowest GNP per capita
MOZAMBIQUE
US$ 70

E
F
G
H
OCEAN
GREENLAND (to Denmark)
Arctic Circle
Alaska (part of US)
CANADA
UNITED STATES
PACIFIC OCEAN
ATLANTIC OCEAN
BERMUDA (to UK)
PUERTO RICO (to US)
DOM. REP.
TURKS & CAICOS ISLANDS (to UK)
CAYMAN ISLANDS (to UK)
BAHAMAS
ST. KITTS & NEVIS
ANTIGUA & BARBUDA
Tropic of Cancer
GUADELOUPE (to France)
DOMINICA
MARTINIQUE (to France)
ST. LUCIA
BARBADOS
ST. VINCENT & THE GRENADINES
GRENADA
TRINIDAD & TOBAGO
MEXICO
HONDURAS
BELIZE
CUBA
JAMAICA
HAITI
NETH. ANT. (to Neth.)
ARUBA (to Neth.)
GUATEMALA
EL SALVADOR
NICARAGUA
COSTA RICA
PANAMA
VENEZUELA
COLOMBIA
FRENCH GUIANA (to France)
GUYANA
SURINAME
Equator
ECUADOR
Hawaii (part of US)
MARSHALL ISLANDS
NAURU
KIRIBATI
TUVALU
TOKELAU (to NZ)
SOLOMON ISLANDS
SAMOA
VANUATU
TONGA
FIJI
NEW CALEDONIA (to France)
FRENCH POLYNESIA (to France)
PITCAIRN ISLANDS (to UK)
PERU
BRAZIL
BOLIVIA
PARAGUAY
Tropic of Capricorn
CHILE
URUGUAY
ARGENTINA
NEW ZEALAND
PACIFIC OCEAN
FALKLAND ISLANDS (to UK)
CHILE
Antarctic Circle
ANTARCTICA
2
3
4
5

HUMAN DEVELOPMENT INDEX (HDI)

High HDI

Low HDI

HDI is one of the best indicators of economic development. The single index is reached by measuring life expectancy at birth, per capita purchasing power, literacy rates and years of schooling

Global Conflict

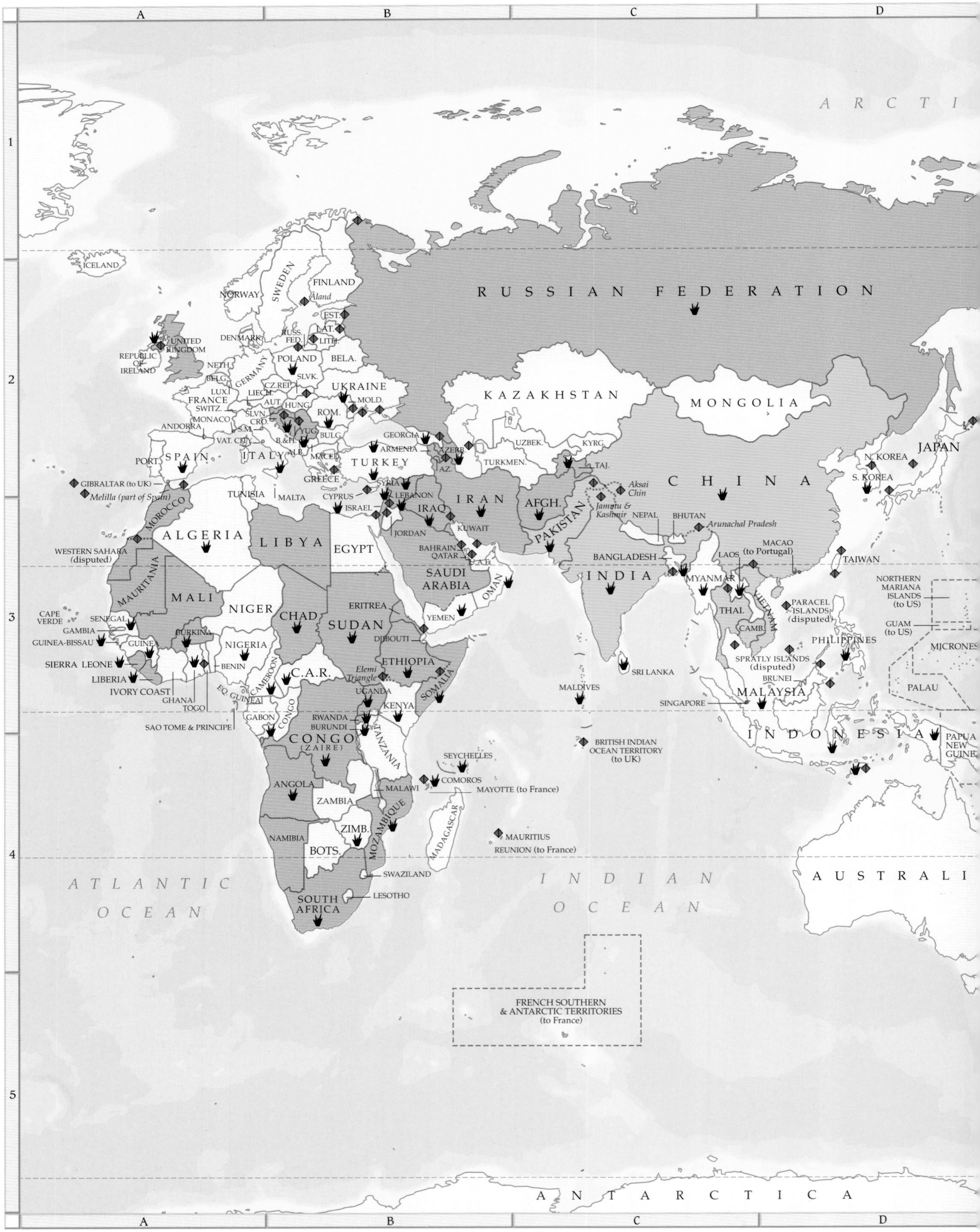
A
B
C
D
1
2
3
4
5
A R C T I
ICELAND
NORWAY
SWEDEN
FINLAND
Aland
EST.
LAT.
LITH.
RUSS. FED.
DENMARK
UNITED KINGDOM
REPUBLIC OF IRELAND
NETH.
BELG.
LUX.
GERMANY
POLAND
BELA.
CZ.REP.
SLVK.
UKRAINE
MOLD.
LIECH.
AUT.
HUNG.
ROM.
FRANCE
SWITZ.
MONACO
SLVN.
CRO.
ANDORRA
S.M.
B.&H.
YUG.
BULG.
VAT. CITY
ALB.
MACED.
PORT.
SPAIN
ITALY
GREECE
TURKEY
GEORGIA
ARMENIA
AZERB.
AZ.
GIBRALTAR (to UK)
Melilla (part of Spain)
TUNISIA
MALTA
CYPRUS
SYRIA
LEBANON
ISRAEL
JORDAN
IRAQ
IRAN
KUWAIT
BAHRAIN
QATAR
U.A.E.
SAUDI ARABIA
OMAN
YEMEN
MOROCCO
ALGERIA
LIBYA
EGYPT
WESTERN SAHARA (disputed)
MAURITANIA
MALI
NIGER
CHAD
SUDAN
ERITREA
DJIBOUTI
ETHIOPIA
SOMALIA
Elemi Triangle
CAPE VERDE
SENEGAL
GAMBIA
GUINEA-BISSAU
GUINEA
BURKINA
SIERRA LEONE
LIBERIA
IVORY COAST
GHANA
TOGO
BENIN
NIGERIA
CAMEROON
C.A.R.
EQ. GUINEA
SAO TOME & PRINCIPE
GABON
CONGO
CONGO (ZAIRE)
UGANDA
KENYA
RWANDA
BURUNDI
TANZANIA
SEYCHELLES
COMOROS
MAYOTTE (to France)
ANGOLA
ZAMBIA
MALAWI
MOZAMBIQUE
ZIMB.
NAMIBIA
BOTS.
MADAGASCAR
MAURITIUS
REUNION (to France)
SWAZILAND
LESOTHO
SOUTH AFRICA
RUSSIAN FEDERATION
KAZAKHSTAN
MONGOLIA
UZBEK.
KYRG.
TURKMEN.
TAJ.
AFGH.
PAKISTAN
Aksai Chin
Jammu & Kashmir
NEPAL
BHUTAN
Arunachal Pradesh
CHINA
N. KOREA
S. KOREA
JAPAN
BANGLADESH
INDIA
MYANMAR
LAOS
MACAO (to Portugal)
TAIWAN
THAI.
VIETNAM
CAMB.
PARACEL ISLANDS (disputed)
PHILIPPINES
SPRATLY ISLANDS (disputed)
BRUNEI
MALAYSIA
SINGAPORE
INDONESIA
PAPUA NEW GUINE
NORTHERN MARIANA ISLANDS (to US)
GUAM (to US)
MICRONES
PALAU
SRI LANKA
MALDIVES
BRITISH INDIAN OCEAN TERRITORY (to UK)
ATLANTIC OCEAN
INDIAN OCEAN
AUSTRALI
FRENCH SOUTHERN & ANTARCTIC TERRITORIES (to France)
ANTARCTICA

STATE POLICY

International conflict since 1975

Civil unrest since 1975

Disputed Territories

Disputed Territories ....

Disputed Territories - - - - -

Origins of major refugee populations (1997)
AFGHANISTAN 2,350,000
RWANDA 1,700,000
BOSNIA & HERZEGOVINA 1,330,000
LIBERIA 750,000
E
F
G
H
2
3
4
5
OCEAN
GREENLAND (to Denmark)
Arctic Circle
Alaska (part of US)
CANADA
Kurile Islands (part of Russ.Fed.)
ST. PIERRE & MIQUELON (to France)
PACIFIC OCEAN
UNITED STATES
ATLANTIC OCEAN
BERMUDA (to UK)
PUERTO RICO (to US)
BRITISH VIRGIN ISLANDS (to UK)
VIRGIN ISLANDS (to US)
ANGUILLA (to UK)
ST. KITTS & NEVIS
ANTIGUA & BARBUDA
MONTSERRAT (to UK)
GUADELOUPE (to France)
DOMINICA
MARTINIQUE (to France)
ST. LUCIA
BARBADOS
ST. VINCENT & THE GRENADINES
GRENADA
TRINIDAD & TOBAGO
DOM. REP.
TURKS & CAICOS ISLANDS (to UK)
CAYMAN ISLANDS (to UK)
BAHAMAS
Tropic of Cancer
MEXICO
HONDURAS
BELIZE
CUBA
JAMAICA
NAVASSA I. (to US)
HAITI
NETH. ANT. (to Neth.)
ARUBA (to Neth.)
GUATEMALA
EL SALVADOR
NICARAGUA
COSTA RICA
PANAMA
Hawaii (part of US)
MARSHALL ISLANDS
WALLIS & FUTUNA (to France)
KINGMAN REEF (to US)
PALMYRA ATOLL (to US)
BAKER & HOWLAND ISLANDS (to US)
JARVIS ISLAND (to US)
NAURU
KIRIBATI
TUVALU
SOLOMON ISLANDS
TOKELAU (to NZ)
VANUATU
COOK ISLANDS (to NZ)
NEW CALEDONIA (to France)
FIJI
FRENCH POLYNESIA (to France)
TONGA
SAMOA
NIUE (to NZ)
AMERICAN SAMOA (to US)
PITCAIRN ISLANDS (to UK)
VENEZUELA
COLOMBIA
FRENCH GUIANA (to France)
Equator
ECUADOR
GUYANA
SURINAME
PERU
BRAZIL
BOLIVIA
PARAGUAY
Tropic of Capricorn
CHILE
URUGUAY
ARGENTINA
NEW ZEALAND
PACIFIC OCEAN
FALKLAND ISLANDS (to UK)
CHILE
Antarctic Circle
ANTARCTICA

Governments of the World

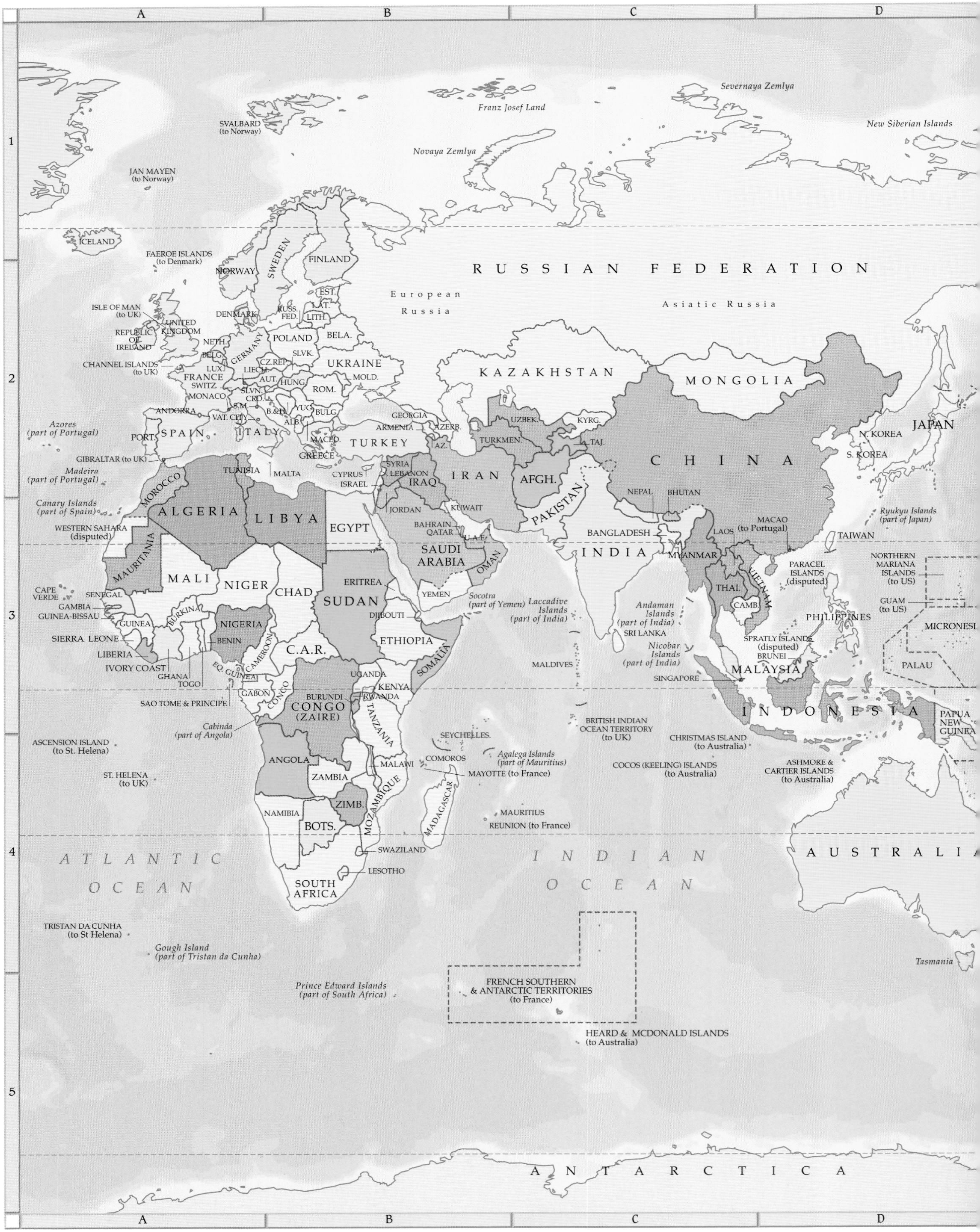
A
B
C
D
1
2
3
4
5
Severnaya Zemlya
Franz Josef Land
New Siberian Islands
SVALBARD (to Norway)
Novaya Zemlya
JAN MAYEN (to Norway)
ICELAND
FAEROE ISLANDS (to Denmark)
NORWAY
SWEDEN
FINLAND
RUSSIAN FEDERATION
European Russia
Asiatic Russia
EST.
LAT.
LITH.
RUSS. FED.
DENMARK
ISLE OF MAN (to UK)
UNITED KINGDOM
REPUBLIC OF IRELAND
NETH.
BELG.
LUX.
GERMANY
POLAND
BELA.
SLVK.
CZ.REP.
LIECH.
UKRAINE
CHANNEL ISLANDS (to UK)
FRANCE
SWITZ.
AUT.
HUNG.
MOLD.
MONACO
SLVN.
CRO.
ROM.
S.M.
B.&H.
YUG.
BULG.
ANDORRA
VAT. CITY
ALB.
Azores (part of Portugal)
PORT.
SPAIN
ITALY
MACED.
GREECE
TURKEY
GEORGIA
ARMENIA
AZERB.
AZ.
KAZAKHSTAN
MONGOLIA
UZBEK.
KYRG.
TURKMEN.
TAJ.
N. KOREA
JAPAN
S. KOREA
CHINA
GIBRALTAR (to UK)
Madeira (part of Portugal)
MOROCCO
TUNISIA
MALTA
CYPRUS
ISRAEL
SYRIA
LEBANON
IRAQ
IRAN
AFGH.
PAKISTAN
NEPAL
BHUTAN
Canary Islands (part of Spain)
ALGERIA
LIBYA
EGYPT
JORDAN
KUWAIT
BAHRAIN
QATAR
U.A.E.
SAUDI ARABIA
OMAN
BANGLADESH
INDIA
MYANMAR
LAOS
MACAO (to Portugal)
TAIWAN
Ryukyu Islands (part of Japan)
WESTERN SAHARA (disputed)
MAURITANIA
MALI
NIGER
CHAD
SUDAN
ERITREA
YEMEN
Socotra (part of Yemen)
Laccadive Islands (part of India)
THAI.
VIETNAM
CAMB.
PARACEL ISLANDS (disputed)
PHILIPPINES
NORTHERN MARIANA ISLANDS (to US)
GUAM (to US)
CAPE VERDE
SENEGAL
GAMBIA
GUINEA-BISSAU
GUINEA
BURKINA
NIGERIA
BENIN
DJIBOUTI
ETHIOPIA
SOMALIA
Andaman Islands (part of India)
SRI LANKA
Nicobar Islands (part of India)
SPRATLY ISLANDS (disputed)
BRUNEI
MALAYSIA
MICRONESIA
PALAU
SIERRA LEONE
LIBERIA
IVORY COAST
GHANA
TOGO
CAMEROON
C.A.R.
EQ. GUINEA
GABON
CONGO
UGANDA
KENYA
MALDIVES
SINGAPORE
SAO TOME & PRINCIPE
BURUNDI
RWANDA
CONGO (ZAIRE)
TANZANIA
INDONESIA
PAPUA NEW GUINEA
Cabinda (part of Angola)
BRITISH INDIAN OCEAN TERRITORY (to UK)
CHRISTMAS ISLAND (to Australia)
ASCENSION ISLAND (to St. Helena)
SEYCHELLES
Agalega Islands (part of Mauritius)
ANGOLA
COMOROS
MALAWI
MAYOTTE (to France)
COCOS (KEELING) ISLANDS (to Australia)
ASHMORE & CARTIER ISLANDS (to Australia)
ST. HELENA (to UK)
ZAMBIA
MOZAMBIQUE
MADAGASCAR
ZIMB.
NAMIBIA
BOTS.
MAURITIUS
REUNION (to France)
SWAZILAND
ATLANTIC OCEAN
INDIAN OCEAN
AUSTRALIA
LESOTHO
SOUTH AFRICA
TRISTAN DA CUNHA (to St Helena)
Gough Island (part of Tristan da Cunha)
Tasmania
Prince Edward Islands (part of South Africa)
FRENCH SOUTHERN & ANTARCTIC TERRITORIES (to France)
HEARD & MCDONALD ISLANDS (to Australia)
ANTARCTICA

TYPES OF GOVERNMENT

- Multiparty Democracy for over 10 years
- Multiparty/Transitional Democracy within last 10 years
- Single Party Government
- Military Regime
- Monarchy or Theocracy
- State of Unrest/Civil War

Newest independent country
PALAU – 1994

Largest political party
COMMUNIST PARTY, CHINA
50.3 million members

Longest term in power
MONGOLIAN PEOPLE'S REVOLUTIONARY PARTY (COMMUNIST PARTY)
In power from 1924 to 1996

Most changes of government
EL SALVADOR
Since independence in 1822, the government has changed on average every 18 months

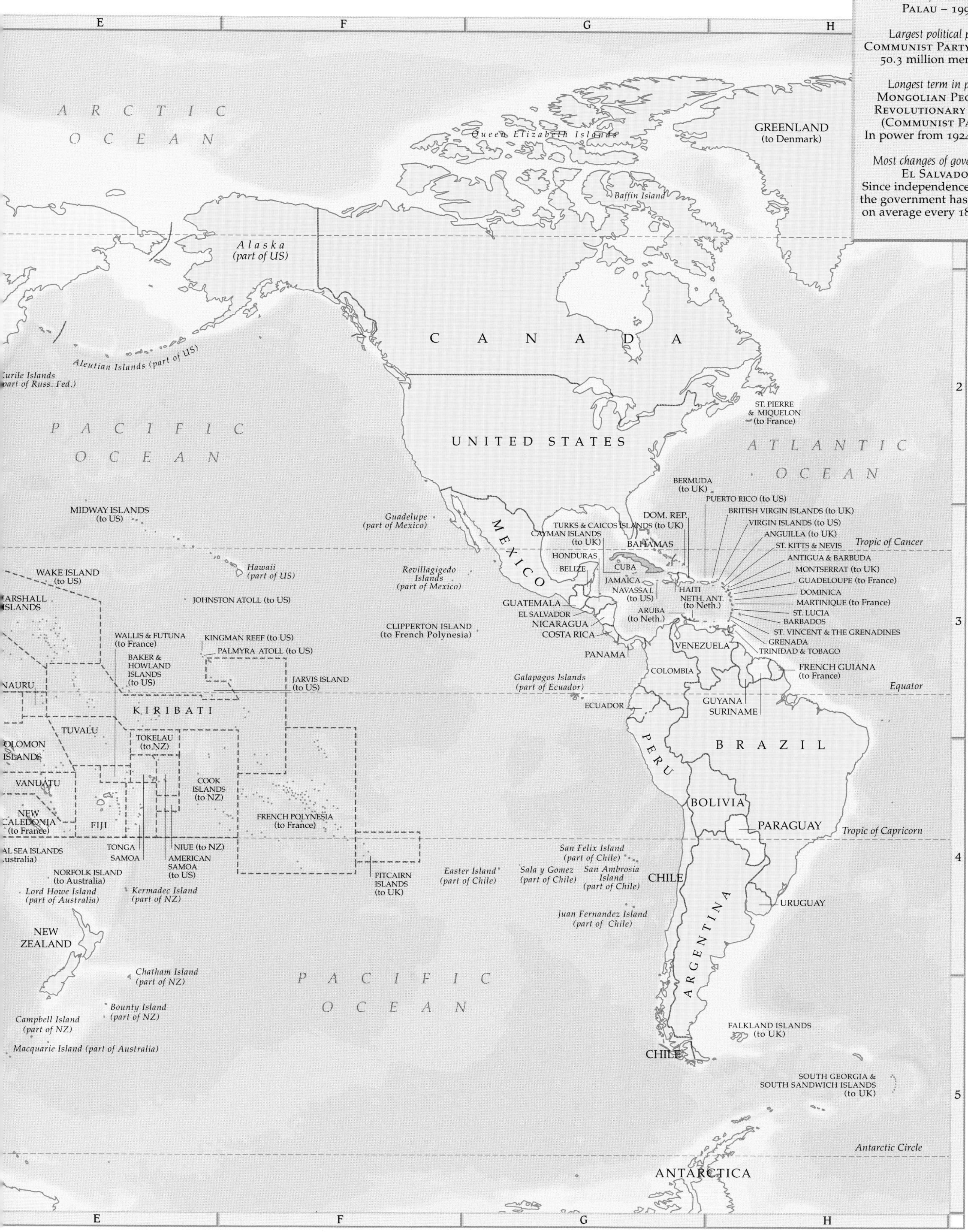
E
F
G
H
ARCTIC OCEAN
Queen Elizabeth Islands
GREENLAND
(to Denmark)
Baffin Island
Alaska
(part of US)
CANADA
Aleutian Islands (part of US)
Kurile Islands
(part of Russ. Fed.)
2
ST. PIERRE & MIQUELON
(to France)
PACIFIC OCEAN
UNITED STATES
ATLANTIC OCEAN
BERMUDA
(to UK)
PUERTO RICO (to US)
DOM. REP.
BRITISH VIRGIN ISLANDS (to UK)
MIDWAY ISLANDS
(to US)
Guadelupe
(part of Mexico)
MEXICO
TURKS & CAICOS ISLANDS (to UK)
VIRGIN ISLANDS (to US)
CAYMAN ISLANDS
(to UK)
ANGUILLA (to UK)
BAHAMAS
ST. KITTS & NEVIS
Tropic of Cancer
HONDURAS
ANTIGUA & BARBUDA
WAKE ISLAND
(to US)
Hawaii
(part of US)
Revillagigedo Islands
(part of Mexico)
BELIZE
CUBA
MONTSERRAT (to UK)
JAMAICA
GUADELOUPE (to France)
HAITI
DOMINICA
NAVASSA I.
(to US)
NETH. ANT.
(to Neth.)
MARTINIQUE (to France)
MARSHALL ISLANDS
JOHNSTON ATOLL (to US)
GUATEMALA
ARUBA
(to Neth.)
ST. LUCIA
EL SALVADOR
BARBADOS
CLIPPERTON ISLAND
(to French Polynesia)
NICARAGUA
ST. VINCENT & THE GRENADINES
3
WALLIS & FUTUNA
(to France)
KINGMAN REEF (to US)
COSTA RICA
GRENADA
VENEZUELA
PALMYRA ATOLL (to US)
PANAMA
TRINIDAD & TOBAGO
BAKER & HOWLAND ISLANDS
(to US)
FRENCH GUIANA
(to France)
JARVIS ISLAND
(to US)
Galapagos Islands
(part of Ecuador)
COLOMBIA
NAURU
Equator
KIRIBATI
GUYANA
ECUADOR
SURINAME
TUVALU
TOKELAU
(to NZ)
SOLOMON ISLANDS
PERU
BRAZIL
VANUATU
COOK ISLANDS
(to NZ)
BOLIVIA
NEW CALEDONIA
(to France)
FRENCH POLYNESIA
(to France)
FIJI
PARAGUAY
Tropic of Capricorn
CORAL SEA ISLANDS
(to Australia)
TONGA
NIUE (to NZ)
San Felix Island
(part of Chile)
SAMOA
AMERICAN SAMOA
(to US)
4
NORFOLK ISLAND
(to Australia)
Easter Island
(part of Chile)
Sala y Gomez
(part of Chile)
San Ambrosia Island
(part of Chile)
CHILE
PITCAIRN ISLANDS
(to UK)
Lord Howe Island
(part of Australia)
Kermadec Island
(part of NZ)
URUGUAY
Juan Fernandez Island
(part of Chile)
ARGENTINA
NEW ZEALAND
Chatham Island
(part of NZ)
PACIFIC OCEAN
Bounty Island
(part of NZ)
Campbell Island
(part of NZ)
FALKLAND ISLANDS
(to UK)
Macquarie Island (part of Australia)
CHILE
SOUTH GEORGIA & SOUTH SANDWICH ISLANDS
(to UK)
5
Antarctic Circle
ANTARCTICA
E
F
G
H

ABBREVIATIONS

AFGH. Afghanistan
ALB. Albania
AUT. Austria
AZ. or AZERB. Azerbaijan
B. & H. Bosnia & Herzegovina
BELG. Belgium
BULG. Bulgaria
BOTS. Botswana
CAMB. Cambodia
CRO. Croatia
CZ. REP. Czech Republic
DOM. REP. Dominican Republic
EST. Estonia
HUNG. Hungary
KYRG. Kyrgyzstan
LAT. Latvia
LIECH. Liechtenstein
LITH. Lithuania
LUX. Luxembourg
MACED. Macedonia
MOLD. Moldova
NETH. Netherlands
NETH. ANT. Netherlands Antilles
PORT. Portugal
ROM. Romania
RUSS. FED. Russian Federation
SLVK. Slovakia
SLVN Slovenia
S. M. San Marino
SWITZ. Switzerland
TAJ. Tajikistan
THAI. Thailand
TURKMEN. Turkmenistan
U. A. E. United Arab Emirates
UZBEK. Uzbekistan
VAT. CITY Vatican City
YUG. Yugoslavia
ZIMB. Zimbabwe

World Tourism

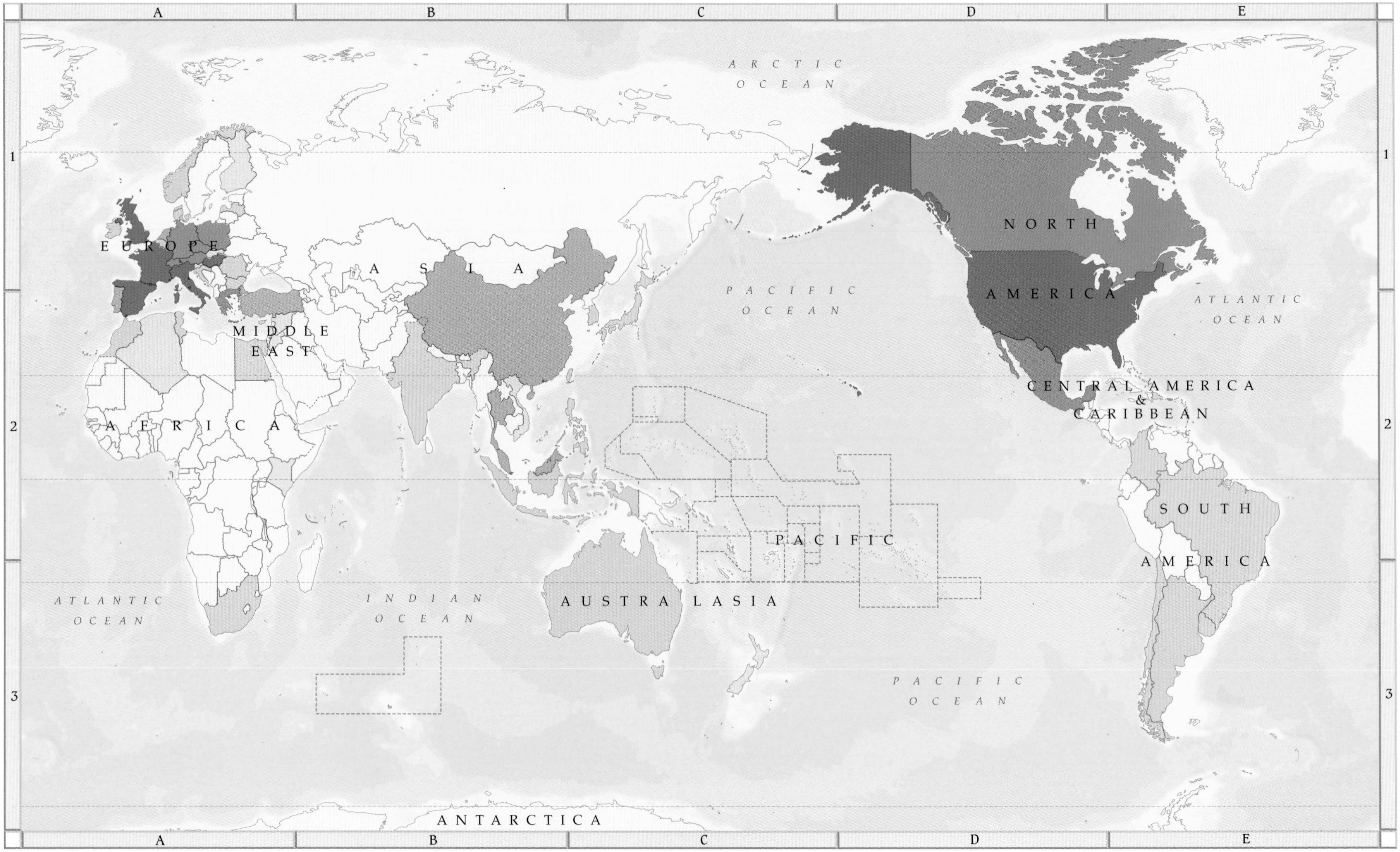
A
B
C
D
E
1
2
3
ARCTIC OCEAN
EUROPE
ASIA
MIDDLE EAST
AFRICA
PACIFIC OCEAN
NORTH AMERICA
ATLANTIC OCEAN
CENTRAL AMERICA & CARIBBEAN
SOUTH AMERICA
PACIFIC
AUSTRALASIA
INDIAN OCEAN
ANTARCTICA

TOURIST ARRIVALS

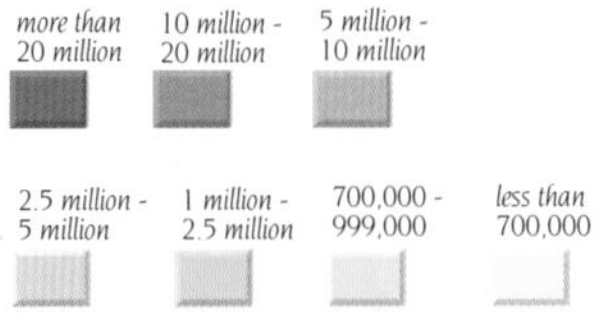
more than 20 million
10 million - 20 million
5 million - 10 million
2.5 million - 5 million
1 million - 2.5 million
700,000 - 999,000
less than 700,000

REGIONAL MARKET SHARE OF GLOBAL TOURIST RECEIPTS

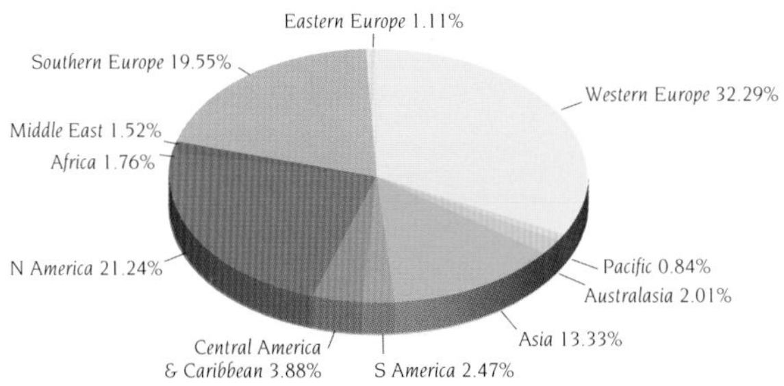
Eastern Europe 1.11%
Southern Europe 19.55%
Western Europe 32.29%
Middle East 1.52%
Africa 1.76%
N America 21.24%
Pacific 0.84%
Australasia 2.01%
Asia 13.33%
Central America & Caribbean 3.88%
S America 2.47%

Most popular tourist destinations
FRANCE, UNITED STATES OF AMERICA, SPAIN, ITALY, UNITED KINGDOM, HUNGARY, MEXICO, POLAND, AUSTRIA, CANADA

Tourists visiting France, 1995
61 MILLION

Number of tourists worldwide, 1995
567 MILLION

Estimated number of tourists, 2010
937 MILLION

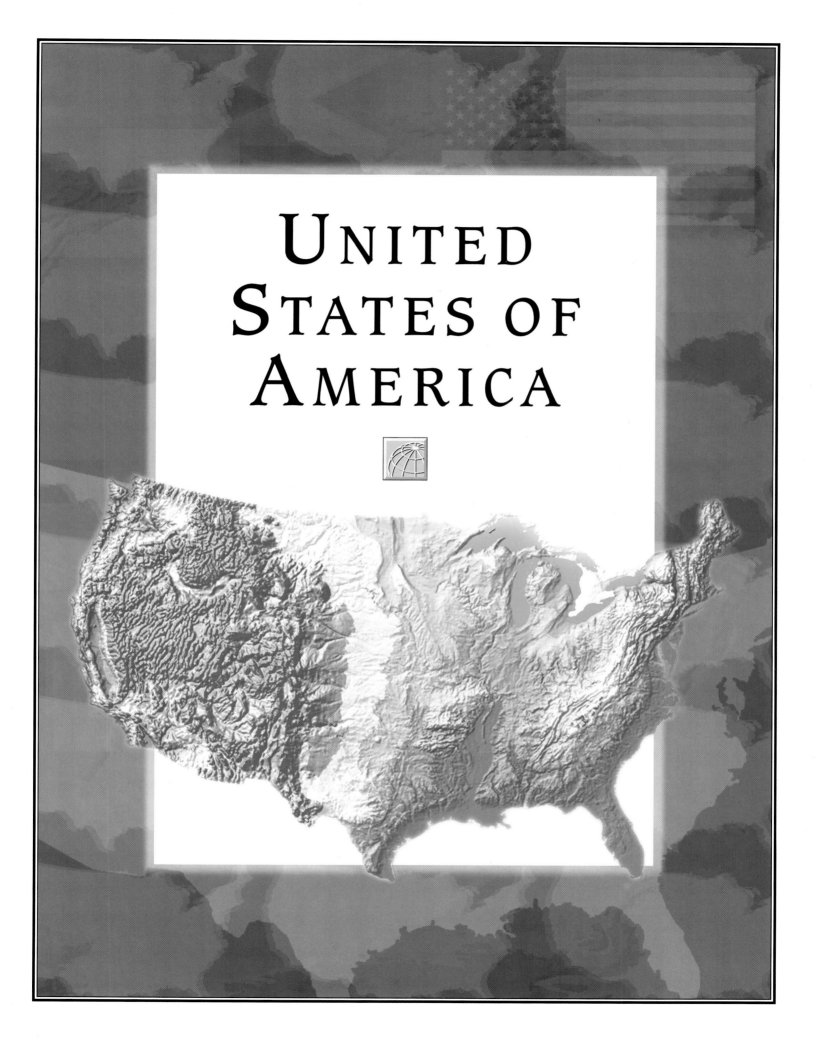

UNITED STATES OF AMERICA

Physical US

The US spans the wide, central part of the North American continent, stretching some 3,125 miles (5,030 km) across its greatest east-west width and 1,548 miles (2,491 km) from north to south. Forty-eight of its 50 states lie in this area; the 49th state, Alaska is in the northwestern corner of North America and the 50th, Hawaii, is a chain of islands in the Pacific Ocean. With its vast open plains, giant rivers, dramatic deserts, rugged mountains, and deep canyons, the US has some of the most spectacular and diverse natural landscapes in the world.

THE LANDSCAPE

A long belt of mountains – including the high Sierra Nevada and Cascade Range, and the lower Coast Ranges – runs along the west coast, dropping inland to the deserts and salt lakes of the Great Basin. Further inland lie the Rocky Mountains, beyond which the land drops again to the interior plains and the Mississippi basin. In the East are the Appalachian Mountains, which are much older and lower than the Rockies. The Great Lakes, among the world's largest freshwater lakes, straddle part of the US-Canada border.

Much of the southwest of the US is very dry, especially the rain-starved areas between the Coast Ranges and the Rocky Mountains, such as the Sonoran Desert (above).

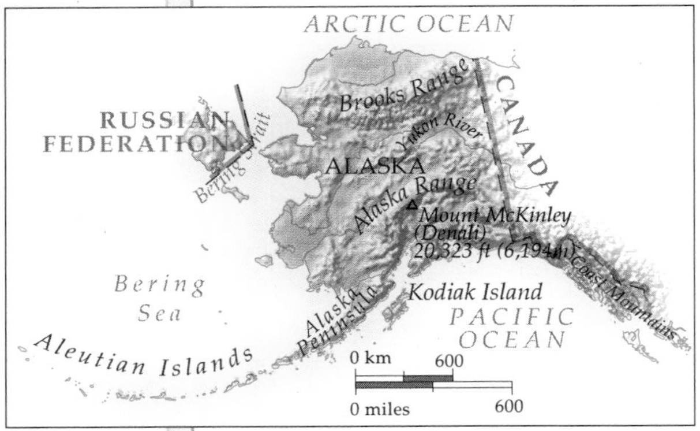
ARCTIC OCEAN
RUSSIAN FEDERATION
Bering Strait
Brooks Range
Yukon River
CANADA
ALASKA
Alaska Range
Mount McKinley (Denali) 20,323 ft (6,194m)
Bering Sea
Kodiak Island
PACIFIC OCEAN
Alaska Peninsula
Aleutian Islands
Coast Mountains
0 km 600
0 miles 600

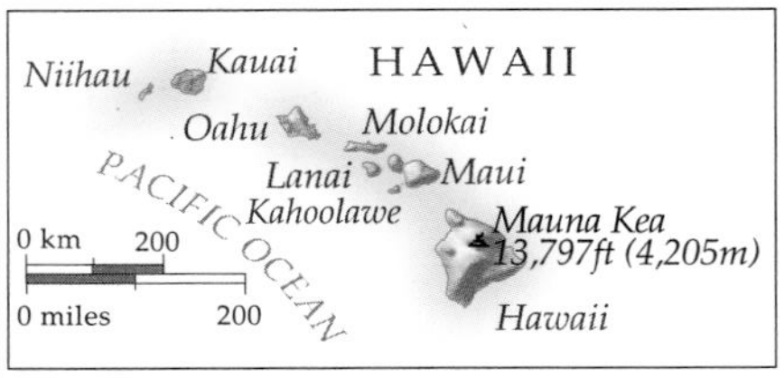
HAWAII
Niihau
Kauai
Oahu
Molokai
Lanai
Maui
Kahoolawe
PACIFIC OCEAN
Mauna Kea 13,797ft (4,205m)
Hawaii
0 km 200
0 miles 200

Cape Flattery
Glacier Peak 10,541ft (3,213m)
CANADA
Mount Rainier 14,409ft (4,392m)
Columbia River
Cascade Range
Columbia Basin
Snake River
Bitterroot Range
Flathead Lake
Missouri River
Fort Peck Lake
Lake Sakakawea
Rocky Mountains
Yellowstone River
Hells Canyon
Salmon River Mountains
Yellowstone Lake
Absaroka Range
Cloud Peak 13,165ft (4,013m)
Harney Basin
Grand Teton 13,769ft (4,197m)
Black Hills
Mount Shasta 14,159ft (4,316m)
Badlands
PACIFIC OCEAN
Cape Mendocino
Great Basin
Humboldt River
Great Salt Lake
Great Divide Basin
North Platte River
Kings Peak 13,526ft (4,123m)
Coast Ranges
Sacramento Valley
Central Valley
Sierra Nevada
Uinta Mountains
South Platte River
Wheeler Peak 13,060ft (3,981m)
Mount Elbert 14,432ft (4,399m)
Colorado River
Bryce Canyon
Colorado Plateau
Arkansas River
Mount Whitney 14,495ft (4,418m)
Death Valley
Lake Mead
Grand Canyon
Mojave Desert
Humphreys Peak 12,634ft (3,851m)
Channel Islands
Colorado River
Canadian River
Baldy Peak 11,404ft (3,476m)
Salton Sea
Sonoran Desert
Gila River
Sacramento Mountains
Llano Estacado
Sierra Blanca Peak 11,972ft (3,649m)
Rio Grande
Pecos River
Edwards Plateau
MEXICO
Emory Peak 7,824ft (2,385m)
Great Plains
Missouri River

CLIMATE

The climate varies hugely, from subarctic in Alaska to tropical in Hawaii. Most of the US is temperate and continental, with hot summers and often harsh winters – especially in the western mountains and plains and in the Midwest, where the Great Lakes can freeze. Southern summers are humid; in the Southwest they are very dry.

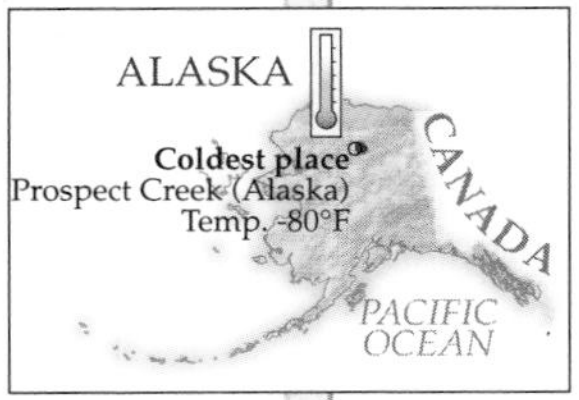
ALASKA
Coldest place
Prospect Creek (Alaska)
Temp. -80°F
CANADA
PACIFIC OCEAN

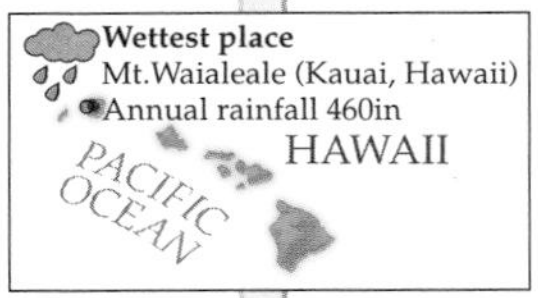
Wettest place
Mt.Waialeale (Kauai, Hawaii)
Annual rainfall 460in
HAWAII
PACIFIC OCEAN

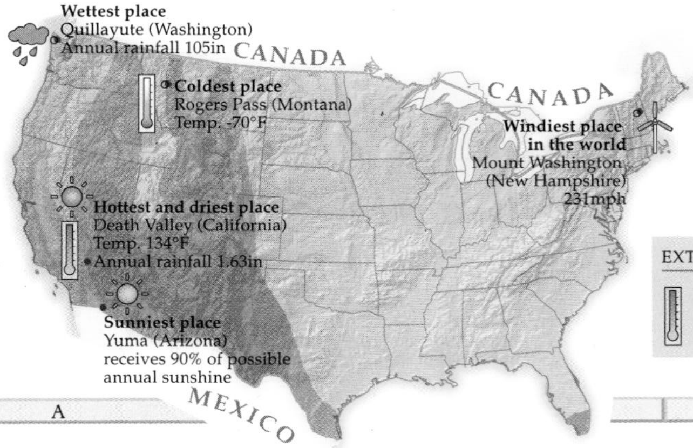
Wettest place
Quillayute (Washington)
Annual rainfall 105in
CANADA
Coldest place
Rogers Pass (Montana)
Temp. -70°F
CANADA
Windiest place in the world
Mount Washington (New Hampshire)
231mph
Hottest and driest place
Death Valley (California)
Temp. 134°F
Annual rainfall 1.63in
Sunniest place
Yuma (Arizona)
receives 90% of possible annual sunshine
MEXICO

CLIMATE
- Subarctic
- Cool continental
- Temperate
- Warm temperate
- Semiarid
- Arid
- Tropical

EXTREME WEATHER EVENTS

Symbols indicate climatic extremes

SCALE 1:17,150,000
0 km 300
0 miles 300

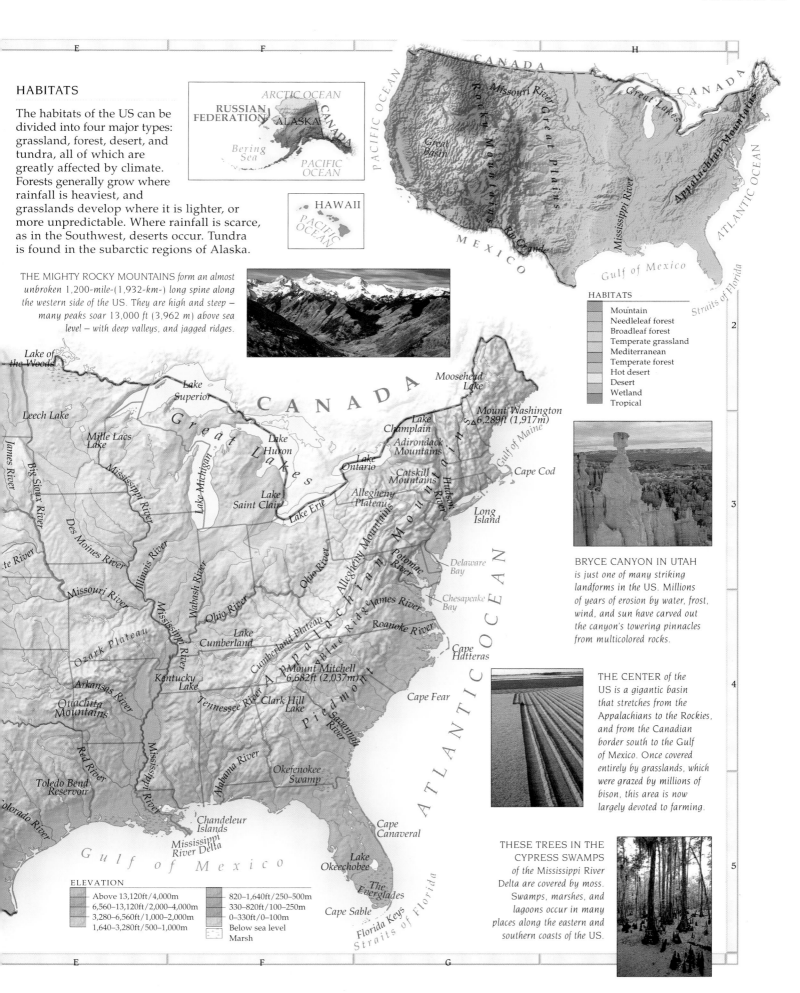

HABITATS

The habitats of the US can be divided into four major types: grassland, forest, desert, and tundra, all of which are greatly affected by climate. Forests generally grow where rainfall is heaviest, and grasslands develop where it is lighter, or more unpredictable. Where rainfall is scarce, as in the Southwest, deserts occur. Tundra is found in the subarctic regions of Alaska.

ARCTIC OCEAN
RUSSIAN FEDERATION
ALASKA
CANADA
Bering Sea
PACIFIC OCEAN

HAWAII
PACIFIC OCEAN

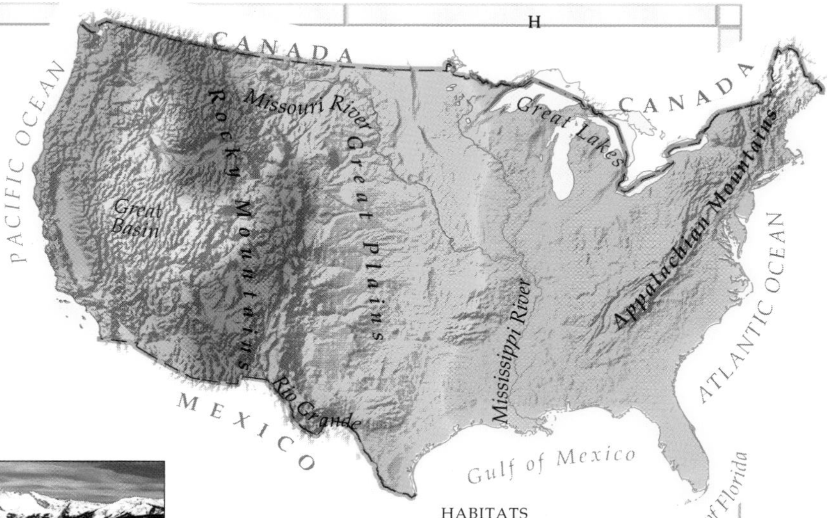
CANADA
Missouri River
Rocky Mountains
Great Plains
Great Lakes
CANADA
Appalachian Mountains
PACIFIC OCEAN
Great Basin
Mississippi River
ATLANTIC OCEAN
MEXICO
Rio Grande
Gulf of Mexico
Straits of Florida

HABITATS
- Mountain
- Needleleaf forest
- Broadleaf forest
- Temperate grassland
- Mediterranean
- Temperate forest
- Hot desert
- Desert
- Wetland
- Tropical

THE MIGHTY ROCKY MOUNTAINS *form an almost unbroken 1,200-mile-(1,932-km-) long spine along the western side of the US. They are high and steep – many peaks soar 13,000 ft (3,962 m) above sea level – with deep valleys, and jagged ridges.*

Lake of the Woods
Lake Superior
CANADA
Moosehead Lake
Leech Lake
Great Lakes
Mount Washington 6,289ft (1,917m)
Lake Champlain
Mille Lacs Lake
Lake Huron
Adirondack Mountains
Gulf of Maine
James River
Big Sioux River
Mississippi River
Lake Michigan
Lake Ontario
Catskill Mountains
Cape Cod
Lake Saint Clair
Lake Erie
Allegheny Plateau
Hudson River
Long Island
Des Moines River
Illinois River
Ohio River
Allegheny Mountains
Appalachian Mountains
Potomac River
Delaware Bay
Missouri River
Wabash River
James River
Chesapeake Bay
Ohio River
Roanoke River
Ozark Plateau
Mississippi River
Lake Cumberland
Cumberland Plateau
Blue Ridge
Cape Hatteras
Mount Mitchell 6,682ft (2,037m)
Kentucky Lake
Arkansas River
Ouachita Mountains
Tennessee River
Clark Hill Lake
Piedmont
Cape Fear
Savannah River
ATLANTIC OCEAN
Red River
Mississippi River
Alabama River
Okefenokee Swamp
Toledo Bend Reservoir
Colorado River
Chandeleur Islands
Mississippi River Delta
Cape Canaveral
Gulf of Mexico
Lake Okeechobee
The Everglades
Cape Sable
Florida Keys
Straits of Florida
ELEVATION
Above 13,120ft/4,000m
6,560–13,120ft/2,000–4,000m
3,280–6,560ft/1,000–2,000m
1,640–3,280ft/500–1,000m
820–1,640ft/250–500m
330–820ft/100–250m
0–330ft/0–100m
Below sea level
Marsh

BRYCE CANYON IN UTAH *is just one of many striking landforms in the US. Millions of years of erosion by water, frost, wind, and sun have carved out the canyon's towering pinnacles from multicolored rocks.*

THE CENTER *of the US is a gigantic basin that stretches from the Appalachians to the Rockies, and from the Canadian border south to the Gulf of Mexico. Once covered entirely by grasslands, which were grazed by millions of bison, this area is now largely devoted to farming.*

THESE TREES IN THE CYPRESS SWAMPS *of the Mississippi River Delta are covered by moss. Swamps, marshes, and lagoons occur in many places along the eastern and southern coasts of the US.*

POLITICAL US

JUST OVER 200 YEARS AGO, the US was a new and undeveloped nation. It occupied a thin strip of land on the Atlantic coast of North America and had a population of about 4 million people. Today, it ranks fourth in the world in both area and population. With fertile land, abundant mineral wealth, and a hugely diverse population, the US has also grown into the richest, most inventive, and most powerful country in the world. Great cities and industries have been established, and vast areas of farmland developed.

GOVERNMENT

The government of the US is organized as laid out in the US Constitution, which was drawn up in 1787. It sets out a federal system in which political power is divided between the national (federal) government, and the governments of each of the 50 states. State governments have the authority to make laws affecting their own residents, while the national government makes decisions on foreign policy and can pass laws that affect the whole country.

WASHINGTON, DC, *was established as the site of the nation's capital in 1790. It is home to the seat of the national government on Capitol Hill, as well as the President's official residence, the White House* (above).

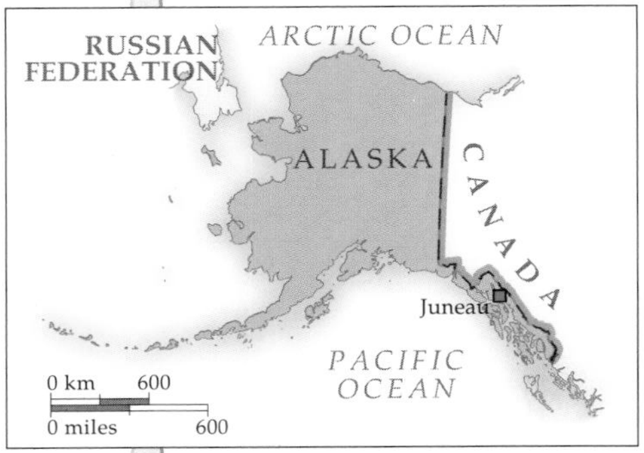
RUSSIAN FEDERATION
ARCTIC OCEAN
ALASKA
CANADA
Juneau
PACIFIC OCEAN
0 km 600
0 miles 600

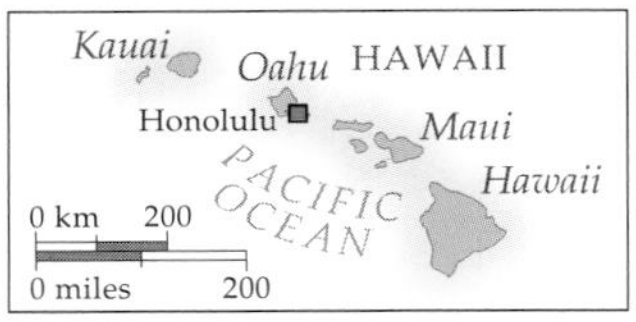
Kauai
Oahu
HAWAII
Honolulu
Maui
Hawaii
PACIFIC OCEAN
0 km 200
0 miles 200

CANADA
PACIFIC OCEAN
MEXICO
Olympia
WASHINGTON
Salem
OREGON
IDAHO
Boise
Helena
MONTANA
NORTH DAKOTA
Bismarck
SOUTH DAKOTA
Pierre
WYOMING
Cheyenne
NEBRASKA
Lincoln
Sacramento
Carson City
NEVADA
Salt Lake City
UTAH
Denver
COLORADO
KANSAS
CALIFORNIA
ARIZONA
Phoenix
Santa Fe
NEW MEXICO
OKLAHOMA
Oklahoma City
TEXAS
Austin

A SEA-TO-SEA NATION

The US began with the 13 former colonies gained from England in the 1783 treaty that ended the Revolutionary War. More states came with land bought from France in 1803 and Spain in 1845. Much of the West was acquired through war and treaties with Mexico and Spain. By 1959, when Alaska and Hawaii were admitted as states, the modern shape of the Union was complete.

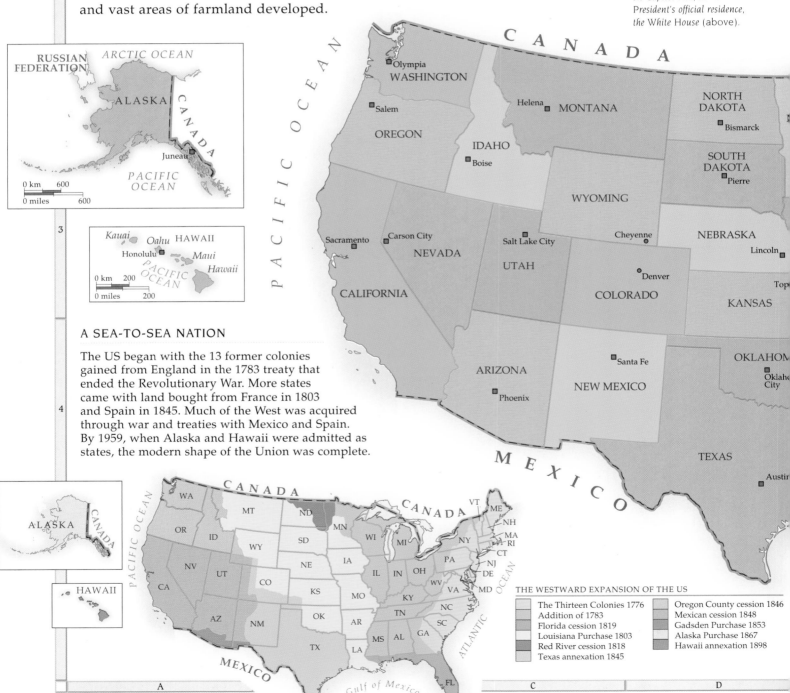

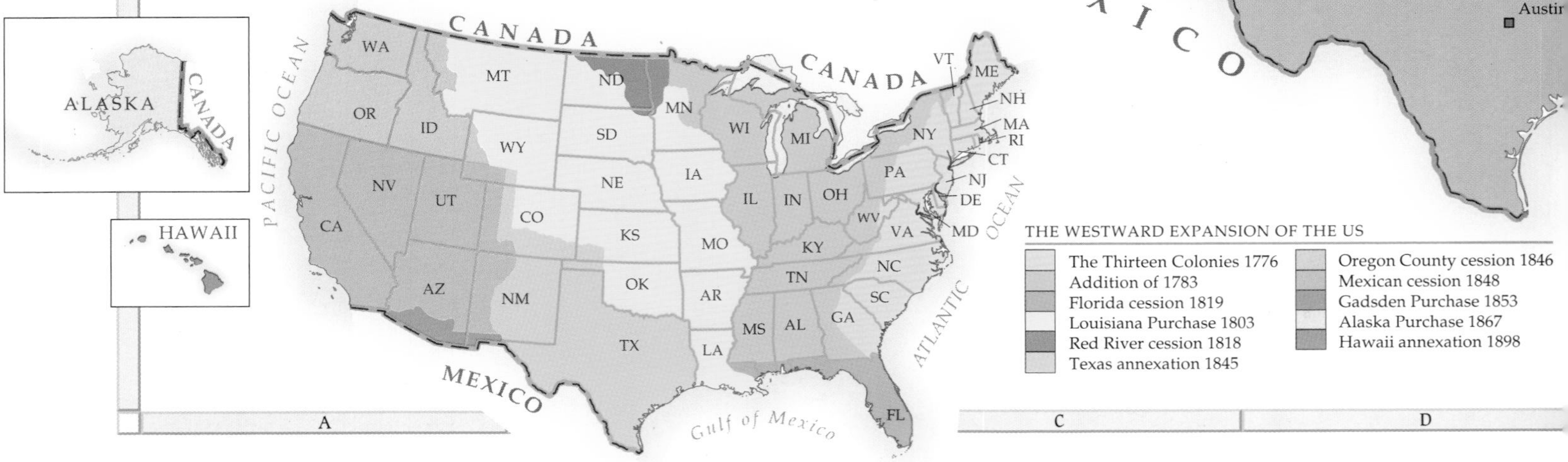
ALASKA
CANADA
HAWAII
PACIFIC OCEAN
CANADA
WA
OR
ID
MT
ND
MN
WY
SD
NE
IA
WI
MI
NY
VT
ME
NH
MA
RI
CT
NJ
DE
MD
PA
OH
IN
IL
NV
UT
CA
CO
KS
MO
KY
WV
VA
NC
TN
SC
GA
AL
MS
AR
LA
OK
TX
NM
AZ
FL
ATLANTIC OCEAN
MEXICO
Gulf of Mexico
THE WESTWARD EXPANSION OF THE US
The Thirteen Colonies 1776
Addition of 1783
Florida cession 1819
Louisiana Purchase 1803
Red River cession 1818
Texas annexation 1845
Oregon County cession 1846
Mexican cession 1848
Gadsden Purchase 1853
Alaska Purchase 1867
Hawaii annexation 1898

E F G H

TRANSPORTATION

Transportation is very highly developed in the US. The country has the world's cheapest, and most extensive internal air network and a 55,000-mile (88,000-km) freeway system, that connects most major cities. The railroads – constructed in the 19th century to open up the country – are now used less than road and air for long-distance passenger travel, but still carry freight. Onland waterways such as the Great Lakes and the Mississippi-Missouri river system – America's first transportation network – move many bulk materials.

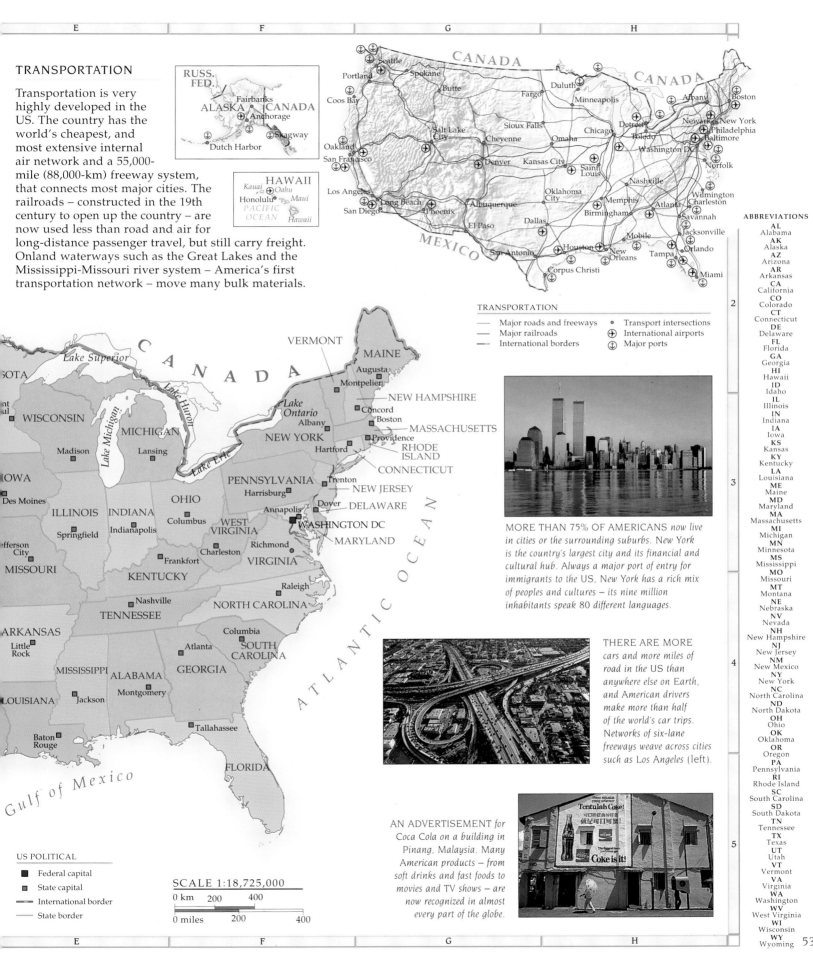

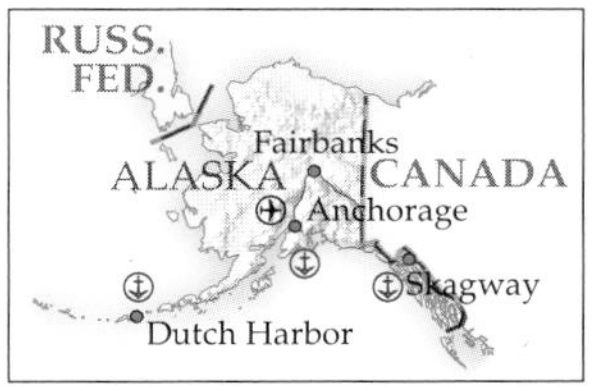

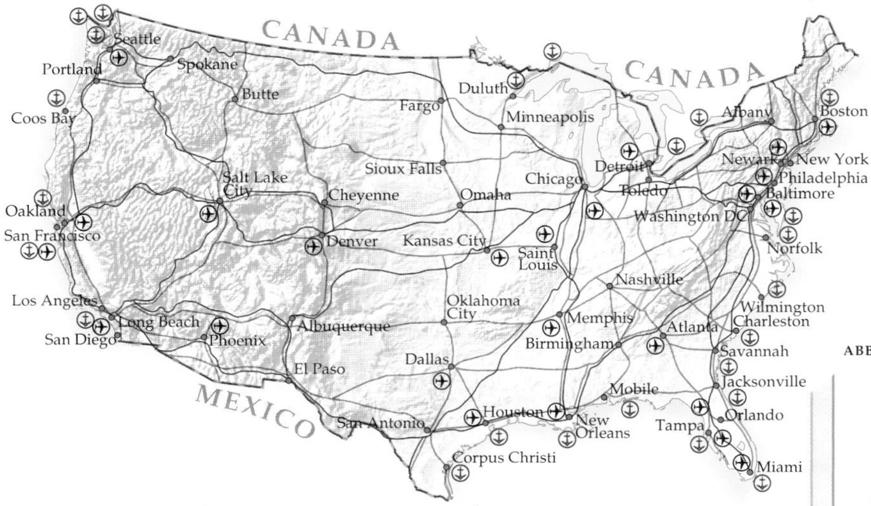

TRANSPORTATION

- Major roads and freeways
- Major railroads
- International borders
- Transport intersections
- International airports
- Major ports

US POLITICAL

- Federal capital
- State capital
- International border
- State border

SCALE 1:18,725,000

0 km 200 400

0 miles 200 400

MORE THAN 75% OF AMERICANS *now live in cities or the surrounding suburbs. New York is the country's largest city and its financial and cultural hub. Always a major port of entry for immigrants to the US, New York has a rich mix of peoples and cultures – its nine million inhabitants speak 80 different languages.*

THERE ARE MORE *cars and more miles of road in the US than anywhere else on Earth, and American drivers make more than half of the world's car trips. Networks of six-lane freeways weave across cities such as Los Angeles (left).*

AN ADVERTISEMENT *for Coca Cola on a building in Pinang, Malaysia. Many American products – from soft drinks and fast foods to movies and TV shows – are now recognized in almost every part of the globe.*

ABBREVIATIONS

AL Alabama
AK Alaska
AZ Arizona
AR Arkansas
CA California
CO Colorado
CT Connecticut
DE Delaware
FL Florida
GA Georgia
HI Hawaii
ID Idaho
IL Illinois
IN Indiana
IA Iowa
KS Kansas
KY Kentucky
LA Louisiana
ME Maine
MD Maryland
MA Massachusetts
MI Michigan
MN Minnesota
MS Mississippi
MO Missouri
MT Montana
NE Nebraska
NV Nevada
NH New Hampshire
NJ New Jersey
NM New Mexico
NY New York
NC North Carolina
ND North Dakota
OH Ohio
OK Oklahoma
OR Oregon
PA Pennsylvania
RI Rhode Island
SC South Carolina
SD South Dakota
TN Tennessee
TX Texas
UT Utah
VT Vermont
VA Virginia
WA Washington
WV West Virginia
WI Wisconsin
WY Wyoming

E F G H

Industry and Resources

A COMBINATION OF exceptional natural resources – including plentiful energy supplies in the form of oil, coal, and natural gas and many minerals needed by modern industry, a highly skilled work force, and an entrepreneurial approach to business have made the US the world's leading economic power. Despite increasing competition from foreign markets, American firms are still at the forefront of technological advances, especially in computers, electronics, medical equipment, and aerospace.

INDUSTRY IN THE US

Together, the northeastern and Great Lakes states form one of the world's biggest industrial zones. Iron and steel production, car manufacturing, chemicals, and heavy engineering are all well established, although newer, service-based, high-tech, and information-processing industries are now the biggest employers. Elsewhere, industry has become more diversified, with traditional industries related to agriculture, such as food-processing, and mineral extraction coexisting with a thriving services sector.

THE GREAT LAKES STATES, *especially Michigan, have long been the center of the American automobile industry, but today, car assembly plants are also found in many other parts of the country.*

THE TWIN TOWERS *of the World Trade Center dominate the Manhattan skyline. New York, and the other great cities of the Atlantic seaboard, Boston and Philadelphia, are international centers of finance and commerce.*

SCALE 1:25,637,500

0 km 500

0 miles 500

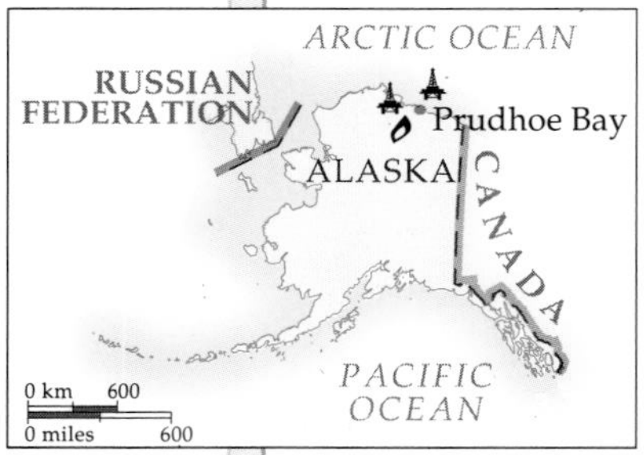

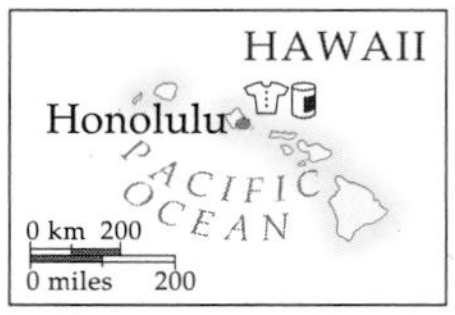

THE SANTA CLARA VALLEY, *south of San Francisco, California, is known as Silicon Valley because it has one of the world's highest concentrations of research institutions and high-tech and electronics industries.*

INDUSTRY

- Aerospace
- Brewing
- Automobile manufacture
- Chemicals
- Defense
- Electronics
- Engineering
- Movie industry
- Finance
- Food processing
- High-tech industry
- Iron and steel
- Pharmaceuticals
- Printing and publishing
- Research and development
- Shipbuilding
- Textiles
- Timber processing
- Coal
- Oil
- Gas
- Industrial cities
- Major industrial areas

MINERAL RESOURCES

The US consumes 25% of the world's energy resources but it is well endowed with energy reserves. Coal is still plentiful and although most production has traditionally taken place in the East, vast open pits now exist in some western states, like Wyoming. Big oil and gas fields are found in Texas, Alaska, Louisiana, and the Gulf of Mexico. In the West, mineral deposits include uranium, copper, and precious metals, and there is iron ore around Lake Superior.

Hawaii has very limited mineral resources

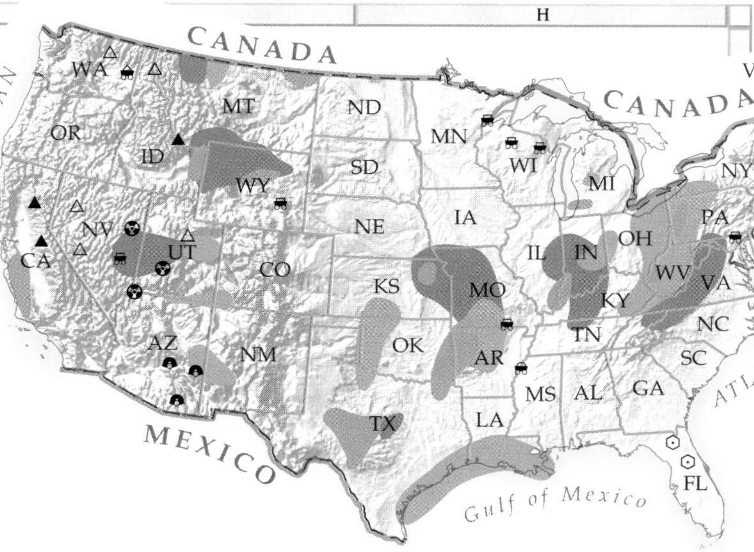

MINERAL RESOURCES

- Oil field
- Gas field
- Coal field
- Bauxite
- Copper
- Gold
- Iron
- Lead
- Nickel
- Phosphates
- Silver
- Uranium

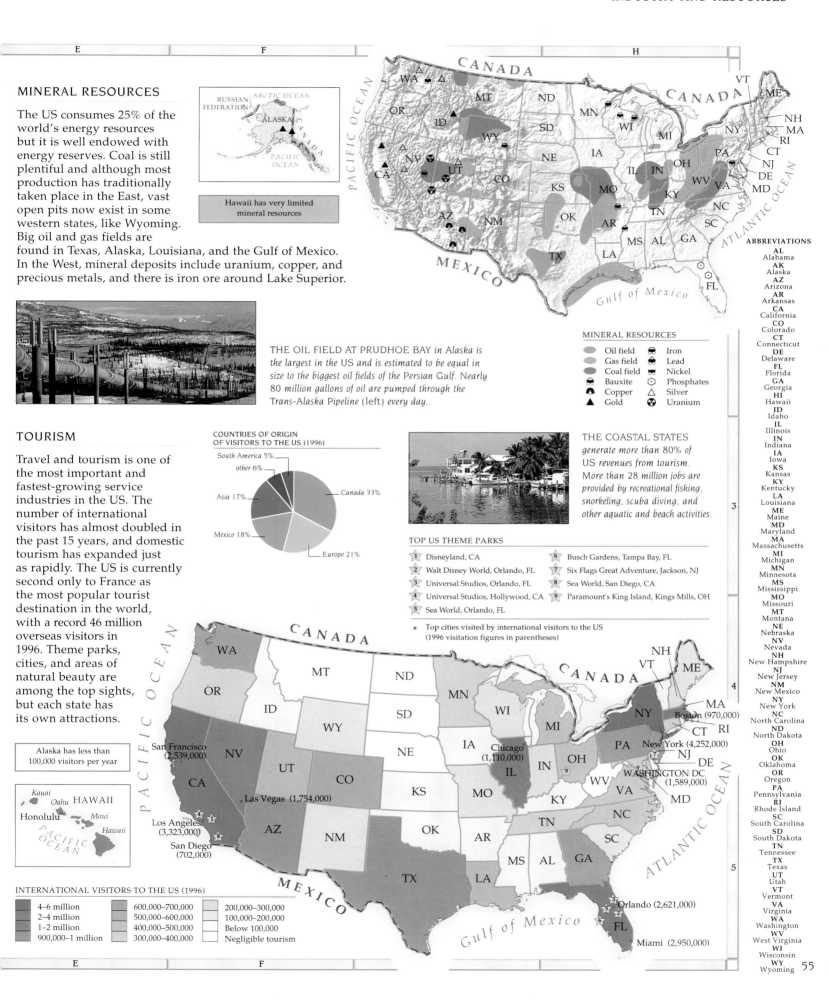

THE OIL FIELD AT PRUDHOE BAY in Alaska is the largest in the US and is estimated to be equal in size to the biggest oil fields of the Persian Gulf. Nearly 80 million gallons of oil are pumped through the Trans-Alaska Pipeline (left) every day..

TOURISM

Travel and tourism is one of the most important and fastest-growing service industries in the US. The number of international visitors has almost doubled in the past 15 years, and domestic tourism has expanded just as rapidly. The US is currently second only to France as the most popular tourist destination in the world, with a record 46 million overseas visitors in 1996. Theme parks, cities, and areas of natural beauty are among the top sights, but each state has its own attractions.

COUNTRIES OF ORIGIN OF VISITORS TO THE US (1996)

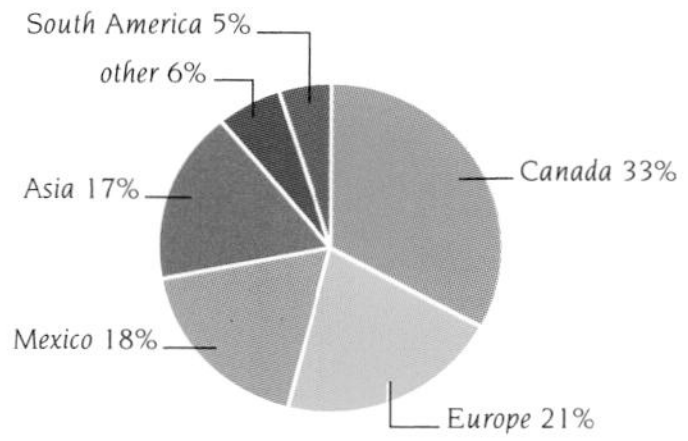

THE COASTAL STATES generate more than 80% of US revenues from tourism. More than 28 million jobs are provided by recreational fishing, snorkeling, scuba diving, and other aquatic and beach activities.

TOP US THEME PARKS

1. Disneyland, CA
2. Walt Disney World, Orlando, FL
3. Universal Studios, Orlando, FL
4. Universal Studios, Hollywood, CA
5. Sea World, Orlando, FL
6. Busch Gardens, Tampa Bay, FL
7. Six Flags Great Adventure, Jackson, NJ
8. Sea World, San Diego, CA
9. Paramount's King Island, Kings Mills, OH

◆ Top cities visited by international visitors to the US (1996 visitation figures in parentheses)

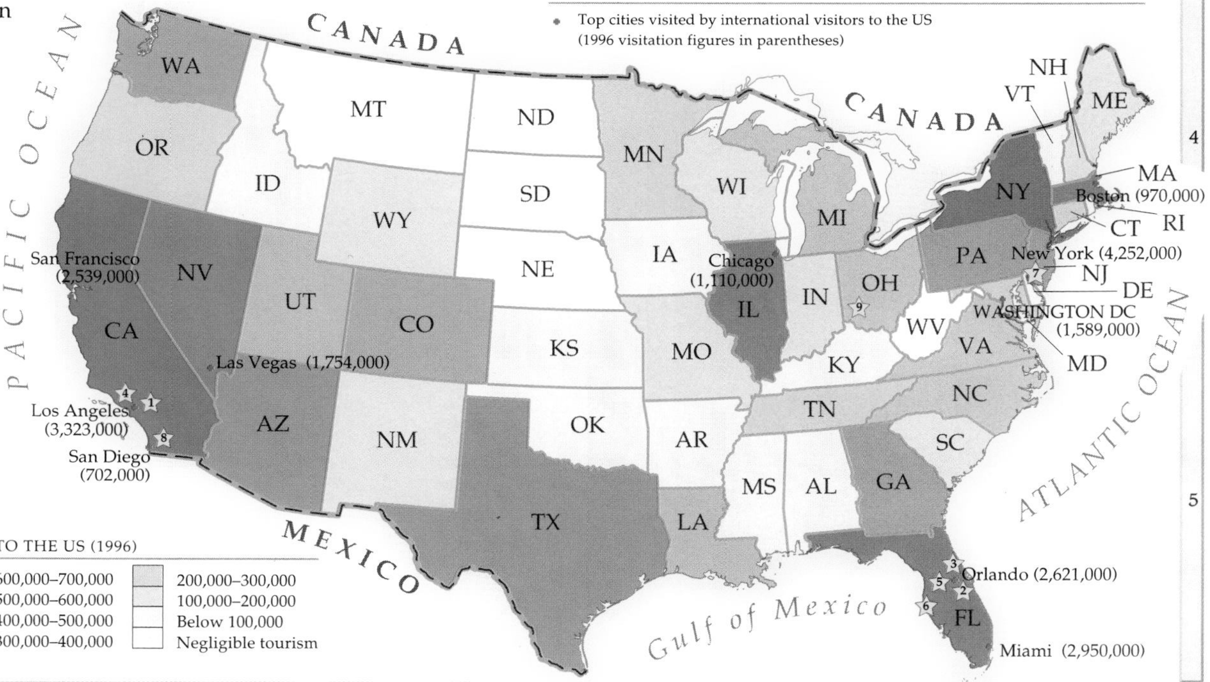

Alaska has less than 100,000 visitors per year

INTERNATIONAL VISITORS TO THE US (1996)

- 4–6 million
- 2–4 million
- 1–2 million
- 900,000–1 million
- 600,000–700,000
- 500,000–600,000
- 400,000–500,000
- 300,000–400,000
- 200,000–300,000
- 100,000–200,000
- Below 100,000
- Negligible tourism

ABBREVIATIONS

AL Alabama
AK Alaska
AZ Arizona
AR Arkansas
CA California
CO Colorado
CT Connecticut
DE Delaware
FL Florida
GA Georgia
HI Hawaii
ID Idaho
IL Illinois
IN Indiana
IA Iowa
KS Kansas
KY Kentucky
LA Louisiana
ME Maine
MD Maryland
MA Massachusetts
MI Michigan
MN Minnesota
MS Mississippi
MO Missouri
MT Montana
NE Nebraska
NV Nevada
NH New Hampshire
NJ New Jersey
NM New Mexico
NY New York
NC North Carolina
ND North Dakota
OH Ohio
OK Oklahoma
OR Oregon
PA Pennsylvania
RI Rhode Island
SC South Carolina
SD South Dakota
TN Tennessee
TX Texas
UT Utah
VT Vermont
VA Virginia
WA Washington
WV West Virginia
WI Wisconsin
WY Wyoming

Agriculture and Land Use

The US is the world's biggest agricultural producer. It not only supplies all its own needs, but has enough surplus to make it the biggest exporter of food, too. In the past 40 years, the American farm has become increasingly mechanized, with farmers using scientific techniques for breeding animals, fertilizing the soil, and controlling pests. As a result, modern farms produce more than ever before, and need a lot less manpower to do so. Today, the US is a world leader in beef, cereals, cotton, and tobacco. It is also a major timber producer and a top fishing nation.

AGRICULTURE IN THE US

The great diversity in climate, terrain, and soils allows American farmers to produce a variety of agricultural products. In the prairie regions of the Great Plains and Midwest, huge farms grow vast quantities of corn and wheat, and raise dairy and beef cattle, pigs, broiler chickens, and other livestock. Further south, many crops used in manufactured products are cultivated, including soybeans – used for vegetable oil, margarine, and livestock feed – cotton, tobacco, peanuts, and sugarcane. Farms in other fertile areas, especially near the Pacific and Atlantic coasts, grow a wide range of fruits and vegetables.

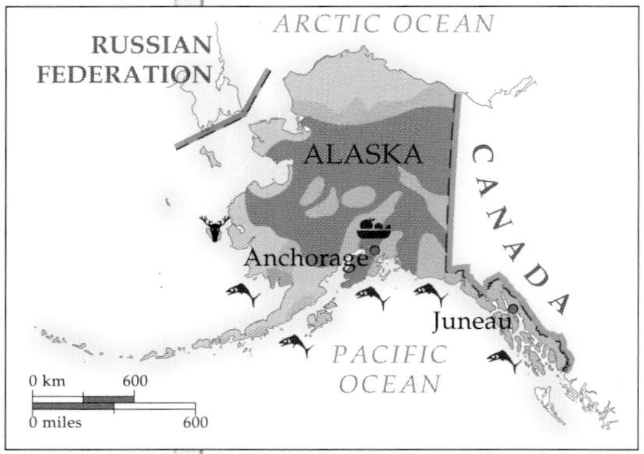

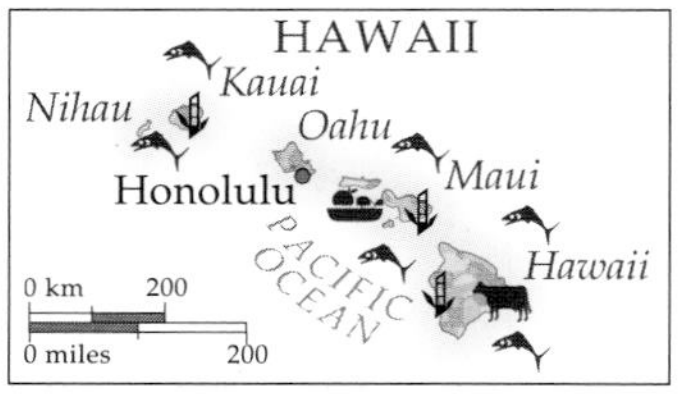

LAND USE AND AGRICULTURAL DISTRIBUTION

- Cattle
- Pigs
- Poultry
- Citrus fruits
- Corn
- Cotton
- Fishing
- Fruit
- Peanuts
- Shellfish
- Soybeans
- Timber
- Tobacco
- Wheat

- Capital city
- Major town

- Barren
- Tundra
- Pasture
- Cropland
- Forest
- Wetland
- Desert
- Mountain region

California is the number one *agricultural state in the US. Its fields and orchards yield more than 200 agricultural products of amazing diversity – from fruits, nuts, and vegetables, nursery and greenhouse products, livestock, and poultry to milk, cheese, and cream. Rich soils, a warm climate, and an almost year-round growing season have contributed to the state's success, but dry conditions mean that most of its farmland has to be irrigated. Over half of California's farm produce comes from the 450-mile- (750-km-) long Central Valley (left), which is irrigated – using a complex system of dams, canals, and power and pumping plants – by water from the Sierra Nevada mountains to the west.*

THE IMMENSE, OPEN, GREAT PLAINS *lie between the Rocky Mountains and the Mississippi River. They were once known as The American Desert because of low rainfall and a lack of trees, but they later proved to be one of the world's greatest agricultural regions; today, much of the land is covered by a giant checkerboard of wheat and cornfields.*

AMERICA'S FORESTS *are among its most valuable resources and commercial forestry is well developed. Washington and Oregon are the country's major producers of forest products. The vast fir, pine, and cedar forests in these two states supply much of the nation's timber, pulp, and paper.*

THE SECOND LARGEST STATE *in the US, Texas has more land for crops, grazing, or pasture than any other, and is second only to California in farm income. Cattle and calves are its main commodity: Texas is the nation's biggest cattle producer, with 14.8 million head. The state's enormous cattle ranches developed during the 19th century, when land was plentiful and could be acquired cheaply.*

IN FLORIDA, *less than two-fifths of the land is farmed, yet the state is the leading agricultural producer in the Southeast. Many types of vegetable are cultivated, and big citrus groves produce 75% of the nation's citrus fruits – including oranges, limes, grapefruit, and tangerines. Florida is also the world's second biggest citrus juice producer.*

POPULATION

THE US has the most racially, ethnically, and culturally diverse population in the world. In addition to the surviving native peoples and the descendants of Africans brought to the Americas as slaves, the nation's character has been constantly redefined by wave after wave of immigrants from all over the world, many of whom came to its shores in the hope of a new and better life. Most of the early settlers were from Europe, but in recent decades large numbers have arrived from Latin America, especially Mexico, and Asia.

ABOUT 21% OF AMERICANS *are under 15 years of age, but the the percentage of older people in the US has increased steadily. Today, the average American citizen can expect to live to about 75 years of age.*

STANDARD OF LIVING

As citizens of one of the world's wealthiest countries, most Americans enjoy a high standard of living, with good-quality, plentiful food supplies, a clean environment, affordable housing, and access to excellent medical care. However, over one-tenth of the population still lives below the poverty level. Members of ethnic minority groups and illegal immigrants – many of whom live in deprived inner-city neighborhoods – and people in some parts of the Northeast, where the decline in heavy industry has led to many job losses, are among the country's less privileged people.

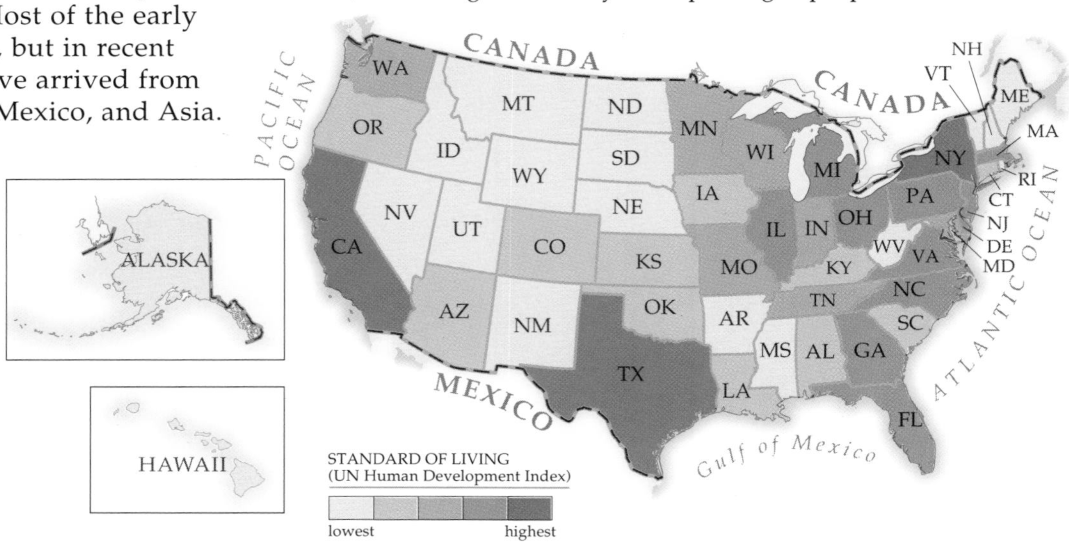
CANADA
PACIFIC OCEAN
ATLANTIC OCEAN
MEXICO
Gulf of Mexico
ALASKA
HAWAII
WA
OR
CA
NV
ID
MT
WY
UT
AZ
CO
NM
ND
SD
NE
KS
OK
TX
MN
IA
MO
AR
LA
WI
IL
MI
IN
OH
KY
TN
MS
AL
GA
FL
SC
NC
VA
WV
PA
NY
VT
NH
ME
MA
RI
CT
NJ
DE
MD
STANDARD OF LIVING
(UN Human Development Index)
lowest
highest

ETHNIC COMPOSITION

Each of the US's ethnic groups contains people with origins in many different countries. The White population includes people of European and southwest Asian ancestry, while the Hispanic population originates from the Spanish-speaking countries of Central and South America. The other ethnic groups are Black, Asian and Pacific Islander, and Native American. Ethnic distribution varies from state to state – for example, in California, one of the most racially mixed states, about 52% of the people are White, whereas in New Hampshire, the figure is 97%. In recent years, mainly because of immigration, Asians and Hispanics have become the fastest-growing ethnic groups.

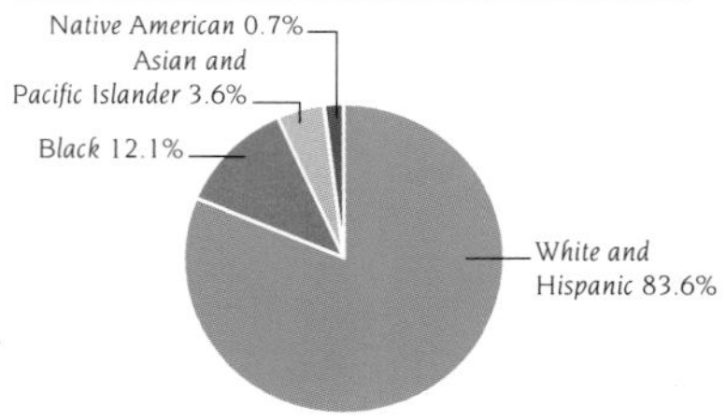
ETHNIC COMPOSITION
Native American 0.7%
Asian and Pacific Islander 3.6%
Black 12.1%
White and Hispanic 83.6%

CANADA
PACIFIC OCEAN
ATLANTIC OCEAN
MEXICO
Gulf of Mexico
WA
OR
CA
NV
ID
MT
WY
UT
AZ
CO
NM
ND
SD
NE
KS
OK
TX
MN
IA
MO
AR
LA
WI
IL
MI
IN
OH
KY
TN
MS
AL
GA
FL
SC
NC
VA
WV
PA
NY
VT
ME
NH
MA
RI
CT
NJ
DE
MD

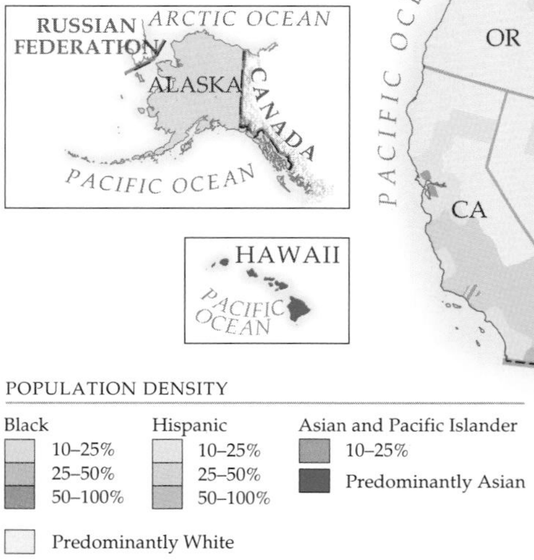
RUSSIAN FEDERATION
ARCTIC OCEAN
ALASKA
CANADA
PACIFIC OCEAN
HAWAII
PACIFIC OCEAN
POPULATION DENSITY
Black
10–25%
25–50%
50–100%
Hispanic
10–25%
25–50%
50–100%
Asian and Pacific Islander
10–25%
Predominantly Asian
Predominantly White

POPULATION DENSITY

The Northeast was the site of the first European settlements. With the Great Lakes region, it still forms the most densely populated part of the US. Since 1900, however, the populations of the southern and western states have grown enormously. In the past 30 years, large numbers of people have moved from the North to the warmer, economically booming "sunbelt" states of Florida, Texas, Arizona, Nevada, and California. With a population of more than 32 million, California is now by far the most populated state in the US.

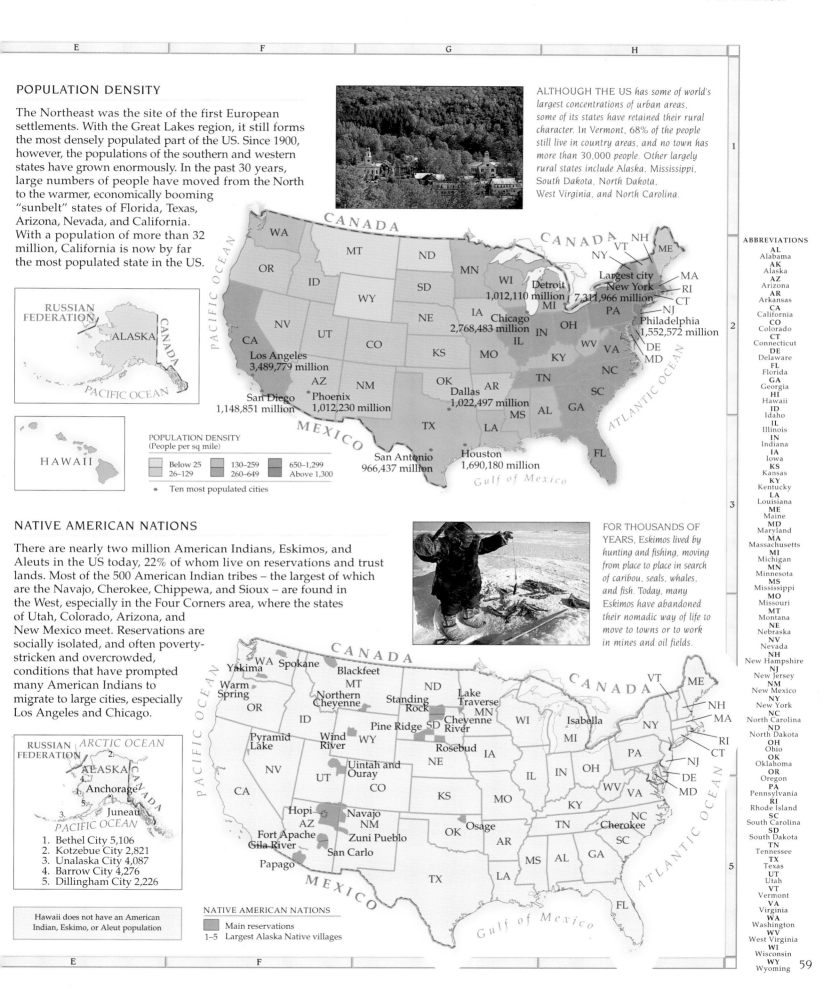

ALTHOUGH THE US has some of world's largest concentrations of urban areas, some of its states have retained their rural character. In Vermont, 68% of the people still live in country areas, and no town has more than 30,000 people. Other largely rural states include Alaska, Mississippi, South Dakota, North Dakota, West Virginia, and North Carolina.

RUSSIAN FEDERATION
ALASKA
CANADA
PACIFIC OCEAN

HAWAII

CANADA
PACIFIC OCEAN
ATLANTIC OCEAN
MEXICO
Gulf of Mexico
WA
OR
CA
NV
ID
MT
WY
UT
CO
AZ
NM
ND
SD
NE
KS
OK
TX
MN
IA
MO
AR
LA
WI
IL
MI
IN
OH
KY
TN
MS
AL
GA
FL
SC
NC
VA
WV
PA
NY
VT
NH
ME
MA
RI
CT
NJ
DE
MD
Los Angeles
3,489,779 million
San Diego
1,148,851 million
Phoenix
1,012,230 million
Dallas
1,022,497 million
San Antonio
966,437 million
Houston
1,690,180 million
Chicago
2,768,483 million
Detroit
1,012,110 million
Largest city
New York
7,311,966 million
Philadelphia
1,552,572 million

POPULATION DENSITY
(People per sq mile)

Below 25	130–259	650–1,299
26–129	260–649	Above 1,300

• Ten most populated cities

NATIVE AMERICAN NATIONS

There are nearly two million American Indians, Eskimos, and Aleuts in the US today, 22% of whom live on reservations and trust lands. Most of the 500 American Indian tribes – the largest of which are the Navajo, Cherokee, Chippewa, and Sioux – are found in the West, especially in the Four Corners area, where the states of Utah, Colorado, Arizona, and New Mexico meet. Reservations are socially isolated, and often poverty-stricken and overcrowded, conditions that have prompted many American Indians to migrate to large cities, especially Los Angeles and Chicago.

FOR THOUSANDS OF YEARS, Eskimos lived by hunting and fishing, moving from place to place in search of caribou, seals, whales, and fish. Today, many Eskimos have abandoned their nomadic way of life to move to towns or to work in mines and oil fields.

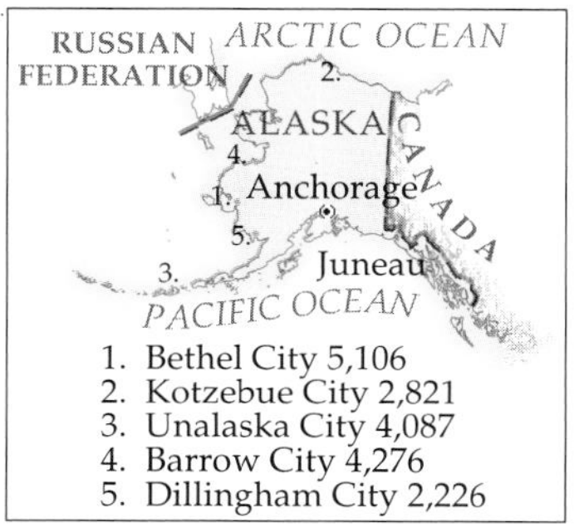
RUSSIAN FEDERATION
ARCTIC OCEAN
ALASKA
CANADA
Anchorage
Juneau
PACIFIC OCEAN
1.
2.
3.
4.
5.

1. Bethel City 5,106
2. Kotzebue City 2,821
3. Unalaska City 4,087
4. Barrow City 4,276
5. Dillingham City 2,226

Hawaii does not have an American Indian, Eskimo, or Aleut population

CANADA
PACIFIC OCEAN
ATLANTIC OCEAN
MEXICO
Gulf of Mexico
Yakima
WA
Spokane
Warm Spring
OR
Blackfeet
MT
Northern Cheyenne
ID
Standing Rock
ND
Lake Traverse
MN
Cheyenne River
SD
Pine Ridge
Rosebud
Wind River
WY
Pyramid Lake
NV
CA
UT
Uintah and Ouray
CO
NE
IA
WI
Isabella
MI
IL
IN
OH
PA
NY
VT
ME
NH
MA
RI
CT
NJ
DE
MD
WV
VA
KY
KS
MO
Osage
OK
AR
TN
NC
Cherokee
SC
GA
AL
MS
LA
TX
FL
Hopi
AZ
Navajo
NM
Zuni Pueblo
Fort Apache
Gila River
San Carlo
Papago

NATIVE AMERICAN NATIONS

▪ Main reservations
1–5 Largest Alaska Native villages

ABBREVIATIONS

AL Alabama
AK Alaska
AZ Arizona
AR Arkansas
CA California
CO Colorado
CT Connecticut
DE Delaware
FL Florida
GA Georgia
HI Hawaii
ID Idaho
IL Illinois
IN Indiana
IA Iowa
KS Kansas
KY Kentucky
LA Louisiana
ME Maine
MD Maryland
MA Massachusetts
MI Michigan
MN Minnesota
MS Mississippi
MO Missouri
MT Montana
NE Nebraska
NV Nevada
NH New Hampshire
NJ New Jersey
NM New Mexico
NY New York
NC North Carolina
ND North Dakota
OH Ohio
OK Oklahoma
OR Oregon
PA Pennsylvania
RI Rhode Island
SC South Carolina
SD South Dakota
TN Tennessee
TX Texas
UT Utah
VT Vermont
VA Virginia
WA Washington
WV West Virginia
WI Wisconsin
WY Wyoming

Environmental Issues

When first colonized by Europeans, the US was still very much a wilderness, with an immense, and largely untapped, wealth of natural resources. Over the past 200 years – and especially in the latter half of the 20th century – rapid population growth and the parallel development of big cities and industries have contributed to enormous environmental changes. Intensive farming and industrial and urban emissions have caused major air and water pollution, damaging habitats and wildlife and threatening the quality of human life. In recent years, awareness of the importance of the environment has led to increasing efforts to protect it.

KEY ENVIRONMENTAL ISSUES IN THE US

In many parts of the US, but especially in the East, the high level of emissions from vehicles, factories, and power stations has led to poor air quality and acid rain. Most rivers in the East, along with the Great Lakes, and coastal waters, have been polluted by industrial and domestic waste discharge, agricultural runoff, and oil spillage, threatening water quality and aquatic life. In the Southwest, overgrazing, along with drought and climatic changes, has turned land that once was pasture into desert.

ENVIRONMENTAL ISSUES

- Acid rain
- Area at risk from desertification
- Existing desert
- Polluted rivers
- Radioactive contamination
- Marine pollution
- Heavy marine pollution
- Poor urban air quality
- Encroaching tourist development

HEAVY INDUSTRY *around the shores of the Great Lakes has led to terrible water pollution. In some regions, fish are unsafe to eat and swimming is dangerous.*

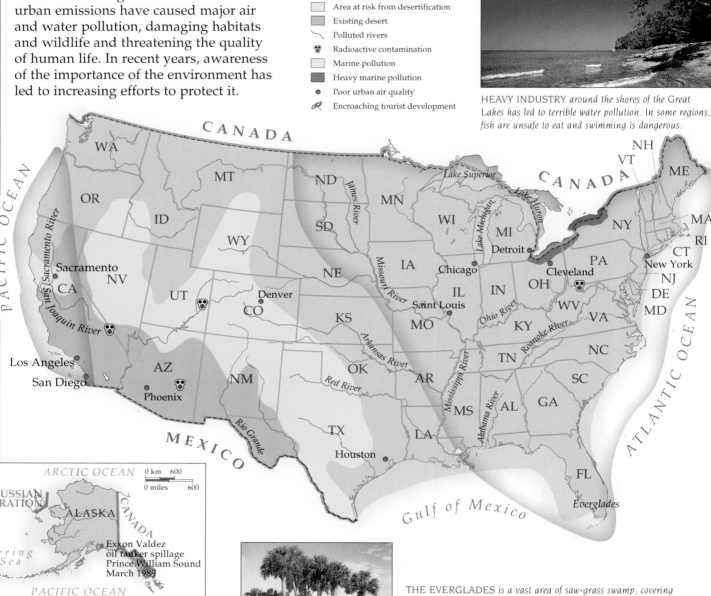

CANADA
PACIFIC OCEAN
ATLANTIC OCEAN
MEXICO
Gulf of Mexico
WA
OR
ID
MT
WY
NV
CA
UT
CO
AZ
NM
ND
SD
NE
KS
OK
TX
MN
IA
MO
AR
LA
WI
IL
MI
IN
OH
KY
TN
MS
AL
GA
FL
SC
NC
VA
WV
PA
NY
VT
NH
ME
MA
RI
CT
NJ
DE
MD
Sacramento
Los Angeles
San Diego
Phoenix
Denver
Houston
Saint Louis
Chicago
Detroit
Cleveland
New York
Everglades
Sacramento River
San Joaquin River
James River
Missouri River
Arkansas River
Red River
Rio Grande
Mississippi River
Ohio River
Roanoke River
Alabama River
Lake Superior
Lake Michigan
Lake Huron
ARCTIC OCEAN
0 km 600
0 miles 600
RUSSIAN FEDERATION
ALASKA
CANADA
Bering Sea
Exxon Valdez oil tanker spillage Prince William Sound March 1989
PACIFIC OCEAN

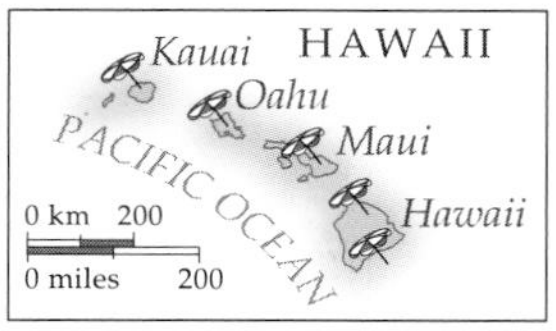
HAWAII
Kauai
Oahu
Maui
Hawaii
PACIFIC OCEAN
0 km 200
0 miles 200

THE EVERGLADES *is a vast area of saw-grass swamp, covering 4,000 sq miles (15,443 sq km) of southern Florida. The swamps support one of the Earth's most varied ecosystems and are home to thousands of species, including many rare birds, fish, alligators, and crocodiles. Unfortunately, humans have disrupted the natural flow of the water that feeds the swamps with dams, locks, canals, and roads, and have polluted the waters with runoff from golf courses and agriculture. In 1994 a state plan was launched to save the remaining wetlands and create new areas of swamp.*

NATURAL HAZARDS

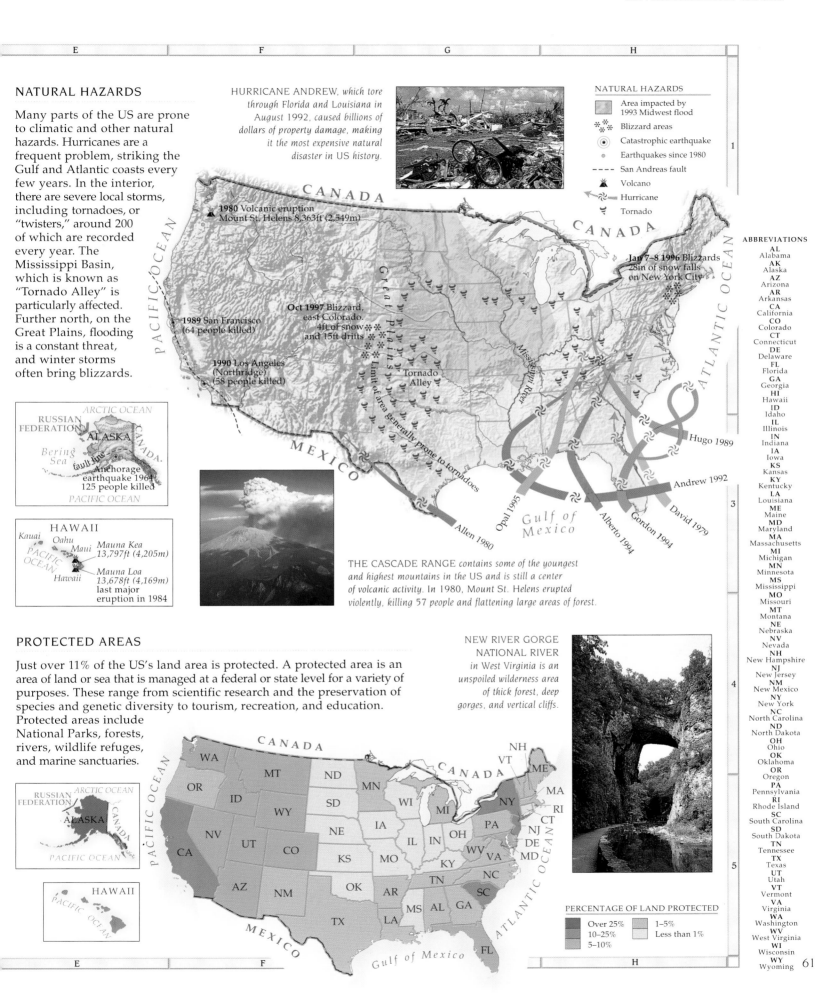

Many parts of the US are prone to climatic and other natural hazards. Hurricanes are a frequent problem, striking the Gulf and Atlantic coasts every few years. In the interior, there are severe local storms, including tornadoes, or "twisters," around 200 of which are recorded every year. The Mississippi Basin, which is known as "Tornado Alley" is particularly affected. Further north, on the Great Plains, flooding is a constant threat, and winter storms often bring blizzards.

HURRICANE ANDREW, which tore through Florida and Louisiana in August 1992, caused billions of dollars of property damage, making it the most expensive natural disaster in US history.

NATURAL HAZARDS
Area impacted by 1993 Midwest flood
Blizzard areas
Catastrophic earthquake
Earthquakes since 1980
San Andreas fault
Volcano
Hurricane
Tornado
CANADA
CANADA
PACIFIC OCEAN
ATLANTIC OCEAN
MEXICO
Gulf of Mexico
1980 Volcanic eruption Mount St. Helens 8,363ft (2,549m)
1989 San Francisco (64 people killed)
1990 Los Angeles (Northridge) (58 people killed)
Oct 1997 Blizzard, east Colorado. 4ft of snow and 15ft drifts
Great Plains
Limit of area generally prone to tornadoes
Tornado Alley
Mississippi River
Jan 7–8 1996 Blizzards 28in of snow falls on New York City
Hugo 1989
Andrew 1992
David 1979
Gordon 1994
Alberto 1994
Opal 1995
Allen 1980

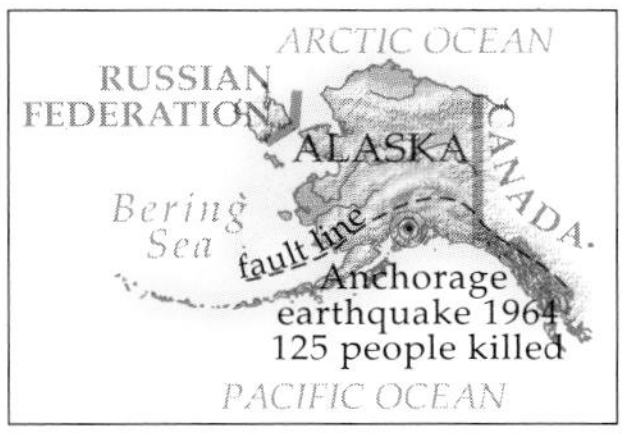
ARCTIC OCEAN
RUSSIAN FEDERATION
ALASKA
CANADA
Bering Sea
fault line
Anchorage earthquake 1964 125 people killed
PACIFIC OCEAN

HAWAII
Kauai
Oahu
Maui
PACIFIC OCEAN
Hawaii
Mauna Kea 13,797ft (4,205m)
Mauna Loa 13,678ft (4,169m) last major eruption in 1984

THE CASCADE RANGE contains some of the youngest and highest mountains in the US and is still a center of volcanic activity. In 1980, Mount St. Helens erupted violently, killing 57 people and flattening large areas of forest.

PROTECTED AREAS

Just over 11% of the US's land area is protected. A protected area is an area of land or sea that is managed at a federal or state level for a variety of purposes. These range from scientific research and the preservation of species and genetic diversity to tourism, recreation, and education. Protected areas include National Parks, forests, rivers, wildlife refuges, and marine sanctuaries.

NEW RIVER GORGE NATIONAL RIVER *in West Virginia is an unspoiled wilderness area of thick forest, deep gorges, and vertical cliffs.*

CANADA
CANADA
PACIFIC OCEAN
ATLANTIC OCEAN
MEXICO
Gulf of Mexico
WA
OR
CA
ID
NV
MT
WY
UT
AZ
CO
NM
ND
SD
NE
KS
OK
TX
MN
IA
MO
AR
LA
WI
IL
MI
IN
OH
KY
TN
MS
AL
GA
FL
SC
NC
VA
WV
PA
NY
VT
NH
ME
MA
RI
CT
NJ
DE
MD
PERCENTAGE OF LAND PROTECTED
Over 25%
10–25%
5–10%
1–5%
Less than 1%

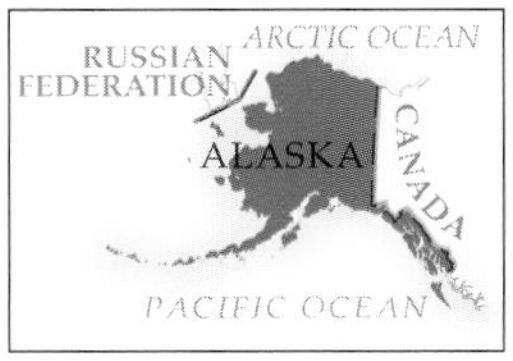
ARCTIC OCEAN
RUSSIAN FEDERATION
ALASKA
CANADA
PACIFIC OCEAN

HAWAII
PACIFIC OCEAN

ABBREVIATIONS

AL Alabama
AK Alaska
AZ Arizona
AR Arkansas
CA California
CO Colorado
CT Connecticut
DE Delaware
FL Florida
GA Georgia
HI Hawaii
ID Idaho
IL Illinois
IN Indiana
IA Iowa
KS Kansas
KY Kentucky
LA Louisiana
ME Maine
MD Maryland
MA Massachusetts
MI Michigan
MN Minnesota
MS Mississippi
MO Missouri
MT Montana
NE Nebraska
NV Nevada
NH New Hampshire
NJ New Jersey
NM New Mexico
NY New York
NC North Carolina
ND North Dakota
OH Ohio
OK Oklahoma
OR Oregon
PA Pennsylvania
RI Rhode Island
SC South Carolina
SD South Dakota
TN Tennessee
TX Texas
UT Utah
VT Vermont
VA Virginia
WA Washington
WV West Virginia
WI Wisconsin
WY Wyoming

NATIONAL PARKS

IN 1872, MILLIONS OF ACRES of magnificent mountain wilderness near the Yellowstone River in Wyoming were set aside by an act of Congress as a "public park or pleasuring ground for the benefit and enjoyment of the people." The area became Yellowstone National Park – the world's first national park. Yosemite and Sequoia National Parks, both in California, followed in 1890. At first, the parks were set up mainly as recreation areas. The idea that they were essential to conserve America's natural, cultural, and historical heritage for future generations became stronger after the US National Parks Service was established in 1916.

THE US NATIONAL PARK SYSTEM

Today, this system is made up of 376 areas covering more than 80 million acres (3.3 million hectares), and attracting around 260 million visitors every year. As well as the 50 national parks, there are 73 national monuments, many of which protect unusual features, such as the giant gypsum sand dune fields at White Sands National Monument in New Mexico, 19 national recreation areas such as the hugely popular Golden Gate National Recreation Area in San Francisco and many other areas, including national preserves, seashores, lakeshores, historic parks and sites, parkways, scenic trails, and battlefields.

YELLOWSTONE National Park is famous for its fantastic thermal features, of which there are around 10,000, including hundreds of hot springs and at least 60% of the world's active geysers. It is also home to the largest concentration of mammals in the lower 48 states. Grizzly and black bear, bison, timber wolves, elk, and bighorn sheep all roam the park.

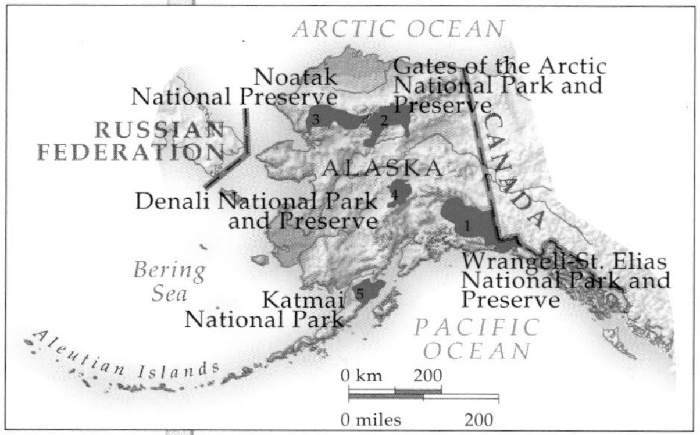

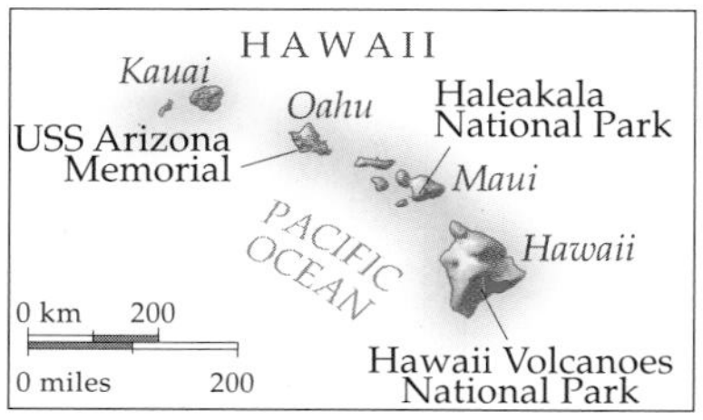

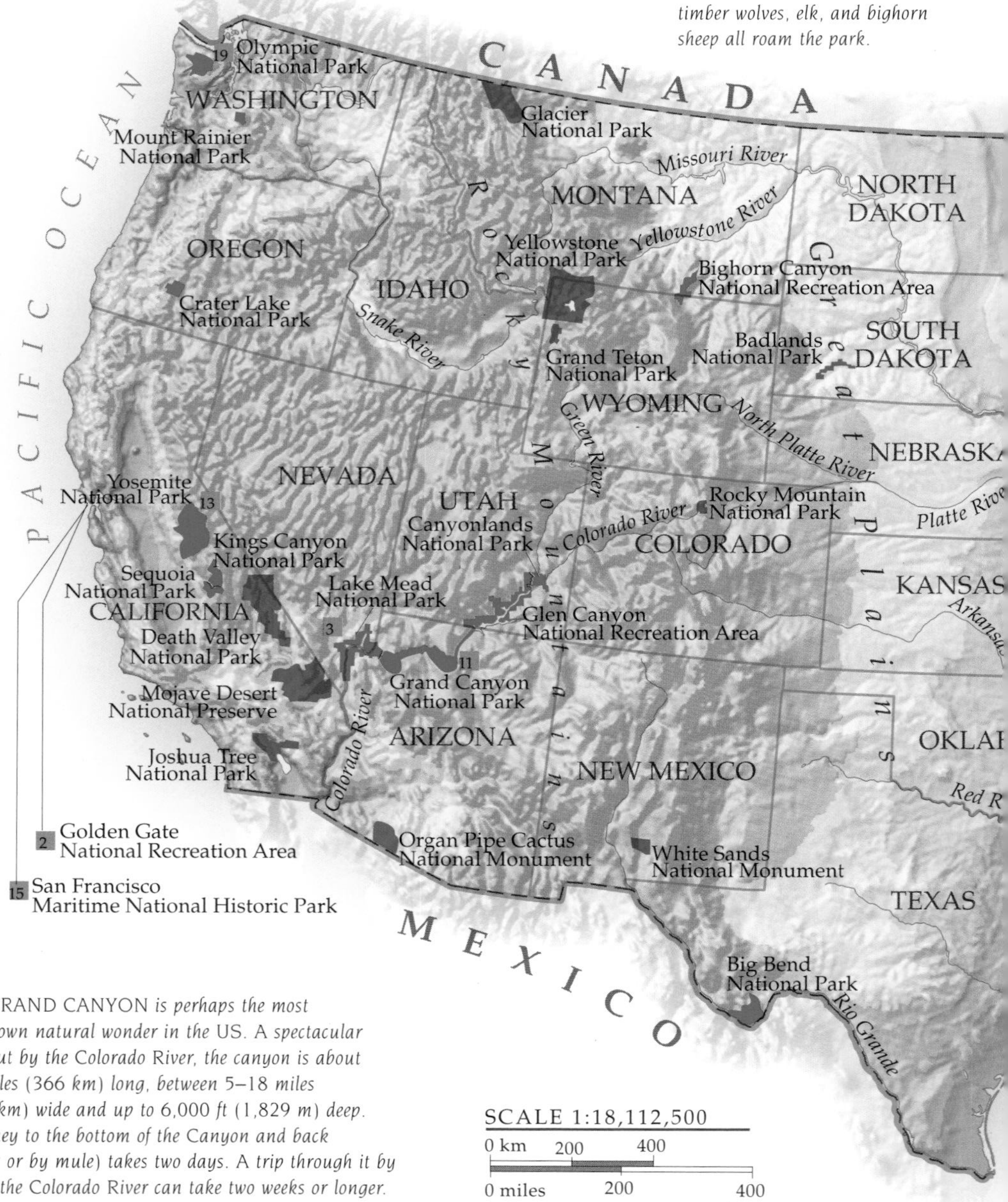

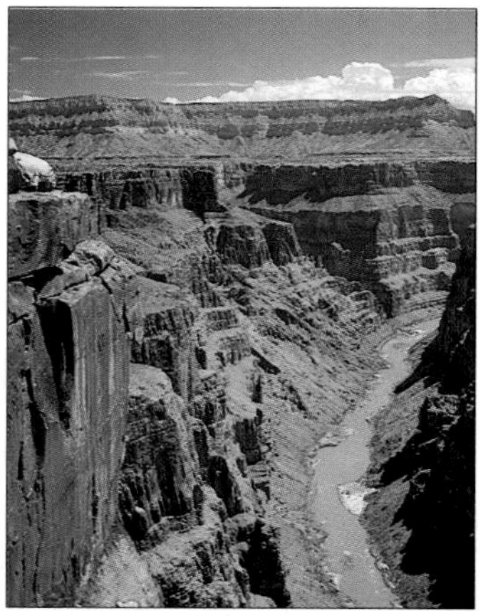

THE GRAND CANYON is perhaps the most well-known natural wonder in the US. A spectacular gorge cut by the Colorado River, the canyon is about 227 miles (366 km) long, between 5–18 miles (8–28 km) wide and up to 6,000 ft (1,829 m) deep. A journey to the bottom of the Canyon and back (on foot or by mule) takes two days. A trip through it by raft on the Colorado River can take two weeks or longer.

WORLD HERITAGE SITES

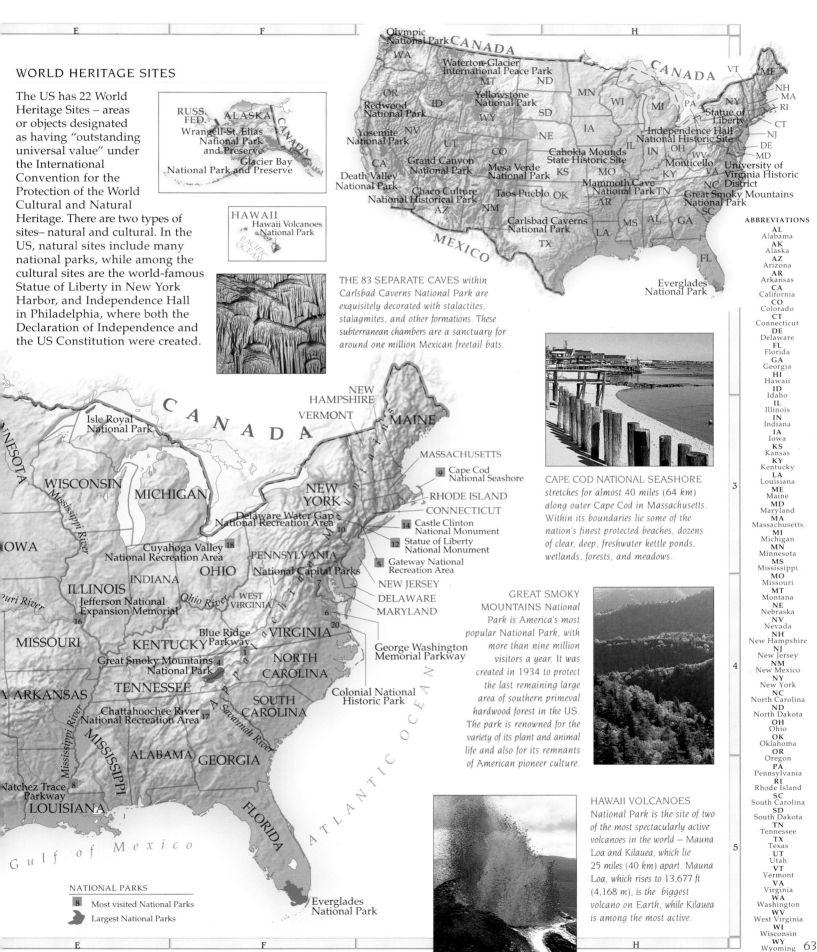

The US has 22 World Heritage Sites – areas or objects designated as having "outstanding universal value" under the International Convention for the Protection of the World Cultural and Natural Heritage. There are two types of sites– natural and cultural. In the US, natural sites include many national parks, while among the cultural sites are the world-famous Statue of Liberty in New York Harbor, and Independence Hall in Philadelphia, where both the Declaration of Independence and the US Constitution were created.

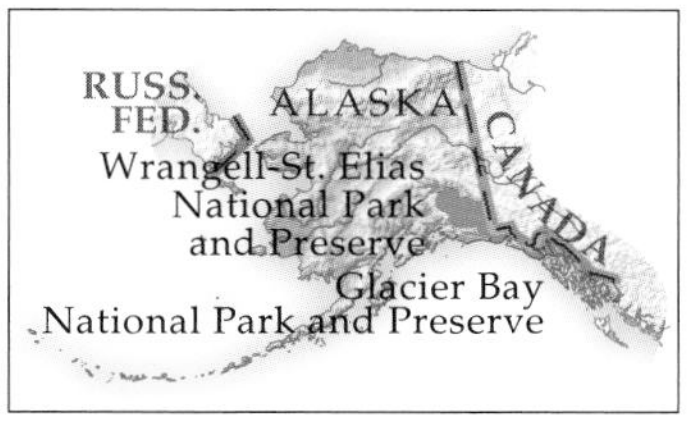

RUSS. FED.
ALASKA
CANADA
Wrangell-St. Elias National Park and Preserve
Glacier Bay National Park and Preserve

HAWAII
Hawaii Volcanoes National Park
PACIFIC OCEAN

Olympic National Park
CANADA
WA
Waterton-Glacier International Peace Park
MT
ND
OR
ID
Redwood National Park
Yellowstone National Park
WY
SD
MN
WI
MI
NY
VT
ME
NH
MA
RI
CT
NJ
DE
MD
PA
Statue of Liberty
Independence Hall National Historic Site
Yosemite National Park
NV
UT
CO
NE
IA
IL
IN
OH
WV
VA
Monticello
University of Virginia Historic District
CA
Grand Canyon National Park
Mesa Verde National Park
Cahokia Mounds State Historic Site
KS
MO
KY
Death Valley National Park
Chaco Culture National Historical Park
AZ
NM
Taos Pueblo
OK
Mammoth Cave National Park
AR
TN
NC
Great Smoky Mountains National Park
SC
Carlsbad Caverns National Park
TX
LA
MS
AL
GA
FL
MEXICO
Everglades National Park

THE 83 SEPARATE CAVES *within Carlsbad Caverns National Park are exquisitely decorated with stalactites, stalagmites, and other formations. These subterranean chambers are a sanctuary for around one million Mexican freetail bats.*

CAPE COD NATIONAL SEASHORE *stretches for almost 40 miles (64 km) along outer Cape Cod in Massachusetts. Within its boundaries lie some of the nation's finest protected beaches, dozens of clear, deep, freshwater kettle ponds, wetlands, forests, and meadows.*

CANADA
Isle Royal National Park
MINNESOTA
WISCONSIN
MICHIGAN
Mississippi River
IOWA
NEW HAMPSHIRE
VERMONT
MAINE
MASSACHUSETTS
9 Cape Cod National Seashore
NEW YORK
RHODE ISLAND
CONNECTICUT
Delaware Water Gap National Recreation Area
10
14 Castle Clinton National Monument
12 Statue of Liberty National Monument
Cuyahoga Valley National Recreation Area 18
PENNSYLVANIA
5 Gateway National Recreation Area
OHIO
National Capital Parks
INDIANA
NEW JERSEY
ILLINOIS
Missouri River
Jefferson National Expansion Memorial
16
Ohio River
WEST VIRGINIA
7
DELAWARE
MARYLAND
6
20
MISSOURI
Blue Ridge Parkway
VIRGINIA
KENTUCKY
1
George Washington Memorial Parkway
Great Smoky Mountains National Park 4
NORTH CAROLINA
ARKANSAS
TENNESSEE
Appalachian Mountains
Colonial National Historic Park
SOUTH CAROLINA
Chattahoochee River National Recreation Area 17
Savannah River
MISSISSIPPI
ALABAMA
GEORGIA
ATLANTIC OCEAN
Natchez Trace Parkway 8
LOUISIANA
FLORIDA
Gulf of Mexico
Everglades National Park
NATIONAL PARKS
8 Most visited National Parks
Largest National Parks

GREAT SMOKY MOUNTAINS *National Park is America's most popular National Park, with more than nine million visitors a year. It was created in 1934 to protect the last remaining large area of southern primeval hardwood forest in the US. The park is renowned for the variety of its plant and animal life and also for its remnants of American pioneer culture.*

HAWAII VOLCANOES *National Park is the site of two of the most spectacularly active volcanoes in the world – Mauna Loa and Kilauea, which lie 25 miles (40 km) apart. Mauna Loa, which rises to 13,677 ft (4,168 m), is the biggest volcano on Earth, while Kilauea is among the most active.*

ABBREVIATIONS

AL Alabama
AK Alaska
AZ Arizona
AR Arkansas
CA California
CO Colorado
CT Connecticut
DE Delaware
FL Florida
GA Georgia
HI Hawaii
ID Idaho
IL Illinois
IN Indiana
IA Iowa
KS Kansas
KY Kentucky
LA Louisiana
ME Maine
MD Maryland
MA Massachusetts
MI Michigan
MN Minnesota
MS Mississippi
MO Missouri
MT Montana
NE Nebraska
NV Nevada
NH New Hampshire
NJ New Jersey
NM New Mexico
NY New York
NC North Carolina
ND North Dakota
OH Ohio
OK Oklahoma
OR Oregon
PA Pennsylvania
RI Rhode Island
SC South Carolina
SD South Dakota
TN Tennessee
TX Texas
UT Utah
VT Vermont
VA Virginia
WA Washington
WV West Virginia
WI Wisconsin
WY Wyoming

STATE FLAGS

The date when each state joined the Union is shown together with the state name.

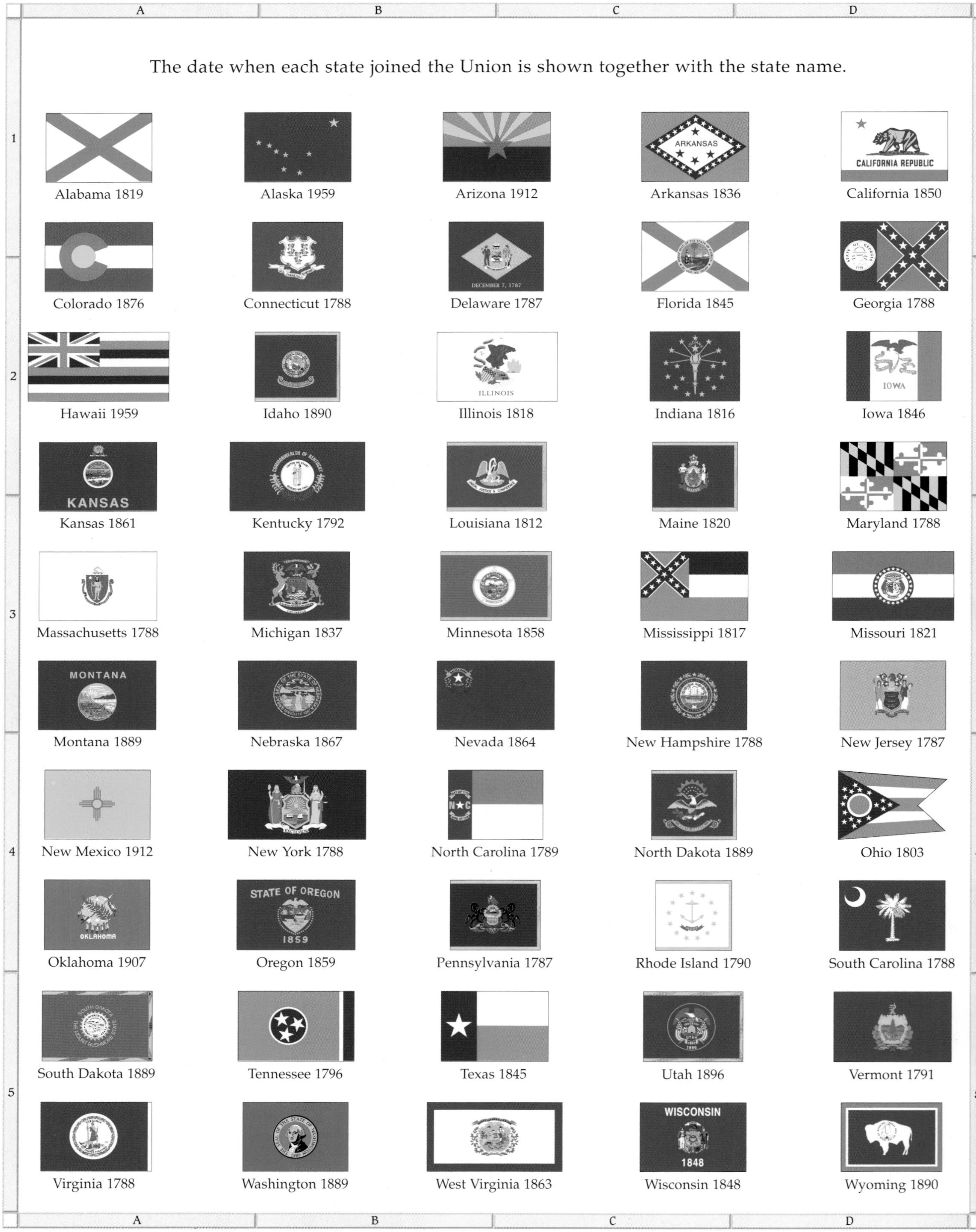

Alabama 1819
Alaska 1959
Arizona 1912
Arkansas 1836
California 1850
Colorado 1876
Connecticut 1788
Delaware 1787
Florida 1845
Georgia 1788
Hawaii 1959
Idaho 1890
Illinois 1818
Indiana 1816
Iowa 1846
Kansas 1861
Kentucky 1792
Louisiana 1812
Maine 1820
Maryland 1788
Massachusetts 1788
Michigan 1837
Minnesota 1858
Mississippi 1817
Missouri 1821
Montana 1889
Nebraska 1867
Nevada 1864
New Hampshire 1788
New Jersey 1787
New Mexico 1912
New York 1788
North Carolina 1789
North Dakota 1889
Ohio 1803
Oklahoma 1907
Oregon 1859
Pennsylvania 1787
Rhode Island 1790
South Carolina 1788
South Dakota 1889
Tennessee 1796
Texas 1845
Utah 1896
Vermont 1791
Virginia 1788
Washington 1889
West Virginia 1863
Wisconsin 1848
Wyoming 1890

THE WORLD ATLAS

THIS ATLAS IS ARRANGED into continental sections, starting at the International Date Line and moving eastward.

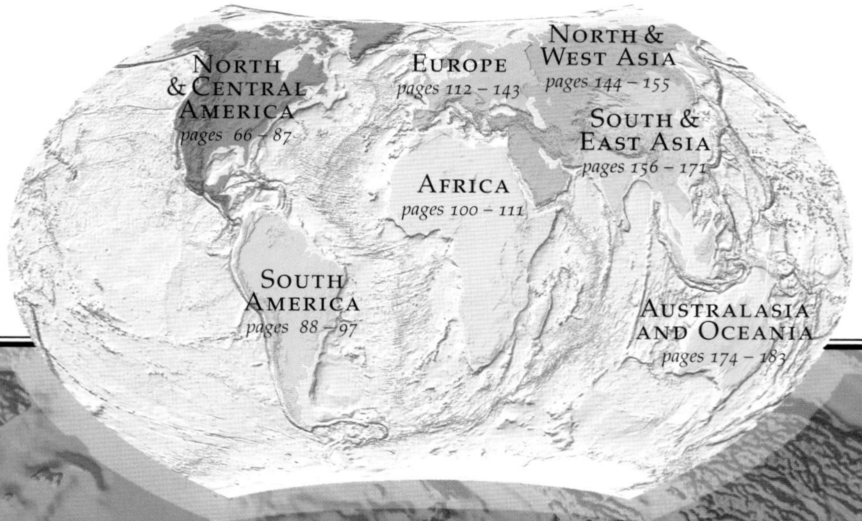

North & Central America

ARCTIC OCEAN
PACIFIC OCEAN
ASIA
EUROPE
CANADA
GREENLAND (to Denmark)
NUUK
SVALBARD (to Norway)
JAN MAYEN (to Norway)
Barents Sea
Greenland Sea
Mohns Ridge
Denmark Strait
Iceland
Reykjanes Basin
Kong Frederik VI Kyst
Kong Christian IX Land
Kong Christian X Land
Kong Frederik VIII Land
Limit of winter pack ice
Labrador Sea
Labrador Basin
North Atlantic Mid-Ocean Canyon
Newfoundland
St. John's
Grand Banks of
Labrador
Smallwood Reservoir
Ungava Bay
Péninsule d'Ungava
Hudson Strait
Davis Strait
Baffin Bay
Baffin Island
Wandel Sea
Lincoln Sea
Kap Morris Jesup
Nansen Basin
Nansen Cordillera
North Pole
Lomonosov Ridge
Makarov Basin
Alpha Cordillera
Mendeleyev Ridge
Laptev Sea
East Siberian Sea
Wrangel Island
Chukchi Sea
Chukchi Plateau
Canada Basin
Beaufort Sea
Ellesmere Island
Queen Elizabeth Islands
Lancaster Sound
Gulf of Boothia
Prince of Wales Island
Victoria Island
Banks Island
Foxe Basin
Southampton Island
Hudson Bay
Belcher Islands
James Bay
Lake Nipigon
Lake Winnipeg
Winnipeg
Reindeer Lake
Lake Athabasca
Great Slave Lake
Great Bear Lake
Athabasca
Saskatoon
Regina
Calgary
Edmonton
Mackenzie
Mackenzie Mountains
Arctic Circle
Rocky Mountains
Coast Mountains
Mount Logan 5959m
Brooks Range
Alaska (part of US)
Mount McKinley 6194m
Alaska Range
Anchorage
Aleutian Range
Kodiak Island
Bristol Bay
Bering Strait
Norton Sound
Yukon
Bering Sea
Saint Lawrence Island
Nunivak Island
Aleutian Basin
Aleutian Islands
Aleutian Trench
Gulf of Alaska
Juneau
Alexander Archipelago
Queen Charlotte Islands
Vancouver Island
Vancouver
Victoria
Seattle
Mount Rainier 4392m
Cascade Range
Cascadia Basin
Eugene
Snake
Boise
113
144
145
185

POPULATION

Less than 50,000

50,000 – 100,000

100,000 – 500,000

Over 500,000

ATLANTIC
OCEAN
UNITED STATES
OF AMERICA
MEXICO
SOUTH
AMERICA
PACIFIC
OCEAN
Sargasso Sea
Nares Plain
Hatteras Plain
Bermuda Rise
BERMUDA
(to UK)
Halifax
(to France)
Georges Bank
Cape Cod
Boston
New York
Philadelphia
Baltimore
WASHINGTON D.C.
Richmond
Raleigh
Columbia
Jacksonville
Blake Plateau
Appalachian Mountains
Montreal
Albany
Lake Ontario
OTTAWA
Lake Huron
Toronto
Niagara Falls
Lake Erie
Detroit
Lansing
Cleveland
Columbus
Milwaukee
Chicago
Madison
Lake Michigan
Saint Paul
Des Moines
Missouri
Lincoln
Topeka
Indianapolis
Ohio
Springfield
Nashville
Atlanta
Montgomery
Memphis
Mississippi
Oklahoma City
Arkansas
Little Rock
Red River
Jackson
Baton Rouge
New Orleans
Mississippi Delta
Dallas
Austin
Houston
San Antonio
Rio Grande
Denver
Salt Lake City
El Paso
Phoenix
Grand Canyon
Colorado
Mount Whitney 4418m
Great Plains
Basin
San Francisco
San Jose
Los Angeles
San Diego
Gulf of California
Lower California
Sierra Madre Occidental
Sierra Madre Oriental
Monterrey
Guadalajara
MEXICO CITY
Volcán Pico de Orizaba 5700m
Acapulco
Middle America Trench
Gulf of Mexico
Tampa
Miami
Florida Straits
HAVANA
CUBA
BAHAMAS
NASSAU
Greater Antilles
TURKS & CAICOS ISLANDS
(to UK)
CAYMAN ISLANDS
(to UK)
JAMAICA
KINGSTON
PORT-AU-PRINCE
HAITI
DOMINICAN REPUBLIC
SANTO DOMINGO
PUERTO RICO
(to US)
VIRGIN ISLANDS (to US)
BRITISH VIRGIN ISLANDS
(to UK)
ANGUILLA (to UK)
ANTIGUA & BARBUDA
ST. KITTS & NEVIS
MONTSERRAT (to UK)
GUADELOUPE
(to France)
DOMINICA
MARTINIQUE (to France)
ST. LUCIA
BARBADOS
ST. VINCENT & THE GRENADINES
GRENADA
TRINIDAD & TOBAGO
PORT-OF-SPAIN
NETHERLANDS ANTILLES
(to Neth.)
ARUBA
(to Neth.)
Lesser Antilles
Caribbean Sea
Colombian Basin
Yucatan Peninsula
BELMOPAN
BELIZE
GUATEMALA
GUATEMALA CITY
HONDURAS
TEGUCIGALPA
SAN SALVADOR
EL SALVADOR
NICARAGUA
MANAGUA
Lake Nicaragua
COSTA RICA
SAN JOSÉ
PANAMA
PANAMA CITY
Andes
Panama Basin
Cocos Ridge
Galapagos Islands
(part of Ecuador)
Guatemala Basin
Colón Ridge
East Pacific Rise
Clarion Fracture Zone
Murray Fracture Zone
Revillagigedo Islands
(part of Mexico)
CLIPPERTON ISLAND
(to French Polynesia)
Gallego Rise
Tropic of Cancer
Equator
0 km
1000
0 miles
1000
N
88
99
185

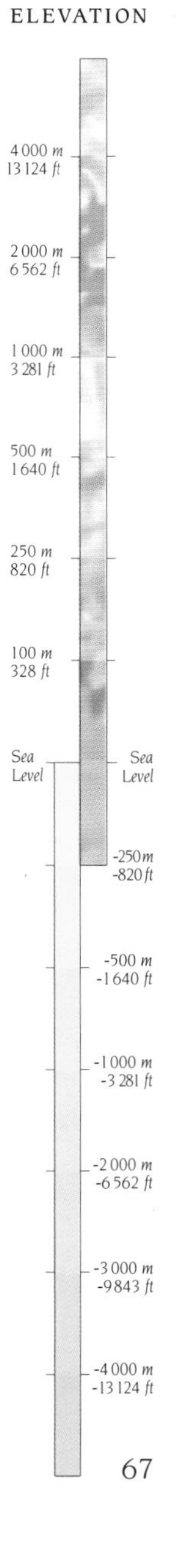
ELEVATION
4000 m
13 124 ft
2000 m
6562 ft
1000 m
3281 ft
500 m
1640 ft
250 m
820 ft
100 m
328 ft
Sea Level
Sea Level
-250 m
-820 ft
-500 m
-1640 ft
-1000 m
-3281 ft
-2000 m
-6562 ft
-3000 m
-9843 ft
-4000 m
-13 124 ft

Western Canada & Alaska

A
B
C
D
1
2
3
4
5
Poluostrov Kamchatka
147
Arctic Circle
RUSSIAN FEDERATION
Ostrov Vrangelya
ARCTI
Chukchi Sea
Attu Island
Near Islands
Bering Sea
Bering Strait
Wevok
Point Lay
Barrow
Kivalina
Wales
Gambell
Saint Lawrence Island
184
Rat Islands
Amchitka Island
Deering
Colville River
Umiat
Prudhoe Bay
Kaktov
Norton Sound
Brooks Range
Alakanuk
Aleutian Islands
Andreanof Islands
Nunivak Island
Grayling
Yukon River
Kokrines
Pribilof Islands
Kwigillingok
ALASKA (part of US)
Fort Yukon
Aklavi
Atka
Kuskokwim Mts
Fairbanks
Yukon River
Fort McPherson
Platinum
Alaska Range
Mount McKinley 6194m
McKinley Park
Umnak Island
Dutch Harbor
Bristol Bay
Iliamna Lake
Susitna
Unalaska Island
Anchorage
YUKON
Macken
Unimak Island
Belkofski
Hope
Gulkana
Alaska Peninsula
Valdez
Chitina
TERRITOR
Shumagin Islands
Kodiak
Cordova
Katalla
Kodiak Island
Mount Logan 5959m
Whitehorse
Yakutat
Gulf of Alaska
Haines
Atlin
Gustavus
Juneau
175
Kake
Alexander Archipelago
BRITIS
Port Alexander
Ketchikan
PACIFIC OCEAN
Prince Rupert
Kitimat
Queen Charlotte Islands
Ocean Falls
Queen Charlotte Sound
Mount Waddington 4016m
Port Hardy
Campbell River
Vancouver Island
Nanaim
Victor
0 km
400
0 miles
400
175

POPULATION

- Less than 50,000
- 50,000 – 100,000
- 100,000 – 500,000
- Over 500,000

E
F
G
H
1
2
3
4
5
OCEAN
Axel Heiberg Island
Ellesmere Island
Alert
187
Knud Rasmussen Land
GREENLAND
(Danish external territory)
Nares Strait
Ellef Ringnes Island
Isachsen
Amund Ringnes Island
Prince Patrick Island
Queen Elizabeth Islands
Mould Bay
Bathurst Island
Devon Island
Melville Island
Cornwallis Island
Lancaster Sound
Resolute
Baffin Bay
Davis Strait
114
Arctic Circle
Beaufort Sea
Banks Island
Viscount Melville Sound
Somerset Island
Brodeur Peninsula
Prince of Wales Island
McClintock Channel
Gulf of Boothia
Baffin Island
Sachs Harbour
Tuktoyaktuk
Amundsen Gulf
Holman
Victoria Island
Boothia Peninsula
Igloolik
Cumberland Sound
Paulatuk
Cambridge Bay
King William Island
Pelly Bay
Gjoa Haven
Melville Peninsula
Foxe Basin
Nettilling Lake
Amadjuak Lake
Iqaluit
Coppermine
Repulse Bay
Fort Good Hope
Hudson Strait
Southampton Island
Great Bear Lake
Mackenzie
Echo Bay
Burnside
Coral Harbour
Garry Lake
Back
Baker Lake
Péninsule d' Ungava
NORTHWEST TERRITORIES
Rankin Inlet
Coats Island
Mansel Island
Whale Cove
Rae-Edzo
Yellowknife
Reliance
QUÉBEC
Fort Simpson
Lutselk'e
Dubawnt
Great Slave Lake
Arviat
Hudson Bay
Fort Providence
Hay River
Fort Liard
Fort Smith
Churchill
Fort Nelson
Lake Athabasca
Belcher Islands
70
COLUMBIA
Reindeer Lake
Wollaston Lake
Fort Vermilion
Southern Indian Lake
Fort McMurray
Fox Mine
Nelson
James Bay
CANADA
Fort St.John
Buffalo Narrows
ALBERTA
Thompson
Grande Prairie
SASKATCHEWAN
Prince George
Athabasca
Flin Flon
Lake Winnipeg
The Pas
North Saskatchewan
Saskatchewan
Edmonton
MANITOBA
Mount Robson 3954m
Leduc
Prince Albert
ONTARIO
Saskatoon
Red Deer
Kindersley
Yorkton
Lake Manitoba
Kamloops
Calgary
Regina
Qu'Appelle
Brandon
Winnipeg
Kelowna
Medicine Hat
Weyburn
Lake of the Woods
Lake Superior
Vancouver
Cranbrook
Lethbridge
Melita
Estevan
Lake Huron
78
Milk River
45
Lake Michigan
UNITED STATES OF AMERICA
ELEVATION
4 000 m
13 124 ft
2 000 m
6 562 ft
1 000 m
3 281 ft
500 m
1 640 ft
250 m
820 ft
100 m
328 ft
Sea Level
-250 m
-820 ft
-500 m
-1 640 ft
-1 000 m
-3 281 ft
-2 000 m
-6 562 ft
-3 000 m
-9 843 ft
-4 000 m
-13 124 ft

EASTERN CANADA

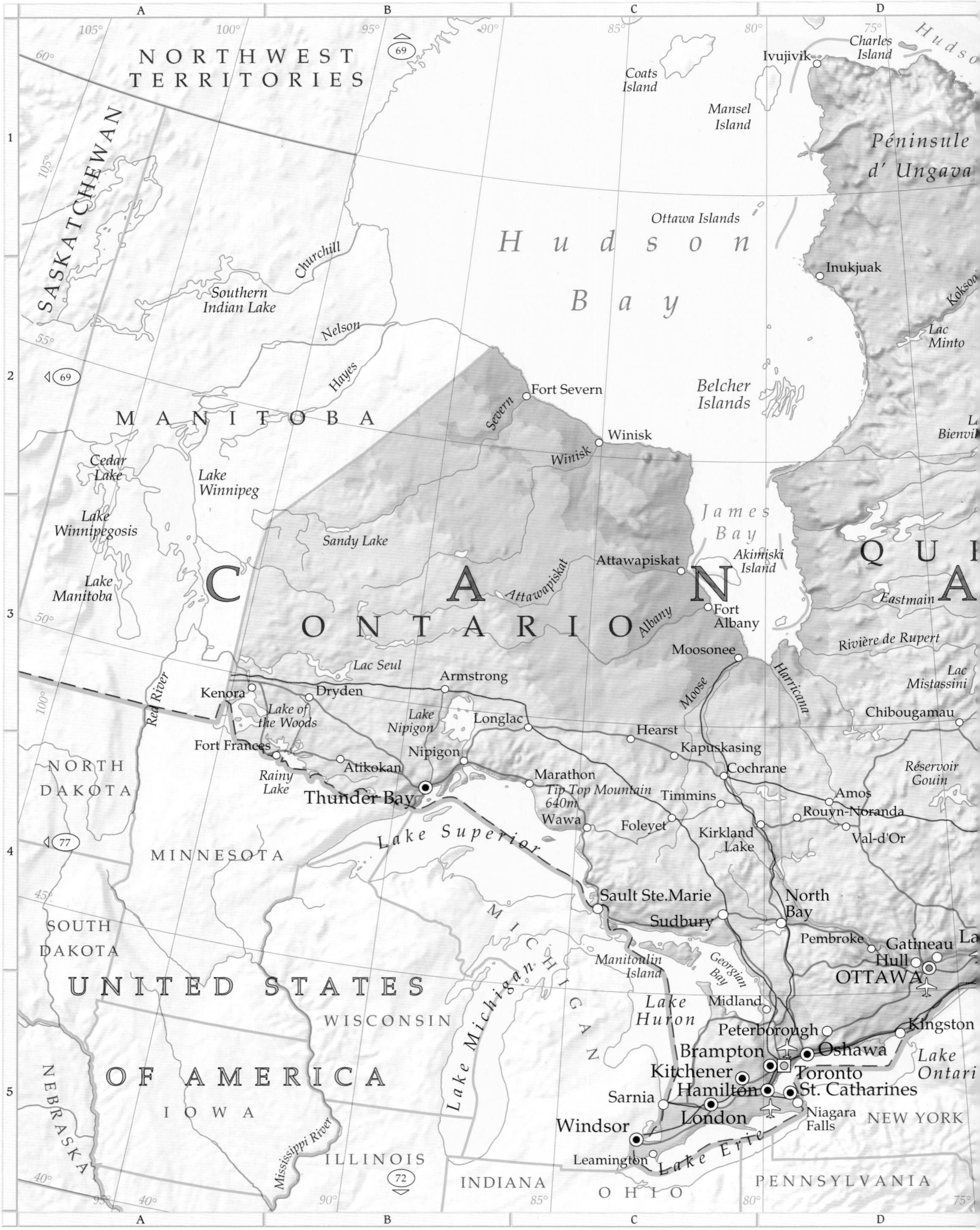
NORTHWEST TERRITORIES
SASKATCHEWAN
MANITOBA
CANADA
ONTARIO
QUÉBEC
NORTH DAKOTA
SOUTH DAKOTA
MINNESOTA
WISCONSIN
MICHIGAN
IOWA
NEBRASKA
ILLINOIS
INDIANA
OHIO
PENNSYLVANIA
NEW YORK
UNITED STATES OF AMERICA
Hudson Bay
James Bay
Coats Island
Mansel Island
Charles Island
Ivujivik
Péninsule d' Ungava
Ottawa Islands
Inukjuak
Lac Minto
Koksoak
Belcher Islands
Akimiski Island
Eastmain
Rivière de Rupert
Lac Mistassini
Chibougamau
Réservoir Gouin
Amos
Rouyn-Noranda
Val-d'Or
Churchill
Southern Indian Lake
Nelson
Hayes
Cedar Lake
Lake Winnipeg
Lake Winnipegosis
Lake Manitoba
Sandy Lake
Fort Severn
Severn
Winisk
Attawapiskat
Fort Albany
Albany
Moosonee
Moose
Harricana
Lac Seul
Armstrong
Kenora
Dryden
Lake of the Woods
Red River
Lake Nipigon
Longlac
Hearst
Kapuskasing
Cochrane
Fort Frances
Nipigon
Atikokan
Rainy Lake
Thunder Bay
Marathon
Tip Top Mountain 640m
Wawa
Timmins
Foleyet
Kirkland Lake
Lake Superior
Sault Ste.Marie
Sudbury
North Bay
Pembroke
Gatineau
Hull
OTTAWA
Manitoulin Island
Georgian Bay
Lake Huron
Midland
Lake Michigan
Peterborough
Kingston
Brampton
Oshawa
Kitchener
Toronto
Hamilton
St. Catharines
Sarnia
London
Niagara Falls
Windsor
Leamington
Lake Erie
Lake Ontario
Mississippi River
69
77
72
A
B
C
D
1
2
3
4
5

POPULATION

Less than 50,000

50,000 – 100,000

100,000 – 500,000

Over 500,000

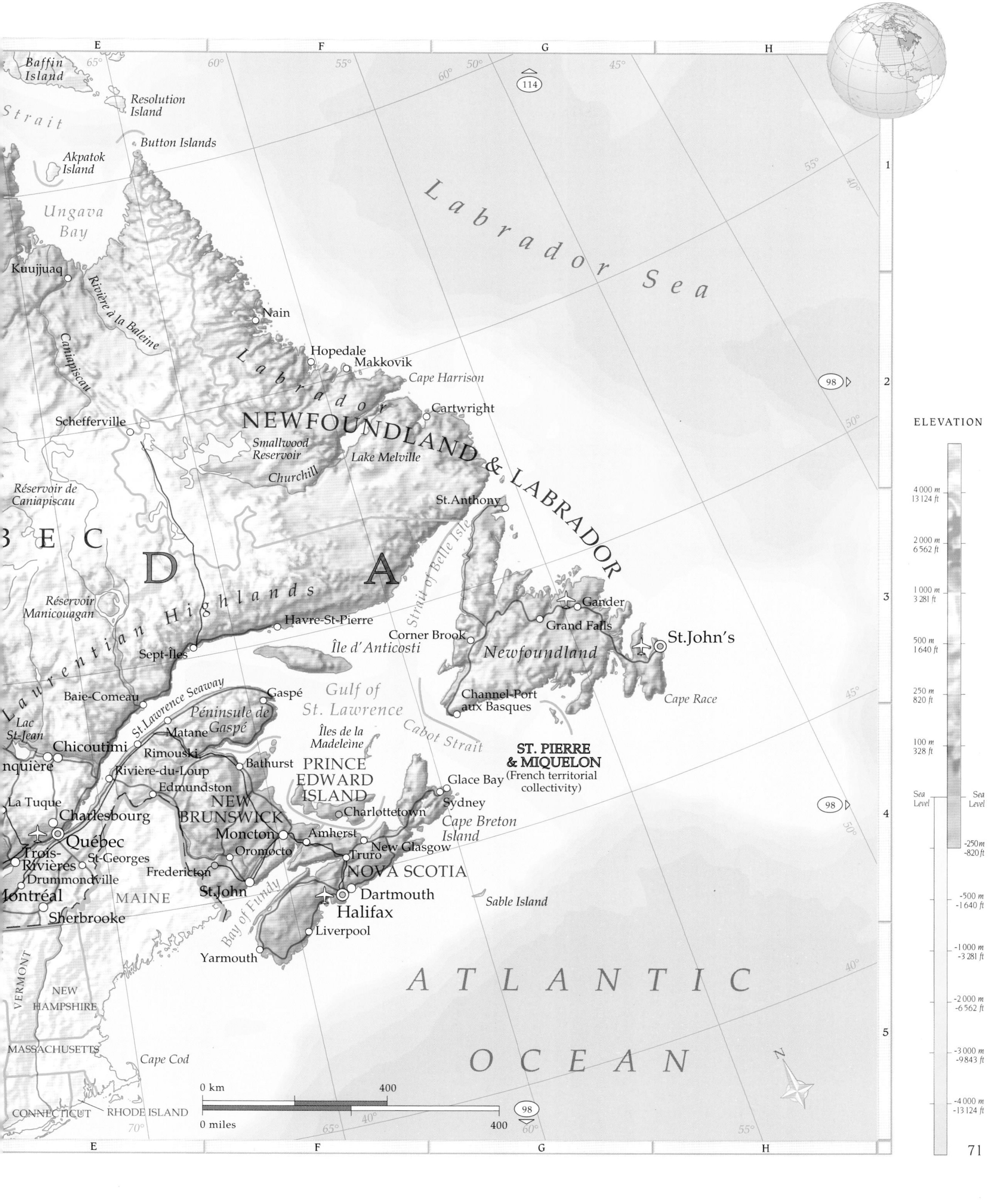
Baffin Island
Resolution Island
Strait
Button Islands
Akpatok Island
Ungava Bay
Kuujjuaq
Rivière à la Baleine
Caniapiscau
Nain
Hopedale
Makkovik
Cape Harrison
Labrador
Labrador Sea
Cartwright
Schefferville
NEWFOUNDLAND & LABRADOR
Smallwood Reservoir
Churchill
Lake Melville
Réservoir de Caniapiscau
St.Anthony
Strait of Belle Isle
Réservoir Manicouagan
Laurentian Highlands
Havre-St-Pierre
Gander
Grand Falls
St.John's
Corner Brook
Newfoundland
Sept-Îles
Île d'Anticosti
Baie-Comeau
St.Lawrence Seaway
Gaspé
Gulf of St. Lawrence
Channel-Port aux Basques
Cape Race
Péninsule de Gaspé
Matane
Lac St-Jean
Chicoutimi
Rimouski
Îles de la Madeleine
Cabot Strait
ST. PIERRE & MIQUELON
(French territorial collectivity)
Bathurst
PRINCE EDWARD ISLAND
Glace Bay
Rivière-du-Loup
Edmundston
Sydney
La Tuque
NEW BRUNSWICK
Charlottetown
Charlesbourg
Cape Breton Island
Moncton
Amherst
Québec
New Glasgow
Oromocto
Trois-Rivières
St-Georges
Truro
Drummondville
Fredericton
NOVA SCOTIA
Montréal
St.John
Dartmouth
MAINE
Halifax
Sable Island
Sherbrooke
Bay of Fundy
Liverpool
Yarmouth
ATLANTIC OCEAN
VERMONT
NEW HAMPSHIRE
MASSACHUSETTS
Cape Cod
CONNECTICUT
RHODE ISLAND
0 km 400
0 miles 400
114
98
E F G H
1 2 3 4 5
ELEVATION
4 000 m 13 124 ft
2 000 m 6 562 ft
1 000 m 3 281 ft
500 m 1 640 ft
250 m 820 ft
100 m 328 ft
Sea Level
-250 m -820 ft
-500 m -1 640 ft
-1 000 m -3 281 ft
-2 000 m -6 562 ft
-3 000 m -9 843 ft
-4 000 m -13 124 ft

Northeast US

POPULATION

Less than 50,000

50,000 – 100,000

100,000 – 500,000

Over 500,000

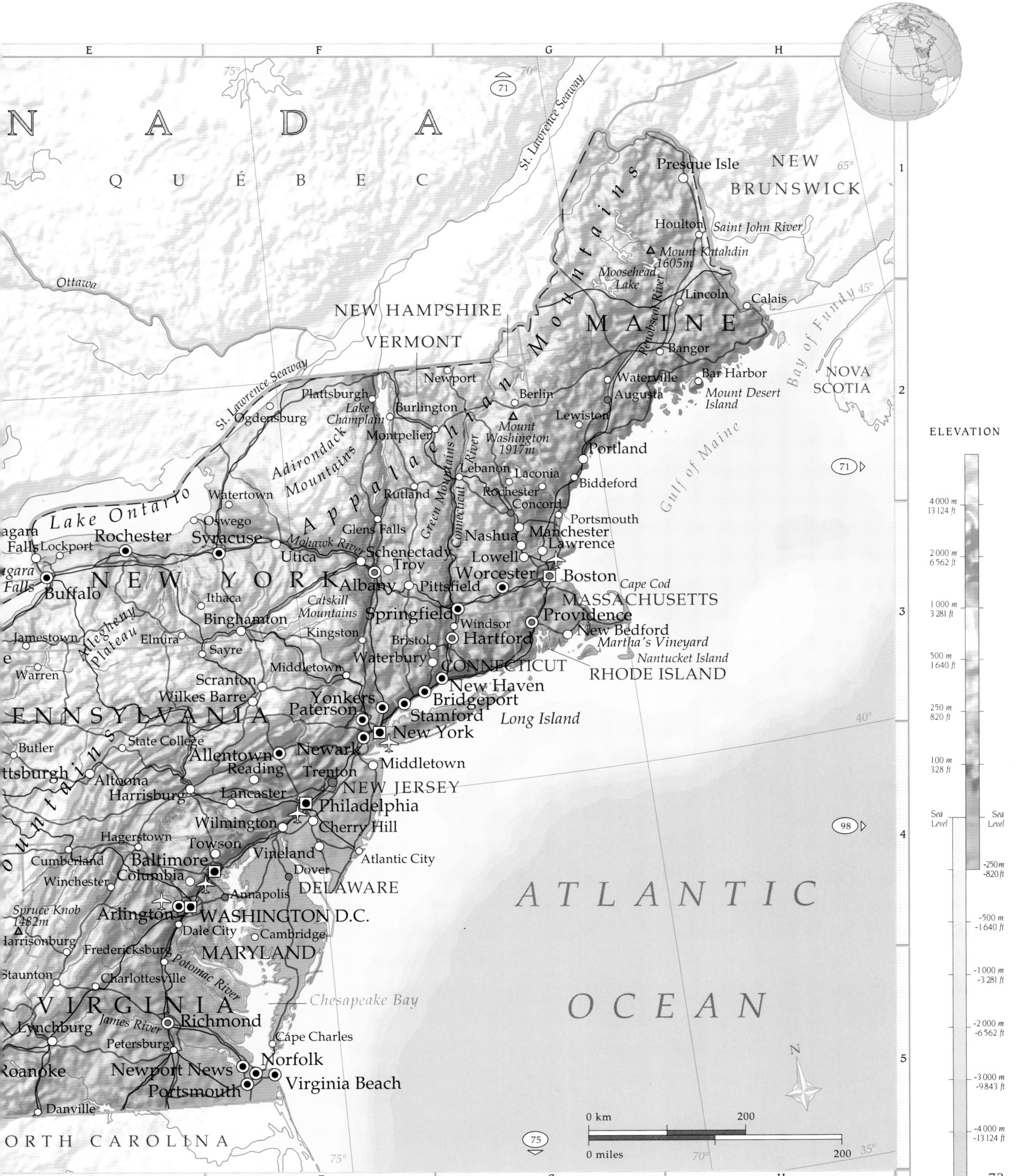
E
F
G
H
1
2
3
4
5
N A D A
Q U É B E C
NEW BRUNSWICK
NOVA SCOTIA
NEW HAMPSHIRE
VERMONT
M A I N E
NEW YORK
PENNSYLVANIA
MASSACHUSETTS
CONNECTICUT
RHODE ISLAND
NEW JERSEY
DELAWARE
MARYLAND
VIRGINIA
NORTH CAROLINA
WASHINGTON D.C.
ATLANTIC
OCEAN
Ottawa
St. Lawrence Seaway
Lake Ontario
Adirondack Mountains
Appalachian Mountains
Allegheny Plateau
Catskill Mountains
Green Mountains
Connecticut River
Mohawk River
Lake Champlain
Moosehead Lake
Penobscot River
Saint John River
Mount Katahdin 1605m
Mount Washington 1917m
Mount Desert Island
Gulf of Maine
Bay of Fundy
Cape Cod
Martha's Vineyard
Nantucket Island
Long Island
Chesapeake Bay
Potomac River
James River
Spruce Knob 1482m
Presque Isle
Houlton
Lincoln
Calais
Bangor
Bar Harbor
Waterville
Augusta
Lewiston
Portland
Biddeford
Berlin
Newport
Burlington
Plattsburgh
Ogdensburg
Montpelier
Lebanon
Laconia
Rochester
Concord
Portsmouth
Manchester
Nashua
Lawrence
Lowell
Boston
Worcester
Providence
New Bedford
Rutland
Glens Falls
Schenectady
Troy
Albany
Pittsfield
Springfield
Windsor
Hartford
Bristol
Waterbury
New Haven
Bridgeport
Stamford
Yonkers
Paterson
New York
Newark
Middletown
Kingston
Watertown
Oswego
Syracuse
Utica
Rochester
Lockport
Niagara Falls
Buffalo
Ithaca
Binghamton
Elmira
Sayre
Jamestown
Warren
Scranton
Wilkes Barre
State College
Butler
Pittsburgh
Altoona
Harrisburg
Allentown
Reading
Lancaster
Trenton
Philadelphia
Cherry Hill
Wilmington
Vineland
Atlantic City
Dover
Hagerstown
Towson
Baltimore
Columbia
Cumberland
Winchester
Annapolis
Arlington
Dale City
Cambridge
Harrisonburg
Fredericksburg
Staunton
Charlottesville
Richmond
Lynchburg
Petersburg
Cape Charles
Norfolk
Newport News
Portsmouth
Virginia Beach
Roanoke
Danville
75°
70°
65°
45°
40°
35°
71
98
75
0 km
200
0 miles
200
N
ELEVATION
4 000 m
13 124 ft
2 000 m
6 562 ft
1 000 m
3 281 ft
500 m
1 640 ft
250 m
820 ft
100 m
328 ft
Sea Level
-250 m
-820 ft
-500 m
-1 640 ft
-1 000 m
-3 281 ft
-2 000 m
-6 562 ft
-3 000 m
-9 843 ft
-4 000 m
-13 124 ft

Southeast US

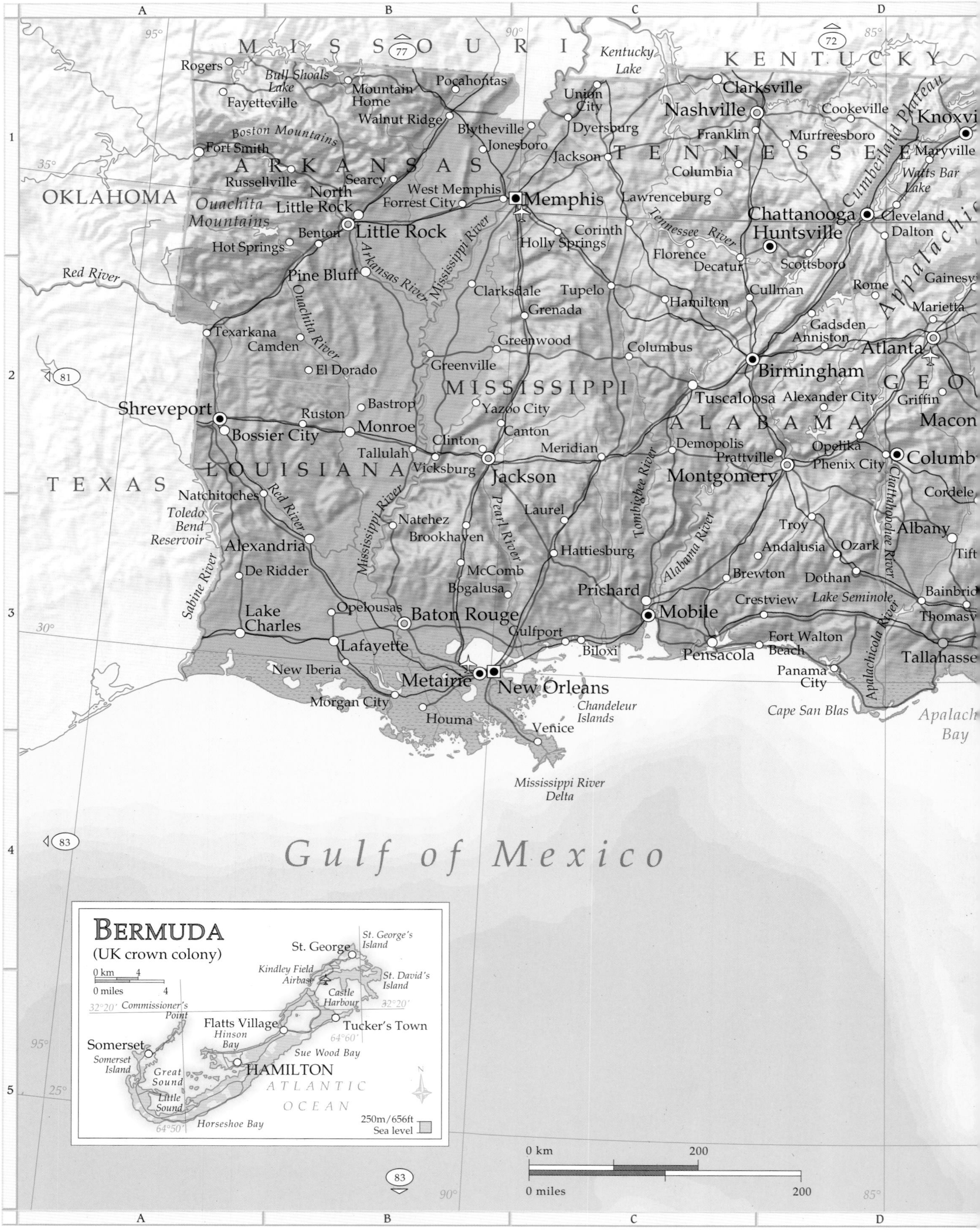
MISSOURI
KENTUCKY
TENNESSEE
ARKANSAS
OKLAHOMA
MISSISSIPPI
ALABAMA
LOUISIANA
TEXAS
GEO
Kentucky Lake
Rogers
Bull Shoals Lake
Fayetteville
Mountain Home
Pocahontas
Walnut Ridge
Boston Mountains
Fort Smith
Russellville
Searcy
North Little Rock
Little Rock
Ouachita Mountains
Hot Springs
Benton
Pine Bluff
Red River
Texarkana
Camden
El Dorado
Ouachita River
Arkansas River
Blytheville
Jonesboro
West Memphis
Forrest City
Memphis
Union City
Dyersburg
Jackson
Clarksville
Nashville
Franklin
Columbia
Cookeville
Murfreesboro
Lawrenceburg
Cumberland Plateau
Knoxvi
Maryville
Watts Bar Lake
Chattanooga
Cleveland
Dalton
Huntsville
Scottsboro
Tennessee River
Florence
Decatur
Corinth
Holly Springs
Mississippi River
Clarksdale
Tupelo
Grenada
Hamilton
Cullman
Rome
Gainesv
Marietta
Appalachi
Gadsden
Anniston
Atlanta
Greenwood
Columbus
Birmingham
Greenville
Tuscaloosa
Alexander City
Griffin
Macon
Yazoo City
Canton
Clinton
Meridian
Demopolis
Prattville
Opelika
Phenix City
Columb
Bastrop
Ruston
Monroe
Shreveport
Bossier City
Tallulah
Vicksburg
Jackson
Montgomery
Cordele
Natchitoches
Toledo Bend Reservoir
Red River
Natchez
Brookhaven
Pearl River
Laurel
Tombigbee River
Troy
Albany
Alexandria
Hattiesburg
Alabama River
Andalusia
Ozark
Tift
Sabine River
De Ridder
McComb
Bogalusa
Brewton
Dothan
Chattahoochee River
Bainbrid
Prichard
Crestview
Lake Seminole
Thomasv
Lake Charles
Opelousas
Baton Rouge
Mobile
Gulfport
Biloxi
Pensacola
Fort Walton Beach
Tallahasse
Lafayette
New Iberia
Metairie
New Orleans
Panama City
Apalachicola River
Morgan City
Houma
Chandeleur Islands
Venice
Cape San Blas
Apalach Bay
Mississippi River Delta
Gulf of Mexico
95°
90°
85°
35°
30°
25°
77
72
81
83
A
B
C
D
1
2
3
4
5
BERMUDA
(UK crown colony)
0 km 4
0 miles 4
St. George
St. George's Island
Kindley Field Airbase
St. David's Island
Castle Harbour
32°20′
Commissioner's Point
Flatts Village
Tucker's Town
Hinson Bay
64°60′
Somerset
Sue Wood Bay
Somerset Island
Great Sound
HAMILTON
Little Sound
ATLANTIC OCEAN
Horseshoe Bay
64°50′
250m/656ft
Sea level
N
0 km 200
0 miles 200

POPULATION

Less than 50,000

50,000 – 100,000

100,000 – 500,000

Over 500,000

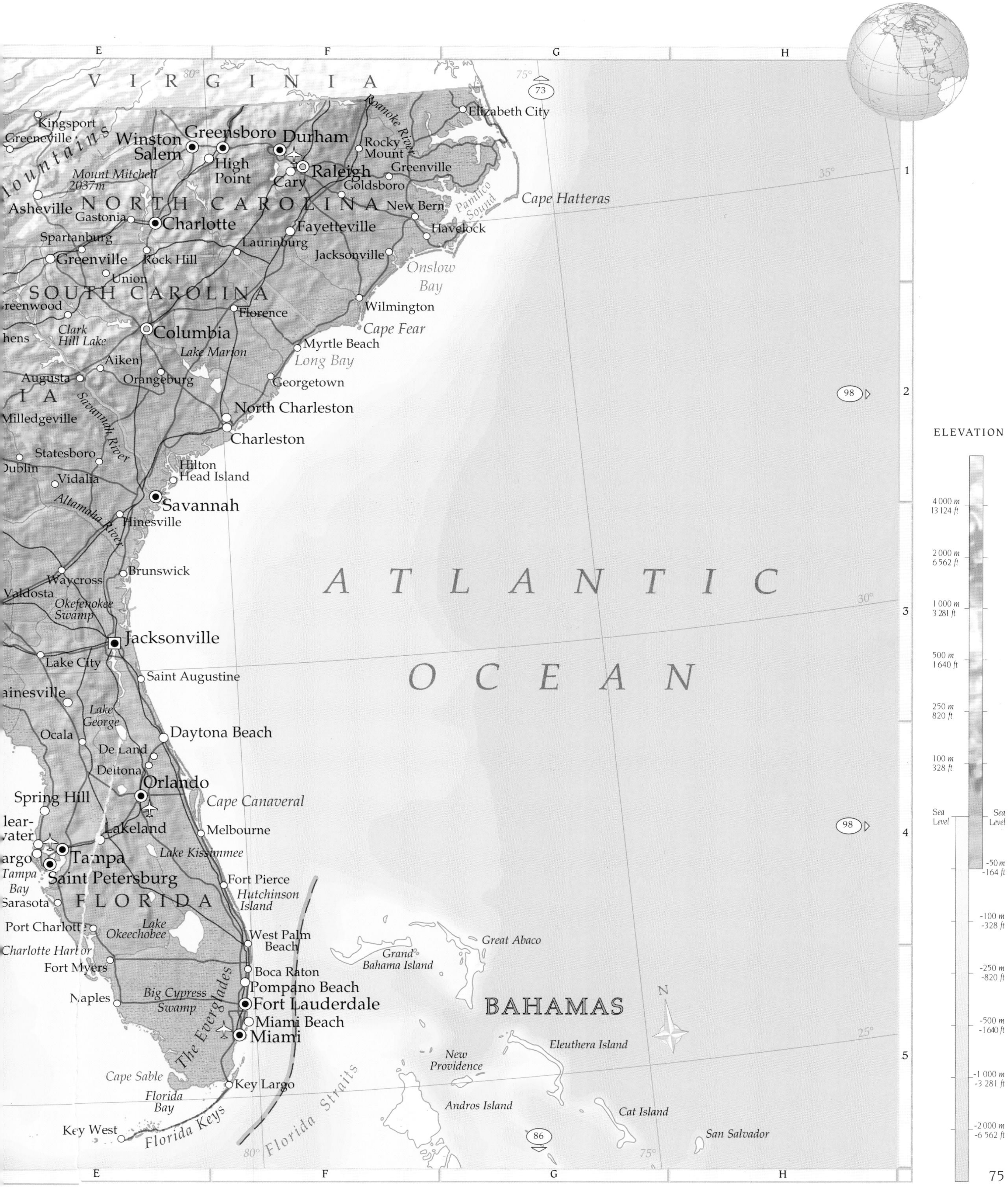
E
F
G
H
VIRGINIA
NORTH CAROLINA
SOUTH CAROLINA
FLORIDA
ATLANTIC
OCEAN
BAHAMAS
Elizabeth City
Kingsport
Greeneville
Winston Salem
Greensboro
Durham
Rocky Mount
High Point
Raleigh
Cary
Greenville
Goldsboro
Mount Mitchell 2037m
Asheville
Gastonia
Charlotte
New Bern
Pamlico Sound
Cape Hatteras
Havelock
Fayetteville
Laurinburg
Jacksonville
Spartanburg
Greenville
Rock Hill
Union
Onslow Bay
Roanoke River
Wilmington
Cape Fear
Florence
Columbia
Clark Hill Lake
Lake Marion
Myrtle Beach
Long Bay
Aiken
Augusta
Orangeburg
Georgetown
Savannah River
North Charleston
Charleston
Milledgeville
Statesboro
Hilton Head Island
Vidalia
Savannah
Altamaha River
Hinesville
Brunswick
Waycross
Valdosta
Okefenokee Swamp
Jacksonville
Lake City
Saint Augustine
Lake George
Ocala
Daytona Beach
De Land
Deltona
Orlando
Spring Hill
Cape Canaveral
Lakeland
Melbourne
Tampa
Lake Kissimmee
Saint Petersburg
Tampa Bay
Sarasota
Fort Pierce
Hutchinson Island
Port Charlotte
Lake Okeechobee
West Palm Beach
Charlotte Harbor
Fort Myers
Boca Raton
Pompano Beach
Naples
Big Cypress Swamp
Fort Lauderdale
Miami Beach
Miami
The Everglades
Cape Sable
Florida Bay
Key Largo
Key West
Florida Keys
Florida Straits
Great Abaco
Grand Bahama Island
Eleuthera Island
New Providence
Andros Island
Cat Island
San Salvador
N
73
98
86
80°
75°
35°
30°
25°
1
2
3
4
5
ELEVATION
4 000 m 13 124 ft
2 000 m 6 562 ft
1 000 m 3 281 ft
500 m 1 640 ft
250 m 820 ft
100 m 328 ft
Sea Level
-50 m -164 ft
-100 m -328 ft
-250 m -820 ft
-500 m -1 640 ft
-1 000 m -3 281 ft
-2 000 m -6 562 ft

Central US

POPULATION

- Less than 50,000
- 50,000 – 100,000
- 100,000 – 500,000
- Over 500,000

E
F
G
H
1
2
3
4
5
0 km
200
0 miles
200
100°
95°
90°
85°
45°
40°
70
72
74
81
MANITOBA
A
D
A
ONTARIO
Lake of the Woods
Rainy Lake
Lake Superior
MICHIGAN
Lake Michigan
WISCONSIN
MINNESOTA
IOWA
ILLINOIS
INDIANA
MISSOURI
KANSAS
KENTUCKY
TENNESSEE
ARKANSAS
OKLAHOMA
NORTH DAKOTA
SOUTH DAKOTA
NEBRASKA
Great Plains
Ozark Plateau
Red River
Souris River
International Falls
Upper Red Lake
Lower Red Lake
Grafton
Thief River Falls
Devils Lake
East Grand Forks
Grand Forks
Crookston
Virginia
Chisholm
Hibbing
Eveleth
Bemidji
Grand Rapids
Leech Lake
Valley City
Jamestown
Fargo
Mandan
Bismarck
West Fargo
Moorhead
Detroit Lakes
Cloquet
Duluth
Brainerd
Mille Lacs Lake
Wahpeton
Fergus Falls
Little Falls
Alexandria
Saint Cloud
Elk River
Coon Rapids
Aberdeen
Morris
Minneapolis
Saint Paul
Montevideo
Bloomington
Burnsville
Watertown
Northfield
Red Wing
Marshall
New Ulm
Faribault
Winona
Pierre
Huron
James River
Big Sioux River
Brookings
Mankato
Owatonna
Rochester
Austin
Mitchell
Madison
Fairmont
Albert Lea
Mississippi River
Sioux Falls
Worthington
Spencer
Lake Francis Case
Mason City
Waverly
Sheldon
Algona
Yankton
Vermillion
Cedar Falls
Waterloo
Dubuque
Niobrara River
Missouri River
Sioux City
Fort Dodge
Evansdale
Iowa Falls
Webster City
Marion
South Sioux City
Cedar Rapids
Denison
Ames
Norfolk
Iowa City
Ankeny
Newton
Illinois River
Harlan
Urbandale
Davenport
Des Moines
Columbus
Fremont
Muscatine
West Des Moines
Oskaloosa
Loup River
Omaha
Council Bluffs
Indianola
Mount Pleasant
North Platte
Papillion
Bellevue
Ottumwa
Platte River
York
Creston
Burlington
Grand Island
Clarinda
Lamoni
Fort Madison
Lexington
Lincoln
Kearney
Nebraska City
Keokuk
Hastings
Maryville
Kirksville
Beatrice
Hannibal
McCook
Macon
Saint Joseph
Moberly
Concordia
Atchison
Excelsior Springs
Mexico
Colby
Wabash River
Manhattan
Kansas City
Independence
Columbia
Florissant
Junction City
Saint Louis
Hays
Salina
Topeka
Kansas City
Kansas River
Kirkwood
Jefferson City
Arnold
Ottawa
McPherson
Emporia
Farmington
Great Bend
Lake of the Ozarks
Rolla
Perryville
Ohio River
Hutchinson
Newton
Iola
Garden City
El Dorado
Jackson
Fort Scott
Lebanon
Cape Girardeau
Dodge City
Pratt
Chanute
Pittsburg
Wichita
Springfield
Carthage
Parsons
Dexter
Sikeston
Wellington
Arkansas City
Joplin
Aurora
Poplar Bluff
Malden
Kentucky Lake
Liberal
Caruthersville
Arkansas River
Kennett

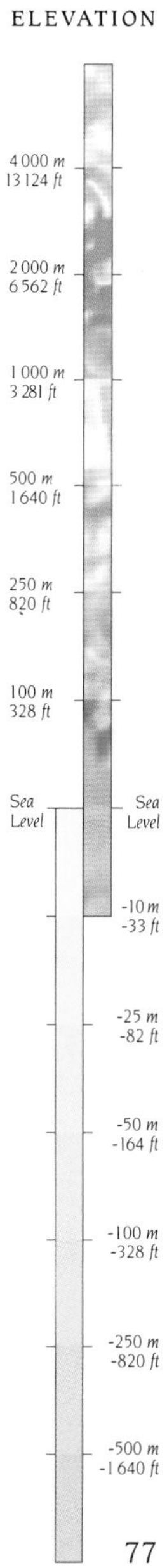
ELEVATION
4 000 m
13 124 ft
2 000 m
6 562 ft
1 000 m
3 281 ft
500 m
1 640 ft
250 m
820 ft
100 m
328 ft
Sea Level
Sea Level
-10 m
-33 ft
-25 m
-82 ft
-50 m
-164 ft
-100 m
-328 ft
-250 m
-820 ft
-500 m
-1 640 ft

West US

POPULATION

Less than 50,000

50,000 – 100,000

100,000 – 500,000

Over 500,000

UTAH
NEVADA
ARIZONA
CALIFORNIA
MEXICO
Great Basin
Desert
Sierra Nevada
Central Valley
San Joaquin Valley
Sacramento Valley
Ruby Mountains
Schell Creek Range
Reese River
Humboldt River
Carson Sink
Pyramid Lake
Honey Lake
Walker Lake
Mono Lake
Lake Tahoe
Lake Powell
Grand Canyon
Colorado River
Lake Mead
Lake Mohave
Gila River
Death Valley
Mount Whitney 4418m
Tulare Lake Bed
Mojave Desert
San Rafael Mountains
Chocolate Mountains
Salton Sea
Santa Lucia Range
Monterey Bay
Channel Islands
Santa Rosa Island
Santa Catalina Island
San Clemente Island
OCEAN
Reno
Sparks
Carson City
South Lake Tahoe
Susanville
Chico
Yuba City
Citrus Heights
Sacramento
Fairfield
Stockton
Manteca
Modesto
Turlock
Oakland
San Jose
Gilroy
Salinas
Madera
Fresno
Hanford
Selma
Visalia
Porterville
Delano
Bakersfield
Ridgecrest
Tonopah
Hawthorne
Ely
Alamo
Las Vegas
Henderson
Barstow
Victorville
Lancaster
Pasadena
San Bernardino
Riverside
Santa Ana
Palm Springs
Blythe
Brawley
El Centro
Escondido
El Cajon
Lakeside
Chula Vista
San Diego
Encinitas
Oceanside
Fallbrook
Huntington Beach
Long Beach
Los Angeles
Oxnard
Santa Barbara
Lompoc
Santa Maria
San Luis Obispo
Atascadero
Monterey
Santa Cruz
Sunnyvale
Palo Alto
San Francisco
Berkeley
Vallejo
Napa
Santa Rosa
Woodland
Ukiah
Redding
Sacramento River
0 km 200
0 miles 200
HAWAII
Niihau
Kauai
Lihue
Oahu
Wahiawa
Honolulu
Kaneohe
Molokai
Maui
Wailuku
Hawaii
Hilo
Mauna Kea 4205m
PACIFIC OCEAN
2000m/6562ft
1000m/3281ft
500m/1640ft
200m/656ft
Sea level
0 km 200
0 miles 200
76
80
82
185
40°
35°
120°
125°
A
B
C
D
E
5
6
7
8

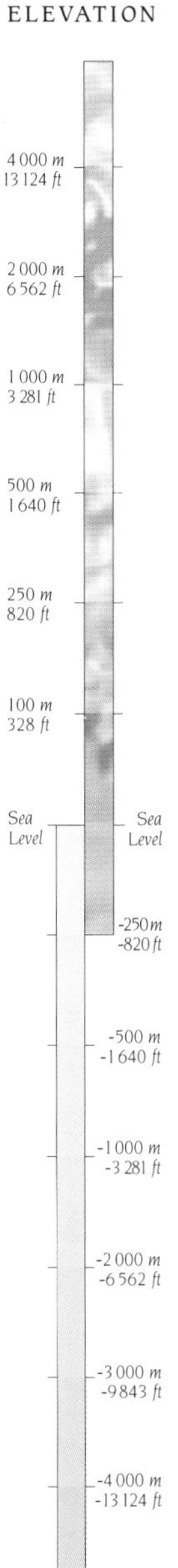
ELEVATION
4 000 m
13 124 ft
2 000 m
6 562 ft
1 000 m
3 281 ft
500 m
1 640 ft
250 m
820 ft
100 m
328 ft
Sea Level
Sea Level
-250 m
-820 ft
-500 m
-1 640 ft
-1 000 m
-3 281 ft
-2 000 m
-6 562 ft
-3 000 m
-9 843 ft
-4 000 m
-13 124 ft

Southwest US

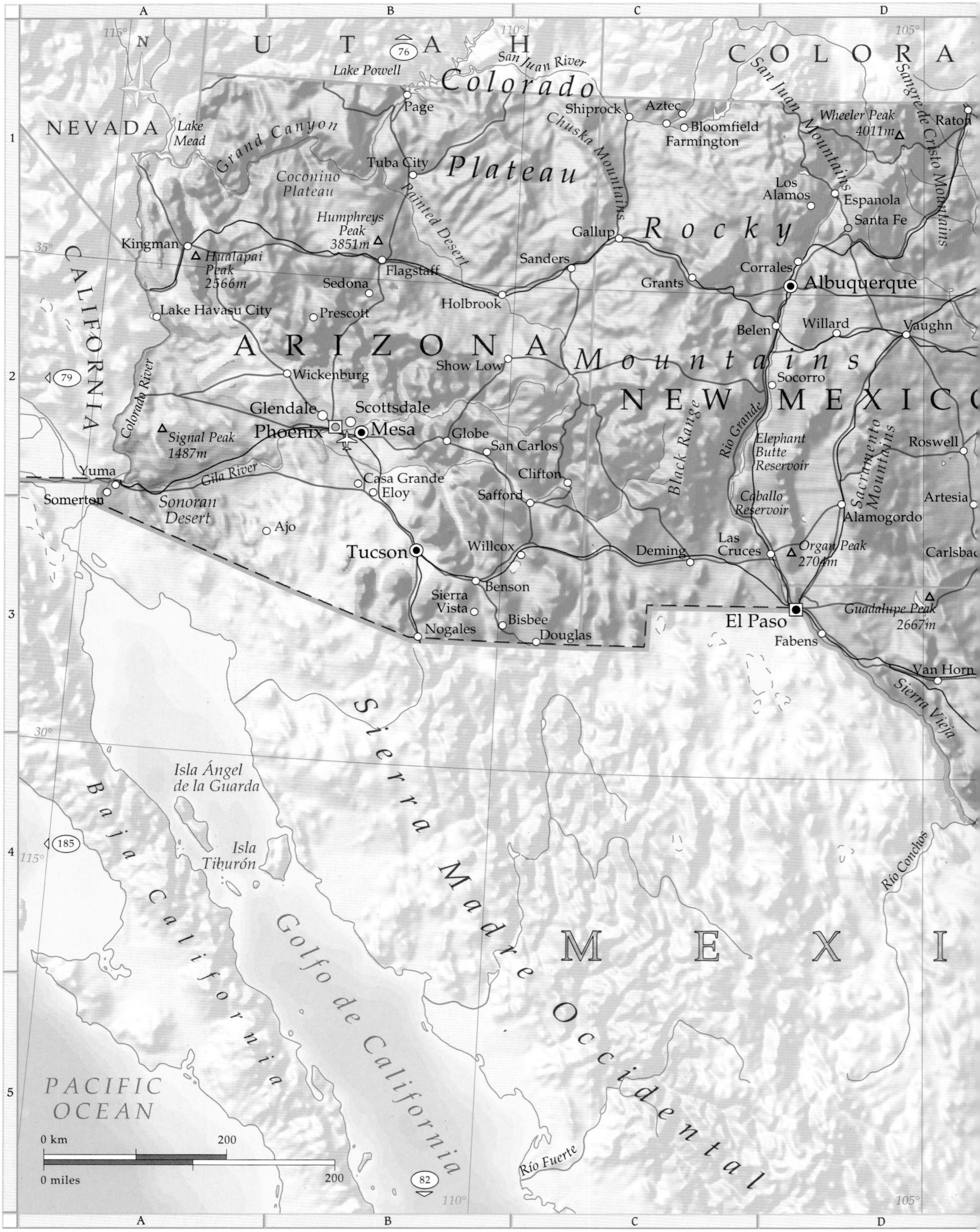

POPULATION

- Less than 50,000
- 50,000 – 100,000
- 100,000 – 500,000
- Over 500,000

E
F
G
H
1
2
3
4
5
100°
95°
35°
30°
K A N S A S
MISSOURI
O K L A H O M A
A R K A N S A S
T E X A S
L O U I S I A N A
C O
77
74
86
83
Table Rock Lake
Beaver Lake
Beaver River
Arkansas River
Canadian River
Red River
Wichita River
Trinity River
Brazos River
Neches River
Sabine River
Colorado River
Guadalupe River
San Antonio River
Pecos River
Rio Grande
Lake Meredith
Lake Texoma
Eufaula Lake
Lake Tawakoni
Toledo Bend Reservoir
Lake Buchanan
Lake Travis
Amistad Reservoir
Llano Estacado
Edwards Plateau
Stockton Plateau
Emory Peak 2385m
Sierra Madre Oriental
Laguna Madre
Padre Island
Gulf of Mexico
Miami
Vinita
Bartlesville
Ponca City
Alva
Enid
Claremore
Tulsa
Sand Springs
Broken Arrow
Tahlequah
Muskogee
Stillwater
Sapulpa
Okmulgee
Boise City
Guymon
Woodward
Perryton
Dalhart
Dumas
Borger
Pampa
Taloga
Clinton
El Reno
The Village
Oklahoma City
Moore
Norman
Shawnee
Warner
Elk City
Chickasha
McAlester
Ada
Amarillo
Canyon
Hereford
Tulia
Altus
Lawton
Duncan
Ardmore
Hugo
Idabel
Childress
Vernon
Burkburnett
Durant
Muleshoe
Plainview
Wichita Falls
Denison
Sherman
Paris
Texarkana
Atlanta
Littlefield
Lubbock
Levelland
Gainesville
Denton
Greenville
Plano
Garland
Sulphur Springs
Brownfield
Mineral Wells
Fort Worth
Dallas
Arlington
Marshall
Snyder
Lamesa
Tyler
Longview
Seminole
Sweetwater
Abilene
Cleburne
Ennis
Henderson
Andrews
Big Spring
Colorado City
Stephenville
Corsicana
Athens
Jacksonville
Midland
Odessa
Coleman
Brownwood
Nacogdoches
Ballinger
Waco
Lufkin
Monahans
San Angelo
Killeen
Pineland
McCamey
Brady
Copperas Cove
Temple
Belton
Livingston
Huntsville
Bryan
College Station
Fort Stockton
Taylor
Davis
Round Rock
Brenham
Conroe
Beaumont
Port Arthur
Austin
Kerrville
Houston
Baytown
New Braunfels
San Marcos
Pasadena
Schertz
Seguin
Rosenberg
Alvin
Texas City
San Antonio
Hondo
El Campo
Angleton
Galveston
Lake Jackson
Del Rio
Uvalde
Edna
Victoria
Bay City
Freeport
Pearsall
Kenedy
Port Lavaca
Port O'Connor
Eagle Pass
Beeville
Portland
Robstown
Alice
Corpus Christi
Kingsville
Laredo
Norias
Edinburg
Mission
McAllen
Harlingen
San Benito
Brownsville

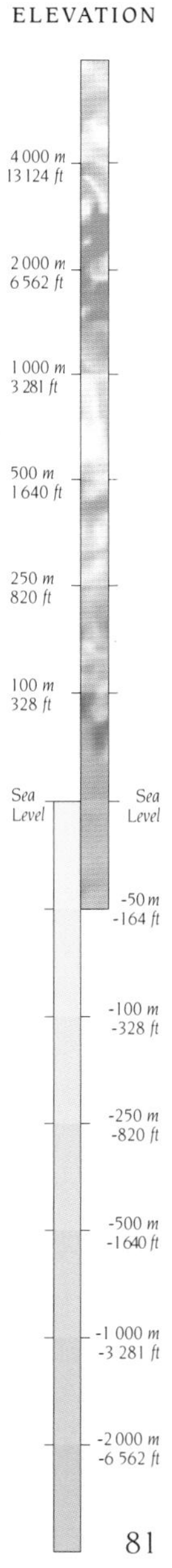
ELEVATION
4 000 m 13 124 ft
2 000 m 6 562 ft
1 000 m 3 281 ft
500 m 1 640 ft
250 m 820 ft
100 m 328 ft
Sea Level
Sea Level
-50 m -164 ft
-100 m -328 ft
-250 m -820 ft
-500 m -1 640 ft
-1 000 m -3 281 ft
-2 000 m -6 562 ft

Mexico

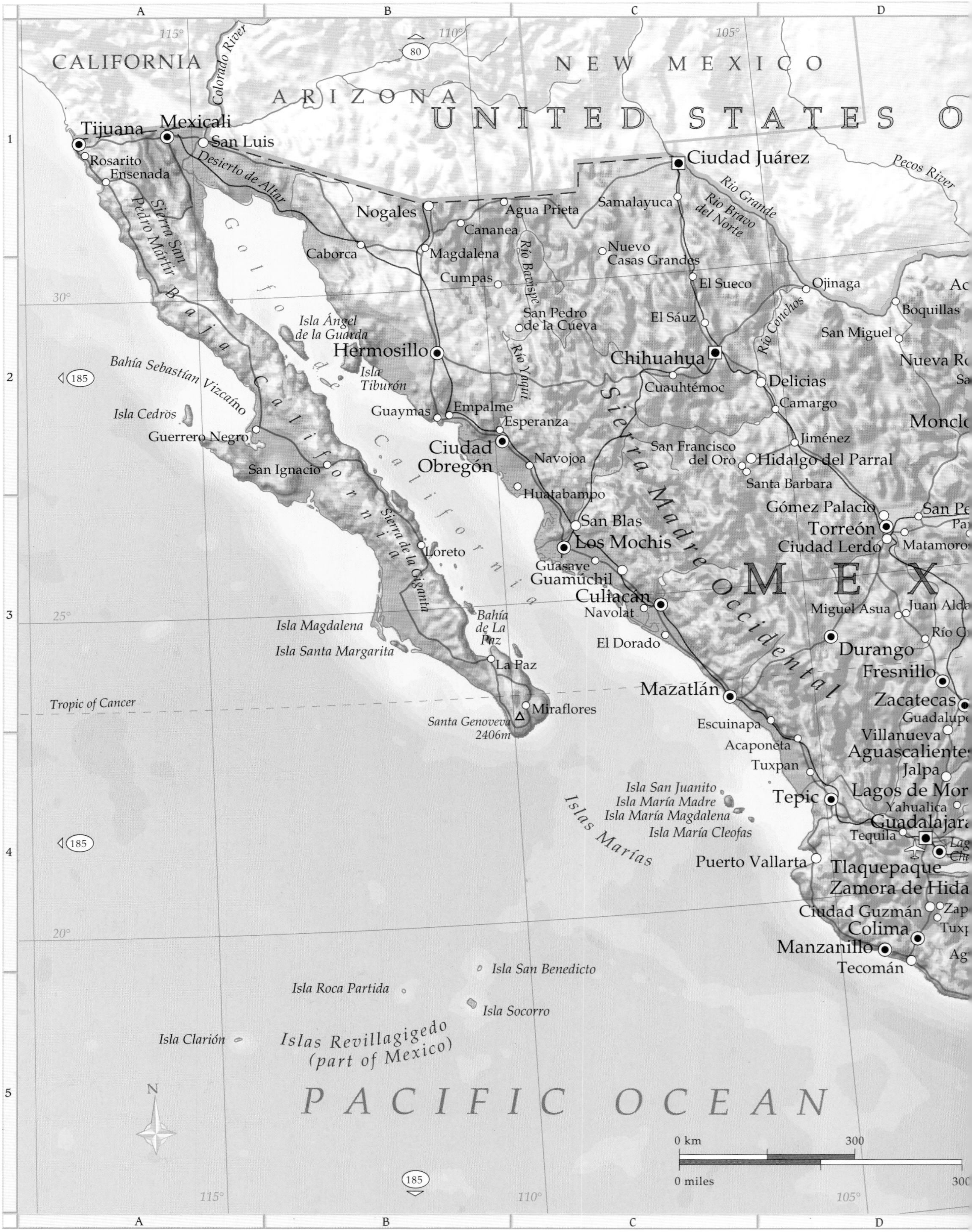

CALIFORNIA
Colorado River
ARIZONA
NEW MEXICO
UNITED STATES O
Pecos River
Rio Grande
Rio Bravo del Norte
Tijuana
Mexicali
San Luis
Rosarito
Ensenada
Desierto de Altar
Sierra San Pedro Mártir
Nogales
Agua Prieta
Cananea
Samalayuca
Ciudad Juárez
Nuevo Casas Grandes
Caborca
Magdalena
Cumpas
Río Bavispe
El Sueco
Ojinaga
Boquillas
Golfo de California
Baja California
Isla Ángel de la Guarda
Hermosillo
San Pedro de la Cueva
El Sáuz
Río Conchos
San Miguel
Nueva Ro
Chihuahua
Río Yaqui
Isla Tiburón
Cuauhtémoc
Delicias
Bahía Sebastián Vizcaíno
Guaymas
Empalme
Camargo
Monclo
Isla Cedros
Esperanza
Guerrero Negro
Ciudad Obregón
Sierra Madre Occidental
San Francisco del Oro
Jiménez
Hidalgo del Parral
Navojoa
San Ignacio
Santa Barbara
Huatabampo
Gómez Palacio
Sierra de la Giganta
San Blas
Torreón
Los Mochis
Ciudad Lerdo
Matamoros
Loreto
Guasave
Guamúchil
MEX
Culiacán
Navolat
Miguel Asua
Juan Alda
Bahía de La Paz
Isla Magdalena
El Dorado
Durango
Isla Santa Margarita
La Paz
Fresnillo
Mazatlán
Zacatecas
Tropic of Cancer
Miraflores
Santa Genoveva 2406m
Escuinapa
Villanueva
Acaponeta
Aguascalientes
Tuxpan
Jalpa
Isla San Juanito
Isla María Madre
Isla María Magdalena
Isla María Cleofas
Islas Marías
Tepic
Lagos de Mor
Yahualica
Guadalajara
Tequila
Puerto Vallarta
Tlaquepaque
Zamora de Hida
Ciudad Guzmán
Colima
Manzanillo
Tecomán
Isla San Benedicto
Isla Roca Partida
Isla Socorro
Isla Clarión
Islas Revillagigedo (part of Mexico)
PACIFIC OCEAN
N
0 km
300
0 miles
115°
110°
105°
30°
25°
20°
80
185
A
B
C
D
1
2
3
4
5

POPULATION

Less than 50,000 ○

50,000 – 100,000 ○

100,000 – 500,000 ◉

Over 500,000 ▣

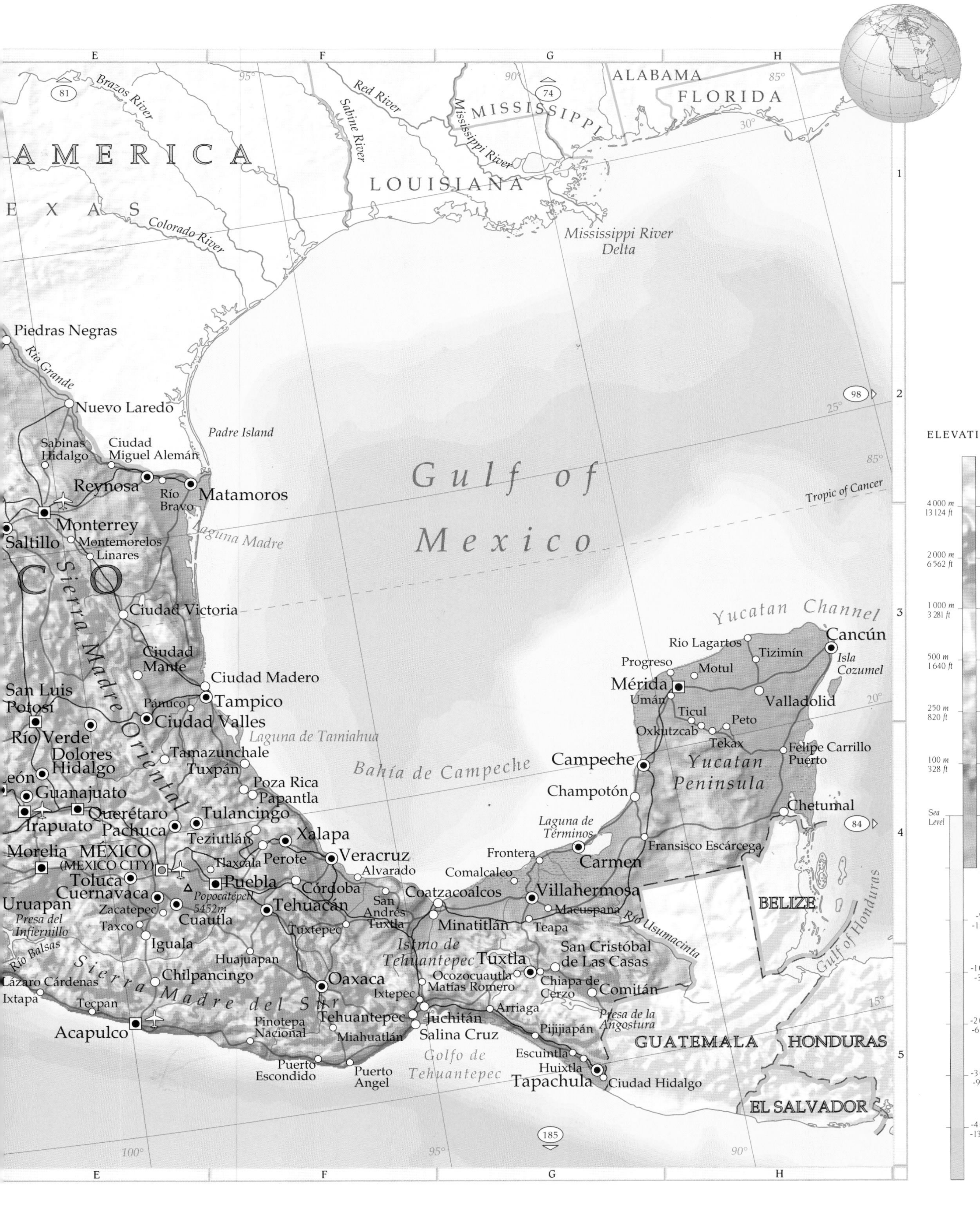
E
F
G
H
1
2
3
4
5
ALABAMA
FLORIDA
MISSISSIPPI
LOUISIANA
AMERICA
TEXAS
95°
90°
85°
30°
25°
20°
15°
100°
81
74
98
84
185
Brazos River
Red River
Sabine River
Mississippi River
Colorado River
Mississippi River Delta
Piedras Negras
Río Grande
Nuevo Laredo
Padre Island
Sabinas Hidalgo
Ciudad Miguel Alemán
Reynosa
Río Bravo
Matamoros
Monterrey
Saltillo
Montemorelos
Linares
Laguna Madre
Gulf of Mexico
Tropic of Cancer
CO
Sierra Madre Oriental
Ciudad Victoria
Ciudad Mante
Ciudad Madero
San Luis Potosí
Tampico
Pánuco
Ciudad Valles
Río Verde
Laguna de Tamiahua
Dolores Hidalgo
Tamazunchale
Tuxpán
León
Guanajuato
Poza Rica
Papantla
Irapuato
Querétaro
Pachuca
Tulancingo
Teziutlán
Xalapa
Morelia
MÉXICO (MEXICO CITY)
Tlaxcala
Perote
Veracruz
Alvarado
Toluca
Puebla
Córdoba
Uruapan
Cuernavaca
Popocatépetl 5452m
Tehuacán
Zacatepec
Cuautla
Presa del Infiernillo
Taxco
Iguala
Tuxtepec
San Andrés Tuxtla
Coatzacoalcos
Minatitlán
Río Balsas
Huajuapan
Istmo de Tehuantepec
Lázaro Cárdenas
Chilpancingo
Oaxaca
Ixtapa
Tecpan
Sierra Madre del Sur
Ixtepec
Acapulco
Pinotepa Nacional
Tehuantepec
Juchitán
Miahuatlán
Salina Cruz
Puerto Escondido
Puerto Angel
Golfo de Tehuantepec
Bahía de Campeche
Yucatan Channel
Rio Lagartos
Cancún
Tizimín
Isla Cozumel
Progreso
Motul
Mérida
Umán
Valladolid
Ticul
Peto
Oxkutzcab
Tekax
Felipe Carrillo Puerto
Campeche
Yucatan Peninsula
Champotón
Chetumal
Laguna de Términos
Fransisco Escárcega
Frontera
Carmen
Comalcalco
Villahermosa
Macuspana
Teapa
Río Usumacinta
BELIZE
Gulf of Honduras
Tuxtla
San Cristóbal de Las Casas
Ocozocuautla
Matías Romero
Chiapa de Corzo
Comitán
Arriaga
Presa de la Angostura
Pijijiapán
GUATEMALA
HONDURAS
Escuintla
Huixtla
Tapachula
Ciudad Hidalgo
EL SALVADOR
ELEVATION
4 000 m 13 124 ft
2 000 m 6 562 ft
1 000 m 3 281 ft
500 m 1 640 ft
250 m 820 ft
100 m 328 ft
Sea Level
Sea Level
-250 m -820 ft
-500 m -1 640 ft
-1 000 m -3 281 ft
-2 000 m -6 562 ft
-3 000 m -9 843 ft
-4 000 m -13 124 ft

Central America

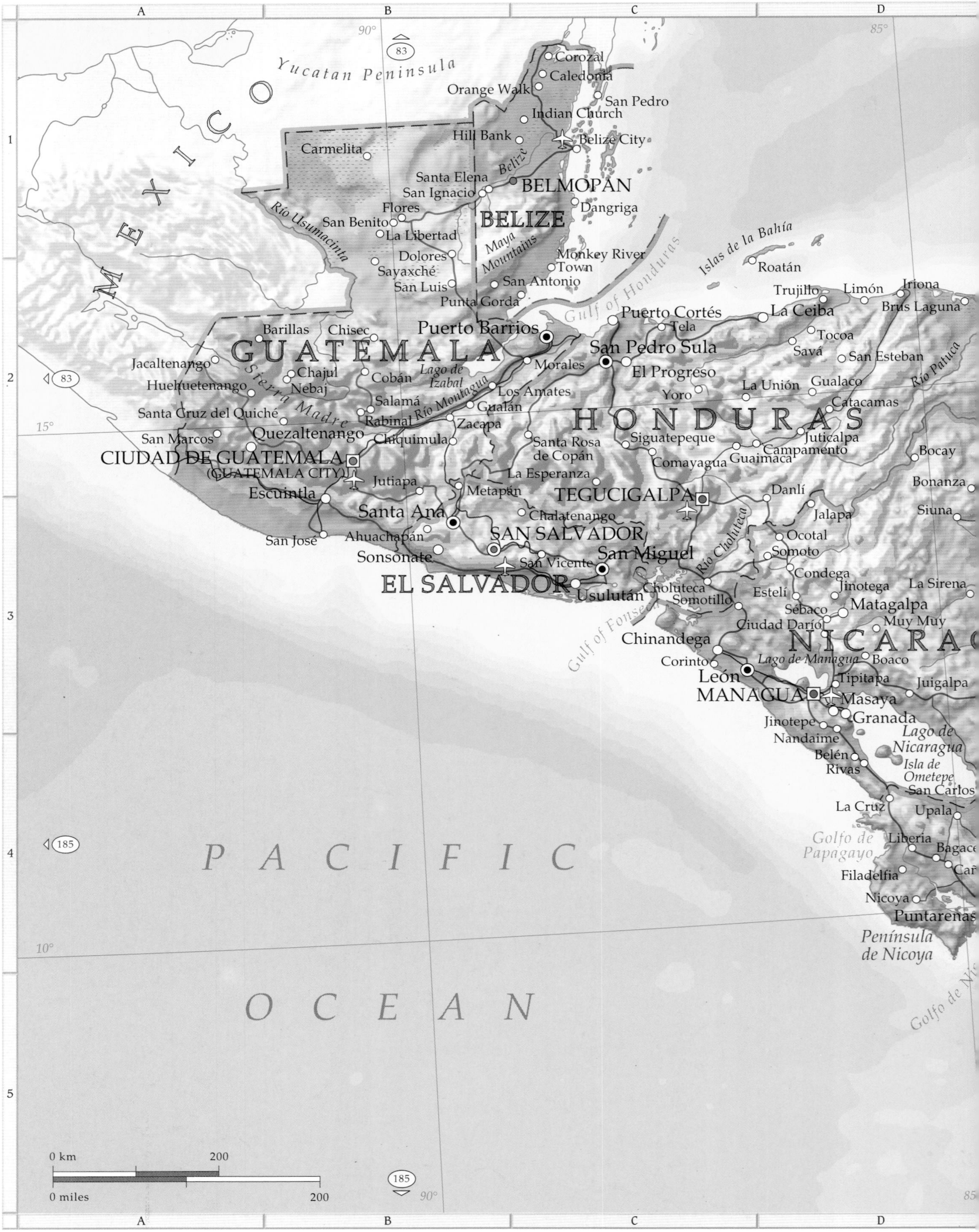

A
B
C
D
1
2
3
4
5
90°
85°
15°
10°
83
185
Yucatan Peninsula
MEXICO
Corozal
Caledonia
Orange Walk
San Pedro
Indian Church
Hill Bank
Belize City
Carmelita
Belize
Santa Elena
San Ignacio
BELMOPAN
Flores
Dangriga
BELIZE
Río Usumacinta
San Benito
La Libertad
Maya Mountains
Dolores
Monkey River Town
Sayaxché
San Antonio
San Luis
Punta Gorda
Islas de la Bahía
Roatán
Gulf of Honduras
Trujillo
Limón
Iriona
La Ceiba
Brus Laguna
Puerto Cortés
Tela
Barillas
Chisec
Puerto Barrios
GUATEMALA
San Pedro Sula
Tocoa
Savá
San Esteban
Jacaltenango
Morales
El Progreso
Chajul
Cobán
Lago de Izabal
Huehuetenango
Nebaj
Sierra Madre
Los Amates
Yoro
La Unión
Gualaco
Río Patuca
Salamá
Gualán
Catacamas
Santa Cruz del Quiché
Rabinal
Río Motagua
Zacapa
HONDURAS
San Marcos
Quezaltenango
Chiquimula
Santa Rosa de Copán
Siguatepeque
Juticalpa
Campamento
Bocay
CIUDAD DE GUATEMALA
(GUATEMALA CITY)
Comayagua
Guaimaca
La Esperanza
Jutiapa
Bonanza
Escuintla
Metapán
TEGUCIGALPA
Danlí
Santa Ana
Chalatenango
Siuna
Jalapa
San José
Ahuachapán
SAN SALVADOR
Ocotal
Río Choluteca
Sonsonate
San Vicente
San Miguel
Somoto
Condega
EL SALVADOR
Usulután
Choluteca
Estelí
Jinotega
La Sirena
Somotillo
Matagalpa
Gulf of Fonseca
Sébaco
Muy Muy
Ciudad Darío
Chinandega
NICARAG
Corinto
Lago de Managua
Boaco
León
Tipitapa
Juigalpa
MANAGUA
Masaya
Granada
Jinotepe
Lago de Nicaragua
Nandaime
Belén
Rivas
Isla de Ometepe
San Carlos
La Cruz
Upala
Golfo de Papagayo
Liberia
Bagace
PACIFIC
Filadelfia
Nicoya
Puntarenas
Península de Nicoya
OCEAN
Golfo de Ni
0 km
200
0 miles
200

POPULATION

- Less than 50,000
- 50,000 – 100,000
- 100,000 – 500,000
- Over 500,000

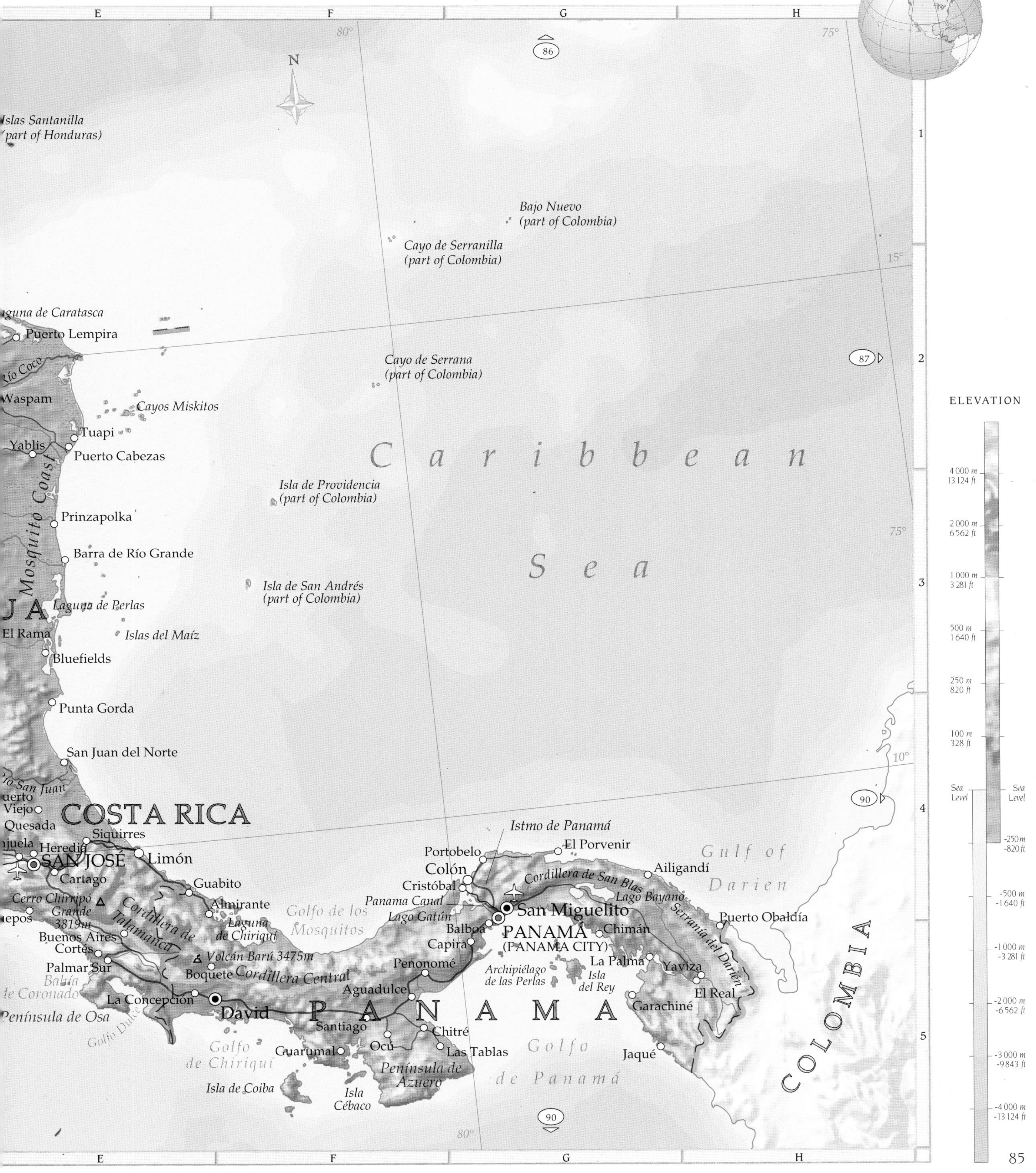
Islas Santanilla
(part of Honduras)
Bajo Nuevo
(part of Colombia)
Cayo de Serranilla
(part of Colombia)
Laguna de Caratasca
Puerto Lempira
Cayo de Serrana
(part of Colombia)
Río Coco
Waspam
Cayos Miskitos
Tuapi
Yablis
Puerto Cabezas
Caribbean
Isla de Providencia
(part of Colombia)
Mosquito Coast
Prinzapolka
Barra de Río Grande
Sea
Isla de San Andrés
(part of Colombia)
Laguna de Perlas
El Rama
Islas del Maíz
Bluefields
Punta Gorda
San Juan del Norte
Río San Juan
Puerto Viejo
COSTA RICA
Quesada
Istmo de Panamá
Siquirres
Heredia
SAN JOSÉ
Limón
Cartago
Portobelo
El Porvenir
Colón
Gulf of Darien
Ailigandí
Cristóbal
Cordillera de San Blas
Guabito
Cerro Chirripó Grande 3819m
Cordillera de Talamanca
Almirante
Golfo de los Mosquitos
Panama Canal
Lago Gatún
San Miguelito
Lago Bayano
Serranía del Darién
Puerto Obaldía
Laguna de Chiriquí
Balboa
PANAMÁ
(PANAMA CITY)
Chimán
Buenos Aires
Cortés
Capira
Volcán Barú 3475m
Penonomé
Archipiélago de las Perlas
La Palma
Isla del Rey
Yaviza
Palmar Sur
Boquete
Cordillera Central
Bahía de Coronado
Aguadulce
El Real
La Concepción
David
PANAMA
Garachiné
Península de Osa
Golfo Dulce
Santiago
Chitré
COLOMBIA
Golfo de Chiriquí
Guarumal
Ocú
Las Tablas
Golfo de Panamá
Jaqué
Península de Azuero
Isla de Coiba
Isla Cébaco
86
87
90
90
80°
75°
15°
10°
E
F
G
H
1
2
3
4
5
ELEVATION
4000 m
13124 ft
2000 m
6562 ft
1000 m
3281 ft
500 m
1640 ft
250 m
820 ft
100 m
328 ft
Sea Level
-250 m
-820 ft
-500 m
-1640 ft
-1000 m
-3281 ft
-2000 m
-6562 ft
-3000 m
-9843 ft
-4000 m
-13124 ft

THE CARIBBEAN

A
B
C
D
1
2
3
4
5
85°
80°
75°
25°
20°
15°
10°
N
75
84
90
UNITED STATES OF AMERICA
The Everglades
Gulf of Mexico
Florida Keys
Florida Straits
Tropic of Cancer
Grand Bahama Island
Freeport
Marsh Harbour
Great Abaco
Bimini Islands
Berry Islands
Northwest Providence Channel
Nicholls Town
NASSAU
New Providence
Eleuthera Island
Rock Sound
Andros Town
Cat Island
Exuma Cays
Exuma Sound
Andros Island
Cay Sal
Anguilla Cays
BAHAMAS
San Salvador
Rum Cay
George Town
Long Island
Great Exuma Island
Clarence Town
Crooked Island Passage
Crooked Island
Acklins Island
Mayaguana Passage
Mayaguana
Caicos Passage
Little Inagua
Lake Rosa
Matthew Town
Great Inagua
Ragged Island Range
Archipiélago de Camagüey
LA HABANA
(HAVANA)
Guanabacoa
Artemisa
Cárdenas
Matanzas
Sagua la Grande
Santa Clara
Placetas
Pinar del Río
Consolación del Sur
La Fé
Cienfuegos
Golfo de Batabanó
Yucatan Channel
Nueva Gerona
Isla de la Juventud
Archipiélago de los Canarreos
Cayo Largo
Bahía de Cochinos
Sancti Spíritus
Morón
Ciego de Avila
CUBA
Camagüey
Nuevitas
Holguín
Las Tunas
Archipiélago de los Jardines de la Reina
Manzanillo
Bayamo
Palma Soriano
Guantánamo
Santiago de Cuba
Windward Passage
Cap-Haïtien
Gonaïves
HAIT
Little Cayman
Cayman Brac
GEORGE TOWN
Grand Cayman
CAYMAN ISLANDS
(UK dependent territory)
NAVASSA ISLAND
(US unincorporated territory)
Île de la Gonâve
Jérémie
PORT-AU-PRINCE
Cayes
Jacme
Montego Bay
Spanish Town
Portmore
KINGSTON
JAMAICA
Pedro Cays
Jamaica Channel
Greater Antilles
Caribbean Sea
HONDURAS
NICARAGUA
COSTA RICA
COLOMBIA
0 km
200
0 miles
200
JAMAICA
Caribbean Sea
78°
77°
18°
Montego Bay
Lucea
Falmouth
Runaway Bay
St Ann's Bay
Ocho Rios
The Cockpit Country
Annotto Bay
Buff Bay
Port Antonio
Cambridge
Ewarton
Savanna-La-Mar
Christiana
Blue Mountain Peak 2258m
Spanish Town
Mandeville
KINGSTON
Black River
May Pen
Old Harbour
Portmore
Morant Bay
Portland Bight
2000m/6562ft
1000m/3281ft
500m/1640ft
200m/656ft
Sea level
0 km
20
0 miles
20

POPULATION

- Less than 50,000 ○
- 50,000 – 100,000 ○
- 100,000 – 500,000 ⊙
- Over 500,000 ▣

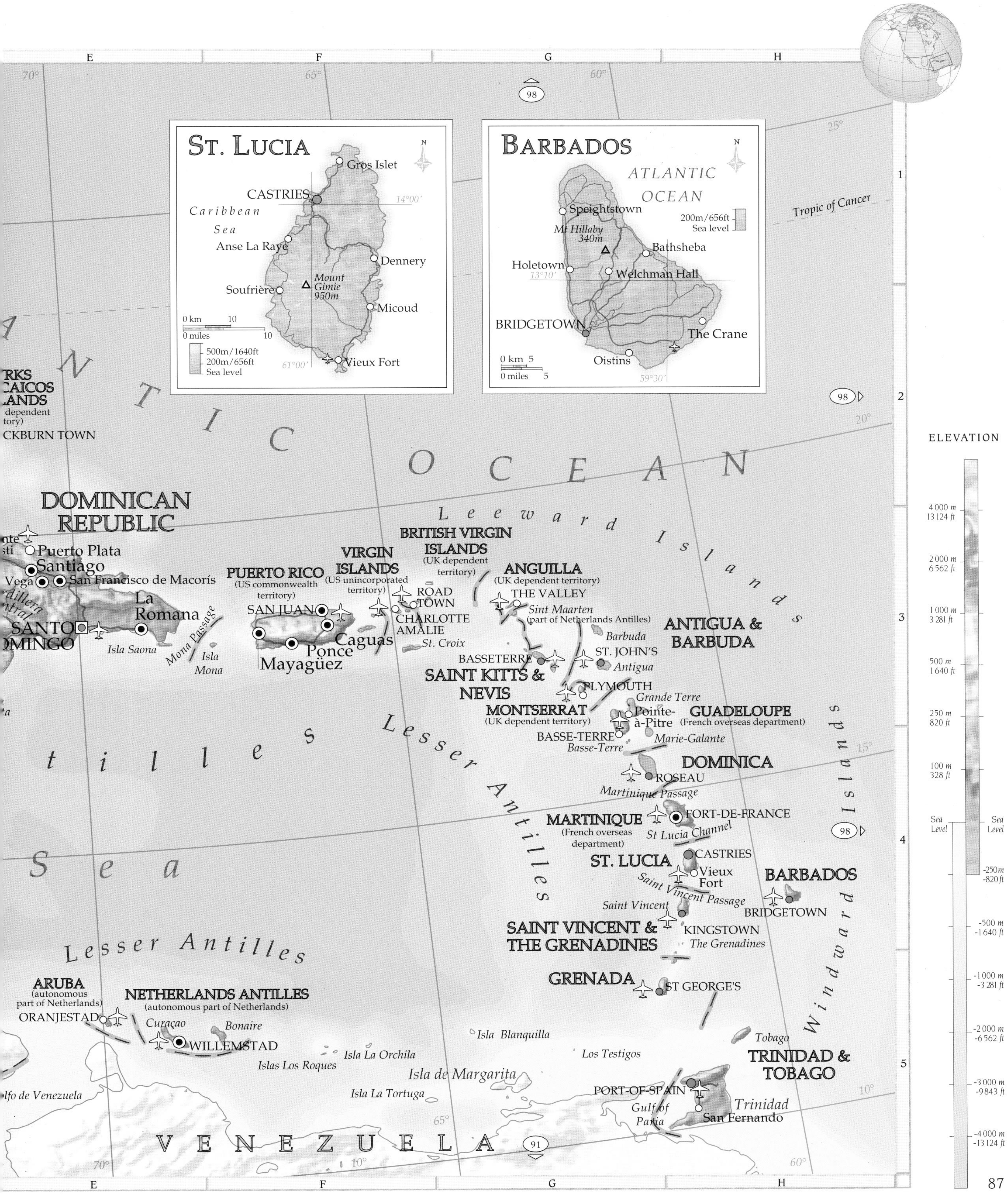

E
F
G
H
70°
65°
60°
25°
20°
15°
10°
98
91
1
2
3
4
5
ST. LUCIA
N
Gros Islet
CASTRIES
14°00′
Caribbean
Sea
Anse La Raye
Dennery
Mount
Gimie
950m
Soufrière
Micoud
0 km 10
0 miles 10
500m/1640ft
200m/656ft
Sea level
61°00′
Vieux Fort
BARBADOS
ATLANTIC
OCEAN
Speightstown
Mt Hillaby
340m
200m/656ft
Sea level
Bathsheba
Holetown
13°10′
Welchman Hall
BRIDGETOWN
The Crane
0 km 5
0 miles 5
Oistins
59°30′
Tropic of Cancer
ATLANTIC OCEAN
TURKS & CAICOS ISLANDS
(UK dependent territory)
COCKBURN TOWN
DOMINICAN REPUBLIC
Puerto Plata
Santiago
Vega
San Francisco de Macorís
La Romana
SANTO DOMINGO
Isla Saona
Mona Passage
Isla Mona
PUERTO RICO
(US commonwealth territory)
SAN JUAN
Caguas
Ponce
Mayagüez
VIRGIN ISLANDS
(US unincorporated territory)
CHARLOTTE AMALIE
St. Croix
BRITISH VIRGIN ISLANDS
(UK dependent territory)
ROAD TOWN
ANGUILLA
(UK dependent territory)
THE VALLEY
Sint Maarten
(part of Netherlands Antilles)
Leeward Islands
Barbuda
ANTIGUA & BARBUDA
BASSETERRE
ST. JOHN'S
Antigua
SAINT KITTS & NEVIS
PLYMOUTH
MONTSERRAT
(UK dependent territory)
Grande Terre
Pointe-à-Pitre
GUADELOUPE
(French overseas department)
BASSE-TERRE
Basse-Terre
Marie-Galante
DOMINICA
ROSEAU
Martinique Passage
FORT-DE-FRANCE
MARTINIQUE
(French overseas department)
St Lucia Channel
CASTRIES
ST. LUCIA
Vieux Fort
BARBADOS
Saint Vincent Passage
Saint Vincent
BRIDGETOWN
SAINT VINCENT & THE GRENADINES
KINGSTOWN
The Grenadines
GRENADA
ST GEORGE'S
Windward Islands
Lesser Antilles
Antilles
Sea
Lesser Antilles
ARUBA
(autonomous part of Netherlands)
ORANJESTAD
NETHERLANDS ANTILLES
(autonomous part of Netherlands)
Curaçao
Bonaire
WILLEMSTAD
Isla Blanquilla
Islas Los Roques
Isla La Orchila
Los Testigos
Tobago
TRINIDAD & TOBAGO
Isla de Margarita
Isla La Tortuga
PORT-OF-SPAIN
Gulf of Paria
Trinidad
San Fernando
Golfo de Venezuela
VENEZUELA
ELEVATION
4000 m
13124 ft
2000 m
6562 ft
1000 m
3281 ft
500 m
1640 ft
250 m
820 ft
100 m
328 ft
Sea Level
-250m
-820 ft
-500 m
-1640 ft
-1000 m
-3281 ft
-2000 m
-6562 ft
-3000 m
-9843 ft
-4000 m
-13124 ft

SOUTH AMERICA

ATLANTIC OCEAN
Mid-Atlantic Ridge
Ceará Plain
Demerara Plain
Amazon Fan
Puerto Rico Trench
Puerto Rico
Lesser Antilles
Greater Antilles
Hispaniola
Jamaica
Caribbean Sea
Venezuelan Basin
Colombian Basin
Panama Basin
Isthmus of Panama
Peru Basin
Peru-Chile Trench
Trinidad
Equator
VENEZUELA
GUYANA
SURINAME
FRENCH GUIANA (to France)
COLOMBIA
ECUADOR
PERU
BRAZIL
BOLIVIA
CARACAS
BOGOTÁ
QUITO
LIMA
LA PAZ
SUCRE
BRASÍLIA
GEORGETOWN
PARAMARIBO
CAYENNE
(claimed by Venezuela)
(claimed by Suriname)
(claimed by Ecuador)
Guiana Highlands
Tumuc-Humac Mountains
Amazon Basin
Brazilian Highlands
Planalto de Mato Grosso
Planalto da Borborema
Chapada dos Parecis
Serra do Cachimbo
Serra Formosa
Serra do Roncador
Andes
Chimborazo 6310m
Gulf of Guayaquil
Lake Titicaca
Represa Balbina
Represa de Sobradinho
Amazon
Orinoco
Magdalena
Cauca
Meta
Guaviare
Caroní
Essequibo
Rio Negro
Branco
Japurá
Caquetá
Putumayo
Napo
Içá
Marañón
Ucayali
Juruá
Purus
Madeira
Madre de Dios
Beni
Tapajós
Xingu
Tocantins
Araguaia
São Francisco
Cumaná
Maracay
Valencia
Barquisimeto
Maracaibo
Barinas
San Cristóbal
Cúcuta
Bucaramanga
Santa Marta
Barranquilla
Cartagena
Montería
Medellín
Manizales
Pereira
Ibagué
Cali
Pasto
Esmeraldas
Portoviejo
Guayaquil
Riobamba
Cuenca
Machala
Piura
Chiclayo
Trujillo
Callao
Arequipa
Cusco
Tacna
Arica
Linden
Santarém
Manaus
Porto Velho
Rio Branco
Belém
São Luís
Teresina
Fortaleza
Mossoró
Natal
João Pessoa
Recife
Maceió
Aracaju
Salvador
Goiânia
Cuiabá
Cochabamba
Oruro
Santa Cruz

POPULATION

- ○ Less than 50,000
- ○ 50,000 – 100,000
- ◉ 100,000 – 500,000
- ▣ Over 500,000

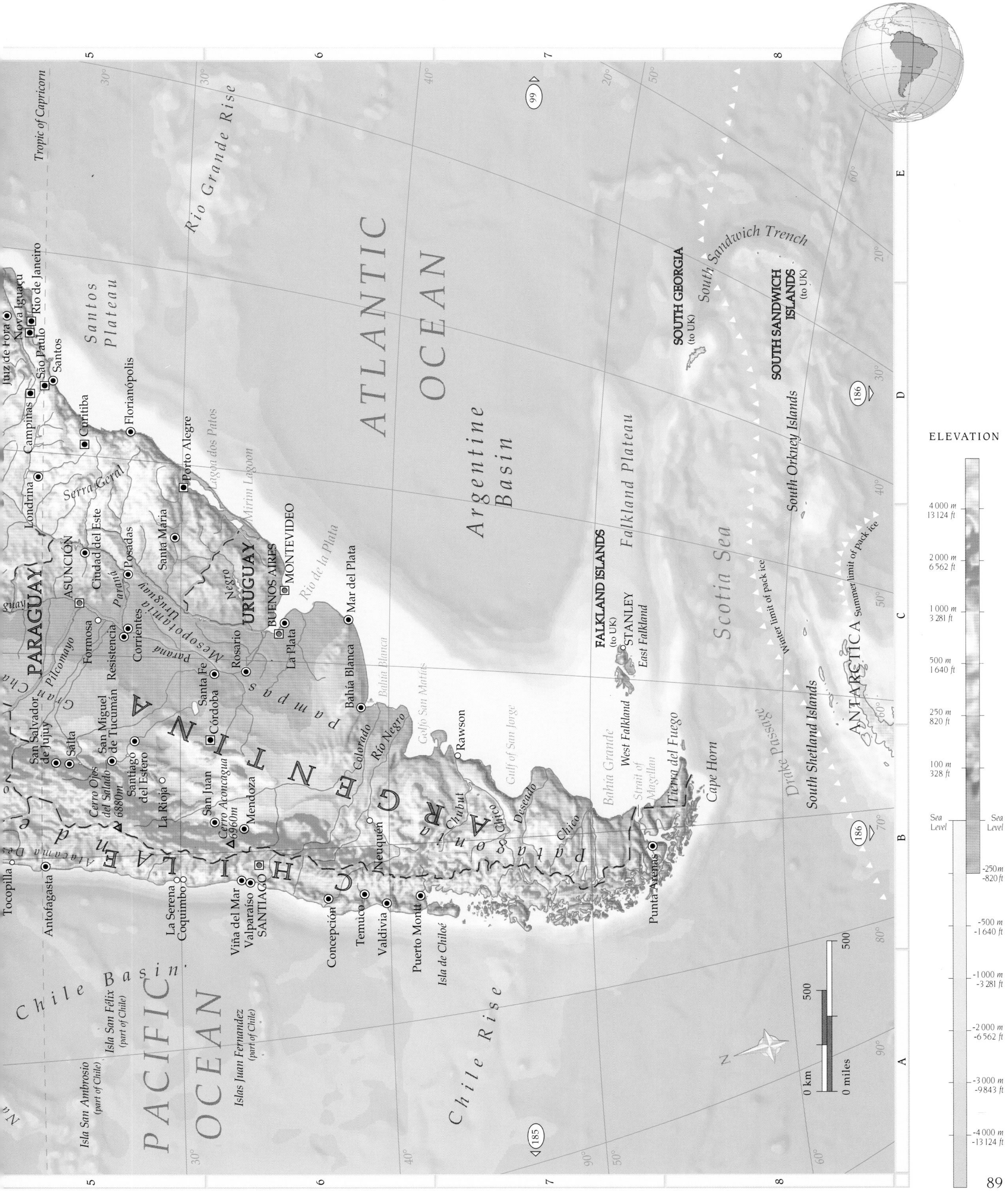
ATLANTIC OCEAN
PACIFIC OCEAN
Argentine Basin
Falkland Plateau
Scotia Sea
Drake Passage
Rio Grande Rise
Santos Plateau
Chile Basin
Chile Rise
South Sandwich Trench
Tropic of Capricorn
PARAGUAY
URUGUAY
ASUNCIÓN
MONTEVIDEO
BUENOS AIRES
SANTIAGO
FALKLAND ISLANDS
(to UK)
STANLEY
East Falkland
West Falkland
SOUTH GEORGIA
(to UK)
SOUTH SANDWICH ISLANDS
(to UK)
South Orkney Islands
South Shetland Islands
ANTARCTICA
Winter limit of pack ice
Summer limit of pack ice
Tierra del Fuego
Cape Horn
Strait of Magellan
Bahía Grande
Gulf of San Jorge
Golfo San Matías
Bahía Blanca
Río de la Plata
Mirim Lagoon
Lagoa dos Patos
Serra Geral
Mesopotamia
Pampas
Patagonia
Gran Chaco
Atacama Desert
Cerro Aconcagua 6960m
Cerro Ojos del Salado 6880m
Isla de Chiloé
Islas Juan Fernandez
(part of Chile)
Isla San Félix
(part of Chile)
Isla San Ambrosio
(part of Chile)
Tocopilla
Antofagasta
La Serena
Coquimbo
Viña del Mar
Valparaíso
Concepción
Temuco
Valdivia
Puerto Montt
Punta Arenas
Rawson
Neuquén
Mendoza
San Juan
La Rioja
Córdoba
Santa Fe
Rosario
La Plata
Mar del Plata
Bahía Blanca
Salta
San Salvador de Jujuy
San Miguel de Tucumán
Santiago del Estero
Formosa
Resistencia
Corrientes
Posadas
Ciudad del Este
Santa Maria
Porto Alegre
Florianópolis
Curitiba
Londrina
Campinas
São Paulo
Santos
Rio de Janeiro
Nova Iguaçu
Juiz de Fora
Pilcomayo
Paraná
Uruguay
Negro
Colorado
Río Negro
Chubut
Chico
Deseado
99
186
185
0 km 500
0 miles 500
N
ELEVATION
4 000 m
13 124 ft
2 000 m
6 562 ft
1 000 m
3 281 ft
500 m
1 640 ft
250 m
820 ft
100 m
328 ft
Sea Level
-250 m
-820 ft
-500 m
-1 640 ft
-1 000 m
-3 281 ft
-2 000 m
-6 562 ft
-3 000 m
-9 843 ft
-4 000 m
-13 124 ft

NORTHERN SOUTH AMERICA

A
B
C
D
1
2
3
4
5
80°
75°
70°
10°
5°
Equator
86
85
92
84
N
Caribbean Sea
Lesser Ant
ARUBA
(autonomous part of Netherlands)
NETHERLANDS ANTILLES
(autonomous part of Netherlands)
Curaçao
Bonaire
Islas Los Roques
Isla La Orch
Península de la Guajira
Puerto López
Punto Fijo
Ríohacha
Maicao
Golfo de Venezuela
Coro
Puerto Cumarebo
Sabaneta
Santa Marta
Barranquilla
Ciénaga
Dabajuro
Pico Cristóbal Colón 5775m
Soledad
Sabanalarga
Cartagena
La Concepción
Maracaibo
Cabimas
San Felipe
Puerto Cabello
CARACA
Valledupar
Ciudad Ojeda
Carora
Valencia
Maracay
San Juan de los Morr
Gulf of Darien
El Carmen de Bolívar
Machiques
Lago de Maracaibo
Barquisimeto
Acarigua
Sincelejo
Magangué
San Carlos del Zulia
Valera
Panama Canal
PANAMA
Montería
Cereté
Guanare
Calabozo
Valle d la Pasc
Mérida
Planeta Rica
Aguachica
El Vigía
Barinas
Pico Bolívar 5007m
Río Guanare
Caucasia
Ocaña
San Fernand
Golfo de Panamá
Cúcuta
San Cristóbal
Río Apure
Pamplona
Río Cauca
Cordillera Occidental
Río Magdalena
Dabeiba
Yarumal
Bucaramanga
Barrancabermeja
Arauca
Río Arauca
Llanos
VENE
Bello
Medellín
Puerto Berrío
Río Meta
Puerto Carreño
Itagüí
Nuquí
Sogamoso
Quibdó
Tunja
Puerto Ayacucho
Manizales
Yopal
Cordillera Oriental
PACIFIC OCEAN
Zipaquira
Pereira
Río Meta
Río Orinoco
Armenia
BOGOTÁ
Cordillera Central
Tuluá
Ibagué
Girardot
Villavicencio
Buenaventura
Buga
Espinal
Río Guaviare
Puerto Inírida
Palmira
COLOMBIA
Cali
Neiva
San José del Guaviare
Popayán
Garzón
Tumaco
Pitalito
Pasto
Florencia
Nevada de Cumbal 4764m
Mocoa
Río Vaupés
Mitú
Ipiales
Orito
Río Apaporis
Andes
Río Putumayo
Río Caquetá
(claimed by Ecuador)
Río Japurá
ECUADOR
Río Napo
Rio Içá
PERU
Amazon
Rio Juruá

POPULATION

- Less than 50,000 ○
- 50,000 – 100,000 ○
- 100,000 – 500,000 ◉
- Over 500,000 ▣

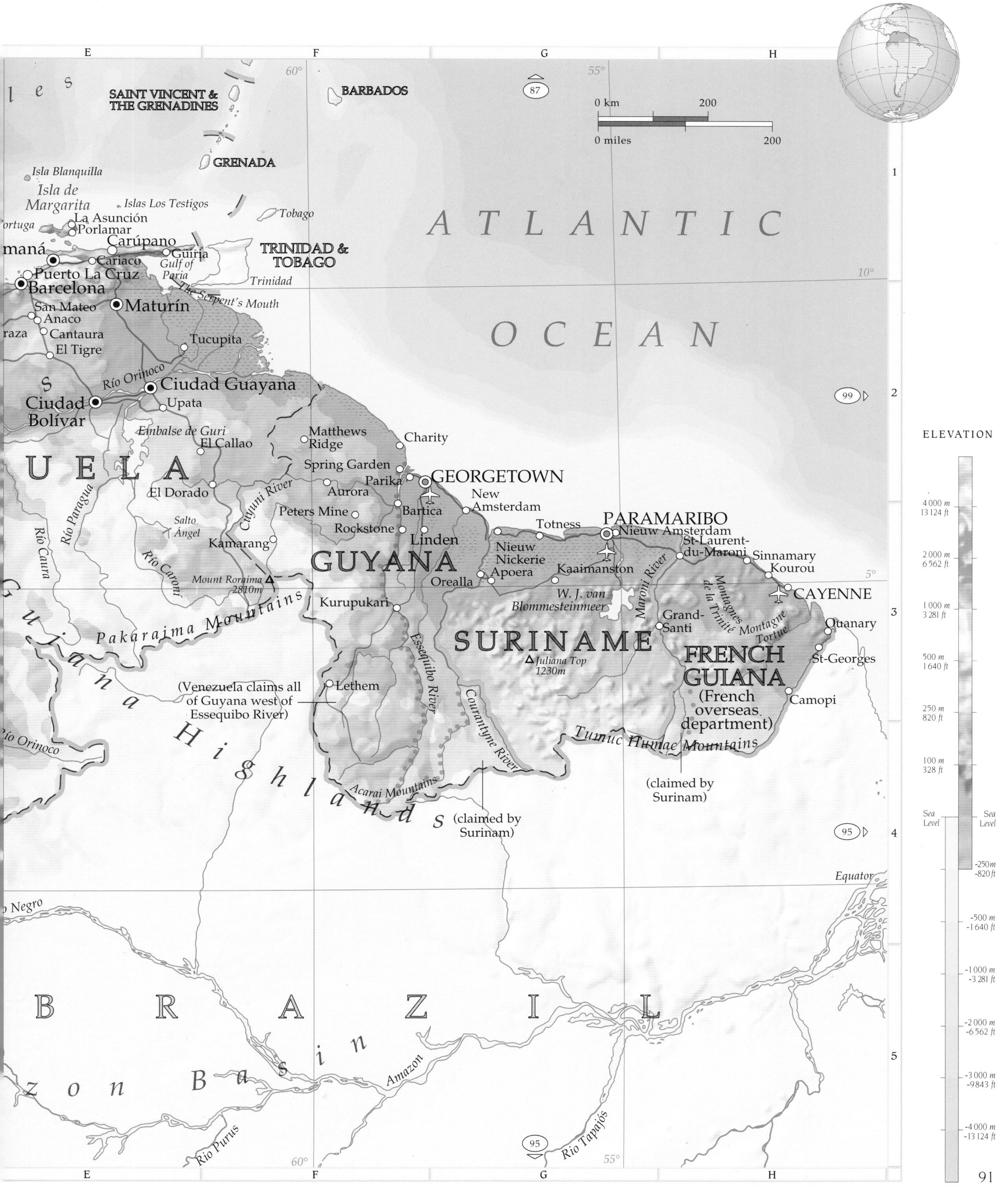

E
F
G
H
60°
55°
10°
5°
Equator
1
2
3
4
5
87
99
95
0 km
200
0 miles
200
SAINT VINCENT & THE GRENADINES
BARBADOS
GRENADA
Isla Blanquilla
Isla de Margarita
Islas Los Testigos
Tobago
La Asunción
Porlamar
Carúpano
Güiria
Cariaco
Gulf of Paria
Puerto La Cruz
Barcelona
Trinidad
TRINIDAD & TOBAGO
The Serpent's Mouth
San Mateo
Maturín
Anaco
Cantaura
El Tigre
Tucupita
Río Orinoco
Ciudad Guayana
Ciudad Bolívar
Upata
Embalse de Guri
El Callao
El Dorado
Río Paragua
Río Caura
Salto Ángel
Kamarang
Cuyuni River
Río Caroní
Mount Roraima 2810m
Pakaraima Mountains
Guiana Highlands
Río Orinoco
(Venezuela claims all of Guyana west of Essequibo River)
ATLANTIC
OCEAN
Matthews Ridge
Charity
Spring Garden
Parika
GEORGETOWN
Aurora
New Amsterdam
Peters Mine
Bartica
Rockstone
Linden
GUYANA
Kurupukari
Lethem
Essequibo River
Courantyne River
Acarai Mountains
(claimed by Surinam)
PARAMARIBO
Totness
Nieuw Amsterdam
Nieuw Nickerie
Apoera
Orealla
Kaaimanston
W. J. van Blommesteinmeer
Maroni River
SURINAME
Juliana Top 1230m
St-Laurent-du-Maroni
Sinnamary
Kourou
CAYENNE
Grand-Santi
Montagnes de la Trinité
Montagne Tortue
Ouanary
St-Georges
FRENCH GUIANA
(French overseas department)
Camopi
Tumuc Humae Mountains
(claimed by Surinam)
BRAZIL
Amazon Basin
Rio Negro
Amazon
Rio Purus
Rio Tapajós
ELEVATION
4 000 m
13 124 ft
2 000 m
6 562 ft
1 000 m
3 281 ft
500 m
1 640 ft
250 m
820 ft
100 m
328 ft
Sea Level
-250 m
-820 ft
-500 m
-1 640 ft
-1 000 m
-3 281 ft
-2 000 m
-6 562 ft
-3 000 m
-9 843 ft
-4 000 m
-13 124 ft

Western South America

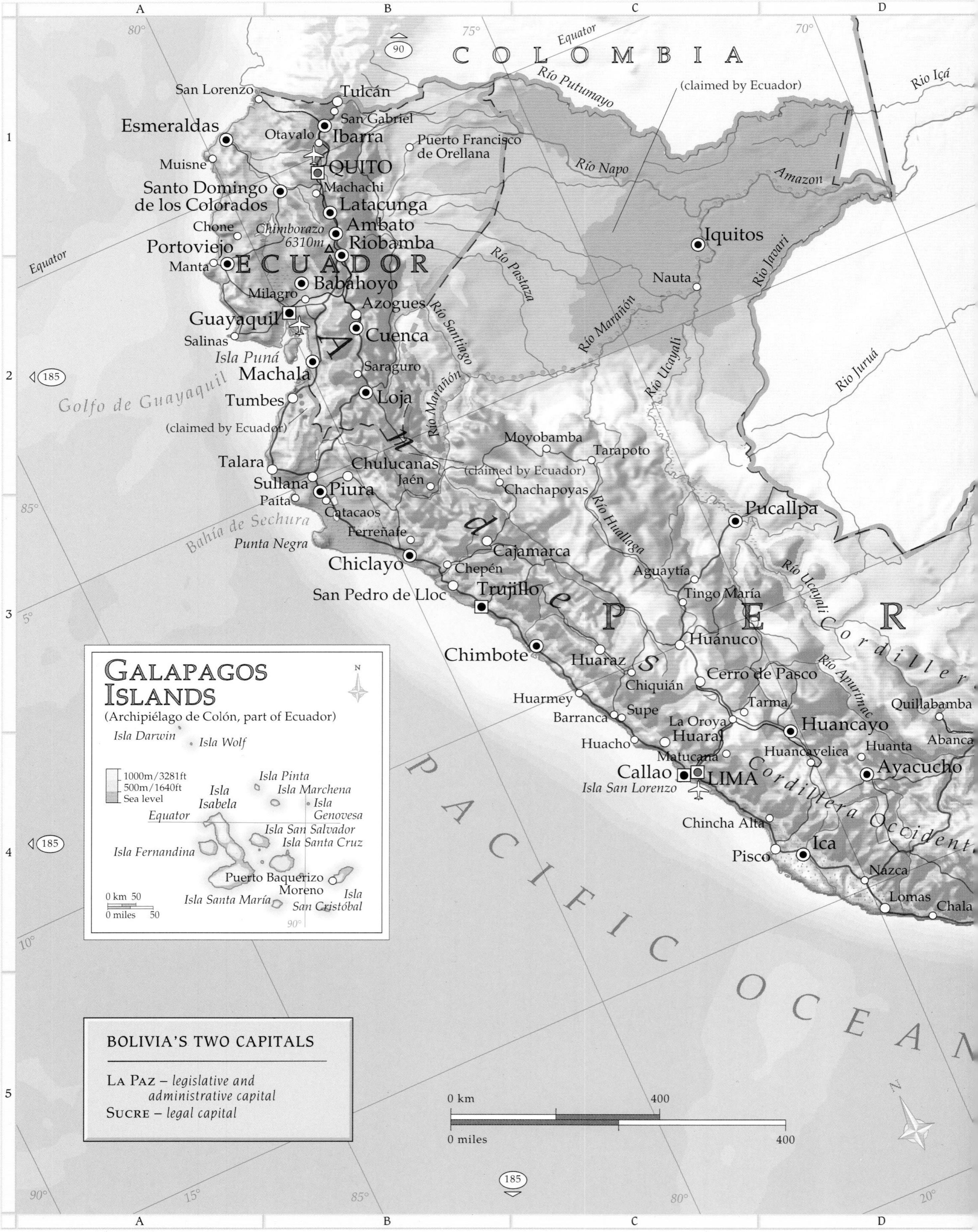
A
B
C
D
1
2
3
4
5
COLOMBIA
Equator
Río Putumayo
(claimed by Ecuador)
Rio Içá
90
185
San Lorenzo
Tulcán
San Gabriel
Esmeraldas
Otavalo
Ibarra
Puerto Francisco de Orellana
Muisne
QUITO
Río Napo
Amazon
Santo Domingo de los Colorados
Machachi
Latacunga
Chone
Chimborazo 6310m
Ambato
Riobamba
Iquitos
Portoviejo
Manta
ECUADOR
Río Pastaza
Nauta
Rio Javari
Milagro
Babahoyo
Azogues
Río Santiago
Guayaquil
Cuenca
Río Marañón
Salinas
Isla Puná
Saraguro
Río Ucayali
Machala
Golfo de Guayaquil
Tumbes
Loja
Rio Juruá
(claimed by Ecuador)
Andes
Moyobamba
Tarapoto
Talara
Chulucanas
(claimed by Ecuador)
Jaén
Sullana
Piura
Chachapoyas
Paita
Catacaos
Río Huallaga
Pucallpa
Bahía de Sechura
Ferreñafe
Punta Negra
Cajamarca
Chiclayo
Chepén
Aguaytía
Río Ucayali
San Pedro de Lloc
Trujillo
Tingo María
PERU
Chimbote
Huaraz
Huánuco
Cordillera
Chiquián
Cerro de Pasco
Río Apurímac
Huarmey
Tarma
Quillabamba
Supe
La Oroya
Barranca
Huancayo
Huara
Huacho
Abanca
Matucana
Huancavelica
Huanta
Callao
LIMA
Ayacucho
Isla San Lorenzo
Cordillera Occidental
Chincha Alta
Ica
Pisco
Nazca
Lomas
Chala
PACIFIC OCEAN
GALAPAGOS ISLANDS
(Archipiélago de Colón, part of Ecuador)
N
Isla Darwin
Isla Wolf
1000m/3281ft
500m/1640ft
Sea level
Isla Pinta
Isla Marchena
Isla Isabela
Isla Genovesa
Equator
Isla San Salvador
Isla Santa Cruz
Isla Fernandina
Puerto Baquerizo Moreno
0 km 50
0 miles 50
Isla Santa María
Isla San Cristóbal
90°
BOLIVIA'S TWO CAPITALS
LA PAZ – legislative and administrative capital
SUCRE – legal capital
0 km 400
0 miles 400
80°
75°
70°
85°
5°
10°
15°
20°
90°

POPULATION

Less than 50,000

50,000 – 100,000

100,000 – 500,000

Over 500,000

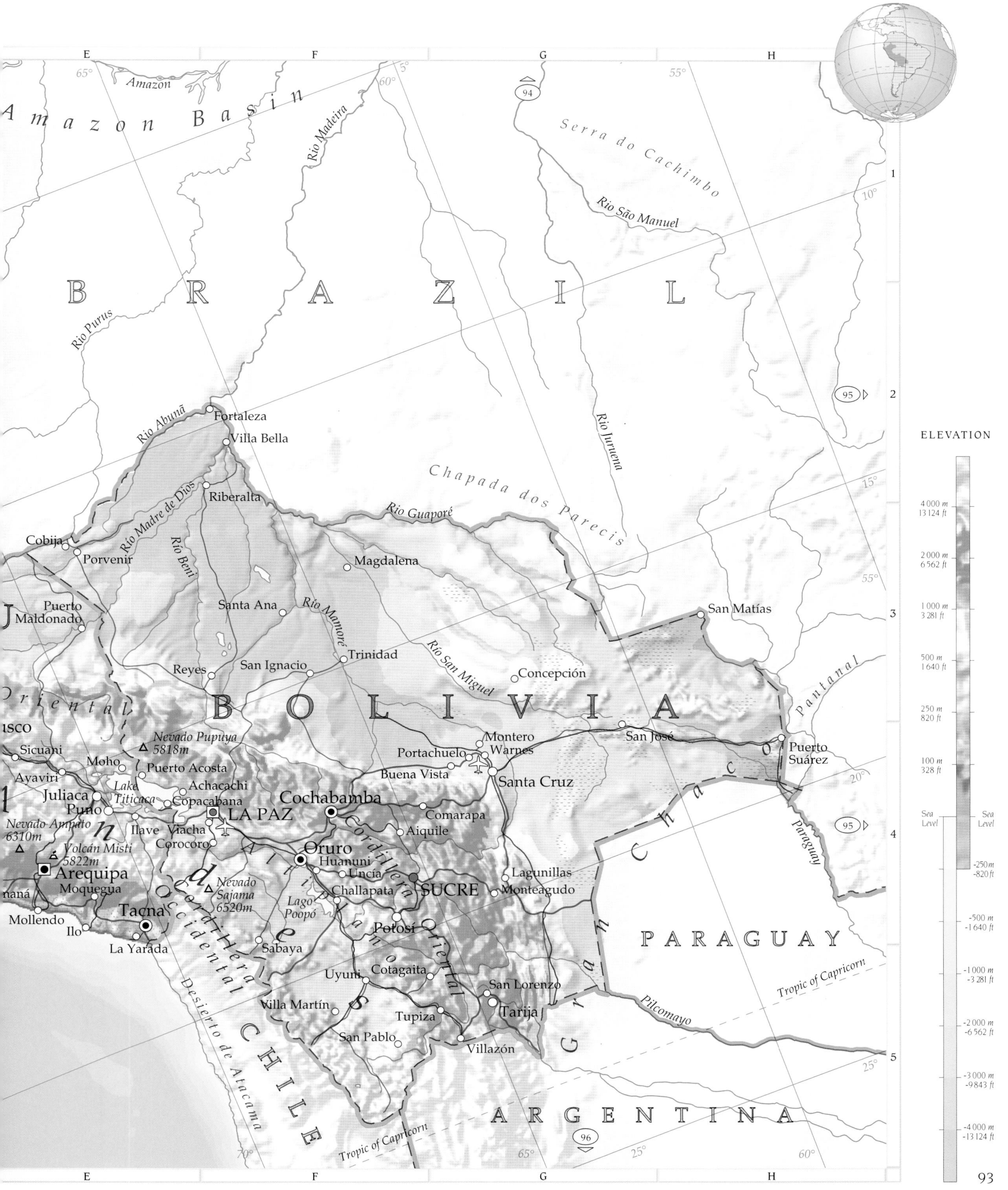
E
F
G
H
1
2
3
4
5
Amazon
Amazon Basin
Rio Madeira
Serra do Cachimbo
Rio São Manuel
BRAZIL
Rio Purus
Rio Abunã
Fortaleza
Villa Bella
Rio Juruena
Chapada dos Parecis
Rio Guaporé
Riberalta
Rio Madre de Dios
Río Beni
Cobija
Porvenir
Magdalena
Puerto Maldonado
Santa Ana
Río Mamoré
San Matías
Trinidad
Río San Miguel
Reyes
San Ignacio
Concepción
Pantanal
BOLIVIA
Nevado Pupuya 5818m
Montero
Warnes
San José
Puerto Suárez
Portachuelo
Sicuani
Moho
Puerto Acosta
Buena Vista
Santa Cruz
Ayaviri
Achacachi
Juliaca
Lake Titicaca
Copacabana
Cochabamba
Puno
LA PAZ
Comarapa
Nevado Ampato 6310m
Ilave
Viacha
Aiquile
Volcán Misti 5822m
Corocoro
Oruro
Huanuni
Uncía
Lagunillas
Arequipa
Nevado Sajama 6520m
SUCRE
Monteagudo
Moquegua
Challapata
Lago Poopó
Cordillera Oriental
Cordillera Occidental
Altiplano
Andes
Tacna
Potosí
Mollendo
Ilo
La Yarada
Sabaya
Gran Chaco
PARAGUAY
Uyuni
Cotagaita
San Lorenzo
Villa Martín
Tarija
Pilcomayo
Tropic of Capricorn
Tupiza
San Pablo
Villazón
Paraguay
Desierto de Atacama
CHILE
ARGENTINA
94
95
96
ELEVATION
4000 m 13124 ft
2000 m 6562 ft
1000 m 3281 ft
500 m 1640 ft
250 m 820 ft
100 m 328 ft
Sea Level
-250 m -820 ft
-500 m -1640 ft
-1000 m -3281 ft
-2000 m -6562 ft
-3000 m -9843 ft
-4000 m -13124 ft

BRAZIL

A
B
C
D
1
2
3
4
5
80°
70°
60°
10°
20°
30°
90°
90
185
96
VENEZUELA
COLOMBIA
ECUADOR
PERU
BOLIVIA
CHILE
ARGENTIN
PARA
BR
Andes
Cordillera Occidental
Cordillera Oriental
Guiana Highlands
Roraima
Uraricoera
Boa Vista
Caracaraí
Pico da Neblina
3014m
Rio Negro
Represa Balb
Río Putumayo
Río Napo
Rio Japurá
Rio Içá
Amazon
Manaus
Tefé
Coari
Rio Juruá
Rio Madeira
Rio Javari
Río Marañón
Amazon Basin
Humaitá
Japiim
Feijó
Rio Purus
Porto Velho
Acre
Rio Abunã
Río Ucayali
Rondônia
Chapada dos Parecis
Guaporé
Vilhe
Río Mamoré
Cordillera
Lake Titicaca
Cordillera Oriental
Cordillera Occidental
Lago Poopó
Desierto de Atacama
Pilcomayo
Río Bermejo
Gran Chaco
Río Salado
Paraguay
Paran
Equator
Galapagos Islands
(Archipiélago de Colón)
(part of Ecuador)
PACIFIC OCEAN
Tropic of Capricorn
N
0 km
600
0 miles
600

POPULATION

- Less than 50,000
- 50,000 – 100,000
- 100,000 – 500,000
- Over 500,000

E
F
G
H
50°
40°
30°
1
2
3
4
5
98
99
10°
20°
30°
FRENCH GUIANA
(French overseas department)
RINAME
Tumuc Humac Mountains
Mouths of the Amazon
Amapá
Macapá
Ilha Caviana de Fora
Baía de Marajó
Ilha de Marajó
Belém
Baía de São Marco
Amazon
Alenquer
Santarém
Altamira
Itaituba
Tapajós
Rio Xingu
Represa de Tucuruí
Marabá
Imperatriz
Pará
ATLANTIC OCEAN
Equator
São Luís
Parnaíba
Camocim
Fortaleza
Bacabal
Piripiri
Teresina
Maranhão
Ceará
Mossoró
Açu
Atol das Rocas
San Fernando de Noronha (part of Brazil)
Cabo de São Roque
Rio Grande do Norte
Natal
Floriano
Carolina
Balsas
Picos
Juazeiro do Norte
Paraíba
João Pessoa
Campina Grande
Serra do Cachimbo
BRAZIL
Piauí
Pernambuco
Recife
Alagoas
Represa de Sobradinho
Juazeiro
Maceió
Serra Formosa
Serra dos Gradaús
Rio Tocantins
Rio São Francisco
Chapada Diamantina
Aracaju
Estância
Tocantins
Taguatinga
Feira de Santana
Salvador
Baía de Todos os Santos
Bahia
Mato Grosso
Rio Araguaia
Goiás
Planalto Central
Cuiabá
Itabuna
BRASÍLIA
Janaúba
Vitória da Conquista
Canavieiras
Anápolis
Montes Claros
Goiânia
Minas Gerais
Araçuai
Jataí
Araguari
Mato Grosso do Sul
Uberlândia
Governador Valadares
Espírito Santo
Uberaba
Campo Grande
Belo Horizonte
Aquidauana
Ribeirão Preto
Divinópolis
Vitória
Presidente Epitácio
Juiz de Fora
Campos
Marília
São Paulo
Campinas
Londrina
Maringá
Nova Iguaçu
Rio de Janeiro
São Paulo
Santos
Tropic of Capricorn
Paraná
Represa de Itaipú
Ponta Grossa
Curitiba
Salto do Iguaçu
Rio Iguaçu
Joinville
Paraná
Blumenau
Santa Catarina
Florianópolis
Passo Fundo
Rio Grande do Sul
Santa Maria
Canoas
Porto Alegre
Bagé
Lagoa dos Patos
Rio Negro
Rio Grande
Mirim Lagoon
URUGUAY

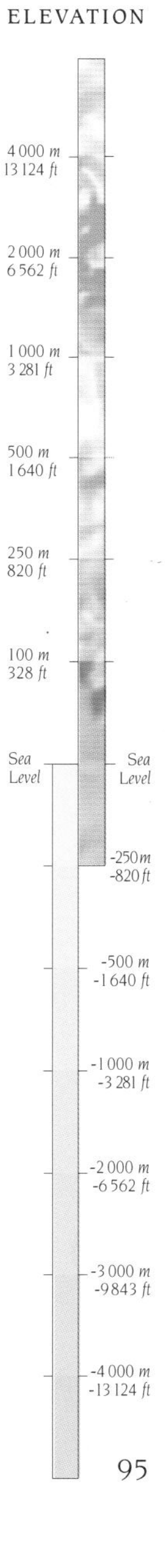
ELEVATION
4 000 m
13 124 ft
2 000 m
6 562 ft
1 000 m
3 281 ft
500 m
1 640 ft
250 m
820 ft
100 m
328 ft
Sea Level
Sea Level
-250 m
-820 ft
-500 m
-1 640 ft
-1 000 m
-3 281 ft
-2 000 m
-6 562 ft
-3 000 m
-9 843 ft
-4 000 m
-13 124 ft

SOUTHERN SOUTH AMERICA

POPULATION

- *Less than* 50,000
- 50,000 – 100,000
- 100,000 – 500,000
- *Over* 500,000

ATLANTIC OCEAN
ARGENTINA
CHILE
Patagonia
FALKLAND ISLANDS
(UK dependent territory)
STANLEY
East Falkland
West Falkland
Goose Green
Drake Passage
Strait of Magellan
Tierra del Fuego
Beagle Channel
Cabo de Hornos
(Cape Horn)
Isla de los Estados
Mar del Plata
Necochea
Balcarce
Tres Arroyos
Coronel Dorrego
Bahía Blanca
Punta Alta
Viedma
San Antonio Oeste
Golfo San Matías
Peninsula Valdés
Golfo Nuevo
Rawson
Trelew
Comodoro Rivadavia
Golfo San Jorge
Caleta Olivia
Puerto Deseado
Puerto San Julián
Bahía Grande
Río Gallegos
Punta Arenas
Porvenir
Ushuaia
Puerto Natales
El Calafate
Río Santa Cruz
Río Chico
Río Deseado
Río Chubut
Río Negro
Río Colorado
Choele Choel
Neuquén
Cipolletti
Zapala
Lago Nahuel Huapi
San Carlos de Bariloche
Esquel
Paso de Indios
Lago Musters
Sarmiento
Lago Buenos Aires
Perito Moreno
Cochrane
Chile Chico
Coihaique
Puerto Aisén
Cerro San Valentín 4058m
Cerro Mellizo Sur 3050m
Cerro Paine 2670m
Isla Wellington
Golfo de Penas
Archipiélago de los Chonos
Golfo Corcovado
Isla de Chiloé
Castro
Ancud
Puerto Montt
Puerto Varas
Osorno
Valdivia
Loncoche
Temuco
Lebu
Concepción
Los Angeles
Río Bío Bío
PACIFIC
0 km 200
0 miles 200
N
A B C D E
5 6 7 8
185 186 99

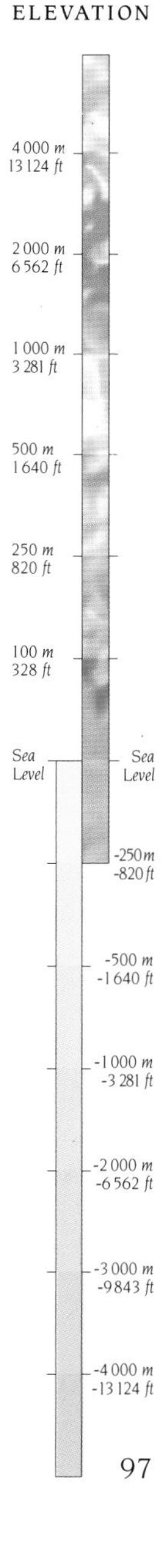

ELEVATION
4000 m 13124 ft
2000 m 6562 ft
1000 m 3281 ft
500 m 1640 ft
250 m 820 ft
100 m 328 ft
Sea Level
-250 m -820 ft
-500 m -1640 ft
-1000 m -3281 ft
-2000 m -6562 ft
-3000 m -9843 ft
-4000 m -13124 ft

The Atlantic Ocean

ARCTIC OCEAN
Lincoln Sea
Ellesmere Island
Baffin Bay
Baffin Island
Davis Strait
Labrador Sea
Labrador Basin
Hudson Bay
GREENLAND
(to Denmark)
Greenland Sea
Denmark Strait
SVALBARD
(to Norway)
Limit of summer pack ice
Limit of winter pack ice
Barents Sea
North Cape
Norwegian Sea
Norwegian Basin
JAN MAYEN
(to Norway)
ICELAND
Reykjavik
FAEROE ISLANDS
(to Denmark)
Iceland Basin
Reykjanes Basin
Scandinavia
Gulf of Bothnia
Baltic Sea
North Sea
British Isles
Gothenburg
Hamburg
Rotterdam
EUROPE
Caspian Sea
Black Sea
Mariupol
Odesa
Danube
Alps
Venice
Adriatic Sea
Mediterranean Sea
Bay of Biscay
Gibraltar
Atlas Mountains
Port Said
Suez
Red Sea
Nile
Sahara
Sahel
AFRICA
Niger
Lagos
Freetown
Dakar
CAPE VERDE
Sierra Leone Rise
Rockall Bank
Charlie-Gibbs Fracture Zone
Mid-Atlantic Ridge
Northwest Atlantic Mid-Ocean Canyon
Newfoundland
Grand Banks of Newfoundland
Newfoundland Basin
Azores
(part of Portugal)
East Azores Fracture Zone
Madeira
(part of Portugal)
Madeira Plain
Great Meteor Tablemount
Canary Islands
(part of Spain)
Cape Verde Plain
Cape Verde Basin
Sohm Plain
Sargasso Sea
Bermuda Rise
BERMUDA
(to UK)
Hatteras Plain
Nares Plain
Kane Fracture Zone
ATLANTIC OCEAN
Doldrums Fracture Zone
Demerara Plain
Puerto Rico Trench
Greater Antilles
Lesser Antilles
Caribbean Sea
Colombian Basin
La Guaira
Cristobal
Panama
Guatemala Basin
Gulf of Mexico
New Orleans
Mississippi
Appalachian Mountains
St. Lawrence Seaway
Montreal
Halifax
New York
Great Lakes
NORTH AMERICA
Arctic Circle
Tropic of Cancer
187
145
66

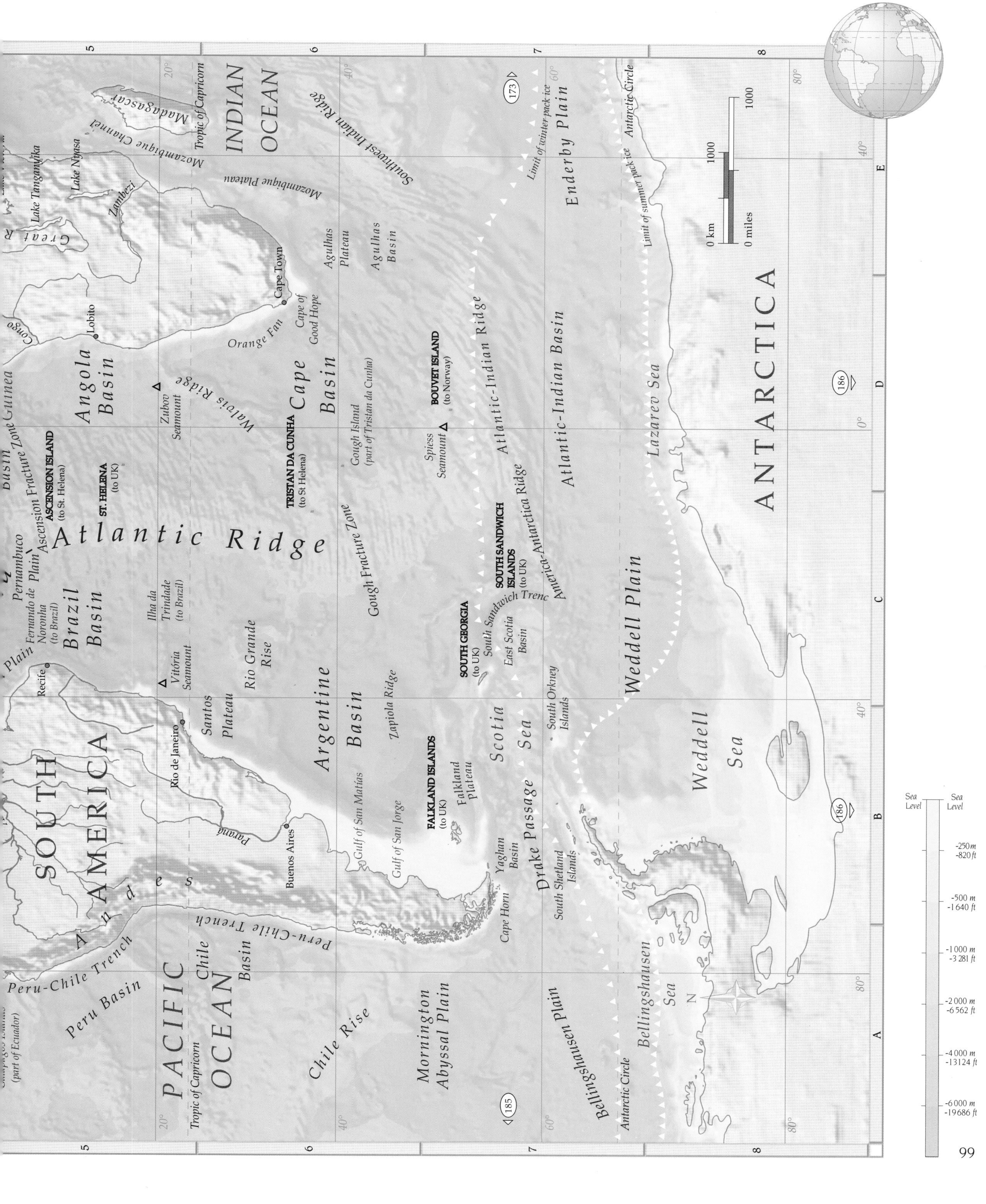
SOUTH AMERICA
Andes
Recife
Rio de Janeiro
Buenos Aires
Paraná
Plain
Fernando de Noronha (to Brazil)
Pernambuco Plain
Ascension Fracture Zone
ASCENSION ISLAND (to St. Helena)
ST. HELENA (to UK)
Atlantic Ridge
Brazil Basin
Ilha da Trindade (to Brazil)
Vitória Seamount
Santos Plateau
Rio Grande Rise
Argentine Basin
Zapiola Ridge
Gulf of San Matías
Gulf of San Jorge
FALKLAND ISLANDS (to UK)
Falkland plateau
Yaghan Basin
Cape Horn
Drake Passage
Scotia Sea
South Orkney Islands
South Shetland Islands
SOUTH GEORGIA (to UK)
South Sandwich Trench
East Scotia Basin
SOUTH SANDWICH ISLANDS (to UK)
America-Antarctica Ridge
Weddell Plain
Weddell Sea
Gough Fracture Zone
TRISTAN DA CUNHA (to St Helena)
Gough Island (part of Tristan da Cunha)
Cape Basin
Walvis Ridge
Zubov Seamount
Angola Basin
Guinea
Basin
Lobito
Congo
Orange Fan
Cape of Good Hope
Cape Town
Agulhas Plateau
Agulhas Basin
BOUVET ISLAND (to Norway)
Spiess Seamount
Atlantic-Indian Ridge
Atlantic-Indian Basin
Lazarev Sea
ANTARCTICA
Enderby Plain
Limit of winter pack ice
Limit of summer pack ice
Antarctic Circle
Southwest Indian Ridge
Mozambique Plateau
Mozambique Channel
Madagascar
Tropic of Capricorn
INDIAN OCEAN
Lake Tanganyika
Lake Nyasa
Zambezi
Great R
(part of Ecuador)
Peru-Chile Trench
Peru Basin
PACIFIC OCEAN
Chile Basin
Chile Rise
Mornington Abyssal Plain
Bellingshausen Plain
Bellingshausen Sea
N
0 km 1000
0 miles 1000
20° 40° 60° 80°
0°
A B C D E
5 6 7 8
173
185
186
Sea Level
-250 m -820 ft
-500 m -1 640 ft
-1 000 m -3 281 ft
-2 000 m -6 562 ft
-4 000 m -13 124 ft
-6 000 m -19 686 ft

AFRICA

POPULATION

Less than 50,000 ○

50,000 – 100,000 ○

100,000 – 500,000 ◉

Over 500,000 ▣

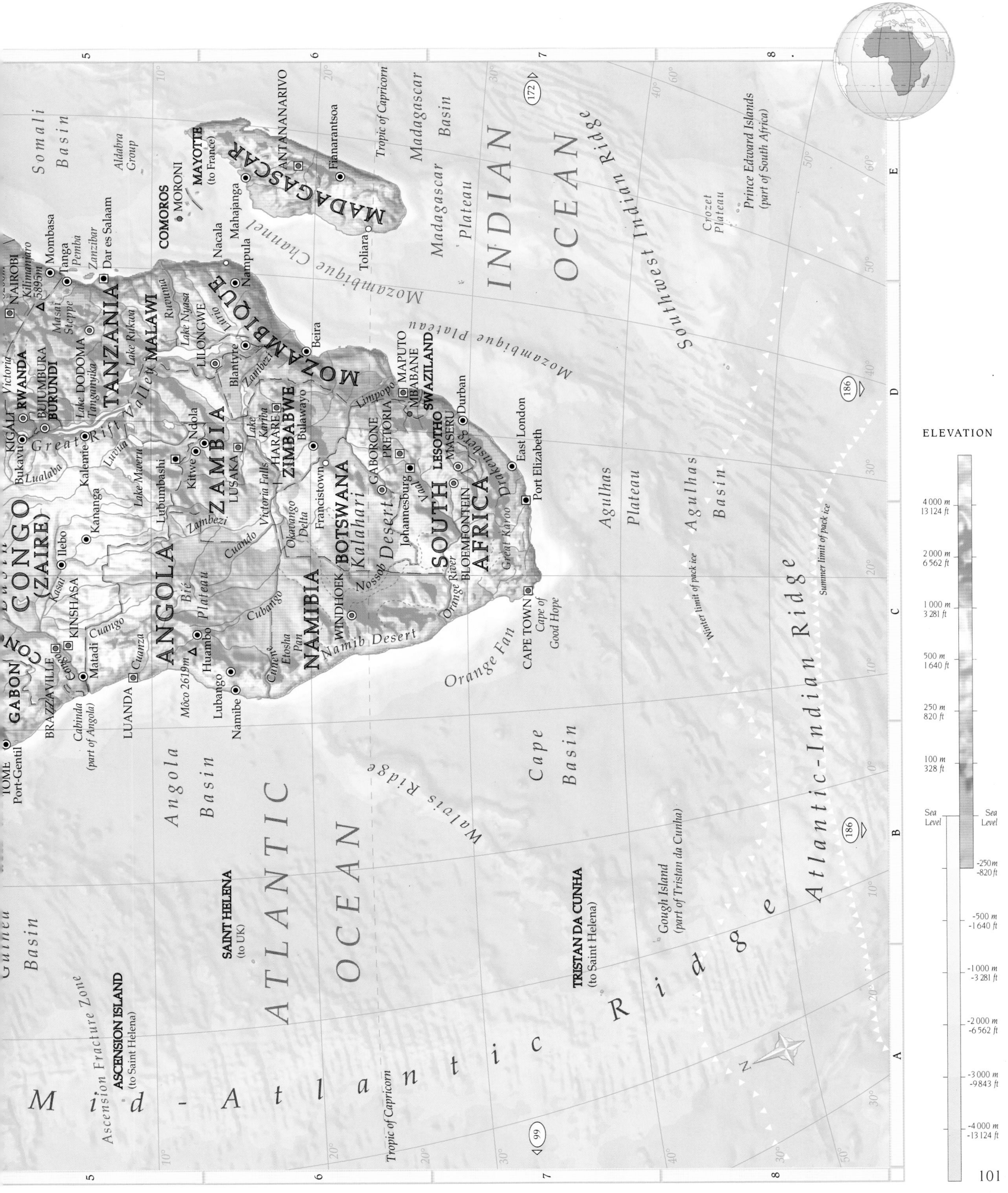

ATLANTIC OCEAN
INDIAN OCEAN
Mid-Atlantic Ridge
Atlantic-Indian Ridge
Southwest Indian Ridge
Walvis Ridge
Angola Basin
Cape Basin
Agulhas Basin
Agulhas Plateau
Madagascar Basin
Madagascar Plateau
Mozambique Plateau
Mozambique Channel
Somali Basin
Guinea Basin
Ascension Fracture Zone
Orange Fan
Crozet Plateau
Winter limit of pack ice
Summer limit of pack ice
Tropic of Capricorn
ASCENSION ISLAND
(to Saint Helena)
SAINT HELENA
(to UK)
TRISTAN DA CUNHA
(to Saint Helena)
Gough Island
(part of Tristan da Cunha)
Prince Edward Islands
(part of South Africa)
GABON
CONGO
CONGO (ZAIRE)
ANGOLA
NAMIBIA
BOTSWANA
SOUTH AFRICA
LESOTHO
SWAZILAND
ZIMBABWE
ZAMBIA
MALAWI
MOZAMBIQUE
TANZANIA
RWANDA
BURUNDI
MADAGASCAR
COMOROS
MAYOTTE
(to France)
Cabinda
(part of Angola)
Port-Gentil
BRAZZAVILLE
KINSHASA
Matadi
LUANDA
Cuanza
Huambo
Môco 2619m
Lubango
Namibe
Bié Plateau
Cubango
Cunene
Etosha Pan
Namib Desert
WINDHOEK
Nossob
Kalahari Desert
Okavango Delta
Francistown
GABORONE
PRETORIA
Johannesburg
Vaal
BLOEMFONTEIN
MASERU
MBABANE
MAPUTO
Durban
East London
Port Elizabeth
CAPE TOWN
Cape of Good Hope
Great Karoo
Drakensberg
Orange River
Limpopo
Bulawayo
HARARE
Lake Kariba
Victoria Falls
LUSAKA
Kitwe
Ndola
Lubumbashi
Zambezi
Cuando
Lake Mweru
Kananga
Ilebo
Kasai
Cuango
Lualaba
Bukavu
KIGALI
BUJUMBURA
Kalemie
Lake Tanganyika
Great Rift Valley
Luvua
Lake Rukwa
Lake Nyasa
LILONGWE
Blantyre
Ruvuma
Lurio
Beira
Nampula
Nacala
DODOMA
Masai Steppe
Kilimanjaro 5895m
NAIROBI
Mombasa
Tanga
Pemba
Zanzibar
Dar es Salaam
MORONI
Mahajanga
ANTANANARIVO
Fianarantsoa
Toliara
Aldabra Group
ELEVATION
4 000 m 13 124 ft
2 000 m 6 562 ft
1 000 m 3 281 ft
500 m 1 640 ft
250 m 820 ft
100 m 328 ft
Sea Level
-250m -820 ft
-500 m -1 640 ft
-1 000 m -3 281 ft
-2 000 m -6 562 ft
-3 000 m -9 843 ft
-4 000 m -13 124 ft

Northwest Africa

A
B
C
D
1
2
3
4
5
0 km
400
0 miles
400
N
ATLANTIC
OCEAN
PORTUGAL
SPAIN
Tagus
Ebro
124
125
Islas Baleares
(Balearic Islands)
Strait of Gibraltar
GIBRALTAR
(UK dependent territory)
Ceuta (part of Spain)
Melilla
(part of Spain)
ALGER
(ALGIERS)
Chlef
Oran
Tanger
Tetouan
Ksar-el-Kebir
Chefchaouen
Mostaganem
Sidi Bel Abbès
Salé
Kénitra
Oujda
Tlemcen
RABAT
Fès
Jerada
Casablanca
El-Jadida
Mohammedia
Khouribga
Safi
Beni-Mellal
Moyen Atlas
Hauts Plateaux
Chott ech Chergui
Atlas Mountains
Atlas Saharien
Laghouat
Marrakech
Figuig
Er-Rachidia
Essaouira
MOROCCO
Béchar
Agadir
Ouarzazate
Haut Atlas
Grand Erg Occidental
El Goléa
Tiznit
Madeira
(part of Portugal)
Madeira
Porto Santo
Funchal
Ilhas Desertas
98
Islas Canarias
(Canary Islands)
(part of Spain)
La Palma
Santa Cruz de Tenerife
Lanzarote
Gomera
Fuerteventura
Hierro
Las Palmas de Gran Canaria
Tenerife
Gran Canaria
Tan-Tan
Hamada du Dra
ALGERIA
LAÂYOUNE
El Mahbas
Tindouf
Plateau du Tademaït
Adrar
Smara
Boujdour
Bou Craa
I-n-Salah
Erg Iguîdi
Reggane
WESTERN SAHARA
(disputed territory under Moroccan occupation)
Galtat-Zemmour
Tropic of Cancer
Ad Dakhla
Erg Chech
Tanezrouft
Ouarâne
Sahara
Lagouira
MAURITANIA
Azaouâd
Senegal
MALI
Niger
SENEGAL
106
107

POPULATION

Less than 50,000

50,000 – 100,000

100,000 – 500,000

Over 500,000

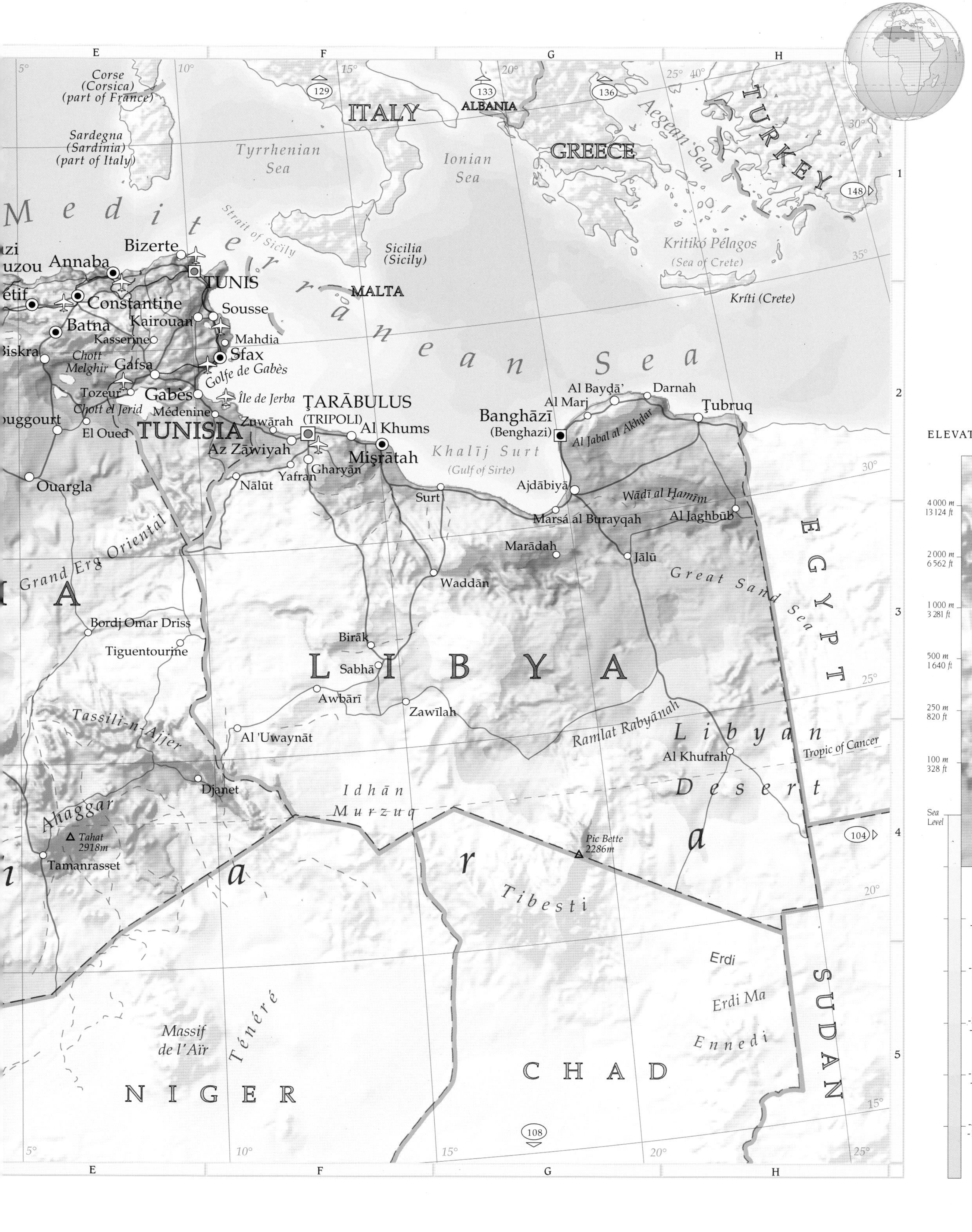
E
F
G
H
Corse
(Corsica)
(part of France)
Sardegna
(Sardinia)
(part of Italy)
ITALY
ALBANIA
GREECE
TURKEY
129
133
136
148
Tyrrhenian Sea
Ionian Sea
Aegean Sea
Strait of Sicily
Sicilia
(Sicily)
MALTA
Kritikó Pélagos
(Sea of Crete)
Kríti (Crete)
Mediterranean Sea
Bizerte
Annaba
TUNIS
Constantine
Batna
Sousse
Kairouan
Mahdia
Kasserine
Sfax
Biskra
Chott Melghir
Gafsa
Golfe de Gabès
Tozeur
Gabès
Île de Jerba
Chott el Jerid
Médenine
El Oued
TUNISIA
Zuwārah
ṬARĀBULUS
(TRIPOLI)
Al Khums
Az Zāwiyah
Miṣrātah
Gharyān
Yafran
Nālūt
Ouargla
Khalīj Surt
(Gulf of Sirte)
Surt
Al Bayḍā'
Darnah
Al Marj
Banghāzī
(Benghazi)
Ṭubruq
Al Jabal al Akhḍar
Ajdābiyā
Wādī al Ḥamīm
Marsá al Burayqah
Al Jaghbūb
Marādah
Jālū
Waddān
Great Sand Sea
EGYPT
Grand Erg Oriental
Bordj Omar Driss
Tiguentourine
Birāk
Sabhā
LIBYA
Awbārī
Zawīlah
Tassili-n-Ajjer
Al 'Uwaynāt
Ramlat Rabyānah
Libyan Desert
Al Khufrah
Tropic of Cancer
Djanet
Idhān Murzuq
Ahaggar
Tahat 2918m
Tamanrasset
Pic Bette 2286m
104
Tibesti
Erdi
Erdi Ma
Ennedi
SUDAN
Massif de l'Aïr
Ténéré
NIGER
CHAD
108
5°
10°
15°
20°
25°
30°
35°
40°
1
2
3
4
5
ELEVATION
4 000 m 13 124 ft
2 000 m 6 562 ft
1 000 m 3 281 ft
500 m 1 640 ft
250 m 820 ft
100 m 328 ft
Sea Level
-250 m -820 ft
-500 m -1 640 ft
-1 000 m -3 281 ft
-2 000 m -6 562 ft
-3 000 m -9 843 ft
-4 000 m -13 124 ft

Northeast Africa

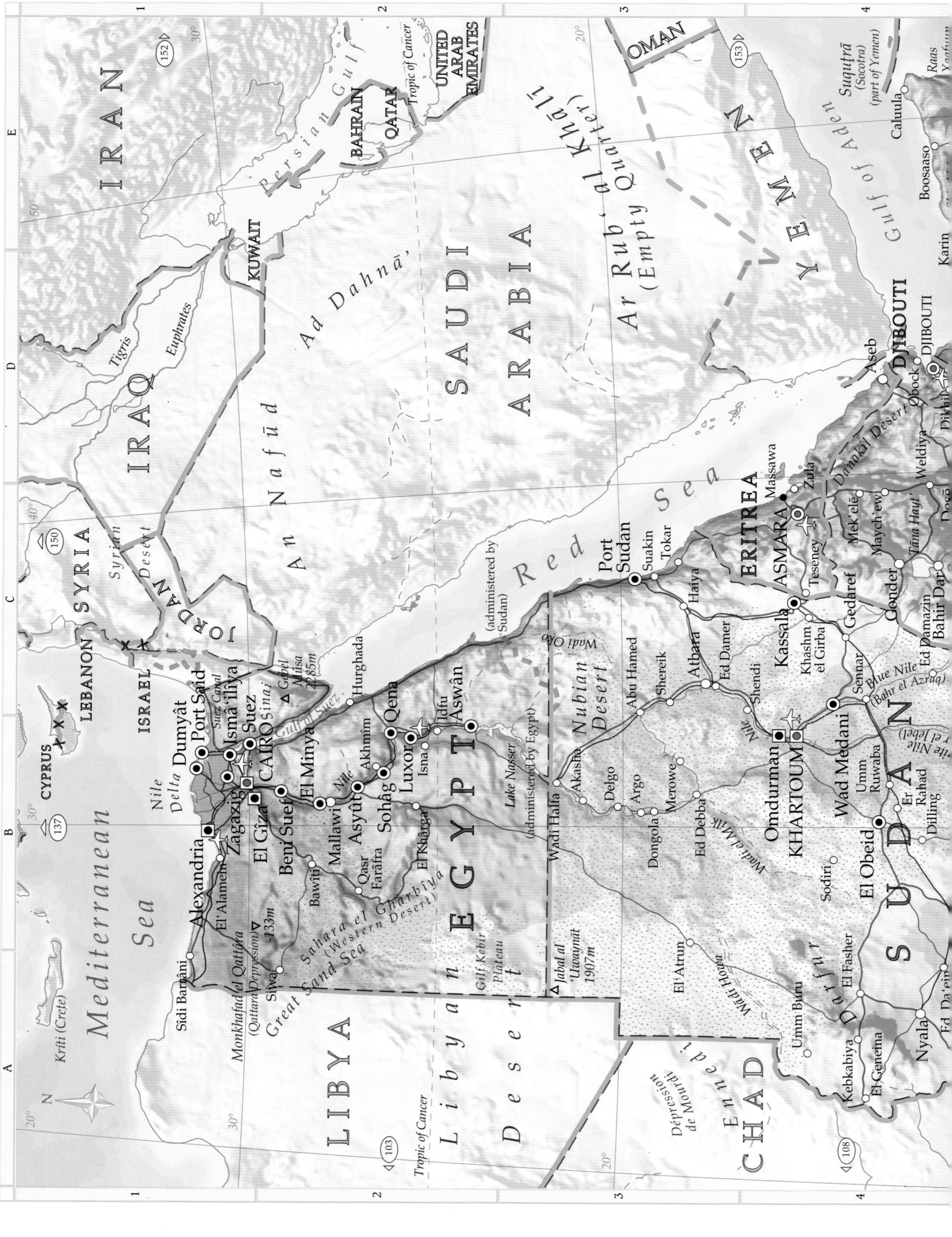
IRAN
IRAQ
KUWAIT
BAHRAIN
QATAR
UNITED ARAB EMIRATES
OMAN
YEMEN
SAUDI ARABIA
SYRIA
JORDAN
LEBANON
ISRAEL
CYPRUS
EGYPT
LIBYA
SUDAN
CHAD
ERITREA
DJIBOUTI
Mediterranean Sea
Red Sea
Persian Gulf
Gulf of Aden
Gulf of Suez
Tigris
Euphrates
Syrian Desert
An Nafūd
Ad Dahnā'
Ar Rub' al Khālī (Empty Quarter)
Libyan Desert
Nubian Desert
Sahara el Gharbîya (Western Desert)
Great Sand Sea
Darfur
Ennedi
Dépression de Mourdi
Nile Delta
Nile
Blue Nile (Bahr el Azraq)
Wadi Howar
Wadi el Milk
Wadi Oko
Lake Nasser (administered by Egypt)
(administered by Sudan)
Suez Canal
Sinai
Gebel Mûsa 2285m
Jabal al 'Uwaynāt 1907m
Gilf Kebir Plateau
Monkhafad el Qattâra (Qattara Depression) -133m
Kriti (Crete)
Suquṭrā (Socotra) (part of Yemen)
Tropic of Cancer
CAIRO
KHARTOUM
ASMARA
DJIBOUTI
Alexandria
Port Said
Dumyât
Ismâ'ilîya
Suez
Zagazig
El Giza
Beni Suef
El Minya
Mallawi
Asyût
Sohâg
Qena
Luxor
Aswân
Idfu
Isna
Akhmîm
Hurghada
El Khârga
Qasr Farâfra
Bawîti
Siwa
Sîdi Barrâni
El 'Alamein
Wadi Halfa
Akasha
Delgo
Argo
Dongola
Merowe
Ed Debba
Abu Hamed
Shereik
Atbara
Ed Damer
Shendi
Omdurman
Port Sudan
Suakin
Tokar
Haiya
Kassala
Khashm el Girba
Gedaref
Sennar
Wad Medani
Ed Damazin
El Obeid
Umm Ruwaba
Er Rahad
Dilling
Sodiri
El Fasher
Nyala
Umm Buru
Kebkabiya
El Geneina
El Atrun
Massawa
Zula
Teseney
Mek'elē
Maych'ew
Gonder
Bahir Dar
Weldiya
Aseb
Obock
Danakil Desert
Boosaaso
Caluula
Karin
Tāna Hāyk'
152
153
150
137
103
108
20°
30°
40°
50°
N

POPULATION

Less than 50,000

50,000 – 100,000

100,000 – 500,000

Over 500,000

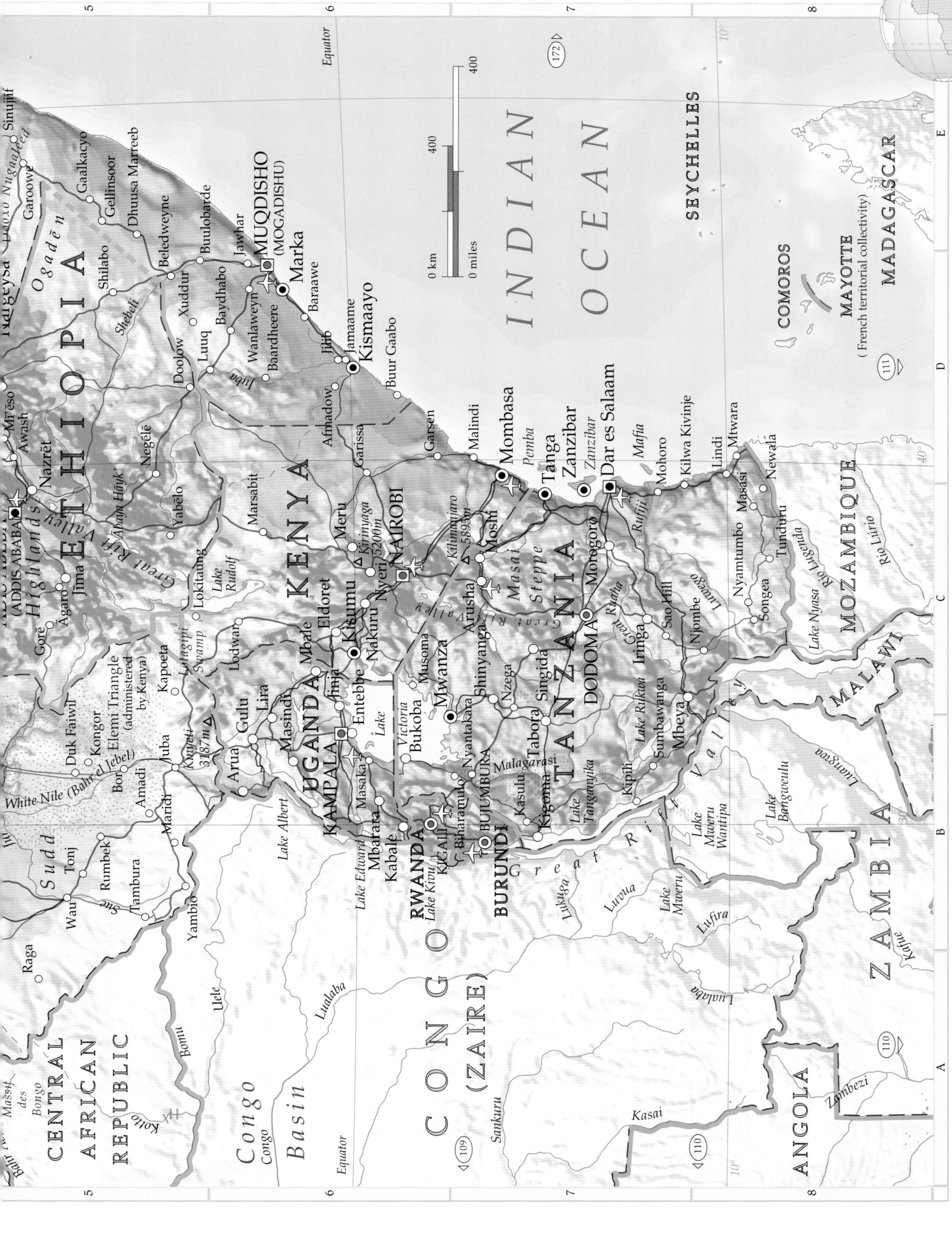
ETHIOPIA
KENYA
UGANDA
TANZANIA
RWANDA
BURUNDI
CONGO (ZAIRE)
CENTRAL AFRICAN REPUBLIC
ANGOLA
ZAMBIA
MALAWI
MOZAMBIQUE
COMOROS
MAYOTTE
(French territorial collectivity)
MADAGASCAR
SEYCHELLES
INDIAN OCEAN
MUQDISHO
(MOGADISHU)
ADDIS ABABA
NAIROBI
KAMPALA
KIGALI
BUJUMBURA
DODOMA
Dar es Salaam
Marka
Kismaayo
Mombasa
Tanga
Zanzibar
Kisumu
Mwanza
Arusha
Moshi
Morogoro
Tabora
Kigoma
Mbeya
Iringa
Juba
Wau
Equator
Great Rift Valley
Lake Victoria
Lake Tanganyika
Lake Nyasa
Lake Rudolf
Lake Albert
Lake Edward
Lake Kivu
Lake Mweru
Kilimanjaro 5895m
Kirinyaga 5200m
Masai Steppe
Ogadēn
Ethiopian Highlands
Congo Basin
0 km 400
0 miles 400
109
110
111
172
5
6
7
8
A
B
C
D
E

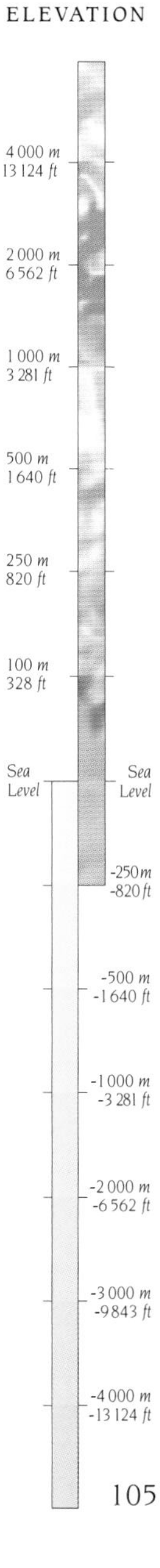
ELEVATION
4 000 m
13 124 ft
2 000 m
6 562 ft
1 000 m
3 281 ft
500 m
1 640 ft
250 m
820 ft
100 m
328 ft
Sea Level
Sea Level
-250 m
-820 ft
-500 m
-1 640 ft
-1 000 m
-3 281 ft
-2 000 m
-6 562 ft
-3 000 m
-9 843 ft
-4 000 m
-13 124 ft

West Africa

A
B
C
D
1
2
3
4
5
WESTERN SAHARA
(disputed territory under Moroccan occupation)
MAURITANIA
SENEGAL
GAMBIA
GUINEA-BISSAU
GUINEA
SIERRA LEONE
LIBERIA
IVORY COAST
CAPE VERDE
ATLANTIC OCEAN
Tropic of Cancer
Ilhas de Barlavento
Ilhas de Sotavento
Santo Antão
Mindelo
Pedra Lume
São Vicente
São Nicolau
Sal
Boa Vista
Santiago
Fogo
Maio
PRAIA
Nouâdhibou
NOUAKCHOTT
Idîni
Boutilimit
Magta Lahjar
Rkîz
Rosso
Richard Toll
Dagana
Aleg
Kaédi
Saint Louis
Louga
Matam
Mékhé
DAKAR
Thiès
Mbaké
Mbour
Diourbel
Kaolack
Sokone
BANJUL
Tambacounda
Bignona
Kolda
Ziguinchor
Sédhiou
Bafatá
BISSAU
Gaoual
Boké
Labé
Pita
Kindia
Mamou
Dinguiraye
Siguiri
Kankan
Faranah
CONAKRY
Tokounou
Makeni
FREETOWN
Bo
Kenema
Kissidougou
Beyla
Nzérékoré
Gbanga
Tubmanburg
MONROVIA
Harbel
Buchanan
Zwedru
Harper
'Aïn Ben Tili
Bîr Mogreïn
Fdérik
Zouérat
Touâjîl
Choûm
Atâr
Chinguetti
Akjoujt
Oujeft
Akchâr
Erg Iguîdi
Kâghet
El Hank
Ouarâne
El Mreyyé
Aoukâr
Tidjikja
Tîchît
Boûmdeïd
Tâmchekket
Kiffa
'Ayoûn el 'Atroûs
Oualâta
Néma
Amourj
Timbedgha
Kobenni
Sélibabi
Nioro
Bassikounou
Kayes
Ténenkou
Toukoto
Kolokani
Kita
Ségou
Koulikoro
BAMAKO
Koutiala
Bougouni
Sikasso
Tengréla
Odienné
Ferkessédougou
Boundiali
Korhogo
Katiola
Danané
YAMOUSSOUKRO
Gagnoa
Divo
Sassandra
San-Pédro
Senegal
Gambia
Bafing
Niger
Bani
Bagoé
Sassandra
Bandama
Cavalla
98
99
102
25°
20°
15°
10°
5°
0 km
400
0 miles
400

POPULATION

- Less than 50,000
- 50,000 – 100,000
- 100,000 – 500,000
- Over 500,000

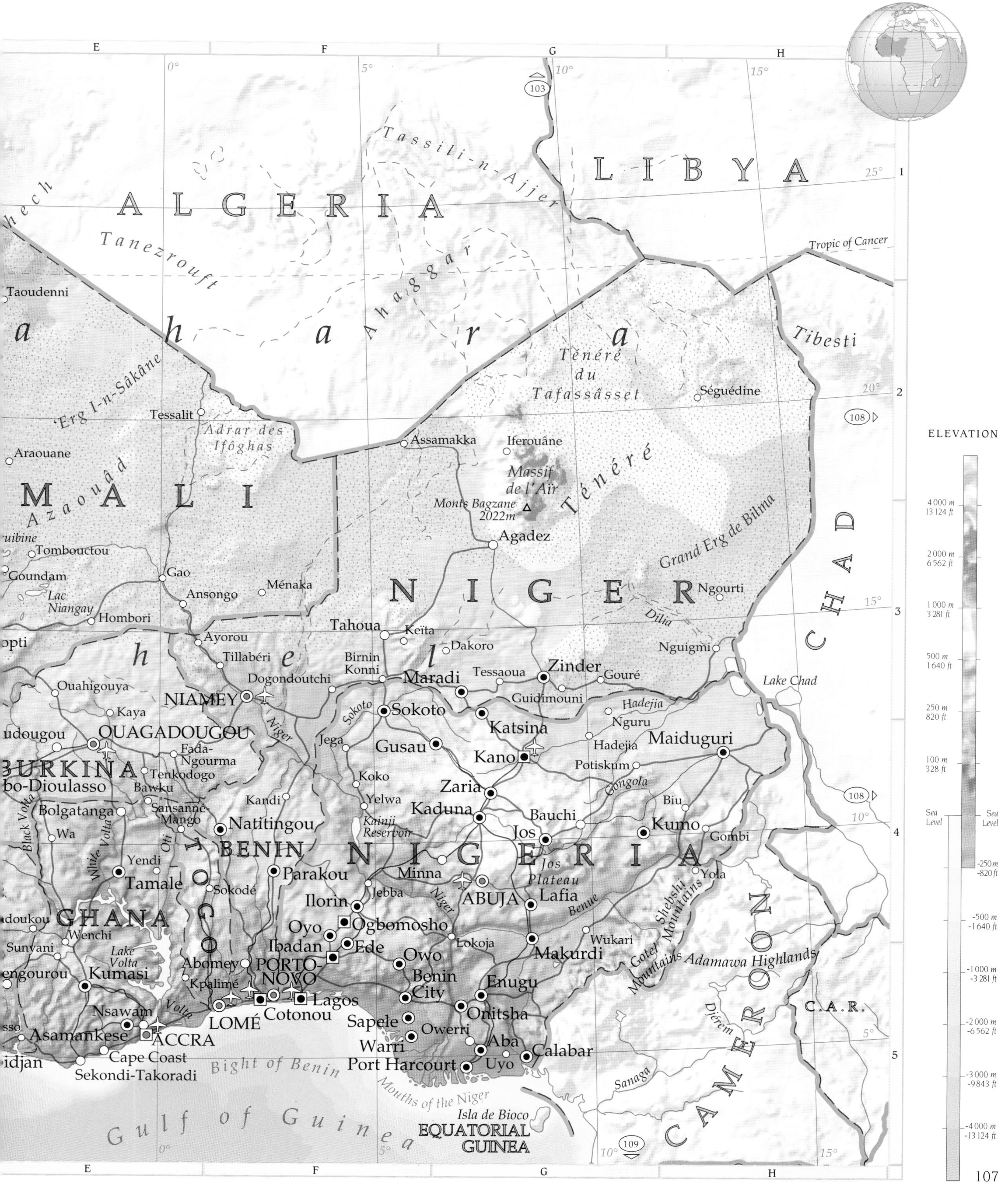
E
F
G
H
0°
5°
10°
15°
103
ALGERIA
LIBYA
Tassili-n-Ajjer
Tanezrouft
Ahaggar
Tropic of Cancer
25°
1
Taoudenni
Sahara
Ténéré du Tafassâsset
Tibesti
Séguédine
20°
2
108
Erg I-n-Sâkâne
Tessalit
Adrar des Ifôghas
Assamakka
Iferouâne
Araouane
Massif de l'Aïr
Ténéré
MALI
Azaouâd
Monts Bagzane 2022m
Agadez
Grand Erg de Bilma
CHAD
Tombouctou
Goundam
Gao
Ménaka
Lac Niangay
Ansongo
NIGER
Ngourti
15°
3
Hombori
Dilia
Tahoua
Keïta
Ayorou
Dakoro
Nguigmi
Sahel
Tillabéri
Birnin Konni
Maradi
Tessaoua
Zinder
Gouré
Dogondoutchi
Guidimouni
Lake Chad
Ouahigouya
NIAMEY
Sokoto
Hadejia
Kaya
Niger
Katsina
Nguru
OUAGADOUGOU
Fada-Ngourma
Jega
Gusau
Hadejia
Maiduguri
BURKINA
Tenkodogo
Kano
Potiskum
Bobo-Dioulasso
Bawku
Koko
Zaria
Gongola
Bolgatanga
Sansanné-Mango
Kandi
Yelwa
Kaduna
Biu
108
Wa
Natitingou
Kainji Reservoir
Bauchi
Kumo
10°
Black Volta
White Volta
Oti
BENIN
NIGERIA
Jos
Gombi
4
Yendi
TOGO
Minna
Jos Plateau
Yola
Tamale
Sokodé
Parakou
Jebba
ABUJA
Lafia
Shebshi Mountains
Ilorin
Benue
GHANA
Oyo
Ogbomosho
Wenchi
Ibadan
Ede
Lokoja
Makurdi
Wukari
Sunyani
Lake Volta
Abomey
PORTO-NOVO
Owo
Gotel Mountains
Adamawa Highlands
Kumasi
Kpalimé
Benin City
Enugu
Volta
Lagos
Onitsha
C.A.R.
Nsawam
LOMÉ
Cotonou
Sapele
Owerri
Asamankese
ACCRA
Warri
Aba
Calabar
Djérem
5°
Cape Coast
Bight of Benin
Port Harcourt
Uyo
5
Sekondi-Takoradi
Mouths of the Niger
Sanaga
CAMEROON
Isla de Bioco
EQUATORIAL GUINEA
Gulf of Guinea
109
ELEVATION
4 000 m
13 124 ft
2 000 m
6 562 ft
1 000 m
3 281 ft
500 m
1 640 ft
250 m
820 ft
100 m
328 ft
Sea Level
-250 m
-820 ft
-500 m
-1 640 ft
-1 000 m
-3 281 ft
-2 000 m
-6 562 ft
-3 000 m
-9 843 ft
-4 000 m
-13 124 ft

CENTRAL AFRICA

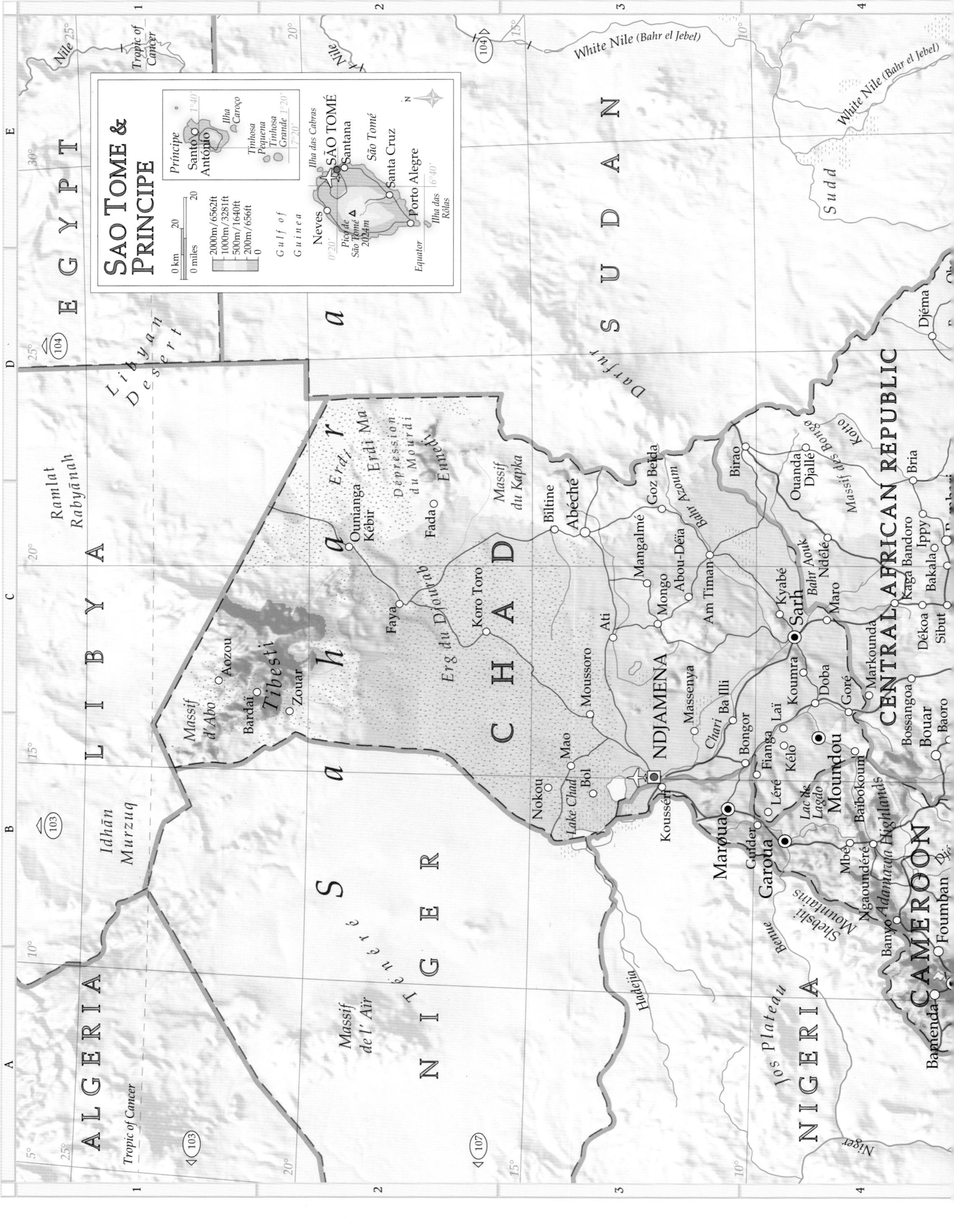
SAO TOME & PRINCIPE
Príncipe
Santo António
Ilha Caroço
Tinhosa Pequena
Tinhosa Grande
Ilha das Cabras
SÃO TOMÉ
Santana
São Tomé
Santa Cruz
Porto Alegre
Neves
Pico de São Tomé 2024m
Ilha das Rôlas
Gulf of Guinea
Equator
2000m/6562ft
1000m/3281ft
500m/1640ft
200m/656ft
0
EGYPT
LIBYA
SUDAN
CHAD
NIGER
ALGERIA
NIGERIA
CAMEROON
CENTRAL AFRICAN REPUBLIC
Sahara
Libyan Desert
Ramlat Rabyānah
Idhān Murzuq
Tibesti
Massif d'Abo
Massif de l'Aïr
Ténéré
Erg du Djourab
Ennedi
Erdi Ma
Massif du Kapka
Darfur
Sudd
Jos Plateau
Adamaoua Highlands
Shebshi Mountains
Tropic of Cancer
White Nile (Bahr el Jebel)
Nile
Lake Chad
Chari
Bahr Aouk
Bahr Azoum
Benue
Niger
Hadejia
NDJAMENA
Abéché
Biltine
Goz Beïda
Faya
Fada
Ounianga Kébir
Koro Toro
Moussoro
Mao
Bol
Nokou
Kousséri
Ati
Mongo
Mangalmé
Abou-Déïa
Am Timan
Massenya
Ba Illi
Bongor
Fianga
Léré
Kélo
Laï
Moundou
Koumra
Doba
Sarh
Kyabé
Maro
Goré
Markounda
Baïbokoum
Bardaï
Zouar
Aozou
Maroua
Guider
Garoua
Mbé
Ngaoundéré
Banyo
Foumban
Bamenda
Bossangoa
Bouar
Baoro
Dékoa
Sibut
Kaga Bandoro
Bakala
Ippy
Bria
Ndélé
Ouanda Djallé
Birao
Djéma
Massif des Bongo
Kotto

POPULATION

○ Less than 50,000

○ 50,000 – 100,000

◉ 100,000 – 500,000

▣ Over 500,000

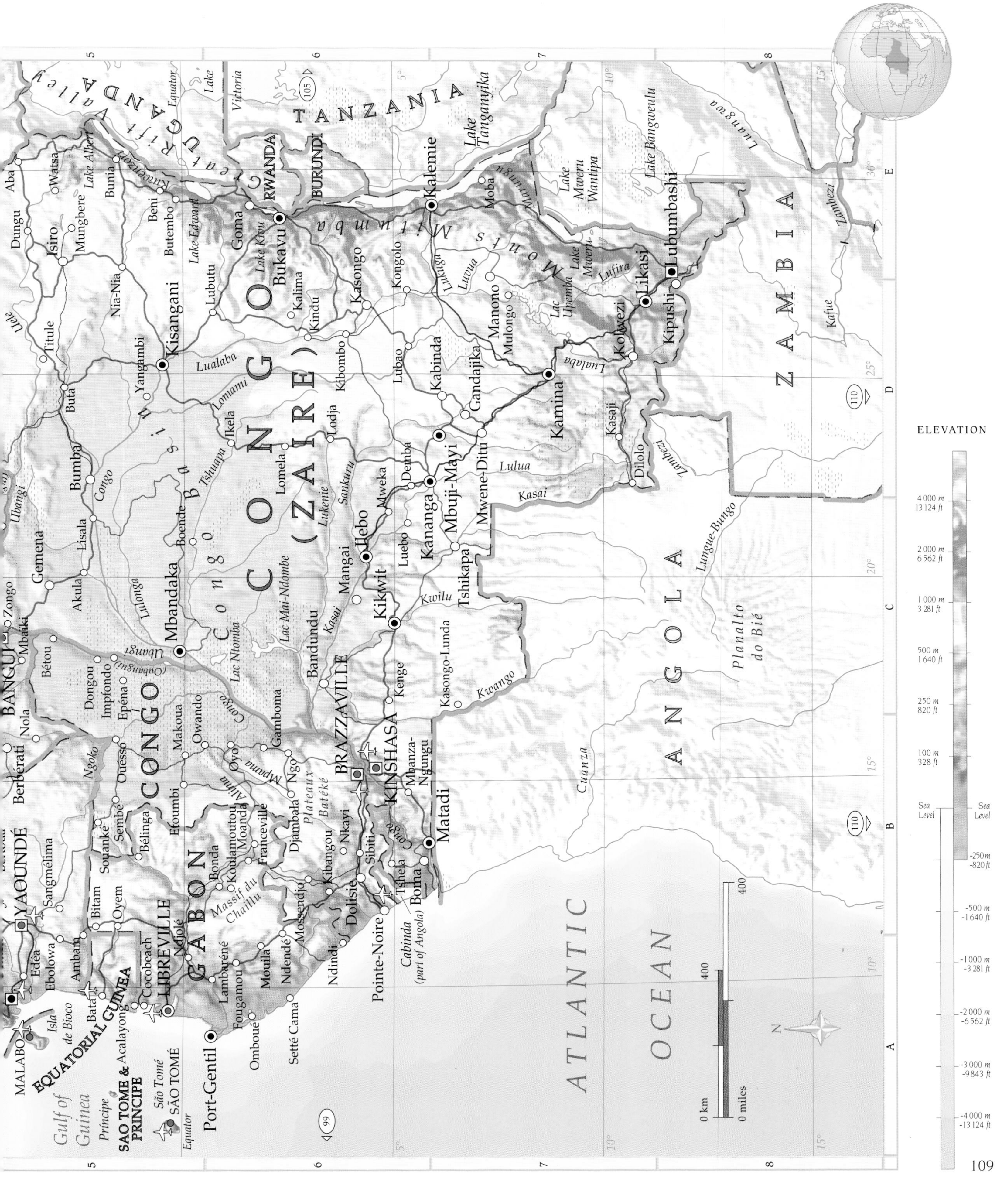
CONGO (ZAIRE)
CONGO
GABON
ANGOLA
ZAMBIA
TANZANIA
UGANDA
RWANDA
BURUNDI
EQUATORIAL GUINEA
SAO TOME & PRINCIPE
ATLANTIC OCEAN
Gulf of Guinea
KINSHASA
BRAZZAVILLE
LIBREVILLE
YAOUNDÉ
BANGUI
MALABO
SÃO TOMÉ
Mbandaka
Kisangani
Kananga
Mbuji-Mayi
Lubumbashi
Likasi
Kolwezi
Kalemie
Bukavu
Goma
Kikwit
Matadi
Boma
Pointe-Noire
Port-Gentil
Kamina
Congo Basin
Mitumba Mountains
Lake Tanganyika
Lake Victoria
Lake Albert
Lake Edward
Lake Kivu
Lake Mweru
Lake Bangweulu
Plateaux Batéké
Massif du Chaillu
Planalto do Bié
Cabinda (part of Angola)
Equator
ELEVATION
4 000 m
13 124 ft
2 000 m
6 562 ft
1 000 m
3 281 ft
500 m
1 640 ft
250 m
820 ft
100 m
328 ft
Sea Level
-250 m
-820 ft
-500 m
-1 640 ft
-1 000 m
-3 281 ft
-2 000 m
-6 562 ft
-3 000 m
-9 843 ft
-4 000 m
-13 124 ft
0 km 400
0 miles 400

Southern Africa

A
B
C
D
1
2
3
4
5
CONGO
CABINDA
(part of Angola)
Cabinda
M'Banza Congo
Congo
109
CONGO
(ZAIRE)
Kwilu
Lake Tanganyika
Lake
Rukwa
N
Uíge
Ambriz
Caxito
LUANDA
Dondo
Cuanza
Malanje
Camabatela
N'Dalatando
Cuango
Lóvua
Chitato
Lucapa
Saurimo
Sankuru
Lualaba
Lake
Mweru
Mbala
Kasama
Mansa
Samfya
Gabela
Sumbe
ANGOLA
Camacupa
Luena
Lunge-Bungo
Zambezi
Solwezi
Chililabombwe
Chingola
Mufulira
Kitwe
Ndola
Luanshya
Serenje
Chipata
Kabompo
Lobito
Benguela
Cubal
Môco 2610m
Caála
Huambo
Kuito
Planalto
do Bié
Caconda
Cubango
Zambezi
ZAMBIA
Kaoma
Mongu
Kafue
Nambala
Kabwe
LUSAKA
Mazabuka
Kafue
Monze
Choma
Albufeira
Cahora Bassa
Vila do
Zumbo
99
Lubango
Namibe
Tombua
Menongue
Huila
Plateau
Cuando
Cubango
Cuito
ATLANTIC OCEAN
Cunene
N'Giva
Olifa
Oshikango
Rundu
Katima Mulilo
Caprivi Strip
Victoria
Falls
Livingstone
Victoria Falls
Hwange
Lake Kariba
Kariba
Nyamapanda
HARARE
Chitungwiza
Kadoma
Kwekwe
Inyangani 2592m
Mutare
Etosha
Pan
Tsumeb
Otavi
Grootfontein
Okavango
Okavango
Delta
Maun
Nata
ZIMBABWE
Bulawayo
Zvishavane
Masvingo
Gwanda
Boteti
Otjiwarongo
Namib Desert
NAMIBIA
Brandberg
2573m
Ghanzi
Francistown
Shashe
BOTSWANA
Wlotzkasbaken
Swakopmund
Walvis Bay
Karibib
Gobabis
WINDHOEK
Mamuno
Serowe
Palapye
Limpopo
Mahalapye
Rehoboth
Kalahari
Tropic of Capricorn
Fish
Mariental
Nosob
Auob
Desert
GABORONE
Mochudi
Jwaneng
Kanye
Werda
Lobatse
Mmabatho
Pietersburg
Nylstroom
PRETORIA
MAPUTO
Johannesburg
Soweto
MBABANE
SWAZILAND
Molopo
Keetmanshoop
Lüderitz
Aus
Klein Karas
Groot Karasberge
Karasburg
Klerksdorp
Vaal
Kroonstad
Dundee
SOUTH
AFRICA
Welkom
Bethlehem
LESOTHO
MASERU
Drakensberg
Oranjemund
Orange River
Upington
Kimberley
BLOEMFONTEIN
Prieska
Pietermaritzburg
Durban
De Aar
Colesberg
Kokstad
Drakensberg
Umtata
Queenstown
Mdantsane
East London
St Helena Bay
Beaufort West
Cradock
Great Karoo
Bellville
Worcester
Uitenhage
George
Port Alfred
CAPE TOWN
Mosselbaai
Port Elizabeth
Cape of
Good Hope
186
10°
20°
30°
SOUTH AFRICA'S
THREE CAPITALS
PRETORIA - administrative capital
CAPE TOWN - legislative capital
BLOEMFONTEIN - judicial capital

POPULATION

Less than 50,000

50,000 – 100,000

100,000 – 500,000

Over 500,000

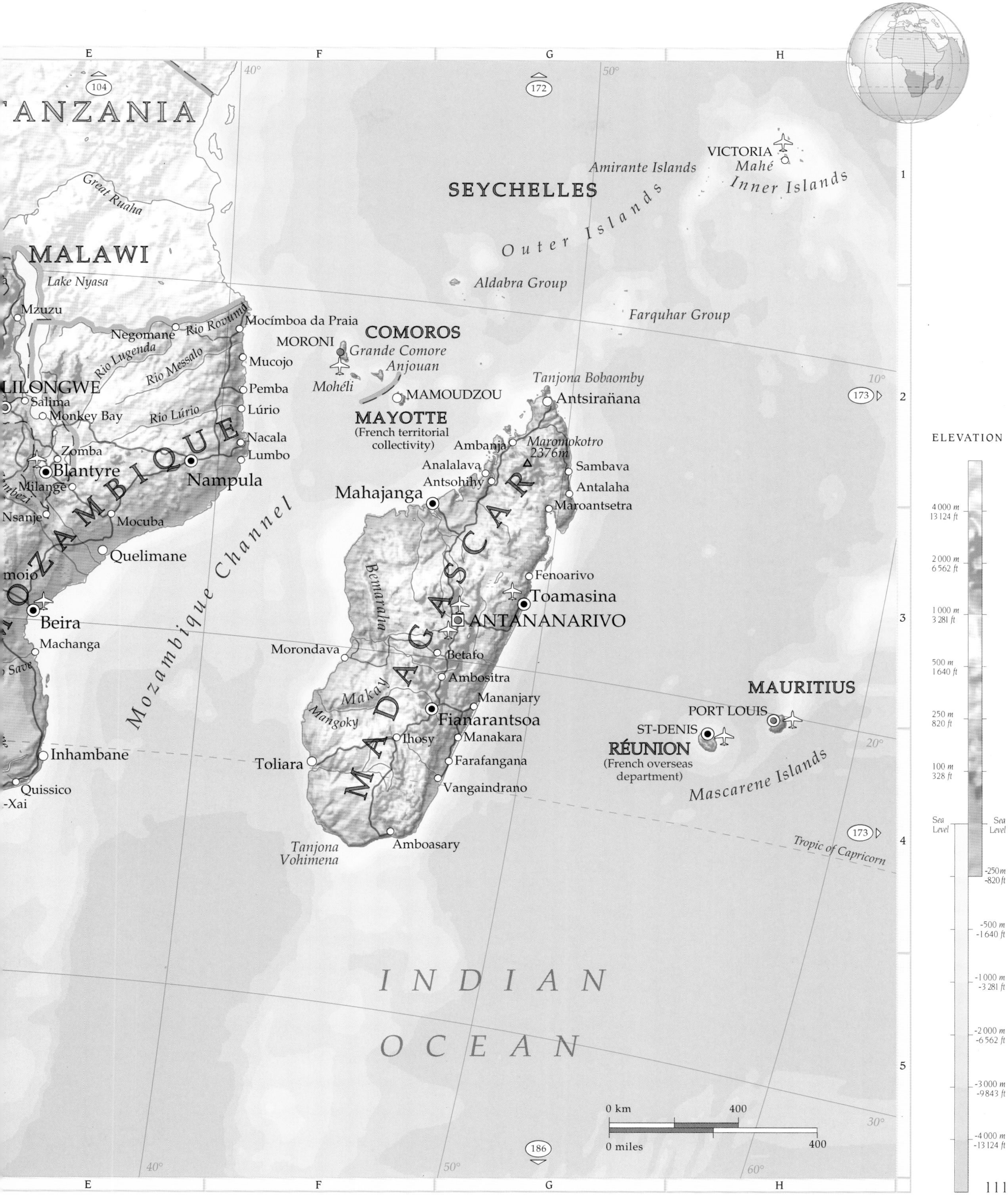
E
F
G
H
1
2
3
4
5
104
172
173
173
186
40°
50°
60°
10°
20°
30°
TANZANIA
Great Ruaha
MALAWI
Lake Nyasa
Mzuzu
LILONGWE
Salima
Monkey Bay
Zomba
Blantyre
Milange
Nsanje
MOZAMBIQUE
Negomane
Rio Rovuma
Rio Lugenda
Rio Messalo
Rio Lúrio
Mocímboa da Praia
Mucojo
Pemba
Lúrio
Nacala
Lumbo
Nampula
Mocuba
Quelimane
Beira
Machanga
Save
Inhambane
Quissico
-Xai
Mozambique Channel
COMOROS
MORONI
Grande Comore
Anjouan
Mohéli
MAMOUDZOU
MAYOTTE
(French territorial collectivity)
SEYCHELLES
Amirante Islands
VICTORIA
Mahé
Inner Islands
Outer Islands
Aldabra Group
Farquhar Group
Tanjona Bobaomby
Antsirañana
Ambanja
Maromokotro 2376m
Sambava
Antalaha
Analalava
Antsohihy
Mahajanga
Maroantsetra
MADAGASCAR
Bemaraha
Fenoarivo
Toamasina
ANTANANARIVO
Betafo
Morondava
Ambositra
Makay
Mangoky
Mananjary
Fianarantsoa
Ihosy
Manakara
Toliara
Farafangana
Vangaindrano
Amboasary
Tanjona Vohimena
MAURITIUS
PORT LOUIS
ST-DENIS
RÉUNION
(French overseas department)
Mascarene Islands
Tropic of Capricorn
INDIAN OCEAN
0 km
400
0 miles
400
ELEVATION
4 000 m
13 124 ft
2 000 m
6 562 ft
1 000 m
3 281 ft
500 m
1 640 ft
250 m
820 ft
100 m
328 ft
Sea Level
Sea Level
-250 m
-820 ft
-500 m
-1 640 ft
-1 000 m
-3 281 ft
-2 000 m
-6 562 ft
-3 000 m
-9 843 ft
-4 000 m
-13 124 ft

Europe

A
B
C
D
1
2
3
4
5
187
98
100
Reykjanes Basin
Reykjanes Ridge
Limit of winter pack ice
REYKJAVÍK
ICELAND
Vatnajökull
Faeroe-Iceland Ridge
Norwegian Basin
Norwegian Sea
Charlie-Gibbs Fracture Zone
Iceland Basin
FAEROE ISLANDS
(to Denmark)
Hatton Ridge
Faeroe-Shetland Trough
Shetland Islands
Mid-Atlantic Ridge
Rockall Bank
Rockall Trough
Outer Hebrides
Orkney Islands
British Isles
Trondheim
Bergen
OSLO
Stavanger
Glasgow
Edinburgh
Ireland
Belfast
REPUBLIC OF IRELAND
DUBLIN
ISLE OF MAN
(to UK)
UNITED KINGDOM
North Sea
Gothenburg
Ålborg
Jylland
DENMARK
Odense
Malmö
Liverpool
Manchester
Britain
Birmingham
ATLANTIC OCEAN
Porcupine Plain
Celtic Sea
Cardiff
LONDON
NETHERLANDS
THE HAGUE
AMSTERDAM
Rotterdam
Hamburg
Elbe
Hannover
BERLIN
Celtic Shelf
English Channel
BELGIUM
BRUSSELS
Channel Islands
(to UK)
le Havre
Seine
Liège
Bonn
GERMANY
Wrocław
LUXEMBOURG
Rennes
PARIS
Frankfurt am Main
LUXEMBOURG
Azores-Biscay Rise
Charcot Seamounts
Biscay Plain
Nantes
Loire
Orléans
Rhine
Stuttgart
CZECH REPUBLIC
Strasbourg
Iberian Plain
Bay of Biscay
FRANCE
Munich
A Coruña
Galicia Bank
Zürich
BERN
LIECH.
Salzburg
Bordeaux
Lyon
SWITZERLAND
Innsbruck
AUSTRIA
Cordillera Cantabrica
Bilbao
Garonne
Massif Central
Mont Blanc 4807m
Alps
SLOVENIA
Porto
Rhône
Milan
Venice
PORTUGAL
Duero
Toulouse
Turin
Po
Trieste
CROATIA
Iberian
Zaragoza
Pyrenees
Nice
Bologna
ANDORRA
Marseille
MONACO
SAN MARINO
Tagus Plain
Tagus
MADRID
Ebro
Pisa
LISBON
Horseshoe Seamounts
SPAIN
Barcelona
Corsica
Adriatic Sea
Peninsula
Apennines
ITALY
Madeira
(part of Portugal)
Guadalquivir
Valencia
VATICAN CITY
ROME
Seville
Strait of Gibraltar
Sardinia
Palma
Balearic Islands
Algerian Basin
Naples
Bari
Málaga
GIBRALTAR
(to UK)
Ceuta
(part of Spain)
Tyrrhenian Sea
Mediterranean
Cagliari
Cosenza
Melilla
(part of Spain)
Palermo
N
Canary Islands
(part of Spain)
Sicily
Mount Etna 3340m
Catania
Atlas Mountains
AFRICA
MALTA
VALLETTA

POPULATION

- ○ Less than 50,000
- ○ 50,000 – 100,000
- ◉ 100,000 – 500,000
- ▣ Over 500,000

E
F
G
H
1
2
3
4
5
187
146
146
150
Barents Sea
North Cape
Ostrov Kolguyev
Murmansk
Kola Peninsula
White Sea
Archangel
Northern Dvina
FINLAND
Gulf of Bothnia
Ural Mountains
Ob'
Irtysh
RUSSIAN FEDERATION
Perm'
Lake Onega
Tampere
Turku
HELSINKI
Åland
Lake Ladoga
Saint Petersburg
Vologda
TALLINN
ESTONIA
Yaroslavl'
Kazan'
Ufa
Nizhniy Novgorod
LATVIA
RĪGA
LITHUANIA
MOSCOW
Ul'yanovsk
Samara
Orenburg
Ural
European Plain
Vitsyebsk
Kaunas
VILNIUS
MINSK
Central Russian Upland
Volga Uplands
Volga
Babruysk
BELARUS
Homyel'
Voronezh
Aral Sea
Syr Darya
WARSAW
Brest
Pripet Marshes
Ural
Don
Dnieper Lowlands
Kharkiv
KIEV
Volgograd
Vistula
Bug
Kraków
L'viv
Dnieper
Amu Darya
Astrakhan'
Carpathian Mountains
Dniester
UKRAINE
Dnipropetrovs'k
Donets'k
Rostov-na-Donu
Chernivtsi
MOLDOVA
CHIŞINĂU
Cluj-Napoca
ROMANIA
Odesa
Sea of Azov
Stavropol'
Caspian Sea
Braşov
Crimea
Simferopol'
Caucasus
El'brus 5642m
BELGRADE
BUCHAREST
Constanţa
Black Sea
Danube
BULGARIA
Varna
Balkan Mountains
SOFIA
Burgas
SKOPJE
MACED.
GREECE
ATHENS
Piraeus
Aegean Sea
Pindus Mountains
Peloponnese
Anatolia
ASIA
0 km
500
0 miles
500
Zāgros Mountains
Tigris
Euphrates
Cyprus
Irákleio
Crete
ELEVATION
4 000 m
13 124 ft
2 000 m
6 562 ft
1 000 m
3 281 ft
500 m
1 640 ft
250 m
820 ft
100 m
328 ft
Sea Level
-250 m
-820 ft
-500 m
-1 640 ft
-1 000 m
-3 281 ft
-2 000 m
-6 562 ft
-3 000 m
-9 843 ft
-4 000 m
-13 124 ft

THE NORTH ATLANTIC

A
B
C
D
1
2
3
4
5
Arctic Circle
69
Gulf of Boothia
Devon Island
Ellesmere Island
NORTHWEST TERRITORIES
Nares Strait
Qaanaaq
Knud Rasmussen L
Hudson Bay
Southampton Island
Innaanganeq
Savissivik
Foxe Basin
Qimusseriarsuaq
Baffin Bay
Kullorsuaq
CANADA
70
Baffin Island
Upernavik
Péninsule d'Ungava
Hudson Strait
Limit of summer pack ice
Uummannaq
QUÉBEC
Davis Strait
Qeqertarsuaq
Qeqertarsuaq
Qeqertarsuup Tunua
Arnaud
Cumberland Sound
Frobisher Bay
Qasigiannguit
GREENLAND
(Danish external territory)
Ungava Bay
Sisimiut
Kong Frederik IX Land
Maniitsoq
George
NUUK
Kong Christian IX Land
Gunnbjørn F
Mont Forel 3360m
Aputitee
71
NEWFOUNDLAND & LABRADOR
Paamiut
Ammassalik
Kong Frederik VI Kyst
Ivittuut
Labrador Sea
Denmar
Qaqortoq
Nanortalik
Uummannarsuaq
Limit of winter pack ice
Reykjanes Basin
ATLANTIC OCEAN
0 km
400
0 miles
400
98
POPULATION
Less than 50,000
50,000 – 100,000
100,000 – 500,000
Over 500,000

ARCTIC OCEAN
Lincoln Sea
Kap Morris Jesup
Wandel Sea
Independence Fjord
Nord
SVALBARD
(Norwegian dependency)
Kvitøya
Nordaustlandet
Kong Karls Land
Spitsbergen
Barentsøya
Edgeøya
LONGYEARBYEN
Barentsberg
Storfjorden
Zemlya Frantsa-Iosifa
Novaya Zemlya
Barents Sea
Kong Frederik VIII Land
Greenland Sea
Limit of winter pack ice
Limit of summer pack ice
Bjørnøya
(part of Norway)
Kong Christian X Land
Daneborg
Petermann Bjerg 2940m
Nordkapp
(North Cape)
Mohns Ridge
Kong Oscar Fjord
Ittoqqortoormiit
Kangertittivaq
Kangikajik
JAN MAYEN
(Norwegian dependency)
FINLAND
Arctic Circle
Norwegian Sea
Vestfjorden
Norwegian Basin
ICELAND
Bolungarvík
Siglufjördhur
Raufarhöfn
Húsavík
Akureyri
Stykkishólmur
Seydhisfjördhur
Neskaupstadhur
REYKJAVÍK
Selfoss
Vatnajökull
Djúpivogur
Hvannadalshnúkur 2119m
Surtsey
Vestmannaeyjar
SWEDEN
Gulf of Bothnia
FAEROE ISLANDS
(Danish external territory)
TÓRSHAVN
NORWAY
Shetland Islands
(part of UK)
187
142
116
117
E
F
G
H
1
2
3
4
5
ELEVATION
4000 m
13124 ft
2000 m
6562 ft
1000 m
3281 ft
500 m
1640 ft
250 m
820 ft
100 m
328 ft
Sea Level
-250 m
-820 ft
-500 m
-1640 ft
-1000 m
-3281 ft
-2000 m
-6562 ft
-3000 m
-9843 ft
-4000 m
-13124 ft

Scandinavia & Finland

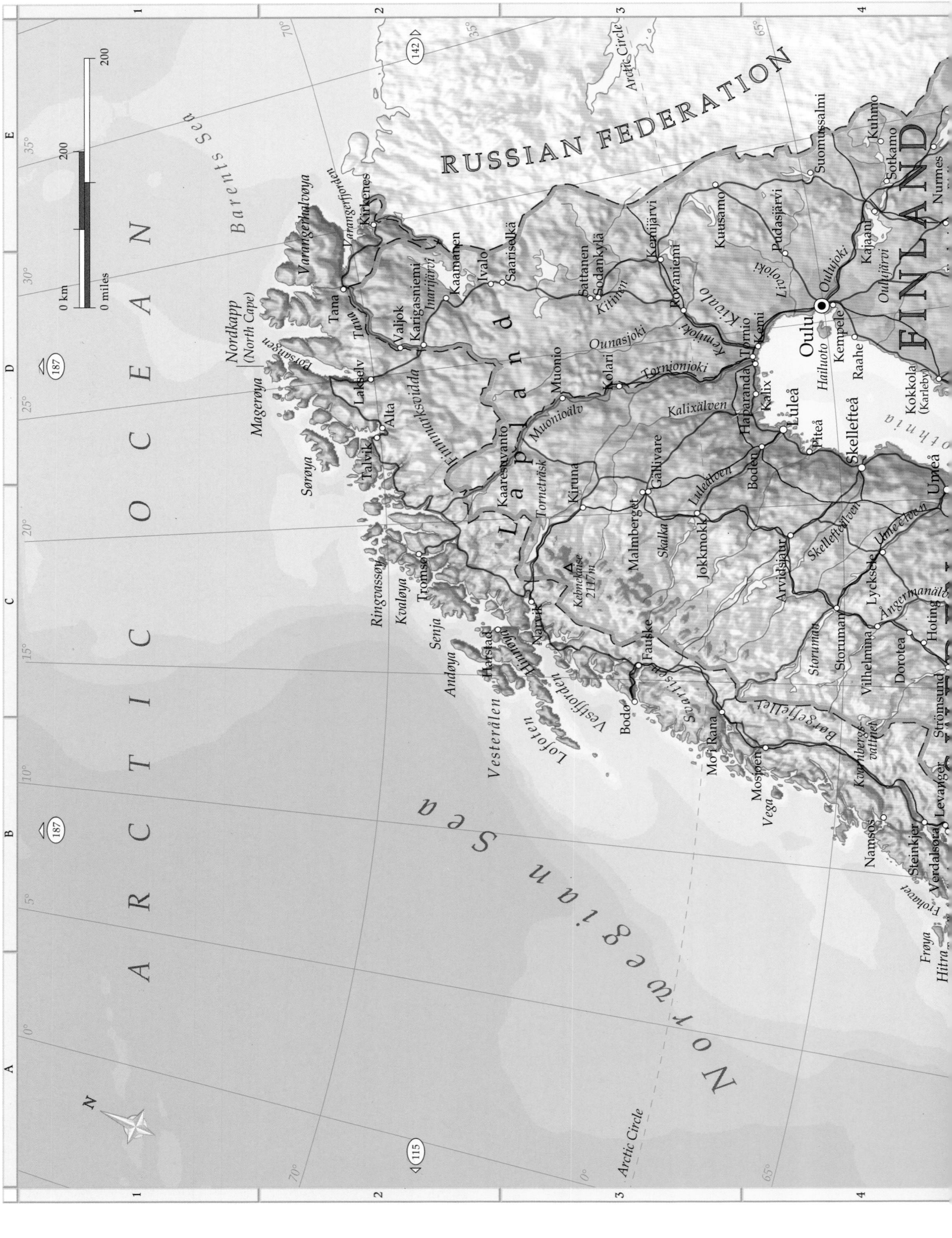
RUSSIAN FEDERATION
FINLAND
ARCTIC OCEAN
Barents Sea
Norwegian Sea
Lapland
Arctic Circle
Nordkapp (North Cape)
Magerøya
Sørøya
Varangerhalvøya
Varangerfjorden
Porsangen
Kirkenes
Tana
Valjok
Karigasniemi
Inarijärvi
Kaamanen
Ivalo
Saariselkä
Sattanen
Sodankylä
Kemijärvi
Kuusamo
Pudasjärvi
Suomussalmi
Kuhmo
Sotkamo
Nurmes
Kajaani
Oulujärvi
Oulujoki
Oulu
Hailuoto
Kempele
Raahe
Kokkola (Karleby)
Rovaniemi
Kitinen
Kemijoki
Kemi
Tornio
Haparanda
Kalix
Kalixälven
Luleå
Piteå
Skellefteå
Umeå
Ounasjoki
Tornionjoki
Kolari
Muonio
Muonioälv
Kaaresuvanto
Lakselv
Alta
Talvik
Finnmarksvidda
Torneträsk
Kiruna
Gällivare
Luleälven
Boden
Malmberget
Jokkmokk
Skalka
Arvidsjaur
Skellefteälven
Umeälven
Lycksele
Ångermanälven
Kebnekaise 2117 m
Ringvassøy
Kvaløya
Tromsø
Senja
Andøya
Harstad
Hinnøya
Narvik
Vesterålen
Vestfjorden
Lofoten
Fauske
Bodø
Saltfjellet
Svartisen
Mo i Rana
Mosjøen
Vega
Børgefjellet
Storuman
Vilhelmina
Dorotea
Hoting
Strömsund
Kultsjön
Namsos
Steinkjer
Levanger
Verdalsøra
Frohavet
Frøya
Hitra
142
187
115
E
D
C
B
A
1
2
3
4
0 km
200
0 miles
200
70°
65°
35°
30°
25°
20°
15°
10°
5°
0°
N

POPULATION

Less than 50,000
○

50,000 – 100,000
○

100,000 – 500,000
◉

Over 500,000
■

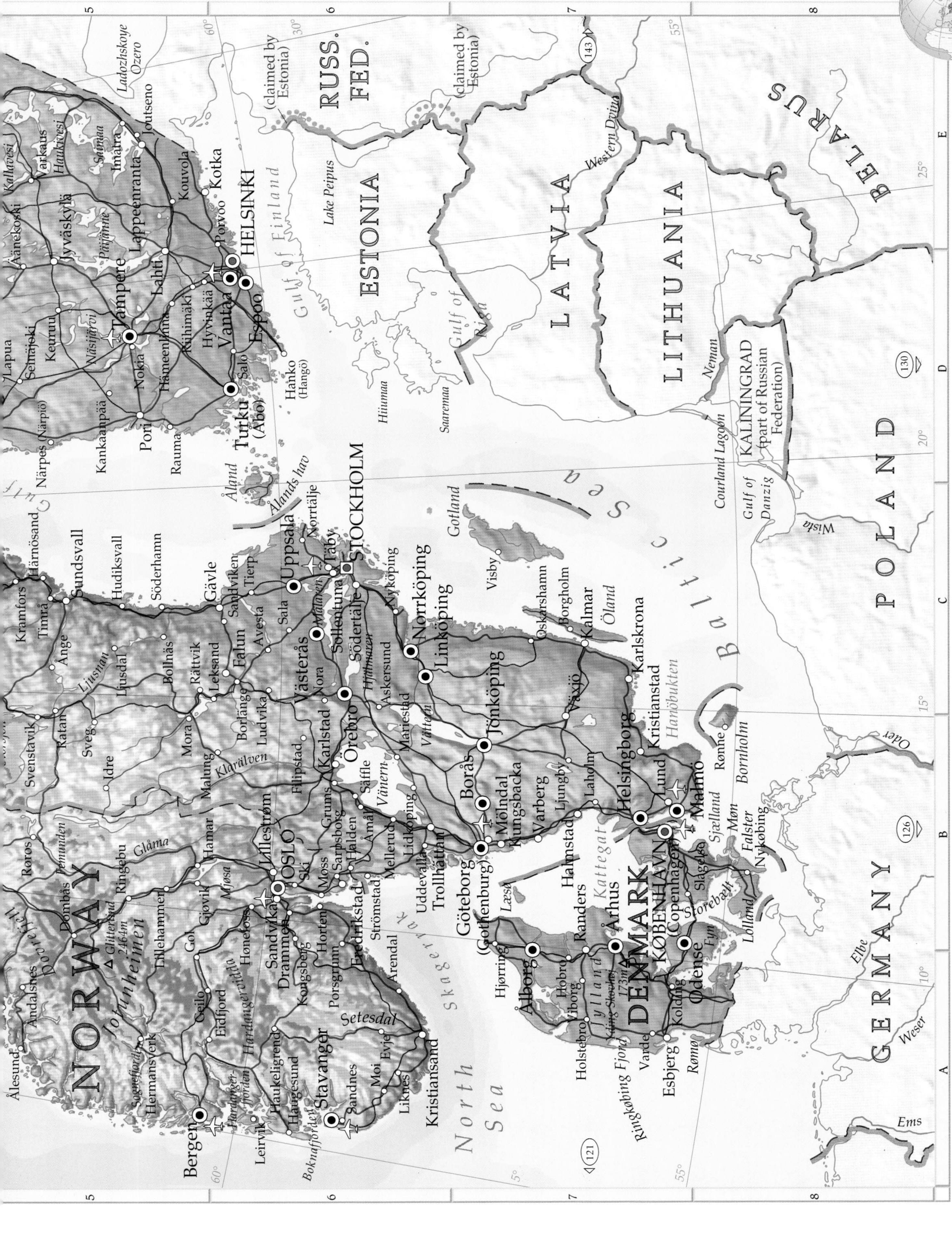
NORWAY
SWEDEN
FINLAND
DENMARK
ESTONIA
LATVIA
LITHUANIA
BELARUS
RUSS. FED.
POLAND
GERMANY
KALININGRAD (part of Russian Federation)
OSLO
STOCKHOLM
HELSINKI
KØBENHAVN (Copenhagen)
Bergen
Stavanger
Kristiansand
Göteborg (Gothenburg)
Malmö
Uppsala
Västerås
Örebro
Norrköping
Linköping
Jönköping
Turku (Åbo)
Tampere
Espoo
Vantaa
Århus
Ålborg
Odense
Baltic Sea
North Sea
Skagerrak
Kattegat
Gulf of Finland
Gulf of Riga
Gotland
Öland
Bornholm
Åland
Saaremaa
Hiiumaa
Lake Peipus
Vänern
Vättern
(claimed by Estonia)
121
126
130
143
5
6
7
8
A
B
C
D
E

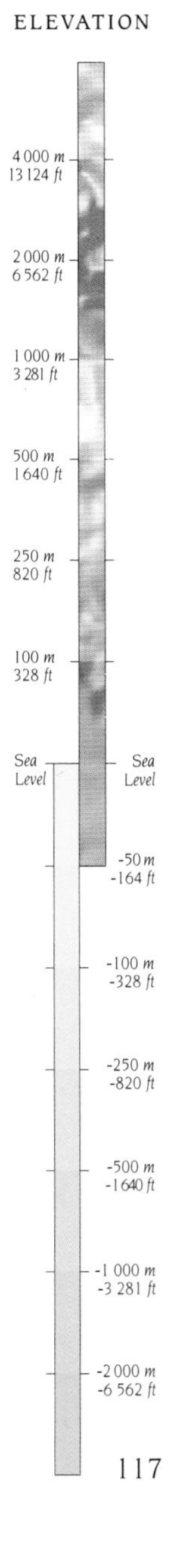
ELEVATION
4 000 m
13 124 ft
2 000 m
6 562 ft
1 000 m
3 281 ft
500 m
1 640 ft
250 m
820 ft
100 m
328 ft
Sea Level
Sea Level
-50 m
-164 ft
-100 m
-328 ft
-250 m
-820 ft
-500 m
-1 640 ft
-1 000 m
-3 281 ft
-2 000 m
-6 562 ft

THE LOW COUNTRIES

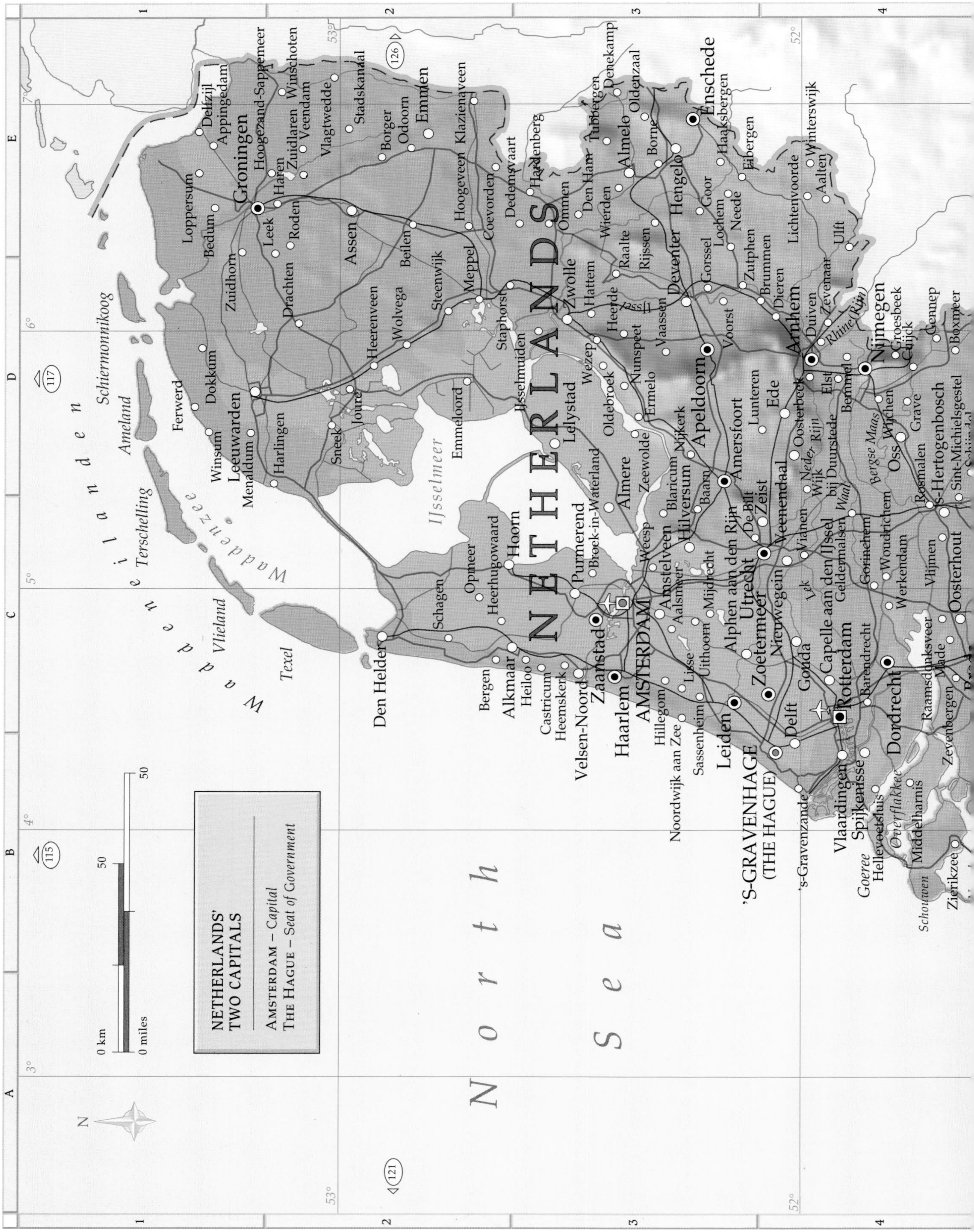

POPULATION

Less than 50,000

50,000 – 100,000

100,000 – 500,000

Over 500,000

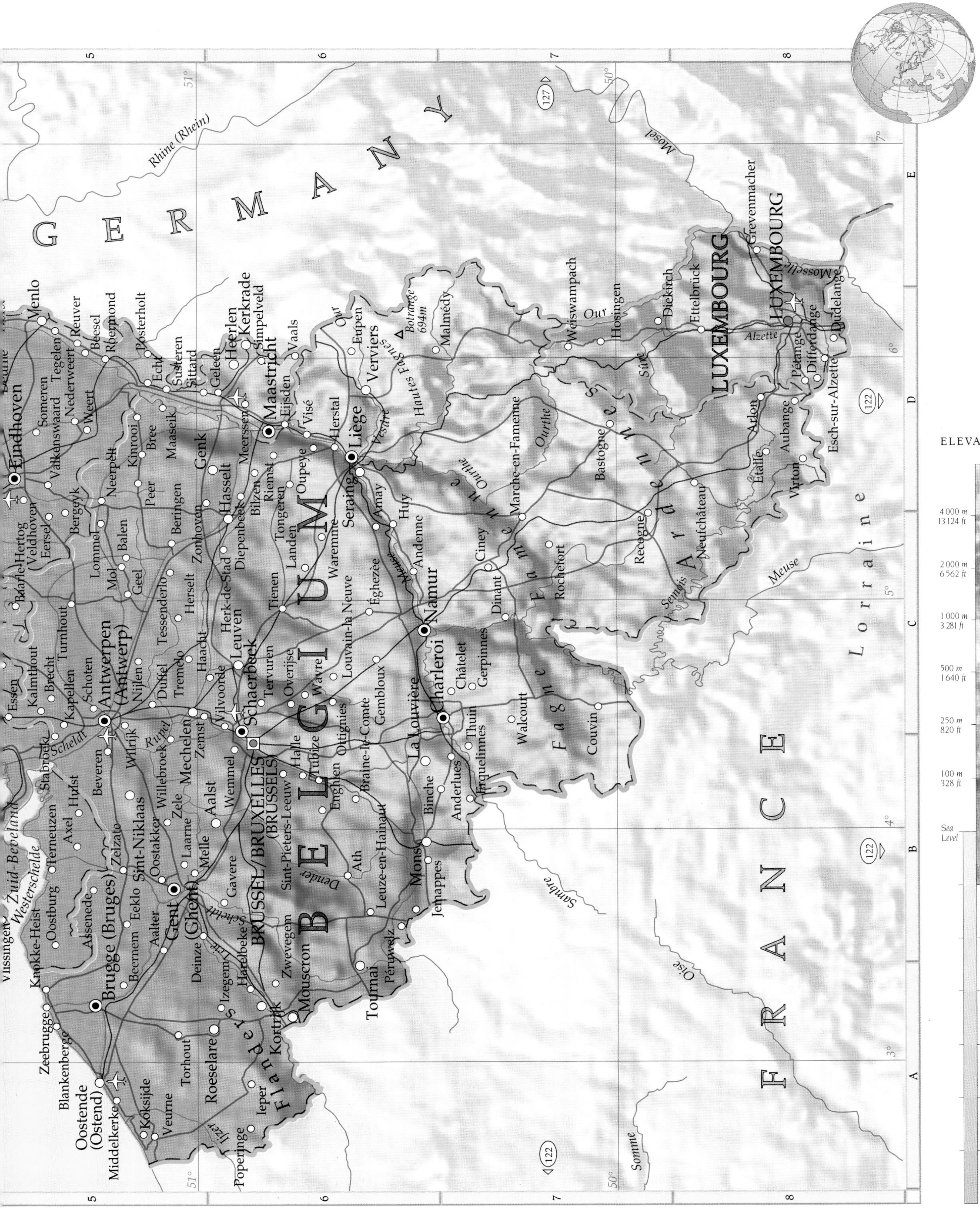
GERMANY
BELGIUM
LUXEMBOURG
FRANCE
Flanders
Ardennes
Famenne
Fagne
Lorraine
Hautes Fagnes
Botrange 694m
BRUSSEL/BRUXELLES (BRUSSELS)
LUXEMBOURG
Antwerpen (Antwerp)
Gent (Ghent)
Brugge (Bruges)
Oostende (Ostend)
Liège
Namur
Charleroi
Mons
Tournai
Kortrijk
Mouscron
Leuven
Mechelen
Hasselt
Genk
Maastricht
Eindhoven
Heerlen
Kerkrade
Verviers
Eupen
Malmédy
Bastogne
Arlon
Dinant
Rochefort
Ciney
Neufchâteau
Virton
Esch-sur-Alzette
Diekirch
Ettelbrück
Grevenmacher
Rhine (Rhein)
Meuse
Mosel
Moselle
Sambre
Scheldt
Oise
Somme
Semois
Ourthe
Sûre
Our
Alzette
Vesdre
Dender
Rupel
Lys
IJzer
Westerschelde
Zuid-Beveland

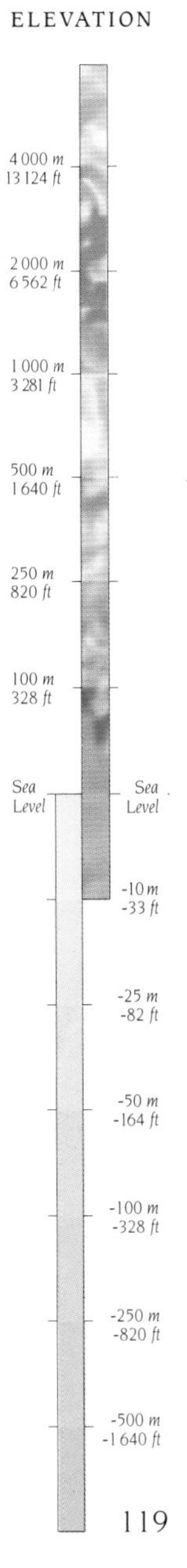
ELEVATION
4 000 m
13 124 ft
2 000 m
6 562 ft
1 000 m
3 281 ft
500 m
1 640 ft
250 m
820 ft
100 m
328 ft
Sea Level
Sea Level
-10 m
-33 ft
-25 m
-82 ft
-50 m
-164 ft
-100 m
-328 ft
-250 m
-820 ft
-500 m
-1 640 ft

THE BRITISH ISLES

North Sea
ATLANTIC OCEAN
Shetland Islands
Unst
Fetlar
Yell
Mainland
Lerwick
Fair Isle
Orkney Islands
Sanday
Kirkwall
Mainland
Hoy
John o'Groats
Thurso
Fraserburgh
Peterhead
Aberdeen
Moray Firth
Elgin
Spey
Dee
Grampian Mountains
Montrose
Arbroath
Dundee
St Andrews
Forfar
Tay
Perth
Firth of Forth
Edinburgh
Dunfermline
Forth
Stirling
Glasgow
Hamilton
Clyde
Berwick-upon-Tweed
Galashiels
Hawick
Cheviot Hills
Southern Uplands
Newcastle upon Tyne
SCOTLAND
North West Highlands
Ben Hope 927 m
Inverness
Loch Ness
Aviemore
Ben Nevis 1343 m
Fort William
Mallaig
Ullapool
The Minch
Isle of Lewis
Stornoway
Harris
North Uist
South Uist
Barra
The Little Minch
Isle of Skye
Stromeferry
Rhum
Eigg
Coll
Tiree
Isle of Mull
Oban
Firth of Lorn
Jura
Islay
Kintyre
Loch Lomond
Greenock
Paisley
East Kilbride
Kilmarnock
Prestwick
Ayr
Isle of Arran
Inner Hebrides
Outer Hebrides
St Kilda
Coleraine
NORTHERN
N
1
2
3
4
A
B
C
D
E
60°
58°
56°
2°
0°
4°
6°
8°
10°
12°
114
117
112

POPULATION

Less than 50,000

50,000 – 100,000

100,000 – 500,000

Over 500,000

UNITED KINGDOM
REPUBLIC OF IRELAND
ENGLAND
WALES
FRANCE
ISLE OF MAN
(UK crown dependency)
DOUGLAS
DUBLIN
LONDON
GUERNSEY
(UK crown dependency)
JERSEY
(UK crown dependency)
ST PETER PORT
ST HELIER
Channel Islands
Irish Sea
Celtic Sea
English Channel
St George's Channel
Bristol Channel
Cardigan Bay
Isles of Scilly
Isle of Wight
Belfast
Cork
Limerick
Galway
Waterford
Wexford
Liverpool
Manchester
Birmingham
Leeds
Bristol
Cardiff
Swansea
Plymouth
Southampton
Portsmouth
Brighton
Norwich
Ipswich
Cambridge
Oxford
Nottingham
Leicester
Coventry
Sheffield
York
Middlesbrough
Kingston upon Hull
LONDON
Watford
Enfield
Barnet
Finchley
Walthamstow
Dagenham
Edgware
Wembley
Hampstead
St Paul's Cathedral
Trafalgar Square
Buckingham Palace
Houses of Parliament
Greenwich
Dartford
Bexley
Richmond
Wandsworth
Wimbledon
Bromley
Orpington
Kingston upon Thames
Croydon
Epsom
Heathrow
Places of interest
Regions/suburbs
0 km 10
0 miles 10

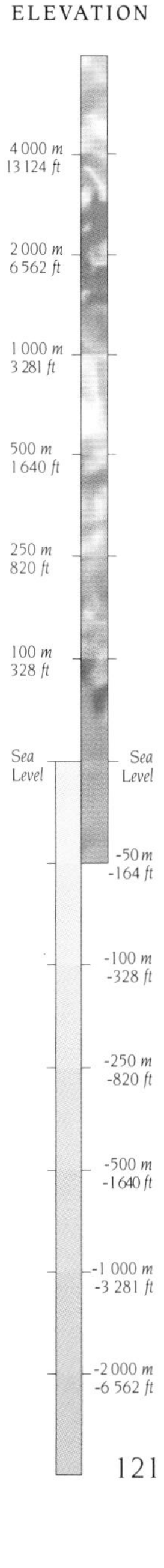
ELEVATION
4 000 m
13 124 ft
2 000 m
6 562 ft
1 000 m
3 281 ft
500 m
1 640 ft
250 m
820 ft
100 m
328 ft
Sea Level
Sea Level
-50 m
-164 ft
-100 m
-328 ft
-250 m
-820 ft
-500 m
-1 640 ft
-1 000 m
-3 281 ft
-2 000 m
-6 562 ft

FRANCE, ANDORRA & MONACO

POPULATION

- Less than 50,000
- 50,000 – 100,000
- 100,000 – 500,000
- Over 500,000

ITALY
MONACO
SPAIN
ANDORRA
Mediterranean Sea
Ligurian Sea
Golfe du Lion
Côte d'Azur
Gulf of Gascony
Corse (Corsica)
Sardinia (part of Italy)
Strait of Bonifacio
Monte Cinto 2706m
Monte Incudine 2136m
Ajaccio
Bastia
Sartène
Bonifacio
Bordeaux
Toulouse
Marseille
Lyon
Montpellier
Nîmes
Perpignan
Nice
Cannes
Antibes
Toulon
Grenoble
Clermont-Ferrand
St-Étienne
Aix-en-Provence
Avignon
Valence
Annecy
Chambéry
Mont Blanc 4807m
Pyrenees
Massif Central
Auvergne
Aquitaine
Gascogne
Languedoc
Roussillon
Provence
Dauphiné
Limousin
Landes
Médoc
Camargue
Îles d'Hyères
ANDORRA LA VELLA
Monaco
Lycée l'Annonciade
Musée Nation
Larvotto
Sporting Club d'Été
Centre de la Culture et d'Expositions
Centre de Congrès
Monte-Carlo
Casino
Port de Monaco
La Condamine
Grand Prix Circuit
Railway Station
Hospitalier Grace
Palais du Prince
Stade Louis II
Cathédrale
Ministère d'Etat
Musée Océanographique
Pontvieille
FRANCE
Côte d'Azur
Mediterranean Sea
Andorra
FRANCE
SPAIN
El Serrat
Pic de Coma Pedrosa 2942m
Arinsal
Ordino
La Massana
Canillo
Soldeu
Encamp
Escaldes
Port d'Envalira
Sant Julià de Lòria
ANDORRA LA VELLA
2000m/6562ft
1000m/3281ft
500m/1640ft

ELEVATION

4 000 m / 13 124 ft
2 000 m / 6 562 ft
1 000 m / 3 281 ft
500 m / 1 640 ft
250 m / 820 ft
100 m / 328 ft
Sea Level
-50 m / -164 ft
-100 m / -328 ft
-250 m / -820 ft
-500 m / -1 640 ft
-1 000 m / -3 281 ft
-2 000 m / -6 562 ft

Spain & Portugal

A
B
C
D
1
2
3
4
5
12°
10°
8°
6°
4°
44°
42°
40°
38°
36°
98
102
N
Bay of Biscay
Costa Verde
ATLANTIC
OCEAN
Ferrol
A Coruña
Laracha
Betanzos
Vilalba
Luarca
Avilés
Gijón
Villaviciosa
Santander
Pravia
Tineo
Oviedo
Mieres
Llanes
Torrelavega
Asturias
Pola de Lena
Cabañaquinta
Cantabria
Santa Comba
Galicia
Cabo Fisterra
Outes
Muros
Santiago
Lugo
Cordillera Cantábrica
Reinosa
Ribeira
Lalín
Chantada
Monforte
Ponferrada
León
Pontevedra
Carballiño
Marín
Vigo
Ourense
Astorga
Burgos
Ponteareas
Xinzo de Limia
Castilla-León
Miño
Minho
Benavente
Palencia
Ponte da Barca
Bragança
Embalse de Ricobayo
Lerma
Viana do Castelo
Chaves
Valladolid
Aranda de Duero
Braga
Póvoa de Varzim
Guimarães
Zamora
Vila do Conde
Toro
Duero
Matosinhos
Vila Real
Porto (Oporto)
Medina del Campo
Vila Nova de Gaia
Douro
Lamego
Embalse de Almendra
Salamanca
Ovar
São João da Madeira
Segovia
Albergaria-a-Velha
Aveiro
Viseu
S
P
Ílhavo
Ciudad-Rodrigo
Ávila
Alto da Torre 1993m
Guarda
Sistema Central
Béjar
Coimbra
Serra da Estrela
Covilhã
Sierra de Gredos
MADRID
Getafe
Figueira da Foz
Plasencia
Talavera de la Reina
PORTUGAL
Aranjuez
Coria
Leiria
Castelo Branco
Toledo
Tomar
Tagus
Embalse de Alcántara
Embalse de Valdecañas
Caldas da Rainha
Entroncamento
Cáceres
Peniche
Abrantes
Trujillo
Torres Vedras
Santarém
Portalegre
Herrera del Duque
Coruche
Extremadura
Sintra
Estremoz
Elvas
Mérida
Villanueva de la Serena
Cascais
LISBOA (LISBON)
Badajoz
Don Benito
Ciudad Real
Almada
Barreiro
Serra d'Ossa
Castuera
Puertollano
Setúbal
Évora
Almendralejo
Guadiana
Villafranca de los Barros
Alcácer do Sal
Zafra
Baía de Setúbal
Azuaga
Pozoblanco
Jeréz de los Caballeros
La Carolina
Sines
Sierra Morena
Bailén
Montoro
Linares
Beja
Cortegana
Córdoba
Bujalance
Jaén
Martos
Ourique
Nerva
Guadalquivir
Palma del Río
Alcaudete
Valverde del Camino
La Algaba
Carmona
Algarve
Sevilla (Seville)
Écija
Andalucía
Ayamonte
Lepe
Lucena
Portimão
Faro
Isla Cristina
Huelva
Dos Hermanas
Osuna
Sistema
Granada
Lagos
Tavira
Olhão
Antequera
Archidona
Cabo de São Vicente
Las Cabezas de San Juan
Olvera
Álora
Golfo de Cádiz
Lebrija
Sierra
Sanlúcar de Barrameda
Ubrique
Ronda
El Puerto de Santa María
Jeréz de la Frontera
Coín
Málaga
Cádiz
Fuengirola
San Fernando
Marbella
Vejer de la Frontera
Estepona
Costa del Sol
Costa de la Luz
Barbate de Franco
GIBRALTAR (UK dependent territory)
Algeciras
Strait of Gibraltar
Ceuta (part of Spain)
MOROCCO
AZORES (part of Portugal)
Corvo
Flores
São Jorge
Graciosa
Terceira
Faial
Pico
São Miguel
Ponta Delgada
Santa Maria
38°
30°
28°
26°
0 km 100
0 miles 100
200m/656ft
Sea level

POPULATION

- Less than 50,000
- 50,000 – 100,000
- 100,000 – 500,000
- Over 500,000

FRANCE
Golfe du Lion
ANDORRA
Pyrenees
Monte Perdido 3348m
Donostia-San Sebastián
Irún
Bermeo
Zarautz
Eibar
Bergara
Tolosa
País Vasco
Vitoria-Gasteiz
Pamplona
Miranda de Ebro
Estella
Navarra
Logroño
Arnedo
Calahorra
La Rioja
Jaca
Huesca
Tudela
Tarazona
Soria
Ejea de los Caballeros
Ebro
Zaragoza
Sistema Ibérico
Calatayud
Aragón
Medinaceli
Daroca
Alcañiz
Sierra de Guadarrama
Guadalajara
Alcalá de Henares
Torrejón de Ardoz
Teruel
Javalambre 2020m
Tagus
Cuenca
Tarancón
Castilla-La Mancha
Mota del Cuervo
Campo de Criptana
Socuéllamos
Tomelloso
La Roda
Júcar
Albacete
Manzanares
La Solana
Valdepeñas
Villanueva de los Infantes
Hellín
Segura
Beas de Segura
Moratalla
Villacarrillo
Cazorla
Cieza
Mula
Murcia
Béticos
Huéscar
Totana
Lorca
Baza
Guadix
Mulhacén 3481m
Sierra Nevada
Berja
Adra
Almería
Mojácar
Águilas
Cartagena
La Unión
Orihuela
Callosa de Segura
Elche
Alicante
San Juan de Alicante
Monóvar
Jumilla
Elda
Villena
Onteniente
Almansa
Alcoy
Villajoyosa
Benidorm
Denia
Oliva
Gandía
Xátiva
Cullera
Algemesí
Sueca
Catarroja
Torrente
Valencia
Burjassot
Sagunto
Vall d' Uxó
Burriana
Onda
Castelló de la Plana
País Valenciano
Costa del Azahar
Costa Blanca
Golfo de Valencia
Vinaròs
Sant Carles de la Ràpita
Amposta
Tortosa
Tarragona
El Vendrell
Sitges
Reus
Valls
Vilafranca del Penedès
Fraga
Lleida (Lérida)
Monzón
Barbastro
Tàrrega
Cervera
Balaguer
Terrassa
Sabadell
Barcelona
L'Hospitalet de Llobregat
Mataró
Arenys de Mar
Blanes
Palamós
Palafrugell
Costa Brava
Girona
Vic
Manlleu
Ripoll
Berga
La Seu d'Urgel
Figueres
Banyoles
Cataluña
Ciutadella de Menorca
Menorca (Minorca)
Mahón
Pollença
Sa Pobla
Palma
Llucmajor
Manacor
Felanitx
Mallorca (Majorca)
Cabrera
Eivissa (Ibiza)
Eivissa
Formentera
Islas Baleares (Balearic Islands)
Mediterranean Sea
ALGERIA
GIBRALTAR (to UK)
SPAIN
Gibraltar Airport
North Mole
Gibraltar Harbour
Catalan Bay
The Rock
Bay of Gibraltar
Sandy Bay
Summit 426m
Rosia
Rosia Bay
Buena Vista
Little Bay
Europa Point
Strait of Gibraltar
200m/656ft
Sea level
0 km 1
0 mile 1
0 km 100
0 miles 100
ELEVATION
4000 m 13124 ft
2000 m 6562 ft
1000 m 3281 ft
500 m 1640 ft
250 m 820 ft
100 m 328 ft
Sea Level
-250m -820 ft
-500 m -1640 ft
-1000 m -3281 ft
-2000 m -6562 ft
-3000 m -9843 ft
-4000 m -13124 ft
122
128
129
103

GERMANY & THE ALPINE STATES

LIECHTENSTEIN
AUSTRIA
SWITZERLAND
Ruggell
Mauren
Planken
Bendern
Schaan
VADUZ
Triesenberg
Triesen
Balzers
Rhine
Samina
Alps
2000m/6562ft
1000m/3281ft
500m/1640ft
250m/820ft
SWEDEN
DENMARK
POLAND
NETHERLANDS
GERMANY
North Sea
Baltic Sea
Jylland
Fyn
Sjælland
Falster
Bornholm
(part of Denmark)
Rügen
Pomeranian Bay
Kieler Bucht
Mecklenburger Bucht
Fehmarn
Fehmarn Belt
North Frisian Islands
(Nordfriesische Inseln)
Helgoländer Bucht
Ostfriesische Inseln
Schleswig-Holstein
Sachsen
Oderhaff
Oder
Noteć
Elbe
Weser
Ems
Rhine
Saale
Spree
Müritz
Ijsselmeer
BERLIN
Hamburg
Bremen
Hannover
Kiel
Lübeck
Rostock
Schwerin
Magdeburg
Potsdam
Leipzig
Dresden
Halle
Erfurt
Weimar
Göttingen
Kassel
Braunschweig
Wolfsburg
Salzgitter
Hildesheim
Bielefeld
Münster
Osnabrück
Oldenburg
Bremerhaven
Wilhelmshaven
Emden
Cuxhaven
Flensburg
Neumünster
Stralsund
Greifswald
Frankfurt an der Oder
Cottbus
Dortmund
Essen
Bochum
Duisburg
Düsseldorf
Wuppertal
Solingen
Köln
Krefeld
Leverkusen
Recklinghausen
Hamm
Paderborn
Dessau
Brandenburg
Neubrandenburg
Wismar
Lüneburg
Celle
Görlitz
Hoyerswerda
Bautzen

POPULATION

Less than 50,000

50,000 – 100,000

100,000 – 500,000

Over 500,000

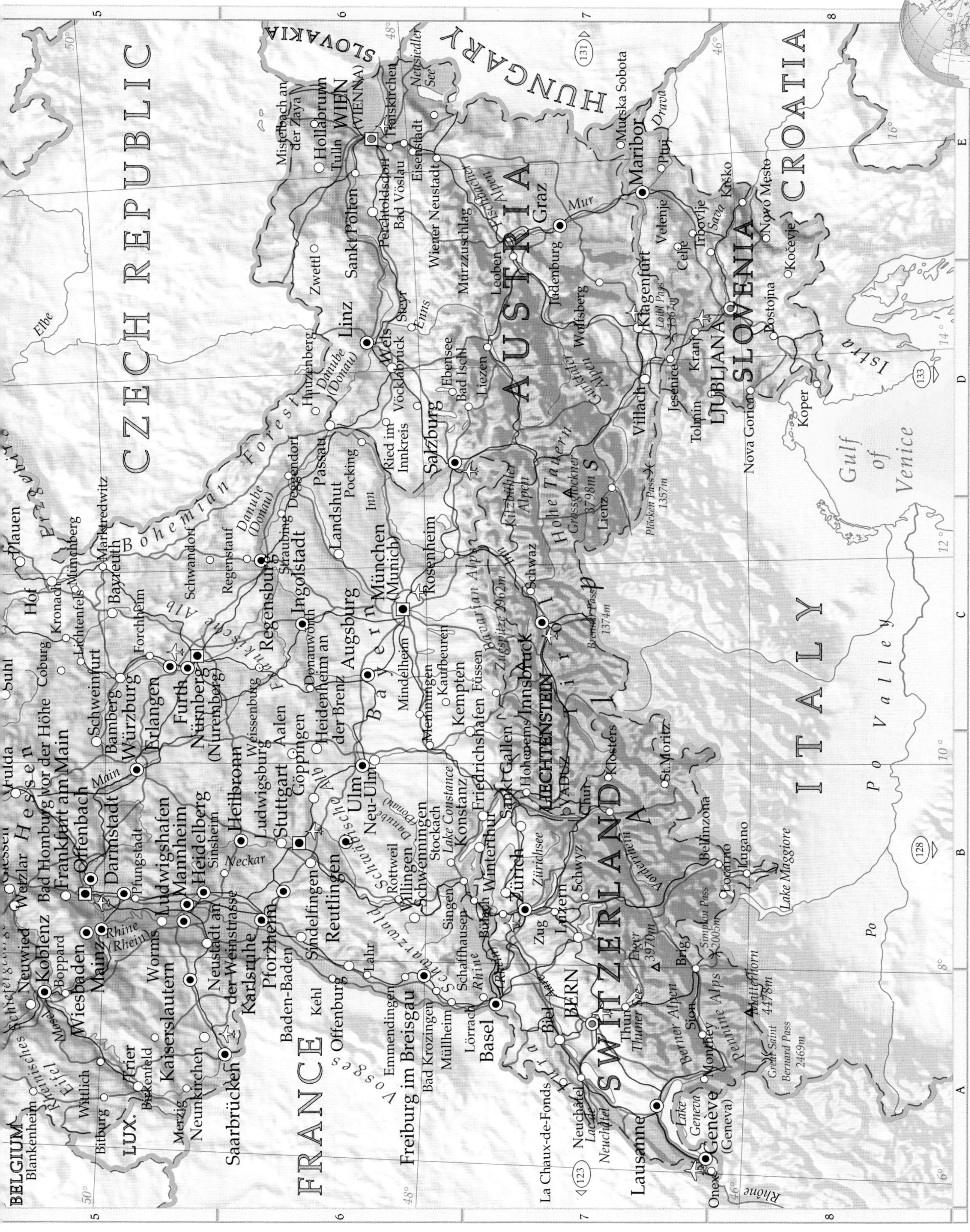
CZECH REPUBLIC
AUSTRIA
SLOVENIA
CROATIA
HUNGARY
SLOVAKIA
ITALY
SWITZERLAND
FRANCE
LIECHTENSTEIN
BELGIUM
LUX.
Gulf of Venice
Po Valley
131
133
128
123

ELEVATION

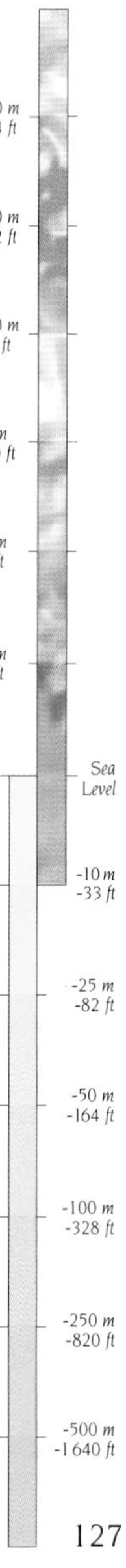
4 000 m
13 124 ft
2 000 m
6 562 ft
1 000 m
3 281 ft
500 m
1 640 ft
250 m
820 ft
100 m
328 ft
Sea Level
Sea Level
-10 m
-33 ft
-25 m
-82 ft
-50 m
-164 ft
-100 m
-328 ft
-250 m
-820 ft
-500 m
-1 640 ft

Italy

GERMANY
AUSTRIA
SWITZERLAND
LIECHTENSTEIN
FRANCE
SLOVENIA
CROATIA
HUNGARY
SLOVAKIA
BOSNIA & HERZEGOVINA
MONACO
SAN MARINO
VATICAN CITY
ROMA
Corse (Corsica) (part of France)
Ligurian Sea
Adriatic Sea
Gulf of Venice
Golfo di Genova
Lake Geneva
Lake Constance
Lake Maggiore
Lago di Como
Lago di Garda
Lago Trasimeno
Mont Blanc 4807m
Gran Paradiso 4061m
Great Saint Bernard Pass 2469m
Little St-Bernard Pass 2188m
Brenner Pass 1374m
Alpi Dolomitiche
Appennino Ligure
Arcipelago Toscano
Isola d'Elba
Strait of Bonifacio
Torino (Turin)
Milano (Milan)
Genova (Genoa)
Venezia (Venice)
Firenze (Florence)
Bologna
Verona
Padova
Trieste
Trento
Bolzano
Brescia
Bergamo
Parma
Modena
Ferrara
Ravenna
Rimini
Ancona
Perugia
Pescara
Livorno
Pisa
La Spezia
Savona
San Remo
Cuneo
Aosta
Novara
Varese
Como
Monza
Pavia
Piacenza
Cremona
Mantova
Vicenza
Treviso
Mestre
Udine
Pordenone
Rovigo
Chioggia
Forlì
Cesena
Pesaro
Fano
Siena
Arezzo
Grosseto
Viterbo
Terni
L'Aquila
Chieti
Teramo
Civitavecchia
Tivoli
Termoli
SAN MARINO
500m/1640ft
200m/656ft
100m/328ft
Monte Titano 739m
Serravalle
Dogana
Borgo Maggiore
Fiorentino
Faetano
Montegiardino
Chiesanuova
Gualdicciolo
0 km
0 miles
100

POPULATION

Less than 50,000

50,000 – 100,000

100,000 – 500,000

Over 500,000

Tyrrhenian Sea
Ionian Sea
Mediterranean Sea
Strait of Sicily
Malta Channel
Strait of Otranto
Stretto di Messina
Golfo di Taranto
Golfo di Salerno
Golfo di Gaeta
Sardegna (Sardinia)
Sicilia (Sicily)
Puglia
Campania
Appennino Lucano
La Sila
Isole Eolie
Isola Stromboli
Isola Lipari
Isola Vulcano
Isola d'Ustica
Isole Ponziane
Isola di Capri
Isole Egadi
Isola di Pantelleria
Isole Pelagie
Gozo
Malta
MALTA
VALLETTA
TUNISIA
Monte Etna 3340m
Vesuvio 1277m
Punta La Marmora 1834m
Napoli (Naples)
Torre del Greco
Salerno
Caserta
Benevento
Avellino
Foggia
Cerignola
Andria
Barletta
Molfetta
Bari
Bitonto
Altamura
Matera
Potenza
Taranto
Brindisi
Lecce
Maglie
Gallipoli
Manduria
Cirò Marina
Crotone
Catanzaro
Cosenza
Rossano
Amantea
Lamezia
Castrovillari
Lauria
Sapri
Sala Consilina
Agropoli
Battipaglia
Gaeta
Terracina
Volturno
Siderno
Reggio di Calabria
Palmi
Messina
Catania
Siracusa
Modica
Ragusa
Pozzallo
Vittoria
Gela
Caltanissetta
Simeto
Cefalù
Palermo
Alcamo
Trapani
Marsala
Castelvetrano
Agrigento
Cagliari
Quartu Sant' Elena
Carbonia
Iglesias
Villacidro
Oristano
Macomer
Nuoro
Ozieri
Siniscola
Alghero
133
137
103
VATICAN CITY
N
ROME
0 m 200
0 yds 250
Main Entrance
Pigna Courtyard
Vatican Museums
Vatican Gardens
Sistine Chapel
Raphael Stanza
Papal Apartments
Saint Peter's Basilica
St Peter's Square
Radio Vatican
Vatican Railway Station
Papal Heliport
Monte Vaticano

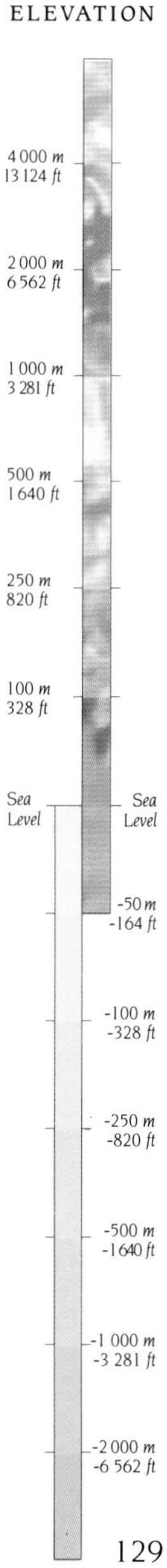

ELEVATION
4 000 m
13 124 ft
2 000 m
6 562 ft
1 000 m
3 281 ft
500 m
1 640 ft
250 m
820 ft
100 m
328 ft
Sea Level
-50 m
-164 ft
-100 m
-328 ft
-250 m
-820 ft
-500 m
-1640 ft
-1 000 m
-3 281 ft
-2 000 m
-6 562 ft

Central Europe

LATVIA
LITHUANIA
BELARUS
KALININGRAD
(part of Russian Federation)
SWEDEN
DENMARK
GERMANY
POLAND
Baltic Sea
Öland
Bornholm
(part of Denmark)
Sjælland
Gulf of Danzig
Courland Lagoon
Vistula Lagoon
Pomeranian Bay
Zalew Szczeciński
Neman
Wisła
Narew
Bug
Noteć
Warta
Oder
Elbe
Mazury
Silesia
Sudety
Śnieżka
Wyżyna Lubelska
WARSZAWA
(Warsaw)
Gdańsk
Gdynia
Sopot
Szczecin
Poznań
Łódź
Wrocław
Kraków
Białystok
Lublin
Bydgoszcz
Toruń
Olsztyn
Elbląg
Koszalin
Słupsk
Kołobrzeg
Świnoujście
Gorzów Wielkopolski
Zielona Góra
Legnica
Kalisz
Płock
Włocławek
Radom
Kielce
Częstochowa
Opole
Siedlce
Biała Podlaska
Suwałki
Łomża
Piła
Ústí nad Labem
Teplice
Děčín
Liberec
Wałbrzych
Jelenia Góra
N
0 miles
100
138
116
126
56°
54°
52°
12°
14°
16°
18°
20°
22°
24°
A
B
C
D
E
1
2
3
4

POPULATION

- Less than 50,000
- 50,000 – 100,000
- 100,000 – 500,000
- Over 500,000

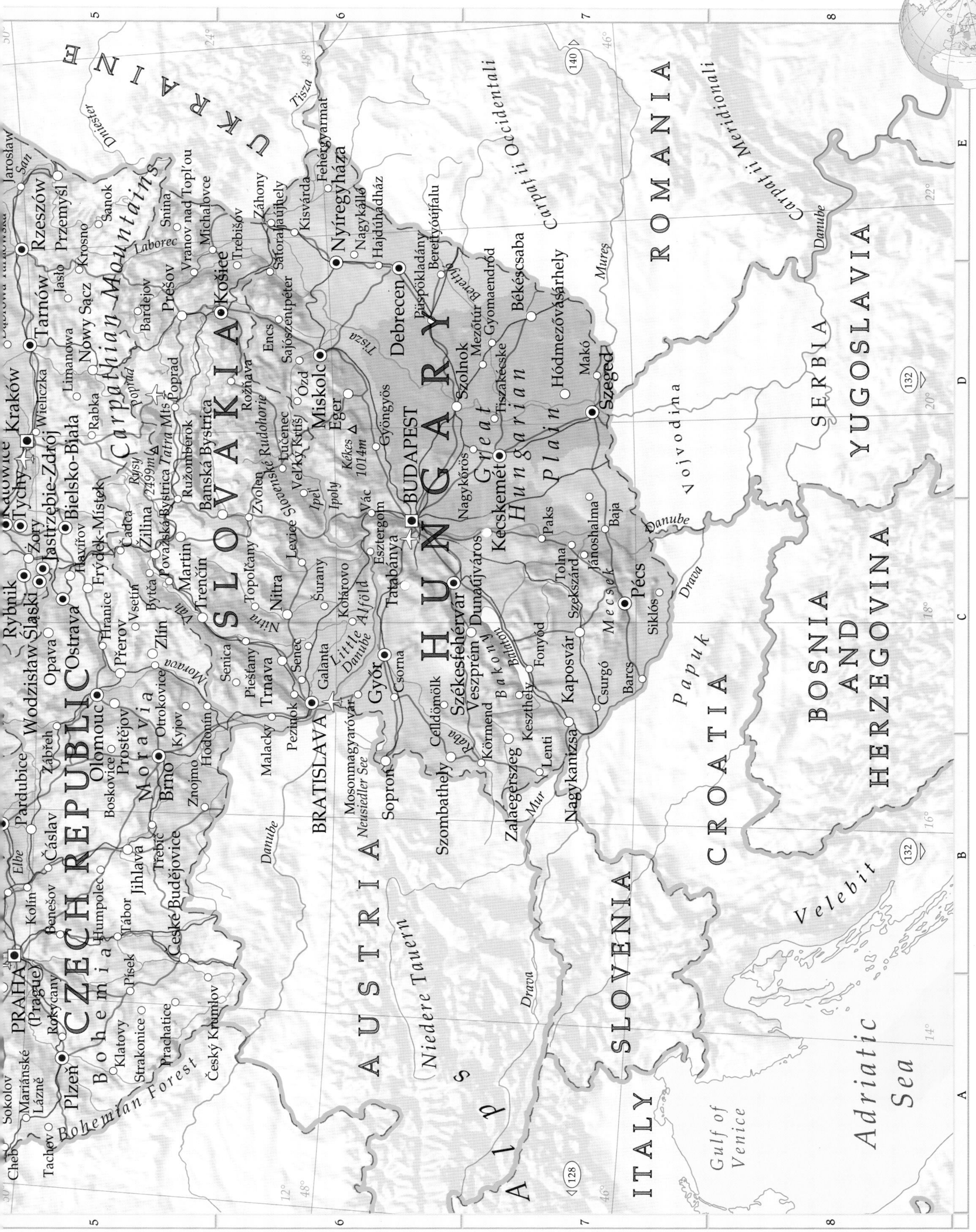

CZECH REPUBLIC
SLOVAKIA
HUNGARY
AUSTRIA
SLOVENIA
CROATIA
BOSNIA AND HERZEGOVINA
YUGOSLAVIA
SERBIA
ROMANIA
UKRAINE
ITALY
PRAHA (Prague)
BRATISLAVA
BUDAPEST
Great Hungarian Plain
Carpathian Mountains
Adriatic Sea
Gulf of Venice
Danube
Tisza

ELEVATION

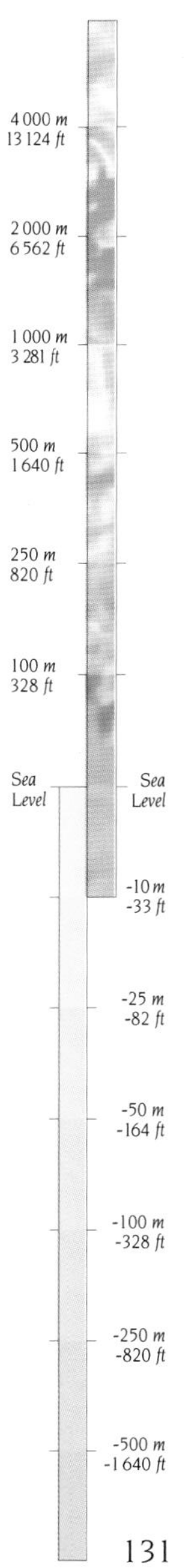

4 000 m
13 124 ft
2 000 m
6 562 ft
1 000 m
3 281 ft
500 m
1 640 ft
250 m
820 ft
100 m
328 ft
Sea Level
-10 m
-33 ft
-25 m
-82 ft
-50 m
-164 ft
-100 m
-328 ft
-250 m
-820 ft
-500 m
-1 640 ft

Western Balkans

SLOVAKIA
HUNGARY
ROMANIA
AUSTRIA
SLOVENIA
CROATIA
BOSNIA & HERZEGOVINA
SERBIA
YUGOSLAVIA
ITALY
GERMANY
UKRAINE
Vojvodina
Transylvania
Great Hungarian Plain
Little Alföld
Carpaţii Meridionali
Alps
Dinaric Alps
Dalmacija
Adriatic
Velebit
Bakony
Mecsek
Papuk
Kozara
Istra
Kvarner
Balaton
Neusiedler See
Danube (Duna)
Danube (Donau)
Danube (Dunaj)
Drava
Sava
Tisza
Mureş
Timiş
Mur
Raab
Kolpa
Una
Unac
Sana
Vrbas
Bosna
Drina
Neretva
Velika Morava
Zapadna Morava
Ibar
Ipel'
Fischbacher Alpen
Troglav 1913m
BEOGRAD (BELGRADE)
ZAGREB
SARAJEVO
Novi Sad
Subotica
Osijek
Rijeka
Split
Banja Luka
Zemun
Pančevo
Smederevo
Kragujevac
Niš
Zrenjanin
Kikinda
Senta
Sombor
Vukovar
Vinkovci
Tuzla
Zenica
Mostar
Zadar
Šibenik
Karlovac
Varaždin
Pula
Bihać
Prijedor
Čakovec
Koprivnica
Bjelovar
Virovitica
Slavonski Brod
Šabac
Valjevo
Čačak
Kraljevo
Jagodina
Bor
Zaječar
Negotin
Vršac
Bela Crkva
Požarevac
Loznica
Bijeljina
Brčko
Zvornik
Doboj
Travnik
Jajce
Livno
Makarska
Brač
Hvar
Vis
Krk
Cres
Pag
Lošinj
Dugi Otok
Gospić
Senj
Crikvenica
Ogulin
Opatija
Rovinj
Poreč
Samobor
Sesvete
Križevci
Sisak
Petrinja
Glina
Kutina
Knin
Sinj
Trogir
Konjic
Foča
Goražde
Rogatica
Višegrad
Srebrenica
Visoko
Priboj
Prijepolje
Užice
Požega
Ćuprija
Paraćin
Trstenik
127
128
131
140
14°
16°
18°
20°
22°
44°
46°
48°
A
B
C
D
E
1
2
3
4

POPULATION

- Less than 50,000 ○
- 50,000 – 100,000 ○
- 100,000 – 500,000 ◉
- Over 500,000 ▣

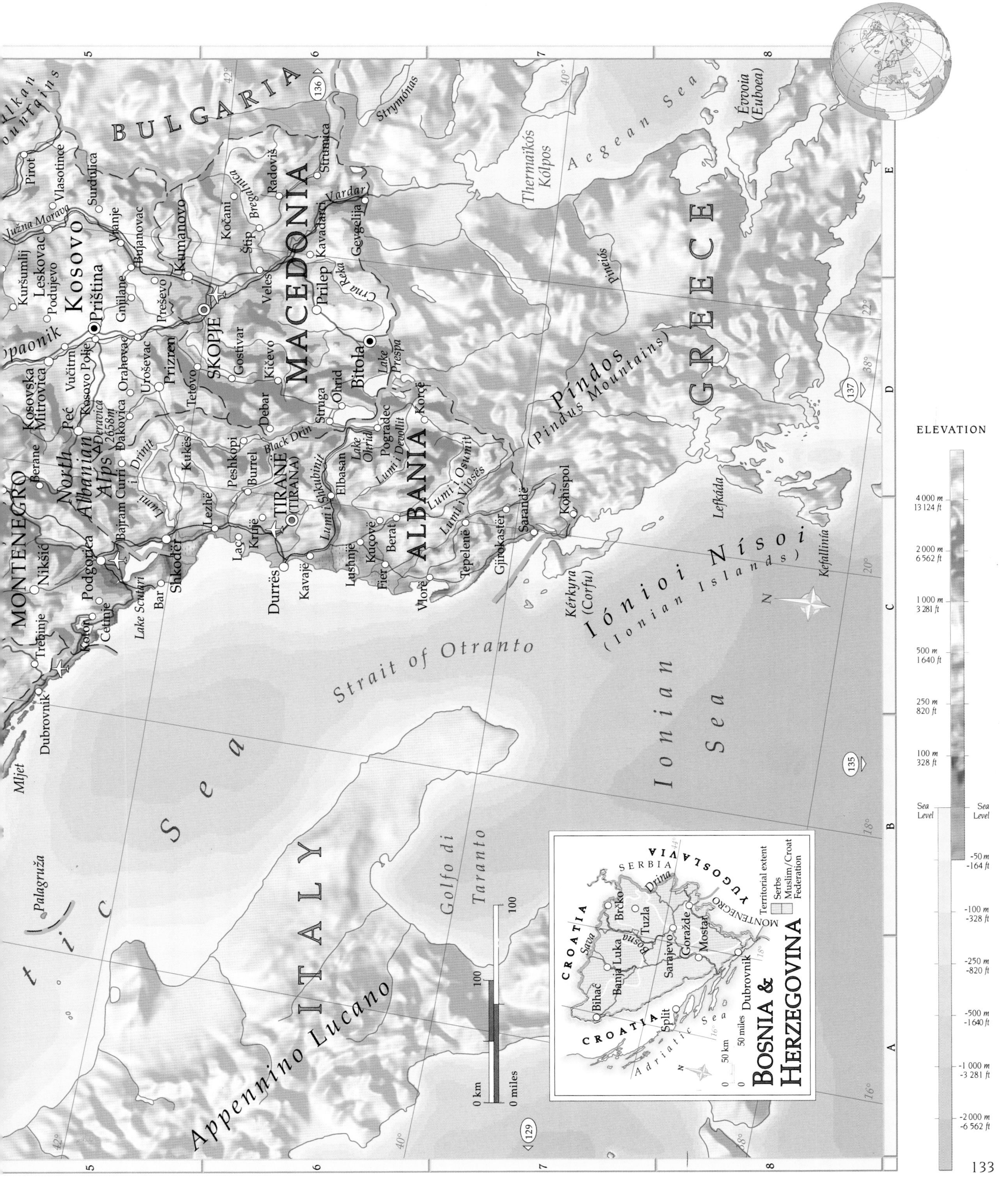
BULGARIA
MACEDONIA
ALBANIA
GREECE
ITALY
MONTENEGRO
KOSOVO
SKOPJE
TIRANË
(TIRANA)
Priština
Adriatic Sea
Ionian Sea
Aegean Sea
Strait of Otranto
Iónioi Nísoi
(Ionian Islands)
Píndos
(Pindus Mountains)
North Albanian Alps
Appennino Lucano
Golfo di Taranto
Thermaïkós Kólpos
Strymónas
Évvoia
(Euboea)
Kérkyra
(Corfu)
Lefkáda
Kefallinía
Palagruža
Mljet
Dubrovnik
Trebinje
Kotor
Cetinje
Podgorica
Nikšić
Berane
Bar
Shkodër
Lake Scutari
Lezhë
Laç
Krujë
Durrës
Kavajë
Lushnjë
Fier
Vlorë
Berat
Kuçovë
Elbasan
Peshkopi
Burrel
Kukës
Bajram Curri
Tepelenë
Gjirokastër
Sarandë
Konispol
Korçë
Pogradec
Lake Ohrid
Lake Prespa
Ohrid
Struga
Debar
Kičevo
Gostivar
Tetovo
Bitola
Prilep
Veles
Kumanovo
Štip
Kočani
Radoviš
Strumica
Kavadarci
Gevgelija
Vardar
Crna Reka
Bregalnica
Prizren
Uroševac
Orahovac
Đakovica
Đeravica 2658m
Peć
Kosovska Mitrovica
Vučitrn
Kosovo Polje
Podujevo
Gnjilane
Preševo
Bujanovac
Vranje
Surdulica
Vlasotince
Pirot
Leskovac
Kuršumlija
Južna Morava
Kopaonik
Balkan Mountains
Black Drin
Lumi i Drinit
Lumi i Shkumbinit
Lumi i Devollit
Lumi i Osumit
Lumi i Vjosës
Pineiós
ELEVATION
4000 m
13124 ft
2000 m
6562 ft
1000 m
3281 ft
500 m
1640 ft
250 m
820 ft
100 m
328 ft
Sea Level
-50 m
-164 ft
-100 m
-328 ft
-250 m
-820 ft
-500 m
-1640 ft
-1000 m
-3281 ft
-2000 m
-6562 ft
0 km
100
0 miles
100
BOSNIA & HERZEGOVINA
CROATIA
SERBIA
YUGOSLAVIA
MONTENEGRO
Adriatic Sea
Bihać
Banja Luka
Brčko
Tuzla
Sarajevo
Goražde
Mostar
Split
Dubrovnik
Sava
Bosna
Drina
Territorial extent
Serbs
Muslim/Croat Federation
0 50 km
0 50 miles
129
135
136
137

The Mediterranean

A
B
C
D
1
2
3
4
5
122
127
98
102
FRANCE
SPAIN
PORTUGAL
MOROCCO
ALGERIA
TUNISIA
GERMANY
SWITZ.
LIECH.
VADUZ
MONACO
ANDORRA
SAN MARI
VATICAN CITY
ATLANTIC OCEAN
Bay of Biscay
Quimper
St-Nazaire
Île d'Yeu
Nantes
Tours
Loire
Seine
Dijon
Zürich
BERN
München (Munich)
Innsbruc
Île de Ré
Île d'Oléron
Limoges
Clermont-Ferrand
Lyon
Lake Geneva
Mont Blanc 4807m
Alps
Milano (Milan)
Alpi Dolomitiche
Venezia (Venice)
Torino (Turin)
Po
Bologna
Dordogne
Massif Central
Bordeaux
Garonne
Rhône
Genova (Genoa)
Golfo di Genova
Nîmes
Montpellier
Marseille
Nice
Côte d'Azur
Ligurian Sea
Pisa
Toulouse
A Coruña
Santander
Bilbao
Pyrenees
Golfe du Lion
Perpignan
Corse (Corsica)
Isola d'Elba
ROMA (ROME)
Tevere
Appennini
Vigo
Cordillera Cantábrica
Sistema Ibérico
Ebro
Zaragoza
Barcelona
Costa Brava
Ajaccio
Duero
Valladolid
Porto
Tarragona
Isola Asinara
Sistema Central
MADRID
Castelló de la Plana
Mallorca (Majorca)
Menorca (Minorca)
Sardegna (Sardinia)
Sassari
Tagus
Palma
Golfo de Valencia
Valencia
Eivissa (Ibiza)
Formentera
Islas Baleares (Balearic Islands)
Tyrrhenian Sea
Cagliari
LISBOA (LISBON)
Sierra Morena
Alicante
Costa Blanca
Mediterranean
Palerm
Sicilia (Sicily)
Guadalquivir
Sevilla (Seville)
Sistemas Béticos
Murcia
Cartagena
Golfe de Tunis
Cap Bon
Cap Bougaroun
Golfo de Cádiz
Cádiz
Málaga
Almería
Costa del Sol
ALGER (ALGIERS)
Tizi Ouzou
Annaba
TUNIS
Isola di Pantell
Strait of Gibraltar
GIBRALTAR (to UK)
Ceuta (part of Spain)
Tétouan
Tangier
Oran
Mostaganem
Atlas Tellien
Sétif
Constantine
Golfe de Hammamet
Sousse
Melilla (part of Spain)
Tlemcen
Massif de l'Aurès
Chott el Hodna
Îles de Kerkenah
Sfax
Oujda
Fès
Chott ech Chergui
RABAT
Casablanca
Haut Plateaux
Chott el Jerid
Golfe de Gabès
Gabès
Chott Melghir
Île de Jerba
Moyen Atlas
Haut Atlas
Atlas Mountains
Safi
ṬARĀBULUS (TRIPOLI)
Gharyān
Sahara
MALTA
Mediterranean Sea
Nadur
Victoria
Gozo
Mġarr
Comino (Kemmuna)
Mellieħa
St Julian's
Sliema
Mosta
VALLETTA
Hamrun
Paola
Malta
Rabat
Birżebbuġa
250m/820ft
100m/328ft
Sea Level
0 km 10
0 miles 10
CYPRUS
Mediterranean Sea
Agialoúsa (Yenierenköy)
TURKISH REPUBLIC OF NORTHERN CYPRUS (recognized only by Turkey)
Lápithos (Lapta)
Kerýneia (Girne)
Mórfou (Güzelyurt)
Kólpos Ammóchostos (Gazimağusa Körfezi)
Pólis
NICOSIA
Dekéleia
Ammóchostos (Gazimağusa) (Famagusta)
Troódos
Lárnaka
Páfos
Sovereign Base Area (to UK)
Lemesós (Limassol)
Akrotírion
0 km 25
0 miles 25
1000m/3281ft
500m/1640ft
250m/820ft
Sea Level

POPULATION

- Less than 50,000
- 50,000 – 100,000
- 100,000 – 500,000
- Over 500,000

E
F
G
H
SLOVAKIA
131
140
141
WIEN
VIENNA)
AUSTRIA
Danube
BUDAPEST
Tisza
Satu Mare
Carpathian Mountains
Bâlti
UKRAINE
Kakhovs'ka
Vodoskhovyshche
HUNGARY
Great
Hungarian
Plain
MOLD.
CHIŞINĂU
Dniester
Târgu Mureş
Odesa
Dnieper
Berdyans'k
Sea of Azov
1
LJUBLJANA
ZAGREB
CROATIA
ROMANIA
Carpaţii Meridonali
Novi Sad
Galaţi
Krymsʹkyy
Pivostrov
Kerch
RUSS.
FED.
Sava
BOSNIA
& HERZ.
BEOGRAD
(BELGRADE)
BUCUREŞTI
(BUCHAREST)
Danube
Constanţa
Sevastopol'
Novorossiysk
Dalmacija
SARAJEVO
Adriatic Sea
YUGOSLAVIA
BULGARIA
Balkan Mountains
Varna
Black Sea
Priština
SOFIYA
(SOFIA)
Burgas
149
2
SKOPJE
MACED.
TIRANË
(TIRANA)
ALBANIA
Rhodope
Mountains
Edirne
İstanbul
Boğazı
(Bosporus)
Küre Dağları
Zonguldak
Samsun
Ordu
Bari
İstanbul
Vesuvio 1277m
Napoli
(Naples)
Lecce
Strait of Otranto
Thessaloniki
(Salonica)
Marmara
Denizi
Kızıl Irmak
Bursa
Golfo di
Taranto
Pindos
(Pindus)
Mts
ANKARA
Límnos
Balıkesir
TURKEY
Cosenza
Kérkyra
(Corfu)
Lárisa
Aegean
Sea
Catanzaro
Ionian
Sea
GREECE
İzmir
Kayseri
Tuz
Gölü
Kefallinía
Chíos
Monte Etna
3340m
ATHÍNA
(ATHENS)
Sámos
Catania
Zákynthos
Dodekánisos
(Dodecanese)
3
Siracusa
Mirtóo
Pelagos
Kykládes
(Cyclades)
Toros Dağları
Antalya
Adana
Gaziantep
Euphrates
Antalya
Körfezi
VALLETTA
MALTA
Kýthira
Kritikó Pélagos
(Sea of Crete)
Ródos
(Rhodes)
Kárpathos
İskenderun Körfezi
Ḩalab
(Aleppo)
Irákleio
NICOSIA
Kríti
(Crete)
CYPRUS
Lárnaka
SYRIA
Lemesós
(Limassol)
LEBANON
Mediterranean Sea
BEYROUTH
(BEIRUT)
DIMASHQ
(DAMASCUS)
Darnah
Hefa
4
Mişrātah
Banghāzī
(Benghazi)
ISRAEL
Tel Aviv-Yafo
'AMMĀN
Khalīj Surt
(Gulf of Sirte)
Ţubruq
JERUSALEM
Gaza
151
Libyan
Plateau
Alexandria
Nile
Delta
Port Said
Dead Sea
Surt
Ajdābiyā
Suez
Canal
JORDAN
Great Sand Sea
Monkhafad al Qattâra
(Qattara Depression)
CAIRO
Suez
El Gîza
Elat
Al 'Aqabah
Waddān
Sinai
Nile
Sahara el Sharqîya
(Eastern Desert)
Gulf of Suez
SAUDI
ARABIA
LIBYA
5
Libyan
Desert
EGYPT
0 km
400
0 miles
400
Red
Sea
103
104
ELEVATION
4 000 m
13 124 ft
2 000 m
6 562 ft
1 000 m
3 281 ft
500 m
1 640 ft
250 m
820 ft
100 m
328 ft
Sea
Level
Sea
Level
-250m
-820 ft
-500 m
-1 640 ft
-1 000 m
-3 281 ft
-2 000 m
-6 562 ft
-3 000 m
-9 843 ft
-4 000 m
-13 124 ft

BULGARIA & GREECE

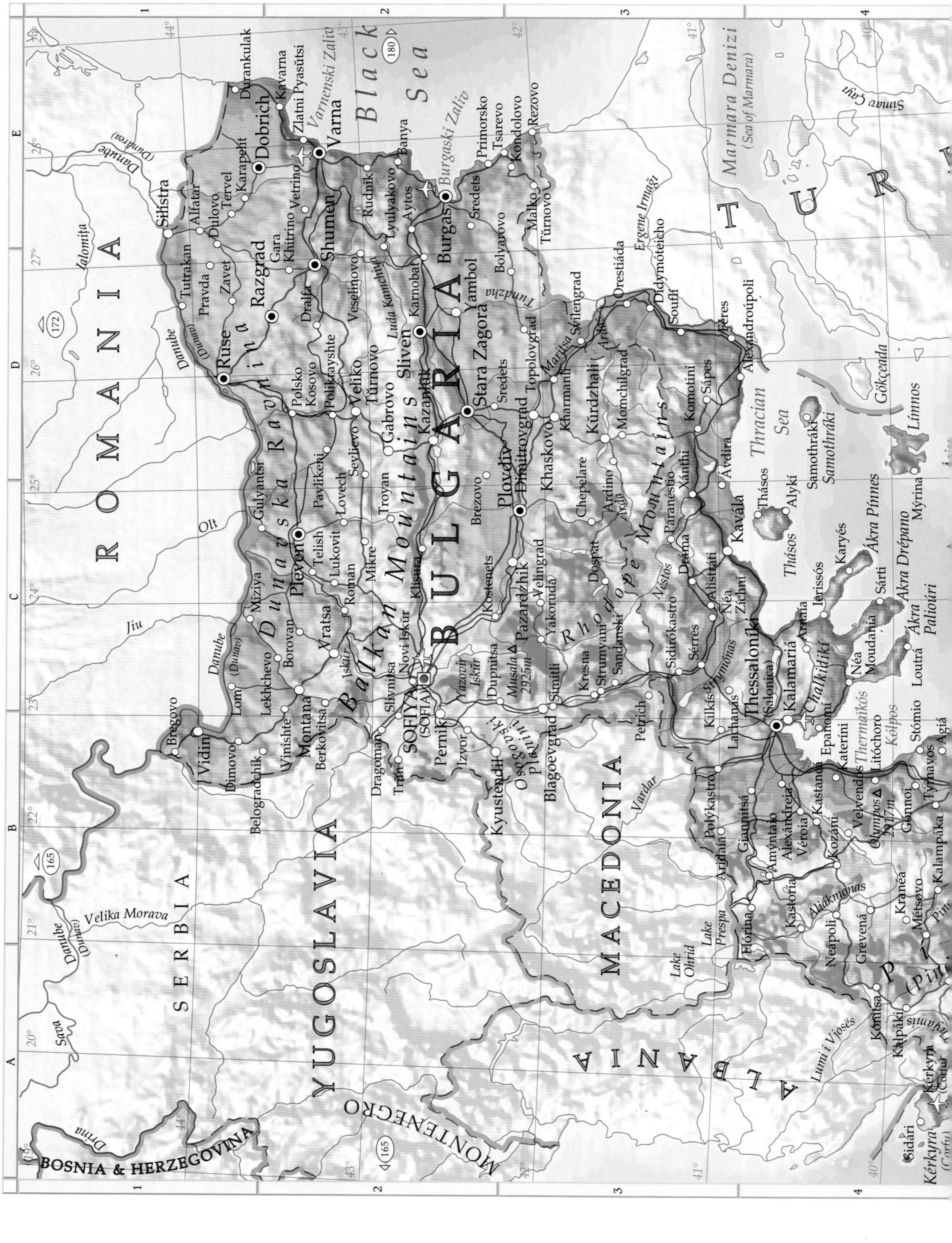

POPULATION

Less than 50,000

50,000 – 100,000

100,000 – 500,000

Over 500,000

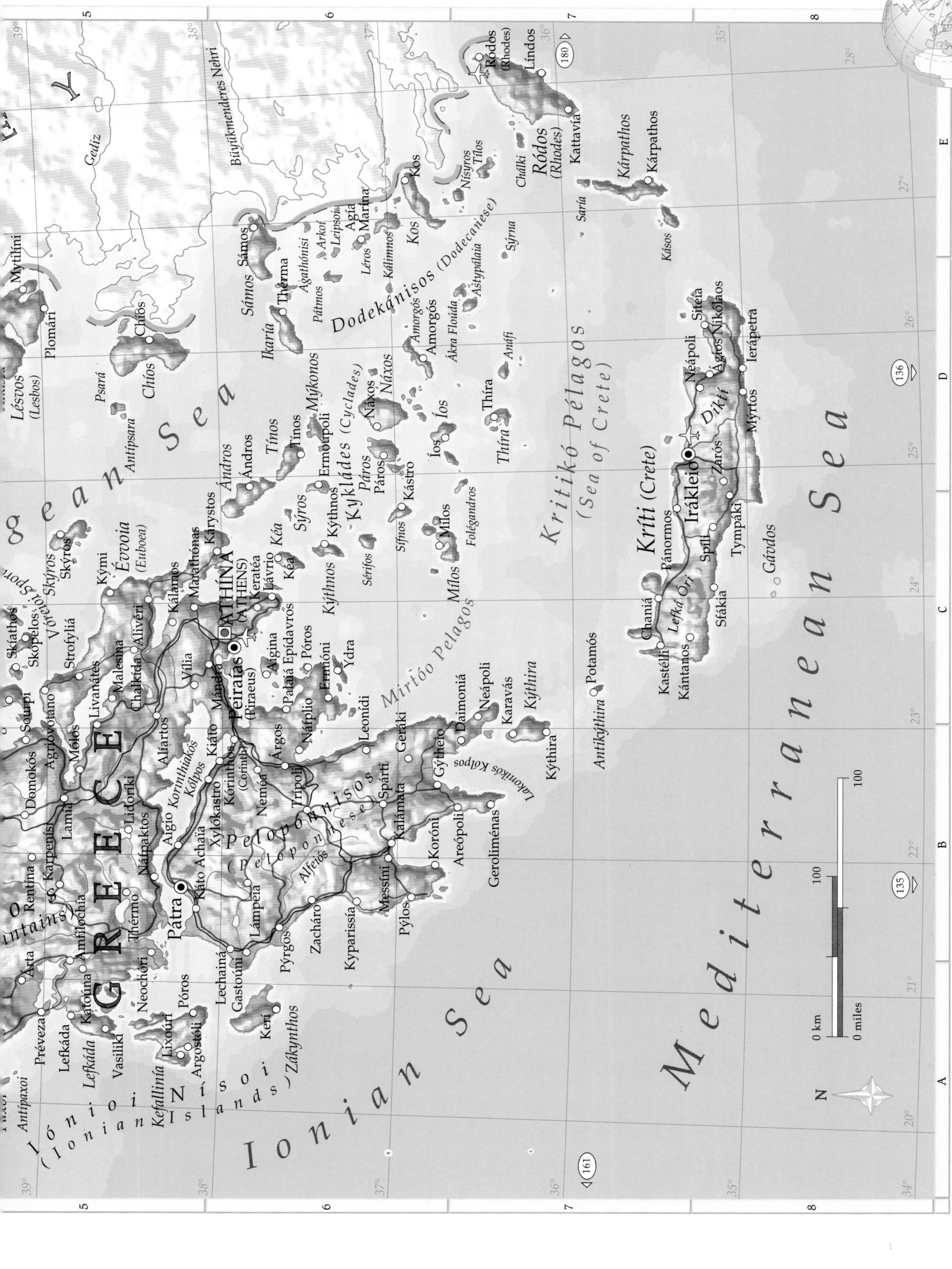
GREECE
Aegean Sea
Ionian Sea
Mediterranean Sea
Kritikó Pélagos
(Sea of Crete)
Mirtóo Pelagos
Lakonikos Kólpos
Korinthiakós Kólpos
Ióonioi Nísoi
(Ionian Islands)
Pelopónnisos
(Peloponnese)
Kykládes (Cyclades)
Dodekánisos (Dodecanese)
Kríti (Crete)
ATHÍNA
(ATHENS)
Peiraias
(Piraeus)
Pátra
Irákleio
Kórinthos
(Corinth)
Lamía
Chalkída
Tripoli
Spárti
Kalámata
Pýrgos
Argostóli
Lefkáda
Préveza
Árta
Chaniá
Réthymno
Ágios Nikólaos
Ierápetra
Siteía
Ródos
(Rhodes)
Líndos
Kárpathos
Kásos
Kos
Sámos
Ikaría
Chíos
Lésvos
(Lesbos)
Mytilíni
Plomári
Psará
Antípsara
Évvoia
(Euboea)
Skýros
Skíathos
Skópelos
Ándros
Tínos
Mýkonos
Sýros
Ermoúpoli
Náxos
Páros
Mílos
Thíra
Íos
Amorgós
Astypálaia
Kýthira
Kýthnos
Kéa
Sérifos
Sífnos
Folégandros
Anáfi
Kefallinía
Zákynthos
Lefkáda
Antipaxoi
Gávdos
Antikýthira
Kálymnos
Léros
Pátmos
Nísyros
Tílos
Chálki
Sýrna
Saría
Gediz
Büyükmenderes Nehri
Alfeiós
Lefká Óri
Díkti
Ýdra
Aígina
Póros
Náfplio
Árgos
Monemvasía
Gýtheio
Kyparissía
Pýlos
Messíni
Koróni
Areópoli
Gerolimenas
Neápoli
Nemea
Kiáto
Aígio
Náfpaktos
Thérmo
Karpenísi
Domokós
Kárystos
Marathónas
Lávrio
Keratéa
Kými
Alivéri
Thíva
Livadeiá
180
136
135
161
0 km
100
0 miles
100
N
A
B
C
D
E
5
6
7
8
20°
21°
22°
23°
24°
25°
26°
27°
28°
34°
35°
36°
37°
38°
39°

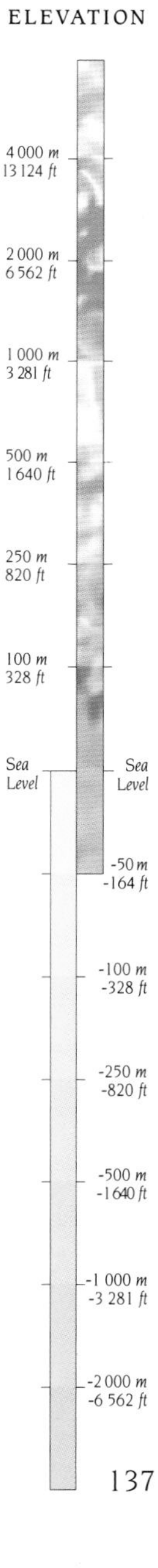
ELEVATION
4000 m
13 124 ft
2000 m
6562 ft
1000 m
3281 ft
500 m
1640 ft
250 m
820 ft
100 m
328 ft
Sea Level
Sea Level
-50 m
-164 ft
-100 m
-328 ft
-250 m
-820 ft
-500 m
-1640 ft
-1000 m
-3281 ft
-2000 m
-6562 ft

The Baltic States & Belarus

SWEDEN
FINLAND
ESTONIA
LATVIA
LITHUANIA
RUSSIAN FEDERATION
KALININGRAD (part of Russian Federation)
Gulf of Finland
Gulf of Riga
Baltic Sea
Narva Bay
Lake Peipus
Lake Pskov
Narva Reservoir (claimed by Estonia)
(claimed by Estonia)
Ålands Hav
Skiftet
Gotland
Gotska Sandön
Öland
Saaremaa
Hiiumaa
Vormsi
Kihnu
Ruhnu
Väinameri
Suur Väin
Pärnu Laht
Kolkasrags
Courland Lagoon
Kurzeme
Žemaičių Aukštumas
Suur Munamägi 318m
Gaiziņa Kalns 311m
Western Dvina
Neman
Venta
Gauja
Velikaya
TALLINN
RIGA
Tartu
Narva
Pärnu
Kohtla-Järve
Sillamäe
Daugavpils
Liepāja
Ventspils
Jelgava
Jūrmala
Klaipėda
Šiauliai
Panevėžys
Kaliningrad
Sovetsk
Chernyakhovsk
Gusev
Baltiysk
Zelenogradsk
Primorsk
Mamonovo
Bagrationovsk
Zheleznodorozhnyy
Gvardeysk
Neman
Valmiera
Cēsis
Valga
Valka
Viljandi
Võru
Haapsalu
Kuressaare
Kärdla
Rēzekne
Jēkabpils
Tukums
Talsi
Kuldīga
Saldus
Bauska
Ogre
Sigulda
Rakvere
Paide
Rapla
Kunda
Loksa
Maardu
Keila
Paldiski
Tapa
Põlva
Otepää
Alūksne
Gulbene
Madona
Balvi
Ludza
Krāslava
Preiļi
Līvāni
Aizkraukle
Dobele
Mažeikiai
Telšiai
Plungė
Kretinga
Palanga
Tauragė
Jurbarkas
Raseiniai
Kelmė
Radviliškis
Joniškis
Pasvalys
Biržai
Rokiškis
Zarasai
Utena
Anykščiai
Kėdainiai
Jonava
Kaunas
Šilutė
Šilalė
Skuodas
117
142
0 km 100
0 miles 100

POPULATION

- ○ Less than 50,000
- ○ 50,000 – 100,000
- ◉ 100,000 – 500,000
- ▣ Over 500,000

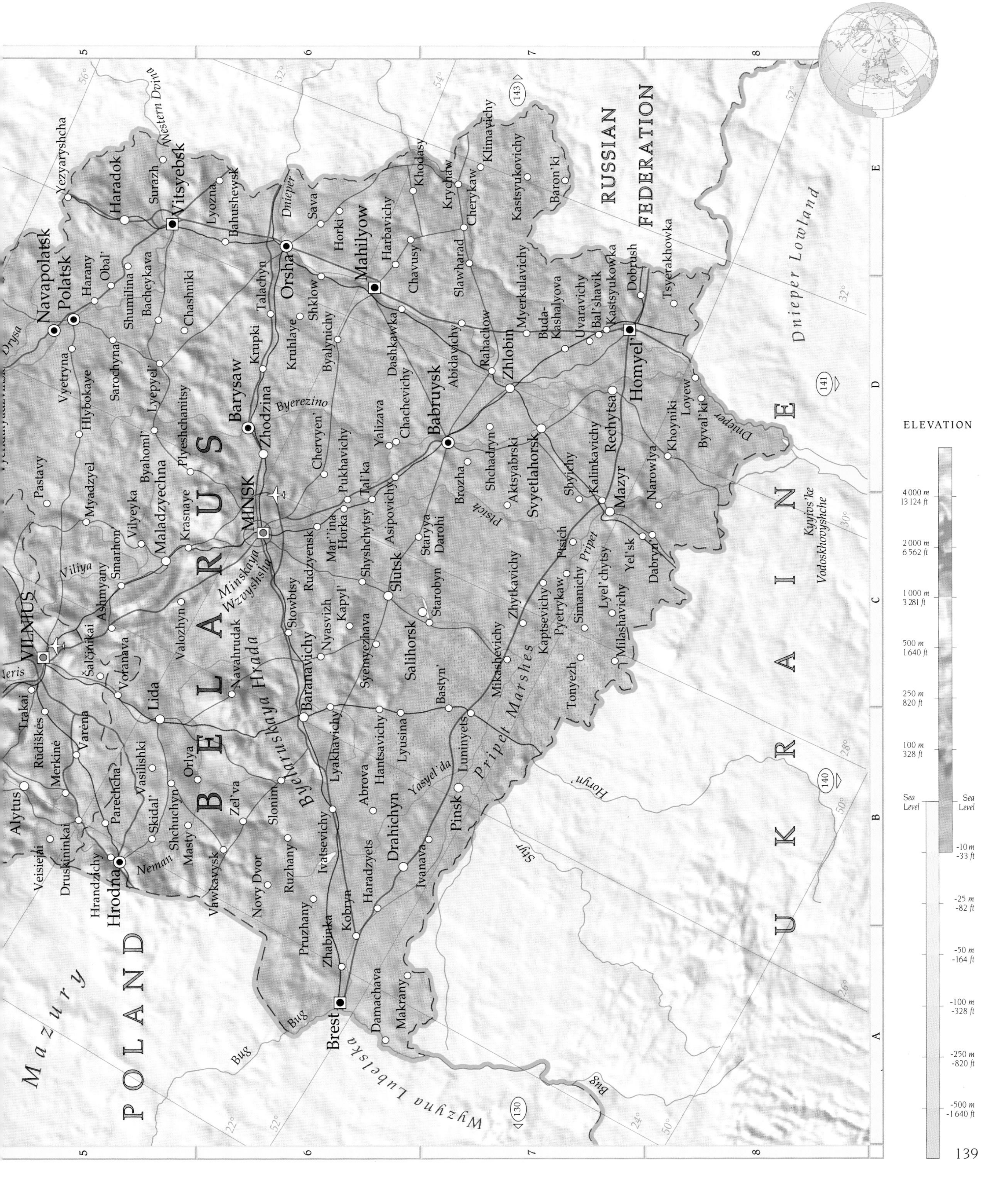
BELARUS
RUSSIAN FEDERATION
UKRAINE
POLAND
MINSK
VILNIUS
Navapolatsk
Polatsk
Haradok
Vitsyebsk
Orsha
Mahilyow
Barysaw
Zhodzina
Babruysk
Zhlobin
Homyel'
Rechytsa
Svyetlahorsk
Mazyr
Slutsk
Salihorsk
Baranavichy
Lida
Hrodna
Brest
Pinsk
Drahichyn
Maladzyechna
Western Dvina
Dnieper
Byerezino
Neman
Neris
Viliya
Pripet
Pripet Marshes
Ptsich
Horyn'
Styr
Bug
Yasyel'da
Drysa
Minskaya Wzvyshsha
Byelaruskaya Hrada
Navahrudak
Dnieper Lowland
Kyyivs'ke Vodoskhovyshche
Wyzyna Lubelska
Mazury
Alytus
Druskininkai
Veisiejai
Trakai
Kobryn
Pruzhany
Zhabinka
Ivanava
Luninyets
Khoyniki
Dobrush
Krychaw
Klimavichy
Horki
Shklow
Asipovichy
Vawkavysk
Slonim
Shchuchyn
Smarhon'
Ashmyany
Pastavy
Hlybokaye
Vilyeyka
Krupki
Chervyen'
Byerazino
143
141
140
130
ELEVATION
4 000 m
13 124 ft
2 000 m
6 562 ft
1 000 m
3 281 ft
500 m
1 640 ft
250 m
820 ft
100 m
328 ft
Sea Level
-10 m
-33 ft
-25 m
-82 ft
-50 m
-164 ft
-100 m
-328 ft
-250 m
-820 ft
-500 m
-1 640 ft

UKRAINE, MOLDOVA, & ROMANIA

A
B
C
D
1
2
3
4
5
130
131
132
136
POLAND
Małopolska
Wisła
Wyżyna Lubelska
BELARUS
Pripet
Pripet Marshes
Styr
Bug
Sluch
Kovel'
Sarny
Olevs'k
Volodymyr-Volyns'kyy
Novovolyns'k
Kivertsi
Luts'k
Rivne
Korosten
Sokal'
Chervonohrad
Dubno
Novohrad-Volyns'kyy
Malyn
Radomyshl
Slavuta
Zhovkva
Kremenets'
Shepetivka
Yavoriv
Izyaslav
Polonne
Zhytomyr
L'viv
Horodok
Zolochiv
Berdychi
Sambir
Zbarazh
Starokostyantyniv
Drohobych
Khodoriv
Ternopil'
Khmel'nyts'kyy
Boryslav
Berezhany
Stryy
Zhydachiv
UKR
Vinnytsya
Kalush
Chortkiv
Lypovets
Dolyna
Ivano-Frankivs'k
Zhmerynka
Nadvirna
Kam''yanets'-Podil's'kyy
Podil's'ka Vysochyna
Haysyn
Kolomyya
Tul'chy
Chernivtsi
Mohyliv-Podil's'kyy
Dniester
Carpathian Mountains
Tatra Mountains
SLOVAKIA
Slovenské Rudohorie
Uzhhorod
Mukacheve
Berehove
Vynohradiv
Khust
Hora Hoverla 2061m
Negrești-Oaș
Satu Mare
Darabani
Soroca
Tisza
HUNGARY
Carei
Baia Mare
Baia Sprie
Borșa
Rădăuți
Dorohoi
Bălți
Rîbnița
Marghita
Someș
Solca
Siret
Botoșani
Suceava
MOLDOVA
Oradea
Zalău
Năsăud
Fălticeni
Aleșd
Dej
Bistrița
Târgu-Neamț
Pașcani
Călărași
Orhei
Great Hungarian Plain
Salonta
Beiuș
Cluj-Napoca
Toplița
Ungheni
Strășeni
Reghin
Bicaz
Roman
Iași
Curtici
Ineu
Transylvania
Piatra-Neamț
CHIȘINĂU
Arad
Turda
Luduș
Gheorgheni
Târgu Mureș
Hîncești
Tighina
Sânnicolau Mare
Mureș
Bacău
Vaslui
Tiraspol
Lipova
Abrud
Aiud
Cristuru Secuiesc
Miercurea-Ciuc
Jimbolia
Alba Iulia
Mediaș
Târgu Ocna
Comrat
Basarabeasca
Deva
Timișoara
ROMANIA
Rupea
Bârlad
Timiș
Lugoj
Hunedoara
Sibiu
Făgăraș
Târgu Secuiesc
Adjud
Prut
Oțelu Roșu
Hațeg
Codlea
Sfântu Gheorghe
Ciadîr-Lunga
Cisnădie
Taraclia
Bocșa
Câmpulung
Vârful Moldoveanu 2544m
Brașov
Cahul
Artsyz
Carpații Meridionali
Râșnov
Tecuci
Petroșani
Focșani
Bolhrad
Reșița
Oravița
Anina
Călimănești
Râmnicu Sărat
Galați
Ozero Yalpuh
Reni
Kiliya
Târgu Jiu
Curtea de Argeș
Sinaia
Danube
Moldova Nouă
Brăila
Izmayil
Orșova
Râmnicu Vâlcea
Câmpina
Măcin
Isaccea
Tulcea
Motru
Pitești
Moreni
Buzău
Drobeta-Turnu Severin
Strehaia
Mizil
Târgoviște
Ploiești
Drăgășani
Babadag
Filiași
Titu
Urziceni
Wallachia
Țăndărei
Hârșova
Lacul Razim
YUGOSLAVIA
Craiova
Slatina
Buftea
Ialomița
Lacul Sinoie
Balș
BUCUREȘTI (BUCHAREST)
Slobozia
Băilești
Caracal
Fetești
Calafat
Medgidia
Jiu
Roșiori de Vede
Alexandria
Oltenița
Călărași
Corabia
Olt
Constanța
Danube (Dunărea)
Turnu Măgurele
Techirghiol
Velika Morava
Giurgiu
Zimnicea
Eforie Sud
SERBIA
Dunavska Ravnina
Mangalia
BULGARIA
18°
20°
22°
24°
26°
28°
44°
46°
48°
50°
52°

POPULATION

Less than 50,000

50,000 – 100,000

100,000 – 500,000

Over 500,000

E
F
G
H
1
2
3
4
5
30°
32°
34°
36°
38°
40°
52°
50°
48°
46°
44°
139
143
148
RUSSIAN FEDERATION
Srednerusskaya Vozvyshennost'
Dnieper (Dnyapro)
Desna
Horodnya
Shchors
Shostka
Hlukhiv
Chernihiv
Krolevets'
Konotop
Bakhmach
Oster
Nizhyn
Nosivka
Romny
Sumy
Brovary
Pryluky
Psel
Lebedyn
Okhtyrka
Yahotyn
Pyryatyn
Vasyl'kiv
Kanivs'ke Vodoskhovyshche
Hrebinka
Lubny
Myrhorod
Zolochiv
Derhachi
Lyubotyn
Kharkiv
Don
Oskil
Kup''yans'k
Bila Tserkva
Kaniv
Bohuslav
Zolotonosha
Dnieper Lowland
Merefa
Poltava
Sivers'kyy Donets
Izyum
Starobil's'k
Horodyshche
Cherkasy
Hlobyne
Kremenchuts'ke Vodoskhovyshche
Smila
Shpola
Chyhyryn
Kremenchuk
Kreminna
Rubizhne
Syeverodonets'k
Tal'ne
Oleksandrivka
Svitlovods'k
Dniprodzerzhyns'ke Vodoskhovyshche
Slov''yans'k
Kramators'k
Lysychans'k
Zolote
Mala Vyska
Znam''yanka
Oleksandriya
Novomoskovs'k
Pavlohrad
Kostyantynivka
Luhans'k
Dniprodzerzhyns'k
Dnipropetrovs'k
Horlivka
Stakhanov
Kirovohrad
Ulyanivka
Zhovti Vody
P''yatykhatky
Synel'nykove
Yenakiyeve
Krasnodon
Vil'shanka
Pervomays'k
Dolyns'ka
Pokrovs'ke
Krasnyy Luch
Torez
Bobrynets'
Kryvyy Rih
Prydniprovs'ka Vysochyna
Donets'k
Makiyivka
Kryve Ozero
Arbyzynka
Novyy Buh
Inhulets'
Zaporizhzhya
Amvrosiyivka
Pivdennyy Buh
Voznesens'k
Ordzhonikidze
Nikopol'
Marhanets'
Orikhiv
Dokuchayevs'k
Volnovakha
Kam''yanka-Dniprovs'ka
Polohy
Dniprorudne
Kakhovs'ka Vodoskhovyshche
Tokmak
Novoazovs'k
Molochans'k
Mariupol'
Mykolayiv
Dnieper (Dnipro)
Black Sea Lowland
Gulf of Taganrog
Zhovtneve
Kakhovka
Melitopol'
Ochakiv
Kherson
Akinovka
Prymors'k
Berdyans'k
Yeya
Odesa
Hola Prystan'
Tsyurupyns'k
Chaplynka
Novotroyits'ke
Illichivs'k
Kalanchak
Armyans'k
Heniches'k
Sea of Azov
Karkinits'ka Zatoka
Krasnoperekops'k
Rozdol'ne
Dzhankoy
Kerch Strait
Chornomors'ke
Krasnohvardiys'ke
Zatoka Syvash
Kerch
Nyzhn'ohirs'kyy
Yevpatoriya
Krym's'kyy Pivostriv
Lenine
Kuban'
Saky
Simferopol'
Feodosiya
Bakhchysaray
Krymś'ki Hory
Sevastopol'
Alushta
Yalta
Alupka
Black Sea
0 km
100
0 miles
100

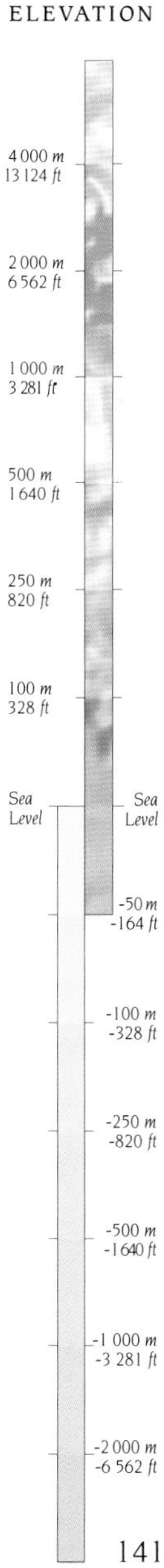
ELEVATION
4 000 m
13 124 ft
2 000 m
6 562 ft
1 000 m
3 281 ft
500 m
1 640 ft
250 m
820 ft
100 m
328 ft
Sea Level
-50 m
-164 ft
-100 m
-328 ft
-250 m
-820 ft
-500 m
-1 640 ft
-1 000 m
-3 281 ft
-2 000 m
-6 562 ft

European Russia

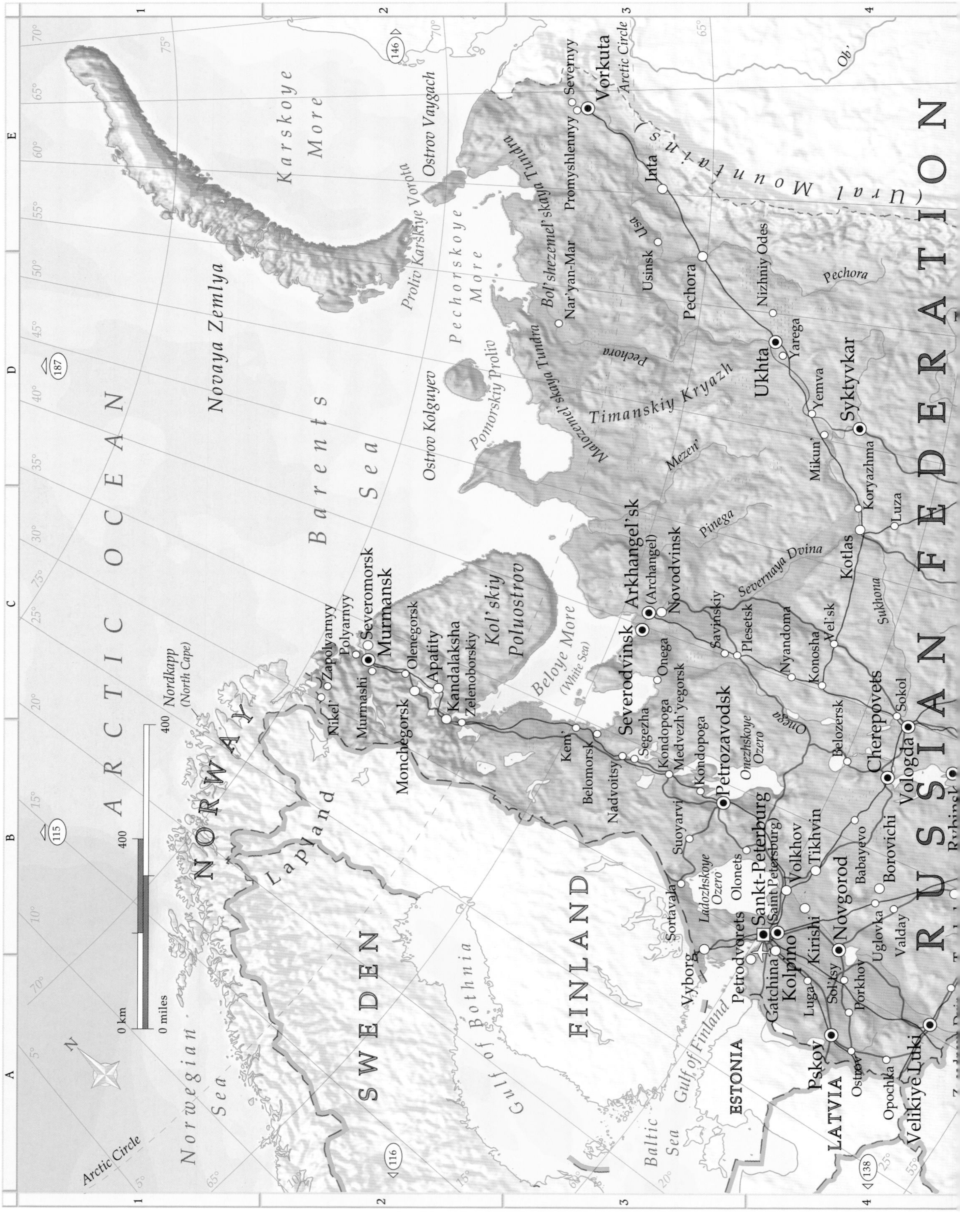
ARCTIC OCEAN
Barents Sea
Karskoye More
Norwegian Sea
Pechorskoye More
Beloye More
(White Sea)
Gulf of Bothnia
Gulf of Finland
Baltic Sea
Novaya Zemlya
Proliv Karskiye Vorota
Ostrov Vaygach
Ostrov Kolguyev
Pomorskiy Proliv
Kol'skiy Poluostrov
Bol'shezemel'skaya Tundra
Malozemel'skaya Tundra
Timanskiy Kryazh
Ural Mountains
Arctic Circle
Nordkapp
(North Cape)
Lapland
NORWAY
SWEDEN
FINLAND
ESTONIA
LATVIA
RUSSIAN FEDERATION
Vorkuta
Severnyy
Promyshlennyy
Inta
Usinsk
Pechora
Nar'yan-Mar
Nizhniy Odes
Ukhta
Yarega
Yemva
Syktyvkar
Mikun'
Koryazhma
Luza
Kotlas
Arkhangel'sk
(Archangel)
Novodvinsk
Severodvinsk
Onega
Savinskiy
Plesetsk
Nyandoma
Konosha
Vel'sk
Murmansk
Severomorsk
Polyarnyy
Zapolyarnyy
Nikel'
Murmashi
Olenegorsk
Monchegorsk
Apatity
Kandalaksha
Zelenoborskiy
Kem'
Belomorsk
Segezha
Nadvoitsy
Medvezh'yegorsk
Kondopoga
Petrozavodsk
Onezhskoye Ozero
Suoyarvi
Sortavala
Ladozhskoye Ozero
Olonets
Sankt-Peterburg
(Saint Petersburg)
Vyborg
Petrodvorets
Gatchina
Kolpino
Kirishi
Volkhov
Tikhvin
Babayevo
Borovichi
Novgorod
Uglovka
Valday
Luga
Sol'tsy
Porkhov
Pskov
Ostrov
Opochka
Velikiye Luki
Belozersk
Sokol
Cherepovets
Vologda
Pechora
Usa
Mezen'
Pinega
Severnaya Dvina
Sukhona
Onega
Ob'
0 km 400
0 miles 400
115
116
138
146
187

POPULATION

Less than 50,000

50,000 – 100,000

100,000 – 500,000

Over 500,000

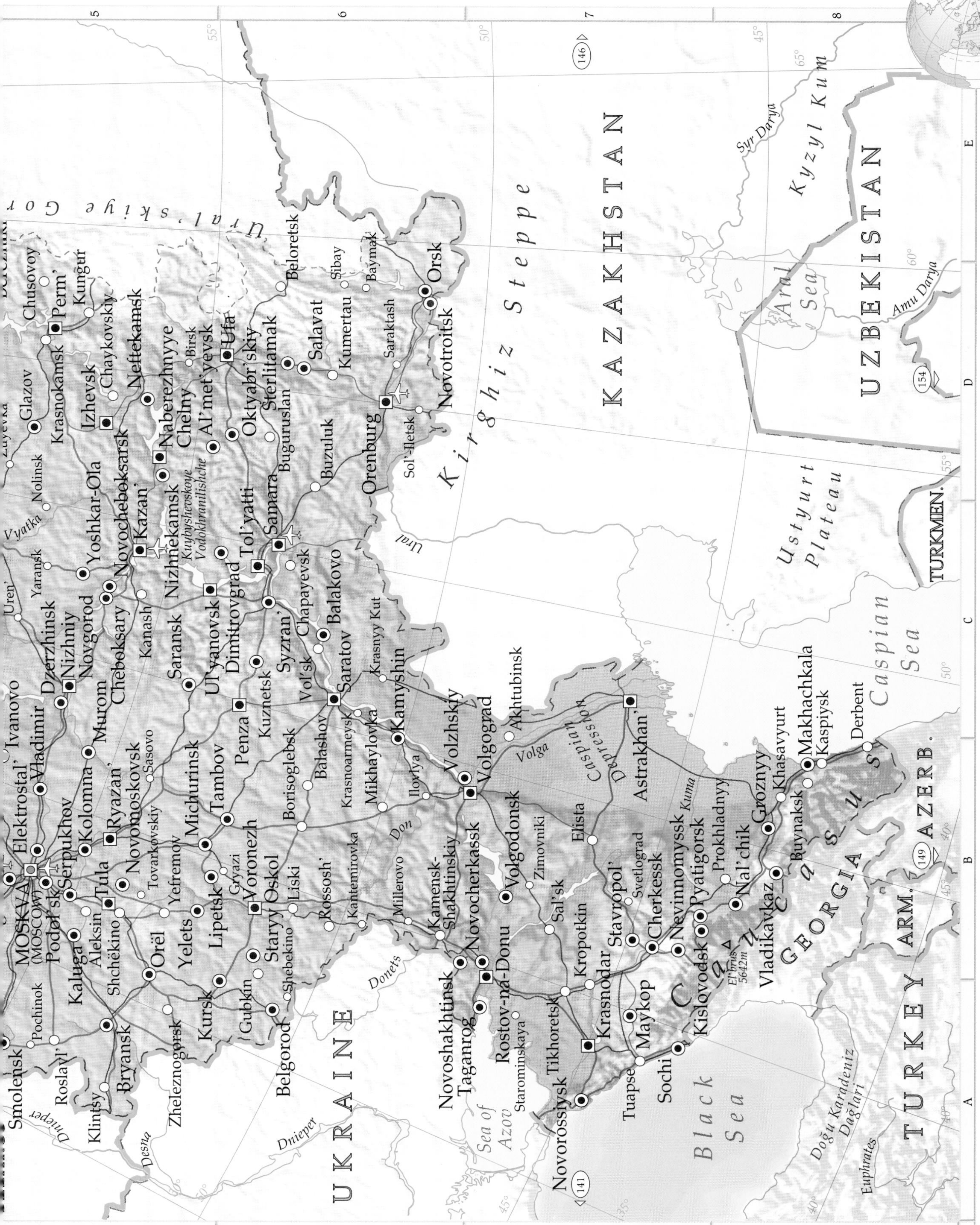

UKRAINE
KAZAKHSTAN
UZBEKISTAN
TURKMEN.
GEORGIA
AZERB.
ARM.
TURKEY
Kirghiz Steppe
Ural'skiye Gory
Kyzyl Kum
Ustyurt Plateau
Caspian Depression
Caucasus
Caspian Sea
Black Sea
Sea of Azov
Aral Sea
Doğu Karadeniz Dağlari
Volga
Don
Donets
Dnieper
Desna
Ural
Kuma
Syr Darya
Amu Darya
Euphrates
Vyatka
Kuybyshevskoye Vodokhranilishche
MOSKVA (MOSCOW)
Smolensk
Roslavl'
Klintsy
Bryansk
Pochinok
Kaluga
Aleksin
Shchëkino
Podol'sk
Serpukhov
Tula
Kolomna
Elektrostal'
Vladimir
Ivanovo
Dzerzhinsk
Nizhniy Novgorod
Murom
Ryazan'
Novomoskovsk
Orël
Yelets
Yefremov
Tovarkovskiy
Michurinsk
Sasovo
Tambov
Lipetsk
Gryazi
Voronezh
Kursk
Zheleznogorsk
Gubkin
Staryy Oskol
Shebekino
Belgorod
Liski
Rossosh'
Kantemirovka
Borisoglebsk
Balashov
Penza
Saransk
Kanash
Cheboksary
Novocheboksarsk
Yoshkar-Ola
Yaransk
Uren'
Kazan'
Nizhnekamsk
Naberezhnyye Chelny
Al'met'yevsk
Ul'yanovsk
Dimitrovgrad
Tol'yatti
Samara
Syzran'
Kuznetsk
Chapayevsk
Balakovo
Vol'sk
Saratov
Krasnyy Kut
Kamyshin
Krasnoarmeysk
Mikhaylovka
Ilovlya
Volzhskiy
Volgograd
Akhtubinsk
Astrakhan'
Millerovo
Kamensk-Shakhtinskiy
Novoshakhtinsk
Taganrog
Novocherkassk
Rostov-na-Donu
Volgodonsk
Zimovniki
Sal'sk
Elista
Starominskaya
Tikhoretsk
Kropotkin
Krasnodar
Novorossiysk
Tuapse
Sochi
Maykop
Stavropol'
Svetlograd
Cherkessk
Nevinnomyssk
Pyatigorsk
Kislovodsk
El'brus 5642m
Prokhladnyy
Nal'chik
Vladikavkaz
Groznyy
Khasavyurt
Buynaksk
Makhachkala
Kaspiysk
Derbent
Nolinsk
Glazov
Izhevsk
Zuyevka
Chusovoy
Krasnokamsk
Perm'
Kungur
Chaykovskiy
Neftekamsk
Birsk
Ufa
Oktyabr'skiy
Sterlitamak
Salavat
Kumertau
Beloretsk
Sibay
Baymak
Saraktash
Orsk
Novotroitsk
Orenburg
Sol'-Iletsk
Buzuluk
Buguruslan
Nizhnekamsk

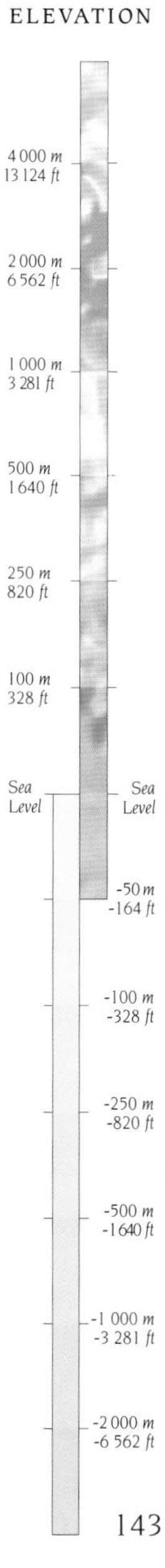

ELEVATION
4 000 m 13 124 ft
2 000 m 6 562 ft
1 000 m 3 281 ft
500 m 1 640 ft
250 m 820 ft
100 m 328 ft
Sea Level
Sea Level
-50 m -164 ft
-100 m -328 ft
-250 m -820 ft
-500 m -1640 ft
-1 000 m -3 281 ft
-2 000 m -6 562 ft

NORTH & WEST ASIA

A
B
C
D
1
2
3
4
5
20°
40°
60°
80°
100°
171
96
85
Franz Josef Land
ARCTI
Severnaya Ze
Ostrov Komsomolets
Ostrov Oktyabr'skoy Revolyutsii
Ostrov Bol'shevik
Summer limit of pack ice
Winter limit of pack ice
Novaya Zemlya
East Novaya Zemlya Trench
Kara Sea
Poluostrov Taymyr
North Siberi
Kheta
Norwegian Sea
North Cape
Barents Sea
Ostrov Kolguyev
Poluostrov Yamal
Gulf of Ob
Noril'sk
Kureyka
Central Siberian Plateau
Murmansk
Kola Peninsula
Arctic Circle
White Sea
Archangel
RUSSIAN F
Ural Mountains
Ob'
West Siberian Plain
Lower Tunguska
Yenisey
Stony Tunguska
Angara
Gulf of Bothnia
Lake Onega
Northern Dvina
Lake Ladoga
Saint Petersburg
Vologda
Yaroslavl'
Perm'
Yekaterinburg
Irtysh
Chulym
Tomsk
Krasnoyarsk
Baltic Sea
Kaliningrad
KALININGRAD
(part of Russ. Fed.)
MOSCOW
Volga
Nizhniy Novgorod
Kazan'
Ufa
Chelyabinsk
Ishim
Omsk
Novosibirsk
Novokuznetsk
Central Russian Upland
Ul'yanovsk
Samara
Orenburg
Voronezh
Saratov
Ural'sk
Ural
Akmola
Karaganda
Semipalatinsk
Sayanskiy Khrebet
EUROPE
Volgograd
Kirghiz Steppe
Kazakh Uplands
Altai Mountains
Ozero Zaysan
Rostov-na-Donu
Don
Astrakhan'
Aral'sk
KAZAKHSTAN
Lake Balkhash
Danube
Stavropol'
Caspian Sea
Aktau
Ustyurt Plateau
Aral Sea
Syr Darya
Kyzyl Kum
Kzyl-Orda
Ili
Zhambyl
ALMA-ATA
Black Sea
El'brus 5642m
Caucasus
GEORGIA
T'BILISI
UZBEKISTAN
BISHKEK
Tien Shan
Istanbul
Küre Dağları
ARMENIA
AZERB.
Dashkhovuz
TASHKENT
KYRGYZSTAN
ANKARA
YEREVAN
BAKU
TURKMENISTAN
Amu Darya
Kara Kum
DUSHANBE
TAJIKISTAN
Anatolia
Lake Van
Mediterranean Sea
TURKEY
Gaziantep
Tabriz
ASHGABAT
Adana
Aleppo
Mosul
TEHRAN
Hindu Kush
Kunlun Mountains
Tripoli
SYRIA
IRAQ
Qom
KABUL
Jalalabad
BEIRUT
DAMASCUS
Herat
Khyber Pass
LEBANON
BAGHDAD
Isfahan
Syrian Desert
Tigris
Iranian Plateau
AFGHANISTAN
ISRAEL
AMMAN
Euphrates
Zagros Mountains
Himalayas
JERUSALEM
JORDAN
Basra
IRAN
Zahedan
An Nafud
KUWAIT
Shiraz
Thar Desert
Persian Gulf
Bandar-e Abbas
MANAMA
BAHRAIN
Dubai
Ganges
RIYADH
DOHA
Gulf of Oman
Indus Fan
QATAR
U.A.E.
MUSCAT
Tropic of Cancer
ABU DHABI
Sur
SAUDI ARABIA
Nile
Red Sea
Arabian Peninsula
Murray Ridge
At Ta'if
OMAN
Ganges Fan
Ar Rub' al Khali
AFRICA
SANA
YEMEN
Arabian Sea
Bay of Bengal
Ta'izz
Aden
Socotra
(part of Yemen)
Gulf of Aden
S
G
A
S
i

POPULATION

- Less than 50,000 ○
- 50,000 – 100,000 ○
- 100,000 – 500,000 ◉
- Over 500,000 ▣

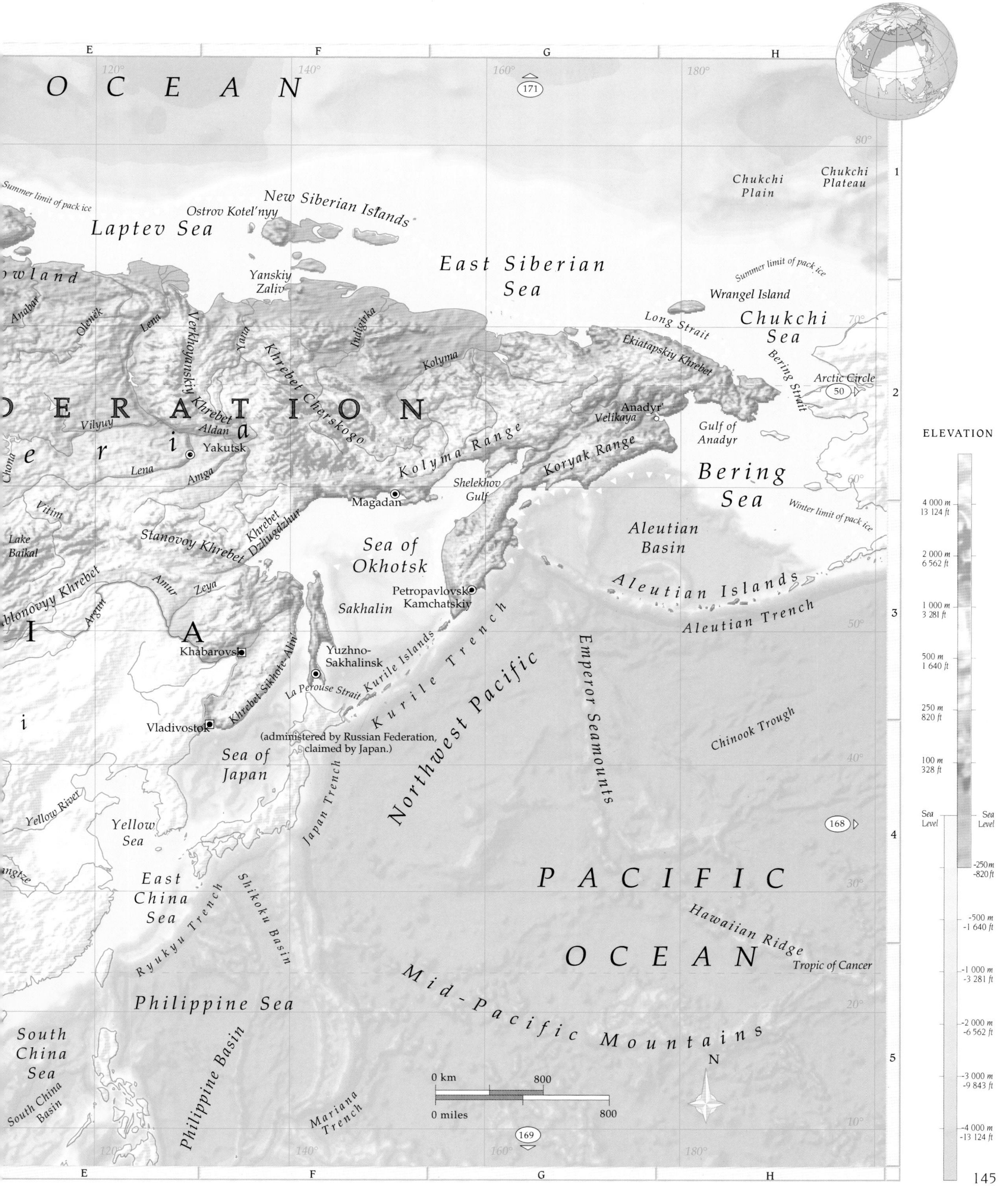
E
F
G
H
120°
140°
160°
180°
80°
70°
60°
50°
40°
30°
20°
10°
1
2
3
4
5
171
168
169
50
O C E A N
Summer limit of pack ice
New Siberian Islands
Ostrov Kotel'nyy
Laptev Sea
owland
Yanskiy Zaliv
East Siberian Sea
Chukchi Plain
Chukchi Plateau
Summer limit of pack ice
Wrangel Island
Long Strait
Chukchi Sea
Anabar
Olenëk
Lena
Verkhoyanskiy Khrebet
Yana
Indigirka
Khrebet Cherskogo
Kolyma
Ekiatapskiy Khrebet
Bering Strait
Arctic Circle
DERATION
Vilyuy
Aldan
Yakutsk
Anadyr'
Velikaya
Gulf of Anadyr
Chona
Lena
Amga
Kolyma Range
Koryak Range
Bering Sea
Shelekhov Gulf
Magadan
Winter limit of pack ice
Vitim
Lake Baikal
Stanovoy Khrebet
Khrebet Dzhugdzhur
Sea of Okhotsk
Aleutian Basin
ablonovyy Khrebet
Amur
Zeya
Petropavlovsk-Kamchatskiy
Aleutian Islands
Argun
Sakhalin
Aleutian Trench
Khabarovsk
Yuzhno-Sakhalinsk
Kurile Islands
Kurile Trench
Emperor Seamounts
Khrebet Sikhote-Alin'
La Perouse Strait
Northwest Pacific
Vladivostok
(administered by Russian Federation, claimed by Japan.)
Chinook Trough
Sea of Japan
Japan Trench
Yellow River
Yellow Sea
angtze
East China Sea
Shikoku Basin
Ryukyu Trench
P A C I F I C
Hawaiian Ridge
O C E A N
Tropic of Cancer
Philippine Sea
Mid-Pacific Mountains
South China Sea
South China Basin
Philippine Basin
Mariana Trench
0 km
800
0 miles
800
N
ELEVATION
4 000 m
13 124 ft
2 000 m
6 562 ft
1 000 m
3 281 ft
500 m
1 640 ft
250 m
820 ft
100 m
328 ft
Sea Level
Sea Level
-250 m
-820 ft
-500 m
-1 640 ft
-1 000 m
-3 281 ft
-2 000 m
-6 562 ft
-3 000 m
-9 843 ft
-4 000 m
-13 124 ft

Russia & Kazakhstan

A
B
C
D
1
2
3
4
5
115
140
152
154
Arctic Circle
SVALBARD
(Norwegian dependency)
NETH.
NORWAY
DENMARK
SWEDEN
GERMANY
Zemlya Frantsa Iosifa
Nordkapp
(North Cape)
Baltic Sea
Gulf of Bothnia
Barents
Sea
KALININGRAD
(part of Russ. Fed.)
Gulf of Finland
FINLAND
Murmansk
Kaliningrad
POLAND
Kandalaksha
Kol'skiy Poluostrov
Novaya Zemlya
EST.
LITH.
LAT.
Sankt-Peterburg
Ladozhskoye Ozero
Beloye More
Karskoye More
Pskov
Novgorod
Petrozavodsk
Onezhskoye Ozero
Severodvinsk
Arkhangel'sk
Ostrov Kolguyev
Ostrov Belyy
Dikson
BELARUS
Smolensk
Cherepovets
Severnaya Dvina
Pechora
Nar'yan-Mar
Poluostrov Yamal
MOSKVA
(MOSCOW)
Tver'
Vel'sk
Vologda
Obskaya Guba
MOLDOVA
Bryansk
Yaroslavl'
Ukhta
Vorkuta
Talna
UKRAINE
Tula
Kineshma
Kotlas
Salekhard
Noril'sk
Syktyvkar
Ural'skiye Gory
Ob'
Belgorod
Ryazan'
Vladimir
Nizhniy Novgorod
Igarka
Voronezh
Tambov
Kirov
Nadym
Taz
Sea of Azov
Penza
Kazan'
Glazov
Solikamsk
Nyagan'
Mikhaylovka
Ul'yanovsk
Izhevsk
Perm'
Serov
Zapadno-
Rostov-na-Donu
Tol'yatti
Khanty-Mansiysk
Yenisey
Black Sea
Saratov
Naberezhnyye Chelny
Krasnodar
Balakovo
Sibirskaya
Sochi
Volgograd
Samara
Ufa
Yekaterinburg
Surgut
Nizhnevartovsk
Stavropol'
Volga
Ravnina
El'brus 5642m
Ural'sk
Ural
Tyumen'
Caucasus
Sterlitamak
Tobol'sk
Orenburg
Chelyabinsk
RUSSIAN
GEORGIA
Nal'chik
Astrakhan'
Magnitogorsk
Ishim
Irtysh
Tobol
Vladikavkaz
Aktyubinsk
Orsk
Petropavlovsk
Chulym
Groznyy
Atyrau
Alga
Rudnyy
Kustanay
ARM.
Makhachkala
Omsk
Tomsk
Strel
Emba
Kokshetau
Fort-Shevchenko
Novosibirsk
Krasnoyar
AZERBAIJAN
Aktau
Atbasar
Shchuchinsk
Kulunda Steppe
Novyy Uzen'
Chelkar
Kemerovo
KAZAKHSTAN
Akmola
Pavlodar
Ustyurt Plateau
Aral Sea
Barnaul
Aral'sk
Temirtau
Novokazalinsk
Novokuznetsk
Caspian Sea
Saran'
Karaganda
Abak
Syr Darya
Zhezkazgan
Semipalatinsk
Kazakhskiy Melkosopochnik
Dzhusaly
Leninogorsk
TURKMENISTAN
Charsk
Zyryanovsk
Kzyl-Orda
Ust'-Kamenogorsk
Gora Belukha 4506m
UZBEKISTAN
Kyzyl Kum
Balkhash
Ayaguz
Altai Mountains
Amu Darya
Turkestan
Kentau
Ozero Balkhash
Ozero Zaysan
Shymkent
Karatau
Arys'
Shu
Taldykorgan
IRAN
Zhambyl
Tekeli
Kirghiz Range
ALMATY
(ALMA-ATA)
TAJIKISTAN
KYRGYZSTAN
CHINA
Tien Shan
AFGHANISTAN

POPULATION

Less than 50,000 ○

50,000 – 100,000 ○

100,000 – 500,000 ◉

Over 500,000 ▣

E
F
G
H
1
2
3
4
5
0 km
800
0 miles
800
ALASKA
(part of US)
Chukchi
Sea
Bering Strait
Arctic Circle
68
Ostrov Vrangelya
Proliv Longa
Ekiatapskiy Khrebet
Anadyrskiy
Zaliv
Anadyr'
Pevek
Anadyr'
O C E A N
Ostrov
Komsomolets
Ostrov Oktyabr'skoy Revolyutsii
Severnaya
Zemlya
Novosibirskiye
Ostrova
Ostrov
Novaya Sibir'
Vostochno-Sibirskoye
More
Ostrov Kotel'nyy
Ostrov Bol'shoy
Lyakhovskiy
Ambarchik
Cherskiy
Bering
Sea
Koryakskoye Nagor'ye
Alazeya
Indigirka
Kolyma
More
Laptevykh
Ozero
Taymyr
184
Ostrov Karaginskiy
Ossora
Tiksi
Kazach'ye
Ust'-Olenëk
Yana
Khrebet Cherskogo
Adycha
Verkhoyanskiy Khrebet
Anabar
Olenëk
Kotuy
Kheta
Zaliv
Shelikhova
Ust'-Kamchatsk
Vulkan Klyucheyskaya
Sopka
4750m
Susuman
Atka
Magadan
Atlasovo
Mil'kovo
Poluostrov
Kamchatka
Petropavlovsk-
Kamchatskiy
Ust'-Olenëk
Lena
Aldan
Srednesibirskoye
Ploskogor'ye
Okhotsk
Yakutsk
Vilyuy
Nyurba
Okhotskoye
More
Pervyy Kuril'skiy Proliv
Ostrov
Paramushir
Mirnyy
Suntar
Lena
Amga
Aldan
Khrebet Dzhugdzhur
Chunya
Olëkminsk
Shantarskiye
Ostrova
EDERATION
Olëkma
Ostrov Sakhalin
Kuril'skiye Ostrova
(Kurile Islands)
Neryungri
Angara
Ust'-Ilimsk
Lena
Bodaybo
Ostrov Urup
Komsomol'sk-
na-Amure
Amur
Ostrov Iturup
Kuril'sk
Tynda
Ust'-Kut
Vitim
Skovorodino
Bratsk
Amur
Khrebet Sikhote-Alin
Yuzhno-Sakhalinsk
Tulun
Ozero
Baykal
Svobodnyy
Khabarovsk
La Perouse
Strait
Usol'ye-Sibirskoye
Angarsk
Yablonovyy Khrebet
Shilka
Chita
Blagoveshchensk
Birobidzhan
Khor
(administered by
Russian Federation,
claimed by Japan)
Bikin
Irkutsk
Ulan-Ude
Olovyannaya
Krasnokamensk
Zabaykal'sk
Kyakhta
CHINA
Ussuriysk
Vladivostok
Nakhodka
MONGOLIA
JAPAN
Sea of
Japan
NORTH
KOREA
N
G o b i
158
160
180°
80°
170°
70°
160°
140°
120°
100°
60°
180°
170°
160°
50°
150°
40°
140°
130°
120°
110°
100°
40°

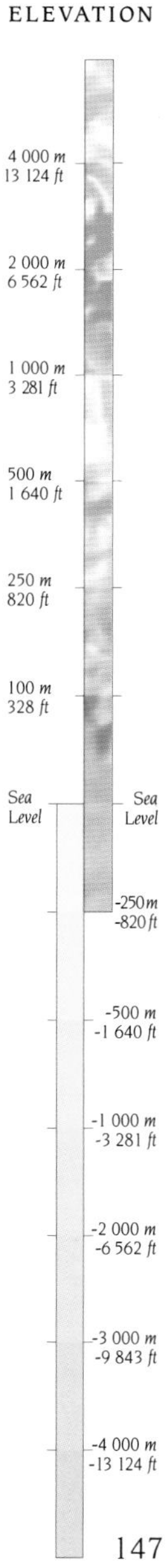
ELEVATION
4 000 m
13 124 ft
2 000 m
6 562 ft
1 000 m
3 281 ft
500 m
1 640 ft
250 m
820 ft
100 m
328 ft
Sea
Level
Sea
Level
-250 m
-820 ft
-500 m
-1 640 ft
-1 000 m
-3 281 ft
-2 000 m
-6 562 ft
-3 000 m
-9 843 ft
-4 000 m
-13 124 ft

Turkey & the Caucasus

A
B
C
D
1
2
3
4
5
140
141
136
137
104
UKRAINE
ROMANIA
Lacul Razim
Lacul Sinoie
Kryms'kyy Pivostriv
Danube
Black Sea
BULGARIA
Varnenski Zaliv
Burgaski Zaliv
Maritsa
Edirne
Kırklareli
İstanbul Boğazı (Bosporus)
Ergene Nehri
Çorlu
Tekirdağ
İstanbul
Marmara Denizi (Sea of Marmara)
İzmit
Adapazarı
Zonguldak
Bartın
Cide
İnebolu
Sinop
Gerze
Küre Dağları
Kastamonu
Karabük
Devrek
Kargı
Bafra
Samsun
Ünye
Canik Dağları
Ordu
Çerkeş
Gerede
Bolu
Merzifon
Kızıl Irmak
Çankırı
Çorum
Tokat
Alaca
Kalecik
Yıldızeli
Sorgun
Sivas
Yalova
İznik Gölü
Bandırma
Bursa
Bilecik
Çanakkale
Çanakkale Boğazı (Dardanelles)
Simav Çayı
Balıkesir
Bozüyük
Eskişehir
ANKARA
Kırıkkale
Edremit
Ayvalık
Kütahya
Polatlı
TURKEY
Şarkışla
Boğazlıyan
Lésvos
Akhisar
Simav
Gediz
Hirfanlı Barajı
Kulu
Menemen
Manisa
Gediz Nehri
Uşak
Afyon
Tuz Gölü
Cihanbeyli
Bünyan
İncesu
Gürün
Chíos
İzmir
Nevşehir
Kayseri
Akşehir
Aksaray
GREECE
Ödemiş
Alaşehir
Anatolia
Sámos
Aydın
Nazilli
Dinar
Göksun
Söke
Büyükmenderes Nehri
Denizli
Beyşehir Gölü
Konya
Niğde
Burdur
Isparta
Kahramanmaraş
Tavas
Milas
Burdur Gölü
Ereğli
Muğla
Suğla Gölü
Bodrum
Toros Dağları
Karaman
Gaziantep
Marmaris
Dalaman
Antalya
Ceyhan
Tarsus
Mersin
Adana
Osmaniye
Manavgat
Fethiye
Alanya
Mut
İskenderun
Kilis
Dodecánese
Ródos (Rhodes)
Kaş
Finike
Antalya Körfezi
Silifke
Kırıkhan
Antakya
Anamur
Kárpathos
TURKISH REPUBLIC OF NORTHERN CYPRUS
(recognised only by Turkey)
CYPRUS
Orantes
Mediterranean Sea
0 km
200
0 miles
200
LEBANON
25°
30°
35°
40°
45°
N

POPULATION

Less than 50,000

50,000 – 100,000

100,000 – 500,000

Over 500,000

RUSSIAN FEDERATION
Caspian Sea
Caucasus
Abkhazia
Gagra
Gudaut'a
Sokhumi
Enguri
Mestia
Kazbek 5047m
Och'amch'ire
South Ossetia
K'ut'aisi
Samtredia
GEORGIA
P'ot'i
Gori
Tsalka
T'BILISI
Rust'avi
K'obulet'i
Lesser Caucasus
Bat'umi
Ajaria
Akhalts'ikhe
Hopa
Artvin
Pazar
Rize
Of
Trabzon
Giresun
Doğu Karadeniz Dağları
Çoruh Nehri
Zaqatala
Greater Caucasus
Xaçmaz
Quba
Siyäzän
Şäki
Kura
Sumqayıt
Mingäçevir
Şamaxı
Gäncä
Yevlax
BAKI (BAKU)
AZERBAIJAN
Vanadzor
Gyumri
Sevan
Art'ik
Kars
ARMENIA
Sarıkamış
İspir
YEREVAN
Sevana Lich
Nagornyy Karabakh
İmişli
Qazimämmäd
Äli-Bayramı
Artashat
Horasan
Aras
Büyükağrı Dağı (Mount Ararat) 5137m
Xankändi
Biläsuvar
Pasinler
Aşkale
Erzurum
Ağrı
Goris
Erzincan
Tercan
Doğubayazıt
AZERBAIJAN
Kemah
Naxçıvan
Länkäran
Patnos
Erciş
Muradiye
Keban Baraji
Bingöl
Muş
Tatvan
Van Gölü
Van
Elâzığ
Bitlis
Malatya
Toroslar
Silvan
Gevaş
Siirt
Daryācheh-ye Orūmīyeh
Reshteh-ye Kūhhā-ye Alborz (Elburz Mountains)
Diyarbakır
Batman
Silverek
Şırnak
Kurdistan
Atatürk Baraji
Mardin
Viranşehir
Şanlıurfa
Ceylanpınar
Nusaybin
IRAN
Tigris
Al Jazīrah
Euphrates
IRAQ
Jabal Bishrī
Kūhhā-ye Zāgros (Zagros Mountains)
Buḩayrat ath Tharthār
ELEVATION
4 000 m 13 124 ft
2 000 m 6 562 ft
1 000 m 3 281 ft
500 m 1 640 ft
250 m 820 ft
100 m 328 ft
Sea Level
-50 m -164 ft
-100 m -328 ft
-250 m -820 ft
-500 m -1640 ft
-1 000 m -3 281 ft
-2 000 m -6 562 ft

THE NEAR EAST

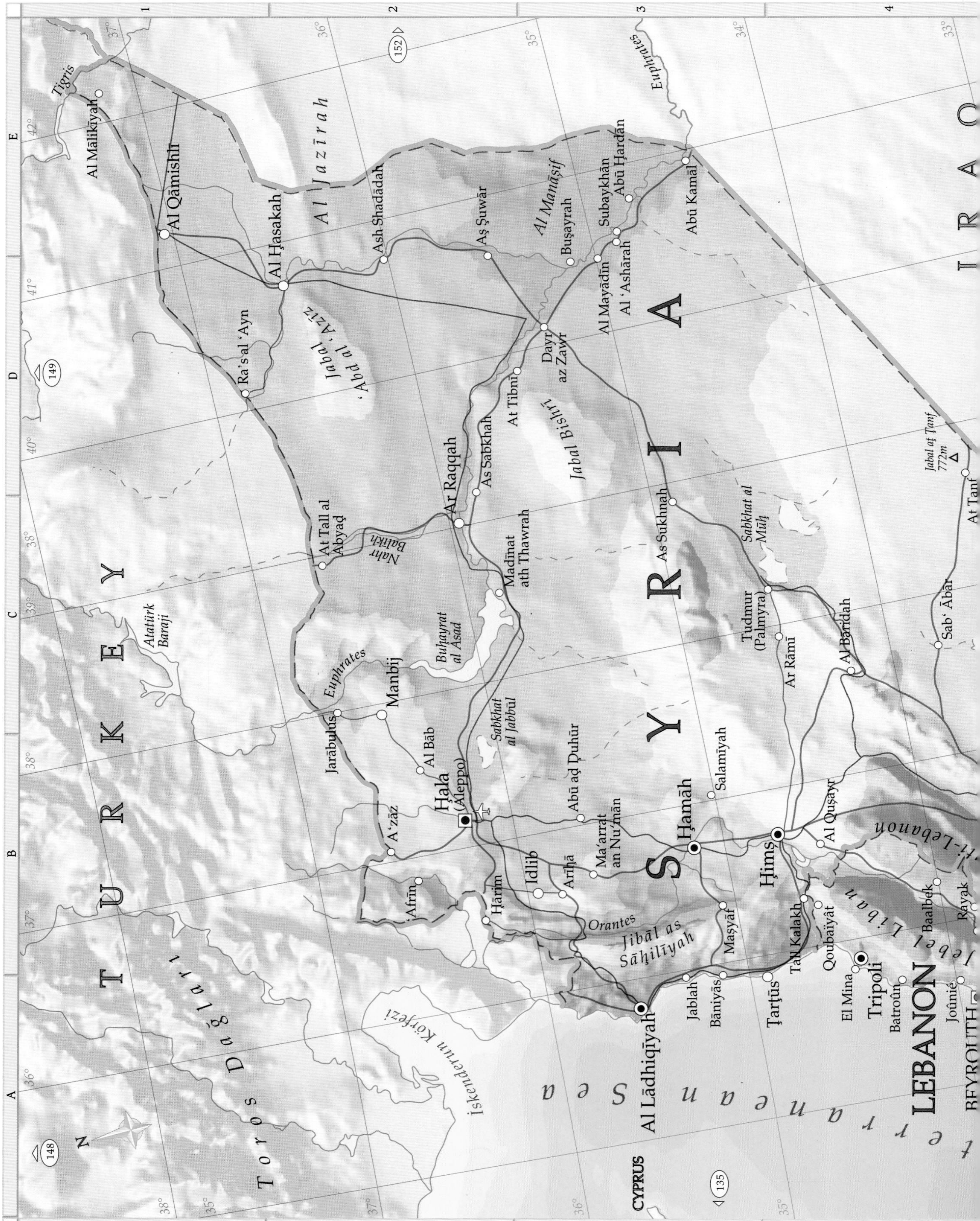
TURKEY
SYRIA
IRAQ
LEBANON
CYPRUS
Mediterranean Sea
Toros Dağları
İskenderun Körfezi
Atatürk Barajı
Euphrates
Tigris
Orantes
Nahr Balīkh
Buḩayrat al Asad
Sabkhat al Jabbūl
Sabkhat al Mūḩ
Al Jazīrah
Jabal 'Abd al 'Azīz
Jabal Bishrī
Al Manāşif
Jibāl as Sāḩilīyah
Jebel Liban
Anti-Lebanon
Jabal aţ Ţanf 772m
Al Mālikīyah
Al Qāmishlī
Al Ḩasakah
Ash Shadādah
Aş Şuwār
Buşayrah
Subaykhān
Abū Ḩardān
Abū Kamāl
Al Mayādīn
Al 'Ashārah
Dayr az Zawr
At Tibnī
As Sabkhah
Ar Raqqah
Ra's al 'Ayn
At Tall al Abyaḑ
Madīnat ath Thawrah
As Sukhnah
Tudmur (Palmyra)
Ar Rāmī
Al Bāridah
Sab' Ābār
At Tanf
Manbij
Jarābulus
Al Bāb
Ḩalab (Aleppo)
A'zāz
'Afrīn
Ḩārim
Idlib
Arīḩā
Ma'arrat an Nu'mān
Abū aḑ Ḑuhūr
Ḩamāh
Salamīyah
Ḩimş
Al Quşayr
Maşyāf
Tall Kalakh
Al Lādhiqīyah
Jablah
Bāniyās
Ţarţūs
Qoubaïyât
El Mina
Tripoli
Batroûn
Baalbek
Rayak
Joûnié
BEYROUTH
152
149
148
135

POPULATION

Less than 50,000

50,000 – 100,000

100,000 – 500,000

Over 500,000

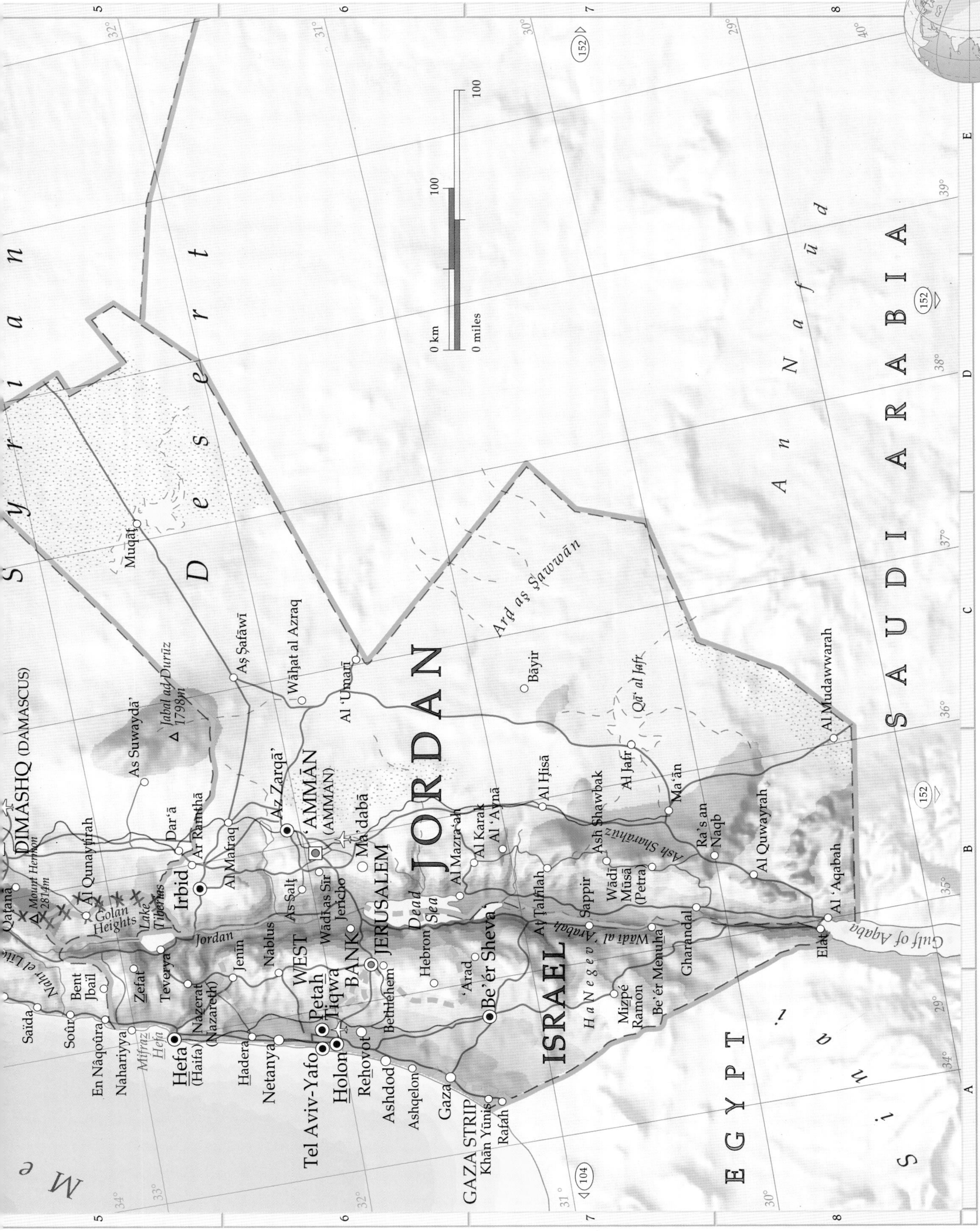
Syrian Desert
JORDAN
ISRAEL
WEST BANK
GAZA STRIP
SAUDI ARABIA
EGYPT
Sinai
An Nafūd
Ard aş Şawwān
Qā' al Jafr
DIMASHQ (DAMASCUS)
'AMMĀN (AMMAN)
JERUSALEM
Az Zarqā'
Irbid
Al Mafraq
Ar Ramthā
Dar'ā
As Suwaydā'
Jabal ad Durūz 1798m
Mount Hermon 2814m
Golan Heights
Lake Tiberias
Jordan
Dead Sea
As Salt
Wādī as Sīr
Jericho
Mā'dabā
Al Mazra'ah
Al Karak
Al 'Aynā
Aţ Ţafīlah
Al Ḩisā
Ash Shawbak
Wādī Mūsā (Petra)
Ma'ān
Al Jafr
Ra's an Naqb
Al Quwayrah
Al 'Aqabah
Al Mudawwarah
Bāyir
Al 'Umarī
Wāḩat al Azraq
Aş Şafāwī
Muqāţ
Ash Sharāh
Wādī al 'Arabah
Gulf of Aqaba
Elat
Gharandal
Be'ér Menuha
Mizpé Ramon
HaNegev
Sappir
'Arad
Be'ér Sheva
Hebron
Bethlehem
Nablus
Jenin
Nazerat (Nazareth)
Teverya
Zefat
Hefa (Haifa)
Mifraz Hefa
Nahariyya
En Nâqoûra
Hadera
Netanya
Petah Tiqwa
Tel Aviv-Yafo
Holon
Rehovot
Ashdod
Ashqelon
Gaza
Khān Yūnis
Rafah
Qatanā
Al Qunayţirah
Bent Jbaïl
Soûr
Saïda
Nahr el Litani
Me
0 km
100
0 miles
100
152
104
A B C D E
5 6 7 8
29° 30° 31° 32° 33° 34° 35° 36° 37° 38° 39° 40°

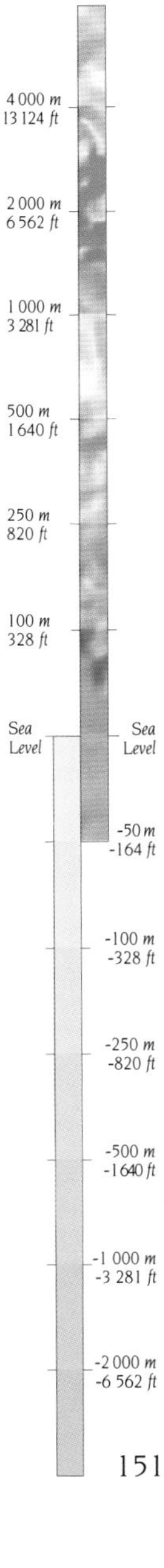
ELEVATION
4 000 m
13 124 ft
2 000 m
6 562 ft
1 000 m
3 281 ft
500 m
1 640 ft
250 m
820 ft
100 m
328 ft
Sea Level
Sea Level
-50 m
-164 ft
-100 m
-328 ft
-250 m
-820 ft
-500 m
-1640 ft
-1 000 m
-3 281 ft
-2 000 m
-6 562 ft

The Middle East

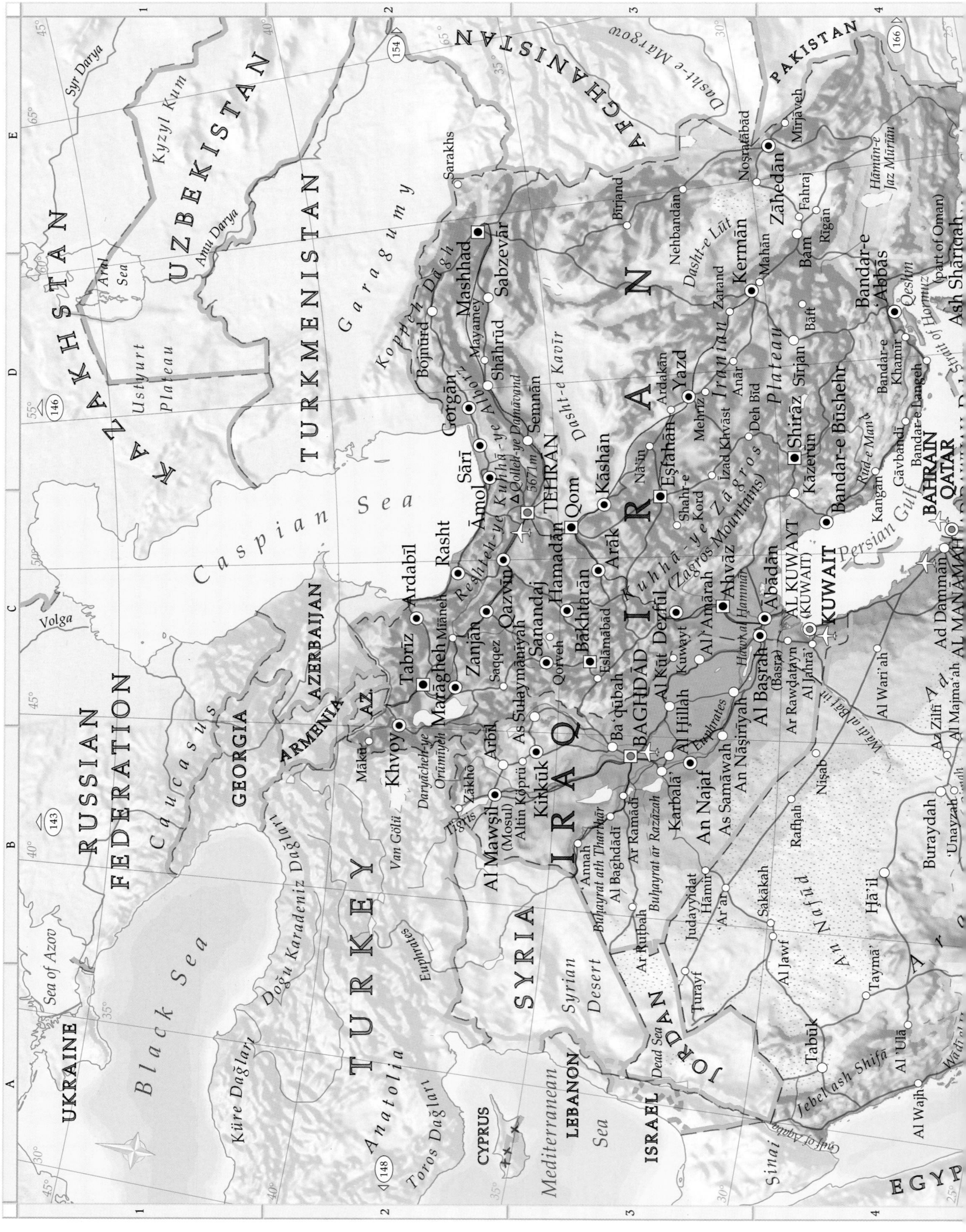
KAZAKHSTAN
UZBEKISTAN
TURKMENISTAN
AFGHANISTAN
PAKISTAN
RUSSIAN FEDERATION
UKRAINE
GEORGIA
ARMENIA
AZERBAIJAN
AZ.
TURKEY
SYRIA
IRAQ
IRAN
LEBANON
ISRAEL
JORDAN
CYPRUS
KUWAIT
BAHRAIN
QATAR
EGYPT
Black Sea
Sea of Azov
Caspian Sea
Aral Sea
Persian Gulf
Mediterranean Sea
Dead Sea
Gulf of Aqaba
Strait of Hormuz
Caucasus
Anatolia
Ustyurt Plateau
Kyzyl Kum
Garagumy
Koppeh Dagh
Dasht-e Kavīr
Dasht-e Lūt
Dasht-e Mārgow
Iranian Plateau
Kuhhā-ye Zāgros (Zagros Mountains)
Reshteh-ye Kuhhā-ye Alborz
Qolleh-ye Damāvand 5671m
Syrian Desert
An Nafūd
Sinai
Volga
Syr Darya
Amu Darya
Tigris
Euphrates
Doğu Karadeniz Dağları
Küre Dağları
Toros Dağları
Van Gölü
Daryācheh-ye Orūmīyeh
TEHRĀN
BAGHDĀD
AL KUWAYT (KUWAIT)
AL MANĀMAH
Mashhad
Sabzevār
Bojnūrd
Gorgān
Sārī
Āmol
Semnān
Shāhrūd
Mayamey
Sarakhs
Bīrjand
Nehbandān
Zāhedān
Mīrjāveh
Nosratābād
Fahraj
Bam
Rīgān
Kermān
Zarand
Māhān
Bāft
Sīrjān
Yazd
Ardakān
Mehrīz
Anār
Deh Bīd
Shīrāz
Kāzerūn
Bandar-e Būshehr
Bandar-e 'Abbās
Bandar-e Khamīr
Bandar-e Lengeh
Kangān
Gāvbandī
Eşfahān
Nā'īn
Shahr-e Kord
Izad Khvāst
Kāshān
Qom
Arāk
Hamadān
Qazvīn
Rasht
Ardabīl
Tabrīz
Mīāneh
Zanjān
Marāgheh
Khvoy
Mākū
Sanandaj
Saqqez
Bakhtarān
Eslāmābād
Qorveh
Dezfūl
Ahvāz
Ābādān
Al Amārah
Al Kūt
Ba'qūbah
Al Ḩillah
Karbalā'
An Najaf
As Samāwah
An Nāşirīyah
Al Başrah (Basra)
As Sulaymānīyah
Kirkūk
Arbīl
Altin Köprü
Zākhō
Al Mawşil (Mosul)
Al Baghdādī
Ar Ramādī
'Annah
Ar Ruţbah
Buḩayrat ath Tharthār
Buḩayrat ar Razāzah
Judayyidat Ḩāmir
'Ar'ar
Sakākah
Al Jawf
Turayf
Tabūk
Taymā'
Ḩā'il
Buraydah
'Unayzah
Az Zilfī
Al Majma'ah
Al Wari'ah
Ad Dammām
Al Jahrā'
Ar Rawdatayn
Nişab
Rafḩah
Al 'Ulā
Al Wajh
Jebel ash Shifā
Wādī al Bāţin
Hawr al Ḩammār
Qeshm
Hāmūn-e Jaz Mūrīān
Rūd-e Mand
Ash Shāriqah
(part of Oman)

POPULATION

Less than 50,000

50,000 – 100,000

100,000 – 500,000

Over 500,000

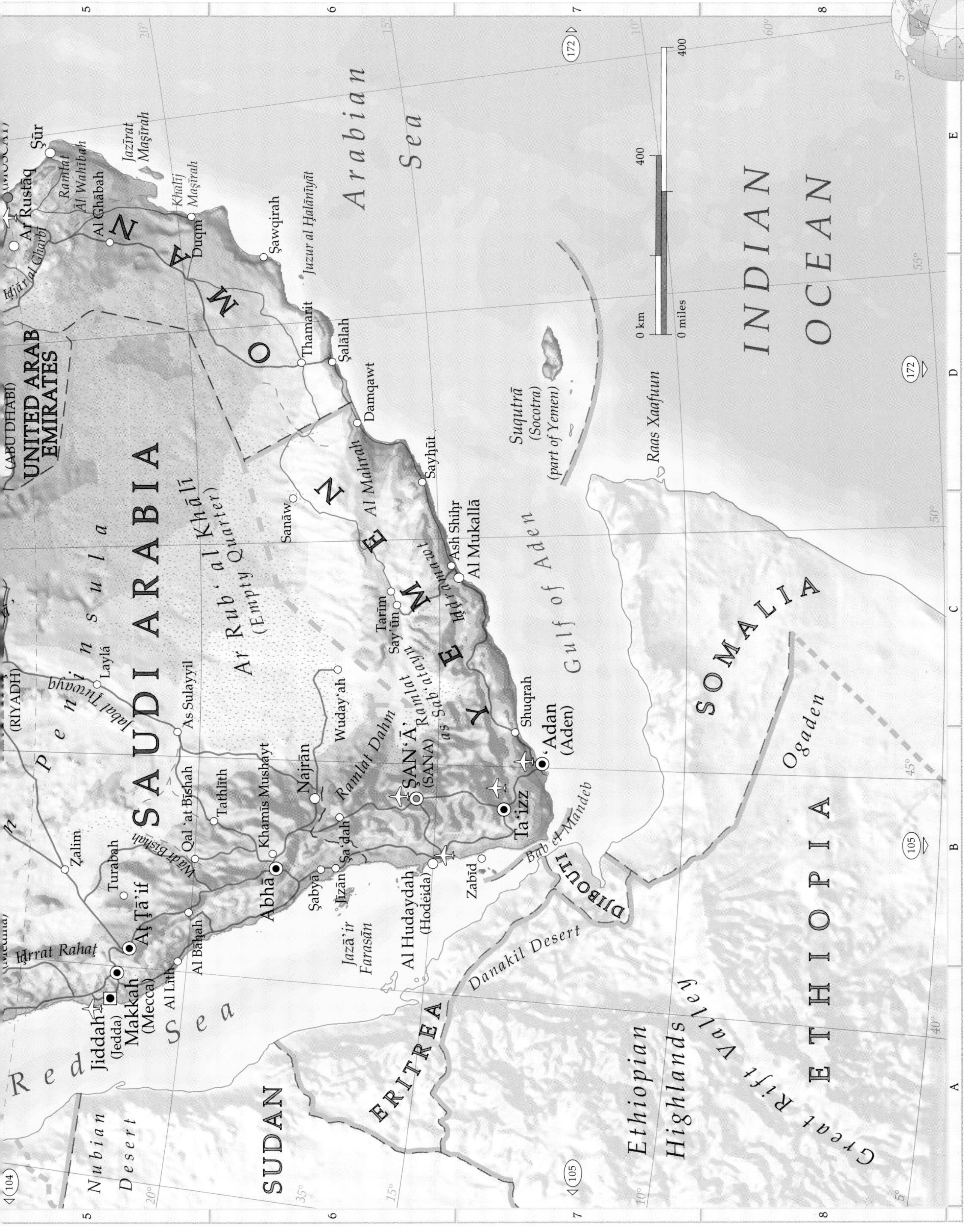
SAUDI ARABIA
UNITED ARAB EMIRATES
(ABU DHABI)
(RIYADH)
OMAN
YEMEN
SOMALIA
ETHIOPIA
ERITREA
DJIBOUTI
SUDAN
Arabian Sea
INDIAN OCEAN
Red Sea
Gulf of Aden
Bab el Mandeb
Peninsula
Ar Rub' al Khālī
(Empty Quarter)
Ramlat Dahm
Ramlat as Sab'atayn
Ḩaḑramawt
Jabal Ţuwayq
Wādī Bīshah
Ḩarrat Rahaţ
Nubian Desert
Danakil Desert
Ethiopian Highlands
Great Rift Valley
Ogaden
Raas Xaafuun
Suquţrā
(Socotra)
(part of Yemen)
Jazīrat Maşīrah
Khalīj Maşīrah
Juzur al Ḩalānīyāt
Ramlat Āl Wahībah
Jazā'ir Farasān
Şūr
Ar Rustāq
Al Ghābah
Duqm
Şawqirah
Thamarīt
Şalālah
Damqawt
Al Mahrah
Sayḩūt
Sanāw
Ash Shiḩr
Al Mukallā
Tarīm
Say'ūn
Shuqrah
'Adan
(Aden)
Ta'izz
ŞAN'Ā'
(SANA)
Wuday'ah
Najrān
Şa'dah
Jīzān
Şabyā
Al Ḩudaydah
(Hodeida)
Zabīd
Abhā
Khamīs Mushayt
Tathlīth
As Sulayyil
Laylā
Qal'at Bīshah
Ţurabah
Z̧alim
Aţ Ţā'if
Al Bāḩah
Al Līth
Makkah
(Mecca)
Jiddah
(Jedda)
0 km 400
0 miles 400
172
105
104
A B C D E
5 6 7 8
5° 10° 15° 20° 35° 40° 45° 50° 55° 60°

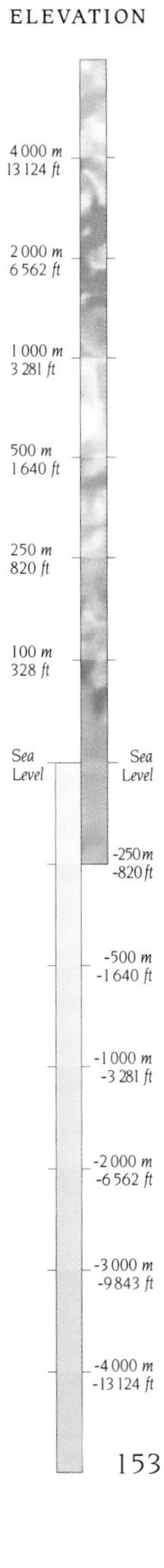
ELEVATION
4 000 m
13 124 ft
2 000 m
6 562 ft
1 000 m
3 281 ft
500 m
1 640 ft
250 m
820 ft
100 m
328 ft
Sea Level
-250 m
-820 ft
-500 m
-1 640 ft
-1 000 m
-3 281 ft
-2 000 m
-6 562 ft
-3 000 m
-9 843 ft
-4 000 m
-13 124 ft

Central Asia

A
B
C
D
1
2
3
4
5
146
152
152
152
45°
50°
55°
60°
65°
40°
35°
30°
RUSSIAN FEDERATION
GEORGIA
AZERBAIJAN
Caspian Sea
Ustyurt Plateau
Aral Sea
Mŭynoq
Turan Lowland
Chimboy
Takhtakŭpir
Këneurgench
Nukus
Takhiatosh
Gubadag
Kyzyl
Il'yaly
Dashkhovuz
Urganch
Uchquduq
UZBEK
Plato Kaplangky
Peski Uchtagan
Tŭrtkŭl
Khiwa
Lebap
Zarafshon
Gaz-Achak
Turkmenbashi
Krasnovodskiy Zaliv
Cheleken
Nebitdag
Zaunguzskiye Garagumy
Darvaza
Amu Darya
Gazandzhyk
Gazli
Turkmenskiy Zaliv
TURKMENISTAN
Ghijduw
Bukhoro
Gyzylarbat
Kopetdag Gershi
Seydi
Kog
Kara-Kala
Bakharden
Garagumy
Deynau
Chardzhev
Byuzmeyin
Sayat
Geok-Tepe
ASHGABAT
Gora Chapan 2889m
Kelifs
Garagumskiy K.
Reshteh-ye Kūhhā-ye Alborz
Tedzhen
Mary
Kaakhka
Bayramaly
Uzbo
Murgab
Murgab
Serakhs
Andkh
Vozvyshennost' Karabil'
Bālā Morghāb
Daryā-ye Morg.
Meyman
Gushgy
Towraghoudī
Selseleh-ye Safīd Kūh
Ghūrīān
Herāt
AFGHAN
Kūhhā-ye Zāgros
Shīndand
IRAN
Iranian Plateau
Farāh Rūd
Farāh
Delārām
Dasht-e Khāsh
Geresh
Hāmūn-e Şāberī
Lashkar Gāh
Chakhānsūr
Zaranj
Dasht-e Mārgow
Kūchnay Darweys
Deh Shū
Daryā-ye Helmand
Rīgest
Chāgai Hills
0 km
200
0 miles
200

POPULATION

Less than 50,000

50,000 – 100,000

100,000 – 500,000

Over 500,000

E
F
G
H
1
2
3
4
5
65°
70°
75°
80°
45°
40°
35°
30°
147
158
158
166
KAZAKHSTAN
Ozero Balkhash
Peski Saryesik-Atyrau
Peski Taukum
Peski Moyynkum
Borohoro Shan
Ili
Syr Darya
BISHKEK
Tokmak
Kara-Balta
Kemin
Talas
Leninpol
Kirghiz Range
Gora Manas 4482m
Chatkal Range
Balykchy
Ozero Issyk-Kul'
Tyup
Dzhergalan
Karakol
Kyzyl-Suu
Kadzhi-Say
Pik Pobedy 7439m
KYRGYZSTAN
Khrebet Moldo-Too
Kara-Say
Naryn
Karakol
Kokshaal-Tau
Chatyr-Tash
Tien Shan
TOSHKENT (TASHKENT)
Chirchiq
Angren
Yangiyŭl
Tash-Kumyr
Namangan
Dzhalal-Abad
Olmaliq
Qŭqon
Andijon
Osh
Nurota
Langar
Guliston
Bekobod
Nawoiy
Jizzakh
Khŭjand
Farghona
Këk-Art
Kattaqŭrghon
Sulyukta
Khaydarkan
Sary-Tash
Samarqand
Ŭroteppa
Daroot-Korgon
Zeravshan
Urgut
Kitob
Qarokŭl
Surkhob
Gissar Range
Qarshi
DUSHANBE
Qullai Kommunizm 7495m
TAJIKISTAN
Sarikol Range
Denow
Norak
Qal'aikhum
Ghŭdara
Murghob
Boysun
Danghara
Qŭrghonteppa
Kŭlob
Bartang
Termiz
Jarqŭrghon
Moskva
Dzhelandy
Dŭsti
Farkhor
Khorugh
Qizilrabot
Pamir
Balkh
Kunduz
Feyzābād
Kholm
Tāloqān
Ishkoshim
Baroghil Pass 3777m
(claimed by India)
Mazār-e Sharīf
Khānābād
Baghlān
Pol-e Khomrī
AKSAI CHIN (administered by China, claimed by India)
Hindu Kush
Karakoram Range
Indus
Aksai Chin
Daryā-ye Kahmard
Barīkowt
Chārīkār
Maḩmūd-e Rāqī
Asadābād
Kūh-e Bābā
KĀBUL
Mehtarlām
Maydān Shahr
Jalālābād
Khyber Pass 1080m
Gardēz
Ghaznī
Khowst
(A 'line of control' was agreed between India and Pakistan in 1972)
DEMCHOK/ DÊMQOG (administered by China, claimed by India)
Xinjiang Uygur Zizhiqu
Taklimakan Shamo
CHINA
Xizang Zizhiqu (Tibet)
Zarghūn Shahr
Kalāt
Indus
Rāvi
Himalayas
Spīn Būldak
Toba Kākar Range
PAKISTAN
INDIA
NEPAL
Sulaimān Range

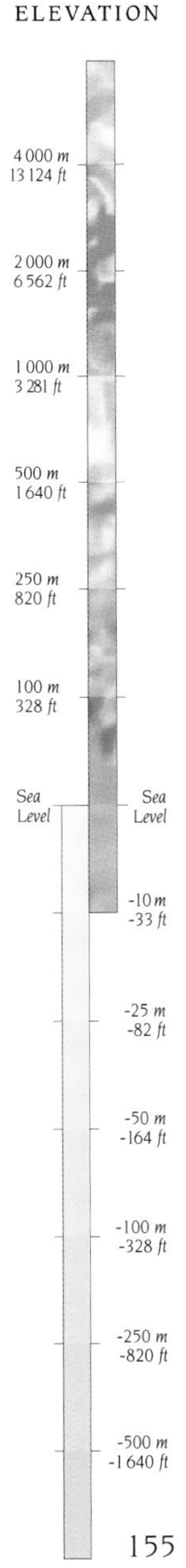
ELEVATION
4 000 m
13 124 ft
2 000 m
6 562 ft
1 000 m
3 281 ft
500 m
1 640 ft
250 m
820 ft
100 m
328 ft
Sea Level
Sea Level
-10 m
-33 ft
-25 m
-82 ft
-50 m
-164 ft
-100 m
-328 ft
-250 m
-820 ft
-500 m
-1 640 ft

SOUTH & EAST ASIA

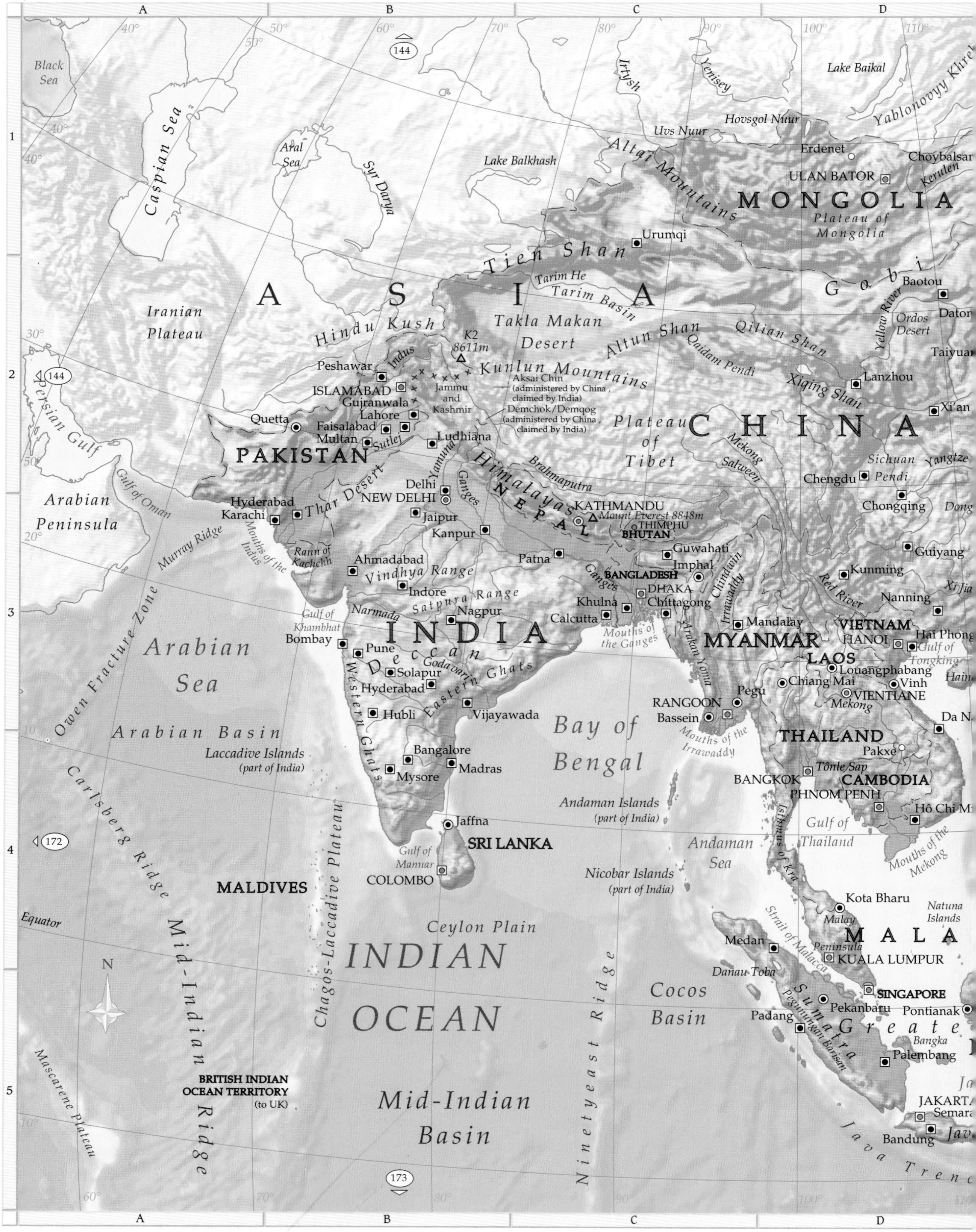
A
B
C
D
1
2
3
4
5
40°
50°
60°
70°
80°
90°
100°
110°
30°
20°
10°
144
172
173
Black Sea
Caspian Sea
Aral Sea
Syr Darya
Lake Balkhash
Irtysh
Yenisey
Lake Baikal
Yablonovyy Khrebet
Hovsgol Nuur
Uvs Nuur
Altai Mountains
Erdenet
Choybalsan
ULAN BATOR
Kerulen
MONGOLIA
Plateau of Mongolia
Urumqi
Tien Shan
Tarim He
Tarim Basin
Gobi
Baotou
Datong
Ordos Desert
Yellow River
Taiyuan
A S I A
Iranian Plateau
Hindu Kush
K2 8611m
Takla Makan Desert
Altun Shan
Qilian Shan
Qaidam Pendi
Lanzhou
Xiqing Shan
Xi'an
Kunlun Mountains
Aksai Chin (administered by China, claimed by India)
Demchok/Demqog (administered by China, claimed by India)
Jammu and Kashmir
Peshawar
Indus
ISLAMABAD
Gujranwala
Lahore
Faisalabad
Multan
Sutlej
Quetta
Persian Gulf
PAKISTAN
Ludhiana
Yamuna
Plateau of Tibet
CHINA
Mekong
Salween
Sichuan Pendi
Yangtze
Chengdu
Chongqing
Brahmaputra
Himalayas
NEPAL
Ganges
Delhi
NEW DELHI
KATHMANDU
Mount Everest 8848m
THIMPHU
BHUTAN
Gulf of Oman
Arabian Peninsula
Hyderabad
Karachi
Thar Desert
Jaipur
Kanpur
Guiyang
Mouths of the Indus
Murray Ridge
Rann of Kachchh
Ahmadabad
Vindhya Range
Patna
Guwahati
Imphal
Chindwin
BANGLADESH
DHAKA
Kunming
Red River
Nanning
Xi Jiang
Owen Fracture Zone
Indore
Satpura Range
Khulna
Chittagong
Irrawaddy
Mandalay
Gulf of Khambhat
Narmada
Nagpur
Calcutta
Mouths of the Ganges
VIETNAM
HANOI
Hai Phong
Gulf of Tongking
Arabian Sea
Bombay
Pune
INDIA
Deccan
Godavari
Solapur
MYANMAR
Arakan Yoma
LAOS
Louangphabang
Chiang Mai
Vinh
Hyderabad
Eastern Ghats
Western Ghats
Pegu
VIENTIANE
Mekong
RANGOON
Bassein
Hubli
Vijayawada
Bay of Bengal
Mouths of the Irrawaddy
Da Nang
Arabian Basin
THAILAND
Pakxe
Laccadive Islands (part of India)
Bangalore
Madras
Mysore
Tônlé Sap
BANGKOK
CAMBODIA
PHNOM PENH
Carlsberg Ridge
Andaman Islands (part of India)
Hô Chi Minh
Jaffna
Gulf of Thailand
SRI LANKA
Andaman Sea
Isthmus of Kra
Mouths of the Mekong
Gulf of Mannar
COLOMBO
MALDIVES
Chagos-Laccadive Plateau
Nicobar Islands (part of India)
Kota Bharu
Natuna Islands
Equator
Malay Peninsula
MALAYSIA
Ceylon Plain
Strait of Malacca
Medan
KUALA LUMPUR
INDIAN OCEAN
Danau Toba
N
Mid-Indian Ridge
Ninetyeast Ridge
Cocos Basin
SINGAPORE
Sumatra
Pekanbaru
Pontianak
Padang
Pegunungan Barisan
Greater
Bangka
Palembang
Mascarene Plateau
BRITISH INDIAN OCEAN TERRITORY (to UK)
Mid-Indian Basin
JAKARTA
Semarang
Bandung
Java
Java Trench

POPULATION

- Less than 50,000
- 50,000 – 100,000
- 100,000 – 500,000
- Over 500,000

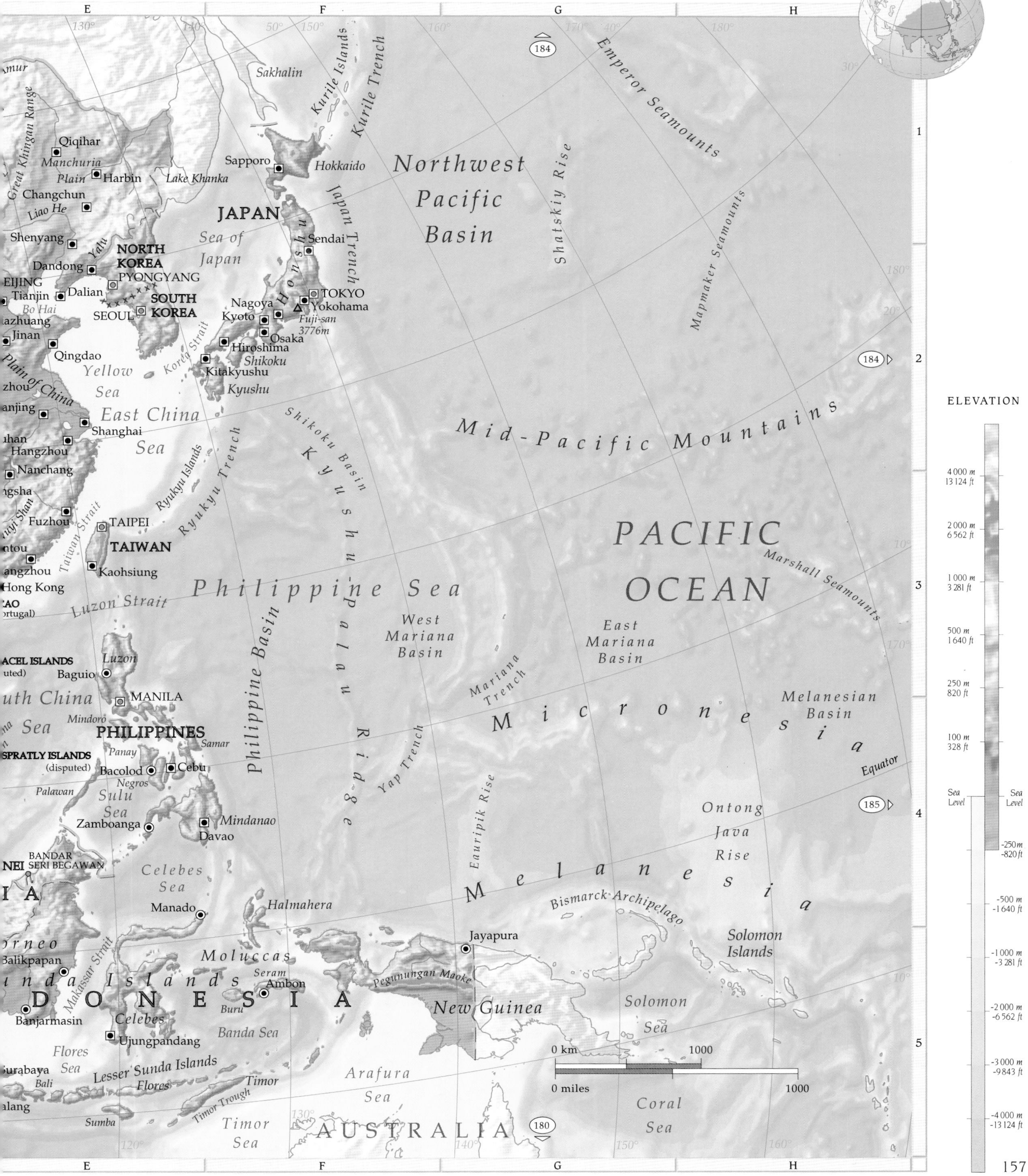
Northwest Pacific Basin
PACIFIC OCEAN
Mid-Pacific Mountains
Philippine Sea
JAPAN
NORTH KOREA
SOUTH KOREA
TAIWAN
PHILIPPINES
Sea of Japan
Yellow Sea
East China Sea
Sakhalin
Kurile Islands
Kurile Trench
Hokkaido
Honshu
Japan Trench
Sapporo
Sendai
TOKYO
Yokohama
Fuji-san 3776m
Nagoya
Kyoto
Osaka
Hiroshima
Shikoku
Kitakyushu
Kyushu
Korea Strait
PYONGYANG
SEOUL
Qiqihar
Manchuria Plain
Harbin
Lake Khanka
Changchun
Liao He
Shenyang
Yalu
Dandong
Dalian
Tianjin
Bo Hai
Jinan
Qingdao
Shanghai
Hangzhou
Nanchang
Fuzhou
TAIPEI
Kaohsiung
Taiwan Strait
Hong Kong
Luzon Strait
Ryukyu Islands
Ryukyu Trench
Shikoku Basin
Kyushu-Palau Ridge
Philippine Basin
West Mariana Basin
East Mariana Basin
Mariana Trench
Yap Trench
Eauripik Rise
Shatskiy Rise
Emperor Seamounts
Mapmaker Seamounts
Marshall Seamounts
Melanesian Basin
Micronesia
Melanesia
Equator
Ontong Java Rise
Bismarck Archipelago
Solomon Islands
Solomon Sea
Coral Sea
Luzon
Baguio
MANILA
Mindoro
Samar
Panay
Negros
Bacolod
Cebu
Palawan
Sulu Sea
Zamboanga
Mindanao
Davao
SPRATLY ISLANDS (disputed)
BANDAR SERI BEGAWAN
Celebes Sea
Manado
Halmahera
Jayapura
Moluccas
Seram
Ambon
Buru
Banda Sea
Pegunungan Maoke
New Guinea
Makassar Strait
Balikpapan
Banjarmasin
Celebes
Ujungpandang
Flores Sea
Lesser Sunda Islands
Bali
Flores
Timor
Timor Trough
Sumba
Timor Sea
Arafura Sea
AUSTRALIA
0 km 1000
0 miles 1000
184
185
180
ELEVATION
4 000 m 13 124 ft
2 000 m 6 562 ft
1 000 m 3 281 ft
500 m 1 640 ft
250 m 820 ft
100 m 328 ft
Sea Level
-250 m -820 ft
-500 m -1 640 ft
-1 000 m -3 281 ft
-2 000 m -6 562 ft
-3 000 m -9 843 ft
-4 000 m -13 124 ft

Western China & Mongolia

A
B
C
D
1
2
3
4
5
65°
70°
75°
80°
55°
85°
90°
95°
100°
50°
45°
35°
30°
25°
N
146
0 km
400
0 miles
400
Kulunda
Steppe
Yenisey
RUSSIAN FE
Zapadnyy Sayan
Hövsgöl Nuur
KAZAKHSTAN
Kazakhskiy
Melkosopochnik
Ozero Balkhash
Ozero Zaysan
Uvs Nuur
Ulaangom
Ölgiy
Altai Mountains
Altay
Charus Nuur
Hyargas Nuur
Har Nuur
Hovd
Mörö
Hangayn Nuruu
Tsetserleg
Ulungur Hu
MON
Altay
Bayanhongor
Karamay
Gurbantünggüt Shamo
Boholo Shan
Kuytun
Yining
Shihezi
Fukang
Jimsar
Ürümqi
Qitai
Aj Bogd Uul 3802m
Atas Bogd 2702m
Ozero Issyk-Kul'
KYRGYZSTAN
Tien Shan
Pik Pobedy 7439m
Turpan
Turpan Pendi
Hami
G
155
Bosten Hu
Korla
Kuruktag
Xingxingxia
Ejin Qi
Kashi
Tarim He
Tarim Basin
Lop Nur
TAJIKISTAN
Yengisar
XINJIANG UYGUR
GANSU
Shache
ZIZHIQU
Qilian Shan
AFGH.
Yecheng
(claimed by India)
Pishan
Taklimakan
Ruoqiang
Altun Shan
Danghe Nanshan
Moyu
Shamo
Hotan
Qira
Qaidam
Karakoram Range
K2 8611m
PAKISTAN
Kashmir
Kunlun Shan
Qinghai Hu
AKSAI CHIN
Golmud
Pendi
Dulan
Burhan Budai Shan
166
JAMMU AND KASHMIR
Indus
AKSAI CHIN (administered by China, claimed by India)
C
H
A'nyêmaqên Shan
Rutog
Qingzang Gaoyuan
QINGHAI
Tongtian He
DEMCHOK/ DÊMQOG (administered by China, claimed by India)
(Plateau of Tibet)
Bayan Har Shan
Gar
XIZANG
Tanggula Shan
Yushu
Mekong
Zanda
Nyima
Siling Co
Amdo
ZIZHIQU
Tangra Yumco
Gyaring Co
Nagqu
Qamdo
(Tibet)
Ngangzê Co
Nam Co
Damxung
Salween
Jinsha Jiang
Himalaya
Brahmaputra
Nyainqêntanglha Shan
Yamuna
Ganges
Lhazê
Xigazê
Maizhokunggar
Lhasa
ARUNÁCHAL PRADESH (claimed by China)
Hengduan Shan
NEPAL
Gonggar
Gyangzê
Mount Everest 8848m
INDIA
BHUTAN
INDIA
167
MYANMAR

POPULATION

- Less than 50,000
- 50,000 – 100,000
- 100,000 – 500,000
- Over 500,000

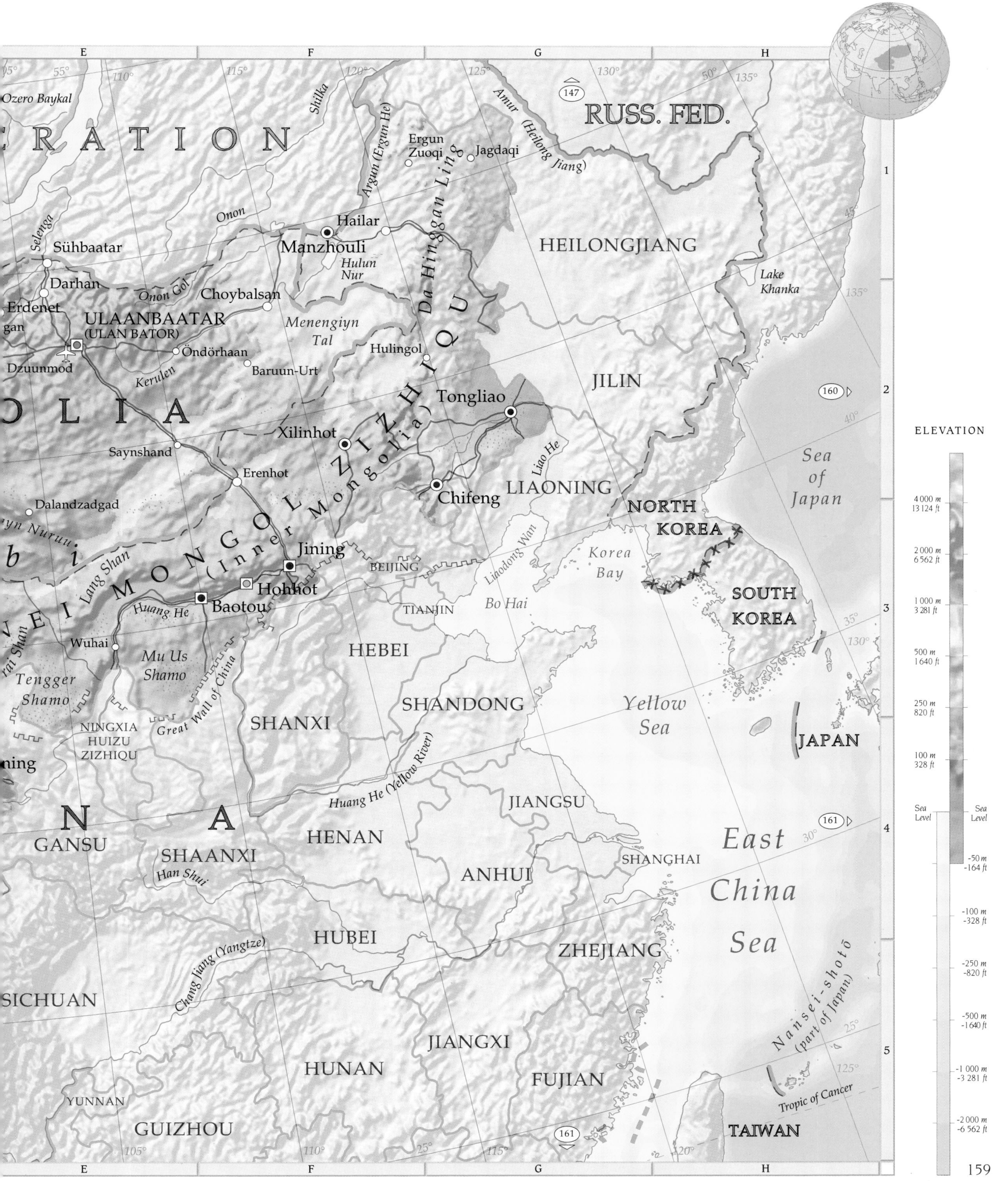
E
F
G
H
1
2
3
4
5
147
160
161
Ozero Baykal
Shilka
RUSS. FED.
Amur (Heilong Jiang)
Argun (Ergun He)
Ergun Zuoqi
Jagdaqi
Da Hinggan Ling
Hailar
Onon
Selenga
Sühbaatar
Manzhouli
Hulun Nur
HEILONGJIANG
Lake Khanka
Darhan
Onon Gol
Choybalsan
Erdenet
ULAANBAATAR (ULAN BATOR)
Menengiyn Tal
Hulingol
Öndörhaan
Baruun-Urt
Dzuunmod
Kerulen
JILIN
Tongliao
Xilinhot
Saynshand
Erenhot
Liao He
Sea of Japan
NEI MONGOL ZIZHIQU (Inner Mongolia)
Chifeng
LIAONING
NORTH KOREA
Dalandzadgad
Jining
BEIJING
Liaodong Wan
Korea Bay
Lang Shan
Hohhot
Baotou
Huang He
Bo Hai
TIANJIN
SOUTH KOREA
Wuhai
Mu Us Shamo
HEBEI
Tengger Shamo
Great Wall of China
SHANDONG
Yellow Sea
SHANXI
NINGXIA HUIZU ZIZHIQU
JAPAN
Huang He (Yellow River)
JIANGSU
GANSU
HENAN
SHAANXI
Han Shui
ANHUI
SHANGHAI
East China Sea
HUBEI
Chang Jiang (Yangtze)
ZHEJIANG
SICHUAN
Nansei-shotō (part of Japan)
JIANGXI
HUNAN
FUJIAN
Tropic of Cancer
YUNNAN
GUIZHOU
TAIWAN
ELEVATION
4 000 m 13 124 ft
2 000 m 6 562 ft
1 000 m 3 281 ft
500 m 1 640 ft
250 m 820 ft
100 m 328 ft
Sea Level
-50 m -164 ft
-100 m -328 ft
-250 m -820 ft
-500 m -1 640 ft
-1 000 m -3 281 ft
-2 000 m -6 562 ft

Eastern China & Korea

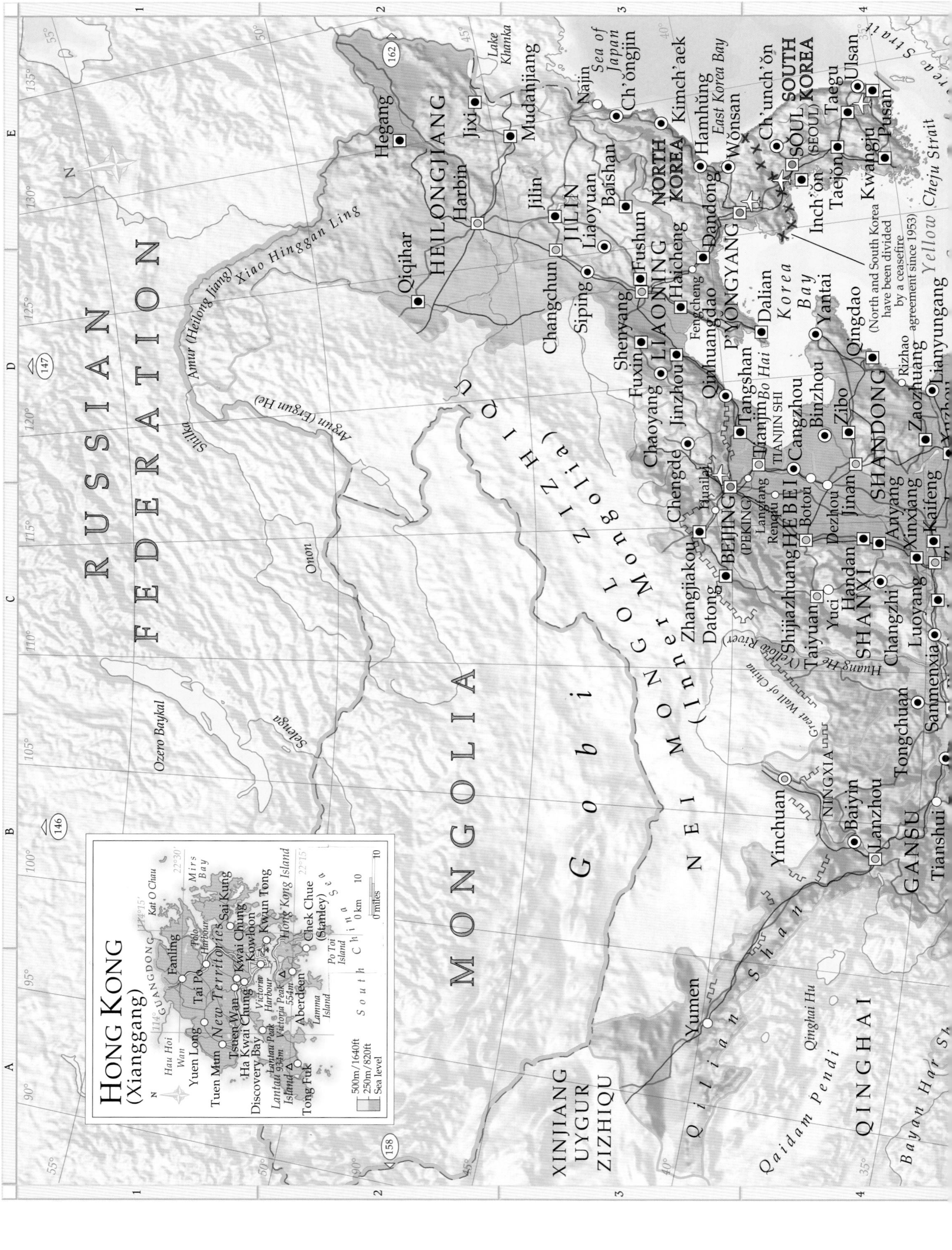
RUSSIAN FEDERATION
MONGOLIA
NEI MONGOL ZIZHIQU (Inner Mongolia)
Gobi
HEILONGJIANG
JILIN
LIAONING
HEBEI
SHANDONG
SHANXI
NINGXIA
GANSU
QINGHAI
XINJIANG UYGUR ZIZHIQU
NORTH KOREA
SOUTH KOREA
BEIJING (PEKING)
TIANJIN SHI
P'YONGYANG
SOUL (SEOUL)
Ozero Baykal
Selenga
Onon
Shilka
Argun (Ergun He)
Amur (Heilong Jiang)
Xiao Hinggan Ling
Lake Khanka
Sea of Japan
East Korea Bay
Korea Bay
Bo Hai
Yellow
Cheju Strait
Huang He (Yellow River)
Great Wall of China
Qilian Shan
Qaidam Pendi
Qinghai Hu
Bayan Har Sh
(North and South Korea have been divided by a ceasefire agreement since 1953)
Hegang
Jixi
Mudanjiang
Harbin
Qiqihar
Jilin
Changchun
Siping
Liaoyuan
Baishan
Fushun
Shenyang
Fuxin
Chaoyang
Jinzhou
Haicheng
Fengcheng
Dandong
Dalian
Yantai
Qingdao
Rizhao
Lianyungang
Najin
Ch'ŏngjin
Kimch'aek
Hamhŭng
Wŏnsan
Ch'unch'ŏn
Inch'ŏn
Taejŏn
Taegu
Ulsan
Kwangju
Pusan
Qinhuangdao
Tangshan
Tianjin
Cangzhou
Binzhou
Zibo
Jinan
Dezhou
Zaozhuang
Chengde
Huailai
Langfang
Renqiu
Botou
Zhangjiakou
Datong
Shijiazhuang
Handan
Anyang
Xinxiang
Kaifeng
Taiyuan
Yuci
Changzhi
Luoyang
Sanmenxia
Tongchuan
Yinchuan
Baiyin
Lanzhou
Tianshui
Yumen
HONG KONG (Xianggang)
GUANGDONG
New Territories
Kat O Chau
Mirs Bay
Hau Hoi Wan
Yuen Long
Tuen Mun
Fanling
Tai Po
Tolo Harbour
Sai Kung
Tsuen Wan
Kwai Chung
Ha Kwai Chung
Kowloon
Kwun Tong
Victoria Harbour
Victoria Peak 554m
Hong Kong Island
Discovery Bay
Lantau Peak 934m
Lantau Island
Aberdeen
Lamma Island
Chek Chue (Stanley)
Po Toi Island
Tong Fuk
South China Sea
500m/1640ft
250m/820ft
Sea level
0 km 10
0 miles 10

POPULATION

- Less than 50,000
- 50,000 – 100,000
- 100,000 – 500,000
- Over 500,000

CHINA
JAPAN
East China Sea
Okinawa
Nansei-shoto (part of Japan)
(China and Taiwan claim all of each others' territory)
Tropic of Cancer
PACIFIC OCEAN
TAIWAN
TAIPEI
Chilung
T'aichung
Chiai
T'ainan
Kaohsiung
Taiwan Strait
Luzon Strait
PHILIPPINES
South China Sea
PARACEL ISLANDS (disputed by China, Taiwan & Vietnam)
Amphitrite Group
Crescent Group
Triton Island
SPRATLY ISLANDS (disputed by China, Malaysia, Philippines, Taiwan & Vietnam)
Flat Island
Nanshan Island
Thitu Island
Loaita Island
Namyit Island
Len Dao
Spratly Island
Hong Kong (Xianggang)
MACAO (Portuguese special territory)
Hainan Dao
HAINAN
Haikou
Xuwen
Danxian
Dongfang
Gulf of Tongking
Gulf of Thailand
VIETNAM
CAMBODIA
THAILAND
LAOS
MYANMAR
INDIA
XIZANG ZIZHIQU (TIBET)
Hengduan Shan
Wuliang Shan
Salween
Mekong
Jinsha Jiang
Chang Jiang (Yangtze)
Red River
Dongting Hu
Sichuan Pendi
SICHUAN
YUNNAN
GUIZHOU
GUANGXI ZHUANGZU ZIZHIQU
GUANGDONG
HUNAN
HUBEI
JIANGXI
FUJIAN
ZHEJIANG
ANHUI
Shanghai
Suzhou
Wuxi
Nanjing
Hefei
Wuhu
Anqing
Jiaxing
Ningbo
Hangzhou
Jinhua
Wenzhou
Huangshi
Huangshan
Jingdezhen
Shangrao
Linchuan
Nanchang
Jiujiang
Wuhan
Xinyang
Yichang
Yueyang
Changsha
Xiangtan
Loudi
Hengyang
Chenzhou
Lengshuitan
Quanzhou
Guilin
Liuzhou
Zhaoqing
Guangzhou
Dongguan
Shaoguan
Ganzhou
Longyan
Zhangzhou
Xiamen
Quanzhou
Yong'an
Nanping
Fuzhou
Shantou
Jiangmen
Maoming
Zhanjiang
Suixi
Yulin
Nanning
Qinzhou
Beihai
Guangyuan
Wanxian
Lichuan
Chongqing
Neijiang
Zigong
Leshan
Chengdu
Ya'an
Mianyang
Zunyi
Huaihua
Guiyang
Anshun
Kunming
Gejiu
Xichang
Litang
Dali
Baoshan
Jinghong
0 km 200
0 miles 200
184
171
168
A B C D E
5 6 7 8
30° 25° 20° 15° 10°
95° 100° 105° 110° 115° 120°

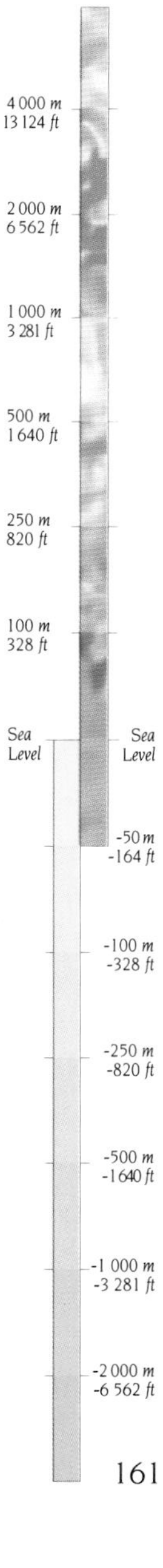
ELEVATION
4 000 m 13 124 ft
2 000 m 6 562 ft
1 000 m 3 281 ft
500 m 1 640 ft
250 m 820 ft
100 m 328 ft
Sea Level
Sea Level
-50 m -164 ft
-100 m -328 ft
-250 m -820 ft
-500 m -1640 ft
-1 000 m -3 281 ft
-2 000 m -6 562 ft

JAPAN

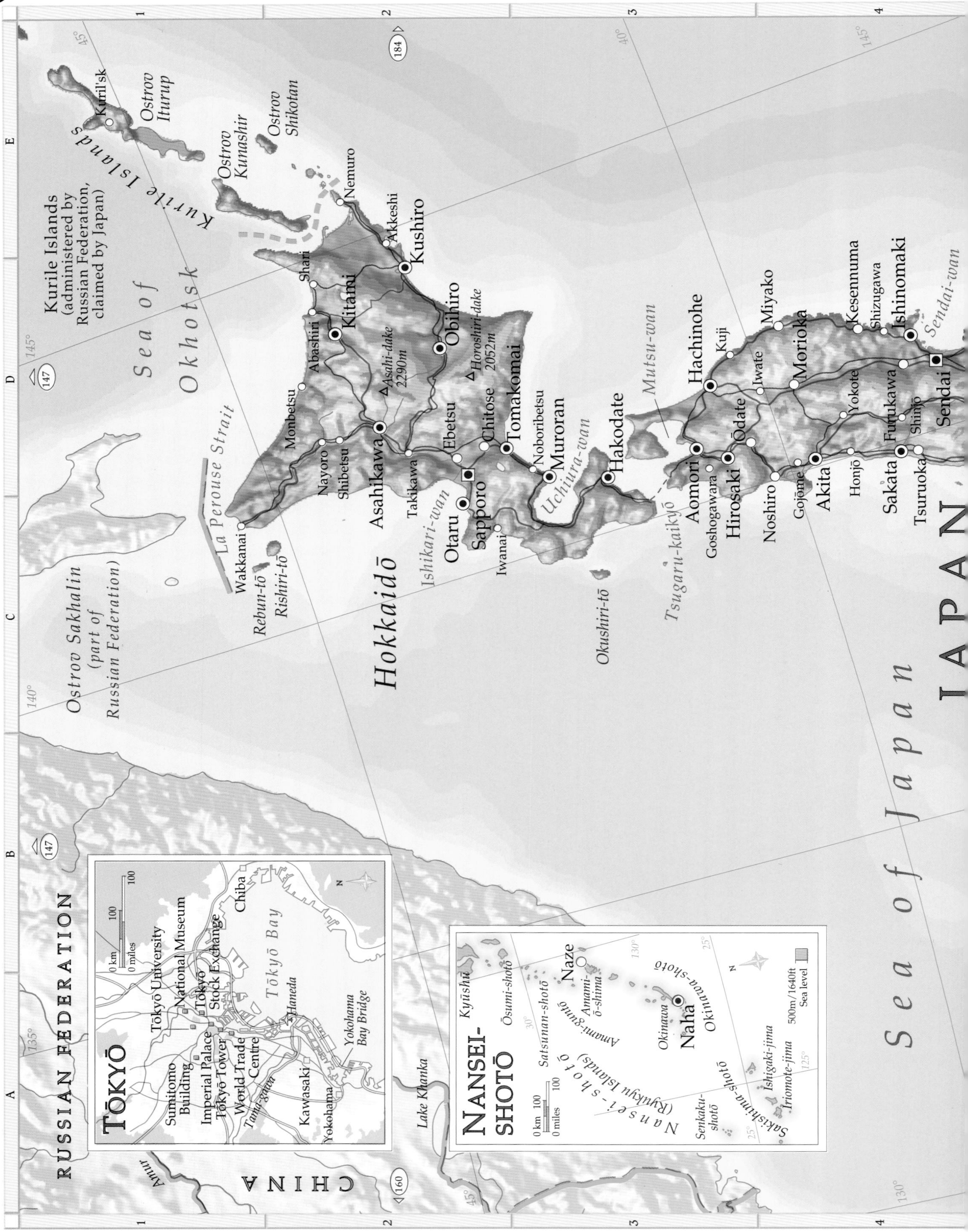

RUSSIAN FEDERATION
CHINA
Amur
Lake Khanka
Ostrov Sakhalin (part of Russian Federation)
Sea of Okhotsk
Kurile Islands
Kurile Islands (administered by Russian Federation, claimed by Japan)
Kuril'sk
Ostrov Iturup
Ostrov Kunashir
Ostrov Shikotan
Nemuro
Akkeshi
Kushiro
Shari
Kitami
Abashiri
Obihiro
Horoshiri-dake 2052m
Asahi-dake 2290m
Monbetsu
La Perouse Strait
Wakkanai
Rebun-tō
Rishiri-tō
Nayoro
Shibetsu
Asahikawa
Takikawa
Hokkaidō
Ishikari-wan
Otaru
Sapporo
Ebetsu
Chitose
Tomakomai
Noboribetsu
Muroran
Uchiura-wan
Iwanai
Hakodate
Okushiri-tō
Mutsu-wan
Tsugaru-kaikyō
Aomori
Goshogawara
Hirosaki
Hachinohe
Kuji
Ōdate
Noshiro
Iwate
Morioka
Miyako
Akita
Gojōme
Yokote
Honjō
Kesennuma
Shizugawa
Ishinomaki
Sendai-wan
Sendai
Furukawa
Shinjō
Sakata
Tsuruoka
Sea of Japan
JAPAN
TŌKYŌ
Sumitomo Building
Imperial Palace
Tōkyō Tower
World Trade Centre
Tama-gawa
Kawasaki
Yokohama
Tōkyō University
National Museum
Tōkyō Stock Exchange
Haneda
Yokohama Bay Bridge
Tōkyō Bay
Chiba
0 km 100
0 miles 100
NANSEI-SHOTŌ
Kyūshū
Ōsumi-shotō
Satsunan-shotō
Naze
Amami-shotō
Amami-ō-shima
Okinawa
Naha
Okinawa-shotō
Nansei-shotō (Ryukyu Islands)
Sakishima-shotō
Ishigaki-jima
Iriomote-jima
Senkaku-shotō
500m/1640ft
Sea level
0 km 100
0 miles 100
147
184
160

POPULATION

Less than 50,000

50,000 – 100,000

100,000 – 500,000

Over 500,000

5
6
7
8
A
B
C
D
E
35°
30°
135°
130°
140°
184
161
Honshū
Shikoku
Kyūshū
PACIFIC
OCEAN
East
China Sea
SOUTH
KOREA
Iwaki
Hitachi
Utsunomiya
Mito
Chōshi
Chiba
Yokohama
Bōsō-hantō
Oyama
Kasumiga-ura
Kawagoe
TŌKYŌ
Kawasaki
Sukagawa
Maebashi
Mikuni-sanmyaku
Nagaoka
Shinano-gawa
Jōetsu
Itoigawa
Nagano
Matsumoto
Kōfu
Fuji-san
3776m
Fuji
Shizuoka
Toyota
Hamamatsu
Izu-hantō
Suruga-wan
Sagami-nada
Ō-shima
Nii-jima
Kōzu-shima
Miyake-jima
Mikura-jima
Hachijō-jima
Izu-shotō
Toyama
Takaoka
Toyama-wan
Hida-sanmyaku
Nakatsugawa
Gifu
Ōgaki
Nagoya
Okazaki
Ise-wan
Ise
Tsu
Owase
Shingū
Ōtsu
Kanazawa
Komatsu
Fukui
Tsuruga
Wakasa-wan
Biwa-ko
Kyōto
Ōsaka
Kōbe
Wakayama
Gobō
Tanabe
Awaji-shima
Kii-suidō
Himeji
Harima-nada
Tottori
Tokushima
Niihama
Kōchi
Tosa-wan
Matsuyama
Nakamura
Sukumo
Okayama
Kurashiki
Yonago
Matsue
Chūgoku-sanchi
Kure
Hiroshima
Iwakuni
Hōfu
Ube
Yamaguchi
Masuda
Hamada
Gōtsu
Nagato
Shimonoseki
Kitakyūshū
Oki-shotō
Dōgo
Dōzen
Liancourt Rocks
(claimed by Japan
& South Korea)
Iyo-nada
Bungo-suidō
Ōita
Nobeoka
Miyazaki
Miyakonojō
Shibushi-wan
Tanega-shima
Yaku-shima
Fukuoka
Kurume
Ōmuta
Kumamoto
Yatsushiro
Sendai
Kagoshima
Kagoshima-wan
Ōsumi-shotō
Sasebo
Nagasaki
Amakusa-nada
Koshikijima-rettō
Gotō-rettō
Iki
Tsushima
Korea Strait
Kō-saki
0 km
200
0 miles
200

ELEVATION

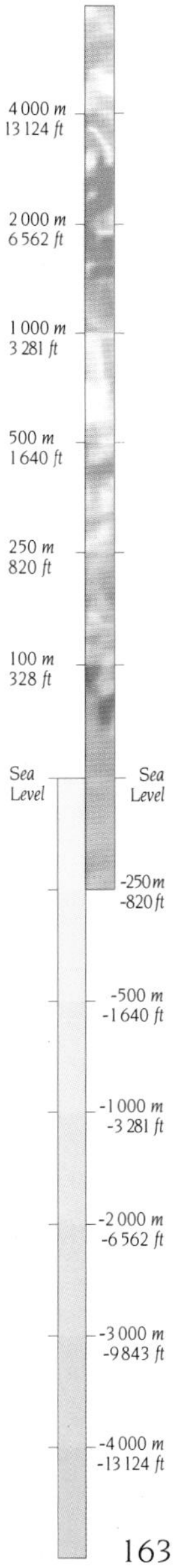

4 000 m
13 124 ft
2 000 m
6 562 ft
1 000 m
3 281 ft
500 m
1 640 ft
250 m
820 ft
100 m
328 ft
Sea Level
Sea Level
-250 m
-820 ft
-500 m
-1 640 ft
-1 000 m
-3 281 ft
-2 000 m
-6 562 ft
-3 000 m
-9 843 ft
-4 000 m
-13 124 ft

SOUTH INDIA & SRI LANKA

A
B
C
D
1
2
3
4
5
70°
75°
80°
15°
10°
5°
166
153
105
172
N
Equator
Arabian
Sea
INDIA
SRI LANKA
MALDIVES
INDIAN
Kalyān
Bombay
(Mumbai)
Pune
Ahmadnagar
Bārāmati
Nānded
Nizāmābād
Karīmnagar
Jagdalpur
Andhra Pradesh
Godāvari
Vizianagaram
Visākhapatnam
Rājahmundry
Kākināda
Solāpur
Sāngli
Secunderābād
Hyderābād
Gulbarga
Kolhāpur
Western Ghats
Deccan
Eastern Ghats
Karnātaka
Krishna
Vijayawāda
Machilīpatnam
Rāichūr
Kurnool
Belgaum
Panaji
(Goa)
Hubli
Gadag
Chīrāla
Ongole
Nandyāl
Tādpatri
Kāvali
Tungabhadra
Reservoir
Dāvangere
Anantapur
Nellore
Cuddapah
Shimoga
Bhadrāvati
Udupi
Tumkūr
Mangalore
Bangalore
Vellore
Madras
Kāsaragod
Mandya
Kānchīpuram
Krishnagiri
Tiruppattūr
Cannanore
Mysore
Coromandel Coast
Pondicherry
Salem
Calicut
Erode
Neyveli
Kerala
Malabār Coast
Coimbatore
Tamil Nādu
Trichūr
Tiruchchirāppalli
Ernākulam
Dindigul
Madurai
Palk Strait
Cochin
Jaffna
Alleppey
Quilon
Rājapālaiyam
Mannar
Vavuniya
Trivandrum
Tuticorin
Trincomalee
Nāgercoil
Puttalam
Anuradhapura
Gulf of
Mannar
Batticaloa
Matale
Negombo
Kandy
COLOMBO
Sri Jayawardanapura
Kalutara
Ratnapura
Galle
Matara
Amīndīvi
Islands
Lakshadweep
(Laccadive Islands)
(part of India)
Kavaratti
Island
Kalpeni
Island
Nine Degree Channel
Minicoy Island
Eight Degree Channel
Ihavandippolhu
Atoll
Faadhippolhu
Atoll
Horsburgh
Atoll
Male'Atoll
MALE'
Ari Atoll
Felidhu Atoll
Mulaku Atoll
Kolhumadulu
Atoll
Hadhdhunmathi Atoll
North Huvadhu Atoll
South Huvadhu
Atoll
Gan
Addu Atoll

POPULATION

- Less than 50,000
- 50,000 – 100,000
- 100,000 – 500,000
- Over 500,000

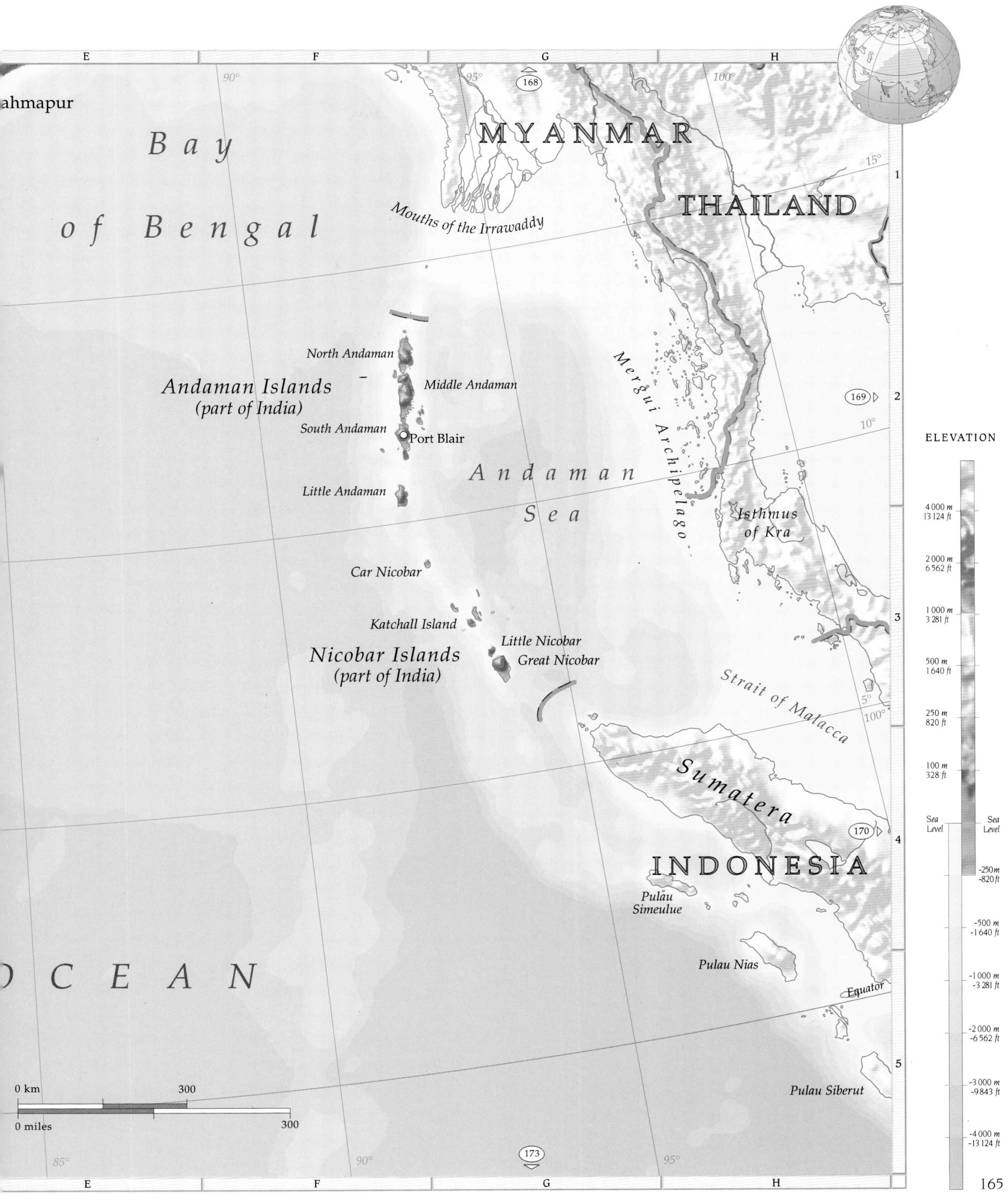
ahmapur
Bay of Bengal
MYANMAR
THAILAND
Mouths of the Irrawaddy
North Andaman
Middle Andaman
Andaman Islands
(part of India)
South Andaman
Port Blair
Little Andaman
Andaman Sea
Mergui Archipelago
Isthmus of Kra
Car Nicobar
Katchall Island
Little Nicobar
Great Nicobar
Nicobar Islands
(part of India)
Strait of Malacca
Sumatera
INDONESIA
Pulau Simeulue
Pulau Nias
Equator
Pulau Siberut
OCEAN
0 km
300
0 miles
300
168
169
170
173
ELEVATION
4 000 m
13 124 ft
2 000 m
6 562 ft
1 000 m
3 281 ft
500 m
1 640 ft
250 m
820 ft
100 m
328 ft
Sea Level
-250 m
-820 ft
-500 m
-1 640 ft
-1 000 m
-3 281 ft
-2 000 m
-6 562 ft
-3 000 m
-9 843 ft
-4 000 m
-13 124 ft

NORTH INDIA, PAKISTAN & BANGLADESH

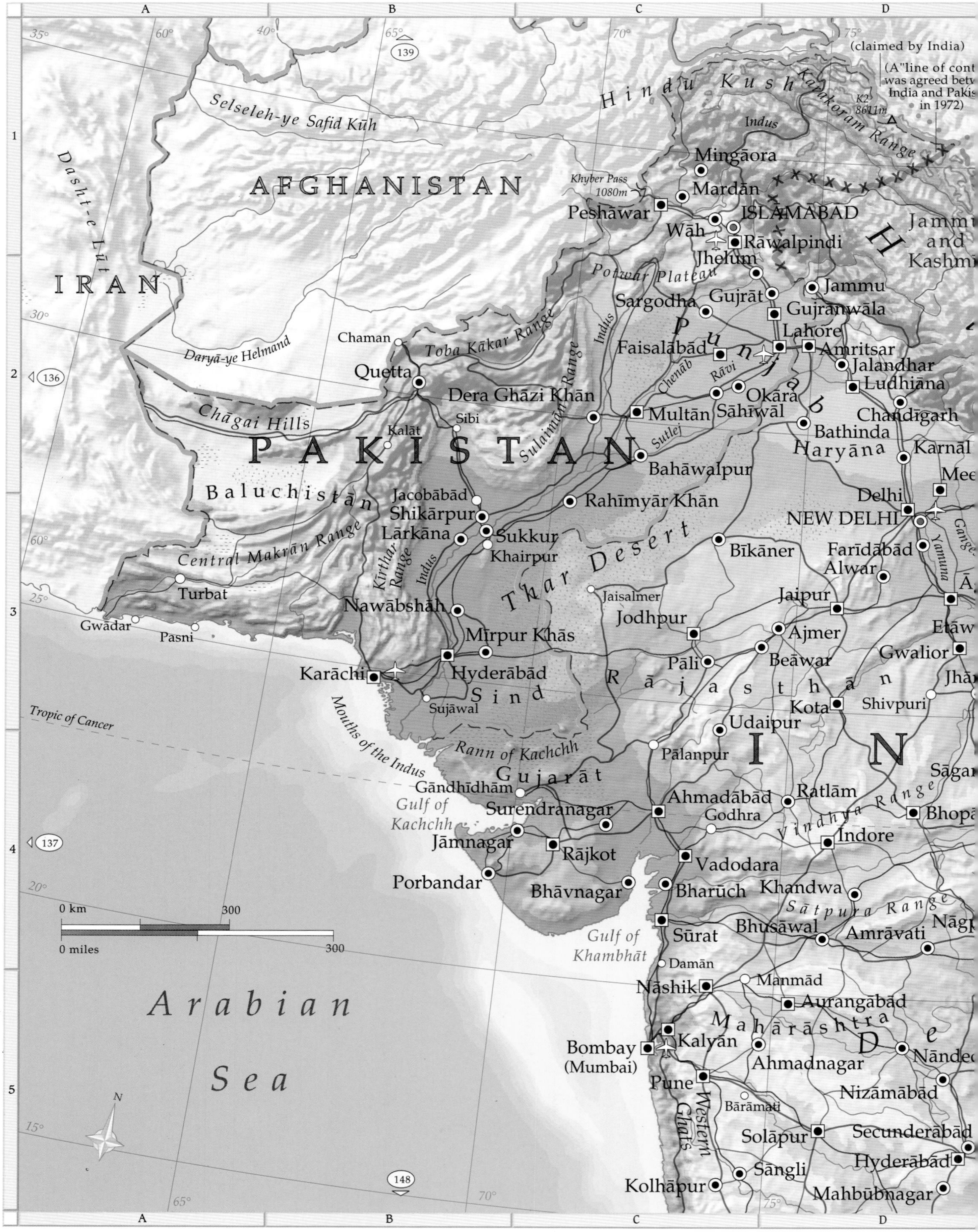

A
B
C
D
1
2
3
4
5
35°
40°
60°
65°
70°
75°
30°
25°
20°
15°
139
136
137
148
(claimed by India)
(A "line of cont
was agreed betw
India and Pakis
in 1972)
Selseleh-ye Safid Kūh
Hindū Kush
Karakoram Range
K2
8611m
Indus
Dasht-e Lūt
AFGHANISTAN
IRAN
Khyber Pass
1080m
Mingāora
Mardān
Peshāwar
ISLAMABAD
Wāh
Rāwalpindi
Jhelum
Jammu and Kashmi
Potwar Plateau
Sargodha
Gujrāt
Jammu
Gujranwāla
Lahore
Chaman
Toba Kākar Range
Darya-ye Helmand
Faisalābād
Amritsar
Jalandhar
Ludhiāna
Quetta
Dera Ghāzi Khān
Sulaimān Range
Chenāb
Rāvi
Okāra
Sāhīwāl
Chāgai Hills
Sibi
Multān
Punjab
Chandīgarh
Kalāt
Bathinda
PAKISTAN
Sutlej
Haryāna
Karnāl
Bahāwalpur
Mee
Baluchistān
Jacobābād
Shikārpur
Rahīmyār Khān
Delhi
NEW DELHI
Lārkāna
Sukkur
Khairpur
Central Makrān Range
Kīrthar Range
Thar Desert
Bīkāner
Farīdābād
Alwar
Yamuna
Turbat
Jaisalmer
Jaipur
Nawābshāh
Jodhpur
Gwādar
Pasni
Mīrpur Khās
Ajmer
Etāw
Beāwar
Gwalior
Pāli
Karāchi
Hyderābād
Sind
Rājasthān
Jhā
Sujāwal
Kota
Shivpuri
Tropic of Cancer
Udaipur
Mouths of the Indus
Rann of Kachchh
Pālanpur
INDIA
Sāgar
Gāndhīdhām
Gujarāt
Ratlām
Ahmadābād
Gulf of Kachchh
Surendranagar
Godhra
Vindhya Range
Bhopā
Jāmnagar
Indore
Rājkot
Vadodara
Porbandar
Bhāvnagar
Bharūch
Khandwa
Sātpura Range
0 km
300
0 miles
300
Bhusāwal
Amrāvati
Nāgp
Sūrat
Gulf of Khambhāt
Damān
Nāshik
Manmād
Aurangābād
Arabian Sea
Mahārāshtra
Kalyān
Bombay
(Mumbai)
Ahmadnagar
Nānded
Pune
Nizāmābād
Bārāmati
Western Ghāts
Solāpur
Secunderābād
N
Hyderābād
Sāngli
Kolhāpur
Mahbūbnagar

POPULATION

- Less than 50,000
- 50,000 – 100,000
- 100,000 – 500,000
- Over 500,000

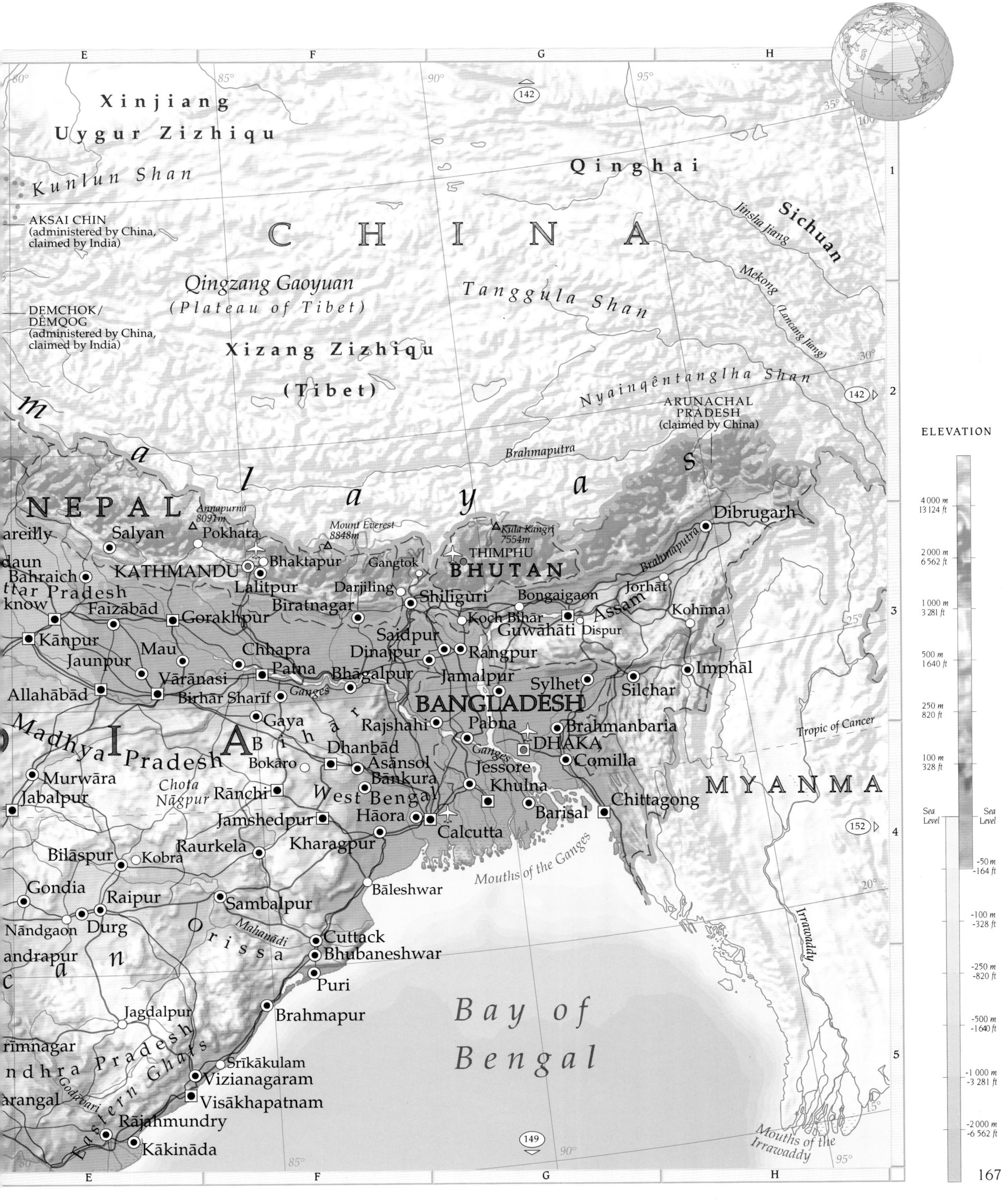
Xinjiang Uygur Zizhiqu
Kunlun Shan
AKSAI CHIN (administered by China, claimed by India)
CHINA
Qinghai
Sichuan
Jinsha Jiang
Mekong (Lancang Jiang)
Qingzang Gaoyuan (Plateau of Tibet)
Tanggula Shan
DEMCHOK/ DÊMQOG (administered by China, claimed by India)
Xizang Zizhiqu (Tibet)
Nyainqêntanglha Shan
ARUNACHAL PRADESH (claimed by China)
Himalayas
Brahmaputra
NEPAL
Annapurna 8091m
Mount Everest 8848m
Kula Kangri 7554m
Dibrugarh
Salyan
Pokhara
Bhaktapur
KATHMANDU
Lalitpur
Gangtok
THIMPHU
BHUTAN
Bahraich
Uttar Pradesh
Faizābād
Gorakhpur
Biratnagar
Darjiling
Shiliguri
Bongaigaon
Jorhat
Assam
Kohīma
Koch Bihar
Guwāhāti
Dispur
Kānpur
Saidpur
Dinajpur
Rangpur
Mau
Chhapra
Jaunpur
Patna
Bhāgalpur
Jamalpur
Sylhet
Silchar
Imphāl
Vārānasi
Allahābād
Birhar Sharīf
Ganges
BANGLADESH
Gaya
Bihar
Rajshahi
Pabna
Brahmanbaria
Madhya Pradesh
INDIA
Dhanbād
DHAKA
Tropic of Cancer
Bokāro
Āsānsol
Comilla
Murwāra
Chota Nāgpur
Rānchi
Bānkura
Jessore
Khulna
MYANMAR
Jabalpur
West Bengal
Barisal
Chittagong
Jamshedpur
Hāora
Calcutta
Raurkela
Kharagpur
Bilāspur
Kobra
Mouths of the Ganges
Bāleshwar
Gondia
Raipur
Sambalpur
Nāndgaon
Durg
Orissa
Mahanādi
Cuttack
Bhubaneshwar
Irrawaddy
Puri
Jagdalpur
Brahmapur
Bay of Bengal
Andhra Pradesh
Eastern Ghats
Godāvari
Srīkākulam
Vizianagaram
Visākhapatnam
Rājahmundry
Kākināda
Mouths of the Irrawaddy
142
149
152
ELEVATION
4 000 m 13 124 ft
2 000 m 6 562 ft
1 000 m 3 281 ft
500 m 1 640 ft
250 m 820 ft
100 m 328 ft
Sea Level
-50 m -164 ft
-100 m -328 ft
-250 m -820 ft
-500 m -1640 ft
-1 000 m -3 281 ft
-2 000 m -6 562 ft

Mainland Southeast Asia

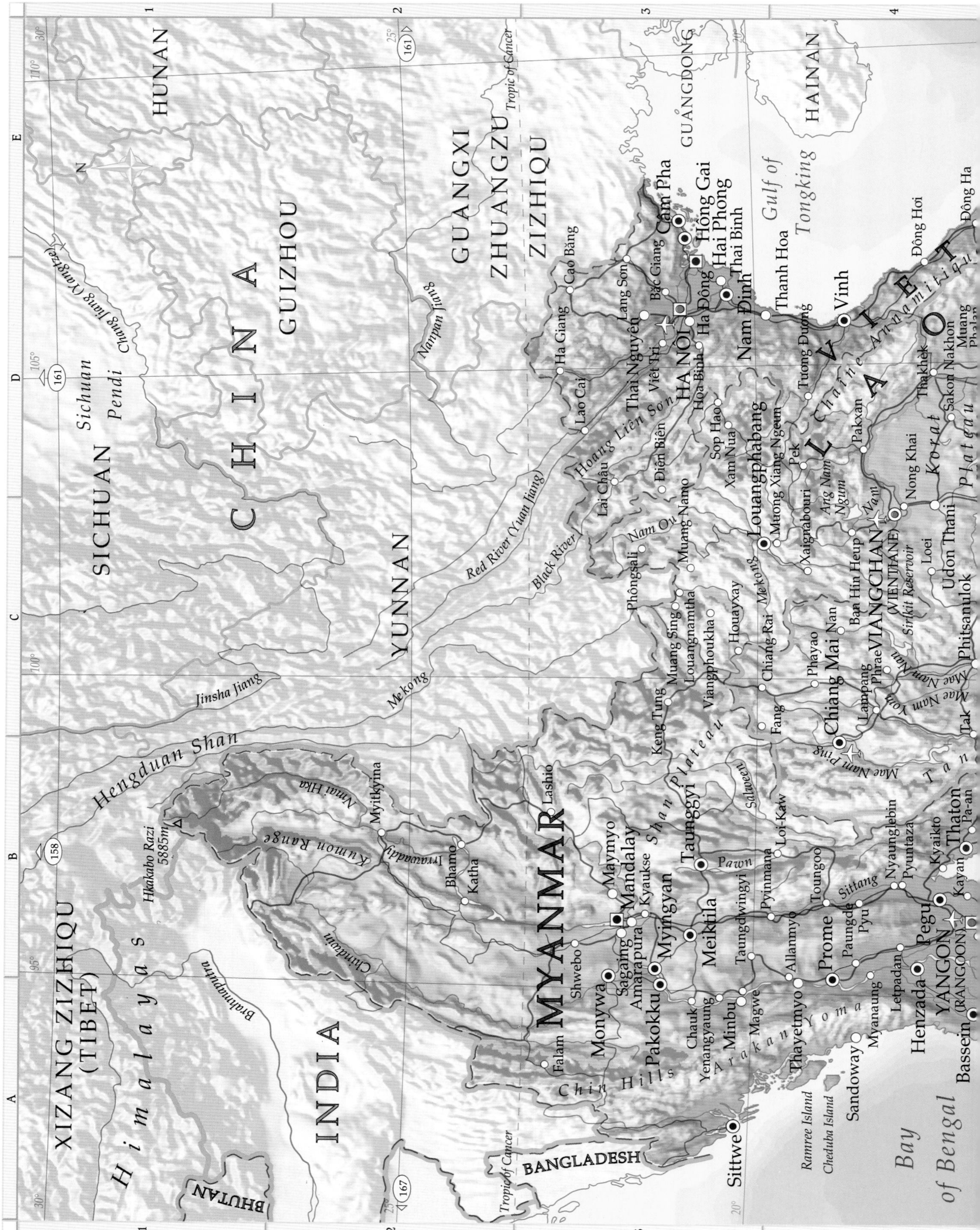

POPULATION

Less than 50,000

50,000 – 100,000

100,000 – 500,000

Over 500,000

CAMBODIA
MALAYSIA
INDONESIA
INDIAN OCEAN
South China Sea
Gulf of Thailand
Andaman Sea
Strait of Malacca
Malay Peninsula
Mergui Archipelago
Sumatera (Sumatra)
KRUNG THEP (BANGKOK)
PHNUM PENH
Hô Chi Minh
Quy Nhon
Cam Ranh
Nha Trang
Đa Lat
Biên Hoa
Vung Tau
My Tho
Cân Tho
Rach Gia
Ca Mau
Bac Liêu
Soc Trăng
Tra Vinh
Long Xuyên
Châu Đôc
Phan Thiêt
Phan Rang-Thap Cham
Tuy Hoa
Quang Ngai
Play Cu
Di Linh
Ubon Ratchathani
Nakhon Ratchasima
Nakhon Sawan
Buriram
Surin
Pakxé
Champasak
Bătdâmbang
Kâmpóng Cham
Kâmpóng Chhnang
Kâmpóng Saôm
Kâmpôt
Pouthisat
Chanthaburi
Rayong
Pattaya
Ayutthaya
Lop Buri
Sara Buri
Samut Prakan
Chon Buri
Nakhon Pathom
Ratchaburi
Phetchaburi
Ban Hua Hin
Chumphon
Lang Suan
Surat Thani
Nakhon Si Thammarat
Pak Phanang
Songkhla
Pattani
Narathiwat
Yala
Hat Yai
Phatthalung
Trang
Phuket
Ko Phuket
Phang-Nga
Ranong
Tavoy
Mergui
Tenasserim
Ye
Isthmus of Kra
Bilauktaung Range
Ko Chang
Ko Phangan
Ko Samui
Ko Lanta
Ko Tarutao
Pulau Langkawi
Pulau Pinang
Thale Luang
Tônlé Sap
Mekong
Mouths of the Mekong
Côn Đao
Andaman Islands (part of India)
North Andaman
Middle Andaman
South Andaman
Little Andaman
Nicobar Islands (part of India)
Car Nicobar
Katchall Island
Little Nicobar
Great Nicobar
Pulau Simeulue
Kepulauan Natuna (part of Indonesia)
Zadetkyi Kyun
Lanbi Kyun
Mali Kyun
Kadan Kyun
Daung Kyun
Letsôk-aw Kyun
Ko Phra Thong
Srinagarind Reservoir
0 km 200
0 miles 200
165
170
171

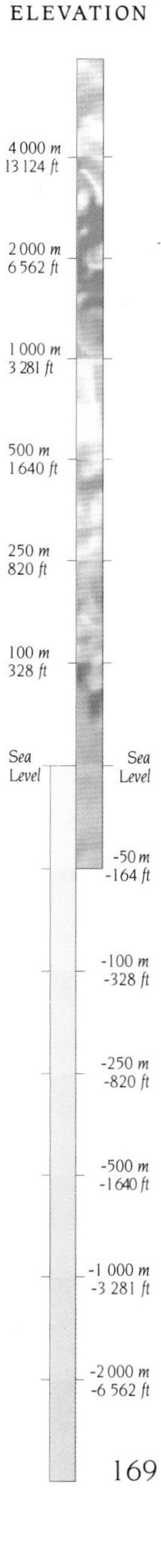
ELEVATION
4 000 m 13 124 ft
2 000 m 6 562 ft
1 000 m 3 281 ft
500 m 1640 ft
250 m 820 ft
100 m 328 ft
Sea Level
-50 m -164 ft
-100 m -328 ft
-250 m -820 ft
-500 m -1640 ft
-1 000 m -3 281 ft
-2 000 m -6 562 ft

Maritime Southeast Asia

A
B
C
D
1
2
3
4
5
MYANMAR
LAOS
VIETNAM
THAILAND
CAMBODIA
Mekong
Gulf of Tongking
Hainan Dao (part of China)
PARACEL ISLANDS (disputed by China, Taiwan and Vietnam)
South China Sea
SPRATLY ISLANDS (disputed by China, Malaysia, Philippines, Taiwan and Vietnam)
Mouths of the Mekong
Gulf of Thailand
Andaman Sea
Nicobar Islands (part of India)
Isthmus of Kra
Strait of Malacca
SINGAPORE
0 km 10
0 miles 10
MALAYSIA
Johore Strait
Causeway
Lim Chu Kang
Pulau Ubin
Pulau Tekong
Hougang New Town
Bukit Panjang
Changi
Choa Chu Kang
Bukit Timah 176m
Queenstown
Bedok New Town
Jurong Industrial Estate
City
Telok Blangah
Selat Pandan
Sentosa
Pulau Sudong
Pulau Pawai
Strait of Singapore
Urban areas
Open areas
Nature reserves
1°20'
104°
103°50'
103°40'
100°
110°
10°
169
165
173
George Town
Pulau Pinang
Butterworth
Taiping
Ipoh
Kota Bharu
Kuala Terengganu
Dungun
Cukai
Kuantan
Klang
KUALA LUMPUR
Seremban
Melaka
Muar
Batu Pahat
Keluang
Johor Bahru
SINGAPORE
MALAYSIA
Kepulauan Natuna
Selat Serasan
Bandaaceh
Sigli
Langsa
Meulaboh
Medan
Tebingtinggi
Pematangsiantar
Pulau Simeulue
Kepulauan Banyak
Danau Toba
Sibolga
Pulau Nias
Pekanbaru
Solok
Rengat
Kepulauan Lingga
Padang
Pulau Siberut
Kepulauan Mentawai
Pegunungan Barisan
Batang Hari
Kualatungkal
Jambi
Sungaipenuh
Pangkalpinang
Bangka
Palembang
Lahat
Bengkulu
Pulau Belitung
Sumatera (Sumatra)
Kotabumi
Bandarlampung
Serang
JAKARTA
Selat Sunda
Bogor
Sukabumi
Bandung
Tasikmalaya
Cirebon
Tegal
Pekalongan
Semarang
Kudus
Cilacap
Magelang
Yogyakarta
Surakarta
Jawa (Java)
Kediri
Madiun
Malang
Pulau Madura
Surabaya
Probolinggo
Jember
Bali
Denpasar
Pulau Lombok
Mataram
Java Sea
INDONESIA
Kota Kinabalu
Gunung Kinabalu 4101
Balabac
BANDAR SERI BEGAWAN
BRUNEI
Miri
Bintulu
Banjaran Tamabo
Sungai Kayan
Sibu
Batang Rajang
Sarawak
Sri Aman
Kuching
Singkawang
Sidas
Sungai Kapuas
Pontianak
Pegunungan Muller
Sungai Mahakam
Borneo
Samarinda
Balikpapan
Kalimantan
Selat Karimata
Sampit
Sungai Barito
Amuntai
Kandangan
Banjarmasin
Pulau Laut
INDIAN OCEAN
0 km 400
0 miles 400
N

POPULATION

Less than 50,000

50,000 – 100,000

100,000 – 500,000

Over 500,000

E
F
G
H
120°
130°
140°
10°
1
2
3
4
5
184
177
178
Luzon Strait
Babuyan Island
Babuyan Channel
Cordillera Central
Tuguegarao
Ilagan
Luzon
aguio
Dagupan
Cabanatuan
geles
ANILA
Lucena
PHILIPPINES
atangas
Naga
Legaspi
Mindoro
Mindoro Strait
Sibuyan Sea
Calbayog
Samar
Roxas City
Cadiz
Tacloban
Leyte
Panay Island
Iloilo
Bacolod City
Cebu
Palawan
uerto rincesa
Negros
Bohol Sea
Butuan
Iligan
Cagayan de Oro
Bislig
Mindanao
Sulu Sea
Zamboanga
Moro Gulf
Davao
Basilan
Lebak
General Santos
Davao Gulf
dakan
Sulu Archipelago
Philippine Sea
NORTHERN MARIANA ISLANDS
(US commonwealth territory)
GUAM
(US unincorporated territory)
PACIFIC OCEAN
Yap
MICRONESIA
Babeldaob
PALAU
Kepulauan Talaud
Kepulauan Sangir
Celebes Sea
Pulau Morotai
Pulau Halmahera
Manado
Bitung
Molucca Sea
Gorontalo
Gulf of Tomini
alu
Pulau Waigeo
Halmahera Sea
Selat Dampier
Sorong
Jazirah Doberai
Pulau Biak
Pulau Yapen
Teluk Cenderawasih
Sungai Mamberamo
Jayapura
Kepulauan Banggai
Sulawesi (Celebes)
Pegunungan Quarles
Kepulauan Sula
Ceram Sea
Maluku (Moluccas)
Pulau Misool
Teluk Berau
Danau Towuti
Waflia
Wahai
Puncak Jaya 5030m
Pegunungan Maoke
PAPUA NEW GUINEA
epare
Teluk Bone
Kendari
Tifu
Pulau Buru
Ambon
Pulau Seram
INDONESIA
Irian Jaya
New Guinea
gkang
Kolaka
Pulau Buton
Watampone
Ujungpandang
Bulukumba
Kepulauan Kai
Kepulauan Aru
Sungai Digul
Banda Sea
Kepulauan Tanimbar
Pulau Yamdena
ores ea
Tenggara
Kepulauan Alor
Pulau Wetar
Flores
Dili
Kepulauan Leti
it Sumba
Savu Sea
Timor
Arafura Sea
Torres Strait
ulau umba
Nikiniki
Kupang
Timor Sea
AUSTRALIA

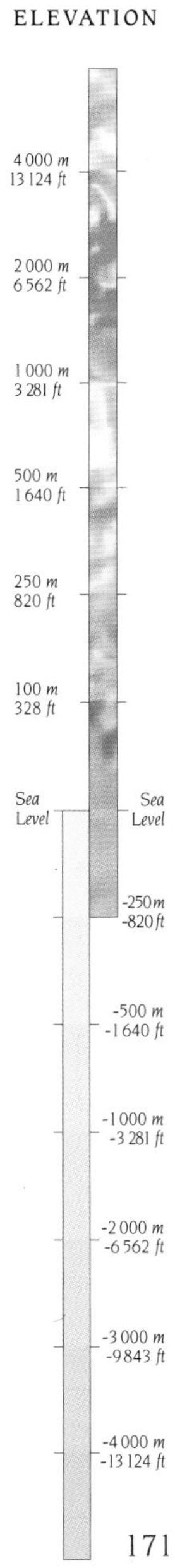
ELEVATION
4000 m
13 124 ft
2000 m
6562 ft
1000 m
3281 ft
500 m
1640 ft
250 m
820 ft
100 m
328 ft
Sea Level
Sea Level
-250m
-820 ft
-500 m
-1640 ft
-1000 m
-3281 ft
-2000 m
-6562 ft
-3000 m
-9843 ft
-4000 m
-13 124 ft

THE INDIAN OCEAN

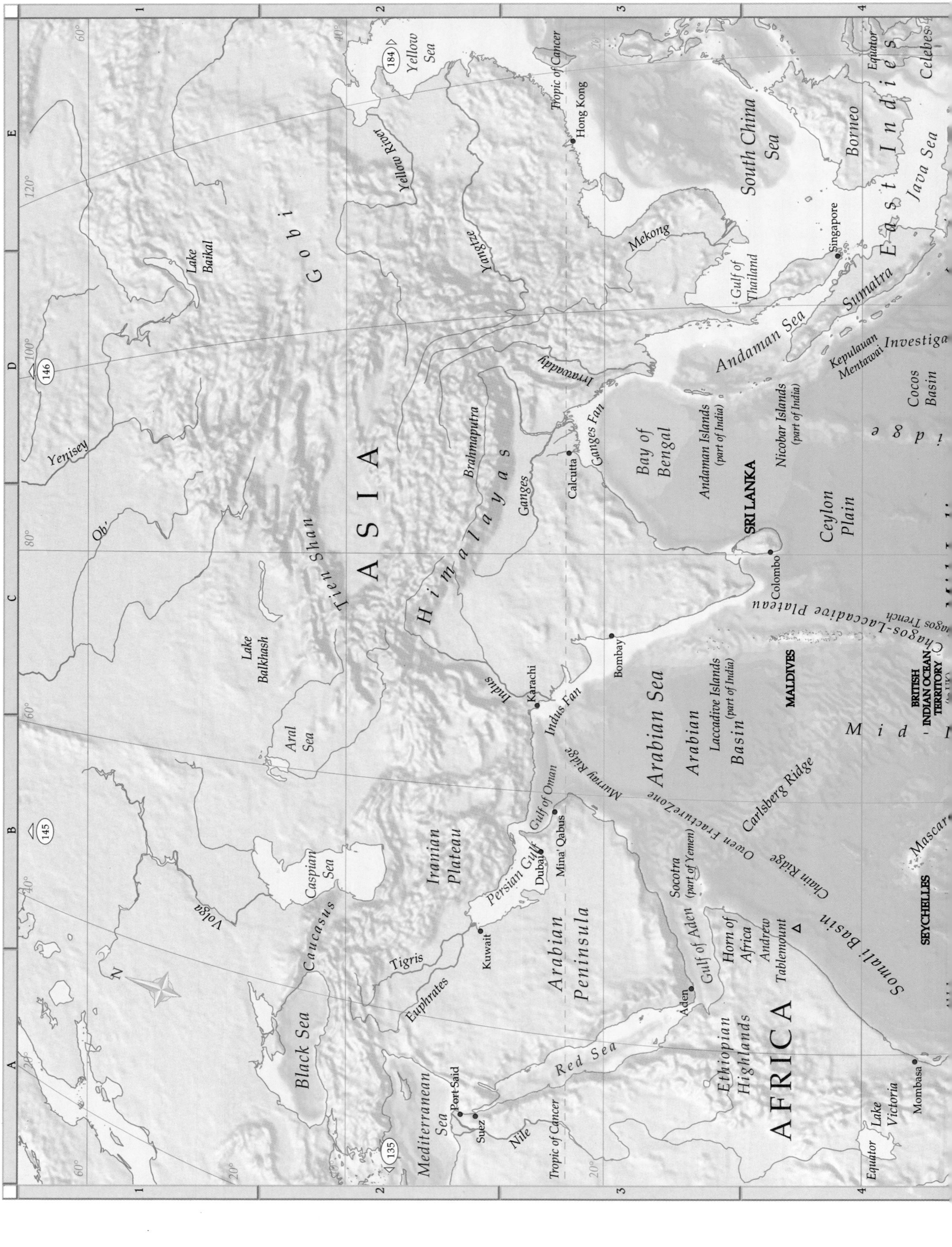
ASIA
AFRICA
Gobi
Lake Baikal
Yellow Sea
Yellow River
Tropic of Cancer
Hong Kong
South China Sea
Borneo
East Indies
Java Sea
Celebes
Equator
Yangtze
Mekong
Gulf of Thailand
Singapore
Sumatra
Andaman Sea
Kepulauan Mentawai
Investiga
Irrawaddy
Brahmaputra
Himalayas
Ganges
Calcutta
Ganges Fan
Bay of Bengal
Andaman Islands (part of India)
Nicobar Islands (part of India)
Cocos Basin
Yenisey
Ob'
Tien Shan
SRI LANKA
Colombo
Ceylon Plain
Chagos-Laccadive Plateau
Chagos Trench
Lake Balkhash
Aral Sea
Indus
Karachi
Indus Fan
Bombay
Arabian Sea
Arabian Basin
Laccadive Islands (part of India)
MALDIVES
BRITISH INDIAN OCEAN TERRITORY
Carlsberg Ridge
Murray Ridge
Gulf of Oman
Mina' Qabus
Owen Fracture Zone
Caspian Sea
Iranian Plateau
Persian Gulf
Dubai
Socotra (part of Yemen)
Chain Ridge
Mascar
Volga
Caucasus
Kuwait
Arabian Peninsula
Gulf of Aden
Horn of Africa
Andrew Tablemount
Somali Basin
SEYCHELLES
Tigris
Euphrates
Black Sea
Aden
Ethiopian Highlands
Red Sea
Mediterranean Sea
Port Said
Suez
Nile
Mombasa
Lake Victoria
N
145
146
184
135

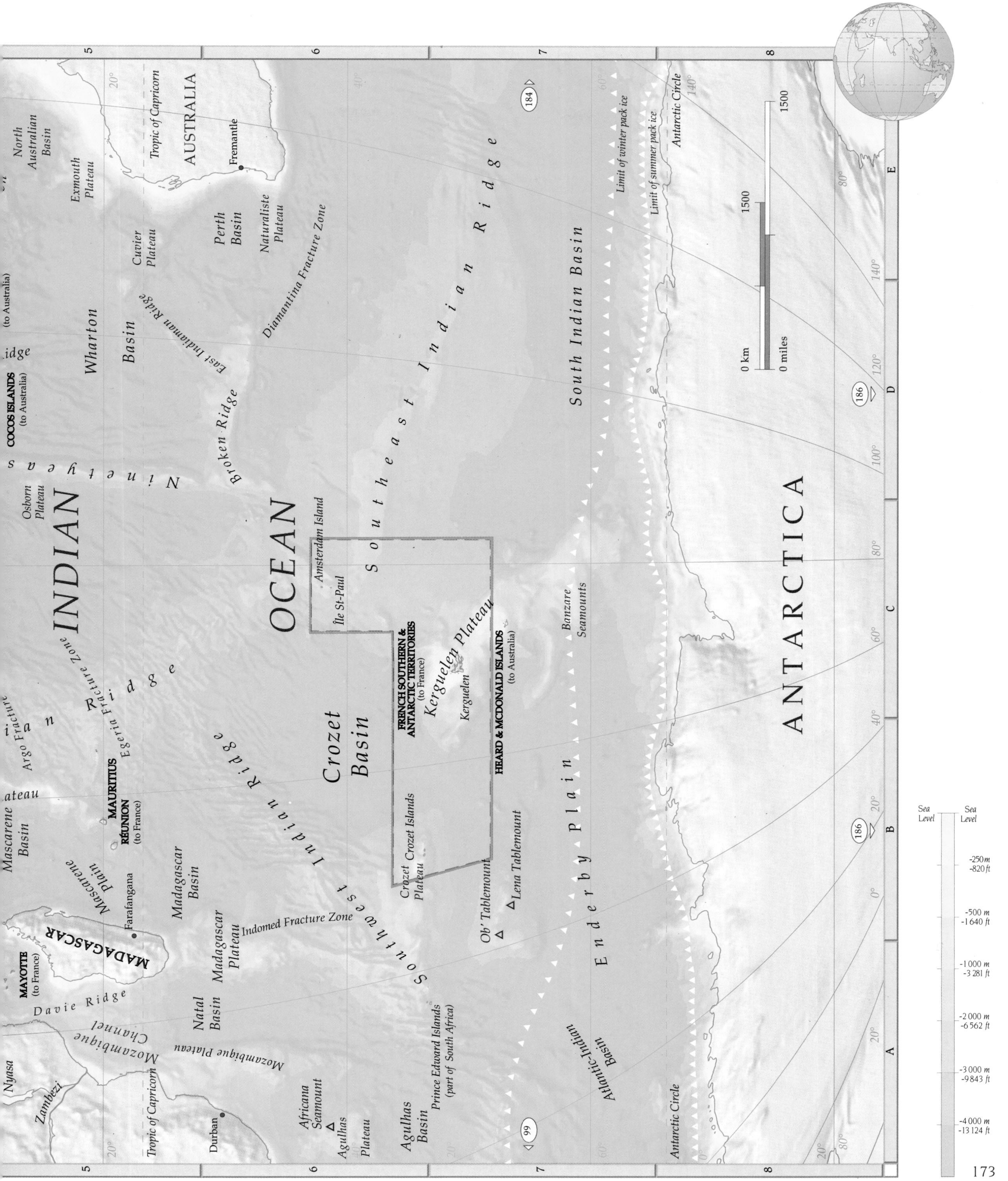
INDIAN
OCEAN
ANTARCTICA
AUSTRALIA
MADAGASCAR
North Australian Basin
Exmouth Plateau
Tropic of Capricorn
Fremantle
Cuvier Plateau
Perth Basin
Naturaliste Plateau
Diamantina Fracture Zone
Wharton Basin
East Indiaman Ridge
Broken Ridge
COCOS ISLANDS (to Australia)
(to Australia)
Ninetyeast Ridge
Osborn Plateau
Amsterdam Island
Île St-Paul
Southeast Indian Ridge
South Indian Basin
Limit of winter pack ice
Limit of summer pack ice
Antarctic Circle
FRENCH SOUTHERN & ANTARCTIC TERRITORIES (to France)
Kerguelen Plateau
Kerguelen
HEARD & MCDONALD ISLANDS (to Australia)
Banzare Seamounts
Crozet Basin
Crozet Islands
Crozet Plateau
Argo Fracture Zone
Egeria Fracture Zone
Mascarene Basin
Mascarene Plain
MAURITIUS
RÉUNION (to France)
Farafangana
Madagascar Basin
Madagascar Plateau
Indomed Fracture Zone
Southwest Indian Ridge
Ob' Tablemount
Lena Tablemount
Enderby Plain
Atlantic-Indian Basin
MAYOTTE (to France)
Davie Ridge
Mozambique Channel
Mozambique Plateau
Natal Basin
Nyasa
Zambezi
Durban
Africana Seamount
Agulhas Plateau
Agulhas Basin
Prince Edward Islands (part of South Africa)
184
186
99
0 km
1500
0 miles
1500
Sea Level
Sea Level
-250 m
-820 ft
-500 m
-1 640 ft
-1 000 m
-3 281 ft
-2 000 m
-6 562 ft
-3 000 m
-9 843 ft
-4 000 m
-13 124 ft

Australasia & Oceania

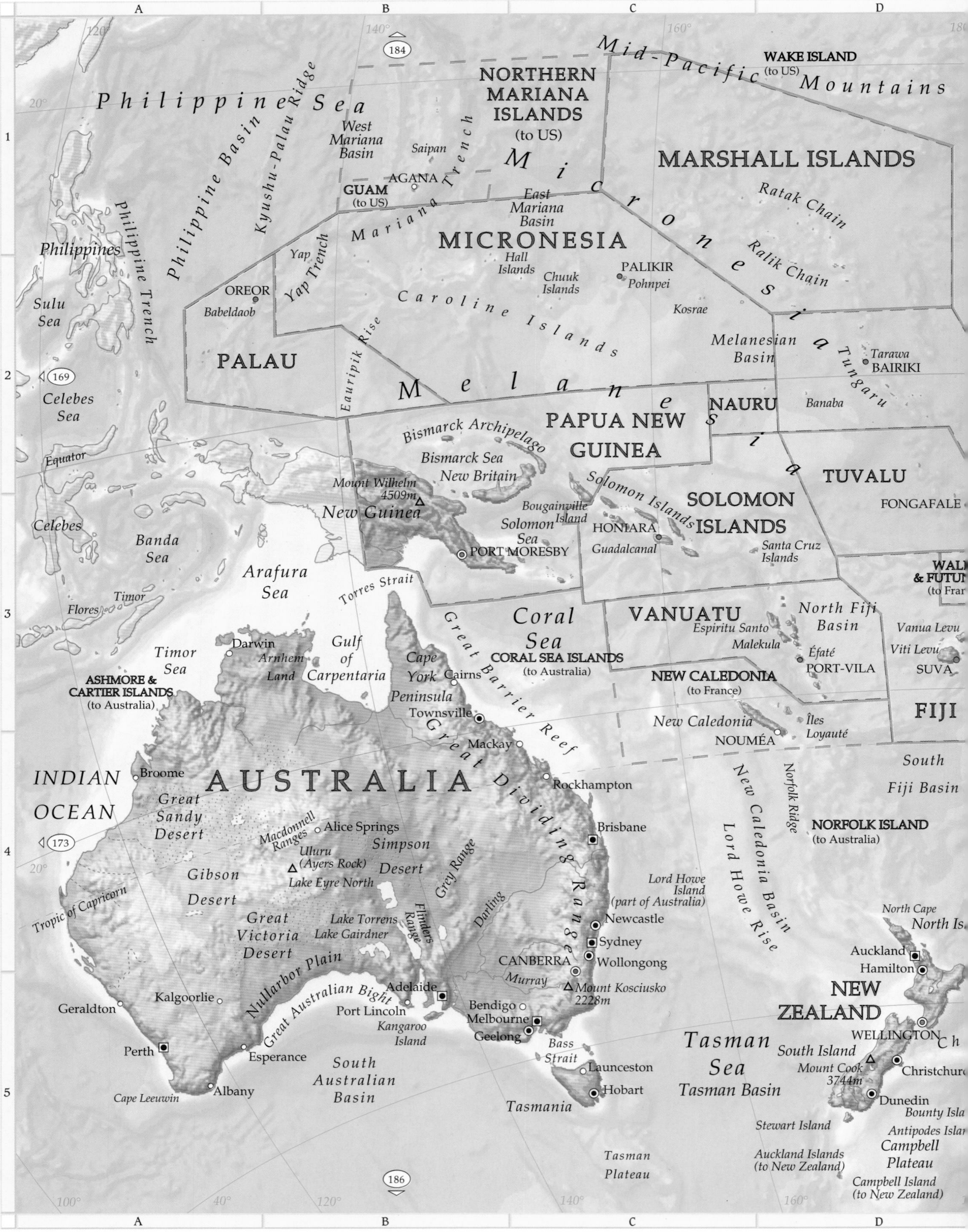
A
B
C
D
1
2
3
4
5
184
169
173
186
Philippine Sea
Philippine Basin
Kyushu-Palau Ridge
West Mariana Basin
Saipan
NORTHERN MARIANA ISLANDS
(to US)
Mariana Trench
Mid-Pacific Mountains
WAKE ISLAND
(to US)
MARSHALL ISLANDS
Micronesia
AGANA
GUAM
(to US)
East Mariana Basin
Ratak Chain
MICRONESIA
Hall Islands
Chuuk Islands
PALIKIR
Pohnpei
Ralik Chain
Philippines
Philippine Trench
Yap
Yap Trench
OREOR
Babeldaob
Caroline Islands
Kosrae
Sulu Sea
PALAU
Eauripik Rise
Melanesian Basin
Tarawa
BAIRIKI
Tungaru
Celebes Sea
Melanesia
NAURU
Banaba
PAPUA NEW GUINEA
Bismarck Archipelago
Bismarck Sea
New Britain
Equator
TUVALU
FONGAFALE
Mount Wilhelm
4509m
Solomon Islands
SOLOMON ISLANDS
Bougainville Island
New Guinea
Solomon Sea
HONIARA
Guadalcanal
Santa Cruz Islands
Celebes
Banda Sea
PORT MORESBY
WALLIS & FUTUNA
Arafura Sea
Torres Strait
Timor
Flores
Coral Sea
VANUATU
North Fiji Basin
Espiritu Santo
Malekula
Vanua Levu
Viti Levu
Great Barrier Reef
Timor Sea
Darwin
Arnhem Land
Gulf of Carpentaria
Cape York Peninsula
Cairns
CORAL SEA ISLANDS
(to Australia)
Éfaté
PORT-VILA
SUVA
ASHMORE & CARTIER ISLANDS
(to Australia)
NEW CALEDONIA
(to France)
Townsville
New Caledonia
Îles Loyauté
FIJI
NOUMÉA
Mackay
Great Dividing Range
South Fiji Basin
INDIAN OCEAN
Broome
AUSTRALIA
Rockhampton
New Caledonia Basin
Norfolk Ridge
Great Sandy Desert
Macdonnell Ranges
Alice Springs
Simpson Desert
Brisbane
NORFOLK ISLAND
(to Australia)
Uluru
(Ayers Rock)
Grey Range
Gibson Desert
Lake Eyre North
Lord Howe Rise
Lord Howe Island
(part of Australia)
Tropic of Capricorn
Flinders Range
Darling
North Cape
North Island
Great Victoria Desert
Lake Torrens
Lake Gairdner
Newcastle
Sydney
Wollongong
Auckland
Nullarbor Plain
CANBERRA
Murray
Hamilton
Adelaide
Mount Kosciusko
2228m
NEW ZEALAND
Kalgoorlie
Great Australian Bight
Port Lincoln
Bendigo
Geraldton
Melbourne
WELLINGTON
Kangaroo Island
Geelong
Tasman Sea
South Island
Perth
Bass Strait
Mount Cook
3744m
Christchurch
Esperance
South Australian Basin
Launceston
Albany
Hobart
Tasman Basin
Dunedin
Cape Leeuwin
Tasmania
Bounty Islands
Stewart Island
Antipodes Islands
Tasman Plateau
Auckland Islands
(to New Zealand)
Campbell Plateau
Campbell Island
(to New Zealand)
100°
120°
140°
160°
180°
20°
40°

POPULATION

- Less than 50,000
- 50,000 – 100,000
- 100,000 – 500,000
- Over 500,000

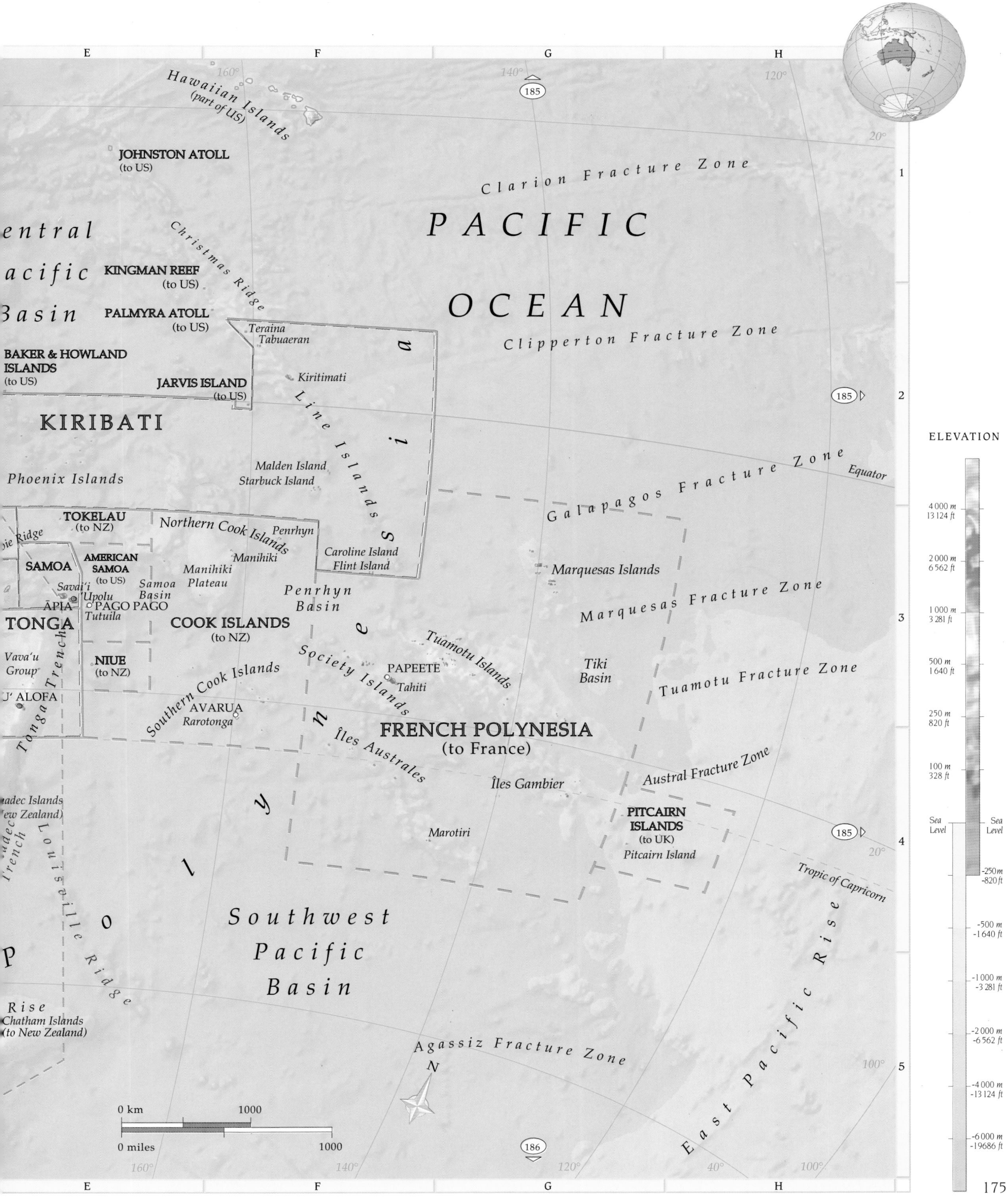
E
F
G
H
1
2
3
4
5
160°
140°
120°
100°
40°
20°
185
186
Hawaiian Islands
(part of US)
JOHNSTON ATOLL
(to US)
Clarion Fracture Zone
PACIFIC
OCEAN
Central
Pacific
Basin
Christmas Ridge
KINGMAN REEF
(to US)
PALMYRA ATOLL
(to US)
Teraina
Tabuaeran
Clipperton Fracture Zone
BAKER & HOWLAND
ISLANDS
(to US)
JARVIS ISLAND
(to US)
Kiritimati
KIRIBATI
Line Islands
Malden Island
Starbuck Island
Phoenix Islands
Galapagos Fracture Zone
Equator
TOKELAU
(to NZ)
Northern Cook Islands
Penrhyn
Caroline Island
Flint Island
Manihiki
AMERICAN
SAMOA
(to US)
SAMOA
Savai'i
Upolu
ĀPIA
PAGO PAGO
Tutuila
Samoa
Basin
Manihiki
Plateau
Penrhyn
Basin
Marquesas Islands
Marquesas Fracture Zone
TONGA
COOK ISLANDS
(to NZ)
Tuamotu Islands
Society Islands
PAPEETE
Tahiti
Tiki
Basin
Tuamotu Fracture Zone
Vava'u
Group
NIUE
(to NZ)
Southern Cook Islands
AVARUA
Rarotonga
Tonga Trench
FRENCH POLYNESIA
(to France)
Îles Australes
Îles Gambier
Austral Fracture Zone
Polynesia
PITCAIRN
ISLANDS
(to UK)
Pitcairn Island
Marotiri
Tropic of Capricorn
Louisville Ridge
Southwest
Pacific
Basin
East Pacific Rise
Rise
Chatham Islands
(to New Zealand)
Agassiz Fracture Zone
N
0 km
1000
0 miles
1000
ELEVATION
4 000 m
13 124 ft
2 000 m
6 562 ft
1 000 m
3 281 ft
500 m
1 640 ft
250 m
820 ft
100 m
328 ft
Sea
Level
-250 m
-820 ft
-500 m
-1 640 ft
-1 000 m
-3 281 ft
-2 000 m
-6 562 ft
-4 000 m
-13 124 ft
-6 000 m
-19686 ft

The Southwest Pacific

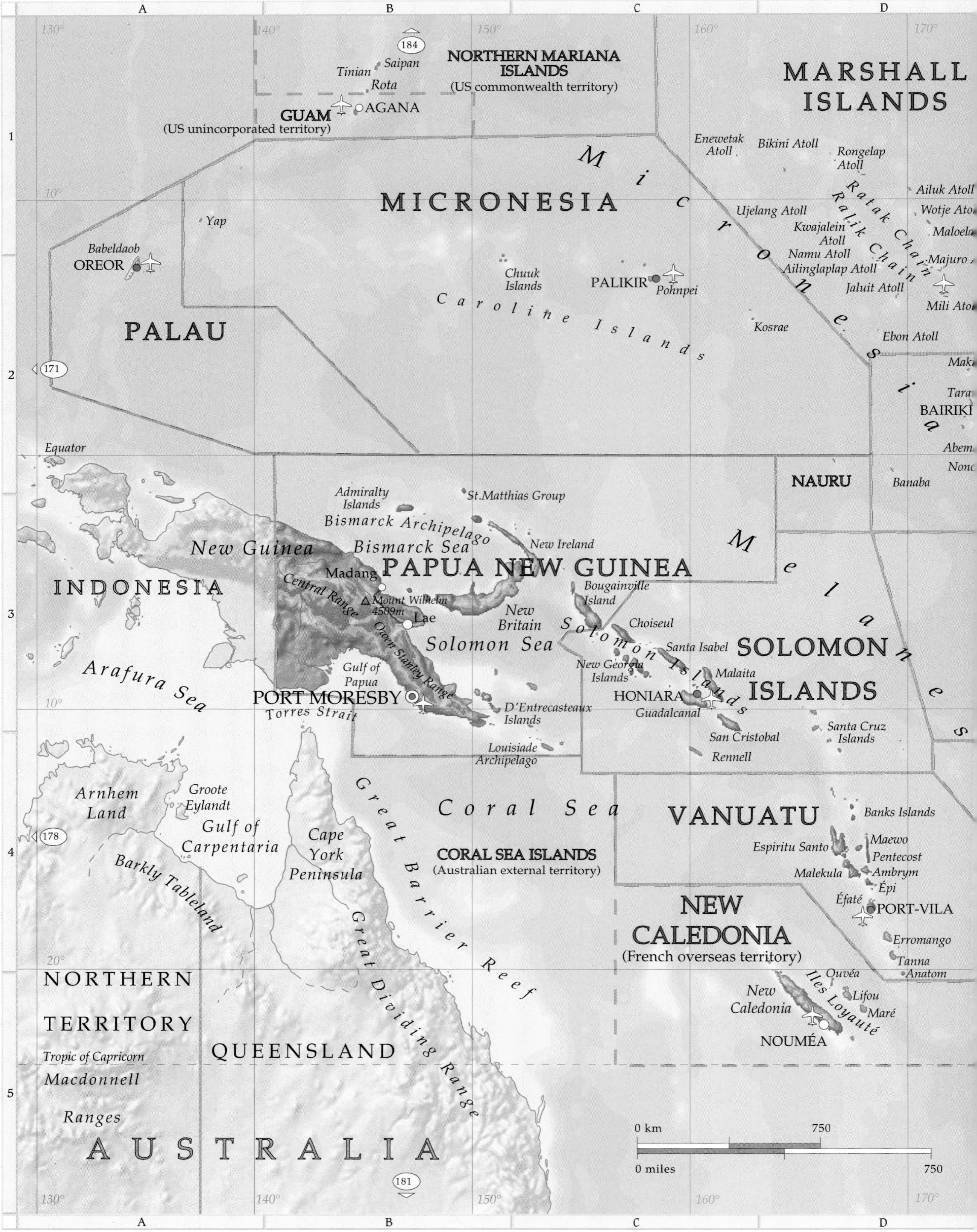

A
B
C
D
1
2
3
4
5
130°
140°
150°
160°
170°
10°
20°
184
171
178
181
NORTHERN MARIANA ISLANDS
(US commonwealth territory)
Saipan
Tinian
Rota
GUAM
(US unincorporated territory)
AGANA
MARSHALL ISLANDS
Enewetak Atoll
Bikini Atoll
Rongelap Atoll
Ailuk Atoll
Ratak Chain
Ralik Chain
Ujelang Atoll
Kwajalein Atoll
Namu Atoll
Ailinglaplap Atoll
Jaluit Atoll
Ebon Atoll
Majuro
Micronesia
MICRONESIA
Yap
Babeldaob
OREOR
PALAU
Chuuk Islands
PALIKIR
Pohnpei
Kosrae
Caroline Islands
BAIRIKI
Banaba
Equator
NAURU
Admiralty Islands
St.Matthias Group
Bismarck Archipelago
Bismarck Sea
New Ireland
New Guinea
PAPUA NEW GUINEA
INDONESIA
Madang
Central Range
Mount Wilhelm 4509m
Lae
New Britain
Owen Stanley Range
Bougainville Island
Solomon Sea
Solomon Islands
Choiseul
Santa Isabel
SOLOMON ISLANDS
New Georgia Islands
Malaita
HONIARA
Guadalcanal
San Cristobal
Rennell
Santa Cruz Islands
Melanesia
Arafura Sea
Gulf of Papua
PORT MORESBY
Torres Strait
D'Entrecasteaux Islands
Louisiade Archipelago
Arnhem Land
Groote Eylandt
Gulf of Carpentaria
Cape York Peninsula
Great Barrier Reef
Coral Sea
CORAL SEA ISLANDS
(Australian external territory)
VANUATU
Banks Islands
Espiritu Santo
Maewo
Pentecost
Malekula
Ambrym
Épi
Éfaté
PORT-VILA
Erromango
Tanna
Anatom
NEW CALEDONIA
(French overseas territory)
Ouvéa
Iles Loyauté
Lifou
Maré
New Caledonia
NOUMÉA
Barkly Tableland
Great Dividing Range
NORTHERN TERRITORY
Tropic of Capricorn
Macdonnell Ranges
QUEENSLAND
AUSTRALIA
0 km
750
0 miles
750

POPULATION

○ Less than 50,000

○ 50,000 – 100,000

◉ 100,000 – 500,000

▣ Over 500,000

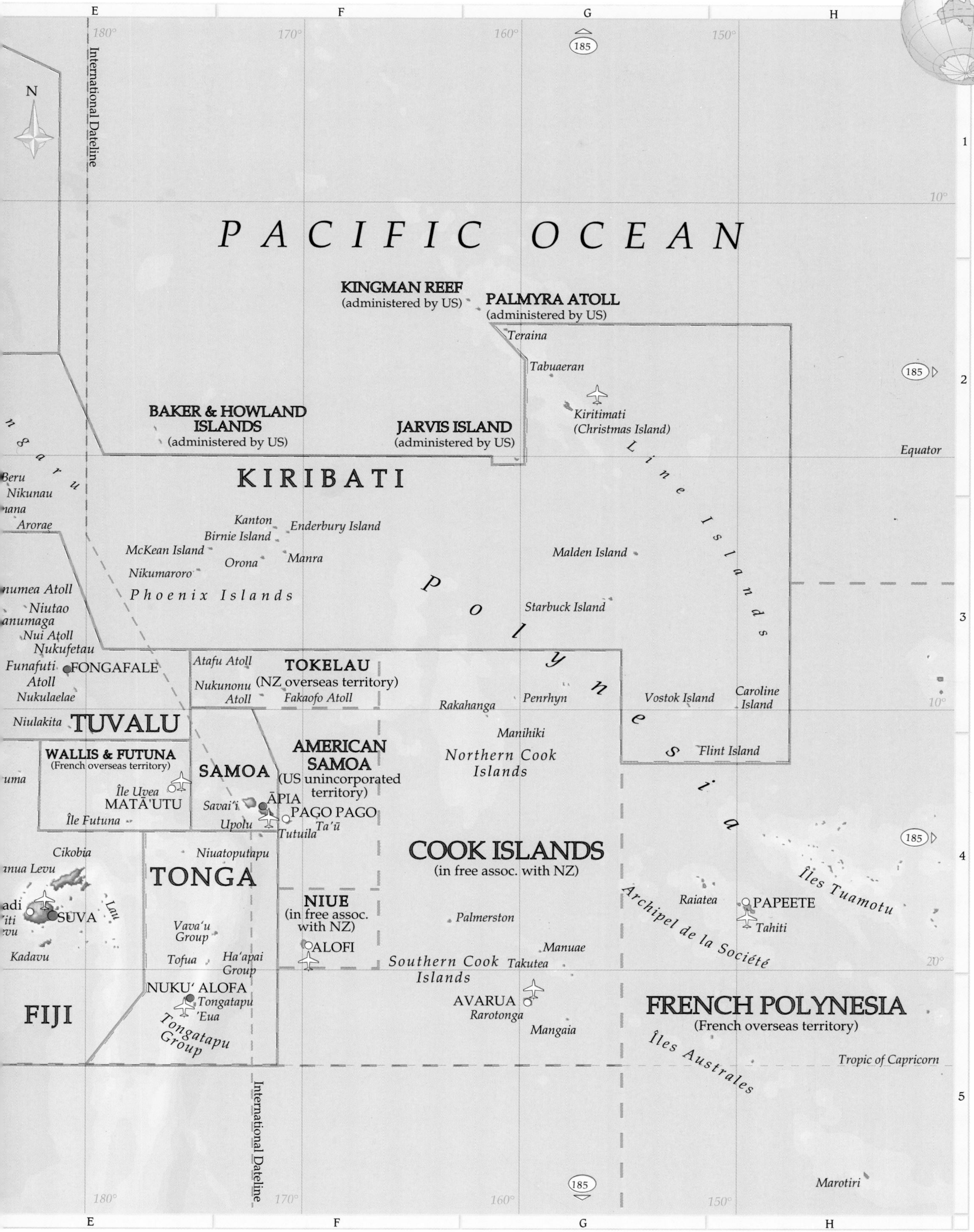
E
F
G
H
180°
170°
160°
150°
185
N
International Dateline
1
10°
PACIFIC OCEAN
KINGMAN REEF
(administered by US)
PALMYRA ATOLL
(administered by US)
Teraina
Tabuaeran
185
2
BAKER & HOWLAND ISLANDS
(administered by US)
JARVIS ISLAND
(administered by US)
Kiritimati
(Christmas Island)
Line Islands
Equator
KIRIBATI
Beru
Nikunau
Arorae
Kanton
Enderbury Island
Birnie Island
McKean Island
Orona
Manra
Nikumaroro
Malden Island
Phoenix Islands
Polynesia
Starbuck Island
3
Niutao
Nui Atoll
Nukufetau
Funafuti
FONGAFALE
Atoll
Nukulaelae
Atafu Atoll
TOKELAU
(NZ overseas territory)
Nukunonu Atoll
Fakaofo Atoll
Rakahanga
Penrhyn
Vostok Island
Caroline Island
Niulakita
TUVALU
Manihiki
WALLIS & FUTUNA
(French overseas territory)
Île Uvea
MATĀ'UTU
Île Futuna
SAMOA
Savai'i
ĀPIA
Upolu
AMERICAN SAMOA
(US unincorporated territory)
PAGO PAGO
Tutuila
Ta'ū
Northern Cook Islands
Flint Island
COOK ISLANDS
(in free assoc. with NZ)
185
4
Cikobia
Niuatoputapu
TONGA
Lau
SUVA
Kadavu
Vava'u Group
Tofua
Ha'apai Group
NIUE
(in free assoc. with NZ)
ALOFI
Palmerston
Manuae
Southern Cook Islands
Takutea
Raiatea
PAPEETE
Tahiti
Îles Tuamotu
Archipel de la Société
20°
FIJI
NUKU' ALOFA
Tongatapu
'Eua
Tongatapu Group
AVARUA
Rarotonga
Mangaia
FRENCH POLYNESIA
(French overseas territory)
Îles Australes
Tropic of Capricorn
5
Marotiri

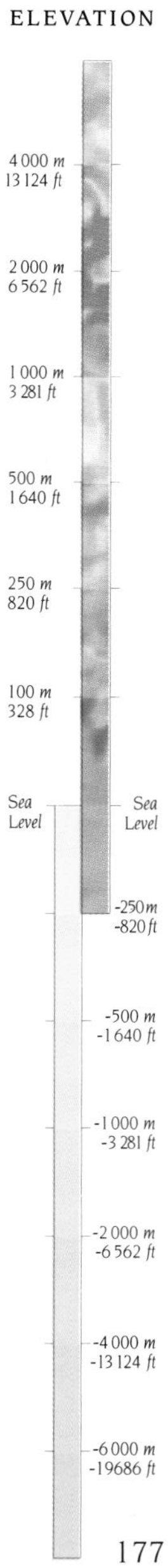
ELEVATION
4 000 m
13 124 ft
2 000 m
6 562 ft
1 000 m
3 281 ft
500 m
1 640 ft
250 m
820 ft
100 m
328 ft
Sea Level
-250 m
-820 ft
-500 m
-1 640 ft
-1 000 m
-3 281 ft
-2 000 m
-6 562 ft
-4 000 m
-13 124 ft
-6 000 m
-19686 ft

Western Australia

INDONESIA
Arafura Sea
Timor Sea
INDIAN OCEAN
NORTHERN TERRITORY
WESTERN
Jawa
Bali
Pulau Lombok
Flores
Pulau Sumba
Pulau Wetar
Timor
Tanimbar Kepulauan
Melville Island
Bathurst Island
Croker Island
South Goulburn Island
Van Diemen Gulf
Arnhem Land
Darwin
Katherine
Pine Creek
Daly Waters
Top Springs Roadhouse
Tennant Creek
Tanami Desert
Victoria River
Kununurra
Wyndham
Joseph Bonaparte Gulf
Halls Creek
Kimberley Plateau
Fitzroy Crossing
Fitzroy River
Cape Londonderry
Bonaparte Archipelago
Bigge Island
Heywood Islands
King Sound
Broome
Eighty Mile Beach
Great Sandy Desert
Percival Lakes
Lake Mackay
Macdonnell Ranges
Tropic of Capricorn
Marble Bar
Newman
Port Hedland
Hamersley Range
Fortescue River
Ashburton River
Dampier
Onslow
Barrow Island
Exmouth Gulf
Exmouth
170
171
173
180

POPULATION

Less than 50,000

50,000 – 100,000

100,000 – 500,000

Over 500,000

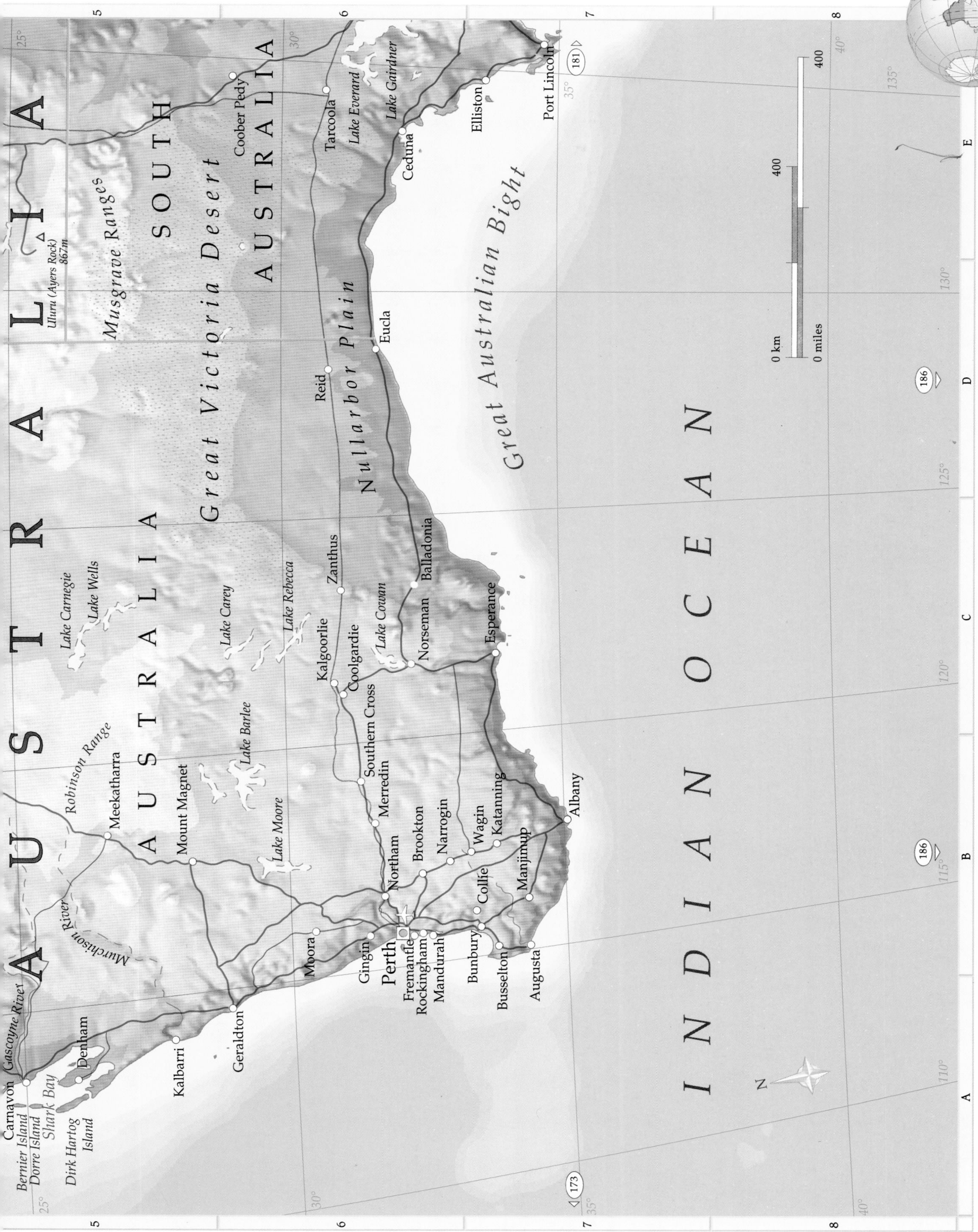
AUSTRALIA
WESTERN AUSTRALIA
SOUTH AUSTRALIA
INDIAN OCEAN
Great Australian Bight
Great Victoria Desert
Nullarbor Plain
Musgrave Ranges
Uluru (Ayers Rock) 867m
Robinson Range
Murchison River
Gascoyne River
Shark Bay
Bernier Island
Dorre Island
Dirk Hartog Island
Lake Carnegie
Lake Wells
Lake Carey
Lake Rebecca
Lake Barlee
Lake Moore
Lake Cowan
Lake Everard
Lake Gairdner
Carnarvon
Denham
Kalbarri
Geraldton
Meekatharra
Mount Magnet
Moora
Gingin
Perth
Fremantle
Rockingham
Mandurah
Bunbury
Busselton
Augusta
Northam
Brookton
Narrogin
Collie
Wagin
Katanning
Manjimup
Albany
Merredin
Southern Cross
Coolgardie
Kalgoorlie
Norseman
Esperance
Zanthus
Balladonia
Reid
Eucla
Tarcoola
Coober Pedy
Ceduna
Elliston
Port Lincoln
0 km
400
0 miles
400
173
181
186
186
A
B
C
D
E
5
6
7
8
25°
30°
35°
40°
110°
115°
120°
125°
130°
135°
N

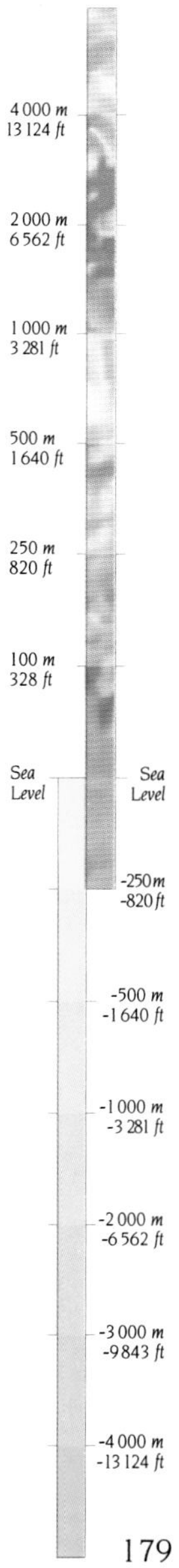
ELEVATION
4 000 m
13 124 ft
2 000 m
6 562 ft
1 000 m
3 281 ft
500 m
1 640 ft
250 m
820 ft
100 m
328 ft
Sea Level
Sea Level
-250 m
-820 ft
-500 m
-1 640 ft
-1 000 m
-3 281 ft
-2 000 m
-6 562 ft
-3 000 m
-9 843 ft
-4 000 m
-13 124 ft

Eastern Australia

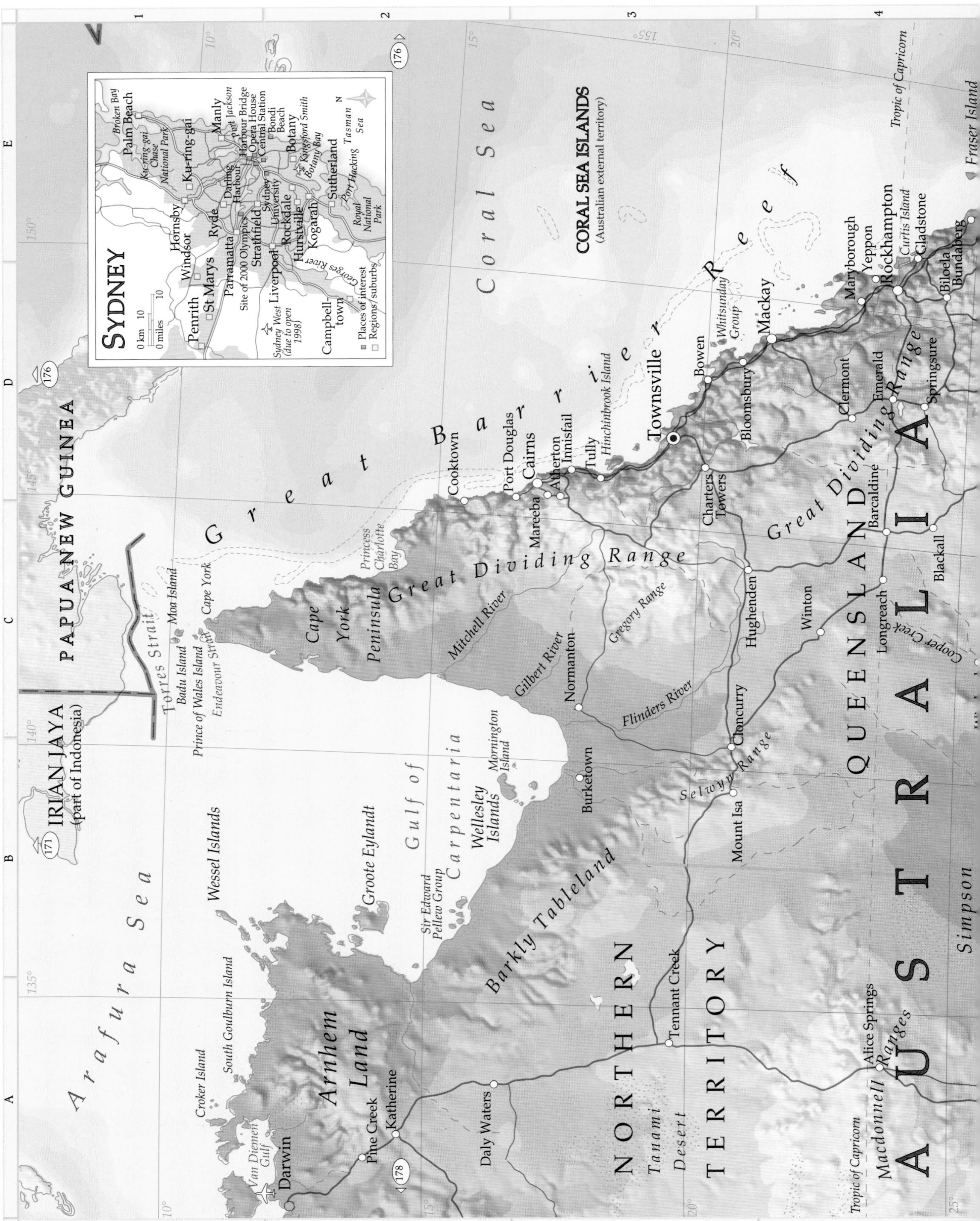

SYDNEY
0 km 10
0 miles 10
Broken Bay
Palm Beach
Ku-ring-gai Chase National Park
Ku-ring-gai
Hornsby
Windsor
Penrith
St Marys
Ryde
Parramatta
Site of 2000 Olympics
Strathfield
Liverpool
Campbelltown
Sydney West (due to open 1998)
Manly
Port Jackson
Harbour Bridge
Opera House
Central Station
Darling Harbour
Sydney University
Rockdale
Hurstville
Kogarah
Georges River
Bondi Beach
Botany
Kingsford Smith
Botany Bay
Sutherland
Port Hacking
Royal National Park
Tasman Sea
Places of interest
Regions/suburbs
Coral Sea
CORAL SEA ISLANDS
(Australian external territory)
Great Barrier Reef
Arafura Sea
PAPUA NEW GUINEA
IRIAN JAYA
(part of Indonesia)
Torres Strait
Moa Island
Badu Island
Prince of Wales Island
Endeavour Strait
Cape York
Cape York Peninsula
Great Dividing Range
Princess Charlotte Bay
Cooktown
Port Douglas
Cairns
Mareeba
Atherton
Innisfail
Tully
Hinchinbrook Island
Townsville
Bowen
Whitsunday Group
Mackay
Bloomsbury
Charters Towers
Clermont
Emerald
Springsure
Maryborough
Yeppon
Rockhampton
Curtis Island
Gladstone
Biloela
Bundaberg
Fraser Island
Tropic of Capricorn
Barcaldine
Blackall
Longreach
Winton
Hughenden
Cooper Creek
Mitchell River
Gilbert River
Gregory Range
Normanton
Flinders River
Cloncurry
Selwyn Range
Mount Isa
Burketown
Gulf of Carpentaria
Mornington Island
Wellesley Islands
Sir Edward Pellew Group
Groote Eylandt
Wessel Islands
Barkly Tableland
QUEENSLAND
AUSTRALIA
NORTHERN TERRITORY
Tennant Creek
Tanami Desert
Simpson
South Goulburn Island
Croker Island
Arnhem Land
Van Diemen Gulf
Darwin
Pine Creek
Katherine
Daly Waters
Alice Springs
Macdonnell Ranges

POPULATION

Less than 50,000

50,000 – 100,000

100,000 – 500,000

Over 500,000

SOUTH AUSTRALIA
NEW SOUTH WALES
VICTORIA
TASMANIA
AUSTRALIAN CAPITAL TERRITORY
Tasman Sea
Bass Strait
Banks Strait
Great Victoria Desert
Great Dividing Range
Grey Range
Barrier Range
Flinders Ranges
Australian Alps
Eyre Peninsula
Spencer Gulf
Investigator Strait
Kangaroo Island
King Island
Hunter Island
Flinders Island
Cape Barren Island
Maria Island
South Bruny Island
South East Point
Lake Eyre North
Lake Eyre South
Lake Blanche
Lake Callabonna
Lake Frome
Lake Torrens
Lake Gairdner
Lake Everard
-16m
Mount Kosciusko 2228m
Darling River
Murray River
Murrumbidgee River
Lachlan River
Warrego River
Barwon River
CANBERRA
Sydney
Melbourne
Brisbane
Adelaide
Hobart
Newcastle
Wollongong
Parramatta
Geelong
Gosford
Gympie
Caloundra
Ipswich
Gold Coast
Surfers Paradise
Murwillumbah
Lismore
Grafton
Coffs Harbour
Port Macquarie
Toowoomba
Warwick
Stanthorpe
Dalby
Miles
Murgon
Roma
Moonie
Goondiwindi
St. George
Mitchell
Bollon
Cunnamulla
Moree
Walgett
Narrabri
Armidale
Tamworth
Gunnedah
Taree
Muswellbrook
Lithgow
Orange
Bathurst
Dubbo
Goulburn
Cooma
Bega
Nyngan
Bourke
Cobar
Parkes
Cootamundra
Wagga Wagga
Albury
Wodonga
Wangaratta
Deniliquin
Hay
Ivanhoe
Wilcannia
Broken Hill
Mildura
Ouyen
Shepparton
Bendigo
Sunbury
Ballarat
Horsham
Moe
Traralgon
Sale
Bairnsdale
Warrnambool
Portland
Mount Gambier
Naracoorte
Keith
Tailem Bend
Gawler
Elizabeth
Crystal Brook
Peterborough
Port Augusta
Port Pirie
Whyalla
Port Lincoln
Elliston
Ceduna
Penong
Tarcoola
Coober Pedy
Marree
Musgrave Ranges
Launceston
Devonport
Burnie
Marrawah
0 km
400
0 miles
400
N
A
B
C
D
E
5
6
7
8
30°
35°
40°
135°
140°
145°
150°
155°
160°
179
185
186

ELEVATION

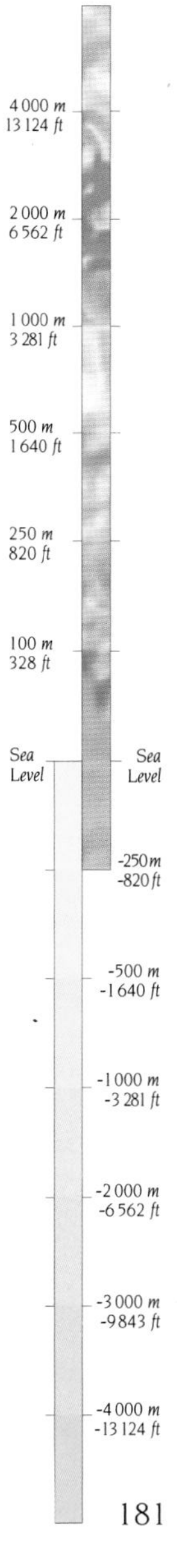
4 000 m
13 124 ft
2 000 m
6 562 ft
1 000 m
3 281 ft
500 m
1 640 ft
250 m
820 ft
100 m
328 ft
Sea Level
Sea Level
-250 m
-820 ft
-500 m
-1 640 ft
-1 000 m
-3 281 ft
-2 000 m
-6 562 ft
-3 000 m
-9 843 ft
-4 000 m
-13 124 ft

NEW ZEALAND

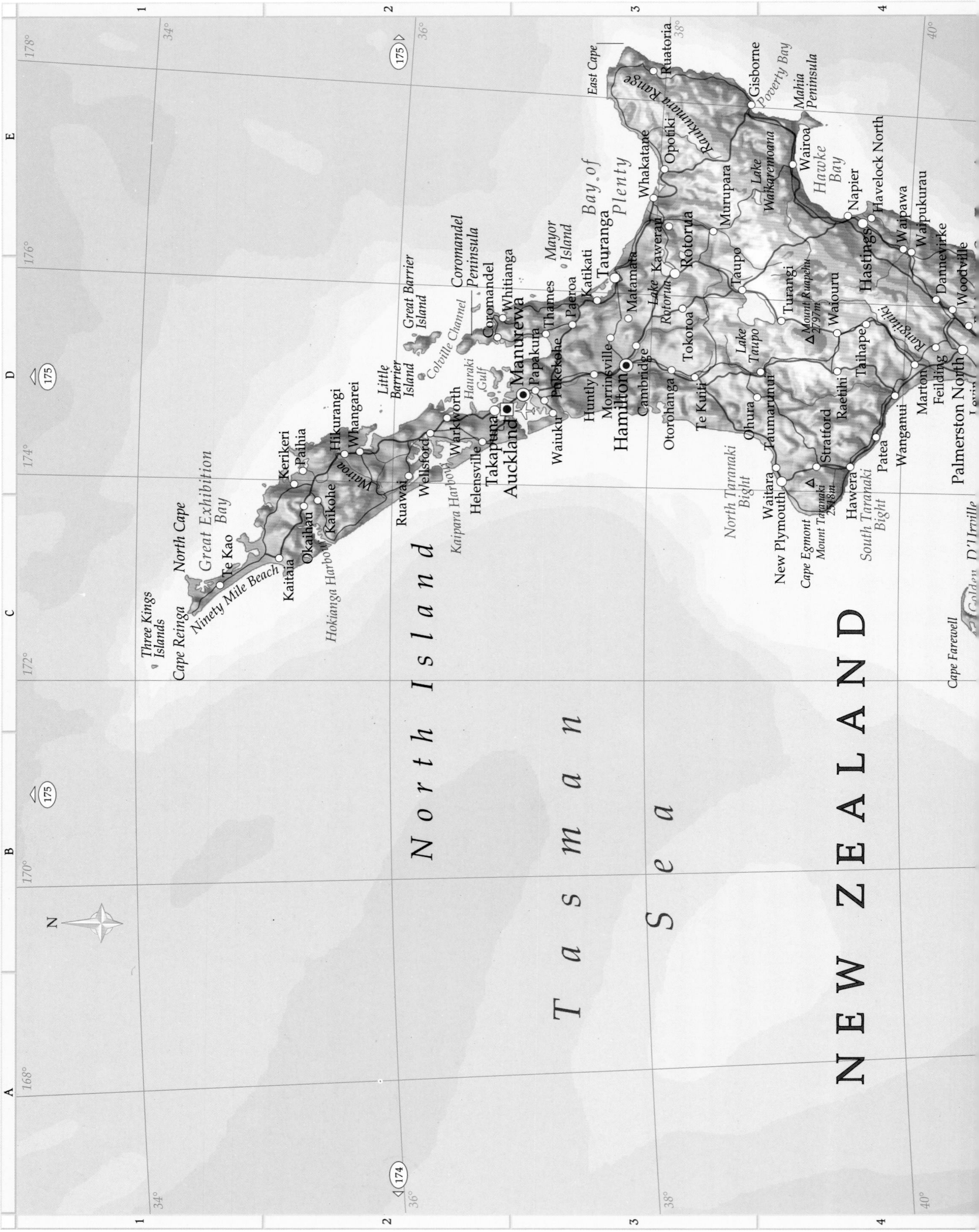
North Island
Tasman Sea
NEW ZEALAND
North Cape
Three Kings Islands
Cape Reinga
Te Kao
Great Exhibition Bay
Ninety Mile Beach
Kaitaia
Okaihau
Kerikeri
Paihia
Kaikohe
Hokianga Harbour
Hikurangi
Whangarei
Wairoa
Ruawai
Wellsford
Warkworth
Little Barrier Island
Great Barrier Island
Kaipara Harbour
Helensville
Takapuna
Auckland
Manurewa
Papakura
Hauraki Gulf
Colville Channel
Coromandel Peninsula
Coromandel
Whitianga
Thames
Pukekohe
Waiuku
Paeroa
Mayor Island
Katikati
Tauranga
Bay of Plenty
Huntly
Morrinsville
Matamata
Hamilton
Cambridge
Lake Rotorua
Rotorua
Kawerau
Whakatane
Opotiki
Raukumara Range
East Cape
Ruatoria
Gisborne
Poverty Bay
Mahia Peninsula
Murupara
Lake Waikaremoana
Wairoa
Hawke Bay
Napier
Havelock North
Hastings
Waipawa
Waipukurau
Dannevirke
Woodville
Tokoroa
Otorohanga
Te Kuiti
Lake Taupo
Taupo
Turangi
Mount Ruapehu 2797m
Waiouru
Taihape
Ruahine
Taumarunui
Ohura
Raetihi
Stratford
North Taranaki Bight
Waitara
New Plymouth
Cape Egmont
Mount Taranaki 2518m
Hawera
Patea
South Taranaki Bight
Wanganui
Marton
Feilding
Palmerston North
Cape Farewell
Golden
D'Urville
175
174
34°
36°
38°
40°
168°
170°
172°
174°
176°
178°
N
A
B
C
D
E
1
2
3
4

POPULATION

- ○ Less than 50,000
- ○ 50,000 – 100,000
- ◉ 100,000 – 500,000
- ▣ Over 500,000

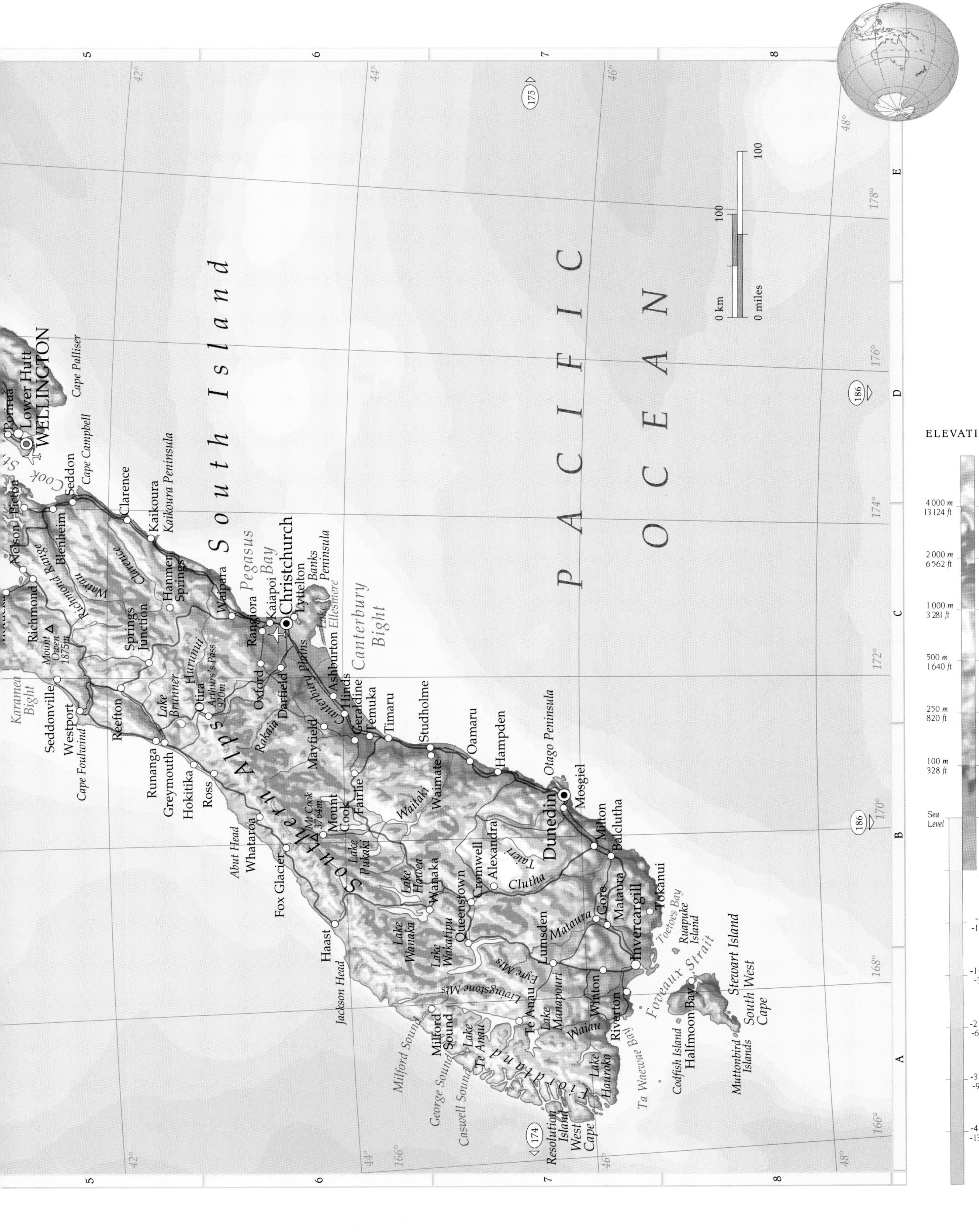
South Island
PACIFIC
OCEAN
Southern Alps
Fiordland
WELLINGTON
Lower Hutt
Porirua
Cook Strait
Cape Palliser
Cape Campbell
Seddon
Picton
Nelson
Blenheim
Richmond
Richmond Range
Wairau
Clarence
Kaikoura
Kaikoura Peninsula
Hanmer Springs
Waipara
Pegasus Bay
Christchurch
Kaiapoi
Rangiora
Lyttelton
Banks Peninsula
Lake Ellesmere
Canterbury Bight
Canterbury Plains
Ashburton
Hinds
Geraldine
Temuka
Timaru
Studholme
Oamaru
Hampden
Otago Peninsula
Dunedin
Mosgiel
Milton
Balclutha
Kaitangata
Tokanui
Toetoes Bay
Invercargill
Mataura
Gore
Lumsden
Winton
Riverton
Foveaux Strait
Ruapuke Island
Stewart Island
Halfmoon Bay
Codfish Island
South West Cape
Muttonbird Islands
Ta Waewae Bay
Lake Hauroko
Waiau
Lake Manapouri
Te Anau
Lake Te Anau
Milford Sound
George Sound
Caswell Sound
Resolution Island
West Cape
Livingstone Mts
Eyre Mts
Queenstown
Lake Wakatipu
Lake Wanaka
Wanaka
Lake Hawea
Cromwell
Alexandra
Clutha
Taieri
Haast
Jackson Head
Fox Glacier
Whataroa
Abut Head
Lake Pukaki
Mt Cook 3764m
Mount Cook
Fairlie
Waitaki
Waimate
Mayfield
Rakaia
Darfield
Oxford
Arthur's Pass 920m
Otira
Hurunui
Springs Junction
Lake Brunner
Ross
Hokitika
Greymouth
Runanga
Reefton
Westport
Cape Foulwind
Seddonville
Karamea Bight
Mount Owen 1875m
Clarence
175
186
174
0 km 100
0 miles 100
ELEVATION
4000 m 13124 ft
2000 m 6562 ft
1000 m 3281 ft
500 m 1640 ft
250 m 820 ft
100 m 328 ft
Sea Level
-250 m -820 ft
-500 m -1640 ft
-1000 m -3281 ft
-2000 m -6562 ft
-3000 m -9843 ft
-4000 m -13124 ft

THE PACIFIC OCEAN

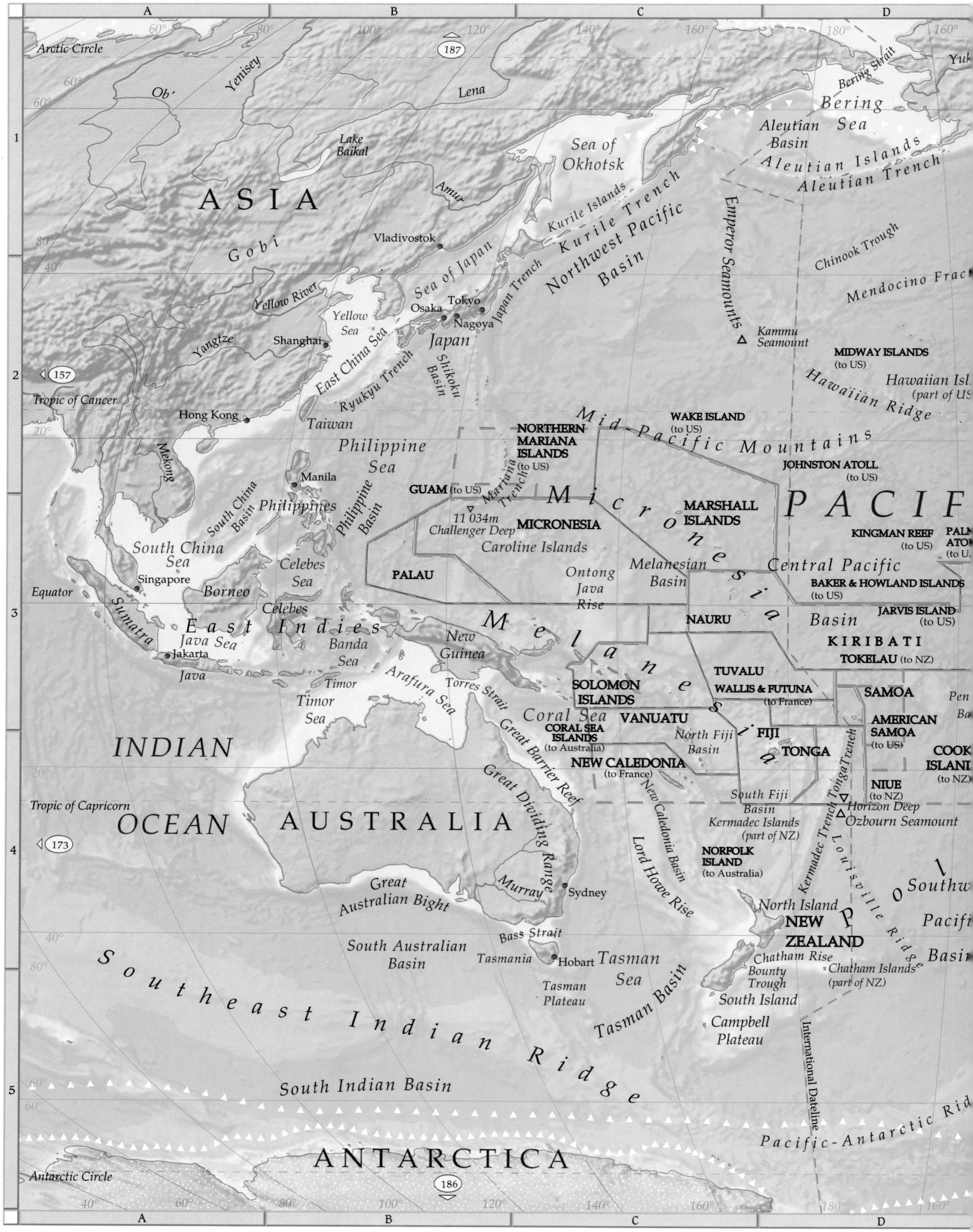
A
B
C
D
1
2
3
4
5
Arctic Circle
60°
80°
100°
120°
140°
160°
180°
187
Yenisey
Ob'
Lena
Lake Baikal
Sea of Okhotsk
Amur
ASIA
Gobi
Vladivostok
Kurile Islands
Kurile Trench
Northwest Pacific Basin
Bering Strait
Bering Sea
Aleutian Basin
Aleutian Islands
Aleutian Trench
Emperor Seamounts
Chinook Trough
Mendocino Frac
Sea of Japan
Japan Trench
Tokyo
Osaka
Nagoya
Japan
Yellow River
Yellow Sea
Shanghai
Yangtze
East China Sea
Ryukyu Trench
Shikoku Basin
Kammu Seamount
MIDWAY ISLANDS
(to US)
Hawaiian Isl.
(part of US
Hawaiian Ridge
157
Tropic of Cancer
Hong Kong
Taiwan
Mekong
Philippine Sea
Mid-Pacific Mountains
WAKE ISLAND
(to US)
NORTHERN MARIANA ISLANDS
(to US)
Mariana Trench
JOHNSTON ATOLL
(to US)
Manila
GUAM (to US)
11 034m
Challenger Deep
Micronesia
MICRONESIA
MARSHALL ISLANDS
PACIF
South China Basin
Philippines
Philippine Basin
Caroline Islands
KINGMAN REEF
(to US)
PALM
ATOL
(to U.
South China Sea
Singapore
Celebes Sea
PALAU
Ontong Java Rise
Melanesian Basin
Central Pacific Basin
BAKER & HOWLAND ISLANDS
(to US)
Equator
Borneo
Celebes
JARVIS ISLAND
(to US)
Sumatra
East Indies
NAURU
KIRIBATI
Java Sea
Jakarta
Banda Sea
New Guinea
Melanesia
TOKELAU (to NZ)
Java
Timor
Arafura Sea
Torres Strait
TUVALU
SOLOMON ISLANDS
WALLIS & FUTUNA
(to France)
SAMOA
Timor Sea
Coral Sea
VANUATU
AMERICAN SAMOA
(to US)
Pen
Ba
CORAL SEA ISLANDS
(to Australia)
North Fiji Basin
FIJI
TONGA
Tonga Trench
COOK ISLANI
(to NZ)
INDIAN
Great Barrier Reef
NEW CALEDONIA
(to France)
NIUE
(to NZ)
Tropic of Capricorn
OCEAN
AUSTRALIA
Great Dividing Range
New Caledonia Basin
South Fiji Basin
Horizon Deep
Ozbourn Seamount
173
Kermadec Islands
(part of NZ)
Kermadec Trench
Lord Howe Rise
NORFOLK ISLAND
(to Australia)
Louisville Ridge
Great Australian Bight
Murray
Sydney
Southw Pacifi Basi
North Island
NEW ZEALAND
Bass Strait
South Australian Basin
Tasmania
Hobart
Tasman Sea
Chatham Rise
Bounty Trough
Chatham Islands
(part of NZ)
Tasman Plateau
South Island
Southeast Indian Ridge
Tasman Basin
Campbell Plateau
International Dateline
South Indian Basin
Pacific-Antarctic Rid
ANTARCTICA
Antarctic Circle
186

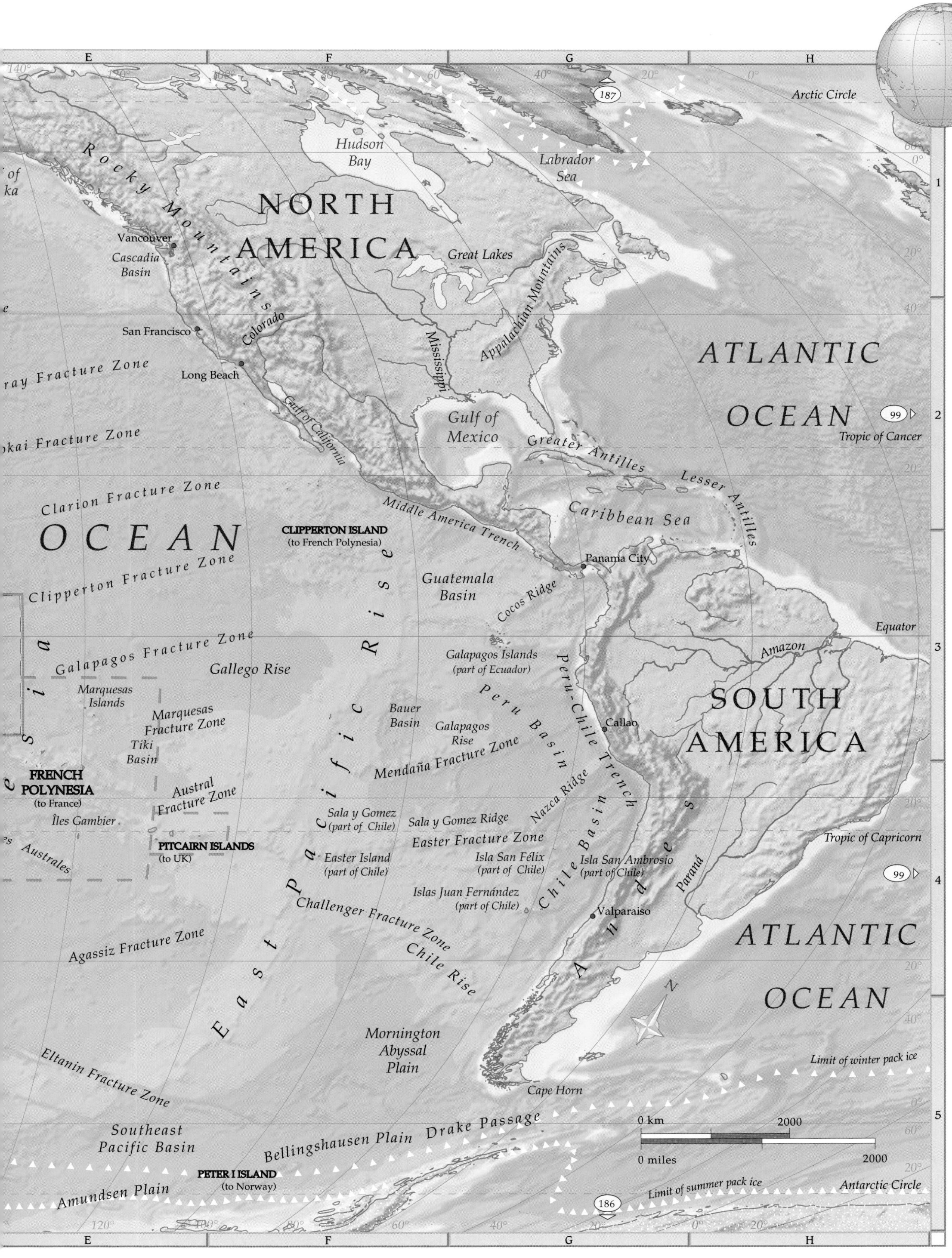
E
F
G
H
140°
120°
100°
60°
40°
20°
0°
187
Arctic Circle
Hudson
Bay
Labrador
Sea
Rocky Mountains
NORTH
AMERICA
Vancouver
Cascadia
Basin
Great Lakes
Appalachian Mountains
San Francisco
Colorado
Mississippi
ATLANTIC
OCEAN
99
Tropic of Cancer
Long Beach
Gulf of California
Gulf of
Mexico
Greater Antilles
Lesser Antilles
Caribbean Sea
Clarion Fracture Zone
Middle America Trench
OCEAN
CLIPPERTON ISLAND
(to French Polynesia)
Clipperton Fracture Zone
Panama City
Guatemala
Basin
Cocos Ridge
Equator
Galapagos Fracture Zone
Gallego Rise
Galapagos Islands
(part of Ecuador)
Amazon
Marquesas
Islands
Marquesas
Fracture Zone
Peru Basin
Peru-Chile Trench
SOUTH
AMERICA
Tiki
Basin
Bauer
Basin
Galapagos
Rise
Callao
FRENCH
POLYNESIA
(to France)
Mendaña Fracture Zone
Austral
Fracture Zone
Nazca Ridge
Îles Gambier
Sala y Gomez
(part of Chile)
Sala y Gomez Ridge
Easter Fracture Zone
Tropic of Capricorn
PITCAIRN ISLANDS
(to UK)
Easter Island
(part of Chile)
Isla San Félix
(part of Chile)
Isla San Ambrosio
(part of Chile)
Chile Basin
Paraná
Islas Juan Fernández
(part of Chile)
Valparaiso
Andes
East Pacific Rise
Challenger Fracture Zone
ATLANTIC
Agassiz Fracture Zone
Chile Rise
OCEAN
N
Mornington
Abyssal
Plain
Eltanin Fracture Zone
Limit of winter pack ice
Cape Horn
Southeast
Pacific Basin
Drake Passage
Bellingshausen Plain
0 km
2000
0 miles
2000
PETER I ISLAND
(to Norway)
Amundsen Plain
Limit of summer pack ice
Antarctic Circle
186
1
2
3
4
5

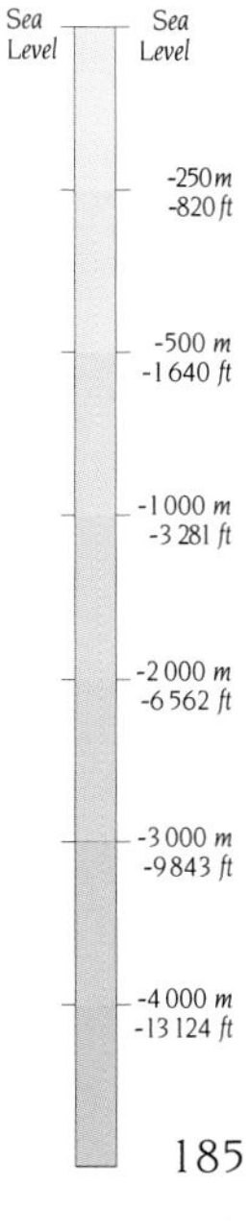
Sea
Level
Sea
Level
-250 m
-820 ft
-500 m
-1 640 ft
-1 000 m
-3 281 ft
-2 000 m
-6 562 ft
-3 000 m
-9 843 ft
-4 000 m
-13 124 ft

Antarctica

ELEVATION

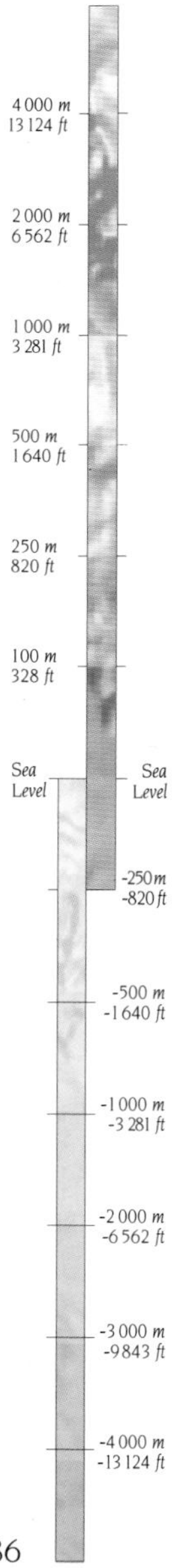
4 000 m
13 124 ft
2 000 m
6 562 ft
1 000 m
3 281 ft
500 m
1 640 ft
250 m
820 ft
100 m
328 ft
Sea Level
Sea Level
-250 m
-820 ft
-500 m
-1 640 ft
-1 000 m
-3 281 ft
-2 000 m
-6 562 ft
-3 000 m
-9 843 ft
-4 000 m
-13 124 ft

A
B
C
D
1
2
3
4
5
ATLANTIC OCEAN
99
SOUTH GEORGIA (to UK)
South Sandwich Trench
America-Antarctica Ridge
SOUTH SANDWICH ISLANDS (to UK)
Atlantic-Indian Basin
Scotia Sea
INDIAN OCEAN
Antarctic Circle
Lazarev Sea
Orcadas (Argentina)
South Orkney Islands
Signy (UK)
Weddell Plain
Sanae (South Africa)
Georg von Neumayer (Germany)
Novolazarevskaya (Russian Federation)
Enderby Plain
Drake Passage
South Shetland Islands
89
Esperanza (Argentina)
Capitán Arturo Prat (Chile)
Dronning Maud Land
Lützow Holmbukta
Molodezhnaya (Russian Federation)
Syowa (Japan)
173
Halley (UK)
Weddell Sea
Enderby Land
Palmer (US)
Graham Land
Antarctic Peninsula
Belgrano II (Argentina)
Coats Land
Mawson (Australia)
Berkner Island
Palmer Land
Rothera (UK)
San Martín (Argentina)
Cape Darnley
Alexander Island
Ronne Ice Shelf
Mackenzie Bay
Prydz Bay
Princess Elizabeth Land
Davis (Australia)
ANTARCTICA
Bellingshausen Sea
PETER I ISLAND (to Norway)
Vinson Massif 4897m
Amundsen-Scott (US)
South Pole
Transantarctic Mountains
Greater Antarctica
Davis Sea
Ellsworth Land
Lesser Antarctica
Mirny (Russian Federation)
Limit of winter pack ice
Limit of summer pack ice
South Geomagnetic Pole
Vostok (Russian Federation)
Shackleton Ice Shelf
Marie Byrd Land
Mount Kirkpatrick 4528m
Mount Markham 4351m
Amundsen Sea
Mount Sidley 4181m
Ross Ice Shelf
Wilkes Land
Casey (Australia)
Mount Siple 3100m
Roosevelt Island
Scott Base (N.Z)
Cape Poinsett
McMurdo Base (US)
Victoria Land
185
Mount Erebus 3794m
Ross Sea
Terre Adélie
PACIFIC OCEAN
Amundsen Plain
South Indian Basin
George V Land
Cape Adare
Dumont d'Urville (France)
Leningradskaya (Russian Federation)
Scott Island
Balleny Islands
Udintsev Fracture Zone
Pacific-Antarctic Ridge
Eltanin Fracture Zone
Macquarie Ridge
0 km
500
0 miles
500
Antarctic Research Stations
185
150°
160°
170°
180°
170°
160°
150°

Arctic Ocean

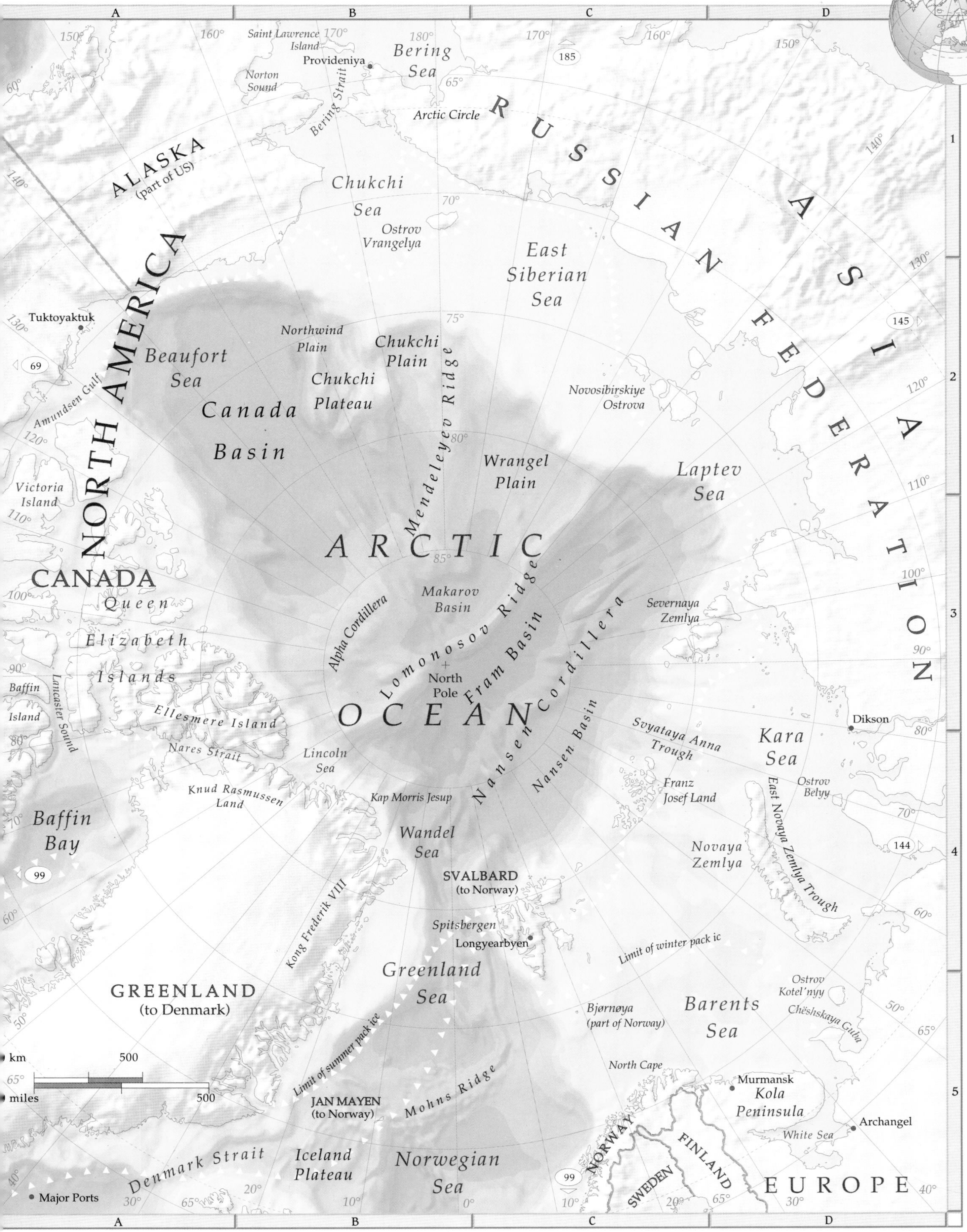
A
B
C
D
1
2
3
4
5
Saint Lawrence Island
Providenia
Bering Sea
Norton Sound
Bering Strait
Arctic Circle
ALASKA (part of US)
RUSSIAN FEDERATION
ASIA
Chukchi Sea
Ostrov Vrangelya
East Siberian Sea
NORTH AMERICA
Tuktoyaktuk
Beaufort Sea
Northwind Plain
Chukchi Plain
Chukchi Plateau
Mendeleyev Ridge
Amundsen Gulf
Canada Basin
Novosibirskiye Ostrova
Wrangel Plain
Laptev Sea
Victoria Island
ARCTIC OCEAN
CANADA
Queen Elizabeth Islands
Makarov Basin
Alpha Cordillera
Lomonosov Ridge
Fram Basin
North Pole
Severnaya Zemlya
Baffin Island
Lancaster Sound
Ellesmere Island
Nares Strait
Lincoln Sea
Nansen Cordillera
Nansen Basin
Svyataya Anna Trough
Dikson
Kara Sea
Franz Josef Land
Ostrov Belyy
East Novaya Zemlya Trough
Knud Rasmussen Land
Kap Morris Jesup
Baffin Bay
Wandel Sea
Novaya Zemlya
SVALBARD (to Norway)
Kong Frederik VIII
Spitsbergen
Longyearbyen
Limit of winter pack ic
Greenland Sea
GREENLAND (to Denmark)
Bjørnøya (part of Norway)
Barents Sea
Ostrov Kotel'nyy
Chëshskaya Guba
Limit of summer pack ice
North Cape
Murmansk
Kola Peninsula
JAN MAYEN (to Norway)
Mohns Ridge
Archangel
White Sea
Denmark Strait
Iceland Plateau
Norwegian Sea
NORWAY
FINLAND
SWEDEN
EUROPE
km
500
miles
500
• Major Ports
185
145
69
144
99

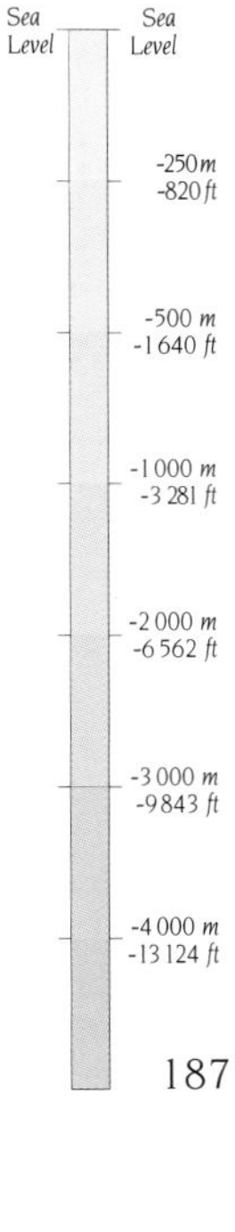
Sea Level
Sea Level
-250m -820ft
-500m -1640ft
-1000m -3281ft
-2000m -6562ft
-3000m -9843ft
-4000m -13124ft

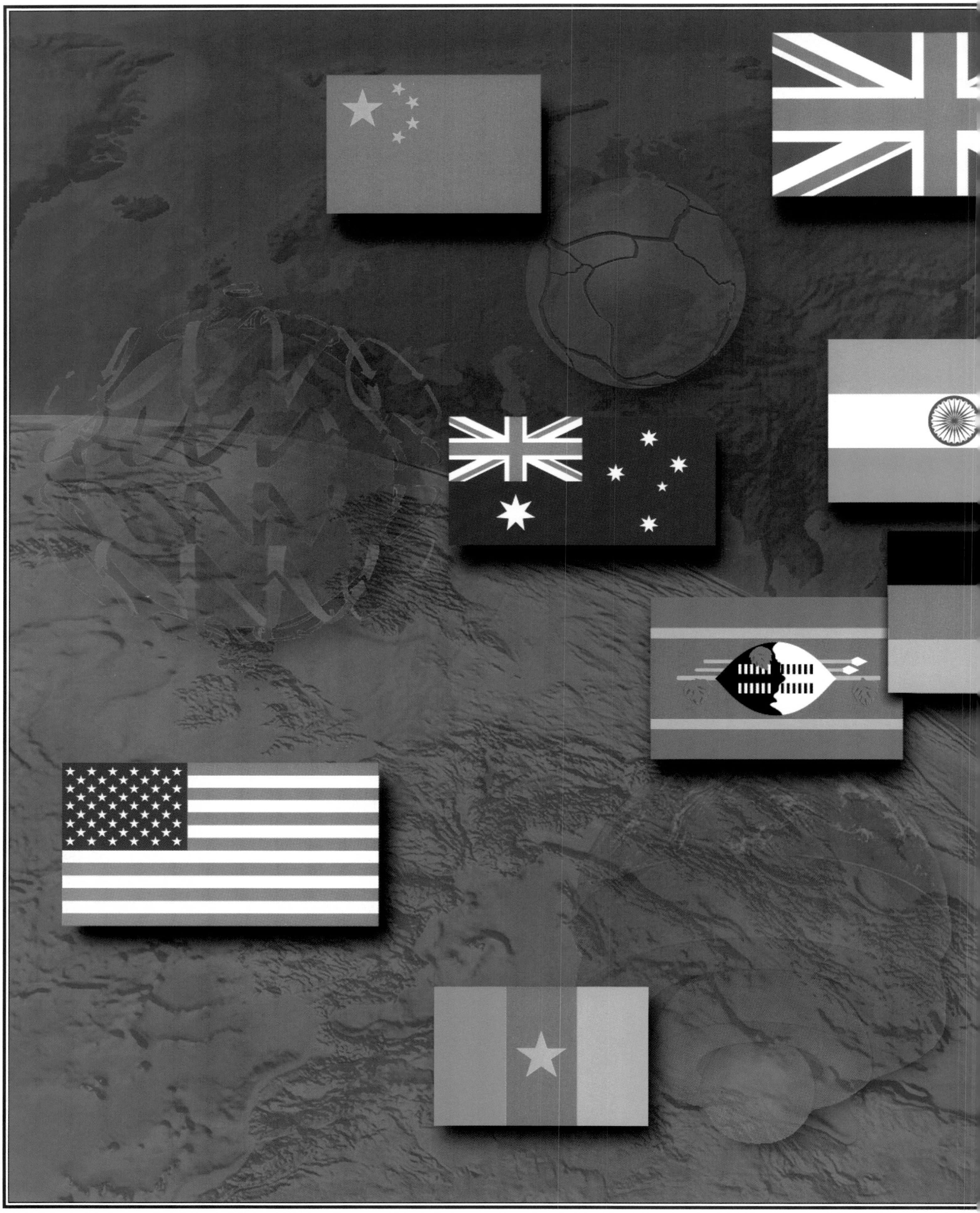

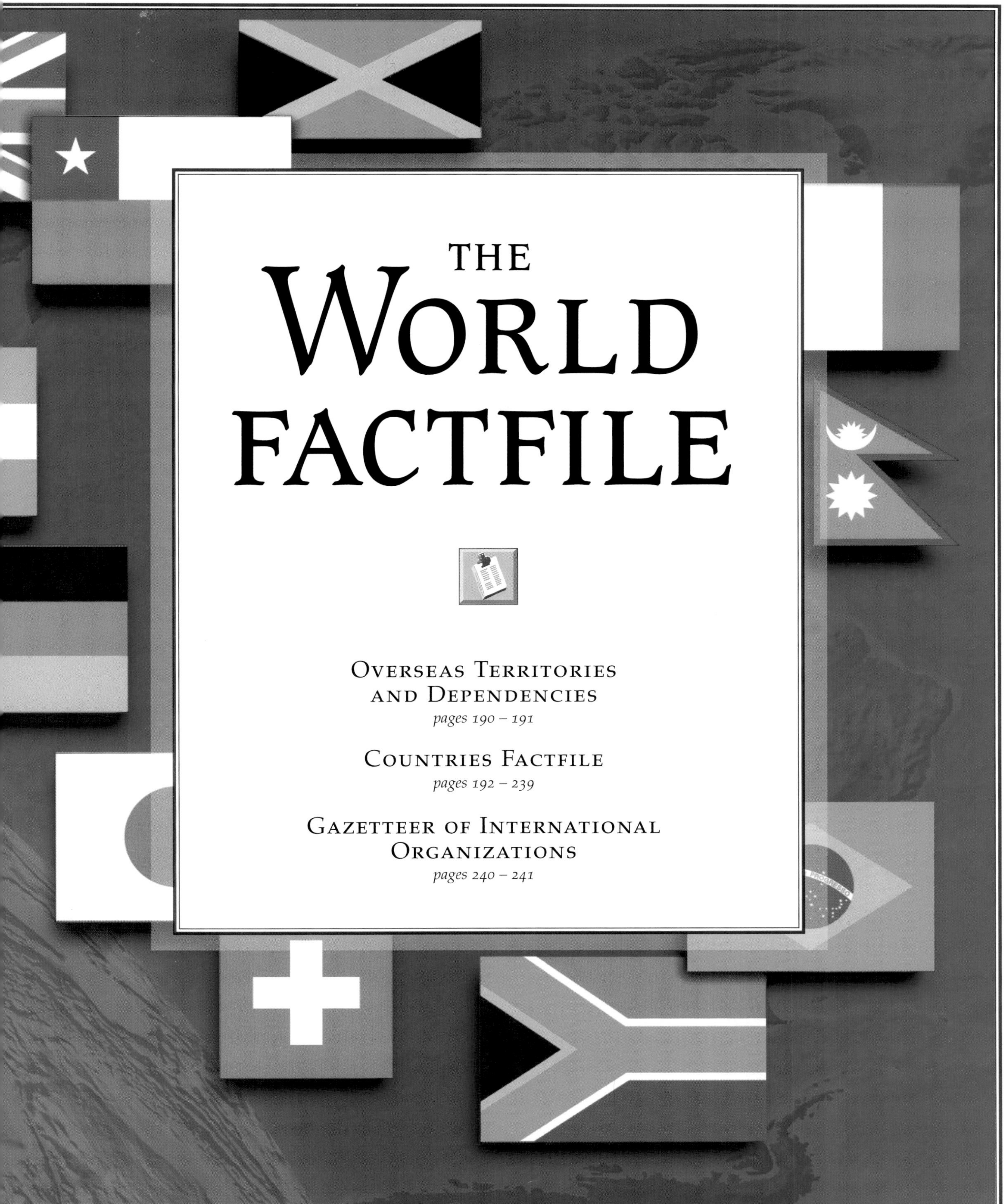

THE WORLD FACTFILE

Overseas Territories and Dependencies

DESPITE THE RAPID PROCESS of decolonization since the end of World War II, around 10 million people in over 50 territories around the world continue to live under the protection of France, Australia, the Netherlands, Denmark, Norway, Portugal, New Zealand, the United Kingdom, or the USA. These remnants of former colonial empires may have persisted for economic, strategic, or political reasons, and are administered in a variety of ways.

Australia

AUSTRALIA'S OVERSEAS territories have not been an issue since Papua New Guinea became independent in 1975. Consequently there is no overriding policy toward them. Some of Norfolk Island is inhabited by descendants of the *HMS Bounty* mutineers and more recent Australian migrants.

Ashmore & Cartier Islands
Indian Ocean

Status External territory
Claimed 1978
Capital *not applicable*
Population None
Area 2 sq miles (5.2 sq km)

Christmas Island
Indian Ocean

Status External territory
Claimed 1958
Capital Flying Fish Cove
Population 2,871
Area 52 sq miles (134.6 sq km)

Cocos Islands
Indian Ocean

Status External territory
Claimed 1955
Capital No official capital
Population 555
Area 5.5 sq miles (14.24 sq km)

Coral Sea Islands
South Pacific

Status External territory
Claimed 1969
Capital None
Population 8 (meteorologists)
Area 1.16 sq miles (Less than 3 sq km)

Heard & McDonald Islands
Indian Ocean

Status External territory
Claimed 1947
Capital *not applicable*
Population None
Area 161 sq miles (417 sq km)

Norfolk Island
South Pacific

Status External territory
Claimed 1913
Capital Kingston
Population 2,637
Area 13.3 sq miles (34.4 sq km)

Denmark

THE FAEROE ISLANDS have been under Danish administration since Queen Margreth I of Denmark inherited Norway in 1380. The Home Rule Act of 1948 gave the Faeroese control over all their internal affairs. Greenland first came under Danish rule in 1380. Today, Denmark remains responsible for the island's foreign affairs and defense.

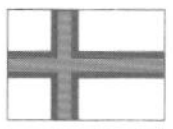

Faeroe Islands
North Atlantic

Status External territory
Claimed 1380
Capital Tórshavn
Population 47,310
Area 540 sq miles (1,399 sq km)

Greenland
North Atlantic

Status External territory
Claimed 1380
Capital Nuuk
Population 55,385
Area 840,000 sq miles (2,175,516 sq km)

France

FRANCE HAS DEVELOPED economic ties with its overseas territories, thereby stressing interdependence over independence. Overseas *départements*, officially part of France, have their own governments. Territorial *collectivités* and overseas *territoires* have varying degrees of autonomy.

Clipperton Island
East Pacific

Status Dependency of French Polynesia
Claimed 1930
Capital *not applicable*
Population None
Area 2.7 sq miles (7 sq km)

French Guiana
South America

Status Overseas department
Claimed 1817
Capital Cayenne
Population 135,000
Area 35,135 sq miles (90,996 sq km)

French Polynesia
South Pacific

Status Overseas territory
Claimed 1843
Capital Papeete
Population 211,000
Area 1,608 sq miles (4,165 sq km)

Guadeloupe
West Indies

Status Overseas department
Claimed 1635
Capital Basse-Terre
Population 413,000
Area 687 sq miles (1,780 sq km)

Martinique
West Indies

Status Overseas department
Claimed 1635
Capital Fort-de-France
Population 371,000
Area 425 sq miles (1,100 sq km)

Mayotte
Indian Ocean

Status Territorial collectivity
Claimed 1843
Capital Mamoudzou
Population 97,088
Area 144 sq miles (374 sq km)

New Caledonia
South Pacific

Status Overseas territory
Claimed 1853
Capital Nouméa
Population 179,000
Area 7,374 sq miles (19,103 sq km)

Réunion
Indian Ocean

Status Overseas department
Claimed 1638
Capital Denis
Population 632,000
Area 970 sq miles (2,512 sq km)

St Pierre & Miquelon
North America

Status Territorial collectivity
Claimed 1604
Capital Saint-Pierre
Population 6,000
Area 93.4 sq miles (242 sq km)

Wallis & Futuna
South Pacific

Status Overseas territory
Claimed 1842
Capital Matā'Utu
Population 14,000
Area 106 sq miles (274 sq km)

Netherlands

THE COUNTRY'S TWO remaining overseas territories were formerly part of the Dutch West Indies. Both are now self-governing, but the Netherlands remains responsible for their defense.

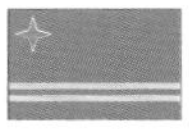

Aruba
West Indies

Status Autonomous part of the Netherlands
Claimed 1643
Capital Oranjestad
Population 69,000
Area 75 sq miles (194 sq km)

Netherlands Antilles
West Indies

Status Autonomous part of the Netherlands
Claimed 1816
Capital Willemstad
Population 195,000
Area 308 sq miles (800 sq km)

New Zealand

NEW ZEALAND'S GOVERNMENT has no desire to retain any overseas territories. However, the economic weakness of its dependent territory, Tokelau and its freely associated states, Niue and the Cook Islands, has forced New Zealand to remain responsible for their foreign policy and defense.

Cook Islands
South Pacific

Status Associated territory
Claimed 1901
Capital Avarua
Population 19,000
Area 113 sq miles (293 sq km)

Niue
South Pacific

Status Associated territory
Claimed 1901
Capital Alofi
Population 2,000
Area 102 sq miles (264 sq km)

Tokelau
South Pacific

Status Dependent territory
Claimed 1926
Capital *not applicable*
Population 2,000
Area 4 sq miles (10.4 sq km)

Norway

IN 1920, 41 nations signed the Spitsbergen treaty recognizing Norwegian sovereignty over Svalbard. There is a NATO base on Jan Mayen. Bouvet Island is a nature reserve.

Bouvet Island
South Atlantic

Status Dependency
Claimed 1928
Capital *not applicable*
Population None
Area 22 sq miles (58 sq km)

Jan Mayen
North Atlantic
Status Dependency
Claimed 1929
Capital *not applicable*
Population None
Area 147 sq miles (381 sq km)

Peter I Island
Southern Ocean
Status Dependency
Claimed 1931
Capital *not applicable*
Population None
Area 69 sq miles (180 sq km)

Svalbard
Arctic Ocean
Status Dependency
Claimed 1920
Capital Longyearbyen
Population 3,431
Area 24,289 sq miles (62,906 sq km)

Portugal

After a coup in 1974, Portugal's overseas possessions were rapidly granted sovereignty. Macao is the only one remaining and it is to become a Special Administrative Region of China in 1999.

Macao
South China
Status Special territory
Claimed 1557
Capital Macao
Population 388,000
Area 7 sq miles (18 sq km)

United Kingdom

The UK still has the largest number of overseas territories. Locally-governed by a mixture of elected representatives and appointed officials, they all enjoy a large measure of internal self-government, but certain powers, such as foreign affairs and defense, are reserved for Governors of the British Crown.

Anguilla
West Indies
Status Dependent territory
Claimed 1650
Capital The Valley
Population 8,960
Area 37 sq miles (96 sq km)

Ascension Island
South Atlantic
Status Dependency of St Helena
Claimed 1673
Capital Georgetown
Population 1,099
Area 34 sq miles (88 sq km)

Bermuda
North Atlantic
Status Crown colony
Claimed 1612
Capital Hamilton
Population 60,686
Area 20.5 sq miles (53 sq km)

British Indian Ocean Territory
Indian Ocean
Status Dependent territory
Claimed 1814
Capital No official capital
Population 3,400
Area 23 sq miles (60 sq km)

British Virgin Islands
West Indies
Status Dependent territory
Claimed 1672
Capital Road Town
Population 16,644
Area 59 sq miles (153 sq km)

Cayman Islands
West Indies
Status Dependent territory
Claimed 1670
Capital George Town
Population 25,355
Area 100 sq miles (259 sq km)

Falkland Islands
South Atlantic
Status Dependent territory
Claimed 1832
Capital Stanley
Population 2,121
Area 4,699 sq miles (12,173 sq km)

Gibraltar
Southwest Europe
Status Crown colony
Claimed 1713
Capital Gibraltar
Population 28,074
Area 2.5 sq miles (6.5 sq km)

Guernsey
Channel Islands
Status Crown dependency
Claimed 1066
Capital St Peter Port
Population 58,000
Area 25 sq miles (65 sq km)

Isle of Man
British Isles
Status Crown dependency
Claimed 1765
Capital Douglas
Population 71,000
Area 221 sq miles (572 sq km)

Jersey
Channel Islands
Status Crown dependency
Claimed 1066
Capital St Helier
Population 84,082
Area 45 sq miles (116 sq km)

Montserrat
West Indies
Status Dependent territory
Claimed 1632
Capital Plymouth (currently uninhabitable)
Population 11,000
Area 40 sq miles (102 sq km)

Pitcairn Islands
South Pacific
Status Dependent territory
Claimed 1887
Capital Adamstown
Population 66
Area 1.35 sq miles (3.5 sq km)

St Helena
South Atlantic
Status Dependent territory
Claimed 1673
Capital Jamestown
Population 6,000
Area 47 sq miles (122 sq km)

South Georgia & the South Sandwich Islands
South Atlantic
Status Dependent territory
Claimed 1775
Population No permanent residents
Area 1,387 sq miles (3,592 sq km)

Tristan da Cunha
South Atlantic
Status Dependency of St Helena
Claimed 1612
Population 297
Area 38 sq miles (98 sq km)

Turks & Caicos Islands
West Indies
Status Dependent territory
Claimed 1766
Capital Cockburn Town
Population 13,000
Area 166 sq miles (430 sq km)

United States of America

America's overseas territories have been seen as strategically useful, if expensive, links with its "backyards." The US has, in most cases, given the local population a say in deciding their own status. A US Commonwealth territory, such as Puerto Rico has a greater level of independence than that of a US unincorporated or external territory.

American Samoa
South Pacific
Status Unincorporated territory
Claimed 1900
Capital Pago Pago
Population 51,000
Area 75 sq miles (195 sq km)

Baker & Howland Islands
South Pacific
Status Unincorporated territory
Claimed 1856
Capital *not applicable*
Population None
Area 0.54 sq miles (1.4 sq km)

Guam
West Pacific
Status Unincorporated territory
Claimed 1898
Capital Agaña
Population 144,000
Area 212 sq miles (549 sq km)

Jarvis Island
South Pacific
Status Unincorporated territory
Claimed 1856
Capital *not applicable*
Population None
Area 1.7 sq miles (4.5 sq km)

Johnston Atoll
Central Pacific
Status Unincorporated territory
Claimed 1858
Capital *not applicable*
Population 327
Area 1 sq mile (2.8 sq km)

Kingman Reef
Central Pacific
Status Administered territory
Claimed 1856
Capital *not applicable*
Population None
Area 0.4 sq miles (1 sq km)

Midway Islands
Central Pacific
Status Administered territory
Claimed 1867
Capital *not applicable*
Population 453
Area 2 sq miles (5.2 sq km)

Navassa Island
West Indies
Status Unincorporated territory
Claimed 1856
Capital *not applicable*
Population None
Area 2 sq miles (5.2 sq km)

Northern Mariana Islands
West Pacific
Status Commonwealth territory
Claimed 1947
Capital No official capital
Population 47,000
Area 177 sq miles (457 sq km)

Palmyra Atoll
Central Pacific
Status Unincorporated territory
Claimed 1898
Capital *not applicable*
Population None
Area 5 sq miles (12 sq km)

Puerto Rico
West Indies
Status Commonwealth territory
Claimed 1898
Capital San Juan
Population 3.6 million
Area 3,458 sq miles (8,959 sq km)

Virgin Islands
West Indies
Status Unincorporated territory
Claimed 1917
Capital Charlotte Amalie
Population 104,000
Area 137 sq miles (355 sq km)

Wake Island
Central Pacific
Status Unincorporated territory
Claimed 1898
Capital *not applicable*
Population 302
Area 2.5 sq miles (6.5 sq km)

North & Central America

Canada

Canada extends from its US border north to the Arctic Ocean. In recent years, French-speaking Québec has sought independence from the rest of the country.

Geography
Arctic tundra and islands give way to forests, interspersed with lakes and rivers, and then central plains, with vast prairies. Rocky Mountains in the west.

Climate
Ranges from polar in the north, to cool in the south. Winters in the interior are colder than on the coast, with freezing temperatures and deep snow.

People and Society
Most people live along narrow strip near US border. Social issues include welfare provision and Commonwealth membership. Government welcomes ethnic diversity among immigrants. Land claims by indigenous peoples settled recently.

The Niagara Falls are situated on the Canada–US border.

The Economy
Wide-ranging resources, providing cheap energy and raw materials for manufactures, underpin high standard of living. Better productivity and rise of high-tech industries have increased unemployment. Concern over primary export prices.

Factfile

Official Name Canada
Date of Formation 1867/1949
Capital Ottawa
Population 27.8 million
Total Area 3,851,788 sq miles (9,976,140 sq km)
Density 7 people per sq mile
Languages English*, French*, Chinese, Italian, German, Portuguese, Cree, Inuktitut
Religions Catholic 46%, Protestant 30%, other 24%
Ethnic Mix British origin 40%, French origin 27%, other European 20%, Indian and Inuit 2%, other 11%
Government Parliamentary state
Currency Canadian $ = 100 cents

North & Central America

United States of America

Stretching across the most temperate part of North America, and with many natural resources, the US is the world's leading economic power.

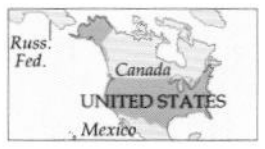

Geography
Central plain, mountains in west, hills and low mountains in east. Forested north and east, southwestern deserts.

Climate
Continental in north, hot summers and mild winters in southeast, desert climate in southwest. Arctic climate in Alaska; Florida and Hawaii tropical.

People and Society
Multiracial population, established through immigration, initially from Europe and Africa, with more recent influxes from Latin America and Asia. Strong sense of nationhood.

The Economy
Innovation, skilled labor and venture capital help high-tech industries replace outdated manufacturing. Global dominance of US culture boosts services, manufactures. Vast agriculture, mining sectors.

Factfile

Official Name United States of America
Date of Formation 1787/1959
Capital Washington DC
Population 265.8 million
Total Area 3,681,760 sq miles (9,372,610 sq km)
Density 72 people per sq mile
Languages English*, Spanish, other
Religions Protestant 56%, Catholic 28%, Jewish 2%, other 14%
Ethnic Mix White (inc. Hispanic) 83%, Black 13%, other 4%
Government Multiparty republic
Currency US $ = 100 cents

North & Central America

Mexico

Located between the United States of America and the Central American states, Mexico was a Spanish colony for 300 years until 1836.

Geography
Coastal plains along Pacific and Atlantic seaboards rise to a high, arid central plateau. To the east and west are Sierra Madre mountain ranges. Limestone lowlands in the Yucatan peninsula.

Climate
Plateau and high mountains are warm for much of year. Pacific coast is tropical: storms occur mostly March–December. Northwest is dry.

People and Society
Faster-growing population than any other large country – it doubled between 1960 and 1980. Most Mexicans are of mixed Spanish and Indian descent. Rural Indians largely segregated from Hispanic society and most live in poverty.

The cathedral of Santa Prisca at Taxco in Guerrero, Mexico.

The Economy
One of the world's largest oil producers. Tropical fruits, vegetables grown as cash crops. US companies poised to move into Mexico and enter competition with Mexican industry.

Factfile

Official Name United Mexican States
Date of Formation 1836/1867
Capital Mexico City
Population 95.5 million
Total Area 756,061 sq miles (1,958,200 sq km)
Density 126 people per sq mile
Languages Spanish*, Mayan dialects
Religions Roman Catholic 89%, Protestant 6%, other 5%
Ethnic Mix *Mestizo* 55%, Indian 30%, White 6%, other 9%
Government Multiparty republic
Currency Peso = 100 centavos

North & Central America

Guatemala

The largest state on the Central American isthmus, Guatemala returned to civilian rule in 1986, after 32 years of repressive military rule.

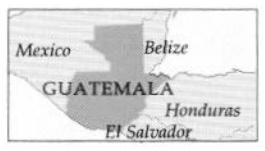

Geography
Narrow Pacific coastal plain. Central highlands with volcanoes. Short, swampy Caribbean coast. Tropical rain forests in the north.

Climate
Tropical, hot and humid in coastal regions and north. More temperate in central highlands

People and Society
Indians form a majority, but power, wealth, and land controlled by *ladino* elite. Highland Indians were main victims of the military's indiscriminate campaign against guerrilla groups 1978–84. Since civilian rule, the level of violence has diminished, but extreme poverty is still widespread.

The Economy
Agriculture is key sector. Sugar, coffee, beef, bananas, and cardamom top exports. Political stability has revived tourism.

Factfile

Official Name Republic of Guatemala
Date of Formation 1838
Capital Guatemala City
Population 10.9 million
Total Area 42,043 sq miles (108,890 sq km)
Density 259 people per sq mile
Languages Spanish*, Quiché, Mam, Kekchí, Cakchiquel
Religions Christian 99%, other 1%
Ethnic Mix Maya Indian 55%, *ladino* (Euro-Indian, White) 45%
Government Multiparty republic
Currency Quetzal = 100 centavos

NORTH & CENTRAL AMERICA

BELIZE

BELIZE LIES on the eastern shore of the Yucatan Peninsula in Central America. A former British colony, it became fully independent in 1981.

GEOGRAPHY

Almost half the land area is forested. Low mountains in south-east. Flat swampy coastal plains.

CLIMATE

Tropical. Very hot and humid, with May–December rainy season.

PEOPLE AND SOCIETY

Spanish-speaking *mestizos* now outnumber black Creoles for the first time. Huge influx of migrants from other states in the region in the past decade. This has caused some tension. Newcomers provide manpower for agriculture, but have put pressure on social services. Creoles have traditionally dominated society. Emigration to US has weakened their influence.

Fishermen near Belize City. More than 500 tons of Caribbean spiny lobster are caught annually.

THE ECONOMY

Agriculture, tourism and remittances from Belizeans living overseas are economic mainstays. Citrus fruit concentrates, lobsters, shrimp, and textiles are exported.

FACTFILE

Official Name Belize
Date of Formation 1981
Capital Belmopan
Population 200,000
Total Area 8,865 sq miles (22,960 sq km)
Density 23 people per sq mile
Languages English*, English Creole, Spanish, Maya, Garifuna
Religions Christian 87%, other 13%
Ethnic Mix *Mestizo* 44%, Creole 30%, Indian 11%, Garifuna 8%, other 7%
Government Parliamentary democracy
Currency Belizean $ = 100 cents

NORTH & CENTRAL AMERICA

EL SALVADOR

EL SALVADOR is Central America's smallest state. A 12-year war between US-backed government troops and left-wing guerrillas ended in 1992.

GEOGRAPHY

Narrow coastal belt backed by mountain ranges with over 20 volcanic peaks. Central plateau.

CLIMATE

Tropical coastal belt is very hot, with seasonal rains. Cooler, temperate climate in highlands.

PEOPLE AND SOCIETY

Population is largely *mestizo*; ethnic tensions are few. The civil war was fought over economic disparities, which still exist, despite some reform. 75,000 people died during the war, many were unarmed civilians. Around 500,000 more were displaced – mainly rural peasant families. In 1992, left-wing movement gave up its arms and joined formal political process.

THE ECONOMY

Civil war caused $2 billion-worth of damage. Huge amounts of foreign aid needed for survival. Over-dependence on coffee, which accounts for 90% of exports.

FACTFILE

Official Name Republic of El Salvador
Date of Formation 1856/1838
Capital San Salvador
Population 5.9 million
Total Area 8,124 sq miles (21,040 sq km)
Density 726 people per sq mile
Languages Spanish*, Nahua
Religions Roman Catholic 75%, other (including Protestant) 25%
Ethnic Mix *Mestizo* (Euro-Indian) 89%, Indian 10%, White 1%
Government Multiparty republic
Currency Colón = 100 centavos

NORTH & CENTRAL AMERICA

HONDURAS

STRADDLING THE Central American isthmus, Honduras returned to democratic civilian rule in 1981, after a succession of military regimes.

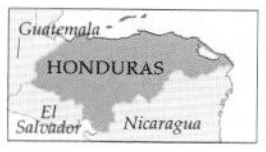

GEOGRAPHY

Narrow plains along both coasts. Mountainous interior, cut by river valleys. Tropical forests, swamps and lagoons in the east.

CLIMATE

Tropical coastal lowlands are hot and humid, with May–October rains. Interior is cooler and drier.

Honduras' main cash crops are bananas and coffee, accounting for 60% of export revenue. Tobacco (above) accounts for 1%.

PEOPLE AND SOCIETY

Majority of population is *mestizo*. Garifunas on Caribbean coast maintain their own language and culture. Indians inhabit the east, and remote mountain areas; their land rights are often violated. Most of the rural population live in poverty. Land reform, and high unemployment are major issues facing the government.

THE ECONOMY

Second poorest country in the region. Bananas are traditional cash crop – production dominated by two US companies. Coffee, timber, and livestock also exported.

FACTFILE

Official Name Republic of Honduras
Date of Formation 1838
Capital Tegucigalpa
Population 5.8 million
Total Area 43,278 sq miles (112,090 sq km)
Density 134 people per sq mile
Languages Spanish*, English Creole, Garifuna, Indian languages
Religions Catholic 97%, other 3%
Ethnic Mix *Mestizo* 90%, Indian 7%, Garifuna (Black Carib) 2%, White 1%
Government Multiparty republic
Currency Lempira = 100 centavos

NORTH & CENTRAL AMERICA

NICARAGUA

NICARAGUA LIES at the heart of Central America. An 11-year war between left-wing Sandinistas and right-wing US-backed Contras ended in 1989.

GEOGRAPHY

Extensive forested plains in the east. Central mountain region with many active volcanoes. Pacific coastlands are dominated by lakes.

CLIMATE

Tropical. Hot all year round in the lowlands. Cooler in the mountains. Occasional hurricanes.

PEOPLE AND SOCIETY

The isolated Atlantic regions, populated by Miskito Indians and blacks, gained limited independence in 1987. Elections in 1990 brought a right-wing pro-US party to power, but the Sandinistas remain a major political force in a country where poverty and unrest are rising.

THE ECONOMY

Coffee, sugar, and cotton are the main exports. All are affected by low world prices. Economy dependent on foreign aid; the US is the largest donor.

FACTFILE

Official Name Republic of Nicaragua
Date of Formation 1838
Capital Managua
Population 4.6 million
Total Area 50,193 sq miles (130,000 sq km)
Density 91 people per sq mile
Languages Spanish*, English Creole, Miskito
Religions Catholic 95%, other 5%
Ethnic Mix *Mestizo* 69%, White 17%, Black 9%, Indian 5%
Government Multiparty republic
Currency Córdoba = 100 pence

NORTH & CENTRAL AMERICA

COSTA RICA

COSTA RICA is the most stable country in Central America. Its neutrality in foreign affairs is long-standing, but it has very strong ties with the US.

GEOGRAPHY

Coastal plains of swamp and savannh rise to a fertile central plateau, which leads to a mountain range with active volcanic peaks.

CLIMATE

Hot and humid in coastal regions. Temperate uplands. High annual rainfall.

PEOPLE AND SOCIETY

Population has a mixture of Spanish, African, and native Indian ancestry. Costa Rica's long democratic tradition, developed public health system and high literacy rates are unrivalled in the region. Plantation-owning families and the US are influential in politics.

The Pan-American Highway runs for 412 miles through Costa Rica, at times as only a simple gravel road.

THE ECONOMY

Traditionally agricultural, but mining and manufacturing are developing rapidly. Bananas, beef, and coffee are the leading exports. Tourist numbers have increased considerably in recent years.

FACTFILE

Official Name Republic of Costa Rica
Date of Formation 1821/1838
Capital San José
Population 3.5 million
Total Area 19,730 sq miles (51,100 sq km)
Density 177 people per sq mile
Languages Spanish*, English Creole, Bribri, Cabecar
Religions Catholic 95%, other 5%
Ethnic Mix White/*mestizo* (Euro-Indian) 96%, Black 2%, Indian 2%
Government Multiparty republic
Currency Colón = 100 centimos

NORTH & CENTRAL AMERICA

JAMAICA

FIRST COLONIZED by the Spanish and then, from 1655, by the English, the Caribbean island of Jamaica achieved independence in 1962.

GEOGRAPHY

Mainly mountainous, with lush tropical vegetation. Inaccessible limestone area in the northwest. Low, irregular coastal plains are broken by hills and plateaus.

CLIMATE

Tropical. Hot and humid, with temperate interior. Hurricanes are likely June–November.

PEOPLE AND SOCIETY

Ethnically diverse, but tensions result from the gulf between rich and poor, rather than race. Economic and political life dominated by a few wealthy, long-established families. Armed crime, much of it drugs-related, is a problem. Large areas of Kingston are ruled by Dons, gang leaders who administer their own violent justice.

THE ECONOMY

Major producer of bauxite (aluminum ore). Tourism well developed. Light industry and data processing for US companies. Sugar, coffee, and rum are exported.

FACTFILE

Official Name Jamaica
Date of Formation 1962
Capital Kingston
Population 2.5 million
Total Area 4,243 sq miles (10,990 sq km)
Density 590 people per sq mile
Languages English*, English Creole, Hindi, Spanish, Chinese
Religions Christian 60%, other 40%
Ethnic Mix Black 75%, mixed 15%, South Asian 5%, other 5%
Government Parliamentary democracy
Currency Jamaican $ = 100 cents

NORTH & CENTRAL AMERICA

PANAMA

PANAMA IS the southernmost country in Central America. The Panama Canal (under US-control until 2000) links the Pacific and Atlantic oceans.

GEOGRAPHY

Lowlands along both coasts, with savanna-covered plains and rolling hills. Mountainous interior. Swamps and rain forests in the east.

CLIMATE

Hot and humid, with heavy rainfall in May–December wet season. Cooler at high altitudes.

PEOPLE AND SOCIETY

Multi-ethnic society, dominated by people of Spanish origin. Indians live in remote areas. The Canal, and US military bases, have given society a cosmopolitan outlook, but the Catholic extended family remains strong. In 1989, US troops invaded to arrest its dictator General Noriega, on drugs charges, and to restore civilian rule.

THE ECONOMY

Important banking sector, plus related financial and insurance services. Earnings from merchant ships sailing under Panamanian flag. Banana and shrimp exports.

FACTFILE

Official Name Republic of Panama
Date of Formation 1903/1914
Capital Panama City
Population 2.7 million
Total Area 29,761 sq miles (77,080 sq km)
Density 90 people per sq mile
Languages Spanish*, English Creole, Indian languages
Religions Catholic 93%, other 7%
Ethnic Mix *Mestizo* 70%, Black 14%, White 10%, Indian 6%
Government Multiparty republic
Currency Balboa = 100 centesimos

NORTH & CENTRAL AMERICA

CUBA

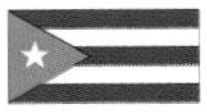

CUBA IS the largest island in the Caribbean and the only Communist country in the Americas. It has been led by Fidel Castro since 1959.

GEOGRAPHY

Mostly fertile plains and basins. Three mountainous areas. Forests of pine and mahogany cover one quarter of the country.

Canefields near Pinar del Río, Cuba. The undulating countryside is ideal for sugar cane.

CLIMATE

Subtropical. Hot all year round, and very hot in summer. Heaviest rainfall in the mountains. Hurricanes can strike in autumn.

PEOPLE AND SOCIETY

Castro's regime has reduced once extreme wealth disparities, given education a high priority and established an efficient health service. Political dissent, however, is not tolerated. Dramatic fall in living standards in recent years has led 30,000 Cubans to flee by boat to the US, to seek asylum.

THE ECONOMY

Main product is sugar. Cuba's economy is in crisis following the loss of its patron and supplier, the former USSR. Recent reforms have allowed small-scale enterprise and use of US dollar. The 30-year-old US trade embargo continues.

FACTFILE

Official Name Republic of Cuba
Date of Formation 1902/1898
Capital Havana
Population 11.1 million
Total Area 42,803 sq miles (110,860 sq km)
Density 259 people per sq mile
Languages Spanish*, English, French, Chinese
Religions Roman Catholic 85%, other 15%
Ethnic Mix White 66%, Afro-European 22%, other 12%
Government Socialist republic
Currency Peso = 100 centavos

NORTH & CENTRAL AMERICA

BAHAMAS

LOCATED IN the western Atlantic, off the Florida coast, the Bahamas comprise some 700 islands and 2,400 keys, 30 of which are inhabited.

GEOGRAPHY

Long, mainly flat coral formations with a few low hills. Some islands have pine forests, lagoons, and mangrove swamps.

CLIMATE

Subtropical. Hot summers, and mild winters. Heavy rainfall, especially in summer. Hurricanes can strike from July–December.

PEOPLE AND SOCIETY

Over half the population live on New Providence. Tourist industry employs 40% of the work force. Remainder are engaged in traditional fishing and agriculture, or in administration. Close ties with US were strained in 1980s, with senior government members implicated in narcotics corruption. In 1993, tough policies instituted to deter settling of Haitian refugees.

Six tourists for every one of the Bahamas' inhabitants visit the islands every year.

THE ECONOMY

Tourism accounts for half of all revenues. Major international financial services sector, including banking and insurance.

FACTFILE

Official Name The Commonwealth of the Bahamas
Date of Formation 1973
Capital Nassau
Population 300,000
Total Area 5,359 sq miles (13,880 sq km)
Density 55 people per sq mile
Languages English*, English Creole
Religions Protestant 76%, Roman Catholic 19%, other 5%
Ethnic Mix Black 85%, White 15%
Government Parliamentary democracy
Currency Bahamian $ = 100 cents

NORTH & CENTRAL AMERICA

HAITI

SHARES THE Caribbean island of Hispaniola with the Dominican Republic. At independence in 1804, it became the world's first black republic.

GEOGRAPHY

Predominantly mountainous, with forests and fertile plains.

CLIMATE

Tropical, with rain throughout the year. Humid in coastal areas, much cooler in the mountains.

PEOPLE AND SOCIETY

Majority of population is of African descent. A few have European roots, primarily French. Rigid class structure maintains vast disparities of wealth. Most Haitians live in extreme poverty. In recent years, political oppression and a collapsing economy led thousands to seek asylum in the US. In 1994, US-led troops reinstated the elected president, who was ousted by the military in 1991.

THE ECONOMY

Few natural resources. In 1994, after three years of UN sanctions, the country's economic links were restored and foreign aid resumed.

FACTFILE

Official Name Republic of Haiti
Date of Formation 1804
Capital Port-au-Prince
Population 7.3 million
Total Area 10,714 sq miles (27,750 sq km)
Density 681 people per sq mile
Languages French*, French Creole*, English
Religions Roman Catholic 80%, Protestant 16%, Voodoo 4%
Ethnic Mix Black 95%, Afro-European 5%
Government Multiparty republic
Currency Gourde = 100 centimes

NORTH & CENTRAL AMERICA

DOMINICAN REPUBLIC

OCCUPIES THE eastern two thirds of the island of Hispaniola in the Caribbean. Frequent coups and a strong US influence mark its recent past.

GEOGRAPHY

Highlands and rain forested mountains – including highest peak in Caribbean, Pico Duarte – interspersed with fertile valleys. Extensive coastal plain in the east.

View south from Pico Duarte, at 10,131 ft, the highest point in the Dominican Republic.

CLIMATE

Hot and humid close to sea level, cooler at altitude. Heavy rainfall, especially in the northeast.

PEOPLE AND SOCIETY

White landowners and the military hold political power. Mixed-race majority control commerce and form bulk of middle classes. Many of the poor are black. White and mixed-race women are starting to enter the professions. Widespread poverty and high unemployment have led some Dominicans to emigrate to the US, or become drug-traffickers.

THE ECONOMY

Mining – mainly of nickel and gold – and sugar are major sectors. Hidden economy based on transshipment of narcotics to the US. Recent dramatic growth in tourism.

FACTFILE

Official Name Dominican Republic
Date of Formation 1865
Capital Santo Domingo
Population 8 million
Total Area 18,815 sq miles (48,730 sq km)
Density 425 people per sq mile
Languages Spanish*, French Creole
Religions Roman Catholic 95%, other (Protestant, Jewish) 5%
Ethnic Mix Afro-European 73%, White 16%, Black 11%
Government Multiparty republic
Currency Peso = 100 centavos

NORTH & CENTRAL AMERICA

ST KITTS & NEVIS

ST KITTS AND NEVIS lies in the northern part of the Leeward Islands chain in the Caribbean. Nevis is the less developed of the two islands.

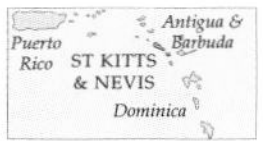

GEOGRAPHY

Volcanic in origin, with forested, mountainous interiors. Nevis has hot and cold springs.

CLIMATE

Tropical, tempered by trade winds. Little seasonal variation in temperature. Moderate rainfall.

PEOPLE AND SOCIETY

Majority of the population is of African descent. Intermarriage has blurred other racial lines and eliminated ethnic tensions. For most people, the extended family is the norm. Wealth disparities are not great, but urban professionals enjoy a higher standard of living than rural sugar cane farmers. Politics is based on the British system; funds are provided by professionals and the trade unions. The proposed Leeward Islands' union is the main political issue.

THE ECONOMY

Sugar industry, currently UK-managed, has preferential access to EU and US markets. Successful and still expanding tourist industry.

FACTFILE

Official Name Federation of Saint Christopher and Nevis
Date of Formation 1983
Capital Basseterre
Population 41,000
Total Area 139 sq miles (360 sq km)
Density 294 people per sq mile
Languages English*, English Creole
Religions Protestant 85%, Roman Catholic 10%, other Christian 5%
Ethnic Mix Black 95%, mixed 5%
Government Parliamentary democracy
Currency E. Caribbean $ = 100 cents

ANTIGUA & BARBUDA

LYING ON the Atlantic edge of the Leeward Islands, Antigua and Barbuda's area includes the uninhabited islet of Redonda.

GEOGRAPHY
Mainly low-lying limestone and coral islands with some higher volcanic areas. Antigua's coast is indented with bays and harbors.

CLIMATE
Tropical, moderated by trade winds and sea breezes. Humidity and rainfall are low for the region.

PEOPLE AND SOCIETY
Population almost entirely of African origin, with small groups of Europeans and South Asians. Women's status has risen as a result of greater access to education. Wealth disparities are small and unemployment is low. Politics dominated for past 30 years by the Bird family.

THE ECONOMY
Tourism is the main source of revenue and the biggest provider of jobs. Fishing and sea-island cotton industries are expanding.

FACTFILE
Official Name Antigua and Barbuda
Date of Formation 1981
Capital St John's
Population 65,000
Total Area 170 sq miles (440 sq km)
Density 382 people per sq mile
Languages English*, English Creole
Religions Protestant 87%, Roman Catholic 10%, other 3%
Ethnic Mix Black 98%, other 2%
Government Parliamentary democracy
Currency E. Caribbean $ = 100 cents

DOMINICA

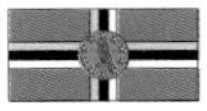

DOMINICA RESISTED European colonization until the 18th century, when it was controlled first by the French, and then, until 1978, by the British.

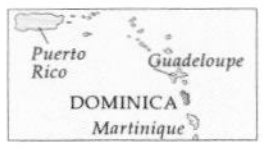

GEOGRAPHY
Mountainous and densely forested. Volcanic activity has given it very fertile soils, hot springs, geysers, and black sand beaches.

CLIMATE
Tropical, cooled by constant trade winds. Heavy annual rainfall. Tropical depressions and hurricanes are likely June–November.

PEOPLE AND SOCIETY
Population mainly of African origin. Small community of Carib Indians – the last remaining in the Caribbean – on the east coast. Most people live in extended families. Electoral system based on British model; politicians tend to come from professional classes, usually doctors or lawyers. For 15 years until 1995, Dominica was governed by Eugenia Charles, the first female prime minister in the Caribbean.

Inshore fishing boats, which mostly supply the domestic market, hauled up on a Dominican beach.

THE ECONOMY
Bananas and tourism are the economic mainstays. Current preferential access to EU and US markets now threatened by moves to deregulate the banana trade.

FACTFILE
Official Name Commonwealth of Dominica
Date of Formation 1978
Capital Roseau
Population 71,000
Total Area 290 sq miles (750 sq km)
Density 244 people per sq mile
Languages English*, French Creole, Carib, Cocoy
Religions Roman Catholic 77%, Protestant 15%, other 8%
Ethnic Mix Black 98%, Indian 2%
Government Multiparty republic
Currency E. Caribbean $ = 100 cents

ST LUCIA

AMONG THE most beautiful of the Caribbean Windward Islands, St Lucia retains both French and British influences from its colonial history.

GEOGRAPHY
Volcanic and mountainous, with some broad fertile valleys. The Pitons, ancient lava cones, rise from the sea on the forested west coast.

CLIMATE
Tropical, moderated by trade winds. May–October wet season brings daily warm showers. Rainfall is highest in the mountains.

PEOPLE AND SOCIETY
Population is a tension-free mixture of descendants of Africans, Europeans and South Asians. Family life and the Church are important to most St Lucians. In rural areas women often head the households, and run much of the farming. There is growing local resistance to over-development of the island by tourism. A proposed union with the other Windward Islands is the main political issue.

THE ECONOMY
Mainly agricultural, some light industry. Bananas are biggest export. Successful tourist industry, but most resorts are foreign-owned.

FACTFILE
Official Name Saint Lucia
Date of Formation 1979
Capital Castries
Population 141,000
Total Area 239 sq miles (620 sq km)
Density 589 people per sq mile
Languages English*, French Creole, Hindi, Urdu
Religions Catholic 90%, other 10%
Ethnic Mix Black 90%, Afro-European 6%, South Asian 4%
Government Parliamentary democracy
Currency E. Caribbean $ = 100 cents

ST VINCENT & THE GRENADINES

INDEPENDENT FROM Britain in 1979, the volcanic islands of St Vincent and the Grenadines form part of the Windward Islands of the Caribbean.

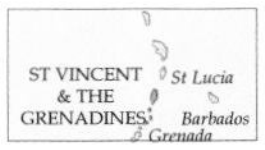

GEOGRAPHY
St Vincent is mountainous and forested, with one of two active volcanoes in the Caribbean, La Soufrière. The Grenadines are 32 islands and keys fringed by beaches.

An aerial view of Union Island in the Grenadines chain. The government is developing the island as a yachting center.

CLIMATE
Tropical, with constant trade winds. Hurricanes are likely during the July–November wet season.

PEOPLE AND SOCIETY
Population is racially diverse, but intermarriage has reduced tensions. Society is informal and relaxed, but family life is strongly influenced by the Anglican Church. Locals fear that their traditional lifestyle is being threatened by the expanding tourist industry.

THE ECONOMY
Dependent on agriculture and tourism. Bananas are the main cash crop. Tourism, targeted at the jet-set and cruise-ship markets, is concentrated on the Grenadines.

FACTFILE
Official Name St Vincent and the Grenadines
Date of Formation 1979
Capital Kingstown
Population 111,000
Total Area 131 sq miles (340 sq km)
Density 847 people per sq mile
Languages English*, English Creole
Religions Protestant 62% Roman Catholic 19%, other 19%
Ethnic Mix Black 82%, mixed 14%, White 3%, South Asian 1%
Government Parliamentary democracy
Currency E. Caribbean $ = 100 cents

NORTH & CENTRAL AMERICA

BARBADOS

BARBADOS IS the most easterly of the Caribbean Windward Islands. Under British rule for 339 years, it became fully independent in 1966.

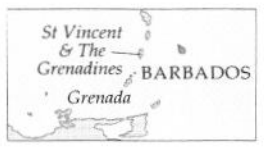

GEOGRAPHY

Encircled by coral reefs. Fertile and predominantly flat, with a few gentle hills to the north.

CLIMATE

Moderate tropical climate. Sunnier and drier than its more mountainous neighbors

PEOPLE AND SOCIETY

Some latent tension between white community, who control politics and much of the economy, and majority black population, but violence is rare. Increasing social mobility has enabled black Bajans to enter the professions. Despite political stability and good welfare and education services, emigration is high, notably to the US and UK.

St George's harbor in Grenada. Most tourist developments are on the beaches south of the capital.

THE ECONOMY

Sugar is the traditional cash crop. Well-developed tourist industry employs almost 40% of the work force. Financial services and information processing are important new growth sectors.

FACTFILE

Official Name Barbados
Date of Formation 1966
Capital Bridgetown
Population 300,000
Total Area 166 sq miles (430 sq km)
Density 1,607 people per sq mile
Languages English*, English Creole
Religions Protestant 94%, Roman Catholic 5%, other 1%
Ethnic Mix Black 80%, mixed 15%, White 4%, other 1%
Government Parliamentary democracy
Currency Barbados $ = 100 cents

NORTH & CENTRAL AMERICA

GRENADA

THE WINDWARD island of Grenada became a focus of attention in 1983, when the US mounted an invasion to sever the growing links with Cuba.

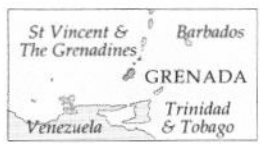

GEOGRAPHY

Volcanic in origin, with densely forested central mountains. Its territory includes the islands of Carriacou and Petite Martinique.

CLIMATE

Tropical, tempered by trade winds. Hurricanes are a hazard in the July–November wet season.

PEOPLE AND SOCIETY

Grenadians are mainly of African origin; their traditions remain strong, especially on Carriacou. Inter-ethnic marriage has reduced tensions between the groups. Extended families, often headed by women, are the norm. The invasion ousted the Marxist regime and restored democracy.

THE ECONOMY

Nutmeg, the most important crop, is currently affected by low world prices. Mace, cocoa, saffron, and cloves are also grown. Tourism has developed in the past decade.

FACTFILE

Official Name Grenada
Date of Formation 1974
Capital St George's
Population 92,000
Total Area 131 sq miles (340 sq km)
Density 702 people per sq mile
Languages English*, English Creole
Religions Roman Catholic 68%, Protestant 32%
Ethnic Mix Black 84%, Afro-European 13%, South Asian 3%
Government Parliamentary democracy
Currency E. Caribbean $ = 100 cents

NORTH & CENTRAL AMERICA

TRINIDAD & TOBAGO

THE FORMER British colony of Trinidad and Tobago is the most southerly of the West Indies, lying just 9 miles (15 km) off the coast of Venezuela.

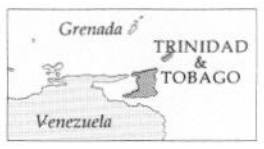

GEOGRAPHY

Both islands are hilly and wooded. Trinidad has a rugged mountain range in the north, and swamps on its east and west coasts

Tobago's white sand beaches, verdant landscape and natural anchorages have encouraged tourist development on the island.

CLIMATE

Tropical, with July–December wet season. Escapes the region's hurricanes, which pass to the north.

PEOPLE AND SOCIETY

Blacks and South Asians are the biggest groups. Minorities of Chinese and Europeans. Politics has recently become fragmented, and dominated by the race issue. An attempted coup by a Muslim sect in 1990 strengthened black opposition to the possibility of a South Asian prime minister.

THE ECONOMY

Oil accounts for 70% of export earnings. Gas is increasingly being exploited to support new industries. Tourism, particularly on Tobago, is being developed.

FACTFILE

Official Name Republic of Trinidad and Tobago
Date of Formation 1962
Capital Port-of-Spain
Population 1.3 million
Total Area 1,981 sq miles (5,130 sq km)
Density 656 people per sq mile
Languages English*, other
Religions Christian 58%, Hindu 30%, Muslim 8%, other 4%
Ethnic Mix Black 43%, South Asian 40%, mixed 14%, other 3%
Government Multiparty republic
Currency Trin. & Tob. $ = 100 cents

SOUTH AMERICA

COLOMBIA

LYING IN northwest South America, Colombia is one of the world's most violent countries, with powerful drugs cartels and guerrilla activity.

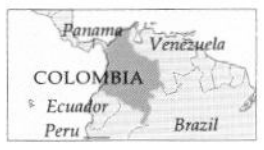

GEOGRAPHY

The densely forested and almost uninhabited east is separated from the western coastal plains by the Andes, which divide into three ranges with intervening valleys.

CLIMATE

Coastal plains are hot and wet. The highlands are cooler. The equatorial east has two wet seasons.

PEOPLE AND SOCIETY

Most Colombians are of mixed blood. Native Indians are concentrated in the southwest and Amazonia. Recent constitutional reform has given them a greater political voice. Blacks are the least represented group. The government, with US help, is engaged in an all-out war against the drugs barons.

THE ECONOMY

Healthy and diversified export sector – especially coffee and coal. Considerable growth potential, but drugs-related violence and corruption deter foreign investors.

FACTFILE

Official Name Republic of Colombia
Date of Formation 1819/1922
Capital Bogotá
Population 35.7 million
Total Area 439,733 sq miles (1,138,910 sq km)
Density 81 people per sq mile
Languages Spanish*, Indian languages, English Creole
Religions Catholic 95%, other 5%
Ethnic Mix *Mestizo* 58%, White 20%, mixed 14%, other 8%
Government Multiparty republic
Currency Peso = 100 centavos

VENEZUELA

LOCATED ON the north coast of South America, Venezuela has the continent's most urbanized society. Most people live in the northern cities.

GEOGRAPHY

Andes mountains and the Maracaibo lowlands in the northwest. Central grassy plains drained by Orinoco river system. Forested Guiana Highlands in the southeast.

CLIMATE

Tropical. Hot and humid. Uplands are cooler. Orinoco plains are alternately parched or flooded.

PEOPLE AND SOCIETY

Latin America's "melting pot" with immigrants from Europe and all over South America. The few indigenous Indians live in remote areas and maintain their traditional lifestyle. Oil wealth has brought prosperity, but many people still live in poverty – there were food riots in 1991. Corruption is a feature of Venezuelan political life.

The Orinoco River, Venezuela. The huge llanos *(plains) close to the river are grazed by five million cattle.*

THE ECONOMY

In addition to oil, Venezuela has vast reserves of coal, bauxite, iron, and gold. Government revenues dented by over-manned and often inefficient state sector, plus widespread tax evasion.

FACTFILE

Official Name Republic of Venezuela
Date of Formation 1830/1929
Capital Caracas
Population 22.3 million
Total Area
352,143 sq miles (912,050 sq km)
Density
63 people per sq mile
Languages
Spanish*, Indian languages
Religions Roman Catholic 96%, Protestant 2%, other 2%
Ethnic Mix *Mestizo* 67%, White 21%, Black 10%, Indian 2%
Government
Multiparty republic
Currency
Bolívar = 100 centimos

SOUTH AMERICA

GUYANA

THE ONLY English-speaking country in South America, Guyana gained independence from Britain in 1966, and became a republic in 1970.

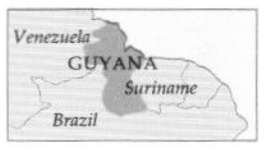

GEOGRAPHY

Mainly artificial coast, reclaimed by dikes and dams from swamps and tidal marshes. Forests cover 85% of the interior, rising to savanna uplands and mountains.

CLIMATE

Tropical. Coast cooled by sea breezes. Lowlands are hot, wet, and humid. Highlands are a little cooler.

PEOPLE AND SOCIETY

Population largely descended from Africans brought over during slave trade, or from South Asian laborers who arrived after slavery was abolished. Racial rivalry exists between the two groups. Small numbers of Chinese and native Indians. Government was once characterized by favoritism toward Afro-Guyanese. This was reversed with the election in 1992 of a South Asian-dominated party.

THE ECONOMY

Free-market economics have improved prospects. Bauxite, gold, rice, and diamonds are produced.

FACTFILE

Official Name Republic of Guyana
Date of Formation 1966
Capital Georgetown
Population 800,000
Total Area
83,000 sq miles (214,970 sq km)
Density
10 people per sq mile
Languages English*, English Creole, Hindi, Urdu, Indian languages
Religions Christian 57%, Hindu 33%, Muslim 9%, other 1%
Ethnic Mix South Asian 51%, Black and mixed 43%, other 6%
Government
Multiparty republic
Currency
Guyana $ =100 cents

SOUTH AMERICA

SURINAME

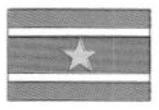

A FORMER Dutch colony on the north coast of South America. Democracy was restored in 1991, after almost 11 years of military rule.

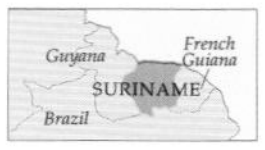

GEOGRAPHY

Mostly covered by tropical rain forest. Coastal plain, central plateaus and the Guiana Highlands.

CLIMATE

Tropical. Hot and humid, cooled by trade winds. High rainfall, especially in the interior.

PEOPLE AND SOCIETY

About 200,000 people have emigrated to the Netherlands since independence. Of those left, 90% live near the coast, the rest live in scattered rain forest communities. Around 7,000 are indigenous Indians. Also *bosnegers* – descendants of runaway African slaves. They fought the Creole-dominated government in the 1980s. Many South Asians and Javanese work in farming. Since return to civilian rule, each group has a political party representing its interests.

Suriname's capital, Paramaribo has fine examples of Dutch 18th and 19th century architecture.

THE ECONOMY

Aluminum and bauxite are the leading exports. Rice and fruit are main cash crops. Oil reserves.

FACTFILE

Official Name Republic of Suriname
Date of Formation 1975
Capital Paramaribo
Population 400,000
Total Area
63,039 sq miles (163,270 sq km)
Density
6 people per sq mile
Languages Dutch*, Pidgin English (Taki-Taki), Hindi, Javanese, Carib
Religions Christian 48%, Hindu 27%, Muslim 20%, other 5%
Ethnic Mix South Asian 37%, Creole 31%, Javanese 15%, other 17%
Government
Multiparty republic
Currency Guilder = 100 cents

SOUTH AMERICA

ECUADOR

ECUADOR SITS high on South America's western coast. Its territory includes the Galapagos Islands, 610 miles (970 km) to the west.

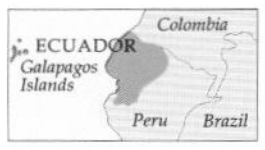

GEOGRAPHY

Broad coastal plain, inter-Andean central highlands, dense jungle in upper Amazon Basin.

CLIMATE

Hot and moist on the coast, cool in the Andes, and hot equatorial in the Amazon Basin.

PEOPLE AND SOCIETY

Most people live in coastal lowlands or Andean highlands. Many have migrated from over-farmed Andean valleys to main port and commercial center, Guayaquil. Strong and unified Indian movement backed by Catholic Church. Amazonian Indians are successfully pressing for recognition of land rights.

THE ECONOMY

World's biggest banana producer. Net oil exporter. Commercial agriculture is main employer. Fishing industry. Ecotourism on Galapagos Islands.

FACTFILE

Official Name Republic of Ecuador
Date of Formation 1830/1942
Capital Quito
Population 11.7 million
Total Area
109,483 sq miles (283,560 sq km)
Density
106 people per sq mile
Languages Spanish*, Quechua* and eight other Indian languages
Religions
Catholic 95%, other 5%
Ethnic Mix *Mestizo* (Euro-Indian) 55%, Indian 25%, Black 10%, White 10%
Government
Multiparty republic
Currency Sucre = 100 centavos

SOUTH AMERICA

PERU

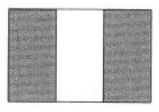

ONCE THE heart of the Inca empire, before the Spanish conquest in the 16th century, Peru lies on the Pacific coast of South America.

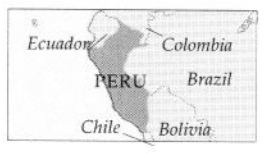

GEOGRAPHY

Coastal plain rises to Andes mountains. Uplands, dissected by fertile valleys, lie east of Andes. Tropical forest in extreme east.

CLIMATE

Coast is mainly arid. Middle slopes of Andes are temperate; higher peaks are snow-covered. East is hot, humid, and very wet.

PEOPLE AND SOCIETY

Populated mainly by Indians or mixed-race *mestizos*, but society is dominated by a small group of Spanish descendants. Indians, together with the small black community, suffer discrimination in the towns. In 1980, *Sendero Luminoso* (Shining Path) guerrillas began armed struggle against the government. Since then, over 25,000 people have died as a result of guerrilla, and army, violence.

With a population of 11 million, the Rio de Janeiro conurbation is Brazil's largest urban area after São Paulo.

THE ECONOMY

Abundant mineral resources. Rich fish stocks. Illegal export of coca leaves for cocaine production.

FACTFILE

Official Name Republic of Peru
Date of Formation 1824/1942
Capital Lima
Population 24.2 million
Total Area 496,223 sq miles (1,285,220 sq km)
Density 48 people per sq mile
Languages Spanish*, Quechua*, Aymará*, other Indian languages
Religions Catholic 95%, other 5%
Ethnic Mix Indian 45%, *mestizo* 37%, White 15%, Black, Japanese, Chinese and other 3%
Government Multiparty republic
Currency New sol = 100 centimos

SOUTH AMERICA

BRAZIL

BRAZIL COVERS more than half of South America and is the site of the world's largest and most important rain forest. The country has immense natural resources.

GEOGRAPHY

Vast, forested Amazon Basin in north. Semiarid scrubland in northeast mountains, fertile highlands in the south. Coastal plain with swampy areas in the southeast. Atlantic coastline is 1,240 miles (2,000 km) long.

CLIMATE

Hot and humid in Amazon Basin. Frequent droughts in northeast. Range of temperature and rainfall on plateau. Hot summers and cool winters in south.

PEOPLE AND SOCIETY

Population includes native Indians, blacks, and people of mixed race. Shanty towns in the cities attract migrants from the northeast. Urban crime, land disputes and unchecked Amazonia development tarnish image. Catholicism and the family remain strong.

THE ECONOMY

Hyperinflation, poor planning and corruption frustrate efforts to harness mineral reserves, diverse industry and agriculture.

FACTFILE

Official Name Federative Republic of Brazil
Date of Formation 1822/1929
Capital Brasília
Population 164.4 million
Total Area 3,286,472 sq miles (8,511,970 sq km)
Density 50 people per sq mile
Languages Portuguese*, German, Italian, English, Spanish, Polish, Japanese, Indian languages
Religions Catholic 90%, other 10%
Ethnic Mix White (Portuguese, Italian, German, Japanese) 55%, mixed 38%, Black 6%, other 1%
Government Multiparty republic
Currency Real = 100 centavos

SOUTH AMERICA

CHILE

EXTENDS IN a ribbon down the west coast of South America. Chile returned to democracy in 1989 after a referendum rejected its military dictator.

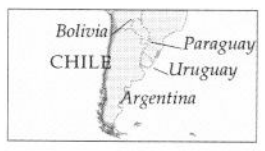

GEOGRAPHY

Pampas (broad grassy plains) between coastal uplands and Andes. Atacama Desert in north. Deep sea channels, lakes, and fiords in south.

CLIMATE

Arid in the north. Hot, dry summers and mild winters in the center. Higher Andean peaks have glaciers and year-round snow. Very wet and stormy in the south.

Lake Titicaca lies on the border between Bolivia and Peru. It is the world's highest lake.

PEOPLE AND SOCIETY

Most people are of European stock, and are highly urbanized. Indigenous Indians live almost exclusively in the south. Poor housing, water, and air pollution are problems in Santiago. General Pinochet's dictatorship was brutally repressive, but the business and middle classes prospered. Growth has continued under civilian rule, but many Chileans live in poverty.

THE ECONOMY

World's biggest producer of copper. Growth in foreign investment due to political stability. Wine, fishmeal, fruits, and salmon are exported.

FACTFILE

Official Name Republic of Chile
Date of Formation 1818/1929
Capital Santiago
Population 14.5 million
Total Area 292,258 sq miles (756,950 sq km)
Density 49 people per sq mile
Languages Spanish*, Indian languages
Religions Roman Catholic 89%, Protestant 11%
Ethnic Mix White and *mestizo* 92%, Indian 6%, other 2%
Government Multiparty republic
Currency Peso = 100 centavos

SOUTH AMERICA

BOLIVIA

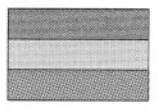

BOLIVIA LIES landlocked high in central South America. Mineral riches once made it the region's wealthiest state. Today, it is the poorest.

GEOGRAPHY

A high windswept plateau, the *altiplano*, lies between two Andean mountain ranges. Semi-arid grasslands to the southeast; dense tropical forests to the north.

CLIMATE

Altiplano has extreme tropical climate, with night frost in winter. North and east are hot and humid.

PEOPLE AND SOCIETY

Indigenous majority is discriminated against at most levels of society. Political process and economy remain under the control of a few wealthy families of Spanish descent. Most Bolivians are poor subsistence farmers or miners. Women have low status.

THE ECONOMY

Gold, silver, zinc, and tin are mined. Recently discovered oil and natural gas deposits. Overseas investors remain deterred by social problems of extreme poverty, and the influence of cocaine barons.

FACTFILE

Official Name Republic of Bolivia
Date of Formation 1825/1938
Capital La Paz
Population 7.6 million
Total Area 424,162 sq miles (1,098,580 sq km)
Density 18 people per sq mile
Languages Spanish*, Quechua*, Aymará*, Tupi-Guaraní
Religions Catholic 95%, other 5%
Ethnic Mix Indian 55%, *mestizo* 27%, White 10%, other 8%
Government Multiparty republic
Currency Boliviano = 100 centavos

South America

Paraguay

Landlocked in central South America. Its post-independence history has included periods of military rule. Free elections were held in 1993.

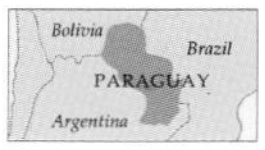

Geography

The River Paraguay divides hilly and forested east from a flat alluvial plain with marsh and semi-desert scrubland in the west.

Climate

Subtropical. Gran Chaco is generally hotter and drier. All areas experience floods and droughts.

People and Society

Population mainly of mixed Spanish and native Indian origin. Most are bilingual, but Guaraní is spoken by preference outside the capital. Gran Chaco is home to small groups of pure Guaraní Indians, cattle-ranchers and Mennonites, a sect of German origin, who live by a cooperative farming system.

The Iguazu Falls lie on the border between Brazil and Paraguay.

The Economy

Agriculture employs 45% of the work force. Soybeans and cotton are main exports. Electricity exporter – earnings cover oil imports. Growth is slow due to remote, landlocked position.

Factfile

Official Name Republic of Paraguay
Date of Formation 1811/1938
Capital Asunción
Population 5.1 million
Total Area 157,046 sq miles (406,750 sq km)
Density 32 people per sq mile
Languages Spanish*, Guaraní*, Plattdeutsch (Low German)
Religions Catholic 90%, other 10%
Ethnic Mix *Mestizo* (Euro-Indian) 95%, White 3%, Indian 2%
Government Multiparty republic
Currency Guaraní = 100 centimos

South America

Uruguay

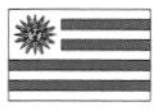

Uruguay is situated in southeastern South America. It returned to civilian government in 1985, after 12 years of military dictatorship.

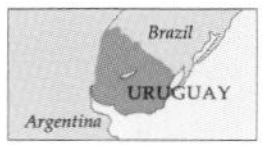

Geography

Low, rolling grasslands cover 80% of the country. Narrow coastal plain. Alluvial flood plain in south-west. Five rivers flow westward and drain into the River Uruguay.

Climate

Temperate throughout the country. Warm summers, mild winters and moderate rainfall.

People and Society

Uruguayans are largely second or third generation Italians or Spaniards. Wealth derived from cattle ranching enabled the country to become the first welfare state in South America. Economic decline since 1960s, but a large, if less prosperous, middle class remains. Although a Roman Catholic country, Uruguay is liberal in its attitude to religion and all forms are tolerated. Divorce is legal.

The Economy

Most land given over to crops and livestock. Wool, meat, and hides are exported. Earnings as offshore banking center. Buoyant tourism.

Factfile

Official Name Republic of Uruguay
Date of Formation 1828/1909
Capital Montevideo
Population 3.2 million
Total Area 68,498 sq miles (177,410 sq km)
Density 46 people per sq mile
Languages Spanish*, other
Religions Catholic 77%, Protestant 3%, Jewish 2%, other 18%
Ethnic Mix White 88%, *mestizo* (Euro-Indian) 8%, Black 4%
Government Multiparty republic
Currency Peso = 100 centesimos

South America

Argentina

Occupying most of the southern half of South America, Argentina extends 2,145 miles (3,460 km) from Bolivia to Tierra del Fuego.

Geography

Andes mountains in the west form a natural border with Chile. East of the Andes are heavily wooded plains in the north, treeless but fertile Pampas plains in the center. Bleak, arid Patagonia in south.

Herding cattle in northeast Argentina, near Corrientes. Beef is still one of the country's major exports.

Climate

Northeast is subtropical. Andes are semiarid in the north, snowy in the south. Western lowlands are arid. Pampas have mild climate.

People and Society

People largely of European descent, mostly from 20th-century migrations from Italy and Germany. Indigenous peoples now in a minority, living mainly in Andean regions or the Gran Chaco. Over 85% of Argentinians are urban dwellers; 40% live in capital.

The Economy

Rich and varied agricultural base. Powerful agribusiness – leading exporter of beef, wheat, and fruit. Important oil and gas reserves still underexploited.

Factfile

Official Name Argentine Republic
Date of Formation 1816/1925
Capital Buenos Aires
Population 35 million
Total Area 1,068,296 sq miles (2,766,890 sq km)
Density 32 people per sq mile
Languages Spanish*, Italian, English, German, French, Indian languages
Religions Catholic 90%, Jewish 2%, other 8%
Ethnic Mix White 85%, other (including *mestizo* and Indian) 15%
Government Multiparty republic
Currency Peso = 100 centavos

Africa

Morocco

A former French colony in northwest Africa, independent in 1956. Morocco has occupied the disputed territory of Western Sahara since 1975.

Geography

Fertile coastal plain is interrupted in the east by the Rif mountains. Atlas Mountain ranges to the south. Beyond lies the outer fringe of the Sahara.

Climate

Ranges from temperate and warm in the north, to semi-arid in the south. Cooler in the mountains.

People and Society

About 35% are descendants of original Berber inhabitants of northwest Africa, and live mainly in mountain villages. Arab majority inhabit lowlands. Large rural–urban gap in wealth. High birth rate. King Hassan heads a powerful monarchy. Government threatened by Islamic militants who fear country is losing its Islamic, Arab identity and becoming too influenced by Europe.

The Economy

World's main exporter of phosphates. Tourism and agriculture have great potential.

Factfile

Official Name Kingdom of Morocco
Date of Formation 1956
Capital Rabat
Population 27.6 million
Total Area 269,757 sq miles (698,670 sq km)
Density 102 people per sq mile
Languages Arabic*, Berber, French
Religions Muslim 99%, other 1%
Ethnic Mix Arab and Berber 99%, European 1%
Government Constitutional monarchy
Currency Dirham = 100 centimes

AFRICA

ALGERIA

ALGERIA ACHIEVED independence from France in 1962. Today, its military-dominated government faces a severe challenge from Islamic extremists.

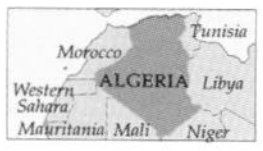

GEOGRAPHY

85% of the country lies within the Sahara. Fertile coastal region with plains and hills rises in the southeast to the Atlas Mountains.

CLIMATE

Coastal areas are warm and temperate, with most rainfall during the mild winters. The south is very hot, with negligible rainfall.

PEOPLE AND SOCIETY

Algerians are predominantly Arab, under 30 years of age and urban. Most indigenous Berbers consider the mountainous Kabylia region in the northeast to be their homeland. The Sahara sustains just 500,000 people, mainly oil workers and Tuareg nomads with goat and camel herds, who move between the irrigated oases. In recent years, political violence has claimed the lives of 3,000 people.

A Saharan town showing the wide range of Algeria's scenery, from irrigated gardens to sandy dunes.

THE ECONOMY

Oil and gas exports. Political turmoil has led to exodus of skilled foreign labor. Limited agriculture.

FACTFILE

Official Name Democratic and Popular Republic of Algeria
Date of Formation 1962
Capital Algiers
Population 28.6 million
Total Area 919,590 sq miles (2,381,740 sq km)
Density 31 people per sq mile
Languages Arabic*, Berber, French
Religions Muslim 99%, Christian and Jewish 1%
Ethnic Mix Arab and Berber 99% European 1%
Government Military regime
Currency Dinar = 100 centimes

AFRICA

TUNISIA

TUNISIA HAS traditionally been one of the more liberal Arab states, but its government is now facing a challenge from Islamic fundamentalists.

GEOGRAPHY

Mountains in the north are surrounded by plains. Vast, low-lying salt pans in the center. To the south lies the Sahara.

CLIMATE

Summer temperatures are high. The north is often wet and windy in winter. Far south is arid.

PEOPLE AND SOCIETY

Population almost entirely of Arab-Berber descent, with Jewish and Christian minorities. Many still live in extended families. Women have better rights than in any other Arab country and make up 25% of the total work force. Politics, however, remains a male preserve. Low birth rate is a result of a long-standing family planning policy.

THE ECONOMY

Well-diversified, despite limited resources. Oil and gas are exported. Expanding manufacturing and tourist industries have been aided by European investment.

FACTFILE

Official Name Republic of Tunisia
Date of Formation 1956
Capital Tunis
Population 9.1 million
Total Area 63,170 sq miles (163,610 sq km)
Density 144 people per sq mile
Languages Arabic*, French
Religions Muslim 98%, Christian 1%, other 1%
Ethnic Mix Arab and Berber 98%, European 1%, other 1%
Government Multiparty republic
Currency Dinar = 1,000 millimes

AFRICA

LIBYA

SITUATED ON the Mediterranean coast of North Africa, Libya is a Muslim dictatorship, politically marginalized by the West for its terrorist links.

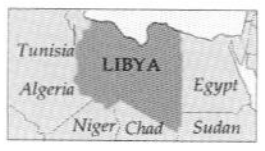

GEOGRAPHY

Apart from the coastal strip and a mountain range in the south, Libya is desert or semidesert. Oases provide agricultural land.

A Roman amphitheater at Sabratah, Libya, reflects the country's strategic importance in classical times.

CLIMATE

Hot and arid. Coastal area has temperate climate, with mild, wet winters and hot, dry summers.

PEOPLE AND SOCIETY

Most Libyans are of Arab and Berber origin. 1969 revolution brought Colonel Gadaffi to power. He stands for Islamic faith, communal lifestyle, and hatred of urban rich. Revolution wiped out private enterprise and middle classes. Jews and European settlers were banished. Libya has changed from being a nation of nomads and livestock herders to 70% city-dwellers.

THE ECONOMY

90% of export earnings come from oil. Subject to fluctuating world prices. Dates, olives, peaches, and grapes are grown in the oases.

FACTFILE

Official Name The Great Socialist People's Libyan Arab Jamahiriya
Date of Formation 1951
Capital Tripoli
Population 5.6 million
Total Area 679,358 sq miles (1,759,540 sq km)
Density 8 people per sq mile
Languages Arabic*, Tuareg
Religions Muslim 97%, other 3%
Ethnic Mix Arab and Berber 97%, other 3%
Government Socialist jamahiriya (state of the masses)
Currency Dinar = 1,000 dirhams

AFRICA

EGYPT

EGYPT OCCUPIES the northeast corner of Africa. Its essentially pro-Western, military-backed regime is being challenged by Islamic fundamentalists.

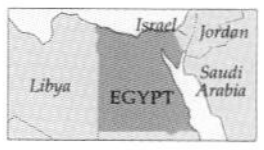

GEOGRAPHY

Fertile Nile valley separates arid Libyan Desert from smaller semiarid eastern desert. Sinai peninsula has mountains in south.

CLIMATE

Summers are very hot, but winters are cooler. Rainfall is negligible, except on the coast.

PEOPLE AND SOCIETY

Continuously inhabited for over 8,000 years, with a tradition of religious and ethnic tolerance. Egyptians are mostly Arabs, Bedouins, and Nubians. Women play full part in education system, politics, and economy. Government is fighting Islamic terrorist groups, whose acts of violence have included attacks on politicians, police, and tourists.

THE ECONOMY

Oil and gas are main sources of revenue. Tolls from the Suez Canal. Successful tourist industry is threatened by security fears.

FACTFILE

Official Name Arab Republic of Egypt
Date of Formation 1936/1982
Capital Cairo
Population 64.2 million
Total Area 386,660 sq miles (1,001,450 sq km)
Density 166 people per sq mile
Languages Arabic*, French, English, Berber, Greek, Armenian
Religions Muslim 94%, other 6%
Ethnic Mix Eastern Hamitic 90%, other (inc. Greek, Armenian) 10%
Government Multiparty republic
Currency Pound = 100 piastres

SUDAN

THE LARGEST country in Africa, Sudan borders the Red Sea. In 1989, an army coup installed a military Islamic fundamentalist regime.

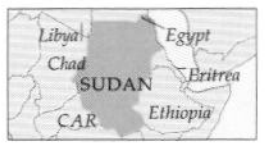

GEOGRAPHY
Lies within the upper Nile basin. Mostly arid plains, with marshes in the south. Highlands border the Red Sea in the northeast.

CLIMATE
North is hot, arid desert with constant dry winds. Rainy season ranging from two months in the center, to eight in the south.

PEOPLE AND SOCIETY
Large number of ethnic and linguistic groups. Two million people are nomads, moving over ancient tribal areas in the south. Major social division is between Arabized Muslims in north, and mostly African, largely Christian or animist peoples in south. Attempts to impose Arab and Islamic values throughout Sudan have been the root cause of the civil war that has ravaged the south since 1983.

Camel caravans in Sudan. Periodic drought and war mean that Sudan requires food aid.

THE ECONOMY
Sudan is frequently affected by drought and food shortages. Sesame seeds, cotton, and gum arabic are main cash crops.

FACTFILE
Official Name Republic of Sudan
Date of Formation 1956
Capital Khartoum
Population 28.9 million
Total Area 967,493 sq miles (2,505,815 sq km)
Density 29 people per sq mile
Languages Arabic*, other
Religions Muslim 70%, traditional beliefs 20%, Christian 5%, other 5%
Ethnic Mix Arab 51%, Dinka 13%, Nuba 9%, Beja 7%, other 20%
Government Military regime
Currency Pound = 100 piastres

ERITREA

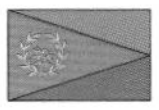

LYING ON the shores of the Red Sea, Eritrea effectively seceded from Ethiopia in 1993, following a 30-year war for independence.

GEOGRAPHY
Mostly rugged mountains, bush, and the Danakil Desert, which falls below sea level.

CLIMATE
Warm in the mountains; desert areas are hot. Droughts from July onward are common.

PEOPLE AND SOCIETY
Nine main ethnic groups. Tigrinya-speakers are the largest in number. Strong sense of nationhood forged by the war. Women played important role in the war, fighting alongside men. Over 80% of people are subsistence farmers. Few live beyond the age of 45. Transitional government will hold multiparty elections in 1997.

THE ECONOMY
Legacy of disruption and destruction from war. Susceptible to drought and famine. Most of the population live at subsistence level. Potential for mining of gold, copper, silver, and zinc. Possible foreign earnings from oil exports.

FACTFILE
Official Name State of Eritrea
Date of Formation 1993
Capital Asmara
Population 3.6 million
Total Area 36,170 sq miles (93,680 sq km)
Density 99 people per sq mile
Languages Tigrinya*, Arabic*, Tigre, Afar, Bilen, Kunama, Nara
Religions Coptic Christian 45%, Muslim 45%, other 10%
Ethnic Mix Nine main ethnic groups
Government Provisional military government
Currency Birr = 100 cents

DJIBOUTI

A CITY STATE with a desert hinterland, Djibouti lies in northeast Africa. Once known as French Somaliland, it became independent in 1977.

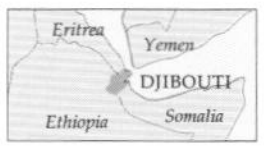

GEOGRAPHY
Mainly low-lying desert and semidesert, with a volcanic mountain range in the north.

CLIMATE
Hot all year round, with June–August temperatures reaching 109°F (45°C). Very low rainfall.

PEOPLE AND SOCIETY
Dominant ethnic groups are the Issas in the south, and the mainly nomadic Afars in the north. Tensions between them developed into a guerrilla war in 1991. Smaller tribal groups make up the rest of the population, together with French and other European expatriates, and Arabs. Population was swelled by 20,000 Somali refugees in 1992. France still exerts considerable influence in Djibouti, supporting it financially and maintaining a naval base and a military garrison.

THE ECONOMY
Djibouti's major asset is its port in a key Red Sea location.

FACTFILE
Official Name Republic of Djibouti
Date of Formation 1977
Capital Djibouti
Population 600,000
Total Area 8,958 sq miles (23,200 sq km)
Density 66 people per sq mile
Languages Arabic*, French*, Somali, Afar, other
Religions Christian 87%, other 13%
Ethnic Mix Issa 35%, Afar 20%, Gadaboursis and Isaaks 28%, other (inc. Arab, European) 17%
Government Single-party republic
Currency Franc = 100 centimes

ETHIOPIA

LOCATED IN northeast Africa, Ethiopia was a Marxist regime from 1974–91. It has suffered a series of economic, civil, and natural crises.

GEOGRAPHY
Great Rift Valley divides mountainous northwest region from desert lowlands in northeast and southeast. Ethiopian Highlands are drained mainly by the Blue Nile.

Lalibela in Ethiopia's central highlands is an important pilgrimage center, famed for its ten 12th century Christian churches.

CLIMATE
Generally moderate with summer rains. Highlands are warm, with night frost and snowfalls on the mountains.

PEOPLE AND SOCIETY
76 Ethiopian nationalities speak 286 languages. Oromo are largest group. In 1995, the first multiparty elections were held, beginning a new nine-state federation.

THE ECONOMY
Most people are subsistence farmers. Despite war-damaged infrastructure and periodic serious droughts, agricultural and industrial output are growing as it moves toward a market economy.

FACTFILE
Official Name Undetermined
Date of Formation 1903/1993
Capital Addis Ababa
Population 56.7 million
Total Area 435,605 sq miles (1,128,221 sq km)
Density 130 people per sq mile
Languages Amharic*, English, Arabic, Tigrinya, Orominga
Religions Muslim 43%, Christian 37%, traditional beliefs, other 20%
Ethnic Mix Oromo 40%, Amhara and Tigrean 32%, other 28%
Government Multiparty republic
Currency Birr = 100 cents

AFRICA

SOMALIA

A SEMIARID state occupying the horn of Africa. Italian Somaliland and British Somaliland were united in 1960 to form an independent Somalia.

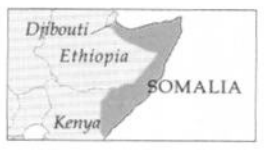

GEOGRAPHY
Highlands in the north, flatter scrub-covered land to the south. Northern coastal areas are hot and humid and are more fertile.

CLIMATE
Very dry, except for the north coast, which is hot and humid. Interior has among world's highest average yearly temperatures.

PEOPLE AND SOCIETY
Clan system forms the basis of all commercial, political, and social activities. Most people are herders (Samaal) while the rest are farmers (Sab). Years of clan-based civil war have resulted in collapse of central government. US-led UN peace-keeping force was deployed to try and bring peace to the country, but it was withdrawn in 1994.

THE ECONOMY
Somalia is heavily reliant on foreign aid, since all commodities, except arms, are in short supply. Formal economy has collapsed due to civil war and drought.

FACTFILE
Official Name Somali Democratic Republic
Date of Formation 1960
Capital Mogadishu
Population 9.5 million
Total Area 246,200 sq miles (637,660 sq km)
Density 39 people per sq mile
Languages Somali*, Arabic*, other
Religions Sunni Muslim 99%, other (inc. Christian) 1%
Ethnic Mix Somali 98%, Bantu, Arab 1.5%, European, other 0.5%
Government Transitional
Currency Shilling = 100 cents

AFRICA

UGANDA

UGANDA LIES landlocked in East Africa. It was ruled by one of Africa's more eccentric leaders, the dictator Idi Amin Dada, from 1971–1980.

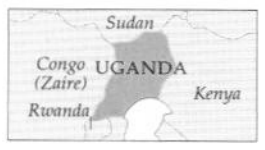

GEOGRAPHY
A large plateau with Great Rift Valley and Ruwenzori mountain range in the west; Lake Victoria in the southeast. Vegetation is of savanna type.

CLIMATE
Altitude and the influence of the lakes modify the equatorial climate. Rain falls throughout the year; spring is the wettest period.

PEOPLE AND SOCIETY
Large rural population with 13 main ethnic groups. President Museveni allowed the restoration of Uganda's four historical monarchies in 1993 to help with the breakdown of traditional animosities. New constitution will use a federal system with boundaries based on those of the old kingdoms.

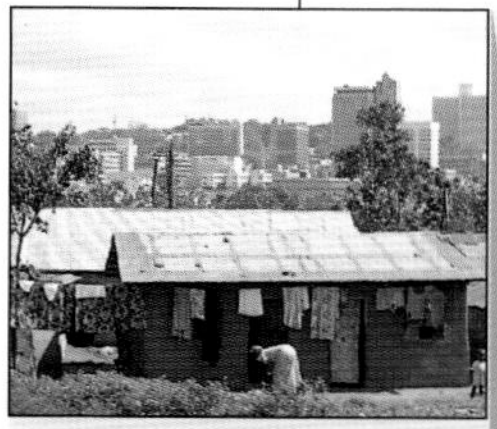

Kampala, the Ugandan capital lies in the country's most populous region, close to Lake Victoria.

THE ECONOMY
Coffee earns 93% of export income. Hydroelectric power planned to replace 50% of oil imports. Reopening of mines should improve the economy.

FACTFILE
Official Name Republic of Uganda
Date of Formation 1962
Capital Kampala
Population 22 million
Total Area 91,073 sq miles (235,880 sq km)
Density 241 people per sq mile
Languages English*, Luganda, Nkole, Chiga, Lango, Acholi, Teso
Religions Catholic/Protestant 66%, traditional beliefs 18%, Muslim 16%
Ethnic Mix Buganda 18%, Banyoro 14%, Teso 9%, other 59%
Government Multiparty republic
Currency Shilling = 100 cents

AFRICA

KENYA

KENYA STRADDLES the Equator on Africa's east coast. It became a multiparty democracy in 1992 and has been led by President Moi since 1978.

GEOGRAPHY
Central plateau divided by Great Rift Valley. North of the Equator is mainly semidesert. To the east lies a fertile coastal belt.

The Kenyan Conference Centre at Nairobi, the country's capital. The modern skyline contrasts sharply with the shacks on its outskirts.

CLIMATE
Coast and Great Rift Valley are hot and humid. Plateau interior is temperate. Northeastern desert is hot and dry. Rain generally falls April–May and October–November.

PEOPLE AND SOCIETY
Kenya's 70 ethnic groups share about 40 languages. Rural majority has strong clan and family links. One of the world's highest population growth rates, together with poverty, has exacerbated the recent surge in ethnic violence.

THE ECONOMY
Tourism is the leading foreign exchange earner. Tea and coffee grown as cash crops. Large and diversified manufacturing sector.

FACTFILE
Official Name Republic of Kenya
Date of Formation 1963
Capital Nairobi
Population 29.1 million
Total Area 224,081 sq miles (580,370 sq km)
Density 130 people per sq mile
Languages Swahili*, English, Kikuyu, Luo, Kamba, other
Religions Catholic/Protestant 66%, animist 26%, Muslim 6%, other 2%
Ethnic Mix Kikuyu 21%, Luhya 14%, Kamba 11%, other 54%
Government Multiparty republic
Currency Shilling = 100 cents

AFRICA

RWANDA

RWANDA LIES just south of the Equator in east central Africa. Since independence from France in 1962, ethnic tensions have dominated politics.

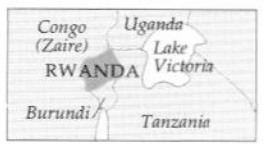

GEOGRAPHY
Series of plateaus descend from ridge of volcanic peaks in the west to Akagera River on eastern border. Great Rift Valley also passes through this region.

CLIMATE
Tropical, tempered by the altitude. Two wet seasons are separated by a dry season, June–August. Heaviest rain in the west.

PEOPLE AND SOCIETY
Rwandans live a subsistence existence. Traditional family and clan structures are strong. For over 500 years Tutsi were politically dominant over the Hutu tribe. In 1959, violent revolt led to a reversal of the roles. In 1994 over 200,000 people died in tribal violence.

THE ECONOMY
Rwanda has few resources, but under peaceful conditions, it produces coffee. Possible oil and gas reserves.

FACTFILE
Official Name Rwandese Republic
Date of Formation 1962
Capital Kigali
Population 8.2 million
Total Area 10,170 sq miles (26,340 sq km)
Density 806 people per sq mile
Languages Kinyarwanda*, French*, Kiswahili
Religions Catholic 65%, Protestant 7%, traditional beliefs 25%, other 1%
Ethnic Mix Hutu 90%, Tutsi 9%, Twa pygmy 1%
Government Multiparty republic
Currency Franc = 100 centimes

BURUNDI

SMALL, DENSELY populated and landlocked, Burundi lies just south of the Equator, on the Nile–Congo watershed in Central Africa.

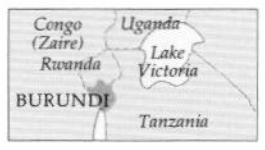

GEOGRAPHY
Hilly with high plateaus in centre and savanna in the east. Great Rift Valley and Lake Tanganyika on western side.

CLIMATE
Temperate, with high humidity. Heavy and frequent rainfall, mostly October–May.

PEOPLE AND SOCIETY
Burundi's postindependence history has been dominated by ethnic conflict – with repeated large-scale massacres – between majority Hutu and the Tutsi, who control the army. Over 120,000 people, mostly Hutu, have been killed since 1992. Twa pygmies are not involved in the conflict. Most people are subsistence farmers. Majority of Burundians are Roman Catholics.

Pig farming and fish ponds in Burundi. Most of the country's population depends on agriculture.

THE ECONOMY
Overwhelmingly agricultural economy. Small quantities of gold and tungsten. Potential of oil in Lake Tanganyika. Burundi has 5% of the world's nickel reserves.

FACTFILE
Official Name Republic of Burundi
Date of Formation 1962
Capital Bujumbura
Population 6.6 million
Total Area 10,750 sq miles (27,830 sq km)
Density 613 people per sq mile
Languages Kirundi*, French*, Swahili, other
Religions Catholic 62%, traditional beliefs 32%, Protestant 6%
Ethnic Mix Hutu 85%, Tutsi 13%, Twa pygmy 1%, other 1%
Government Multiparty republic
Currency Franc = 100 centimes

CENTRAL AFRICAN REPUBLIC

A LANDLOCKED country lying between the basins of the Chad and Congo rivers. Its arid north sustains less than 2% of the population.

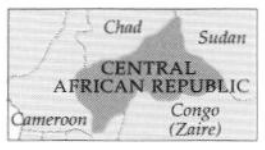

GEOGRAPHY
Comprises a low plateau, covered by scrub or savanna. Rain forests in the south. One of Africa's great rivers, the Ubangi, forms the border with Congo (Zaire).

CLIMATE
The south is equatorial; the north is hot and dry. Rain occurs all year round, with heaviest falls between July and October.

PEOPLE AND SOCIETY
Baya and Banda are largest ethnic groups, but Sangho, spoken by minority river peoples in the south, is the *lingua franca*. Most political leaders since independence have come from the south. Women, as in other non-Muslim African countries, have considerable power. Large number of ethnic groups helps limit disputes.

THE ECONOMY
Dominated by subsistence farming. Exports include gold, diamonds, cotton, and timber. Country is self-sufficient in food production. Poor infrastructure.

FACTFILE
Official Name Central African Republic
Date of Formation 1960
Capital Bangui
Population 3.4 million
Total Area 240,530 sq miles (622,980 sq km)
Density 14 people per sq mile
Languages French*, Sangho, Banda
Religions Christian 50%, traditional beliefs 27%, Muslim 15%, other 8%
Ethnic Mix Baya 34%, Banda 27%, Mandjia 21%, Sara 10%, other 8%
Government Multiparty republic
Currency CFA franc = 100 centimes

CONGO [ZAIRE]

STRADDLING THE Equator in east central Africa, Congo (Zaire) is one of Africa's largest countries. It achieved independence from Belgium in 1960.

GEOGRAPHY
Rain forested basin of River Congo occupies 60% of the land. High mountain ranges stretch down the eastern border.

The Congo River is navigable for 994 miles and provides one of the most convenient ways of travelling in the country.

CLIMATE
Tropical and humid. Distinct wet and dry seasons south of the Equator. The north is mainly wet.

PEOPLE AND SOCIETY
12 main groups and around 190 smaller ones. Original inhabitants, Forest Pygmies, are now a marginalized group. Ethnic tensions inherited from colonial period were contained until 1990, since when outbreaks of ethnic violence have occurred. Despotic regime of President Mobutu overthrown by rebel forces in 1997.

THE ECONOMY
25 years of mismanagement have brought economy near to collapse. Hyperinflation. Minerals, including copper and diamonds, provide 85% of export earnings

FACTFILE
Official Name Democratic Republic of Congo
Date of Formation 1960
Capital Kinshasa
Population 45.3 million
Total Area 905,563 sq miles (2,345,410 sq km)
Density 50 people per sq mile
Languages French*, Kiswahili, Tshiluba, Kikongo, Lingala
Religions Christian 70%, traditional beliefs 20%, Muslim 10%
Ethnic Mix Bantu 23%, Hamitic 23%, other (inc. Pygmy) 54%
Government Single party republic
Currency New zaire = 100 makuta

NIGER

NIGER LIES landlocked in West Africa, but it is linked to the sea by its one permanent river, the Niger. It became independent of France in 1960.

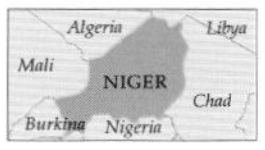

GEOGRAPHY
North and northeast regions are part of Sahara and Sahel. Aïr mountains in center rise high above the desert. Savanna in the south.

CLIMATE
High temperatures for most of the year – around 95°F (35°C). The north is virtually rainless.

PEOPLE AND SOCIETY
A largely Islamic society. Women have limited rights, and restricted access to education. Considerable tensions exist between Tuareg nomads in the north and groups in the south. Tuaregs have felt alienated from mainstream politics. They mounted a low-key revolt in 1990. Sense of community and egalitarianism among southern peoples helps to combat economic difficulties.

THE ECONOMY
Vast uranium deposits. Frequent droughts and southwest expansion of Sahara are problems.

FACTFILE
Official Name Republic of Niger
Date of Formation 1960
Capital Niamey
Population 9.5 million
Total Area 489,188 sq miles (1,267,000 sq km)
Density 19 people per sq mile
Languages French*, Hausa, Djerma, Fulani, Tuareg, Teda
Religions Muslim 85%, traditional beliefs 14%, Christian 1%
Ethnic Mix Hausa 56%, Djerma 22%, Fulani 9%, other 13%
Government Multiparty republic
Currency CFA franc = 100 centimes

AFRICA

CHAD

LANDLOCKED in north central Africa, Chad has been torn by intermittent periods of civil war since independence from France in 1960.

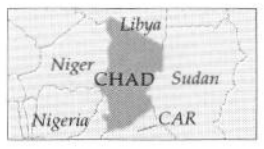

GEOGRAPHY
Mostly plateaux sloping westwards to Lake Chad. Northern third is Sahara. Tibesti mountains in north rise to 10,826 ft (3,300 m).

CLIMATE
Three distinct zones: desert in north, semiarid region in center and tropics in south.

PEOPLE AND SOCIETY
Half the population live in southern fifth of the country. Northern third has only 100,000 people, mainly Muslim Toubeu nomads. Political strife between Muslims in north and Christians in south. Recent attempts to introduce multi-party system, after 30 years of military and one-party rule.

THE ECONOMY
One of Africa's poorest states. Arid lands not suitable for commercial agriculture. Vast majority of people involved in subsistence agriculture, notably cotton and cattle herding. Recent discovery of large oil deposits.

FACTFILE
Official Name Republic of Chad
Date of Formation 1960
Capital Ndjamena
Population 6.5 million
Total Area 495,752 sq miles (1,284,000 sq km)
Density 13 people per sq mile
Languages French*, Sara, Maba
Religions Muslim 44%, Christian 33%, traditional beliefs 23%
Ethnic Mix Bagirmi, Sara and Kreish 31%, Sudanic Arab 26%, Teda 7%, other 36%
Government Transitional
Currency CFA franc = 100 centimes

AFRICA

MAURITANIA

SITUATED IN northwest Africa, two thirds of Mauritania's territory is desert. A former French colony, it achieved independence in 1960.

GEOGRAPHY
The Sahara, barren with scattered oases, covers the north. Savanna lands to the south.

CLIMATE
Generally hot and dry, aggravated by dusty *harmattan* wind. Summer rain in the south, virtually none in the north.

PEOPLE AND SOCIETY
The Maures, who make up two thirds of the population, control political life and dominate the minority black population. Ethnic tension centers on the oppression of blacks by Maures. Tens of thousands of blacks are estimated to be in slavery. Tensions came to a head in 1989 when over 200,000 Maures fled from Senegal. Family solidarity among nomadic peoples is particularly strong.

Only 1% of Mauritania's land is suitable for grain crops. Two thirds of the country is Sahara.

THE ECONOMY
Agriculture and herding are main agricultural activities. Iron and copper mining. World's largest gypsum deposits. Rich fishing grounds. Large foreign debt.

FACTFILE
Official Name Islamic Republic of Mauritania
Date of Formation 1960
Capital Nouakchott
Population 2.3 million
Total Area 395,953 sq miles (1,025,520 sq km)
Density 6 people per sq mile
Languages French*, Hassaniyah Arabic, Wolof
Religions Muslim 100%
Ethnic Mix Maure 80%, Wolof 7%, Tukulor 5%, other 8%
Government Multiparty republic
Currency Ouguiya = 5 khoums

AFRICA

MALI

LANDLOCKED in the heart of West Africa, Mali held its first free elections in 1992, more than 30 years after it gained independence from France.

GEOGRAPHY
Landlocked nation. Northern half lies in the Sahara. Inland delta of River Niger flows through grassy savannah region in the south.

A village near Bandiagara in eastern Mali. The low broken hills are typical of the region, the homeland of the Dogon people.

CLIMATE
In the south, intensely hot, dry weather precedes the westerly rains. The north is almost rainless.

PEOPLE AND SOCIETY
Most people live in southern savanna region. Bambara are politically dominant. A few nomadic Fulani and Tuareg herders travel northern plains. Extended family provides social security. Tension between peoples of the south and Tuaregs in north. 80% of population are Muslim.

THE ECONOMY
One of the poorest countries in the world. Less than 2% of land can be cultivated. Most people are farmers, herders or river fishermen. Gold deposits now being mined.

FACTFILE
Official Name Republic of Mali
Date of Formation 1960
Capital Bamako
Population 11.1 million
Total Area 478,837 sq miles (1,240,190 sq km)
Density 23 people per sq mile
Languages French*, Bambara, Fulani, Senufo, Soninké
Religions Muslim 80%, traditional beliefs 18%, Christian 2%
Ethnic Mix Bambara 31%, Fulani 13%, Senufo 12%, other 44%
Government Multiparty republic
Currency CFA franc = 100 centimes

AFRICA

SENEGAL

A FORMER French colony, Senegal achieved independence in 1960. Its capital, Dakar, stands on the westernmost cape of Africa.

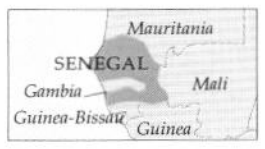

GEOGRAPHY
Arid semidesert in the north. The south is mainly savanna bushland. Plains in the southeast.

CLIMATE
Tropical, with humid rainy conditions June–October, and drier season December–May. Coast is cooled by northern trade winds.

PEOPLE AND SOCIETY
Little ethnic tension, due to significant intermarriage. Groups can be identified regionally. Dakar is a Wolof area, the Senegal River is dominated by the Toucouleur, and the Malinke mostly live in the east. The Diola in Casamance have felt politically excluded and this has led to unrest. French-influenced class system still exists and has become more obvious recently.

THE ECONOMY
70% of people are farmers – groundnuts are main export crop. Phosphate is mined. More industry than most West African countries.

FACTFILE
Official Name Republic of Senegal
Date of Formation 1960
Capital Dakar
Population 8.5 million
Total Area 75,950 sq miles (196,720 sq km)
Density 111 people per sq mile
Languages French*, Wolof, Fulani, Serer, Diola, Malinke, Soninke
Religions Muslim 92%, traditional beliefs 6%, Christian 2%
Ethnic Mix Wolof 46%, Fulani 25%, Serer 16%, Diola 7%, Malinke 6%
Government Multiparty republic
Currency CFA franc = 100 centimes

THE GAMBIA

A NARROW state on the west coast of Africa, The Gambia was renowned for its stability until its government was overthrown in a coup in 1994.

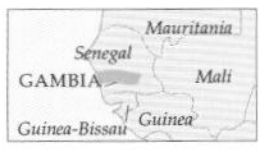

GEOGRAPHY

Narrow strip of land which borders River Gambia. Long, sandy beaches backed by mangrove swamps along river. Savanna and tropical forests higher up.

CLIMATE

Sub-tropical, with wet, humid months July–October and warm, dry season November–May

PEOPLE AND SOCIETY

Little tension between various ethnic groups. Creole community – the Aku, is small but socially prominent. People leaving rural areas for the towns, where average incomes are four times higher. Each year seasonal immigrants from neighboring states come to farm groundnuts. Women are active as traders.

A fish market in Gambia.

THE ECONOMY

80% of the labor force is involved in agriculture. Groundnuts are the principal crop. The fisheries sector is being improved. Growth in tourism now halted by political instability.

FACTFILE

Official Name Republic of The Gambia
Date of Formation 1965
Capital Banjul
Population 1.2 million
Total Area 4,363 sq miles (11,300 sq km)
Density 275 people per sq mile
Languages English*, other
Religions Muslim 85%, Christian 9%, traditional beliefs 6%
Ethnic Mix Mandinka 41%, Fulani 14%, Wolof 13%, other 32%
Government Military regime
Currency Dalasi = 100 butut

CAPE VERDE

OFF THE west coast of Africa, in the Atlantic Ocean, lies the group of islands that make up Cape Verde, a Portuguese colony until 1975.

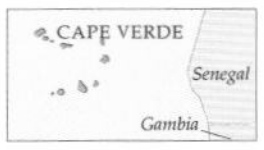

GEOGRAPHY

Ten main islands and eight smaller islets, all of volcanic origin. Mostly mountainous, with steep cliffs and rocky headlands.

CLIMATE

Warm, and very dry. Subject to droughts that may last for years at a time.

PEOPLE AND SOCIETY

Most people are of mixed Portuguese-African origin; the rest are largely African, descended from slaves or from more recent immigrants from the mainland. 50% of the population live on Santiago. Strong Roman Catholic influences. Some ethnic tension between islands. Peaceful transition to multiparty democracy in 1991.

THE ECONOMY

Most people are subsistence farmers. Fish is the main export. Only minerals produced are salt, and volcanic rock for cement. Experiments with natural energy taking place.

FACTFILE

Official Name Republic of Cape Verde
Date of Formation 1975
Capital Praia
Population 400,000
Total Area 1,556 sq miles (4,030 sq km)
Density 257 people per sq mile
Languages Portuguese*, Creole
Religions Roman Catholic 98%, Protestant 2%
Ethnic Mix Creole (mestiço) 71%, Black 28%, White 1%
Government Multiparty republic
Currency Escudo = 100 centavos

GUINEA-BISSAU

KNOWN AS Portuguese Guinea during its days as a colony, Guinea-Bissau is situated on Africa's west coast, bordered by Senegal and Guinea.

GEOGRAPHY

Low-lying, apart from savanna highlands in northeast. Rain forests and swamps are found along coastal areas.

Bafatá, in central Guinea-Bissau lies on the Gêba River and is an important inland port.

CLIMATE

Tropical, with wet season May–November and dry season December–April. Hot *harmattan* wind blows during dry season

PEOPLE AND SOCIETY

Largest ethnic group is Balante, who live in the south. Mixed Portuguese-African mestiços dominate top ranks of government and bureaucracy but comprise less than 2% of population. Most people live on small family farms in self-contained villages. First multiparty elections held in 1994.

THE ECONOMY

Mostly subsistence farming – corn, sweet potatoes, cassava. Main cash crops are cashews, groundnuts, and palm kernels. Offshore oil as yet untapped.

FACTFILE

Official Name Republic of Guinea-Bissau
Date of Formation 1974
Capital Bissau
Population 1.1 million
Total Area 13,940 sq miles (36,120 sq km)
Density 79 people per sq mile
Languages Portuguese*, other
Religions Traditional beliefs 54%, Muslim 38%, Christian 8%
Ethnic Mix Balante 27%, Fulani 22%, Malinke 12%, other 39%
Government Multiparty republic
Currency Peso = 100 centavos

GUINEA

FACING THE Atlantic Ocean, on the west coast of Africa, Guinea became the first French colony in Africa to gain independence, in 1958.

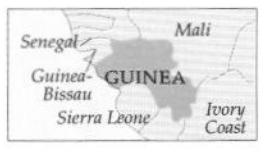

GEOGRAPHY

Coastal plains and mangrove swamps in west rise to forested or savanna highlands in the south. Semidesert in the north.

CLIMATE

Tropical, with wet season April–October. Heavy annual rainfall. In dry season, hot *harmattan* wind blows from the Sahara.

PEOPLE AND SOCIETY

Malinke and Fulani make up most of the population, but traditional rivalries between them have allowed coastal peoples such as the Susu to dominate politics. Women gained influence under Marxist party rule from 1958–84, but Muslim revival since then has reversed the trend. First multiparty elections held in 1995.

THE ECONOMY

Two thirds of people are farmers. Cash crops are palm oil, bananas, pineapples, and rice. Gold, diamond, and bauxite reserves.

FACTFILE

Official Name Republic of Guinea
Date of Formation 1958
Capital Conakry
Population 6.9 million
Total Area 94,926 sq miles (245,860 sq km)
Density 72 people per sq mile
Languages French*, Fulani, Malinke, Susu, Kissi, other
Religions Muslim 85%, Christian 8%, traditional beliefs 7%
Ethnic Mix Fulani 40%, Malinke 25%, Susu 12%, Kissi 7%, other 16%
Government Multiparty republic
Currency Franc = 100 centimes

AFRICA

SIERRA LEONE

THE WEST AFRICAN state of Sierra Leone achieved independence from the British in 1961. Today, it is one of the world's poorest nations.

GEOGRAPHY

Flat plain, running the length of the coast, stretches inland for 83 miles (133 km). Forests rise to highlands near neighboring Guinea in the northeast.

CLIMATE

Hot tropical climate, with very high rainfall and humidity. Dusty, northeastern *harmattan* wind blows November–April.

PEOPLE AND SOCIETY

Mende and Temne are major ethnic groups. Freetown's citizens descended from slaves freed from Britain and the US, resulting in a strongly anglicized Creole culture. A military coup in 1992 halted plans to turn the government into a multiparty democracy. Rebel forces have been fighting the government since 1991; leading to a coup in 1997.

A village near Gbanga, Liberia. The largest of Liberia's indigenous groups, the Kpelle, live in this area.

THE ECONOMY

Vast majority of people are subsistance farmers. Cash crops include palm kernels, cocoa beans, and kola. Main export is diamonds.

FACTFILE

Official Name Republic of Sierra Leone
Date of Formation 1961
Capital Freetown
Population 4.6 million
Total Area 27,699 sq miles (71,740 sq km)
Density 166 people per sq mile
Languages English*, Krio (Creole)
Religions Traditional beliefs 52%, Muslim 40%, Christian 8%
Ethnic Mix Mende 34%, Temne 31%, Limba 9%, Kono 5%, other 21%
Government Military regime
Currency Leone = 100 cents

AFRICA

LIBERIA

LIBERIA FACES the Atlantic Ocean in equatorial West Africa. Africa's oldest republic, it was established in 1847. Today it is torn by civil war.

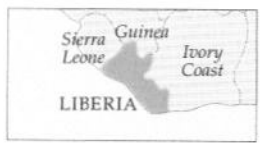

GEOGRAPHY

Coastline of beaches and mangrove swamps rises to forested plateaus and highlands inland.

CLIMATE

High temperatures. Except in extreme southeast, there is only one wet season, May–October.

PEOPLE AND SOCIETY

Key social distinction has been between Americo-Liberians – descendants of freed slaves – and the indigenous tribal peoples. However, political assimilation and intermarriage have eased tensions. Inter-tribal tension is now a problem. A civil war has ravaged the country since 1990, with private armies competing for power.

THE ECONOMY

Civil war has led to collapse of economy – little commercial activity. Only 1% of land is arable. Estimated one billion tonnes of iron-ore reserves at Mount Nimba, but current state of world demand does not justify their exploitation.

FACTFILE

Official Name Republic of Liberia
Date of Formation 1847/1907
Capital Monrovia
Population 3.1 million
Total Area 43,000 sq miles (111,370 sq km)
Density 72 people per sq mile
Languages English*, Kpelle, Bassa Vai, Grebo, Kru, Kissi, Gola
Religions Traditional beliefs 70%, Muslim 20%, Christian 10%
Ethnic Mix Kpelle 20%, Bassa 14%, Americo-Liberians 5%, other 61%
Government Transitional
Currency Liberian $ = 100 cents

AFRICA

IVORY COAST

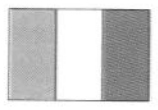

ONE OF the larger nations along the coast of West Africa, the Ivory Coast remains under the influence of its former colonial ruler, France.

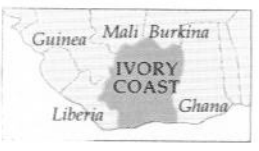

GEOGRAPHY

Sandy coastal strip backed by a largely rain forested interior, and a savanna plateau in the north.

A camel being used to plow fields in Burkina. The poor soil quality and frequent droughts leads to seasonal emigration.

CLIMATE

High temperatures all year round. South has two wet seasons; north has one, with lower rainfall.

PEOPLE AND SOCIETY

More than 60 ethnic groups. President Houphouët-Boigny, who ruled from independence until 1993, promoted his own group, the Baoule. Succession of Konan Bedic, another Baoule, has annoyed other tribes. The extended family keeps laborers who migrate to the cities in contact with their villages. Improved education means that many women now hold top jobs.

THE ECONOMY

Cash crops include cocoa, coffee, palm oil, bananas, and rubber. Teak, mahogany, and ebony in rain forests. Oil reserves.

FACTFILE

Official Name Republic of the Ivory Coast
Date of Formation 1960
Capital Yamoussoukro
Population 14.7 million
Total Area 124,503 sq miles (322,463 sq km)
Density 118 people per sq mile
Languages French*, Akran, other
Religions Traditional beliefs 63%, Muslim 25%, Christian 12%
Ethnic Mix Baoule 23%, Bété 18%, Kru 17%, Malinke 15%, other 27%
Government Multiparty republic
Currency CFA franc = 100 centimes

AFRICA

BURKINA

KNOWN AS Upper Volta until 1984, the West African state of Burkina has been under military rule for most of its post-independence history.

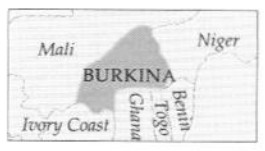

GEOGRAPHY

North of country is covered by the Sahara. South is largely savanna. Three main rivers are Black, White and Red Voltas

CLIMATE

Tropical. Dry, cool weather November-February. Erratic rain March-April, mostly in southeast.

PEOPLE AND SOCIETY

No ethnic group is dominant, but the Mossi have always played an important part in government. Extreme poverty has led to a strong sense of egalitarianism. The extended family is important, and reaches from villages into towns and cities. Women wield considerable power and influence within this system, but most are still denied access to education

THE ECONOMY

Based on agriculture – cotton is most valuable cash crop – but not self-sufficient in food. Gold is the leading nonagricultural export.

FACTFILE

Official Name Burkina
Date of Formation 1960
Capital Ouagadougou
Population 10.6 million
Total Area 105,870 sq miles (274,200 sq km)
Density 100 people per sq mile
Languages French*, Mossi, Fulani, Tuareg, Dyula, Songhai
Religions Traditional beliefs 65%, Muslim 25%, Christian 10%
Ethnic Mix Mossi 45%, Mande 10%, Fulani 10%, others 35%
Government Multiparty republic
Currency CFA franc = 100 centimes

Africa

Ghana

Once known as the Gold Coast, Ghana in West Africa has experienced intermittent periods of military rule since independence in 1957.

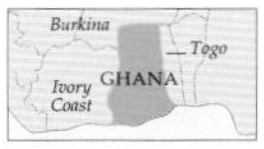

Geography

Mostly low-lying. West is covered by rain forest. Lake Volta – the world's third largest artificial lake – was created by damming the White Volta River.

Climate

Tropical. Two wet seasons in the south; one in the north.

People and Society

Around 75 ethnic groups of which the largest is the Akan. Over 100 languages and dialects are spoken. Southern peoples are richer and more urbanized than those of the north. In recent years, tension between groups in the north has erupted into violence. Multiparty elections in 1992 confirmed former military leader Jerry Rawlings in power.

The Economy

Ghana produces 15% of the world's cocoa. Good-quality hardwood trees such as maple and sapele are exploited for timber. Gold, diamonds, bauxite, and manganese are major exports.

Factfile

Official Name Republic of Ghana
Date of Formation 1957
Capital Accra
Population 18 million
Total Area 92,100 sq miles (238,540 sq km)
Density 195 people per sq mile
Languages English*, Akan, Mossi, Ewe, Ga, Twi, Fanti, Gurma, other
Religions Traditional beliefs 38%, Muslim 30%, Christian 24%, other 8%
Ethnic Mix Akan 52%, Mossi 15%, Ewe 12%, Ga 8%, other 13%
Government Multiparty republic
Currency Cedi = 100 pesewas

Africa

Togo

Togo lies sandwiched between Ghana and Benin in West Africa. The 1993–94 elections were the first since its independence in 1960.

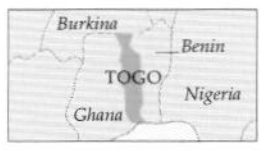

Geography

Central forested region bounded by savanna lands to the north and south. Mountain range stretches southwest to northeast.

Climate

Coast hot and humid; drier inland. Rainy season March–July, with heaviest falls in the west.

People and Society

Harsh resentment between Ewe in the south and Kabye in the north. Kabye control military, but are far less developed than people of the south. Extended family is important. Tribalism and nepotism are key factors in everyday life. Some ethnic groups, such as the Mina, have matriarchal societies.

Kabye cultivation near Kara, northern Togo. The main crops are cassava, yams, and corn.

The Economy

Most people are farmers. Self-sufficient in basic foodstuffs. Main export crops are coffee, cocoa, and cotton. Half of all export revenues come from phosphate deposits with the world's highest mineral content.

Factfile

Official Name Togolese Republic
Date of Formation 1960
Capital Lomé
Population 4.3 million
Total Area 21,927 sq miles (56,790 sq km)
Density 196 people per sq mile
Languages French*, Ewe, Kabye, Gurma, other
Religions Traditional beliefs 70%, Christian 20%, Muslim 10%
Ethnic Mix Ewe 43%, Kabye 26%, Gurma 16%, other 15%
Government Multiparty republic
Currency CFA franc = 100 centimes

Africa

Benin

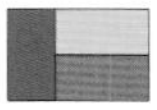

Stretches north from the West African coast. In 1990, it became one of the pioneers of African democratization, ending years of military rule.

Geography

Long, sandy coastal region. Numerous lagoons lie just behind the shoreline. Forested plateaus inland. Mountains in the northwest.

Fishing boats near Cotonou, on the Benin coast. There are numerous small lagoons clustered behind the short (62-mile) coastline.

Climate

Hot and humid in the south. Two rainy seasons. Hot, dusty *harmattan* winds blow during December-February dry season.

People and Society

Around 50 ethnic groups. Fon people in the south dominate politics. Other major groups are Adja and Yoruba. In the far north, Fulani are nomadic. Tension between north and south, partly reflects Muslim–Christian divide, and greater development of south. Women hold positions of power in retail trade.

The Economy

Mostly subsistence farming. Cash crops include cotton, cocoa beans, and coffee. Some oil and limestone are produced. France is the main aid donor.

Factfile

Official Name Republic of Benin
Date of Formation 1960
Capital Porto-Novo
Population 5.6 million
Total Area 43,480 sq miles (112,620 sq km)
Density 128 people per sq mile
Languages French*, Fon, Bariba, Yoruba, Adja, Houeda, Fulani
Religions Traditional beliefs 70%, Muslim 15%, Christian 15%
Ethnic Mix Fon 39%, Yoruba 12%, Adja 10%, other 39%
Government Multiparty republic
Currency CFA franc = 100 centimes

Africa

Nigeria

Four times the size of the United Kingdom, from which it gained independence in 1960, Nigeria in West Africa is a federation of 30 states.

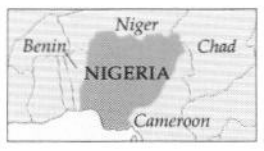

Geography

Coastal area of beaches, swamps and lagoons gives way to rain forest, and then to savanna on high plateaus. Semidesert in north.

Climate

South is hot, rainy and humid for most of the year. Arid north has one very humid wet season. Jos plateau and highlands are cooler.

People and Society

Some 250 ethnic groups: the largest are Hausa, Yoruba, Ibo, and Fulani. Tensions between groups threaten national unity, although this has been largely contained in recent years. International condemnation over govenment treatment of dissidents. Except in the Islamic north, women are allowed economic independence.

The Economy

Oil has been the economic mainstay since 1970s, accounting for 90% of export earnings.

Factfile

Official Name Federal Republic of Nigeria
Date of Formation 1960
Capital Abuja
Population 115 million
Total Area 356,668 sq miles (923,770 sq km)
Density 322 people per sq mile
Languages English*, Hausa, Yoruba
Religions Muslim 50%, Christian 40%, traditional beliefs 10%
Ethnic Mix Hausa 21%, Yoruba 20%, Ibo 17%, Fulani 9%, other 33%
Government Military regime
Currency Naira = 100 kobo

AFRICA

CAMEROON

SITUATED ON the central West African coast, Cameroon was effectively a one-party state for 30 years. Multiparty elections were held in 1992.

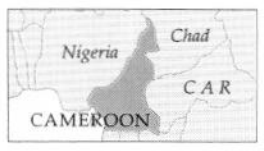

GEOGRAPHY
Over half the land is forested: equatorial rain forest in north, evergreen forest and wooded savanna in south. Mountains in the west.

CLIMATE
South is equatorial, with plentiful rainfall, declining inland. Far north is beset by drought.

PEOPLE AND SOCIETY
Around 230 ethnic groups; no single group is dominant. Bamileke is the largest, but it has never held political power. Some tension between more affluent south and poorer north, albeit diminished by the ethnic diversity. Also rivalry between majority French-speakers and minority English-speakers, with sections of the latter group demanding autonomy.

The steep slopes of Mindif Pic flatten out into a savanna landscape in Cameroon's far north.

THE ECONOMY
Moderate oil reserves. Very diversified agricultural economy – timber, cocoa, coffee, rubber. Self-sufficient in food. Growing national debt owing to failure to adjust to falling oil revenues.

FACTFILE
Official Name Republic of Cameroon
Date of Formation 1960
Capital Yaoundé
Population 13.6 million
Total Area 183,570 sq miles (475,440 sq km)
Density 74 people per sq mile
Languages English*, French*, Fang, Bulu, Yaunde, Duala, Mbum
Religions Traditional beliefs 51%, Christian 33%, Muslim 16%
Ethnic Mix Bamileke and Manum 20%, Fang 19%, other 61%
Government Multiparty republic
Currency CFA franc = 100 centimes

AFRICA

EQUATORIAL GUINEA

COMPRISES THE mainland territory of Rio Muni and five islands on the west coast of central Africa. In 1993, the first free elections were held.

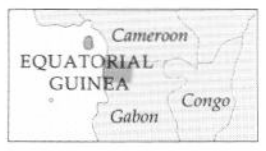

GEOGRAPHY
Islands are mountainous and volcanic. Mainland is lower, with mangrove swamps along coast.

CLIMATE
The Isla de Bioco is extremely wet and humid. The mainland is only marginally drier and cooler.

PEOPLE AND SOCIETY
The mainland is sparsely populated. Most people are Fang, the dominant group in politics. The ruling Mongomo clan hold most of the country's wealth. The Isla de Bioco is populated mostly by Bubi people and a minority of Creoles known as Fernandinos. Extended family ties have remained strong despite disruptive social pressure during the years of the Macías dictatorship.

THE ECONOMY
The Isla de Bioco generates the most income. Main exports are tropical timber and cocoa is the major cash crop. Oil and gas reserves are yet to be fully exploited.

FACTFILE
Official Name Republic of Equatorial Guinea
Date of Formation 1968
Capital Malabo
Population 400,000
Total Area 10,830 sq miles (28,050 sq km)
Density 36 people per sq mile
Languages Spanish*, Fang, other
Religions Christian (mainly Roman Catholic) 89%, other 11%
Ethnic Mix Fang 72%, Bubi 14%, Duala 3%, Ibibio 2%, other 9%
Government Multiparty republic
Currency CFA franc = 100 centimes

AFRICA

SAO TOME & PRINCIPE

A FORMER Portuguese colony off Africa's west coast, comprising two main islands and smaller islets. 1991 elections ended 15 years of Marxism.

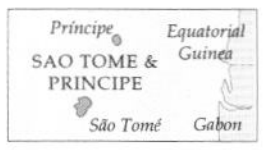

GEOGRAPHY
Islands are scattered across Equator. São Tomé and Príncipe are heavily forested and mountainous.

CLIMATE
Hot and humid, slightly cooled by Benguela Current. Plentiful rainfall, but dry July–August.

The Albert Schweitzer Hospital at Lambaréné, on the lower Ogooué River, Gabon. Schweitzer won a Nobel Prize for his work in Africa.

PEOPLE AND SOCIETY
Population is entirely descended from immigrants as islands were uninhabited when Portuguese arrived in 1470. People mostly black, although Portuguese culture predominates. Blacks run the political parties. Society is well integrated and free of racial prejudice. Growing business class. Extended family offers main form of social security. Príncipe assumed autonomous status in April 1995.

THE ECONOMY
Cocoa provides for 90% of export earnings. Palm oil, pepper, and coffee are also farmed. One of Africa's highest aid-to-population ratios.

FACTFILE
Official Name Democratic Republic of Sao Tome and Principe
Date of Formation 1975
Capital São Tomé
Population 125,000
Total Area 372 sq miles (964 sq km)
Density 336 people per sq mile
Languages Portuguese*, Portuguese Creole, other
Religions Roman Catholic 90%, other Christian 10%
Ethnic Mix Black 90%, Portuguese and Creole 10%
Government Multiparty republic
Currency Dobra = 100 centimos

AFRICA

GABON

A FORMER French colony straddling the Equator on Africa's west coast. It returned to multiparty politics in 1990, after 22 years of one-party rule.

GEOGRAPHY
Low plateaus and mountains lie beyond the coastal strip. Two thirds of the land is rain forested.

CLIMATE
Hot and tropical, with little distinction between seasons. Cold Benguela Current cools the coast.

PEOPLE AND SOCIETY
Some 40 different languages are spoken. The Fang, who live mainly in the north, are the largest ethnic group, but have yet to gain control of the government. Oil wealth has led to growth of an affluent middle class. Menial jobs are done by immigrant workers. Education follows the French system. Gabon is one of Africa's most urbanized countries. The government is encouraging population growth.

THE ECONOMY
Oil is the main source of revenue. Tropical hardwoods are being exploited. Cocoa beans, coffee, and rice grown for export.

FACTFILE
Official Name The Gabonese Republic
Date of Formation 1960
Capital Libreville
Population 1.4 million
Total Area 103,347 sq miles (267,670 sq km)
Density 13 people per sq mile
Languages French*, Fang, other
Religions Catholic, other Christian 96%, Muslim 2%, other 2%
Ethnic Mix Fang 36%, Mpongwe 15%, Mbete 14%, other 35%
Government Multiparty republic
Currency CFA franc = 100 centimes

Africa

Congo

Astride the Equator in west central Africa, this former French colony emerged from 20 years of Marxist-Leninist rule in 1990.

Geography

Mostly forest- or savanna-covered plateaus, drained by Ubangi and Congo River systems. Narrow coastal plain is lined with sand dunes and lagoons.

Climate

Hot, tropical. Temperatures rarely fall below 86°F (30°C). Two wet and two dry seasons. Rainfall is heaviest south of the Equator.

People and Society

One of the most tribally conscious nations in Africa. Four main ethnic groups Bakongo, Sangha, Teke, and Mboshi. Main tensions between Bakongo in the north and Mboshi in the south. Middle class is sustained by oil wealth. Schools are run according to the French system and are still subject to inspection from Paris. Multiparty elections held in 1992.

The Economy

Oil is main source of revenue. Cash crops include sugar, coffee, cocoa, and palm oil. Substantial industrial base. Large foreign debt.

Factfile

Official Name The Republic of the Congo
Date of Formation 1960
Capital Brazzaville
Population 2.7 million
Total Area 132,040 sq miles (342,000 sq km)
Density 20 people per sq mile
Languages French*, Kongo, other
Religions Catholic 50%, traditional beliefs 48%, other (inc. Muslim) 2%
Ethnic Mix Bakongo 48%, Teke 17%, Mboshi 17%, Sangha 5%, other 13%
Government Multiparty republic
Currency CFA franc = 100 centimes

Africa

Angola

Located in southwest Africa, Angola was in an almost continuous state of civil war from 1975–94, following independence from Portugal.

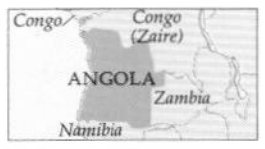

Geography

Most of the land is hilly and grass-covered. Desert in the south. Mountains in the center and north.

Climate

Varies from temperate to tropical. Rainfall decreases north to south. Coast is cooler and dry.

People and Society

Civil war was fought by two groups. UNITA cast itself as sole representative of the Ovimbundu, in order to attack ruling Kimbundu-dominated MPLA. In 1991–92, MPLA abandoned Marxist rule and held free elections. UNITA lost, and resumed civil war. Up to 500,000 people died as a result. In 1995, UN troops were deployed to begin a phased demilitarization operation.

Luanda, the Angolan capital, was founded in 1573 by Portuguese colonists.

The Economy

Rich mineral resources give Angola the potential to be one of Africa's richest countries, but civil war has severely hampered economic development. Oil and diamonds are exported.

Factfile

Official Name Republic of Angola
Date of Formation 1975
Capital Luanda
Population 11.5 million
Total Area 481,551 sq miles (1,246,700 sq km)
Density 23 people per sq mile
Languages Portuguese*, other
Religions Catholic/Protestant 64%, traditional beliefs 34%, other 2%
Ethnic Mix Ovimbundu 37%, Kimbundu 25%, Bakongo 13%, mixed 1%, other 24%
Government Multiparty republic
Currency Kwanza = 100 lwei

Africa

Zambia

Zambia lies landlocked at the heart of southern Africa. In 1991, it made a peaceful transition from single-party rule to multiparty democracy.

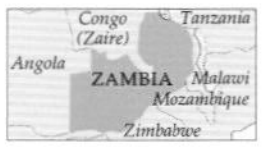

Geography

A high savanna plateau, broken by mountains in northeast. Vegetation mainly trees and scrub

Climate

Tropical, with three seasons cool and dry, hot and dry, and wet. Southwest is prone to drought.

People and Society

One of the continent's most urbanized countries. Although there are more than 70 different ethnic groups, Zambia has been less affected by ethnic tensions than many African states. Largest group is Bemba in northeast. Other major groups are Tonga in the south, and Lozi in the west. Women still have subordinate role in the family and politics. Rural population live by subsistence farming.

The Economy

Copper mining is the main industry – exports bring in 80% of foreign income. However, domestic reserves are declining rapidly.

Factfile

Official Name Republic of Zambia
Date of Formation 1964
Capital Lusaka
Population 9.7 million
Total Area 290,563 sq miles (752,610 sq km)
Density 33 people per sq mile
Languages English*, Bemba, Tonga, Nyanja, Lozi, Lunda
Religions Christian 63%, traditional beliefs 35%, other 2%
Ethnic Mix Bemba 36%, Maravi 18%, Tonga 15%, other 31%
Government Multiparty republic
Currency Kwacha = 100 ngwee

Africa

Tanzania

The East African state of Tanzania was formed in 1964 by the union of Tanganyika and Zanzibar. A third of its area is game reserve or national park.

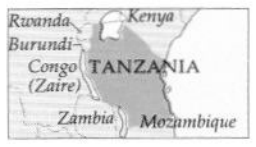

Geography

Mainland is mostly a high plateau lying to the east of the Great Rift Valley. Forested coastal plain. Highlands in the north and south.

Tanzania's Arusha National Park lies in the Ngurdoto volcanic crater. Herds of buffalo, rhino, elephant, and giraffe live in the park.

Climate

Tropical on the coast and Zanzibar. Semi-arid on central plateau, semi-temperate in the highlands. March-May rains.

People and Society

99% of people belong to one of 120 small ethnic Bantu groups. Arabs, Asians, and Europeans make up remaining population. Use of Swahili as *lingua franca* has eliminated ethnic rivalries. Family is still the focus of traditional rural life. Politics is moving toward democracy, though separatists in Zanzibar are a growing force.

The Economy

Reliant on agriculture, including forestry and livestock. Cotton, coffee, tea, and cloves are cash crops. Diamonds are mined.

Factfile

Official Name United Republic of Tanzania
Date of Formation 1964
Capital Dodoma
Population 30.5 million
Total Area 364,900 sq miles (945,090 sq km)
Density 83 people per sq mile
Languages English*, Swahili*
Religions Traditional beliefs 42%, Muslim 31%, Christian 27%
Ethnic Mix 120 ethnic Bantu groups 99%, other 1%
Government Single-party republic
Currency Shilling = 100 cents

AFRICA

MALAWI

A FORMER British colony, Malawi lies landlocked in southeast Africa. Its name means "the land where the sun is reflected in the water like fire."

GEOGRAPHY
Lake Nyasa takes up one fifth of the country. Highlands lie west of the lake. Much of the land is covered by forests and savanna.

CLIMATE
Mainly subtropical. South is hot and humid. Highlands are cooler. May–October dry season.

PEOPLE AND SOCIETY
Few ethnic tensions as most people share common Bantu origin. However, tensions between north and south have arisen in recent years. Northerners are increasingly disaffected by their lack of political representation but the new government has strived to reduce tensions. Many Asians are involved in the retail trade. Multi-party politics introduced in 1993.

The building of the Kariba Dam, created the vast Lake Kariba on the Zambezi River.

THE ECONOMY
Tobacco accounts for 76% of export earnings. Tea and sugar production. Coal, bauxite reserves. Fishing takes place on Lake Nyasa.

FACTFILE
Official Name Republic of Malawi
Date of Formation 1964
Capital Lilongwe
Population 11.4 million
Total Area 45,745 sq miles (118,480 sq km)
Density 249 people per sq mile
Languages English*, Chewa*, other
Religions Protestant/Catholic 66%, traditional beliefs 18%, other 16%
Ethnic Mix Maravi 55%, Lomwe 17%, Yao 13%, Ngoni 7%, other (including Asian) 8%
Government Multiparty republic
Currency Kwacha = 100 tambala

AFRICA

ZIMBABWE

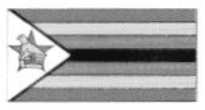

THE FORMER British colony of Southern Rhodesia became fully independent as Zimbabwe in 1980, after 15 years of troubled white minority rule.

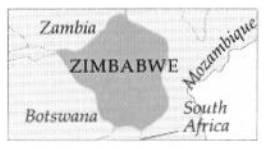

GEOGRAPHY
High plateaus in center bordered by Zambezi River in the north and Limpopo in the south. Rivers criss-cross central area.

CLIMATE
Tropical, though moderated by the altitude. Wet season November–March. Drought is common in eastern highlands.

PEOPLE AND SOCIETY
Two main ethnic groups, Ndebele in the north, and Shona in the south. Shona outnumber Ndebele by four to one. Whites make up just 1% of the population, but are generally far more affluent than blacks. Recent government policies aim at increasing black education and employment. Families are large and 45% of people are under 15.

THE ECONOMY
Most broadly based African economy after South Africa. Virtually self-sufficient in food and energy. Tobacco is main cash crop.

FACTFILE
Official Name Republic of Zimbabwe
Date of Formation 1980
Capital Harare
Population 11.5 million
Total Area 150,800 sq miles (390,580 sq km)
Density 76 people per sq mile
Languages English*, Shona, Ndebele
Religions Syncretic (Christian and traditional beliefs) 50%, Christian 26%, traditional beliefs 24%
Ethnic Mix Shona 71%, Ndebele 16%, other 11%, White, Asian 2%
Government Multiparty republic
Currency Zimbabwe $ = 100 cents

AFRICA

MOZAMBIQUE

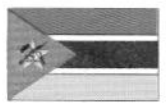

MOZAMBIQUE LIES on the southeast African coast. It was torn by a civil war between the Marxist government and a rebel group from 1977–1992.

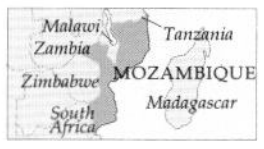

GEOGRAPHY
Largely a savanna-covered plateau. Coast is fringed by coral reefs and lagoons. Zambezi River bisects country from east to west.

CLIMATE
Tropical. Hottest along the coast. Wet season usually March–October, but rains frequently fail.

Tea is an important cash crop in Mozambique. Other cash crops include cashew nuts, cotton, sugar, copra, and citrus fruits.

PEOPLE AND SOCIETY
Racially diverse, but tensions in society are between northerners and southerners, rather than ethnic groups. Life is based around the extended family, which in some regions is matriarchal. Polygamy is fairly common. Government has faced huge task of re-settling the one million refugees from civil war. 90% of the population live in severe poverty.

THE ECONOMY
The country is almost entirely dependent on foreign aid. 85% of the population is engaged in agriculture.

FACTFILE
Official Name Republic of Mozambique
Date of Formation 1975
Capital Maputo
Population 16.5 million
Total Area 309,493 sq miles (801,590 sq km)
Density 53 people per sq mile
Languages Portuguese*, other
Religions Traditional beliefs 60%, Christian 30%, Muslim 10%
Ethnic Mix Makua-Lomwe 47%, Tsonga 23%, Malawi 12%, other 18%
Government Multiparty republic
Currency Metical = 100 centavos

AFRICA

NAMIBIA

LOCATED IN southwestern Africa, Namibia became free of South African control in 1990, after years of uncertainty and guerrilla activity.

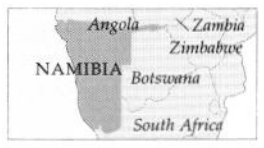

GEOGRAPHY
Namib Desert stretches along coastal strip. Inland, a ridge of mountains rises to 8,200 ft (2,500 m). Kalahari Desert lies in the east.

CLIMATE
Almost rainless. Coast usually shrouded in thick fog, unless hot dry *berg* wind blows.

PEOPLE AND SOCIETY
Largest ethnic group, the Ovambo, live mainly in the north. Whites, including a large German community, are centered around Windhoek. Ethnic strife predicted at time of independence has not materialized. High illiteracy among blacks due to legacy of apartheid. Whites still control the economy.

THE ECONOMY
Third wealthiest country in sub-Saharan Africa. Varied mineral resources, including uranium and diamonds. Rich offshore fishing grounds. Lack of skilled labor inhibits economic development.

FACTFILE
Official Name Republic of Namibia
Date of Formation 1990/1994
Capital Windhoek
Population 1.6 million
Total Area 318,260 sq miles (824,290 sq km)
Density 5 people per sq mile
Languages English*, Afrikaans, Ovambo, Kavango, German, other
Religions Christian 90%, other 10%
Ethnic Mix Ovambo 50%, Kavango 9%, Herero 7%, Damara 7%, White 6%, other 21%
Government Multiparty republic
Currency Rand = 100 cents

BOTSWANA

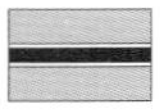

ONCE THE British protectorate of Bechuanaland, Botswana lies landlocked in southern Africa. Diamonds provide it with a prosperous economy.

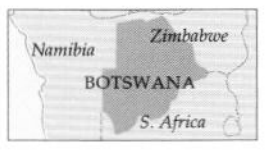

GEOGRAPHY
Lies on vast plateau, high above sea-level. Hills in the east. Kalahari Desert in center and southwest. Swamps and saltpans elsewhere and in Okavango basin.

CLIMATE
Dry and prone to drought. Summer wet season, April–October. Winters are warm, with cold nights.

PEOPLE AND SOCIETY
Tswana make up 75% of the population. San, or Kalahari Bushmen, the first inhabitants, have been marginalized. 72% of people live in rural areas. Traditional forms of authority such as the village *kgotla*, or parliament, remain important.

Botswana's Okavango Delta is home to a vast range of wildlife and rare plant species.

THE ECONOMY
Diamonds are the leading export and contribute by a 50% state-owned company. Deposits of copper, nickel, coal, salt, and soda ash are also exported. Beef is exported to Europe. Tourism aimed at wealthy wildlife enthusiasts.

FACTFILE
Official Name Republic of Botswana
Date of Formation 1966
Capital Gaborone
Population 1.5 million
Total Area 224,600 sq miles (581,730 sq km)
Density 7 people per sq mile
Languages Tswana, Shona, San, Khoikhoi, Ndebele
Religions Traditional beliefs 50%, Christian (mostly Anglican) 50%
Ethnic Mix Tswana 75%, Shona 12%, San 3%, White 1%, other 9%
Government Multiparty republic
Currency Pula = 100 thebe

LESOTHO

THE LANDLOCKED kingdom of Lesotho is entirely surrounded by South Africa, which provides all its land transportation links with the outside world.

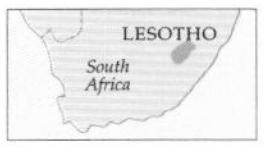

GEOGRAPHY
High mountainous plateau, cut by valleys and ravines. Maluti range in center. Drakensberg range in the east. Lowlands in the west.

CLIMATE
Temperate. Summers are hot and wet. Snow is frequent in the mountains in winter.

PEOPLE AND SOCIETY
Almost everyone is Basotho, although there are some Europeans, South Asians, and Taiwanese. Strong sense of national identity has tended to minimize ethnic tensions. Many men work as migrant laborers in South Africa, leaving 72% of households, and most of the farms, run by women.

THE ECONOMY
Few natural resources and so is heavily reliant on the incomes of its migrant workers. Subsistence farming is the main activity. Exports include livestock, wool, mohair from goat herds.

FACTFILE
Official Name Kingdom of Lesotho
Date of Formation 1966
Capital Maseru
Population 2.1 million
Total Area 11,718 sq miles (30,350 sq km)
Density 179 people per sq mile
Languages English*, Sesotho*, Zulu
Religions Roman Catholic and other Christian 93%, other 7%
Ethnic Mix Basotho 99%, other 1%
Government Constitutional monarchy
Currency Loti = 100 lisente

SWAZILAND

THE SOUTHERN African kingdom of Swaziland gained independence from Britain in 1968. It is economically dependent on South Africa.

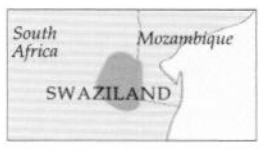

GEOGRAPHY
Mainly high plateaus and mountains. Rolling grasslands and low scrub plains to the east. Pine forests on western border.

The town of Mbabane lies on the high veld of Swaziland, where traditional cattle farming has led to soil erosion through overgrazing.

CLIMATE
Temperatures rise and rainfall declines as land descends eastward, from high to low veld.

PEOPLE AND SOCIETY
One of Africa's most homogenous states. Also among its most conservative, although it is now coming under pressure from urban-based modernizers. Political system promotes Swazi tradition and is dominated by a powerful monarchy. Society is patriarchal and focused around various clans and chiefs.

THE ECONOMY
Sugar cane is the main cash crop. Others are pineapples, cotton, rice, and tobacco. Asbestos, coal, and wood pulp are also exported.

FACTFILE
Official Name Kingdom of Swaziland
Date of Formation 1968
Capital Mbabane
Population 900,000
Total Area 6,703 sq miles (17,360 sq km)
Density 134 people per sq mile
Languages Siswati*, English*, Zulu
Religions Protestant and other Christian 60%, traditional beliefs 40%
Ethnic Mix Swazi 95%, other 5%
Government Executive monarchy
Currency Lilangeni = 100 cents

SOUTH AFRICA

SOUTH AFRICA is the most southerly nation on the African continent. The multiracial, multiparty elections of 1994 overturned 80 years of minority rule.

GEOGRAPHY
Large grassland plateaus, drained by the Orange and Limpopo rivers. Drakensberg mountains overshadow eastern coastal lowlands.

CLIMATE
Warm, temperate and dry. Interior of country gets most rain in summer. Coast around Cape Town has mediterranean climate.

PEOPLE AND SOCIETY
Dismantling of apartheid in early 1990s ended racial segregation. Some Zulus and whites have made demands for independent homelands. Racial imbalance to be addressed by focus on education, housing, land reform.

THE ECONOMY
Highly diversified economy with modern infrastructure. Growing manufacturing sector. Diamonds, gold, platinum, coal, silver, uranium, copper, and asbestos mined.

FACTFILE
Official Name Republic of South Africa
Date of Formation 1910/1934
Capital Pretoria, Cape Town, Bloemfontein
Population 42.4 million
Total Area 471,443 sq miles (1,221,040 sq km)
Density 89 people per sq mile
Languages Afrikaans*, English, 9 African languages
Religions Protestant 55%, Catholic 9%, Hindu 1%, Muslim 1%, other 34%
Ethnic Mix Black 75%, White 14%, mixed 9%, South Asian 2%
Government Multiparty republic
Currency Rand = 100 cents

Africa

Comoros

In the Indian Ocean between Mozambique and Madagascar lie the Comoros, comprising three main islands and a number of smaller islets.

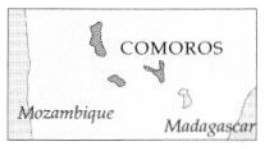

Geography

Main islands are of volcanic origin and are heavily forested. The remainder are coral atolls

Climate

Hot and humid all year round. November–May is hottest and wettest period.

People and Society

Country has absorbed a diversity of people over the years Africans, Arabs, Polynesians, and Persians. Also Portuguese, Dutch, French, and Indian immigrants. Ethnic tension is rare. Wealth concentrated among political and business elite. Schools equipped to teach only basic literacy, hygiene, and agricultural skills. Politically unstable – frequent coup attempts have been made during 1990s

Moroni, the Comoros capital, lies on the island of Grande Comore. The islands are fertile and forested.

The Economy

One of the world's poorest countries. 80% of the people are farmers Vanilla and cloves are main cash crops. Lack of basic infrastructure.

Factfile

Official Name Federal Islamic Republic of the Comoros

Date of Formation 1975

Capital Moroni

Population 700,000

Total Area 861 sq miles (2,230 sq km)

Density 813 people per sq mile

Languages Arabic*, French*, other

Religions Muslim 86%, Roman Catholic 14%

Ethnic Mix Comorian 96%, Makua 2%, other (inc. French) 2%

Government Islamic republic

Currency Franc = 100 centimes

Africa

Madagascar

Lying in the Indian Ocean, Madagascar is the world's fourth largest island. Free elections in 1993 ended 18 years of socialist government.

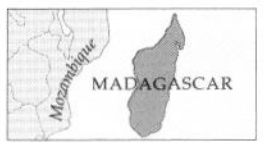

Geography

two-thirds of country is a savanna-covered plateau, which drops sharply to narrow coastal belt in the east.

Climate

Tropical, often hit by cyclones. East coast affected by monsoons. Southwest is drier.

People and Society

People are Malay-Indonesian in origin, intermixed with later migrants from African mainland. Main ethnic division is between Merina of the central plateau and the poorer *côtier* (coastal) peoples. Merina were the country's historic rulers. They remain the social elite, and largely run the government

The Economy

80% of the people are farmers. Coffee is the most important cash crop. World's largest producer of vanilla. Prawns are a valuable export commodity.

Factfile

Official Name Democratic Republic of Madagascar

Date of Formation 1960

Capital Antananarivo

Population 15.2 million

Total Area 226,660 sq miles (587,040 sq km)

Density 67 people per sq mile

Languages Malagasy*, French*

Religions Traditional beliefs 52%, Catholic/Protestant 41%, Muslim 7%

Ethnic Mix Merina 26%, Betsimisaraka 15%, Betsileo 12%, other 47%

Government Multiparty republic

Currency Franc = 100 centimes

Africa

Seychelles

A former British colony, comprising 115 islands in the Indian Ocean. Under one-party rule for 16 years, it became a multiparty democracy in 1993.

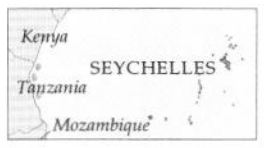

Geography

Mostly low-lying coral atolls, but 40 islands, including the largest, Mahé, are mountainous and are the only granitic islands in the world.

The Seychelles, like many islands in the Indian Ocean are threatened by rising sea levels.

Climate

Tropical oceanic climate. Hot and humid all year round. Rainy season December–May.

People and Society

The islands were uninhabited when French settlers arrived in the 18th century. Today, the population is homogeneous – a result of intermarriage between ethnic groups. Almost 90% of people live on Mahé. Living standards are among Africa's highest. Poverty is rare and the welfare system caters for all.

The Economy

Tourism is main source of income, based on appeal of beaches and exotic plants and animals. Tuna fished and canned for export. Virtually no mineral resources. All domestic requirements imported.

Factfile

Official Name Republic of the Seychelles

Date of Formation 1976

Capital Victoria

Population 74,000

Total Area 108 sq miles (280 sq km)

Density 685 people per sq mile

Languages Creole*, French, English

Religions Catholic 90%, other 10%

Ethnic Mix Seychellois (mixed African, South Asian and European) 95%, Chinese and South Asian 5%

Government Multiparty republic

Currency Rupee = 100 cents

Africa

Mauritius

Located to the east of Madagascar in the Indian Ocean. Independent in 1968, as part of the Commonwealth, it became a republic in 1993.

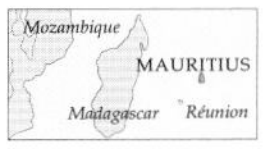

Geography

Main island, of volcanic origin, is ringed by coral reefs. Rises from coast to fertile central plateau. Outer islands lie some 311 miles (500 km) to the north

Climate

Warm and humid. March–December are hottest and wettest months, with tropical storms.

People and Society

Most people are descendants of laborers brought over from India in the 19th century. Small minority of French descent are the wealthiest group. Literacy rate for under-30s is 95%. Crime rates on main island are fairly low; outer islands are virtually crime free.

The Economy

Sugar, tourism, and clothing manufacture are main sources of income. Sugar accounts for 30% of exports. Potential as offshore financial center is being developed.

Factfile

Official Name Mauritius

Date of Formation 1968

Capital Port Louis

Population 1.1 million

Total Area 718 sq miles (1,860 sq km)

Density 1,532 people per sq mile

Languages English*, French Creole, Hindi, Bhojpuri, Chinese

Religions Hindu 52%, Catholic 26%, Muslim 17%, other 5%

Ethnic Mix Creole 55%, South Asian 40%, Chinese 3%, other 2%

Government Multiparty republic

Currency Rupee = 100 cents

EUROPE

ICELAND

EUROPE'S WESTERNMOST country, Iceland lies in the north Atlantic, straddling the Mid-Atlantic ridge. Its spectacular landscape is largely uninhabited.

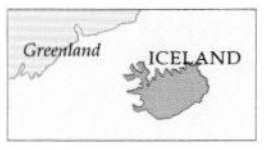

GEOGRAPHY
Grassy coastal lowlands, with fiords in the north. Central plateau of cold lava desert, glaciers, and geothermal springs. Around 200 volcanoes.

CLIMATE
Location in middle of Gulf Stream moderates climate. Mild winters and brief, cool summers.

PEOPLE AND SOCIETY
Prosperous and homogeneous society includes only 4,000 foreign residents. High social mobility, free health care and heating (using geothermal power). Longevity rates are among the highest in the world. Equivocal attitude toward Europe accompanies increasing US influence. Strong emphasis on education and reading. Low crime rate, but concerns about alcohol abuse.

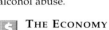

THE ECONOMY
Fish products make up 80% of exports. Light industries produce knitwear, textiles, paint. Ecotourism potential.

FACTFILE

Official Name Republic of Iceland
Date of Formation 1944
Capital Reykjavík
Population 300,000
Total Area 39,770 sq miles (103,000 sq km)
Density 8 people per sq mile
Languages Icelandic*, other
Religions Evangelical Lutheran 96%, other Christian 3%, other 1%
Ethnic Mix Icelandic (Norwegian-Celtic descent) 98%, other 2%
Government Constitutional republic
Currency Krona = 100 aurar

EUROPE

NORWAY

THE KINGDOM of Norway traces the rugged western coast of Scandinavia. Settlements are largely restricted to southern and coastal areas.

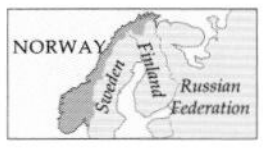

GEOGRAPHY
Highly indented Atlantic coast with fiords and tens of thousands of islands. Rugged mountains and plateaus cover most of the country.

CLIMATE
Mild coastal climate. Inland east is more extreme, with warm summers, and cold, snowy winters.

PEOPLE AND SOCIETY
Homogeneous, with some recent refugees from Bosnian conflict. Strong family tradition despite high divorce rate. Fair-minded consensus promotes female equality, boosted by generous childcare provision. Wealth more evenly distributed than in most developed countries. Most people have high standard of living.

The village of Reine on Moskenesøya, in Norway's Lofoten islands is a popular vacation resort.

THE ECONOMY
Europe's largest producer and exporter of oil and gas. Engineering, chemical, and metal industries. Fishing and forestry are also significant industries.

FACTFILE

Official Name Kingdom of Norway
Date of Formation 1905/1930
Capital Oslo
Population 4.4 million
Total Area 125,060 sq miles (323,900 sq km)
Density 35 people per sq mile
Languages Norwegian* (Bokmal and Nynorsk), Lappish
Religions Evangelical Lutheran 88%, other Christian 12%
Ethnic Mix Norwegian 95%, Lapp 1%, other 4%
Government Constitutional monarchy
Currency Krone = 100 øre

EUROPE

DENMARK

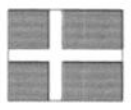

OCCUPIES THE Jutland peninsula and over 400 islands in Scandinavia. Greenland and the Faeroe Islands are self-governing associated territories.

GEOGRAPHY
Fertile farmland covers two-thirds of the terrain, which is among the flattest in the world. About 100 islands are inhabited.

The island of Fyn, like most of Denmark, is flat – lying barely above sea level. Coastal defenses are needed to prevent flooding.

CLIMATE
Damp, temperate climate with mild summers and cold, wet winters. Rainfall is moderate.

PEOPLE AND SOCIETY
Prosperous population maintains traditions of tolerance and welfare provision. High rates of divorce and cohabiting mean that almost 40% of children are brought up by unmarried couples or single parents. Over 75% of women work, due to generous state-funded childcare.

THE ECONOMY
Few natural resources but a diverse manufacturing base. The skilled work force is the key to high-tech industrial success. Bacon, ham, and dairy products are major agricultural exports.

FACTFILE

Official Name Kingdom of Denmark
Date of Formation AD 960/1953
Capital Copenhagen
Population 5.2 million
Total Area 16,629 sq miles (43,069 sq km)
Density 312 people per sq mile
Languages Danish*, other
Religions Evangelical Lutheran 91% other Protestant and Catholic 9%
Ethnic Mix Danish 96%, Faeroese and Inuit 1%, other 3%
Government Constitutional monarchy
Currency Krone = 100 øre

EUROPE

SWEDEN

THE LARGEST Scandinavian country in both population and area, Sweden's strong industrial base helps to fund its extensive welfare system.

GEOGRAPHY
Heavily forested, with many lakes. Northern plateau extends beyond the Arctic Circle. Southern lowlands are widely cultivated.

CLIMATE
Southern coasts warmed by Gulf Stream. North has more extreme continental climate.

PEOPLE AND SOCIETY
Traditions of hard work and economic success are balanced by permissiveness and egalitarianism. High taxes pay for extensive child-care provision, medical protection, and state education. Bulk of population and industry based in and around the southern cities. A 15,000-strong minority of Sami (Lapps) live in the north.

THE ECONOMY
Global companies, including Volvo, Saab, SFK, Ericsson. Highly developed infrastructure. Up-to-date technology Skilled labor force.

FACTFILE

Official Name Kingdom of Sweden
Date of Formation 1809/1905
Capital Stockholm
Population 8.8 million
Total Area 173,730 sq miles (449,960 sq km)
Density 51 people per sq mile
Languages Swedish*, Finnish, Lappish, other
Religions Evangelical Lutheran 94%, Catholic 2%, other 4%
Ethnic Mix Swedish 87%, Finnish and Lapp 1%, other European 12%
Government Constitutional monarchy
Currency Krona = 100 öre

EUROPE

FINLAND

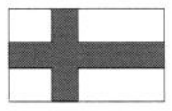

FINLAND'S DISTINCTIVE language and national identity have been influenced by both its Scandinavian and its Russian neighbors.

GEOGRAPHY

South and center are flat, with low hills and many lakes. Uplands and low mountains in the north. 60% of the land area is forested.

CLIMATE

Long, harsh winters with frequent snowfalls. Short, warmer summers. Rainfall is low, and decreases northward.

PEOPLE AND SOCIETY

More than half the population live in the five districts around Helsinki. The Swedish minority live mainly in the Åland Islands in the southwest. The Sami (Lapps) lead a semi-nomadic existence in the north. Over 50% of women go out to work, continuing a tradition of equality between the sexes.

Kilpisjarvi – "The Way of the Four Winds," where the borders of Finland, Sweden, and Norway meet.

THE ECONOMY

Wood-based industries account for 40% of exports. Strong engineering and electronics sectors.

FACTFILE

Official Name Republic of Finland
Date of Formation 1917/1920
Capital Helsinki
Population 5.1 million
Total Area 130,552 sq miles (338,130 sq km)
Density 39 people per sq mile
Languages Finnish*, Swedish, Lappish
Religions Evangelical Lutheran 89%, Greek Orthodox 1%, other 10%
Ethnic Mix Finnish 93%, Swedish 6%, other (inc. Sami) 1%
Government Multiparty republic
Currency Markka = 100 pennia

EUROPE

ESTONIA

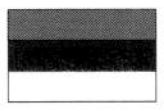

ESTONIA IS the smallest and most developed of the three Baltic states and has the highest standard of living of any former Soviet republic.

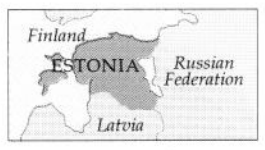

GEOGRAPHY

Flat, boggy and partly forested, with over 1,500 islands. Lake Peipus forms much of the eastern border with Russia.

CLIMATE

Maritime, with some continental extremes. Harsh winters, cool summers, and damp springs.

PEOPLE AND SOCIETY

The Estonians are related linguistically and ethnically to the Finns. Friction between ethnic Estonians and the large Russian minority has led to reassertion of Estonian culture and language, as well as job discrimination. Some post-independence political upheaval reflects disenchantment with free-market economics. Families are small; divorce rates are high.

THE ECONOMY

Agricultural machinery, electric motors, and ships are the leading manufactures. Strong timber industry. Increased trade links with Finland and Germany.

FACTFILE

Official Name Republic of Estonia
Date of Formation 1991
Capital Tallinn
Population 1.5 million
Total Area 17,423 sq miles (45,125 sq km)
Density 86 people per sq mile
Languages Estonian*, Russian
Religions Evangelical Lutheran 98%, Eastern Orthodox, Baptist 2%
Ethnic Mix Estonian 62%, Russian 30%, Ukrainian 3%, other 5%
Government Multiparty republic
Currency Kroon = 100 cents

EUROPE

LATVIA

SITUATED ON the east coast of the Baltic Sea. Like its Baltic neighbors, it became independent in 1991. It retains a large Russian population.

GEOGRAPHY

Flat coastal plain deeply indented by the Gulf of Riga. Poor drainage creates many bogs and swamps in the forested interior.

CLIMATE

Temperate warm summers and cold winters. Steady rainfall throughout the year.

The Russian Orthodox cathedral in Riga, the Latvian capital, was used as a planetarium during the Soviet era, but is now being restored.

PEOPLE AND SOCIETY

Latvia is the most urbanized of the three Baltic states, with more than 70% of the population living in cities and towns. Delicate relations with Russia are dictated by a large Russian minority, and energy and infrastructure investment dating from the Soviet period. The status of women is on a par with that in western Europe. The divorce rate is high.

THE ECONOMY

Transportation and defense equipment lead strong industrial sector. Developed paper-making industry. Good ports. Russia remains main trading partner.

FACTFILE

Official Name Republic of Latvia
Date of Formation 1991
Capital Riga
Population 2.5 million
Total Area 24,938 sq miles (64,589 sq km)
Density 100 people per sq mile
Languages Latvian*, Russian
Religions Evangelical Lutheran 85%, other Christian 15%
Ethnic Mix Latvian 52%, Russian 34%, Belorussian 5%, Ukrainian 4%, Polish 3%, other 2%
Government Multiparty republic
Currency Lats = 100 santimi

EUROPE

LITHUANIA

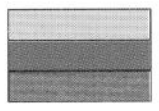

THE LARGEST and most powerful of the Baltic states, Lithuania was the first Baltic country to declare independence from Moscow, in 1991.

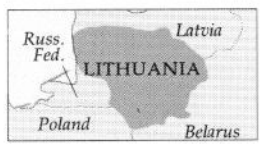

GEOGRAPHY

Mostly flat with moors, bogs, and an intensively farmed central lowland. Numerous lakes, and forested sandy ridges in the east.

CLIMATE

Coastal location moderates continental extremes. Cold winters, cool summers, and steady rainfall.

PEOPLE AND SOCIETY

Homogeneous population, with Lithuanians forming a large majority. Strong Roman Catholic tradition and historical links with Poland. Better relations among ethnic groups than in other Baltic states and interethnic marriages are fairly common. However, some ethnic Russians and Poles see a threat of "Lithuanianization." Russian army presence until 1993, when all troops were withdrawn.

THE ECONOMY

Wide range of high-tech and heavy industries, includes textiles, engineering, shipbuilding, and food processing. Agricultural surpluses.

FACTFILE

Official Name Republic of Lithuania
Date of Formation 1991
Capital Vilnius
Population 3.7 million
Total Area 25,174 sq miles (65,200 sq km)
Density 146 people per sq mile
Languages Lithuanian*, Russian
Religions Roman Catholic 87%, Russian Orthodox 10%, other 3%
Ethnic Mix Lithuanian 80%, Russian 9%, Polish 8%, other 3%
Government Multiparty republic
Currency Litas = 100 centas

EUROPE

POLAND

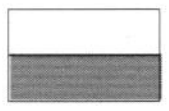

WITH ITS seven international borders and strategic location, Poland has always played an important role in European affairs.

GEOGRAPHY
Lowlands, part of the North European Plain, cover most of the country. Carpathian Mountains run along the southern borders.

CLIMATE
Peak rainfall during hot summers. Cold winters with snow, especially in mountains

PEOPLE AND SOCIETY
Ethnic homogeneity masks a number of tensions. Secular liberals criticize semiofficial status of Catholic Church; emerging wealth disparities resented by those unaffected by free-market reforms. German minority presses for action on Green issues. Many women hold policy-making posts

THE ECONOMY
High growth, with foreign investment linked to government privatization program. Heavy industries still dominate, but service sector is quickly emerging.

FACTFILE

Official Name Republic of Poland
Date of Formation 1918/1945
Capital Warsaw
Population 38.4 million
Total Area 120,720 sq miles (312,680 sq km)
Density 318 people per sq mile
Languages Polish*, German, other
Religions Roman Catholic 95%, other (inc. Protestant and Eastern Orthodox) 5%
Ethnic Mix Polish 98%, other 2%
Government Multiparty republic
Currency Zloty = 100 groszy

EUROPE

GERMANY

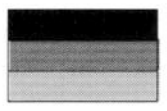

EUROPE'S STRONGEST economic power, Germany's democratic west and communist east were reunified in 1990, after the fall of the east's regime.

GEOGRAPHY
Coastal plains in the north, rising to rolling hills of central region. Alpine region in the south.

CLIMATE
Damp, temperate in northern and central regions. Continental extremes in mountainous south.

PEOPLE AND SOCIETY
Social and economic differences reflect former divisions. Some prosperous western Germans resent added taxes since reunification. Far-right political groups have emerged. Immigrant "guest workers" – mainly Turks – face citizenship problems and occasional racial attacks. Strong feminist and Green movements.

Neuschwanstein Castle, built for the eccentric King Ludwig II of Bavaria.

THE ECONOMY
Massive exports of cars, heavy engineering, electronics, and chemicals. Postwar "miracle" powered by efficiency and good labor relations.

FACTFILE

Official Name Federal Republic of Germany
Date of Formation 1871/1990
Capital Berlin
Population 81.8 million
Total Area 137,800 sq miles (356,910 sq km)
Density 593 people per sq mile
Languages German*, Sorbian, other
Religions Protestant 45%, Roman Catholic 37%, other 18%
Ethnic Mix German 92%, other 8%
Government Multiparty republic
Currency Deutsche Mark = 100 pfennigs

EUROPE

NETHERLANDS

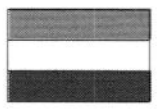

ASTRIDE THE delta of five major rivers in northwest Europe, the Netherlands has a long trading tradition. Rotterdam is the world's largest port.

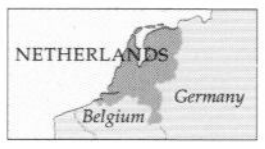

GEOGRAPHY
Mainly flat, with 27% of the land below sea level and protected by dunes, dikes, and canals. Low hills in the south and east.

A century ago there were more than 10,000 windmills in the Netherlands. Today, there are only about 100 lremaining.

CLIMATE
Mild, rainy winters and cool summers. Gales from the North Sea are common in autumn and winter.

PEOPLE AND SOCIETY
The Dutch see their country as the most tolerant in Europe. This reflects a long history of welcoming refugees and immigrants. Large urban concentration (89%) accounts for high population density. Laws concerning issues such as sexuality, euthanasia, and drug-taking are among the world's most liberal.

THE ECONOMY
Diverse industrial sector exports metals, machinery, chemicals, and electronics. Many high-profile multinationals.

FACTFILE

Official Name Kingdom of the Netherlands
Date of Formation 1815/1890
Capital Amsterdam, The Hague
Population 15.6 million
Total Area 14,410 sq miles (37,330 sq km)
Density 1,082 people per sq mile
Languages Dutch*, Frisian, other
Religions Catholic 36%, Protestant 27%, other (inc. unaffiliated) 37%
Ethnic Mix Dutch 96%, other 4%
Government Constitutional monarchy
Currency Guilder = 100 cents

EUROPE

BELGIUM

BELGIUM LIES in northwestern Europe. Its history has been marked by the division between its Flemish- and French-speaking communities.

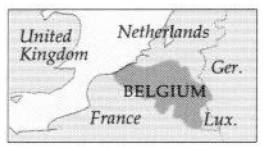

GEOGRAPHY
Low-lying coastal plain covers two-thirds of the country. Land becomes hilly and forested in southeast (Ardennes) region.

CLIMATE
Maritime climate with Gulf Stream influences. Temperatures are mild, with heavy cloud cover and rain. More rainfall and weather fluctuations on coast.

PEOPLE AND SOCIETY
Since 1970, Flemish-speaking regions have become more prosperous than those of the minority French-speakers (Walloons), overturning the traditional roles and increasing friction. In order to contain tensions, Belgium began to move toward federalism in 1980. Both groups now have their own governments and control most of their own affairs

THE ECONOMY
Variety of industrial exports, including steel, glassware, cut diamonds, and textiles. Many foreign multinationals.

FACTFILE

Official Name Kingdom of Belgium
Date of Formation 1830
Capital Brussels
Population 10.1 million
Total Area 12,780 sq miles (33,100 sq km)
Density 790 people per sq mile
Languages French*, Dutch*, Flemish
Religions Catholic 75%, other 25%
Ethnic Mix Flemish 58%, Walloon 32%, other European 6%, other 4%
Government Constitutional monarchy
Currency Franc = 100 centimes

EUROPE

IRELAND

THE REPUBLIC of Ireland occupies 85% of the island of Ireland, with the remainder (Northern Ireland) being part of the United Kingdom.

GEOGRAPHY

Low mountain ranges along an irregular coastline surround an inland plain punctuated by lakes, undulating hills, and peat bogs.

CLIMATE

The Gulf Stream accounts for the mild and wet climate. Snow is rare, except in the mountains.

PEOPLE AND SOCIETY

Although homogeneous in ethnicity and Catholic religion, the population shows signs of change. Younger Irish question Vatican teachings on birth control, divorce, abortion. Many people still emigrate to find jobs. 1994 terrorist ceasefire in Northern Ireland tempered the traditional aim of reunification.

Clew Bay in County Mayo on the western coast of Ireland.

THE ECONOMY

High unemployment tarnishes high-tech export successes and trade surplus. Highly educated work force. Efficient agriculture and food-processing industries.

FACTFILE

Official Name Republic of Ireland
Date of Formation 1921/1922
Capital Dublin
Population 3.6 million
Total Area 27,155 sq miles (70,280 sq km)
Density 133 people per sq mile
Languages English*, Irish Gaelic*
Religions Catholic 93%, Protestant (mainly Anglican) 5%, other 2%
Ethnic Mix Irish 95%, other (mainly British) 5%
Government Multiparty republic
Currency Irish pound = 100 pence

EUROPE

FRANCE

STRADDLING WESTERN Europe from the English Channel to the Mediterranean Sea, France is one of the world's leading industrial powers.

GEOGRAPHY

Broad plain covers northern half of the country. Tall mountain ranges in the east and southwest. Mountainous plateau in the center.

CLIMATE

Three main climates temperate and damp northwest; continental east; and Mediterranean south.

PEOPLE AND SOCIETY

Strong French national identity coexists with pronounced regional differences, including local languages. Long tradition of absorbing immigrants (European Jews, North African Muslims, economic migrants from Southern Europe). Catholic Church is no longer central to daily life.

THE ECONOMY

Steel, chemicals, electronics, heavy engineering, wine, and aircraft typify a strong and diversified export sector.

FACTFILE

Official Name The French Republic
Date of Formation 1685/1920
Capital Paris
Population 58.2 million
Total Area 212,930 sq miles (551,500 sq km)
Density 273 people per sq mile
Languages French*, Provençal, German, Breton, Catalan, Basque
Religions Catholic 90%, Protestant 2%, Jewish 1%, Muslim 1%, other 6%
Ethnic Mix French 92%, North African 3%, German 2%, other 3%
Government Multiparty republic
Currency Franc = 100 centimes

EUROPE

UNITED KINGDOM

SEPARATED FROM continental Europe by the North Sea and the English Channel, the UK comprises England, Wales, Scotland and Northern Ireland.

GEOGRAPHY

Mountainous in the north and west, undulating hills and lowlands in the south and east.

CLIMATE

Generally mild and temperate. Rainfall is heaviest in the west. Winter snow in mountainous areas.

PEOPLE AND SOCIETY

Although of mixed stock themselves, the British have an insular and ambivalent attitude toward Europe. The Welsh and Scottish are ethnically and culturally distinct. Asian and West Indian minorities in most cities. Class, the traditional source of division, is fading in the face of popular culture.

Black Mount at Rannoch Moor in the Scottish Highlands – one of the UK's wildest regions.

THE ECONOMY

World leader in financial services, pharmaceuticals, and defense industries. Exports of steel, vehicles, aircraft, high-tech goods.

FACTFILE

Official Name United Kingdom of Great Britain and Northern Ireland
Date of Formation 1801/1922
Capital London
Population 58.4 million
Total Area 94,550 sq miles (244,880 sq km)
Density 617 people per sq mile
Languages English*, other
Religions Protestant 52%, Catholic 9%, Muslim 3%, other 36%
Ethnic Mix English 81%, Scottish 10%, Welsh 2%, other 7%
Government Constitutional monarchy
Currency Pound sterling = 100 pence

EUROPE

LUXEMBOURG

MAKING UP part of the plateau of the Ardennes in Western Europe, Luxembourg is Europe's last independent duchy and one of its richest states.

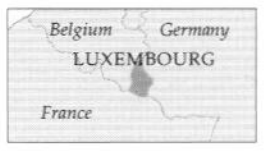

GEOGRAPHY

Dense Ardennes forests in the north, low, open southern plateau. Undulating terrain throughout.

CLIMATE

Moist climate with warm summers and mild winters. Snow is common only in the Ardennes.

PEOPLE AND SOCIETY

Society is peaceable, despite large proportion of foreigners (half the work force and one-third of the residents). Integration has been straightforward; most are fellow Western Europeans and Catholics, mainly from Italy and Portugal. High salaries and very low unemployment promote stability.

THE ECONOMY

Traditional industries such as steel-making have given way in recent years to a thriving banking and service sector. Tax-haven status attracts foreign companies.

FACTFILE

Official Name Grand Duchy of Luxembourg
Date of Formation 1890
Capital Luxembourg
Population 400,000
Total Area 998 sq miles (2,586 sq km)
Density 400 people per sq mile
Languages Letzeburgish*, French*, German*, Italian, Portuguese, other
Religions Catholic 97%, other 3%
Ethnic Mix Luxemburger 72%, Portuguese 9%, Italian 5%, other 14%
Government Constitutional monarchy
Currency Franc = 100 centimes

MONACO

A JET-SET image and a thriving service sector define the modern identity of this tiny enclave on the Côte d'Azur in southeastern France.

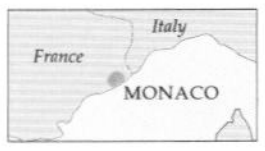

GEOGRAPHY
A rocky promontory overlooking a narrow coastal strip that has been enlarged through land reclamation.

CLIMATE
Mediterranean. Summers are hot and dry; days with 12 hours of sunshine are not uncommon. Winters are mild and sunny.

PEOPLE AND SOCIETY
Less than 20% of residents are Monégasques. The rest are Europeans – mainly French – attracted by the tax-haven, upscale lifestyle. Nationals enjoy considerable privileges, including housing benefits to protect them from high housing prices, and the right of first refusal before foreigners can take a job. Women have equal status but only acquired the vote in 1962.

Monte-Carlo is one of the world's most densely populated places.

THE ECONOMY
Tourism and gambling are the mainstays. Banking secrecy laws and tax-haven conditions attract foreign investment. Almost totally dependent on imports due to lack of natural resources.

FACTFILE
Official Name Principality of Monaco
Date of Formation 1861
Capital Monaco
Population 31,000
Total Area 0.75 sq miles (1.95 sq km)
Density 41,333 people per sq mile
Languages French*, Italian, other
Religions Catholic 95%, other 5%
Ethnic Mix French 47%, Monégasque 17%, Italian 16%, other 20%
Government Constitutional monarchy
Currency French franc = 100 centimes

ANDORRA

A TINY landlocked principality, Andorra lies high in the eastern Pyrenees between France and Spain. It held its first full elections in 1993.

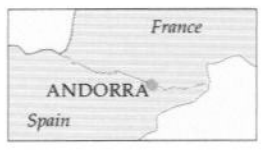

GEOGRAPHY
High mountains, and six deep, glaciated valleys that drain into the River Valira as it flows into Spain.

CLIMATE
Cool, wet springs followed by dry, warm summers. Mountain snows linger until March.

PEOPLE AND SOCIETY
Immigration is strictly monitored and restricted by quota to French and Spanish nationals seeking employment. A referendum in 1993 ended 715 years of semi-feudal status but society remains conservative. Divorce is illegal.

THE ECONOMY
Tourism and duty-free sales dominate the economy. Banking secrecy laws and low consumer taxes promote investment and commerce. Dependence on imported food and raw materials.

FACTFILE
Official Name Principality of Andorra
Date of Formation 1278
Capital Andorra la Vella
Population 65,000
Total Area 181 sq miles (468 sq km)
Density 359 people per sq mile
Languages Catalan*, Spanish, other
Religions Catholic 86%, other 14%
Ethnic Mix Catalan 61%, Spanish Castilian 30%, other 9%
Government Parliamentary democracy
Currency French franc, Spanish peseta

PORTUGAL

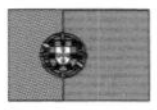

FACING THE Atlantic on the western side of the Iberian Peninsula, Portugal is the most westerly country on the European mainland.

GEOGRAPHY
The River Tagus runs through the country roughly east to west, dividing mountainous north from lower and more undulating south.

CLIMATE
North is cool and moist. South is warmer with dry, mild winters.

PEOPLE AND SOCIETY
Homogeneous and stable society, losing some of its conservative traditions. Small, well-assimilated immigrant population, mainly from former colonies. Urban areas and south are more socially progressive. North is more responsive to traditional Catholic values. Family ties remain all-important.

THE ECONOMY
Agricultural exports include grain, vegetables, fruits, and wine, but farming methods are outdated. Strong banking and tourism sectors.

FACTFILE
Official Name Republic of Portugal
Date of Formation 1140/1640
Capital Lisbon
Population 9.8 million
Total Area 35,670 sq miles (92,390 sq km)
Density 274 people per sq mile
Languages Portuguese*
Religions Catholic 97%, Protestant 1%, other 2%
Ethnic Mix Portuguese 98%, African 1%, other 1%
Government Multiparty republic
Currency Escudo = 100 centavos

SPAIN

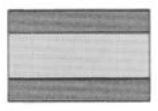

LODGED BETWEEN Europe and Africa, the Atlantic and the Mediterranean, Spain has occupied a pivotal position since it was united in 1492.

GEOGRAPHY
Mountain ranges in north, center and south. Huge central plateau. Verdant valleys in north-west, Mediterranean lowlands

A ruined Moorish castle at Alcaudete, in Spain's Andalucían mountains between Granada and the River Guadalquivir.

CLIMATE
Maritime in north. Hotter and drier in south. Central plateau has an extreme climate.

PEOPLE AND SOCIETY
Ethnic regionalism, suppressed under General Franco's regime (1936–75), is increasing. 17 regions are now autonomous. People remain church-going, although Catholic teachings on social issues are often flouted. Status of women rising quickly, with strong political representation.

THE ECONOMY
Outdated labor practices and low investment hinder growth. Heavy industry, textiles, and food-processing lead exports. Tourism and agriculture are important.

FACTFILE
Official Name Kingdom of Spain
Date of Formation 1492/1713
Capital Madrid
Population 39.7 million
Total Area 194,900 sq miles (504,780 sq km)
Density 203 people per sq mile
Languages Castilian Spanish*, Catalan*, Galician*, Basque*, other
Religions Catholic 99%, other 1%
Ethnic Mix Castilian Spanish 72%, Catalan 16%, Galician 7%, Basque 2%, Gypsy 1%, other 2%
Government Constitutional monarchy
Currency Peseta = 100 céntimos

EUROPE

ITALY

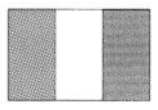

PROJECTING INTO the Mediterranean Sea in Southern Europe, Italy is an ancient land but also one of the continent's newest unified states.

GEOGRAPHY

Appennino form the backbone of a rugged peninsula, extending from the Alps into the Mediterranean Sea. Alluvial plain in the north.

CLIMATE

Mediterranean in the south. Seasonal extremes in mountains and on northern plain.

PEOPLE AND SOCIETY

Ethnically homogeneous, but gulf between prosperous, industrial north and poorer, agricultural south. Strong regional identities, especially on islands of Sicily and Sardinia. State institutions viewed as inefficient and corrupt. Allegiance to the family survives lessened influence of the Church.

The church of Santa Maria della Salute marks the entrance to the historic city of Venice.

THE ECONOMY

World leader in industrial and product design and textiles. Strong tourism and agriculture sectors. Weak currency. Large public sector debt.

FACTFILE

Official Name Italian Republic
Date of Formation 1871/1954
Capital Rome
Population 57.2 million
Total Area 116,320 sq miles (301,270 sq km)
Density 491 people per sq mile
Languages Italian*, German, French, Rhaeto-Romanic, Sardinian
Religions Catholic 99%, other 1%
Ethnic Mix Italian 98%, other (inc. German, French, Greek, Slovenian, Albanian) 2%
Government Multiparty republic
Currency Lira = 100 centesimi

EUROPE

MALTA

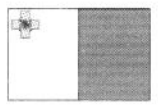

THE MALTESE archipelago lies off southern Sicily, midway between Europe and Africa. The only inhabited islands are Malta, Gozo and Kemmuna.

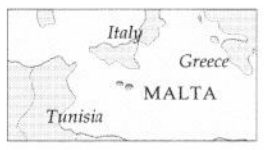

GEOGRAPHY

The main island of Malta has low hills and a ragged coastline with numerous harbors, bays, sandy beaches, and rocky coves. Gozo is more densely vegetated.

CLIMATE

Mediterranean climate. Many hours of sunshine throughout the year but very low rainfall.

PEOPLE AND SOCIETY

Over the centuries, the Maltese have been subject to Arab, Sicilian, Spanish, French, and English influences. Today, the population is socially conservative and devoutly Roman Catholic. Divorce is illegal. Many young Maltese go abroad to find work – notably to the US and Australia – as opportunities for them on the islands are few.

THE ECONOMY

Tourism is the chief source of income. Offshore banking potential. Schemes to attract foreign high-tech industry. Almost all requirements have to be imported.

FACTFILE

Official Name Republic of Malta
Date of Formation 1964
Capital Valletta
Population 400,000
Total Area 124 sq miles (320 sq km)
Density 3.225 people per sq mile
Languages Maltese*, English
Religions Catholic 98%, other (mostly Anglican) 2%
Ethnic Mix Maltese (mixed Arab, Sicilian, Norman, Spanish, Italian, English) 98%, other 2%
Government Multiparty republic
Currency Lira = 100 cents

EUROPE

VATICAN CITY

THE VATICAN City, the seat of the Roman Catholic Church, is a walled enclave in the city of Rome. It is the world's smallest fully independent state.

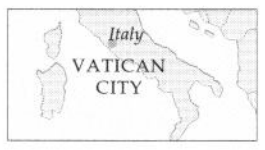

GEOGRAPHY

Territory includes ten other buildings in Rome, plus the papal residence. The Vatican Gardens cover half the City's area.

CLIMATE

Mild winters with regular rainfall. Hot, dry summers with occasional thunderstorms.

PEOPLE AND SOCIETY

The Vatican has about 1,000 permanent inhabitants, including several hundred lay persons, and employs a further 3,400 lay staff. Citizenship can be acquired through stable residence and holding an office or job within the City. Reigning Pope has supreme legislative and judicial powers, and holds office for life. State maintains a neutral stance in world affairs and has observer status in many international organizations.

THE ECONOMY

Investments and voluntary contributions by Catholics worldwide (known as Peter's Pence), backed up by tourist revenue and issue of Vatican stamps and coins.

FACTFILE

Official Name State of the Vatican City
Date of Formation 1929
Capital Not applicable
Population 1,000
Total Area 0.17 sq miles (0.44 sq km)
Density 5,882 people per sq mile
Languages Italian*, Latin*, other
Religions Catholic 100%
Ethnic Mix Italian 90%, Swiss 10% (including the Swiss Guard, which is responsible for papal security)
Government Papal Commission
Currency Italian lira = 100 centesimi

EUROPE

SAN MARINO

PERCHED ON the slopes of Monte Titano in the Italian Appennino, San Marino has maintained its independence since the 4th century AD.

GEOGRAPHY

Distinctive limestone outcrop of Monte Titano dominates wooded hills and pastures near Italy's Adriatic coast.

San Marino's 13th century fortress, the Cesta.

CLIMATE

Altitude and sea breezes moderate Mediterranean climate. Hot summers and cool, wet winters.

PEOPLE AND SOCIETY

Territory is divided into nine "castles," or districts. Tightly knit society, with 16 centuries of tradition. Strict immigration rules require 30-year residence before applying for citizenship. Catholic Church remains a more powerful influence than in neighboring Italy. Living standards are similar to those in northern Italy.

THE ECONOMY

Tourism provides 60% of government income. Light industries – led by mechanical engineering and high-quality clothing – generate export revenue. Italian infrastructure is a boon.

FACTFILE

Official Name Republic of San Marino
Date of Formation AD 301/1862
Capital San Marino
Population 25,000
Total Area 24 sq miles (61 sq km)
Density 1,041 people per sq mile
Languages Italian*, other
Religions Catholic 96%, Protestant 2%, other 2%
Ethnic Mix Sammarinese 95%, Italian 4%, other 1%
Government Multiparty republic
Currency Italian lira = 100 centesimi

EUROPE

SWITZERLAND

ONE OF the world's most prosperous countries, with a long tradition of neutrality in foreign affairs, it lies at the center of Western Europe.

GEOGRAPHY
Mostly mountainous, with river valleys. Alps cover 60% of its area; Jura in west cover 10%. Lowlands lie along east-west axis.

CLIMATE
Most rain falls in the warm summer months. Snowy winters, but milder and foggy away from the mountains.

PEOPLE AND SOCIETY
Composed of distinct Swiss-German, Swiss-French, and Swiss-Italian linguistic groups, but national identity is strong. Country divided into 26 autonomous cantons (states), each with control over housing and economic policy. Tensions over membership of EU, drug abuse, and role of guest workers in economy. Some young see society as regimented and conformist.

THE ECONOMY
Diversified economy relies on services – with strong tourism and banking sectors – and specialized industries (engineering, watches).

FACTFILE
Official Name Swiss Confederation
Date of Formation 1815
Capital Bern
Population 7.3 million
Total Area 15,940 sq miles (41,290 sq km)
Density 457 people per sq mile
Languages German*, French*, Italian*, Romansch*, other
Religions Catholic 48%, Protestant 44%, other 8%
Ethnic Mix German 65%, French 18%, Italian 10%, other 7%
Government Federal republic
Currency Franc = 100 centimes

EUROPE

LIECHTENSTEIN

TUCKED IN the Alps between Switzerland and Austria, Liechtenstein became an independent principality of the Holy Roman Empire in 1719.

GEOGRAPHY
Upper Rhine valley covers western third. Mountains and narrow valleys of the eastern Alps make up the remainder.

CLIMATE
Warm, dry summers. Cold winters, with heavy snow in mountains December–March.

PEOPLE AND SOCIETY
Country's role as a financial center accounts for its many foreign residents (over 35% of the population), of whom half are Swiss and the rest mostly German. High standard of living results in few social tensions. Sovereignty cherished, despite close alliance with Switzerland, which handles its foreign relations and defense.

Liechtenstein allocates 2% of its state budget to restoring mountain vegetation and coordinating land use.

THE ECONOMY
Banking secrecy and low taxes attract foreign investment. Well-diversified exports include dental products, furniture, and chemicals.

FACTFILE
Official Name Principality of Liechtenstein
Date of Formation 1719
Capital Vaduz
Population 31,000
Total Area 62 sq miles (160 sq km)
Density 500 people per sq mile
Languages German*, Alemannish
Religions Catholic 87%, Protestant 8%, other 5%
Ethnic Mix Liechtensteiner 63%, Swiss 15%, German 9%, other 13%
Government Constitutional monarchy
Currency Swiss franc = 100 centimes

EUROPE

AUSTRIA

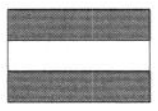

BORDERING EIGHT countries in the heart of Europe, Austria was created in 1920 after the collapse of the Austro-Hungarian Empire the previous year.

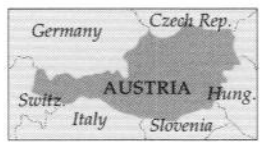

GEOGRAPHY
Mainly mountainous. Alps and foothills cover the west and south. Lowlands in the east are part of the Danube River basin.

CLIMATE
Temperate continental climate. Western Alpine regions have colder winters and more rainfall.

PEOPLE AND SOCIETY
Although all are German-speaking, Austrians consider themselves ethnically distinct from Germans. Minorities are few; there are a small number of Hungarians, Slovenes, and Croats, plus refugees from conflict in former Yugoslavia. Some Austrians are beginning to challenge patriarchal and class-conscious social values. Legislation reflects strong environmental concerns.

THE ECONOMY
Large manufacturing base, despite lack of energy resources. Skilled labor force the key to high-tech exports. Strong tourism sector.

FACTFILE
Official Name Republic of Austria
Date of Formation 1918/1945
Capital Vienna
Population 8 million
Total Area 32,375 sq miles (83,850 sq km)
Density 247 people per sq mile
Languages German*, Croatian, Slovene, Hungarian (Magyar)
Religions Catholic 85%, Protestant 6%, other 9%
Ethnic Mix German 99%, other (inc. Hungarian, Slovene, Croat) 1%
Government Multiparty republic
Currency Schilling = 100 groschen

EUROPE

HUNGARY

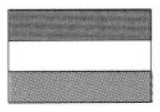

HUNGARY IS bordered by seven states in Central Europe. It has changed its economic and political policies to develop closer ties with the EU.

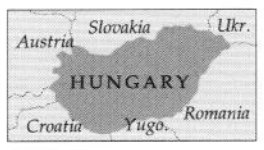

GEOGRAPHY
Fertile plains in east and northwest; west and north are hilly. River Danube bisects the country from north to south.

The Hungarian capital, Budapest is actually two cities, Buda and Pest which lie on opposing banks of the River Danube.

CLIMATE
Continental. Wet springs; late, but very hot summers, and cold, cloudy winters.

PEOPLE AND SOCIETY
Ethnically homogenous and stable society, showing signs of stress since change to market economy. Most homes are overcrowded, due to a severe housing shortage. Since 1989, a middle class has emerged, but life for the unemployed and unskilled is harder than under communism. Concern over treatment of Hungarian nationals in neighboring states.

THE ECONOMY
Weak banking sector and unemployment hamper moves to open economy. Heavy industries and agriculture remain strong. Growing tourism and services.

FACTFILE
Official Name Republic of Hungary
Date of Formation 1918/1945
Capital Budapest
Population 10.1 million
Total Area 35,919 sq miles (93,030 sq km)
Density 281 people per sq mile
Languages Hungarian (Magyar)*, German, Slovak, other
Religions Catholic 68%, Protestant 25%, other 7%
Ethnic Mix Hungarian (Magyar) 90%, German 2%, other 8%
Government Multiparty republic
Currency Forint = 100 filler.

EUROPE

CZECH REPUBLIC

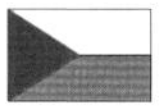

ONCE PART of Czechoslovakia in Central Europe, it became independent in 1993, after peacefully dissolving its federal union with Slovakia.

GEOGRAPHY

Western territory of Bohemia is a plateau surrounded by mountains. Moravia, in the east, has hills and lowlands.

CLIMATE

Cool, sometimes cold winters, and warm summer months, which bring most of the annual rainfall.

PEOPLE AND SOCIETY

Secular and urban society, with high divorce rates. Czechs make up the vast majority of the population. The 300,000 Slovaks left after partition now form largest ethnic minority. Ethnic tensions are few, but there is some hostility toward the Gypsy community. A new commercial elite is emerging alongside ex-communist entrepreneurs.

The Vltava River in Prague. Millions of tourists, mainly from Europe and the USA visit each year.

THE ECONOMY

Traditional heavy industries (machinery, iron, car-making) have been successfully privatized. Large tourism revenues. Skilled labor force. Rising unemployment.

FACTFILE

- *Official Name:* Czech Republic
- *Date of Formation:* 1993
- *Capital:* Prague
- *Population:* 10.3 million
- *Total Area:* 30,260 sq miles (78,370 sq km)
- *Density:* 340 people per sq mile
- *Languages:* Czech*, Slovak, Romany, other
- *Religions:* Catholic 44%, Protestant 6%, other Christian 12%, other 38%
- *Ethnic Mix:* Czech 85%, Moravian 13%, other (inc. Slovak, Gypsy) 2%
- *Government:* Multiparty republic
- *Currency:* Koruna = 100 halura

EUROPE

SLOVAKIA

LANDLOCKED in Central Europe, Slovakia has been independent since 1993. It is the less-developed half of the former Czechoslovakia.

GEOGRAPHY

Carpathian Mountains stretch along northern border with Poland. Southern lowlands include the fertile Danube plain.

CLIMATE

Continental. Moderately warm summers and steady rainfall. Cold winters with heavy snowfalls.

PEOPLE AND SOCIETY

Slovaks are largest and most dominant group. Tension between them and the Hungarian minority has increased, particularly over directive that Hungarians should adopt Slovak name endings. Before partition, many skilled Slovaks took jobs in Prague, but few have returned to help structure the new Slovakia. Catholic Church remains influential.

THE ECONOMY

Narrow emphasis on heavy industry, with poor record on innovation and capital investment. High inflation and unemployment. Growing tourism sector.

FACTFILE

- *Official Name:* Slovak Republic
- *Date of Formation:* 1993
- *Capital:* Bratislava
- *Population:* 5.4 million
- *Total Area:* 19,100 sq miles (49,500 sq km)
- *Density:* 282 people per sq mile
- *Languages:* Slovak*, Hungarian (Magyar), Romany, Czech, other
- *Religions:* Catholic 80%, Protestant 12%, other 8%
- *Ethnic Mix:* Slovak 85%, Hungarian 9%, Czech 1%, other (inc. Gypsy) 5%
- *Government:* Multiparty republic
- *Currency:* Koruna = 100 halura

EUROPE

SLOVENIA

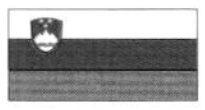

NORTHERNMOST of the former Yugoslav republics, Slovenia has the closest links with Western Europe. In 1991, it gained independence with little violence.

GEOGRAPHY

Alpine terrain with hills and mountains. Forests cover almost half the country's area. Short Adriatic coastline.

Lake Bled in the Julian Alps, which lie astride the Slovenian–Italian border. The lake is a popular tourist destination.

CLIMATE

Mediterranean climate on small coastal strip. Alpine interior has continental extremes.

PEOPLE AND SOCIETY

Homogeneous population accounts for relatively peaceful transition to independence. Traditional links with Austria and Italy, each with Slovene populations, account for the "Alpine" rather than "Balkan" outlook. Wages are the highest in Central Europe, but unemployment is rising. Institutional change is proceeding slowly.

THE ECONOMY

Competitive manufacturing industry. Prospects for growth in electronics industry. Well-developed tourist sector. Czech demand for Slovenia's consumer goods exports.

FACTFILE

- *Official Name:* Republic of Slovenia
- *Date of Formation:* 1991
- *Capital:* Ljubljana
- *Population:* 1.9 million
- *Total Area:* 7,820 sq miles (20,250 sq km)
- *Density:* 242 people per sq mile
- *Languages:* Slovene*, Serbo-Croatian
- *Religions:* Roman Catholic 96%, Muslim 1%, other 3%
- *Ethnic Mix:* Slovene 92%, Croat 3%, Serb 1%, other 4%
- *Government:* Multiparty republic
- *Currency:* Tolar = 100 stotins

EUROPE

CROATIA

A FORMER Yugoslav republic. Postindependence fighting thwarted its plans to capitalize on its prime location along the east Adriatic coast.

GEOGRAPHY

Rocky, mountainous Adriatic coastline is dotted with islands. Interior is a mixture of wooded mountains and broad valleys.

CLIMATE

The interior has a temperate continental climate. Mediterranean climate along the Adriatic coast.

PEOPLE AND SOCIETY

Turbulence was triggered by long-held ethnic hostilities. Open warfare between Croats and Serbs began in 1990. Some areas with local Serb majorities achieved *de facto* autonomy, after fierce fighting in 1992. Destruction was widespread; thousands of people were made homeless.

THE ECONOMY

Economy was severely strained by fighting and influx of refugees. Potential for renewed success in manufacturing, tourism. Exports to the West have grown, despite conflict.

FACTFILE

- *Official Name:* Republic of Croatia
- *Date of Formation:* 1991
- *Capital:* Zagreb
- *Population:* 4.5 million
- *Total Area:* 21,830 sq miles (56,540 sq km)
- *Density:* 206 people per sq mile
- *Languages:* Croatian*, Serbian
- *Religions:* Roman Catholic 77%, Orthodox Catholic 11%, Protestant 1%, Muslim 1%, other 10%
- *Ethnic Mix:* Croat 80%, Serb 12%, Hungarian, Slovenian, other 8%
- *Government:* Multiparty republic
- *Currency:* Kuna = 100 para

BOSNIA & HERZEGOVINA

DOMINATING THE western Balkans, Bosnia and Herzegovina was the focus of the bitter conflict surrounding the breakup of former Yugoslavia.

GEOGRAPHY
Hills and mountains, with narrow river valleys. Lowlands in the north. Mainly deciduous forest covers about half of the total area.

CLIMATE
Continental. Hot summers and cold, often snowy winters.

PEOPLE AND SOCIETY
Early 1990s civil war between rival ethnic groups. Ethnic Bosnians (mainly Muslim) form the largest group, with large minorities of Serbs and Croats. Communities have been destroyed or uprooted ("ethnic cleansing") as Serbs and Croats established separate ethnic areas. The UN and NATO were involved as peacekeepers.

THE ECONOMY
Before 1991, Bosnia was home to five of former Yugoslavia's largest companies. It has the potential to become a thriving market economy with a strong manufacturing base.

FACTFILE

Official Name: The Republic of Bosnia and Herzegovina
Date of Formation: 1992
Capital: Sarajevo
Population: 3.5 million
Total Area: 19,741 sq miles (51,130 sq km)
Density: 177 people per sq mile
Languages: Serbo-Croatian*, other
Religions: Muslim 40%, Orthodox Catholic 31%, other 29%
Ethnic Mix: Bosnian 44%, Serb 31%, Croat 17%, other 8%
Government: Multiparty republic
Currency: Dinar = 100 para

YUGOSLAVIA [SERBIA & MONTENEGRO]

THE FEDERAL Republic of Yugoslavia, comprising Serbia and Montenegro, is the successor state to the former Yugoslavia.

GEOGRAPHY
Fertile Danube plain in north, rolling uplands in center. Mountains in south, and behind narrow Adriatic coastal plain.

CLIMATE
Mediterranean along coast, continental inland. Hot summers and cold winters, with heavy snow.

PEOPLE AND SOCIETY
Social order has disintegrated since dissolution of the former Yugoslavia. Serbia was vilified in the international community for its role in the conflict in the region. Serbian concerns over Bosnia and Croatia have masked domestic tensions, particularly unrest among the Albanian population in the southern region of Kosovo.

Prior to 1991, the glorious scenery of Serbia and Montenegro attracted over five million tourists annually.

THE ECONOMY
Bosnian war and UN trade sanctions crippled the economy. Fuel and food shortages. Hyper-inflation created a barter economy.

FACTFILE

Official Name: Federal Republic of Yugoslavia
Date of Formation: 1992
Capital: Belgrade
Population: 10.9 million
Total Area: 9,929 sq miles (25,715 sq km)
Density: 1,097 people per sq mile
Languages: Serbo-Croatian*, other
Religions: Orthodox Catholic 65%, Muslim 19%, other 16%
Ethnic Mix: Serb 63%, Albanian 14%, Montenegrin 6%, other 17%
Government: Multiparty republic
Currency: Dinar = 100 para

ALBANIA

LYING AT the southeastern end of the Adriatic Sea, Albania held its first multiparty elections in 1991, after nearly five decades of communism.

GEOGRAPHY
Narrow coastal plain. Interior is mostly hills and mountains. Forest and scrub cover over 40% of the land. Large lakes in the east.

CLIMATE
Mediterranean coastal climate, with warm summers and cool winters. Mountains receive heavy rains or snows in winter.

PEOPLE AND SOCIETY
Last eastern European country to move toward Western economic liberalism – pace of change remains a sensitive issue. Mosques and churches have reopened in what was once the world's only officially atheist state. Greek minority in the south suffers much discrimination.

Berat, in Albania, the "city of a thousand windows" was preserved as a museum city while a new town was built further down the valley.

THE ECONOMY
Oil and gas reserves plus high growth rate have potential to offset rudimentary infrastructure and lack of foreign investment.

FACTFILE

Official Name: Republic of Albania
Date of Formation: 1912/1913
Capital: Tirana
Population: 3.5 million
Total Area: 11,100 sq miles (28,750 sq km)
Density: 315 people per sq mile
Languages: Albanian*, Greek
Religions: Muslim 70%, Greek Orthodox 20%, Roman Catholic 10%
Ethnic Mix: Albanian 96%, Greek 2%, other (inc. Macedonian) 2%
Government: Multiparty republic
Currency: Lek = 100 qindars

MACEDONIA

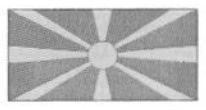

LANDLOCKED in the southern Balkans, Macedonia is affected by sanctions imposed on its northern trading partners and by Greek antagonism.

GEOGRAPHY
Mainly mountainous or hilly, with deep river basins in center. Plains in northeast and southwest.

CLIMATE
Continental climate with wet springs and dry autumns. Heavy snowfalls in northern mountains.

PEOPLE AND SOCIETY
Slav Macedonians comprise two-thirds of the population. Officially 20% are Albanian, although Albanians claim they account for 40%. Tensions between the two groups have so far been restrained. Greek government is hostile toward the state because it suspects it may try to absorb northern Greece – also called Macedonia – in a "Greater Macedonia." Social structures remain essentially socialist.

THE ECONOMY
Serbian sanctions paralyse exports, but foreign aid and grants boost foreign exchange reserves. Growing private sector. Thriving black market in the capital.

FACTFILE

Official Name: Former Yugoslav Republic of Macedonia
Date of Formation: 1991
Capital: Skopje
Population: 2.2 million
Total Area: 9,929 sq miles (25,715 sq km)
Density: 221 people per sq mile
Languages: Macedonian, Serbo-Croatian (no official language)
Religions: Christian 80%, Muslim 20%
Ethnic Mix: Macedonian 67%, Albanian 20%, Turkish 4%, other 9%
Government: Multiparty republic
Currency: Denar = 100 deni

EUROPE

BULGARIA

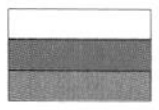

LOCATED IN southeastern Europe, Bulgaria has made slow progress towards democracy since the fall of its communist regime in 1990.

GEOGRAPHY
Mountains run east–west across center and along southern border. Danube plain in north, Thracian plain in southeast.

CLIMATE
Warm summers and snowy winters, especially in mountains. East winds bring seasonal extremes.

PEOPLE AND SOCIETY
Government has sought to assimilate separate ethnic groups, thereby suppressing cultural identities. Large exodus of Bulgarian Turks in 1989. Recent privatization program has left many Turks landless and prompted further emigration. Gypsies suffer much discrimination. Female equality exists only in theory. Ruling party, mainly ex-communists, have resisted change.

Rila monastery in Bulgaria's Rila Mountains is famous for its 1,200 frescoes dating from the 19th century.

THE ECONOMY
Political and technical delays hinder privatization program. Good agricultural production, including grapes for well-developed wine industry, and tobacco.

FACTFILE
Official Name Republic of Bulgaria
Date of Formation 1908/1923
Capital Sofia
Population 8.7 million
Total Area 42,822 sq miles (110,910 sq km)
Density 203 people per sq mile
Languages Bulgarian*, Turkish, Macedonian, Romany, Armenian
Religions Christian 85%, Muslim 13%, Jewish 1%, other 1%
Ethnic Mix Bulgarian 85%, Turkish 9%, Macedonian 3%, Gypsy 3%
Government Multiparty republic
Currency Lev = 100 stotinki

EUROPE

GREECE

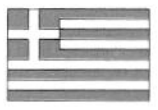

GREECE IS the southernmost Balkan nation. Surrounded by the Mediterranean, Aegean and Ionian seas, it has a strong seafaring tradition.

GEOGRAPHY
Mountainous peninsula with over 2,000 islands. Large central plain along the Aegean coast.

CLIMATE
Mainly Mediterranean with dry, hot summers. Alpine climate in northern mountain areas.

PEOPLE AND SOCIETY
Postwar industrial development altered the dominance of agriculture and seafaring. Rural exodus to industrial cities has been stemmed, but over half the population now live in the two largest cities. Age-old culture and Greek Orthodox Church balance social mobility.

THE ECONOMY
High inflation and poor investment work against strong economic sectors: tourism, shipping, agriculture. Thriving black economy.

FACTFILE
Official Name Hellenic Republic
Date of Formation 1830/1947
Capital Athens
Population 10.5 million
Total Area 50,961 sq miles (131,990 sq km)
Density 206 people per sq mile
Languages Greek*, Turkish, Albanian, Macedonian
Religions Greek Orthodox 98%, Muslim 1%, other (mainly Roman Catholic and Jewish) 1%
Ethnic Mix Greek 98%, other 2%
Government Multiparty republic
Currency Drachma = 100 lepta

EUROPE

ROMANIA

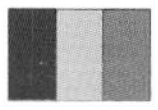

ROMANIA LIES on the Black Sea coast. Since the overthrow of its communist regime in 1989, it has been slowly converting to a free-market economy.

GEOGRAPHY
Carpathian Mountains encircle Transylvanian plateau. Wide plains to the south and east. River Danube on southern border.

Moldova's warm summers and even rainfall are ideal for growing a wide range of crops.

CLIMATE
Continental. Hot, humid summers and cold, snowy winters. Very heavy spring rains.

PEOPLE AND SOCIETY
Since 1989, there has been a rise in Romanian nationalism, aggravated by the hardships brought by economic reform. Incidence of ethnic violence has also risen, particularly toward Hungarians and Gypsies. Decrease in population in recent years due to emigration and falling birth rate.

THE ECONOMY
Outdated, polluting heavy industries and unmechanized agricultural sector. Wages have fallen since demise of communism. High number of small-scale foreign joint ventures. Tourism potential.

FACTFILE
Official Name Romania
Date of Formation 1947
Capital Bucharest
Population 22.8 million
Total Area 91,700 sq miles (237,500 sq km)
Density 249 people per sq mile
Languages Romanian*, Hungarian
Religions Romanian Orthodox 70%, Roman Catholic 6%, Protestant 6%, Greek Catholic 3%, other 15%
Ethnic Mix Romanian 89%, Hungarian 8%, other (inc. Gypsy) 3%
Government Multiparty republic
Currency Leu = 100 bani

EUROPE

MOLDOVA

THE SMALLEST AND most densely populated of the ex-Soviet republics, Moldova has strong linguistic and cultural links with Romania to the west.

GEOGRAPHY
Steppes and hilly plains, drained by Dniester and Prut rivers.

CLIMATE
Warm summers and relatively mild winters. Moderate rainfall, evenly spread throughout the year.

PEOPLE AND SOCIETY
Shared heritage with Romania defines national identity, although in 1994 Moldovans voted against possible unification with Romania. Most of the population is engaged in intensive agriculture. The 1994 constitution granted special autonomous status to the Gagauz people in the south (Orthodox Christian Turks), and to the Slav peoples on the east bank of the River Dniester.

THE ECONOMY
Well-developed agricultural sector: wine, tobacco, cotton, food processing. Light manufacturing. Progress in establishing markets for exports. High unemployment.

FACTFILE
Official Name Republic of Moldova
Date of Formation 1991
Capital Chişinău
Population 4.4 million
Total Area 13,000 sq miles (33,700 sq km)
Density 338 people per sq mile
Languages Moldovan*, Russian
Religions Romanian Orthodox 98%, Jewish 1%, other 1%
Ethnic Mix Moldovan (Romanian) 65%, Ukrainian 14%, Russian 13%, Gagauz 4%, other 4%
Government Multiparty republic
Currency Leu = 100 bani

EUROPE

BELARUS

FORMERLY KNOWN as White Russia, Belarus lies landlocked in eastern Europe. It reluctantly became independent of the USSR in 1991.

GEOGRAPHY

Mainly plains and low hills. Dnieper and Dvina rivers drain eastern lowlands. Vast Pripet Marshes in the southwest.

CLIMATE

Extreme continental climate. Long, subfreezing, but mainly dry winters, and hot summers.

PEOPLE AND SOCIETY

Only 2% of people are non-Slav, ethnic tension is minimal. Entire population have right to Belarussian citizenship, although only 11% are fluent in Belarussian. Post-Soviet constitution was not adopted until 1994. Wealth is held by a small ex-communist elite. Fallout from 1986 Chornobyl' nuclear disaster in Ukraine affected Belorussians' health and environment.

Much of southern Belarus is marshy and sparsely populated. It includes the vast Pripet Marshes.

THE ECONOMY

Food processing and heavy industries stagnate while politicians argue over market reforms. Low unemployment but high inflation.

FACTFILE

Official Name Republic of Belarus
Date of Formation 1991
Capital Minsk
Population 10.1 million
Total Area 80,154 sq miles (207,600 sq km)
Density 127 people per sq mile
Languages Belorussian*, Russian
Religions Russian Orthodox 60%, Catholic 8%, other (including Uniate, Protestant, Muslim, Jewish) 32%
Ethnic Mix Belorussian 78%, Russian 13%, Polish 4%, other 5%
Government Multiparty republic
Currency Rouble = 100 kopeks

EUROPE

UKRAINE

THE FORMER "breadbasket of the Soviet Union," Ukraine balances assertive nationalism with concerns over its relations with Russia.

GEOGRAPHY

Mainly fertile steppes and forests. Carpathian Mountains in southwest, Crimean chain in south. Pripet Marshes in northwest.

CLIMATE

Mainly continental climate, with distinct seasons. Southern Crimea has Mediterranean climate.

PEOPLE AND SOCIETY

Over 90% of the population in western Ukraine is Ukrainian. However, in several cities in the east and south, Russians form a majority. In the Crimea, the Tartars comprise around 10% of the population. At independence in 1991, most Russians accepted Ukrainian sovereignty. However, tensions are now rising as both groups adopt more extremist nationalist policies.

THE ECONOMY

Hyperinflation, corruption, and hostility from economic elite stifle any reforms. Heavy industries and agriculture largely unchanged since independence.

FACTFILE

Official Name Ukraine
Date of Formation 1991
Capital Kiev
Population 51.3 million
Total Area 223,090 sq miles (603,700 sq km)
Density 229 people per sq mile
Languages Ukrainian*, Russian, Tartar
Religions Mostly Ukrainian Orthodox, with Roman Catholic, Protestant and Jewish minorities
Ethnic Mix Ukrainian 73%, Russian 22%, other (inc. Tartar) 5%
Government Multiparty republic
Currency Karbovanets (coupons)

EUROPE

RUSSIAN FEDERATION

STILL THE world's largest state, despite the breakup of the USSR in 1991, the Russian Federation is struggling to capitalize on its diversity.

GEOGRAPHY

Ural Mountains divide European steppes and forests from tundra and forests of Siberia. South-central deserts and mountains.

CLIMATE

Continental in European Russia. Elsewhere from subarctic to Mediterranean and hot desert.

The Kremlin, in Moscow is the home of the Russian parliament. It is enclosed by walls 1.5 miles long.

PEOPLE AND SOCIETY

Ethnic Russians make up 80% of the population, but many minorities. 57 nationalities have territorial status, a further 95 lack their own territory. 1994 war with Chechnya indicated potential for ethnic crisis. Wealth disparities, rising crime, and black market activity have accompanied reform. Recent return to religious practice.

THE ECONOMY

Inefficiencies since transition to market economy. Natural resources, include oil and gas, precious metals, timber, and hydrocarbons. Enormous engineering and scientific base.

FACTFILE

Official Name Russian Federation
Date of Formation 1991
Capital Moscow
Population 146.7 million
Total Area 6,592,800 sq miles (17,075,400 sq km)
Density 22 people per sq mile
Languages Russian*, other
Religions Russian Orthodox 80%, other (inc. Jewish, Muslim) 20%
Ethnic Mix Russian 80%, Tatar 4%, Ukrainian 3%, other 13%
Government Multiparty republic
Currency Rouble = 100 kopeks

ASIA

AZERBAIJAN

SITUATED ON the western coast of the Caspian Sea, Azerbaijan was the first Soviet republic to declare independence from Moscow in 1991.

GEOGRAPHY

Caucasus mountains in north and Naxçivan enclave to south of Armenia. Flat, low-lying terrain on the coast of the Caspian Sea.

CLIMATE

Continental with pronounced seasonal extremes. Low rainfall, with peak months during summer.

PEOPLE AND SOCIETY

Azerbaijanis now form a large majority. Thousands of Armenians, Russians and Jews have left as a result of rising nationalism among Azerbaijanis. Racial hostility against those who remain is increasing. Influx of half a million Azerbaijani refugees fleeing war with Armenia over the disputed enclave of Nagornoyy Karabakh. Once effective social security system has collapsed.

THE ECONOMY

Oil and gas have considerable potential. War is a major drain on state resources. Market reforms attract foreign interest.

FACTFILE

Official Name Republic of Azerbaijan
Date of Formation 1991
Capital Baku
Population 7.6 million
Total Area 33,436 sq miles (86,600 sq km)
Density 227 people per sq mile
Languages Azerbaijani*, Russian, Armenian, other
Religions Muslim 83%, Armenian Apostolic, Russian Orthodox 17%
Ethnic Mix Azerbaijani 83%, Russian 6%, Armenian 6%, other 5%
Government Multiparty republic
Currency Manat = 100 gopik

ASIA

ARMENIA

SMALLEST OF the former USSR's republics, Armenia lies in the Lesser Caucasus mountains. Since 1988, it has been at war with Azerbaijan.

GEOGRAPHY

Rugged and mountainous, with expanses of semidesert and a large lake in the east, Sevana Lich.

CLIMATE

Continental climate, little rainfall in the lowlands. Winters are often bitterly cold.

PEOPLE AND SOCIETY

Strong commitment to Christianity, and to Armenian culture. Minority groups are well integrated. War with Azerbaijan over the enclave of Nagornyy Karabakh has meant 100,000 Armenians living in Azerbaijan forced to return home to live in poverty. In 1988, 25,000 people died in an earthquake in the west.

The island of Akdamar, in eastern Anatolia, surrounded by Lake Van is the site of the 10th-century Church of the Holy Cross.

THE ECONOMY

Few natural resources, though lead, copper, and zinc are mined. Main agricultural products are wine, tobacco, olives, and rice. Well-developed machine-building and manufacturing – includes textiles, and bottling of mineral water.

FACTFILE

Official Name Republic of Armenia
Date of Formation 1991
Capital Yerevan
Population 3.6 million
Total Area 11,505 sq miles (29,000 sq km)
Density 312 people per sq mile
Languages Armenian*, Azerbaijani, Russian, Kurdish
Religions Armenian Apostolic 90%, other Christian and Muslim 10%
Ethnic Mix Armenian 93%, Azerbaijani 3%, Russian, Kurdish 4%
Government Multiparty republic
Currency Dram = 100 louma

ASIA

TURKEY

LYING PARTLY in Europe, but mostly in Asia, Turkey's position gives it significant influence in the Mediterranean, Black Sea and Middle East.

GEOGRAPHY

Asian Turkey (Anatolia) is dominated by two mountain ranges, separated by a high, semi-desert plateau. Coastal regions are fertile.

CLIMATE

Coast has a Mediterranean climate. Interior has cold, snowy winters and hot, dry summers.

PEOPLE AND SOCIETY

The Turks are racially diverse. Many are refugees or descendants of refugees, often from the Balkans or other territories once under Russian rule. However, the sense of national identity is strong. Since 1984, southeastern region has been the scene of a civil war waged by the Kurdish minority, demanding their rights within the country.

THE ECONOMY

Since the early 1980s, textiles, manufacturing, and construction sectors all booming. Tourism is also a major foreign currency earner.

FACTFILE

Official Name Republic of Turkey
Date of Formation 1923/1939
Capital Ankara
Population 63.1 million
Total Area 300,950 sq miles (779,450 sq km)
Density 210 people per sq mile
Languages Turkish*, Kurdish, Arabic, Circassian, Armenian
Religions Muslim 99%, other 1%
Ethnic Mix Turkish 80%, Kurdish 17%, other 3%
Government Multiparty republic
Currency Turkish lira = 100 krural

ASIA

GEORGIA

LOCATED ON the eastern shore of the Black Sea, Georgia has been torn by civil war since achieving independence from the USSR in 1991.

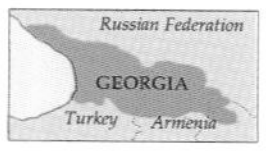

GEOGRAPHY

Kura valley lies between Caucasus mountains in the north and Lesser Caucasus range in south. Lowlands along the Black Sea coast.

CLIMATE

Subtropical along the coast, changing to continental extremes at high altitudes. Rainfall is moderate.

Beirut's seafront, the Corniche, damaged in the civil war, is due to be rebuilt by US engineers and architects.

PEOPLE AND SOCIETY

Paternalistic society, with strong family, cultural, and literary traditions. One in five live in poverty. Georgians majority group. An uneasy truce has followed the 1990–93 civil war, and the political scene remains volatile. In 1994, another civil war was fought, as ethnic Abkhazians attempted to secede from Georgia.

THE ECONOMY

Food processing and wine production are main industries. Economy has broken down due to war and severance of links with other former Soviet republics.

FACTFILE

Official Name Republic of Georgia
Date of Formation 1991
Capital Tbilisi
Population 5.5 million
Total Area 26,911 sq miles (69,700 sq km)
Density 204 people per sq mile
Languages Georgian*, Russian, other
Religions Georgian Orthodox 70%, Russian Orthodox 10%, other 20%
Ethnic Mix Georgian 69%, Armenian 9%, Russian 6%, Azerbaijani 5%, other 11%
Government Republic
Currency Coupons

ASIA

LEBANON

LEBANON IS dwarfed by its two powerful neighbors, Syria and Israel. The state is rebuilding after 14 years of civil war.

GEOGRAPHY

Behind a narrow coastal plain, two parallel mountain ranges run the length of the country, separated by the fertile El Beqaa valley.

CLIMATE

Hot summers, with high humidity on the coast. Mild winters.

PEOPLE AND SOCIETY

Population is split between Christians and Muslims. Although in the minority, Christians have been the traditional rulers. In 1975, civil war broke out between the two groups. A settlement, which gave the Muslims more power, was reached in 1989. Elections in 1992 brought hope of greater stability. A huge gulf exists between the poor and a small, immensely rich elite.

THE ECONOMY

Infrastructure wrecked by civil war. Postwar opportunity to regain position as Arab center for banking and services. Potentially a major producer of wine and fruit.

FACTFILE

Official Name Republic of Lebanon
Date of Formation 1944
Capital Beirut
Population 3.1 million
Total Area 4,015 sq miles (10,400 sq km)
Density 772 people per sq mile
Languages Arabic*, French, Armenian, English
Religions Muslim (mainly Shi'a) 57%, Christian (mainly Maronite) 43%
Ethnic Mix Arab 93% (Lebanese 83%, Palestinian 10%), other 7%
Government Multiparty republic
Currency Pound = 100 piastres

SYRIA

STRETCHING FROM the eastern Mediterranean to the River Tigris, Syria's borders were created on its independence from France in 1946.

GEOGRAPHY
Northern coastal plain is backed by a low range of hills. The River Euphrates cuts through a vast interior desert plateau.

CLIMATE
Mediterranean coastal climate. Inland areas are arid. In winter, snow is common on the mountains.

PEOPLE AND SOCIETY
Most Syrians live near the coast, where the biggest cities are sited. 90% are Muslim, including the politically dominant Alawis. In the north and west are groups of Kurds, Armenians and Turkish-speaking peoples. Some 300,000 Palestinian refugees have also settled in Syria. They, together with the urban unemployed, make up the poorest groups in a growing gulf between rich and poor.

The city of Palmyra, in central Syria, possesses some of the Middle East's finest classical monuments.

THE ECONOMY
High defense spending is major drain on economy. Exporter of crude oil. Agriculture is thriving: crops include cotton, wheat, olives.

FACTFILE
Official Name Syrian Arab Republic
Date of Formation 1946
Capital Damascus
Population 15.2 million
Total Area 71,500 sq miles (185,180 sq km)
Density 212 people per sq mile
Languages Arabic*, French, Kurdish, Armenian, Circassian, Aramaic
Religions Sunni Muslim 74%, other Muslim 16%, Christian 10%
Ethnic Mix Arab 90%, other 10%
Government Single-party republic
Currency Pound = 100 piastres

CYPRUS

CYPRUS LIES in the eastern Mediterranean. Since 1974, it has been partitioned between the Turkish-occupied north and the Greek south.

GEOGRAPHY
Mountains in the center-west give way to a fertile plain in the east, flanked by hills to the northeast.

CLIMATE
Mediterranean. Summers are hot and dry. Winters are mild, with snow in the mountains.

PEOPLE AND SOCIETY
Majority of the population is Greek Christian. Since the 16th century, a minority community of Turkish Muslims has lived in the north of the island. In 1974 Turkish troops occupied the north, which was proclaimed the Turkish Republic of Northern Cyprus, but is recognized only by Turkey. The north remains poor, while the south, where the tourist industry is booming, is richer.

THE ECONOMY
In the south, tourism is the key industry. Shipping and light manufacturing also important. In the north, the main exports are citrus fruits and live animals.

FACTFILE
Official Name Republic of Cyprus
Date of Formation 1960/1983
Capital Nicosia
Population 800,000
Total Area 3,572 sq miles (9,251 sq km)
Density 223 people per sq mile
Languages Greek*, Turkish, other
Religions Greek Orthodox 77%, Muslim 18%, other 5%
Ethnic Mix Greek 77%, Turkish 18%, other (mainly British) 5%
Government Multiparty republic
Currency Cypriot £/Turkish lira

ISRAEL

CREATED AS a new state in 1948, on the east coast of the Mediterranean. Following wars with its Arab neighbors, it has extended its boundaries.

GEOGRAPHY
Coastal plain. Desert in the south. In the east lie the Great Rift Valley and the Dead Sea – the lowest point on the Earth's surface.

CLIMATE
Summers are hot and dry. Wet season, March–November, is mild.

PEOPLE AND SOCIETY
Large numbers of Jews settled in Palestine before Israel was founded. After World War II there was a huge increase in immigration. Sephardi Jews from the Middle East and Mediterranean are now in the majority, but Ashkenazi Jews from Central Europe still dominate business and politics. Palestinians in Gaza and Jericho gained limited autonomy in 1994.

THE ECONOMY
Huge potential of industrial, agricultural, and manufacturing products. Major exporter of mineral salts. Important banking sector.

FACTFILE
Official Name State of Israel
Date of Formation 1948/1982
Capital Jerusalem
Population 5.8 million
Total Area 7,992 sq miles (20,700 sq km)
Density 726 people per sq mile
Languages Hebrew*, Arabic, Yiddish, German, Russian, Polish, Romanian, Persian, English
Religions Jewish 83%, Muslim 13%, Christian 2%, other 2%
Ethnic Mix Jewish 83%, Arab 17%
Government Multiparty republic
Currency New shekel = 100 agorat

JORDAN

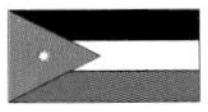

THE KINGDOM of Jordan lies east of Israel. In 1993, King Hussein responded to calls for greater democracy by agreeing to multiparty elections.

GEOGRAPHY
Mostly desert plateaus, with occasional salt pans. Lowest parts lie along eastern shore of Dead Sea and east bank of the River Jordan.

Jordan's King's Highway, seen from the castle at Al Karak. This strategic fortress was built by Crusader knights in the 12th century.

CLIMATE
Hot, dry summers. Cool, wet winters. Areas below sea level very hot in summer, and warm in winter.

PEOPLE AND SOCIETY
A predominantly Muslim country with a strong national identity, Jordan's population has Bedouin roots. There is a Christian minority and a large Palestinian population who have moved to Jordan from Israeli-occupied territory. Jordan gave up its claim to the West Bank to the PLO in 1988. The monarchy's power base lies among the rural tribes, which also provide the backbone of the military.

THE ECONOMY
Phosphates, chemicals, and fertilizers are principal exports. Skilled, educated work force.

FACTFILE
Official Name Hashemite Kingdom of Jordan
Date of Formation 1946/1976
Capital Amman
Population 5.7 million
Total Area 34,440 sq miles (89,210 sq km)
Density 165 people per sq mile
Languages Arabic*, other
Religions Muslim 95%, Christian 5%
Ethnic Mix Arab 98% (Palestinian 49%), Armenian 1%, Circassian 1%
Government Constitutional monarchy
Currency Dinar = 1,000 fils

ASIA

SAUDI ARABIA

OCCUPYING MOST of the Arabian Peninsula, the oil- and gas-rich kingdom of Saudi Arabia covers an area the size of Western Europe.

GEOGRAPHY

Mostly desert or semidesert plateau. Mountain ranges in the west run parallel to the Red Sea and drop steeply to a coastal plain.

CLIMATE

In summer, temperatures often soar above 118°F (48°C), but in winter they may fall below freezing. Rainfall is rare.

PEOPLE AND SOCIETY

Most Saudis are Sunni Muslims who follow the strictly orthodox *wahabi* interpretation of Islam and embrace *sharia* (Islamic law) in their daily lives. Women are obliged to wear the veil, cannot hold drivers' licenses, and have no role in public life. The Al-Saud family have been absolutist rulers since 1932. With the support of the religious establishment, they control all political life.

THE ECONOMY

Vast oil and gas reserves. Other minerals include coal, iron, and gold. Most food is imported.

FACTFILE

Official Name Kingdom of Saudi Arabia
Date of Formation 1932/1981
Capital Riyadh
Population 18.4 million
Total Area 829,995 sq miles (2,149,690 sq km)
Density 22 people per sq mile
Languages Arabic*, other
Religions Sunni Muslim 85%, Shi'a Muslim 14%, Christian 1%
Ethnic Mix Arab 90%, Yemeni 8%, other Arab 1%, other 1%
Government Absolute monarchy
Currency Riyal = 100 malalah

ASIA

YEMEN

LOCATED IN southern Arabia, Yemen was formerly two countries – a socialist regime in the south, and a republic in the north, which united in 1990.

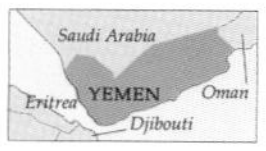

GEOGRAPHY

Mountainous north with fertile strip along the Red Sea. Arid desert and mountains in south and east.

CLIMATE

Desert climate, modified by altitude, which affects temperatures by as much as 54°F (12°C).

PEOPLE AND SOCIETY

Yemenis are almost entirely of Arab and Bedouin descent. The majority are Sunni Muslims, of the Shafi sect. In rural areas and in the north, Islamic orthodoxy is strong and most women wear the veil. Tension continues to exist between the south, led by the cosmopolitan city of Aden, and the more conservative north. Clashes between their former armies escalated into a brief civil war in 1994.

Hilltop village in northern Yemen, showing traditionally decorated, multi-storey houses built from mud bricks.

THE ECONOMY

Poor economic development due to political instability. Large oil and gas reserves were discovered in 1984. Agriculture is the largest employer.

FACTFILE

Official Name Republic of Yemen
Date of Formation 1990
Capital Sana
Population 15.1 million
Total Area 203,849 sq miles (527,970 sq km)
Density 74 people per sq mile
Languages Arabic*, other
Religions Sunni Muslim 55%, Shi'a Muslim 42%, other 3%
Ethnic Mix Arab 95%, Afro-Arab 3%, South Asian, African, European 2%
Government Multiparty republic
Currency Rial (North), Dinar (South) – both are legal currency

ASIA

OMAN

SITUATED ON the eastern coast of the Arabian Peninsula, Oman is the least developed of the Gulf states, despite modest oil exports.

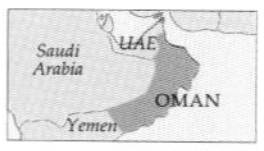

GEOGRAPHY

Mostly gravelly desert, with mountains in the north and south. Some narrow fertile coastal strips.

CLIMATE

Blistering heat in the north. Summer temperatures often climb above 113°F (45°C). Southern uplands receive rains June–September.

PEOPLE AND SOCIETY

Most Omanis still live on the land, especially in the south. The majority are Ibadi Muslims who follow an appointed leader, the Imam. Ibadism is not opposed to freedom for women, and a few women hold positions of authority. Baluchis from Pakistan are the largest group of foreign workers.

THE ECONOMY

Oil accounts for most export revenue. Gas is set to eventually supplant oil. Other exports include fish, dates, limes, and coconuts.

FACTFILE

Official Name Sultanate of Oman
Date of Formation 1650
Capital Muscat
Population 1.7 million
Total Area 82,030 sq miles (212,460 sq km)
Density 21 people per sq mile
Languages Arabic*, Baluchi, other
Religions Ibadi Muslim 75%, other Muslim 11% Hindu 14%
Ethnic Mix Arab 75%, Baluchi 15%, other (mainly South Asian) 10%
Government Monarchy with Consulative Council
Currency Rial = 1,000 baizas

ASIA

UNITED ARAB EMIRATES

BORDERING THE GULF on the northern coast of the Arabian Peninsula is the United Arab Emirates, a federation of seven states.

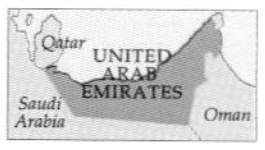

GEOGRAPHY

Mostly flat, semiarid desert with sand dunes, salt pans and occasional oases. Cities are watered by extensive irrigation systems.

CLIMATE

Summers are humid, despite minimal rainfall. Sand-laden *shamal* winds blow in winter and spring.

PEOPLE AND SOCIETY

People are mostly Sunni Muslims of Bedouin descent, and largely city-dwellers. In theory, women enjoy equal rights with men. Emirians make up one fifth of the population. They are outnumbered by immigrants who arrived during the 1970s oil boom. Western expatriates are permitted a virtually unrestricted lifestyle. Islamic fundamentalism is growing among the young.

An oasis village near Al Fujayrah in the northeast UAE is now accessible through a network of new roads.

THE ECONOMY

Major exported of oil and natural gas. Fish and shellfish are caught in the Gulf, as well as oysters for pearls.

FACTFILE

Official Name United Arab Emirates
Date of Formation 1971
Capital Abu Dhabi
Population 1.9 million
Total Area 32,278 sq miles (83,600 sq km)
Density 58 people per sq mile
Languages Arabic*, Farsi (Persian), Urdu, Hindi, English
Religions Sunni Muslim 77%, Shi'a Muslim 19% other 4%
Ethnic Mix South Asian 50%, Emirian 19%, other Arab 23%, other 8%
Government Federation of monarchs
Currency Dirham = 100 fils

QATAR

PROJECTING NORTH from the Arabian Peninsula into The Gulf, Qatar's reserves of oil and gas make it one of the region's wealthiest states.

GEOGRAPHY

Flat, semiarid desert with sand dunes and salt pans. Vegetation limited to small patches of scrub.

CLIMATE

Hot and humid. Summer temperatures soar to over 104°F (40°C). Rainfall is rare.

PEOPLE AND SOCIETY

Only one in five Qataris is native-born. Most of the population are guest workers from the Indian subcontinent, Iran, and North Africa. Qataris were once nomadic Bedouins, but since advent of oil wealth, have become city-dwellers. As a result, the north is dotted with abandoned villages. Political and religious life is dominated by the ruling Al-Thani family

THE ECONOMY

Steady supply of crude oil and huge gas reserves, plus related industries. Economy is heavily dependent on foreign work force. All raw materials and most foods, except vegetables, are imported.

FACTFILE

Official Name State of Qatar
Date of Formation 1971
Capital Doha
Population 600,000
Total Area 4,247 sq miles (11,000 sq km)
Density 141 people per sq mile
Languages Arabic*, Farsi (Persian), Urdu, Hindi, English
Religions Sunni Muslim 86%, Hindu 10%, Christian 4%
Ethnic Mix Arab 40%, South Asian 35%, Persian 12%, other 13%
Government Absolute monarchy
Currency Riyal = 100 dirhams

BAHRAIN

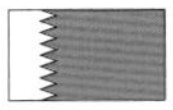

BAHRAIN IS an archipelago of 33 islands between the Qatar peninsula and the Saudi Arabian mainland. Only three islands are inhabited.

GEOGRAPHY

All islands are low-lying. The largest, Bahrain island, is mainly sandy plains and salt marshes.

CLIMATE

Summers are hot and humid. Winters are mild. Low rainfall.

PEOPLE AND SOCIETY

Largely Muslim population is divided between Shi'a majority and Sunni minority. Tensions between the two groups. Ruling Sunni class hold the best jobs in bureaucracy and business. Shi'ites tend to do menial work. Al-Khalifa family has ruled since 1783. Regime is autocratic and political dissent is not tolerated. Bahrain is the most liberal of the Gulf states. Women have access to education and jobs.

The Grand Mosque, Manama, is the largest building in Bahrain.

THE ECONOMY

Main exports are refined petroleum and aluminum products. As oil reserves run out, gas is of increasing importance. Bahrain is also the Arab world's major offshore banking center.

FACTFILE

Official Name State of Bahrain
Date of Formation 1971
Capital Manama
Population 600,000
Total Area 263 sq miles (680 sq km)
Density 2,281 people per sq mile
Languages Arabic*, English, Urdu
Religions Muslim (Shi'a majority) 85%, Christian 7%, other 8%
Ethnic Mix Arab 73%, South Asian 14%, Persian 8%, other 5%
Government Absolute monarchy (emirate)
Currency Dinar = 1,000 fils

KUWAIT

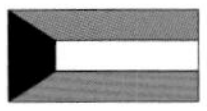

KUWAIT LIES on the north of The Gulf. The state was a British protectorate from 1914 until 1961, when full independence was granted.

GEOGRAPHY

Low-lying desert. Lowest land in the north. Cultivation is only possible along the coast.

CLIMATE

Summers are very hot and dry. Winters are cooler, with some rain and occasional frost.

Saffar Towers in the business center of Kuwait. The country is re-building its economy following the 1991 Gulf War.

PEOPLE AND SOCIETY

Oil-rich monarchy, ruled by the Al-Sabah family. Oil wealth attracted workers from India, Pakistan, and other Arab states. Iraqi invasion of 1990 overcome with aid of US-led alliance with UN backing following a short war in 1991. Many foreign workers expelled after the war, in attempt to ensure Kuwaiti majority.

THE ECONOMY

Oil and gas production restored to pre-invasion levels. Skilled labor, raw materials and food have to be imported. Vulnerability to Iraqi attack deters Western industrial investment.

FACTFILE

Official Name State of Kuwait
Date of Formation 1961/1981
Capital Kuwait
Population 1.5 million
Total Area 6,880 sq miles (17,820 sq km)
Density 218 people per sq mile
Languages Arabic*, English, other
Religions Muslim 92%, Christian 6%, other 2%
Ethnic Mix Arab 85%, South Asian 9%, Persian 4%, other 2%
Government Constitutional monarchy
Currency Dinar = 1,000 fils

IRAQ

IRAQ IS situated in the central Middle East. Since the removal of the monarchy in 1958, it has experienced considerable political turmoil.

GEOGRAPHY

Mainly desert. Rivers Tigris and Euphrates water fertile regions and create southern marshland. Mountains along northeast border.

CLIMATE

South has hot, dry summers and mild winters. North has dry summers, but winters can be harsh in the mountains. Rainfall is low.

PEOPLE AND SOCIETY

Population mainly Arab and Kurdish. Small minorities of Turks and Persians. President Saddam Hussein has led the country into an inconclusive war with Iran (1980–88) and 1990 invasion of Kuwait precipitated the Gulf War against UN forces. Drainage schemes in the southern marshlands threaten unique lifestyle of the Marsh Arabs.

THE ECONOMY

Gulf War and resulting UN sanctions mean Iraq cannot sell its oil on the international market.

FACTFILE

Official Name Republic of Iraq
Date of Formation 1932/1981
Capital Baghdad
Population 21 million
Total Area 169,235 sq miles (438,320 sq km)
Density 124 people per sq mile
Languages Arabic*, Kurdish, Turkish, Farsi (Persian)
Religions Shi'a Muslim 63%, Sunni Muslim 34%, other 3%
Ethnic Mix Arab 79%, Kurdish 16%, Persian 3%, Turkish 2%
Government Single-party republic
Currency Dinar = 1,000 fils

ASIA

IRAN

SINCE THE 1979 revolution led by Ayatollah Khomeini, the Middle Eastern country of Iran has become the world's largest theocracy.

GEOGRAPHY
High desert plateau with large salt pans in the east. West and north are mountainous. Fertile coastal land borders Caspian Sea.

CLIMATE
Mostly desert climate. Hot summers, and bitterly cold winters. Area around the Caspian Sea is more temperate.

PEOPLE AND SOCIETY
Many ethnic groups, including Persians, Azerbaijanis and Kurds. Large number of refugees, mainly from Afghanistan. Since 1979 Islamic revolution, political life has been dominated by militant Islamic idealism. Mullahs' belief that adherence to religious values is more important than economic welfare has resulted in declining living standards. The role of women in public life is restricted.

THE ECONOMY
One of the world's biggest oil producers. Government restricts contact with the West, blocking acquisition of vital technology. High unemployment and inflation.

FACTFILE
Official Name Islamic Republic of Iran
Date of Formation 1906
Capital Tehran
Population 68.7 million
Total Area 636,293 sq miles (1,648,000 sq km)
Density 108 people per sq mile
Languages Farsi (Persian)*, other
Religions Shi'a Muslim 95%, Sunni Muslim 4%, other 1%
Ethnic Mix Persian 52%, Azerbaijani 24%, Kurdish 9%, other 15%
Government Islamic republic
Currency Rial = 100 dinars

ASIA

TURKMENISTAN

STRETCHING FROM the Caspian Sea into the deserts of Central Asia, the ex-Soviet state of Turkmenistan has adjusted better than most to independence.

GEOGRAPHY
Low Kara Kum desert covers 80% of the country. Mountains on southern border with Iran. Fertile Amu Darya valley in north.

CLIMATE
Arid desert climate with extreme summer heat, but sub-freezing winter temperatures.

PEOPLE AND SOCIETY
Before Tsarist Russia annexed the country in 1884, the Turkmen were a largely nomadic tribal people. Today, the tribal unit remains strong, with most of the population clustered around desert oases. Generally peaceful relations between Turkmen and Uzbek and Russian minorities. Resurgence of Islam fosters ties with its Muslim neighbors to the south.

Salt flats near the Kara Kum Canal zone in the Kara Kum desert in Turkmenistan.

THE ECONOMY
Abundant reserves of natural gas. Least industrialized of the ex-Soviet states. Large cotton crop, but most food has to be imported.

FACTFILE
Official Name Republic of Turkmenistan
Date of Formation 1991
Capital Ashgabat
Population 4.2 million
Total Area 188,455 sq miles (488,100 sq km)
Density 22 people per sq mile
Languages Turkmen*, Uzbek, other
Religions Muslim 85%, Eastern Orthodox 10%, other 5%
Ethnic Mix Turkmen 72%, Russian 9%, Uzbek 9%, other 10%
Government Single-party republic
Currency Manat = 100 tenge

ASIA

UZBEKISTAN

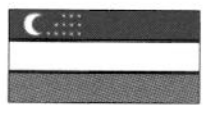

SHARING THE Aral Sea coastline with its northern neighbor, Kazakhstan, Uzbekistan lies on the ancient Silk Road between Asia and Europe.

GEOGRAPHY
Arid and semiarid plains in much of the west. Fertile, irrigated eastern farmland below peaks of the western Pamirs.

CLIMATE
Harsh continental climate. Summers can be extremely hot and dry; winters are cold.

PEOPLE AND SOCIETY
Complex ethnic makeup, with potential for racial and regional conflict. Ex-communists are in firm control, but traditional social patterns based on family, religion, clan, and region have reemerged. Population is concentrated in the fertile east. High birth rates, continued low status of women. Constitutional measures aim to control influence of Islam.

THE ECONOMY
Strong agricultural sector, led by widespread cotton production. Large unexploited deposits of oil and natural gas, gold, and uranium. Very limited economic reform.

FACTFILE
Official Name Republic of Uzbekistan
Date of Formation 1991
Capital Tashkent
Population 23.3 million
Total Area 439,733 sq miles (1,138,910 sq km)
Density 52 people per sq mile
Languages Uzbek*, Russian, other
Religions Muslim 88%, other (mostly Eastern Orthodox) 12%
Ethnic Mix Uzbek 71%, Russian 8%, Tajik 5%, Kazakh 4%, other 12%
Government Single-party republic
Currency Sum = 100 teen

ASIA

KAZAKHSTAN

LARGEST OF the former Soviet republics, mineral-rich Kazakhstan has the potential to become the major Central Asian economic power.

GEOGRAPHY
Mainly steppe. Caspian Sea in the west. Central plateau. Mountains in the east. Semi-desert in the south.

The Altai Mountains in eastern Kazakhstan are cold and inhospitable. Rivers carry melt-water down onto the vast steppe.

CLIMATE
Dry continental. Hottest summers in desert south, coldest winters in northern steppes.

PEOPLE AND SOCIETY
Kazakhs only just outnumber Russians in a multiethnic society. Stable relations with Russia, plus increased international profile, preserve relative harmony. Few Kazakhs maintain a nomadic lifestyle, but Islam and loyalty to the three Hordes (clan federations) remain strong. Wealth is concentrated among former communists in the capital.

THE ECONOMY
Vast mineral resources, notably gas, oil, coal, uranium, and gold. Increasing foreign investment, but living standards have fallen with market reforms to date.

FACTFILE
Official Name Republic of Kazakhstan
Date of Formation 1991
Capital Akmola
Population 17.2 million
Total Area 1,049,150 sq miles (2,717,300 sq km)
Density 16 people per sq mile
Languages Kazakh*, Russian, other
Religions Muslim 47%, other 53% (mostly Russian Orthodox, Lutheran)
Ethnic Mix Kazakh 40%, Russian 38%, Ukrainian 6%, other 16%
Government Multiparty republic
Currency Tenge = 100 tein

MONGOLIA

LYING BETWEEN Russia and China, Mongolia is a vast and isolated country with a tiny population. Over two-thirds of the country is desert.

GEOGRAPHY
High steppe plateau, with mountains in the north. Lakes in the north and west. Desert region of the Gobi dominates the south.

CLIMATE
Continental. Mild summers, and long, dry, very cold winters, with heavy snowfall. Temperatures can drop to −22°F (−30°C).

PEOPLE AND SOCIETY
Mongolia was unified by Genghis Khan in 1206 and was later absorbed into Manchu China. It became a communist People's Republic in 1924, and after 66 years of Soviet-style communist rule, introduced democracy in 1990. Most Mongolians still follow a traditional nomadic way of life, living in circular felt tents called *gers*. Others live on state-run farms.

THE ECONOMY
Rich in oil, coal, copper and other minerals, which were barely exploited under communism. In 1990s, some shift in agriculture away from traditional herding and toward a market economy.

FACTFILE
Official Name Mongolia
Date of Formation 1924
Capital Ulan Bator
Population 2.5 million
Total Area 604,247 sq miles (1,565,000 sq km)
Density 4 people per sq mile
Languages Khalkha Mongol*, Turkic, Russian, Chinese
Religions Predominantly Tibetan Buddhist, with a Muslim minority
Ethnic Mix Khalkha Mongol 90%, Kazakh 4%, Chinese 2%, other 4%
Government Multiparty republic
Currency Tughrik = 100 möngös

ASIA

KYRGYZSTAN

A MOUNTAINOUS, landlocked state in Central Asia. The most rural of the ex-Soviet republics, it only gradually developed its own cultural nationalism.

GEOGRAPHY
Mountainous spurs of Tien Shan range have glaciers, alpine meadows, forests and narrow valleys. Semidesert in the west.

CLIMATE
Varies from permanent snow and cold deserts at altitude, to hot deserts in low regions.

PEOPLE AND SOCIETY
Ethnic Kyrgyz majority status dates only from the late 1980s, and is due to their higher birth rate. Considerable tension between Kyrgyz and other groups, particularly Uzbeks. Large Russian community no longer wields power, but is seen as necessary for transfer of skills. Concerns over rising crime rate and opium poppy cultivation accompany political reforms.

The Naryn valley in eastern Kyrgyzstan.

THE ECONOMY
Still dominated by the state, and tradition of collective farming. Small quantities of commercially exploitable coal, oil, and gas. Great hydroelectric power potential.

FACTFILE
Official Name Kyrgyz Republic
Date of Formation 1991
Capital Bishkek
Population 4.8 million
Total Area 76,640 sq miles (198,500 sq km)
Density 63 people per sq mile
Languages Kyrgyz*, Russian, Uzbek
Religions Muslim 65%, other (mostly Russian Orthodox) 35%
Ethnic Mix Kyrgyz 52%, Russian 21%, Uzbek 13%, other (mostly Kazakh and Tajik) 14%
Government Mutiparty republic
Currency Som = 100 teen

ASIA

TAJIKISTAN

LIES LANDLOCKED on the western slopes of the Pamirs in Central Asia. The Tajiks' language and traditions are similiar to those of Iran.

GEOGRAPHY
Mainly mountainous: bare slopes of Pamir ranges cover most of the country. Small, but fertile Fergana Valley in northwest.

CLIMATE
Continental extremes in valleys. Bitterly cold winters in mountains. Low rainfall.

PEOPLE AND SOCIETY
Conflict between Tajiks, a Persian people, and minority Uzbeks (of Turkic origin), coupled with civil war between supporters of the government and Tajik Islamic rebels. Despite a cease-fire in late 1994, clashes continued in 1995. Already low living standards have been worsened by the conflict. Many Russians have left, to escape discrimination.

THE ECONOMY
Formal economy crippled by conflict. All sectors in decline, barter economy is widespread. Uranium potential and hydro-electric schemes depend on peace.

FACTFILE
Official Name Republic of Tajikistan
Date of Formation 1991
Capital Dushanbe
Population 6.3 million
Total Area 55,251 sq miles (143,100 sq km)
Density 114 people per sq mile
Languages Tajik*, Uzbek, Russian
Religions Sunni Muslim 85%, Shi'a Muslim 5%, other 10%
Ethnic Mix Tajik 62%, Uzbek 24%, Russian 4%, Tatar 2%, other 8%
Government Single-party republic
Currency Tajik rouble = 100 kopeks

ASIA

AFGHANISTAN

LANDLOCKED in southwestern Asia, about three quarters of Afghanistan is inaccessible. Civil war means the country effectively has no government.

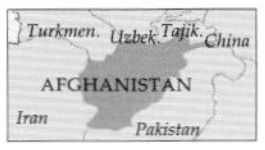

GEOGRAPHY
Predominantly mountainous. Highest range is the Hindu Kush. Mountains are bordered by fertile plains. Desert plateau in the south.

The Band-i-Amir River in the Hindu Kush. Afghanistan is mountainous and arid. Many Afghans are nomadic sheep farmers.

CLIMATE
Harsh continental. Hot, dry summers. Cold winters with heavy snow, especially in Hindu Kush.

PEOPLE AND SOCIETY
In 1979, Soviet forces invaded to support communist government against Islamic guerrillas. Last Soviet troops pulled out in 1989. Civil war continues between Pashtuns, the country's traditional rulers, and minority groups of Tajiks, Hazaras and Uzbeks. Health and education systems have collapsed. Many Afghans are nomadic sheep farmers and live in extreme poverty

THE ECONOMY
Economy has collapsed. The largest sector, agriculture, has been damaged. Illicit opium trade is the main currency earner.

FACTFILE
Official Name Islamic State of Afghanistan
Date of Formation 1919
Capital Kabul
Population 21.5 million
Total Area 251,770 sq miles (652,090 sq km)
Density 85 people per sq mile
Languages Persian*, Pashtu*, other
Religions Sunni Muslim 84%, Shi'a Muslim 15%, other 1%
Ethnic Mix Pashtun 38%, Tajik 25%, Hazara 19%, Uzbek 6%, other 12%
Government Mujahideen coalition
Currency Afghani = 100 puls

ASIA

PAKISTAN

ONCE A part of British India, Pakistan was created in 1947 as an independent Muslim state. Today, it is divided into four provinces.

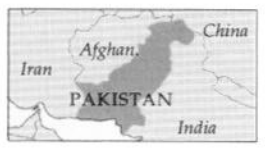

GEOGRAPHY
East and south is great flood plain drained by River Indus. Hindu Kush range in north. West is semidesert plateau and mountains.

CLIMATE
Temperatures can soar to 122°F (50°C) in south and west, and fall to –4°F (–20°C) in the Hindu Kush.

PEOPLE AND SOCIETY
Majority Punjabis control bureaucracy and the army. Many tensions with minority groups. Vast gap between rich and poor. Bonded laborers, often recent converts to Islam, or Christians, form the underclass. Strong family ties, reflected in dynastic and nepotistic political system.

THE ECONOMY
Leading producer of cotton and rice, but unpredictable weather conditions often affect the crop. Oil, gas reserves. Inefficient, haphazard government economic policies.

FACTFILE
Official Name Islamic Republic of Pakistan
Date of Formation 1947/1972
Capital Islamabad
Population 144.5 million
Total Area 307,374 sq miles (796,100 sq km)
Density 470 people per sq mile
Languages Urdu*, Punjabi, other
Religions Sunni Muslim 77%, Shi'a Muslim 20%, Hindu 2%, Christian 1%
Ethnic Mix Punjabi 56%, Sindhi 13%, Pashtun 8%, other 23%
Government Multiparty republic
Currency Rupee = 100 paisa

ASIA

NEPAL

NEPAL LIES between India and China, on the shoulder of the southern Himalayan mountains. It is one of the world's poorest countries.

GEOGRAPHY
Mainly mountainous. Includes some of the highest mountains in the world, such as Everest. Flat, fertile river plains in the south.

CLIMATE
July–October warm monsoon. Rest of year dry, sunny, mild. Valley temperatures in Himalayas may average 14°F (–10°C).

PEOPLE AND SOCIETY
Few ethnic tensions, despite the variety of ethnic groups, including the Sherpas in the north, Terai peoples in the south, and the Newars, found mostly in the Kathmandu valley. Women's subordinate position enshrined in law. Hindu women are the most restricted. In 1991, first democratic elections for over 30 years ended period of absolute rule by the king.

Collecting the harvest in a Nepalese village. Around 90% of Nepalis are farmers.

THE ECONOMY
90% of the people work on the land. Crops include rice, corn, and millet. Dependent on foreign aid. Tourism is growing. Great potential for hydroelectric power.

FACTFILE
Official Name Kingdom of Nepal
Date of Formation 1769
Capital Kathmandu
Population 22.5 million
Total Area 54,363 sq miles (140,800 sq km)
Density 414 people per sq mile
Languages Nepali*, Maithilli, other
Religions Hindu 90%, Buddhist 5%, Muslim 3%, other 2%
Ethnic Mix Nepalese 58%, Bihari 19%, Tamang 6%, other 17%
Government Constitutional monarchy
Currency Rupee = 100 paisa

ASIA

BHUTAN

PERCHED IN the eastern Himalayas between India and China, the landlocked kingdom of Bhutan is largely closed to the outside world.

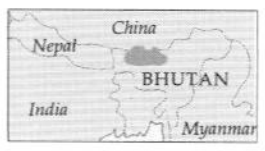

GEOGRAPHY
Low, tropical southern strip rising through fertile central valleys to high Himalayas in the north. two-thirds of the land is forested.

CLIMATE
South is tropical, north is alpine, cold and harsh. Central valleys warmer in east than west.

A Hindu festival in India. Festivals take place frequently and are an important part of the Hindu culture.

PEOPLE AND SOCIETY
The king is absolute monarch, head of both state and government. Most people devoutly Buddhist. 24% Hindu Nepalese, who settled in the south. Twenty languages. In 1988, Dzongkha (a Tibetan dialect) was made the official language and Nepali was banned. Many southerners deported as illegal immigrants, creating fierce ethnic tensions.

THE ECONOMY
80% of people farm their own plots of land and herd cattle and yaks. Development of cash crops for Asian markets.

FACTFILE
Official Name Kingdom of Bhutan
Date of Formation 1949/1865
Capital Thimphu
Population 1.7 million
Total Area 18,147 sq miles (47,000 sq km)
Density 94 people per sq mile
Languages Dzongkha*, Nepali, other
Religions Mahayana Buddhist 70%, Hindu 24%, Muslim 5%, other 1%
Ethnic Mix Bhutia 61%, Gurung 15%, Assamese 13%, other 11%
Government Constitutional monarchy
Currency Ngultrum = 100 chetrum

ASIA

INDIA

SEPARATED FROM the rest of Asia by the Himalayan mountain range, India forms a subcontinent. It is the world's second most populous country.

GEOGRAPHY
Three main regions Himalayan mountains; northern plain between Himalayas and Vindhya Range; southern Deccan plateau.

CLIMATE
Most of India has three seasons: hot, wet and cool. In summer, the north is usually hotter than the south, with temperatures often over 104°F (40°C).

PEOPLE AND SOCIETY
Most Indians are Hindu, born into one of thousands of castes and subcastes, which determine their future status and occupation. Middle class enjoy comfortable lifestyle, but at least 30% of Indians live in extreme poverty.

THE ECONOMY
Protectionist mixed economy moving to free market. Foreign investment. High-tech industries. Exports are clothing, jewelry, gems, and engineering products.

FACTFILE
Official Name Republic of India
Date of Formation 1947/1961
Capital New Delhi
Population 953 million
Total Area 1,269,338 sq miles (3,287,590 sq km)
Density 751 people per sq mile
Languages Hindi*, English*, other
Religions Hindu 83%, Muslim 11%, Christian 2%, Sikh 2%, other 2%
Ethnic Mix Indo-Aryan 72%, Dravidian 25%, Mongoloid and other 3%
Government Multiparty republic
Currency Rupee = 100 paisa

MALDIVES

THE MALDIVES is an archipelago of 1,190 small coral islands set in the Indian Ocean, southwest of Sri Lanka. Only 202 islands are inhabited.

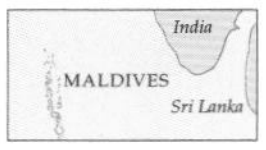

GEOGRAPHY

Low-lying islands and coral atolls. The larger ones are covered in lush, tropical vegetation.

CLIMATE

Tropical. Rain in all months, but heaviest June–November, during monsoon. Violent storms occasionally hit northern islands.

PEOPLE AND SOCIETY

Maldivians are descended from Sinhalese, Dravidian, Arab, and black ancestors. About 25% of the population, who are all Sunni Muslim, live on Male'. Tourism has grown in recent years, but resort islands are separate from settler islands. Politics is restricted to a small group of influential families, and is based around family and clan loyalties rather than formal parties. New young elite is pressing for a liberal political system.

THE ECONOMY

Too dependent on fluctuating tourist industry, which is the economic mainstay. Fish, especially bonito and tuna, are the leading exports.

FACTFILE

Official Name Republic of Maldives
Date of Formation 1965
Capital Male'
Population 300,000
Total Area 116 sq miles (300 sq km)
Density 2,586 people per sq mile
Languages Dhivehi (Maldivian)*, Sinhala, Tamil
Religions Sunni Muslim 100%
Ethnic Mix Maldivian 99%, Sinhalese and other South Asian 1%
Government Republic
Currency Rufiyaa = 100 laari

SRI LANKA

SEPARATED FROM India by the narrow Palk Strait, Sri Lanka comprises one large island and several coral islets to the northwest.

GEOGRAPHY

Main island is dominated by rugged central highlands. Fertile northern plains dissected by rivers. Much of the land is tropical jungle.

CLIMATE

Tropical, with breezes on the coast and cooler air in highlands. Northeast is driest and hottest.

PEOPLE AND SOCIETY

Majority Sinhalese are mostly Buddhist, minority Tamils are mostly Muslim or Hindu. Since independence from Britain in 1948, Tamils have felt sidelined, and support for secession has grown. Long-standing tensions between the groups erupted into civil war in 1983. Tamils demand an independent state in the north and east.

A hilltop village in central Sri Lanka, close to Pidurutalagala, the country's highest peak.

THE ECONOMY

World's largest tea exporter. Manufacturing now accounts for 60% of export earnings. Civil war is a drain on government funds and deters investors and tourists.

FACTFILE

Official Name Democratic Socialist Republic of Sri Lanka
Date of Formation 1948
Capital Colombo
Population 18.6 million
Total Area 25,332 sq miles (65,610 sq km)
Density 734 people per sq mile
Languages Sinhala*, Tamil, English
Religions Buddhist 70%, Hindu 15%, Christian 8%, Muslim 7%
Ethnic Mix Sinhalese 74%, Tamil 18%, Sri Lankan Moor 7%, other 1%
Government Multiparty republic
Currency Rupee = 100 cents

BANGLADESH

BANGLADESH LIES at the north of the Bay of Bengal. It seceded from Pakistan in 1971 and, after much political instability, returned to democracy in 1991.

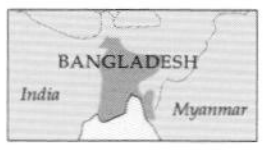

GEOGRAPHY

Mostly flat alluvial plains and deltas of the Brahmaputra and Ganges rivers. Southeast coasts are fringed with mangrove forests.

Traders on the Meghna River, which flows from the Padma. Bangladesh's flood plains are among the world's most fertile.

CLIMATE

Hot and humid. During the monsoon, water level can rise 20 feet above sea level, flooding two thirds of the country.

PEOPLE AND SOCIETY

Bangladesh has suffered from a cycle of floods, cyclones, famine, political corruption, and military coups. Although 55% of people still live below the poverty line, living standards have improved in past decade. By providing independent income, textile trade is a factor in growing emancipation of women.

THE ECONOMY

Heavily dependent on foreign aid. Agriculture is vulnerable to unpredictable climate. Bangladesh accounts for 80% of world jute fiber exports. Expanding textile industry.

FACTFILE

Official Name People's Republic of Bangladesh
Date of Formation 1971
Capital Dhaka
Population 123.1 million
Total Area 55,598 sq miles (143,998 sq km)
Density 2,214 people per sq mile
Languages Bangla*, Urdu, Chakma, Marma (Margh), other
Religions Muslim 83%, Hindu 16%, other (Buddhist, Christian) 1%
Ethnic Mix Bengali 98%, other 2%
Government Multiparty republic
Currency Taka = 100 paisa

MYANMAR

MYANMAR FORMS the eastern shores of the Bay of Bengal and the Andaman Sea in Southeast Asia. It gained independence from Britain in 1948.

GEOGRAPHY

Fertile Irrawaddy basin in the center. Mountains to the west, Shan plateau to the east. Tropical rain forest covers much of the land.

CLIMATE

Tropical. Hot summers, with high humidity, and warm winters.

PEOPLE AND SOCIETY

Under socialist military rule since 1962, Myanmar has suffered widespread political repression and ethnic conflict. Minority groups maintain low-level guerrilla activity against the state. 1990 election was won by opposition democratic party. Its leader, Aung San Suu Kyi, was placed under house arrest. She was released in 1995.

THE ECONOMY

Under socialism, Myanmar has plunged from prosperity to poverty. Nationwide black market, on which prices are soaring. Main products are teak, rice, and gems.

FACTFILE

Official Name Union of Myanmar
Date of Formation 1948
Capital Rangoon (Yangon)
Population 47.5 million
Total Area 261,200 sq miles (676,550 sq km)
Density 182 people per sq mile
Languages Burmese*, Karen, Shan, Chin, Kachin, Mon, Palaung, Wa
Religions Buddhist 89%, Muslim 4%, Baptist 3%, other 4%
Ethnic Mix Burman 68%, Shan 9%, Karen 6%, Rakhine 4%, other 13%
Government Military regime
Currency Kyat = 100 pyas

ASIA

THAILAND

THAILAND LIES at the heart of mainland Southeast Asia. Continuing rapid industrialization has resulted in massive congestion in the capital.

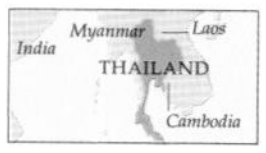

GEOGRAPHY

One third is occupied by a low plateau, drained by tributaries of the Mekong River. Fertile central plain. Mountains in the north.

CLIMATE

Tropical. Hot, humid March–May, monsoon rains May–October, cooler season November–March.

PEOPLE AND SOCIETY

The king is head of state. Criticism of him is not tolerated. Buddhism is national binding force. North and northeast are home to about 600,000 hill tribespeople, with their own languages and culture. Sex tourism is a problem. Women from the poor northeast enter prostitution in Bangkok and Pattaya.

THE ECONOMY

Rapid economic growth. Rise in manufacturing. Chief world exporter of rice and rubber. Gas reserves. Successful tourist industry.

FACTFILE

Official Name Kingdom of Thailand
Date of Formation 1822/1887
Capital Bangkok
Population 59.4 million
Total Area 198,116 sq miles (513,120 sq km)
Density 299 people per sq mile
Languages Thai*, Chinese, Malay, Khmer, Mon, Karen, Miao, English
Religions Buddhist 95%, Muslim 4%, other (inc. Hindu, Christian) 1%
Ethnic Mix Thai 75%, Chinese 14%, Malay 4%, Khmer 3%, other 4%
Government Constitutional monarchy
Currency Baht = 100 stangs

ASIA

LAOS

A FORMER French colony, independent in 1953, Laos lies landlocked in Southeast Asia. It has been under communist rule since 1975.

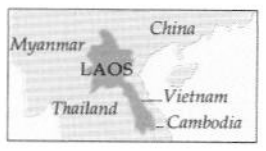

GEOGRAPHY

Largely forested mountains, broadening in the north to a plateau. Lowlands along Mekong valley.

CLIMATE

Monsoon rains September–May. Rest of the year is hot and dry.

PEOPLE AND SOCIETY

Over 60 ethnic groups. Lowland Laotians (*Lao Loum*), live along Mekong River and are wet-rice farmers. Upland Laotians (*Lao Theung*) and mountain-top Laotians (*Lao Soung*) practice slash-and-burn farming. Government efforts to halt this traditional farming method, which can destroy forests and watersheds, have been resisted.

A farm in northeastern Laos. Three quarters of Laotians are subsistence farmers.

THE ECONOMY

One of the world's 20 least-developed nations. Government began to introduce market-oriented reforms in 1986. Potential for timber, mining, garment manufacturing.

FACTFILE

Official Name Lao People's Democratic Republic
Date of Formation 1953
Capital Vientiane
Population 5 million
Total Area 91,428 sq miles (236,800 sq km)
Density 55 people per sq mile
Languages Lao*, Miao, Yao, other
Religions Buddhist 85%, Christian 2%, Muslim 1%, other 12%
Ethnic Mix Lao Loum 56%, Lao Theung 34%, Lao Soung 10%
Government Single-party republic
Currency Kip = 100 cents

ASIA

CAMBODIA

LOCATED in mainland Southeast Asia, Cambodia has emerged from two decades of civil war and invasion from Vietnam.

GEOGRAPHY

Mostly low-lying basin. Tonle Sap (Great Lake) drains into the Mekong River. Forested mountains and plateau east of the Mekong.

Angkor Wat stands in the ruins of the ancient city of Angkor, once the capital of the Khmer empire.

CLIMATE

Tropical. High temperatures throughout the year. Heavy rainfall during May–October monsoon.

PEOPLE AND SOCIETY

Under Pol Pot's Marxist Khmer Rouge regime between 1975 and 1979, over one million Cambodians died. Half a million more went into exile in Thailand. Effects of revolution and civil war are still felt and are reflected in the world's highest rate of orphans and widows. Free elections held under UN supervision in 1993 brought fragile stability, although the Khmer Rouge, still led by Pol Pot, continues its armed struggle.

THE ECONOMY

Economy is still recovering from civil war. Loss of skilled workers as result of Khmer Rouge anti-bourgeois atrocities in 1970s. Modest trade in rubber and timber.

FACTFILE

Official Name State of Cambodia
Date of Formation 1953
Capital Phnom Penh
Population 10.5 million
Total Area 69,000 sq miles (181,040 sq km)
Density 152 people per sq mile
Languages Khmer*, French, other
Religions Buddhist 88%, Muslim 2%, Christian 1%, other 9%
Ethnic Mix Khmer 94%, Chinese 4%, Vietnamese 1%, other 1%
Government Constitutional monarchy
Currency Riel = 100 sen

ASIA

VIETNAM

SITUATED IN the far east of mainland Southeast Asia, the country is still rebuilding after the devastating 1962–1975 Vietnam War.

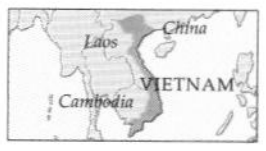

GEOGRAPHY

Heavily forested mountain range separates northern Red River delta lowlands from southern Mekong delta in the south.

CLIMATE

Cool winters in north; south is tropical, with mainly even temperatures. Typhoons in central provinces.

PEOPLE AND SOCIETY

Partitioned in 1954, the communist north reunited the nation after the Vietnam War, in which two million people died. Women outnumber men, largely because of war deaths. Resettling of lowlanders in mountain regions has put pressure on farming and forest resources. Family life is based on kinship groups within village clans.

THE ECONOMY

After years of stagnation, the economy is recovering. Government seeking transfer to market economy. Growing steel, oil, gas, car industries.

FACTFILE

Official Name Socialist Republic of Viet-Nam
Date of Formation 1976
Capital Hanoi
Population 76.2 million
Total Area 127,243 sq miles (329,560 sq km)
Density 599 people per sq mile
Languages Vietnamese*, other
Religions Buddhist 55%, Catholic 7%, Muslim 1%, other 37%
Ethnic Mix Vietnamese 88%, Chinese 4%, Thai 2%, other 6%
Government Single-party republic
Currency Dong = 10 hao = 100 xu

MALAYSIA

MALAYSIA'S THREE separate territories stretch over 1,240 miles (2,000 km) from the Malay Peninsula to the northern area of the island of Borneo.

GEOGRAPHY

Peninsular Malaysia (Malaya) has mountain ranges along its axis. Almost three quarters of the land is tropical rain forest or swamp forest. States of Sabah and Sarawak in Borneo are rugged and forested.

CLIMATE

Equatorial. Warm, with year-round rainfall. Heaviest rain March–May and September–November.

PEOPLE AND SOCIETY

Indigenous Malays are the largest ethnic group, but Chinese have traditionally controlled most economic activity. Malays favored in education and jobs since 1970s, in order to address imbalance. Labor shortages attract many immigrants from other Southeast Asian states.

THE ECONOMY

Rapid growth since 1980s. Successful electronics, car industries. Leading producer of rubber, palm oil, pepper, tin, tropical hardwoods.

FACTFILE

Official Name Malaysia
Date of Formation 1957/1965
Capital Kuala Lumpur
Population 20.6 million
Total Area 127,317 sq miles (329,750 sq km)
Density 161 people per sq mile
Languages Malay*, Chinese*, Tamil
Religions Muslim 53%, Buddhist and Confucian 30%, other 17%
Ethnic Mix Malay and aborigine 60%, Chinese 30%, Indian 8%, other 2%
Government Federal constitutional monarchy
Currency Ringgit = 100 cents

ASIA

INDONESIA

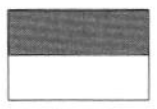

THE WORLD'S largest archipelago, Indonesia's 13,677 islands are scattered over 3,000 miles (5,000 km), from the Indian Ocean to the Pacific Ocean.

GEOGRAPHY

Mountains, tropical swamps, rain forests and over 200 volcanoes, many still active. Most larger islands have coastal lowlands.

CLIMATE

Predominantly tropical monsoon. Hilly areas are cooler. June–September dry season.

PEOPLE AND SOCIETY

A mosaic of different cultures and languages. Islam, urbanization and national language, Bahasa Indonesia, are unifying factors. Papuans of Irian Jaya, East Timorese and Aceh of north Sumatra, denied autonomy, are all in conflict with government.

Rice terraces on Bali, one of Indonesia's 13,677 islands.

THE ECONOMY

Varied resources, especially oil, coal, and gas. Timber, minerals (bauxite and nickel), fishing, are all important. Rice is main cash and subsistence crop for the rural population.

FACTFILE

Official Name Republic of Indonesia
Date of Formation 1949/1963
Capital Jakarta
Population 200.6 million
Total Area 735,555 sq miles (1,904,570 sq km)
Density 273 people per sq mile
Languages Bahasa Indonesia*, 250 (est.) languages or dialects
Religions Muslim 87%, Christian 10%, Hindu 2%, Buddhist 1%
Ethnic Mix Javanese 45%, Sundanese 14%, Madurese 8%, other 33%
Government Multiparty republic
Currency Rupiah = 100 sen

ASIA

SINGAPORE

A CITY STATE linked to the southernmost tip of the Malay Peninsula by a causeway, Singapore is one of Asia's most important commercial centers.

GEOGRAPHY

Little remains of the original vegetation on Singapore island. The other 54 much smaller islands are swampy jungle.

Singapore's financial centre. More than a quarter of Singapore's GDP is generated by financial and business services.

CLIMATE

Equatorial. Hot and humid, with heavy rainfall all year round.

PEOPLE AND SOCIETY

Dominated by the Chinese, who make up three quarters of the community. English-speaking Straits Chinese and newer Mandarin-speakers are now well integrated. There is a significant foreign work force. Society is highly regulated and government campaigns to improve public behaviour are frequent. Crime is limited and punishment can be severe.

THE ECONOMY

Highly successful financial, banking, and manufacturing sectors. Produces 50% of the world's computer disk drives. All food and energy has to be imported.

FACTFILE

Official Name Republic of Singapore
Date of Formation 1965
Capital Singapore
Population 2.9 million
Total Area 239 sq miles (620 sq km)
Density 12,133 people per sq mile
Languages Malay*, Chinese*, other
Religions Buddhist 30%, Christian 20%, Muslim 17%, other 33%
Ethnic Mix Chinese 76%, Malay 15%, South Asian 7%, other 2%
Government Multiparty republic
Currency Singapore $ = 100 cents

ASIA

BRUNEI

LYING ON the northwestern coast of the island of Borneo, Brunei is surrounded and divided in two by the Malaysian state of Sarawak.

GEOGRAPHY

Mostly dense lowland rain forest and mangrove swamps. Mountains in the southeast.

CLIMATE

Tropical. Six-month rainy season with very high humidity.

PEOPLE AND SOCIETY

Malays benefit from positive discrimination. Many in Chinese community are stateless. Independent from the UK since 1984, Brunei is ruled by decree of the Sultan. In 1990, "Malay Muslim Monarchy" was introduced, promoting Islamic values as state ideology. Women less restricted than in some Muslim states.

THE ECONOMY

Oil and natural gas reserves have brought one of the world's highest standards of living. Massive overseas investments. Major consumer of high-tech audio equipment, VCR's, and Western designer clothes.

FACTFILE

Official Name The Sultanate of Brunei
Date of Formation 1984
Capital Bandar Seri Begawan
Population 300,000
Total Area 2,228 sq miles (5,770 sq km)
Density 134 people per sq mile
Languages Malay*, English, Chinese
Religions Muslim 63%, Buddhist 14%, Christian 10%, other 13%
Ethnic Mix Malay 69%, Chinese 18%, other 13%
Government Absolute monarchy
Currency Brunei $ = 100 cents

ASIA

PHILIPPINES

AN ARCHIPELAGO of 7,107 islands between the South China Sea and the Pacific. After 21 years of dictatorship, democracy was restored in 1986.

GEOGRAPHY
Larger islands are forested and mountainous. Over 20 active volcanoes. Frequent earthquakes.

CLIMATE
Tropical. Warm and humid all year round. Typhoons occur in rainy season, June–October.

PEOPLE AND SOCIETY
Over 100 ethnic groups. Most Filipinos are of Malay origin, and Christian. Catholic Church is the dominant cultural force. It opposes state-sponsored family planning programs designed to curb accelerating population growth. Women have traditionally played a prominent part in society. Many enter the professions. Half the population live on the poverty line.

THE ECONOMY
Now open to considerable outside investment. Agricultural productivity is generally rising. Power failures limit scope for expansion. Weak infrastructure.

FACTFILE
Official Name Republic of the Philippines
Date of Formation 1946
Capital Manila
Population 69 million
Total Area 115,831 sq miles (300,000 sq km)
Density 566 people per sq mile
Languages Pilipino*, English*, other
Religions Catholic 83%, Protestant 9%, Muslim 5%, other 3%
Ethnic Mix Filipino 96%, Chinese 2%, other 2%
Government Multiparty republic
Currency Peso = 100 centavos

ASIA

TAIWAN

THE ISLAND republic of Taiwan lies 80 miles (130 km) off the southeast coast of mainland China. China considers it to be one of its provinces.

GEOGRAPHY
Mountain region covers two-thirds of the island. Highly fertile lowlands and coastal plains.

CLIMATE
Tropical monsoon. Hot and humid. Typhoons July–September. Snow falls in mountains in winter.

PEOPLE AND SOCIETY
Most Taiwanese are Han Chinese, descendants of 17th-century settlers from the mainland. Taiwan came into existence in 1949, when the government was expelled from Beijing (then Peking) by the communists under Mao. 100,000 Nationalists arrived and established themselves as ruling class. Taiwan is diplomatically isolated and cannot gain representation at the UN.

Wen Wu temple lies on the shores of Sun Moon Lake in the mountains of central Taiwan.

THE ECONOMY
One of the world's most successful economies, based on small, adaptable manufacturing companies. Goods include televisions, calculators, footwear.

FACTFILE
Official Name Republic of China (Taiwan)
Date of Formation 1949
Capital Taipei
Population 21.1 million
Total Area 13,969 sq miles (36,179 sq km)
Density 1,510 people per sq mile
Languages Mandarin*, other
Religions Buddhist, Confucian and Taoist 93%, Christian 5%, other 2%
Ethnic Mix Taiwanese 84%, mainland Chinese 14%, other 2%
Government Multiparty republic
Currency New Taiwan $ = 100 cents

ASIA

CHINA

CHINA COVERS a vast area of East Asia. From the founding of Communist China in 1949, until his death in 1976, Mao Zedong dominated the nation.

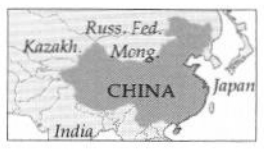

GEOGRAPHY
Great mountains and plateau in west. Arid basin in north and northeast. Deserts in northwest. South is mountainous. Rolling hills and plains in east.

The famous limestone hills of Guilin in southern China.

CLIMATE
North and west are mainly arid. South and east warmer and more humid, with year-round rainfall. Summer temperatures above 70°F (26°C).

PEOPLE AND SOCIETY
Most people are Han Chinese. Rest of population belong to one of 55 minority nationalities, or recognized ethnic groups. One-child family policy no longer applies to minorities after some small groups brought close to extinction. Han still face controls.

THE ECONOMY
Moving rapidly toward a market-oriented economy. Vast mineral reserves. Increasingly diversified industrial sector. Low wage costs. Self-sufficient in food.

FACTFILE
Official Name People's Republic of China
Date of Formation 1949/1950
Capital Beijing
Population 1234.3 million
Total Area 3,628,166 sq miles (3,628,166 sq km)
Density 340 people per sq mile
Languages Mandarin*, other
Religions Confucianist 20%, Buddhist 6%, Taoist 2%, other 72%
Ethnic Mix Han 93%, Zhaung 1%, Hui 1%, other 5%
Government Single-party republic
Currency Yuan = 10 jiao = 100 fen

ASIA

NORTH KOREA

NORTH KOREA comprises the northern half of the Korean peninsula. A communist state since 1948, it is largely isolated from the outside world.

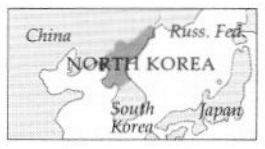

GEOGRAPHY
Mostly mountainous, with fertile plains in the southwest.

CLIMATE
Continental. Warm summers and cold winters, especially in the north, where snow is common.

PEOPLE AND SOCIETY
People live severely regulated lives. Divorce is non-existent and extra-marital sex highly frowned upon. Women form 57% of the work force, but are also expected to run the home. From an early age, children are looked after in state-run nurseries. Korean Workers' Party is only legal political party. Membership is essential for advancement. The political elite enjoy a privileged lifestyle.

THE ECONOMY
Economy has suffered badly in 1990s, since end of aid from China and former Soviet Union. Manufacturing, agriculture and mining all in decline. Electricity shortage is a problem.

FACTFILE
Official Name Democratic People's Republic of Korea
Date of Formation 1948
Capital Pyongyang
Population 24.3 million
Total Area 46,540 sq miles (120,540 sq km)
Density 522 people per sq mile
Languages Korean*, Chinese
Religions Traditional beliefs 16%, Ch'ondogyo 14%, Buddhist 2%, non-religious 68%
Ethnic Mix Korean 99%, other 1%
Government Single-party republic
Currency Won = 100 chon

SOUTH KOREA

SOUTH KOREA occupies the southern half of the Korean peninsula. Under US sponsorship, it was separated from the communist North in 1948.

GEOGRAPHY

Over 80% is mountainous and two-thirds is forested. Flattest and most populous parts lie along west coast and in the extreme south.

CLIMATE

Four distinct seasons. Winters are dry, and bitterly cold. Summers are hot and humid.

PEOPLE AND SOCIETY

Inhabited by a single ethnic group for the last 2,000 years. Tiny Chinese community. Family life is a central and clearly defined part of Korean society. Women's role is traditional; it is not respectable for those who are married to have jobs. Since the inconclusive Korean War (1950–53), North and South Korea have remained mutually hostile

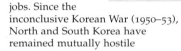

The Ginza District of central Tokyo lit by neon signs at night. Japan's cities are among the world's safest.

THE ECONOMY

World's biggest shipbuilder. High demand from China for Korean goods, especially cars. Electronics, household appliances also important.

FACTFILE

Official Name Republic of Korea

Date of Formation 1948

Capital Seoul

Population 45.4 million

Total Area 38,232 sq miles (99,020 sq km)

Density 1,187 people per sq mile

Languages Korean*, Chinese

Religions Mahayana Buddhist 47%, Protestant 38%, Catholic 11%, Confucian 3%, other 1%

Ethnic Mix Korean 99.9%, other (mainly Chinese) 0.1%

Government Multiparty republic

Currency Won = 100 chon

JAPAN

JAPAN COMPRISES four principal islands and over 3,000 smaller ones. With the emperor as constitutional head, Japan is now one of the world's most powerful nations.

GEOGRAPHY

Predominantly mountainous, and wooded, with small fertile areas. Lies on a fault line. Frequent earthquakes and volcanic eruptions. Pacific coast vulnerable to *tsunamis* – giant waves.

CLIMATE

Generally temperate oceanic. Spring is warm and sunny, summer hot and humid, with high rainfall. In northwest, winters are very cold, with heavy snowfall.

PEOPLE AND SOCIETY

Racially homogenous society. People define themselves by the company they work for, not the job they do. Women mostly play a traditional role running the home. Education system is highly pressurized.

THE ECONOMY

World's most competitive producer of high-tech electronic products and cars. Commitment to long-term research and development. Revolutionary management and production methods.

FACTFILE

Official Name Japan

Date of Formation 1868/1945

Capital Tokyo

Population 125.4 million

Total Area 145,869 sq miles (377,800 sq km)

Density 861 people per sq mile

Languages Japanese*, Korean, Chinese

Religions Shinto and Buddhist 76%, Buddhist 16%, other (including Christian) 8%

Ethnic Mix Japanese 99.4%, other (mostly Korean) 0.6%

Government Constitutional monarchy

Currency Yen = 100 sen

AUSTRALIA

AN ISLAND continent located between the Indian and Pacific oceans, Australia was settled by Europeans 200 years ago. The focus has shifted away from Europe toward Asia.

GEOGRAPHY

Western half arid plateaus, and vast deserts. Eastern lowlands and river systems drain into Lake Eyre. Great Dividing Range in east. In the north are tropical rain forests.

CLIMATE

Interior, west and south are arid and very hot in summer. Central desert areas can reach 120°F (50°C). The north is hot throughout the year. East, southeast and southwest coasts are temperate.

PEOPLE AND SOCIETY

Immigration after 1945 brought many Europeans to Australia. Since 1970s, 50% of immigrants have been Asian. Aborigines, the first inhabitants, are sidelined economically and socially. 1990s recession increased gap between rich and poor.

Green Island on Australia's Great Barrier Reef in the far north of Queensland. The reef stretches more than 124 miles down the coast.

THE ECONOMY

Efficient mining and agricultural industries. Successful tourist industry. Investor in booming Southeast Asian economies.

FACTFILE

Official Name Commonwealth of Australia

Date of Formation 1901

Capital Canberra

Population 18.3 million

Total Area 2,967,893 sq miles (7,686,850 sq km)

Density 6 people per sq mile

Languages English*, Greek, Italian, Malay, Bahasa Indonesia, Vietnamese, Aboriginal, other

Religions Protestant 60%, Catholic 26%, other 14%

Ethnic Mix Caucasian 95%, Asian 4%, Aboriginal and other 1%

Government Parliamentary democracy

Currency Australian $ = 100 cents

VANUATU

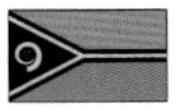

AN ARCHIPELAGO of 82 islands and islets in the Pacific Ocean, it was ruled jointly by Britain and France from 1906 until independence in 1980.

GEOGRAPHY

Mountainous and volcanic, with coral beaches and dense rain forest. Cultivated land along coasts.

CLIMATE

Tropical. Temperatures and rainfall decline from north to south.

PEOPLE AND SOCIETY

Indigenous Melanesians form a majority. 80% of the population live on 16 main islands. People are among the most traditional in the Pacific local social and religious customs are strong, despite centuries of missionary influence. Subsistence farming and fishing are the main activities. Women have lower social status than men and payment of bride-price is common.

THE ECONOMY

Copra and cocoa are the largest exports. Recent upsurge in tourist industry. Offshore financial services are also important.

FACTFILE

Official Name Republic of Vanuatu

Date of Formation 1980

Capital Port-Vila

Population 200,000

Total Area 4,706 sq miles (2,190 sq km)

Density 42 people per sq mile

Languages Bislama (Melanesian pidgin)*, English*, French*, other

Religions Protestant 77%, Catholic 15%, traditional beliefs 8%

Ethnic Mix Ni-Vanuatu 98%, European 1%, other 1%

Government Multiparty republic

Currency Vatu = 100 centimes

AUSTRALASIA & OCEANIA

FIJI

A VOLCANIC archipelago in the southern Pacific Ocean, Fiji comprises two large islands and 880 islets. From 1874 to 1970, it was a British colony.

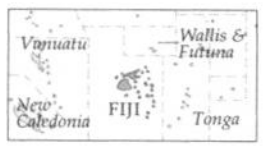

GEOGRAPHY

Main islands are mountainous, fringed by coral reefs. Remainder are limestone and coral formations.

CLIMATE

Tropical. High temperatures year round. Cyclones are a hazard.

PEOPLE AND SOCIETY

The British introduced workers from India in the late 19th century, and by 1946 their descendants outnumbered the Native Fijian population. In 1987, the Indian-dominated government was overthrown by Native Fijians. Many Indo-Fijians left the country. Civilian rule returned in 1990, and a new constitution discriminating against Indo-Fijians was introduced.

THE ECONOMY

Well-diversified economy based on sugar production, gold mining, timber, and commercial fishing. Tourists are returning after a drop in numbers after the coups.

FACTFILE

Official Name Republic of Fiji
Date of Formation 1970
Capital Suva
Population 800,000
Total Area 7,054 sq miles (18,270 sq km)
Density 113 people per sq mile
Languages English*, Fijian*, Hindi, Urdu, Tamil, Telugu
Religions Christian 52%, Hindu 38%, Muslim 8%, other 2%
Ethnic Mix Native Fijian 49%, Indo-Fijian 46%, other 5%
Government Multiparty republic
Currency Fiji $ = 100 cents

AUSTRALASIA & OCEANIA

PAPUA NEW GUINEA

ACHIEVING INDEPENDENCE from Australia in 1975, PNG occupies the eastern section of the island of New Guinea and several other island groups.

GEOGRAPHY

Mountainous and forested mainland, with broad, swampy river valleys. 40 active volcanoes in the north. Around 600 outer islands.

Papua New Guinea's 600 outer islands are mainly high, volcanic islands, fringed by coral reefs.

CLIMATE

Hot and humid in lowlands, cooling toward highlands, where snow can fall on highest peaks.

PEOPLE AND SOCIETY

Around 750 language groups – the highest number in the world – and even more tribes. Main social distinction is between lowlanders, who have frequent contact with the outside world, and the very isolated, but increasingly threatened, highlanders who live by hunter-gathering. Great tensions exist between highland tribes – anyone who is not a *wontok* (of one's tribe) is seen as potentially hostile.

THE ECONOMY

Significant quantities of gold, copper, silver. Oil and natural gas reserves. Secessionist violence on Bougainville deters investors.

FACTFILE

Official Name The Independent State of Papua New Guinea
Date of Formation 1975
Capital Port Moresby
Population 4.4 million
Total Area 178,700 sq miles (462,840 sq km)
Density 24 people per sq mile
Languages Pidgin English*, Motu*, Papuan, 750 (est.) native languages
Religions Christian 66%, other 34%
Ethnic Mix Papuan 85%, other 15%
Government Parliamentary democracy
Currency Kina = 100 toea

AUSTRALASIA & OCEANIA

SOLOMON ISLANDS

THE SOLOMONS archipelago comprises several hundred islands scattered in the southwestern Pacific. Independence from Britain came in 1978.

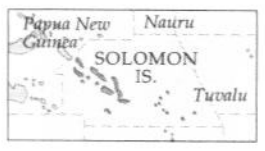

GEOGRAPHY

The six largest islands are volcanic, mountainous, and thickly forested. Flat coastal plains provide the only cultivable land.

CLIMATE

Northern islands are hot and humid all year round; further south a cool season develops. November–April wet season brings cyclones.

PEOPLE AND SOCIETY

Most Solomon Islanders are Melanesian. Around 87 native languages are spoken, but Pidgin English is used as a contact language between tribes. Most people live by shifting, subsistence agriculture in small rural villages. Villagers work collectively on community projects and there is much sharing among clans. Animist beliefs exist alongside Christianity.

Unloading seed coconuts near Munda on New Georgia in the Solomons' southern chain.

THE ECONOMY

Main products are palm oil, copra, cocoa, fish ,and timber. Bauxite deposits found on Rennell island, but islanders persuaded the government that exploiting them would destroy the island.

FACTFILE

Official Name Solomon Islands
Date of Formation 1978
Capital Honiara
Population 400,000
Total Area 111,583 sq miles (289,000 sq km)
Density 35 people per sq mile
Languages English*, Pidgin English, 87 (est.) native languages
Religions Christian 91%, other 9%
Ethnic Mix Melanesian 94%, other (Polynesian, Chinese, European) 6%
Government Parliamentary democracy
Currency Solomon Is. $ = 100 cents

AUSTRALASIA & OCEANIA

PALAU

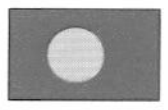

THE PALAU archipelago, a group of over 300 islands, lies in the western Pacific Ocean. In 1994, it became the world's newest independent state.

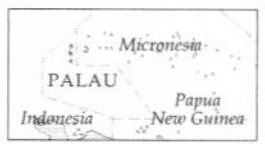

GEOGRAPHY

Terrain varies from thickly-forested mountains to limestone and coral reefs. Babeldaob, the largest island, is volcanic, with many rivers and waterfalls.

CLIMATE

Hot and wet. Little variation in daily and seasonal temperatures. February–April is the dry season.

PEOPLE AND SOCIETY

Palau was the last remaining US-administered UN Trust Territory of the Pacific Islands, until 1994. Only nine islands are inhabited and two-thirds of the population live in Oreor. Society is matrilineal; women choose which males will be the clan chiefs. Local traditions remain strong, despite US influence.

THE ECONOMY

Subsistence level. Main crops are coconuts and cassava. Revenue from fishing licenses and tourism. Heavily reliant on US aid.

FACTFILE

Official Name Republic of Palau
Date of Formation 1994
Capital Oreor
Population 16,500
Total Area 192 sq miles (497 sq km)
Density 85 people per sq mile
Languages Palauan*, English*, Sonsorolese-Tobian, other
Religions Christian (mainly Catholic) 70%, traditional beliefs 30%
Ethnic Mix Palaun 99%, other (mainly Filipino) 1%
Government Multiparty republic
Currency US $ = 100 cents

MICRONESIA

THE FEDERATED States of Micronesia, situated in the western Pacific, comprise 607 islands and atolls grouped into four main island states.

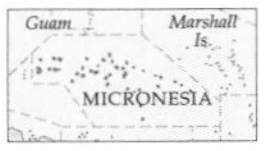

GEOGRAPHY
Mixture of high volcanic islands with forested interiors, and low-lying coral atolls. Some islands have coastal mangrove swamps.

CLIMATE
Tropical, with high humidity. Very heavy rainfall outside the January–March dry season.

PEOPLE AND SOCIETY
Part of the US-administered UN Trust Territory of the Pacific Islands, until independence in 1979, but it still relies on US aid, which funds food stamps, schools and hospitals. Most islanders live without electricity or running water. Society is traditionally matrilineal.

Ebeye Island in the Marshalls where population pressures have led to the disappearance of most tree and grass cover.

THE ECONOMY
Fishing and copra production are the mainstays. Construction industry is largest private-sector activity. High unemployment.

FACTFILE
Official Name Federated States of Micronesia
Date of Formation 1986
Capital Palikir
Population 104,000
Total Area 1,120 sq miles (2,900 sq km)
Density 92 people per sq mile
Languages English*, Trukese, Pohnpeian, Mortlockese, other
Religions Catholic 50%, Protestant 48%, other 2%
Ethnic Mix Micronesian 99%, other 1%
Government Republic
Currency US $ = 100 cents

MARSHALL ISLANDS

UNDER US rule as part of the UN Trust Territory of the Pacific Islands until independence in 1986, the Marshall Islands comprise a group of 34 atolls.

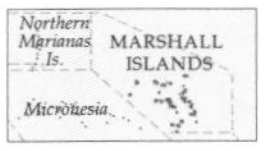

GEOGRAPHY
Narrow coral rings with sandy beaches enclosing lagoons. Those in the south have thicker vegetation. Kwajalein is the world's largest atoll.

CLIMATE
Tropical oceanic, cooled year-round by northeast trade winds.

PEOPLE AND SOCIETY
Majuro Atoll is the main commercial center, and is home to almost half the population. Tensions are high due to poor living conditions. Life on the outlying islands is still traditional, based around subsistence agriculture and fishing. Society is matrilineal; chiefly titles descend through the mother.

THE ECONOMY
Almost totally dependent on US aid and the rent paid by the US for its missile base on Kwajalein Atoll. Revenue from Japan for use of Marshallese waters for tuna fishing. Copra and coconut oil are the only significant agricultural exports.

FACTFILE
Official Name Republic of the Marshall Islands
Date of Formation 1986
Capital No official capital
Population 54,000
Total Area 70 sq miles (181 sq km)
Density 771 people per sq mile
Languages English*, Marshallese*
Religions Protestant 80%, Catholic 15%, other 5%
Ethnic Mix Marshallese 90%, other Pacific islanders 10%
Government Republic
Currency US $ = 100 cents

NAURU

NAURU LIES in the Pacific, 2,480 miles (4,000 km) northeast of Australia. Phosphate deposits have made its citizens among the richest in the world.

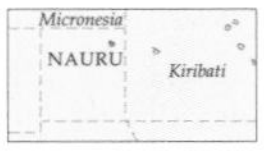

GEOGRAPHY
Low-lying coral atoll, with a fertile coastal belt. Coral cliffs encircle an elevated interior plateau.

Nauru is almost circular with a single 11-mile ring road.

CLIMATE
Equatorial, moderated by sea breezes. Occasional long droughts.

PEOPLE AND SOCIETY
Native Nauruans are of mixed Micronesian and Polynesian origin. Most live in simple, traditional houses and spend their money on luxury cars and consumer goods. Government provides free welfare and education. Diet of imported processed foods has caused widespread obesity and diabetes. Mining is left to an imported labor force, mainly from Kiribati. Many young attend boarding school in Australia.

THE ECONOMY
Phosphate, the only resource, is sold to Pacific Rim countries for use as a fertilizer. Deposits are near exhaustion. Huge investments in Australian and Hawaiian property. Possible future as a tax haven.

FACTFILE
Official Name Republic of Nauru
Date of Formation 1968
Capital No official capital
Population 11,000
Total Area 8.2 sq miles (21.2 sq km)
Density 1,341 people per sq mile
Languages Nauruan*, English, other
Religions Christian 95%, other 5%
Ethnic Mix Nauruan 58%, other Pacific islanders 26%, Chinese 8%, European 8%
Government Parliamentary democracy
Currency Australian $ = 100 cents

KIRIBATI

PART OF the British colony of the Gilbert and Ellice Islands until independence in 1979, Kiribati comprises 33 islands in the mid-Pacific Ocean.

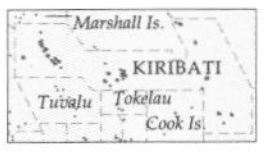

GEOGRAPHY
Three groups of tiny, very low-lying coral atolls scattered across 1,930,000 sq miles (5 million sq km) of ocean. Most have central lagoons.

CLIMATE
Central islands have maritime equatorial climate. Those to north and south are tropical, with constant high temperatures.

PEOPLE AND SOCIETY
Locals still refer to themselves as Gilbertese. Apart from the inhabitants of Banaba, who employed anthropologists to establish their racial distinction, almost all people are Micronesian. Most are poor subsistence farmers. The islands are effectively ruled by traditional chiefs, though there is a party system based on the British model.

THE ECONOMY
Until 1980, when deposits ran out, phosphate from Banaba provided 80% of exports. Since then, coconuts, copra, fish, have become main exports, but the islands are heavily dependent on foreign aid.

FACTFILE
Official Name Republic of Kiribati
Date of Formation 1979
Capital Bairiki
Population 77,000
Total Area 274 sq miles (710 sq km)
Density 281 people per sq mile
Languages English*, Kiribati, other
Religions Catholic 53%, Protestant (mainly Congregational) 40%, other Christian 4%, other 3%
Ethnic Mix I-Kiribati 98%, other 2%
Government Multiparty republic
Currency Australian $ = 100 cents

AUSTRALASIA & OCEANIA

TUVALU

A TINY isolated state, linked to the Gilbert Islands as a British colony until independence in 1978, Tuvalu's nine islands lie in the central Pacific.

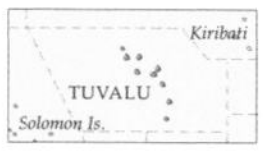

GEOGRAPHY

Coral atolls, none more than 15 feet (4.6 meters) above sea level. Poor soils restrict vegetation to bush, coconut palms, and breadfruit trees.

CLIMATE

Hot all year round. Heavy annual rainfall. Hurricane season brings many violent storms.

PEOPLE AND SOCIETY

People are mostly Polynesian, related to the Samoans and Tongans. Almost half the population live on Funafuti Atoll, where government jobs are centered. Life is communal and traditional. Most people live by subsistence farming, digging pits out of the coral to grow crops. Fresh water is precious due to frequent droughts.

THE ECONOMY

World's smallest economy. Fish stocks exploited mainly by foreign boats in return for licensing fees. Exports are few; copra, stamps, and garments. Aid is crucial.

FACTFILE

Official Name Tuvalu
Date of Formation 1978
Capital Fongafale
Population 9,000
Total Area 10 sq miles (26 sq km)
Density 900 people per sq mile
Languages Tuvaluan, Kiribati, other (no official language)
Religions Protestant 97%, other 3%
Ethnic Mix Tuvaluan 95%, other (inc. Micronesian, I-Kiribati) 5%
Government Constitutional monarchy
Currency Australian $ = 100 cents

AUSTRALASIA & OCEANIA

SAMOA

THE SOUTHERN Pacific islands of Samoa gained independence from New Zealand in 1962. Four of the nine islands are inhabited.

GEOGRAPHY

Comprises two large islands and seven smaller ones. Two largest islands have rain forested, mountainous interiors surrounded by coastal lowlands and coral reefs.

CLIMATE

Tropical, with high humidity. Cooler May–November. Hurricane season December–March.

PEOPLE AND SOCIETY

Ethnic Samoans are world's second largest Polynesian group, after the Maoris. Extended family groups own 80% of the land. Each family has an elected chief, who looks after its political and social interests. Large-scale migration to the US and New Zealand reflects lack of jobs and attractions of Western lifestyle.

The capital of Samoa, Apia, lies on Upolu, the second largest island.

THE ECONOMY

Agricultural products include taro, coconut cream, cocoa, and copra. Growth of service sector since 1989 launch of offshore banking. Dependent on aid and expatriate remittances.

FACTFILE

Official Name Independent State of Samoa
Date of Formation 1962
Capital Apia
Population 200,000
Total Area 1,027 sq miles (2,840 sq km)
Density 195 people per sq mile
Languages Samoan*, English*
Religions Protestant (mostly Congregational) 74%, Catholic 26%
Ethnic Mix Samoan 93%, mixed European and Polynesian 7%
Government Parliamentary state
Currency Tala = 100 sene

AUSTRALASIA & OCEANIA

TONGA

TONGA IS an archipelago of 170 islands, 45 of which are inhabited, in the South Pacific. Politics is effectively controlled by the king.

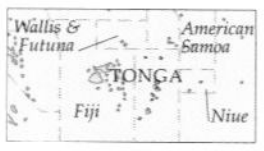

GEOGRAPHY

Easterly islands are generally low and fertile. Those in the west are higher and volcanic in origin.

CLIMATE

Tropical oceanic. Temperatures range between 68°F (20°C) and 86°F (30°C) all year round. Heavy rainfall, especially February–March.

PEOPLE AND SOCIETY

The last remaining Polynesian monarchy, and the only Pacific state never brought under foreign rule. All land is property of the crown, but is administered by nobles who allot it to the common people. Respect for traditional institutions and values remains high, although younger, Westernized Tongans are starting to question some attitudes.

THE ECONOMY

Most people are subsistence farmers. Commercial production of coconuts, cassava, and passion fruit. Tourism is increasing slowly.

FACTFILE

Official Name Kingdom of Tonga
Date of Formation 1970
Capital Nuku'alofa
Population 98,000
Total Area 290 sq miles (750 sq km)
Density 337 people per sq mile
Languages Tongan*, English
Religions Protestant 82% (mainly Methodist), Catholic 18%
Ethnic Mix Tongan 98%, mixed European and Polynesian 2%
Government Constitutional monarchy
Currency Pa'anga = 100 seniti

AUSTRALASIA & OCEANIA

NEW ZEALAND

LYING SOUTHEAST of Australia, New Zealand comprises the North and South Islands, separated by the Cook Strait, and many smaller islands.

GEOGRAPHY

North Island has mountain ranges, valleys and volcanic central plateau. South Island is mostly mountainous, with eastern lowlands.

New Zealand has many volcanoes, some of which are still active. Mount Taranaki on North Island is now extinct.

CLIMATE

Generally temperate and damp. Extreme north is almost subtropical; southern winters are cold.

PEOPLE AND SOCIETY

Maoris were the first settlers, 1,200 years ago. Today's majority European population is descended mainly from British migrants who settled after 1840. Maoris' living and education standards are generally lower than average. Tense relations beween the two groups in recent years. Government now negotiating settlement of Maori land claims.

THE ECONOMY

Modern agricultural sector; world's biggest exporter of wool, cheese, butter, and meat. Growing manufacturing industry. Tourism.

FACTFILE

Official Name The Dominion of New Zealand
Date of Formation 1947
Capital Wellington
Population 3.6 million
Total Area 103,730 sq miles (268,680 sq km)
Density 34 people per sq mile
Languages English*, Maori, other
Religions Protestant 62%, Catholic 18%, other 20%
Ethnic Mix European 88%, Maori 9%, other (inc. Malay, Chinese) 3%
Government Constitutional monarchy
Currency NZ $ = 100 cents

Gazetteer of International Organizations

THIS LISTING GIVES the full names of a number of international organizations. Most have been set up for the purpose of fostering social and economic ties between countries – usually with close geographic links. The full names are followed by the date of establishment or foundation, an indication of membership where appropriate and a summary of the organization's aims and functions.

ACC
Arab Cooperation Council
Established 1989
Members – Egypt, Iraq, Jordan, Yemen; promotes Arab economic cooperation

ACP
African, Caribbean and Pacific Countries
Established 1976
Members – 70 developing countries; preferential economic and aid relationship with the EU

ACS
Association of Caribbean States
Established 1994
Members – 24 Caribbean countries; promotes economic, scientific , and cultural cooperation in the region

ADB
Asian Development Bank
Established 1966
Members – 39 Asian-Pacific countries and territories, 16 non-regional countries; encourages regional development

AfDB
African Development Bank
Established 1963
Members – 52 African countries, 24 non-African countries; encourages African economic development

AFESD **Arab Fund for Economic and Social Development**
Established 1968
Members – 20 Arab countries and the PLO; promotes social and economic development in Arab states

AL
Arab League
Established 1945
Members – 21 Arab countries and the PLO; forum to promote Arabic cooperation on social, political and military issues

ALADI
Latin American Integration Association
Established 1960
Members – 11 South American countries; promotes trade and regional integration

Amazon Pact
Established 1978
Members – Bolivia, Brazil, Colombia, Ecuador, Guyana, Peru, Suriname, Venezuela; promotes the harmonious development of the Amazon region

AG
Andean Pact (Acuerdo de Cartegena)
Established 1969
Members – Bolivia, Colombia, Ecuador, Peru and Venezuela; promotes development through integration

AMF
Arab Monetary Fund
Established 1977
Members – 19 countries and the PLO; promotes monetary and economic cooperation

AMU
Arab Maghreb Union
Established 1989
Members – Algeria, Libya, Mauritania, Morocco, Tunisia; promotes integration and economic cooperation among North African Arab states

APEC
Asia-Pacific Economic Cooperation
Established 1989
Members – 18 Pacific Rim countries; promotes regional economic cooperation

ASEAN
Association of Southeast Asian Nations
Established 1967
Members – Brunei, Myanmar, Indonesia, Laos, Malaysia, Philippines, Singapore, Thailand, Vietnam; promotes economic, social and cultural cooperation

BADEA **Arab Bank for Economic Development in Africa**
Established 1974 (as an agency of the Arab League)
Members – 17 Arab countries and the PLO; promotes economic development in Africa

BDEAC **Central African States Development Bank**
Established 1976
Members – Cameroon, Central African Republic, Chad, Congo, Equatorial Guinea, France, Gabon, Germany, Kuwait; furthers economic development

Benelux
Benelux Economic Union
Established 1958
Members – Belgium, Luxembourg, Netherlands; develops economic ties between member countries

BOAD
West African Development Bank
Established 1973
Members – Benin, Burkina, Ivory Coast, Mali, Niger, Senegal, Togo; promotes economic development and integration

BSEC
Black Sea Economic Co-operation Group
Established 1992
Members – Albania, Armenia, Azerbaijan, Bulgaria, Georgia, Greece, Moldova, Romania, Russia, Turkey, Ukraine; furthers regional stability through economic cooperation

CACM
Central American Common Market
Established 1960
Members – Costa Rica, El Salvador, Guatemala, Honduras, Nicaragua; furthers economic ties between members; one of its institutions is the BCIE – Central American Bank for Economic Integration

CAEU
Council of Arab Economic Unity
Established 1964
Members – 11 Arab countries and the PLO; encourages economic integration

CARICOM **Caribbean Community and Common Market**
Established 1973
Members – 13 Caribbean countries and Montserrat; fosters economic ties in the Caribbean

CBSS
Council of the Baltic Sea States
Established 1992
Members – Denmark, Estonia, Finland, Germany, Latvia, Lithuania, Norway, Poland, Russia, Sweden; promotes cooperation among Baltic Sea states

CDB
Caribbean Development Bank
Established 1969
Members – 20 Caribbean countries, 5 non-Caribbean countries; promotes regional development

CE
Council of Europe
Established 1949
Members – 40 European countries; promotes unity and quality of life in Europe

CEEAC **Economic Community of Central African States**
Established 1983
Members – 10 Central African countries; promotes regional cooperation, and aims to establish a Central African common market

CEFTA **Central European Free Trade Agreement**
Established 1992
Members – Czech Republic, Hungary, Poland, Romania, Slovakia, Slovenia; promotes trade and cooperation

CEI **Central European Initiative**
Established 1991 (evolved from Hexagonal Group)
Members – Austria, Bosnia & Herzegovina, Bulgaria, Belarus, Croatia, Czech Republic, Hungary, Italy, Moldova, Poland, Slovakia, Slovenia, Ukraine, Yugoslavia; promotes economic and political cooperation, within the OSCE

CEMAC **Economic and Monetary Community of Central Africa**
Established 1994
Members – 6 Central African members of the franc zone; customs union (replaced UDEAC)

CEPGL **Economic Community of the Great Lakes Countries**
Established 1976
Members – Burundi, Congo (Zaire), Rwanda; promotes regional economic cooperation

CERN **European Organization for Nuclear Research**
Established 1953
Members – 23 European countries; provides for collaboration in nuclear research for peaceful purposes

CILSS **Permanent Interstate Committee for Drought Control in the Sahel**
Established 1973
Members – 9 African countries in the Sahel region; promotes prevention of drought and crop failure in the region

CIS
Commonwealth of Independent States
Established 1991 (as successor of the Soviet Union)
Members – Armenia, Azerbaijan, Belarus, Georgia, Kazakhstan, Kyrgyzstan, Moldova, Russia, Tajikistan, Turkmenistan, Ukraine, Uzbekistan; promotes interstate relationships

COMESA **Common Market for Eastern and Southern Africa**
Established 1993 (replacing PTA)
Members – 24 African countries; promotes economic development and cooperation

Commonwealth
(evolved from British Empire)
Established 1931
Members – 53 countries; develops relationships and contacts between its members (Nigeria suspended 1995, Fiji re-admitted in 1997)

CP **Colombo Plan**
Established 1951
Members – Australia, Japan, New Zealand, USA (donors) and 20 Asia-Pacific countries; encourages economic and social development in Asia-Pacific region

Damascus Declaration
Established 1991
Members – Bahrain, Egypt, Kuwait, Oman, Qatar, Saudi Arabia, Syria, UAE; a loose association, formed after the Gulf War, which aims to secure the stability of the region

EBRD **European Bank for Reconstruction and Development**
Established 1991
Members – 58 countries; helps transition of former communist European states to market economies

ECO
Economic Cooperation Organization
Established 1985
Members – Iran, Pakistan, Turkey and 7 Central Asian states; aims at cooperation in economic, social, and cultural affairs

ECOWAS **Economic Community of West African States**
Established 1975
Members – 16 West African countries; promotes regional economic cooperation

EEA **European Economic Area**
Established 1994
Members – the 15 members of the EU and all the members of EFTA, except Switzerland; aims to include EFTA members in the EU single market

EFTA
European Free Trade Association
Established 1960
Members – Iceland, Norway, Liechtenstein, Switzerland; promotes economic cooperation

ESA
European Space Agency
Established 1973
Members – 14 European countries; promotes cooperation in space research for peaceful purposes

EU European Union
Established 1992;
Members – 15 countries; aims to integrate the economies of member states and promote cooperation and coordination of policies

FZ Franc zone
Members – 15 African states, France and Monaco; aims to form monetary union among countries whose currencies are linked to the French franc.

GCC Gulf Co-operation Council
Established 1981
Members – Bahrain, Kuwait, Oman, Qatar, Saudi Arabia, UAE; promotes cooperation in economic, political and social affairs

G3 Group of 3
Established 1987
Members – Colombia, Mexico, Venezuela; aims to remove trade restrictions

G5 Group of 5
Finance ministers of France, Germany, Japan, UK, USA, meeting informally to establish agenda of G7

G7 Group of 7
Established 1975
Members – Canada, France, Germany, Italy, Japan, UK, USA; the seven major industrialized countries

G10 Group of 10
Established 1962
Members – G7 members, plus Belgium, the Netherlands, Sweden and Switzerland (now 11 members); ministers meet to discuss monetary issues

G15 Group of 15
Established 1989
Members – 15 developing countries; meets annually to further cooperation among developing countries

G24 Group of 24
Members – the 24 countries within the IMF which represent the interests of developing countries

GEPLACEA Latin American and Caribbean Sugar Exporting Countries
Established 1974
Members – 23 countries; a forum for consultation on the production and sale of sugar

IMF International Monetary Fund
Established 1945
Members – 181 countries (voting rights of Congo (Zaire) and Sudan are currently suspended); promotes international monetary cooperation, balanced growth of trade and exchange rate stability; provides credit resources to members experiencing balance-of-trade difficulties

IBRD International Bank for Reconstruction and Development (also known as the World Bank)
Established 1945
Members – 178 countries; UN agency providing economic development loans

IDB Islamic Development Bank
Established 1975 (agency of the OIC)
Members – 47 countries and the PLO; promotes economic development on Islamic principles among Muslim communities

IGADD Intergovernmental Authority on Drought and Development
Established 1986
Members – Djibouti, Eritrea, Ethiopia, Kenya, Somalia, Sudan, Uganda; promotes cooperation on drought-related matters

IOC
Indian Ocean Commission
Established 1982
Members – Comoros, France (representing Réunion), Madagascar, Mauritius, Seychelles; promotes regional cooperation

IWC
International Whaling Commission
Established 1946
Members – 40 countries; reviews conduct of whaling throughout world; coordinates and funds whale research

LCBC
Lake Chad Basin Commission
Established 1964
Members – Cameroon, CAR, Chad, Niger, Nigeria; encourages economic and environmental development in Lake Chad region

MEKONG RIVER COMMISSION
Established 1995 (replacing the 1958 interim Mekong Secretariat)
Members – Cambodia, Laos, Thailand, Vietnam; accord on the sustainable development of Mekong River basin

MERCOSUR
Southern Common Market
Established 1991
Members – Argentina, Brazil, Paraguay, Uruguay; promotes economic cooperation

MRU Mano River Union
Established 1973
Members – Guinea, Liberia, Sierra Leone; aims to create customs and economic union

NACC
North Atlantic Cooperation Council
Established 1991
Members – 36 countries (members of NATO and former members of Warsaw Pact); forum for cooperation on political and security issues

NAFTA
North American Free Trade Agreement
Established 1994
Members – Canada, Mexico, USA; free-trade zone

NAM Non-Aligned Movement
Established 1961
Members – 111 countries; fosters political and military cooperation away from traditional Eastern or Western blocs

NATO
North Atlantic Treaty Organization
Established 1949
Members – 16 countries; promotes mutual defense cooperation. Since January 1994, NATO's *Partnerships for Peace* program has provided a loose framework for cooperation with former members of the Warsaw Pact and the ex-Soviet republics. In 1997, Czech Republic, Hungary, and Poland were the first former Warsaw Pact members invited to join.

NC Nordic Council
Established 1952
Members – Denmark, Finland, Iceland, Norway, Sweden; promotes cultural and environmental cooperation in Scandinavia

OAPEC Organization of Arab Petroleum Exporting Countries
Established 1968
Members – Algeria, Bahrain, Egypt, Iraq, Kuwait, Libya, Qatar, Saudi Arabia, Syria, UAE; aims to promote the interests of member countries and increase cooperation in the petroleum industry

OAS
Organization of American States
Established 1948
Members – 34 American countries; promotes security, economic, and social development in the Americas

OAU
Organization of African Unity
Established 1963
Members – 53 African countries; promotes unity and cooperation

OECD Organization for Economic Cooperation and Development
Established 1961
Members – 29 industrialized democracies; forum for coordinating economic policies

OECS
Organization of Eastern Caribbean States
Established 1981
Members – Antigua & Barbuda, Dominica, Grenada, Montserrat, St Kitts & Nevis, St Lucia, St Vincent & the Grenadines; promotes political, economic, and defense cooperation

OIC
Organization of the Islamic Conference
Established 1971
Members – 53 Islamic countries; furthers Islamic solidarity and cooperation

OMVG Gambia River Development Organization
Established 1978
Members – The Gambia, Guinea, Guinea-Bissau, Senegal; promotes integrated development of the Gambia River basin

OPANAL Agency for the Prohibition of Nuclear Weapons in Latin America and the Caribbean
Established 1969
Members – 26 countries; aims to ensure compliance with the Treaty of Tlatelolco (banning nuclear weapons from South America and the Caribbean)

OPEC Organization of the Petroleum Exporting Countries
Established 1960
Members – Algeria, Gabon, Indonesia, Iran, Iraq, Kuwait, Libya, Nigeria, Qatar, Saudi Arabia, UAE, Venezuela; aims to coordinate oil policies to ensure fair and stable prices

OSCE Organization for Security and Cooperation in Europe
Established 1972 (as CSCE; renamed 1994)
Members – 53 countries; aims to strengthen democracy and human rights, and settle disputes peacefully

PARTNERSHIPS FOR PEACE (PfP)
see NATO

RG
Rio Group
Established 1987 (evolved from Contadora Group, established 1948)
Members – Argentina, Bolivia, Brazil, Chile, Colombia, Ecuador, Mexico, Paraguay, Peru, Uruguay, Venezuela; forum for Latin American issues

SAARC South Asian Association for Regional Co-operation
Established 1985
Members – Bangladesh, Bhutan, India, Maldives, Nepal, Pakistan, Sri Lanka; encourages economic, social and cultural cooperation

SACU
Southern African Customs Union
Established 1969
Members – 5 countries; promotes cooperation in trade and customs matters among southern African states

SADC Southern African Development Community
Established 1992
Members – Angola, Botswana, Lesotho, Malawi, Mauritius, Mozambique, Namibia, South Africa, Swaziland, Tanzania, Zambia, Zimbabwe; promotes economic integration

SAN JOSÉ GROUP
Established 1988
Members – Costa Rica, El Salvador, Guatemala, Honduras, Nicaragua, Panama; a "complementary, voluntary and gradual" economic union

SELA
Latin American Economic System
Established 1975
Members – 27 countries; promotes economic and social development through regional cooperation

SPC
South Pacific Commission
Established 1948
Members – 28 countries and territories; a forum for dialogue between Pacific countries and powers administering Pacific territories

SPF
South Pacific Forum
Established 1971
Members – 15 countries and territories; develops regional political cooperation

UEMOA West African Economic and Monetary Union
Established 1994
Members – 7 countries; aims for convergence of monetary policies and economic union

UN
United Nations
Established 1945
Members – 184 countries; permanent members of the Security Council – China, France, Russia, UK, USA; aims to maintain international peace and security and to promote cooperation over economic, social, cultural, and humanitarian problems. Agencies include the regional commissions of the UN's Economic and Social Council: ECA (Economic Commission for Africa – established 1958); ECE (Economic Commission for Europe – established 1947); ECLAC (Economic Commission for Latin America and the Caribbean – established 1948); ESCAP (Economic and Social Commission for Asia and the Pacific – established 1947); ESCWA (Economic and Social Commission for Western Asia – established 1973)

WEU
Western European Union
Established 1954
Members – 10 countries; a forum for European military cooperation

WTO
World Trade Organisation
Established 1995 (as the successor to GATT – General Agreement on Tariffs and Trade)
Members – 131 countries; aims to liberalize trade through multilateral trade agreements

INDEX

GLOSSARY OF ABBREVIATIONS

This Glossary provides a comprehensive guide to the abbreviations used in this Atlas, and in the Index.

abbrev abbreviation
Afr. Afrikaans
Alb. Albanian
Amh. Amharic
anc. ancient
Ar. Arabic
Arm. Armenian
Az. Azerbaijani

B
Basq. Basque
Bel. Belorussian
Ben. Bengali
Bibl. Biblical
Bret. Breton
Bul. Bulgarian
Bur. Burmese

C
Cam. Cambodian
Cant. Cantonese
Cast. Castilian
Cat. Catalan
Chin. Chinese
Cro. Croat
Cz. Czech

D
Dan. Danish
Dut. Dutch

E
Eng. English
Est. Estonian
est. estimated

F
Faer. Faeroese
Fij. Fijian
Fin. Finnish
Flem. Flemish
Fr. French
Fris. Frisian

G
Geor. Georgian
Ger. German
Gk. Greek
Guj. Gujarati

H
Haw. Hawaiian
Heb. Hebrew
Hind. Hindi
hist. historical
Hung. Hungarian

I
Icel. Icelandic
Ind. Indonesian
Inuit Inuit
Ir. Irish
It. Italian

J
Jap. Japanese

K
Kaz. Kazakh
Kir. Kirghiz
Kor. Korean
Kurd. Kurdish

L
Lao. Laotian
Lapp. Lappis
Lat. Latin
Latv. Latvian
Lith. Lithanian
Lus. Lusatian

M
Mac. Macedonian
Mal. Malay
Malg. Mahilgasy
Malt. Maltese
Mong. Mongolia

N
Nepali. Nepali
Nor. Norwegian

O
off. officially

P
Pash. Pashtu
Per. Persian
Pol. Polish
Port. Portuguese
prev. previously

R
Rmsch. Romansch
Roman. Romanian
Rus. Russian

S
SCr. Serbian & Croatian
Serb. Serbian
Slvk. Slovak
Slvn. Slovene
Som. Somali
Sp. Spanish
Swa. Swahili
Swe. Swedish

T
Taj. Tajik
Th. Thai
Tib. Tibetan
Turk. Turkish
Turkm. Turkmenistan

U
Uigh. Uighur
Ukr. Ukrainian
Uzb. Uzbek

V
var. variant
Vtn. Vietnamese

W
Wel. Welsh

X
Xh. Xhosa

Y
Yugo. Yugoslavia

A

Aachen 126 A4 *Dut.* Aken, *Fr.* Aix-la-Chapelle; *anc.* Aquae Grani, Aquisgranum. Nordrhein-Westfalen, W Germany
Aaiún *see* Laâyoune
Aalborg *see* Ålborg
Aalen 127 B6 Baden-Württemberg, S Germany
Aalsmeer 118 C3 Noord-Holland, C Netherlands
Aalst 119 B6 *Fr.* Alost. Oost-Vlaanderen, C Belgium
Aalten 118 E4 Gelderland, E Netherlands
Aalter 119 B5 Oost-Vlaanderen, NW Belgium
Äänekoski 117 D5 Keski-Suomi, C Finland
Aar *see* Aare
Aare 127 A7 *var.* Aar. *River* W Switzerland
Aarhus *see* Århus
Aat *see* Ath
Aba 107 G5 Abia, S Nigeria
Aba 109 E5 Haut-Zaïre, NE Congo (Zaire)
Abā as Su'ūd *see* Najrān
Abaco Island *see* Great Abaco
Ābādān 152 C4 Khūzestān, SW Iran
Abai *see* Blue Nile
Abakan 146 D4 Respublika Khakasiya, S Russian Federation
Abancay 92 D4 Apurímac, SE Peru
Abariringa *see* Kanton
Abashiri 162 D2 *var.* Abasiri. Hokkaidō, NE Japan
Abasiri *see* Abashiri
Ābaya Hāyk' 105 C5 *Eng.* Lake Margherita, *It.* Abbaia. *Lake* SW Ethiopia
Ābay Wenz *see* Blue Nile
Abbeville 122 C2 *anc.* Abbatis Villa. Somme, N France
'Abd al 'Azīz, Jabal 150 D2 *mountain range* NE Syria
Abéché 108 C3 *var.* Abécher, Abeshr. Ouaddaï, SE Chad
Abécher *see* Abéché
Abela *see* Ávila
Abemama 176 D2 *var.* Apamama; *prev.* Roger Simpson Island. *Atoll* Tungaru, W Kiribati
Abengourou 107 E5 E Ivory Coast
Aberdeen 120 D3 *anc.* Devana. NE Scotland, UK
Aberdeen 77 E2 South Dakota, N USA
Aberdeen 78 B2 Washington, NW USA
Abergwaun *see* Fishguard
Abertawe *see* Swansea
Aberystwyth 121 C6 W Wales, UK
Abeshr *see* Abéché
Abhā 153 B6 'Asīr, SW Saudi Arabia
Abidavichy 139 D7 *Rus.* Obidovichi. Mahilyowskaya Voblasts', E Belarus
Abidjan 107 E5 S Ivory Coast
Abilene 81 F3 Texas, SW USA
Abingdon *see* Pinta, Isla
Abkhazia 149 E1 *autonomous republic* NW Georgia
Åbo 117 D6 Turku-Pori, SW Finland
Aboisso 107 E5 SE Ivory Coast
Abo, Massif d' 108 B1 *mountain range* NW Chad
Abomey 107 F5 S Benin
Abou-Déïa 108 C3 Salamat, SE Chad
Abrantes 124 B3 *var.* Abrántes. Santarém, C Portugal
Abrolhos Bank 88 E4 *undersea feature* W Atlantic Ocean
Abrova 139 B6 *Rus.* Obrovo. Brestskaya Voblasts', SW Belarus
Abrud 140 B4 *Ger.* Gross-Schlatten, *Hung.* Abrudbánya. Alba, SW Romania
Abruzzese, Appennino 128 C4 *mountain range* C Italy
Absaroka Range 76 B2 *mountain range* Montana/Wyoming, NW USA
Abū aḍ Ḍuhūr 150 B3 *Fr.* Aboudouhour. Idlib, NW Syria
Abu Dhabi 144 *see* Abū Ẓaby
Abu Hamed 104 C3 River Nile, N Sudan
Abū Ḥardān 150 E3 *var.* Hajîne. Dayr az Zawr, E Syria
Abuja 107 G4 *country capital* (Nigeria) Federal Capital District, C Nigeria
Abū Kamāl 150 E3 *Fr.* Abou Kémal. Dayr az Zawr, E Syria
Abula *see* Ávila
Abunã, Rio 94 C2 *var.* Río Abuná. *River* Bolivia/Brazil
Abut Head 183 B6 *headland* South Island, NZ
Ābuyē Mēda 104 D4 *mountain* C Ethiopia
Abū Ẓabī *see* Abū Ẓaby
Abū Ẓaby 153 C5 *var.* Abū Ẓabī, *Eng.* Abu Dhabi. *Country capital* (UAE) Abū Ẓaby, C UAE
Abyla *see* Ávila
Acalayong 109 A5 SW Equatorial Guinea
Acaponeta 82 D4 Nayarit, C Mexico
Acapulco 83 E5 *var.* Acapulco de Juárez. Guerrero, S Mexico
Acapulco de Juárez *see* Acapulco
Acarai Mountains 91 F4 *Sp.* Serra Acaraí. *Mountain range* Brazil/Guyana
Acarigua 90 D2 Portuguesa, N Venezuela
Accra 107 E5 *country capital* (Ghana) SE Ghana
Achacachi 93 E4 La Paz, W Bolivia
Acklins Island 86 C2 *island* SE Bahamas
Aconcagua, Cerro 96 B4 *mountain* W Argentina
Açores *see* Azores
A Coruña 124 B1 *Cast.* La Coruña, *Eng.* Corunna; *anc.* Caronium. Galicia, NW Spain
Acre 94 C2 *off.* Estado do Acre. *State* W Brazil
Açu 95 G2 *var.* Assu. Rio Grande do Norte, E Brazil
Acuña 82 D2 *var.* Villa Acuña. Coahuila de Zaragoza, NE Mexico
Ada 81 G2 Oklahoma, C USA
Ada 132 D3 Serbia, N Yugoslavia
Adalia, Gulf of *see* Antalya Körfezi
Adama *see* Nazrēt
Adamawa Highlands 108 B4 *plateau* NW Cameroon
'Adan 153 B7 *Eng.* Aden. SW Yemen
Adana 148 D4 *var.* Seyhan. Adana, S Turkey
Adapazarı 148 B2 *prev.* Ada Bazar. Sakarya, NW Turkey
Adare, Cape 186 B4 *headland* Antarctica
Ad Dahnā' 152 C4 *desert* E Saudi Arabia
Ad Dakhla 102 A4 *var.* Dakhla. SW Western Sahara
Ad Dalanj *see* Dilling
Ad Damar *see* Ed Damer
Ad Damazīn *see* Ed Damazin
Ad Dāmir *see* Ed Damer
Ad Dammān 152 C4 *var.* Dammām. Ash Sharqīyah, NE Saudi Arabia
Ad Dāmūr *see* Damoûr
Ad Dawḥah 152 C4 *Eng.* Doha. *Country capital* (Qatar) C Qatar
Aḍ Ḍiffah *see* Libyan Plateau
Addis Ababa 100 *see* Ādīs Ābeba
Addu Atoll 164 A5 *atoll* S Maldives
Adelaide 181 B6 *state capital* South Australia
Aden 144 *see* 'Adan
Aden, Gulf of 153 C7 *gulf* SW Arabian Sea
Adige 128 C2 *Ger.* Etsch. *River* N Italy
Adirondack Mountains 73 F2 *mountain range* New York, NE USA
Ādīs Ābeba 105 C5 *Eng.* Addis Ababa. *Country capital* (Ethiopia) C Ethiopia
Adıyaman 149 E4 Adıyaman, SE Turkey
Adjud 140 C4 Vrancea, E Romania
Admiralty Islands 176 B3 *island group* N PNG
Adra 125 E5 Andalucía, S Spain
Adrar 102 D3 C Algeria
Adrar des Iforas *see* Ifôghas, Adrar des
Adrian 72 C3 Michigan, N USA
Adriatic Sea 135 E2 *Alb.* Deti Adriatik, *It.* Mare Adriatico, *SCr.* Jadransko More, *Slvn.* Jadransko Morje. *Sea* N Mediterranean Sea
Adycha 147 F2 *river* NE Russian Federation
Aegean Sea 137 C5 *Gk.* Aigaíon Pélagos, Aigaío Pélagos, *Turk.* Ege Denizi. *Sea* NE Mediterranean Sea
Aegviidu 138 D2 *Ger.* Charlottenhof. Harjumaa, NW Estonia
Aelana *see* Al 'Aqabah
Aelok *see* Ailuk Atoll
Aelōnlaplap *see* Ailinglaplap Atoll
Aeolian Islands *see* Eolie, Isole
Afar Depression *see* Danakil Desert
Afghanistan 154 C4 *off.* Islamic State of Afghanistan, *Per.* Dowlat-e Eslāmī-ye Afghānestān; *prev.* Republic of Afghanistan. *Country* C Asia
Afmadow 105 D6 Jubbada Hoose, S Somalia
Africa 100 *continent*
Africa, Horn of 100 E4 *physical region* Ethiopia/Somalia
Africana Seamount 173 A6 *undersea feature* SW Indian Ocean
'Afrīn 150 B2 Ḥalab, N Syria
Afyon 148 B3 *prev.* Afyonkarahisar. Afyon, W Turkey
Agadez 107 G3 *prev.* Agadès. Agadez, C Niger
Agadir 102 B3 SW Morocco
Agana 176 B1 *var.* Agaña. *Dependent territory capital* (Guam) NW Guam
Āgaro 105 C5 W Ethiopia
Agassiz Fracture Zone 175 G5 *tectonic feature* S Pacific Ocean
Agathónisi 137 D6 *island* Dodekánisos, Greece, Aegean Sea
Agde 123 C6 *anc.* Agatha. Hérault, S France
Agedabia *see* Ajdābiyā
Agen 123 B5 *anc.* Aginnum. Lot-et-Garonne, SW France
Aghri Dagh *see* Büyükağrı Dağı
Agiá 136 B4 *var.* Ayiá. Thessalía, C Greece
Agialoúsa 134 D4 *var.* Yenierenköy. NE Cyprus
Agía Marína 137 E6 Léros, Dodekánisos, Greece, Aegean Sea
Ágios Nikólaos 137 D8 *var.* Áyios Nikólaos. Kríti, Greece, E Mediterranean Sea
Āgra 166 D3 Uttar Pradesh, N India
Ağrı 149 F3 *var.* Karaköse; *prev.* Karakılısse. Ağrı, NE Turkey
Agri Dagi *see* Büyükağrı Dağı
Agrigento 129 C7 *Gk.* Akragas; *prev.* Girgenti. Sicilia, Italy, C Mediterranean Sea
Agriovótano 137 C5 Évvoia, C Greece
Agropoli 129 D5 Campania, S Italy
Aguachica 90 B2 Cesar, N Colombia
Aguadulce 85 F5 Coclé, S Panama
Agua Prieta 82 B1 Sonora, NW Mexico
Aguascalientes 82 D4 Aguascalientes, C Mexico
Aguaytía 92 C3 Ucayali, C Peru
Aguilas 125 E4 Murcia, SE Spain
Aguililla 82 D4 Michoacán de Ocampo, SW Mexico
Agulhas Basin 101 D8 *undersea feature* SW Indian Ocean
Agulhas Plateau 99 D6 *undersea feature* SW Indian Ocean
Ahaggar 107 F2 *high plateau region* SE Algeria
Ahlen 126 B4 Nordrhein-Westfalen, W Germany
Ahmadābād 166 C4 *var.* Ahmedabad. Gujarāt, W India
Ahmadnagar 166 C5 *var.* Ahmednagar. Mahārāshtra, W India
Ahmedabad *see* Ahmadābād
Ahmednagar *see* Ahmadnagar
Ahuachapán 84 B3 Ahuachapán, W El Salvador
Ahvāz 152 C3 *var.* Ahwāz; *prev.* Nāsiri. Khūzestān, SW Iran
Ahvenanmaa *see* Åland
Ahwāz *see* Ahvāz
Aïdin *see* Aydın
Aígina 137 C6 *var.* Aíyina, Egina. Aígina, C Greece
Aígio 137 B5 *var.* Egio; *prev.* Aíyion. Dytikí Ellás, S Greece
Aiken 75 E2 South Carolina, SE USA
Ailigandí 85 G4 San Blas, NE Panama
Ailinglaplap Atoll 176 D2 *var.* Aelōnlaplap. *Atoll* Ralik Chain, S Marshall Islands
Ailuk Atoll 176 D1 *var.* Aelok. *Atoll* Ratak Chain, NE Marshall Islands
Ainaži 138 D3 *Est.* Heinaste, *Ger.* Hainasch. Limbaži, N Latvia
'Aïn Ben Tili 106 D1 Tiris Zemmour, N Mauritania
Aintab *see* Gaziantep
Aïoun el Atrous *see* 'Ayoûn el 'Atroûs
Aïoun el Atroûss *see* 'Ayoûn el 'Atroûs
Aiquile 93 F4 Cochabamba, C Bolivia
Aïr *see* Aïr, Massif de l'
Air du Azbine *see* Aïr, Massif de l'
Aïr, Massif de l' 107 G2 *var.* Aïr, Air du Azbine, Asben. *Mountain range* NC Niger
Aiud 140 B4 *Ger.* Strassburg, *Hung.* Nagyenyed; *prev.* Engeten. Alba, SW Romania
Aix *see* Aix-en-Provence
Aix-en-Provence 123 D6 *var.* Aix; *anc.* Aquae Sextiae. Bouches-du-Rhône, SE France
Aíyina *see* Aígina
Aíyion *see* Aígio
Aizkraukle 138 C4 Aizkraukle, S Latvia
Ajaccio 123 E7 Corse, France, C Mediterranean Sea
Ajaria 149 F2 *autonomous republic* SW Georgia
Aj Bogd Uul 158 D2 *mountain* SW Mongolia
Ajdābiyā 103 G2 *var.* Agedabia, Ajdābiyah. NE Libya
Ajdābiyah *see* Ajdābiyā
Ajjinena *see* El Geneina
Ajmer 166 D3 *var.* Ajmere. Rājasthān, N India
Ajmere *see* Ajmer
Ajo 80 A3 Arizona, SW USA
Akaba *see* Al 'Aqabah
Akamagaseki *see* Shimonoseki
Akasha 104 B3 Northern, N Sudan
Akchâr 106 C2 *desert* W Mauritania
Akhalts'ikhe 149 F2 SW Georgia
Akhisar 148 A3 Manisa, W Turkey
Akhmîm 104 B2 *anc.* Panopolis. C Egypt
Akhtubinsk 143 C7 Astrakhanskaya Oblast', SW Russian Federation
Akimiski Island 70 C3 *island* Northwest Territories, C Canada
Akinovka 141 F4 Zaporiz'ka Oblast', S Ukraine
Akita 162 D4 Akita, Honshū, C Japan
Akjoujt 106 C2 *prev.* Fort-Repoux. Inchiri, W Mauritania
Akkeshi 162 E2 Hokkaidō, NE Japan
Aklavik 68 D3 Northwest Territories, NW Canada
Akmola 146 C4 *Kaz.* Aqmola; *prev.* Akmolinsk, Tselinograd. Akmola, N Kazakhstan
Akpatok Island 71 E1 *island* Northwest Territories, E Canada
Akra Dhrepanon *see* Drépano, Ákra
Akra Kanestron *see* Palioúri, Ákra
Akron 72 D4 Ohio, N USA
Akrotiri *see* Akrotírion
Akrotírion 134 C5 *var.* Akrotiri. *UK air base* S Cyprus
Aksai Chin 156 B2 *Chin.* Aksayqin. *Disputed region* China/India
Aksaray 148 C4 Aksaray, C Turkey
Akşehir 148 B4 Konya, W Turkey
Aktau 146 A4 *Kaz.* Aqtaū; *prev.* Shevchenko. Mangistau, W Kazakhstan
Aktsyabrski 139 C7 *Rus.* Oktyabr'skiy; *prev.* Karpilovka. Homyel'skaya Voblasts', SE Belarus
Aktyubinsk 146 B4 *Kaz.* Aqtöbe. Aktyubinsk, NW Kazakhstan
Akula 109 C5 Equateur, NW Congo (Zaire)
Akureyri 115 E4 Nordhurland Eystra, N Iceland
Akyab *see* Sittwe
Alabama 83 G1 *off.* State of Alabama; also known as Camellia State, Heart of Dixie, The Cotton State, Yellowhammer State. *State* S USA
Alabama River 74 C3 *river* Alabama, S USA
Alaca 148 C3 Çorum, N Turkey
Alagoas 95 G2 *off.* Estado de Alagoas. *State* E Brazil
Alajuela 85 E4 Alajuela, C Costa Rica
Alakanuk 68 C2 Alaska, USA
Al 'Alamayn *see* El 'Alamein
Al 'Amārah 152 C3 *var.* Amara. E Iraq
Alamo 79 D6 Nevada, W USA
Alamogordo 80 D3 New Mexico, SW USA
Alamosa 76 C5 Colorado, C USA
Åland 117 C6 *var.* Aland Islands, *Fin.* Ahvenanmaa. *Island group* SW Finland
Aland Islands *see* Åland
Aland Sea *see* Ålands Hav
Ålands Hav 117 C6 *var.* Aland Sea. *Strait* Baltic Sea/Gulf of Bothnia
Alanya 148 C4 Antalya, S Turkey
Alappuzha *see* Alleppey
Al 'Aqabah 151 B8 *var.* Akaba, Aqaba, 'Aqaba; *anc.* Aelana, Elath. Ma'ān, SW Jordan
Alaşehir 138 A4 Manisa, W Turkey
Al 'Ashārah 150 E3 *var.* Ashara. Dayr az Zawr, E Syria
Alaska 68 C3 *off.* State of Alaska; also known as Land of the Midnight Sun, The Last Frontier, Seward's Folly; *prev.* Russian America. *State* NW USA
Alaska, Gulf of 68 C4 *var.* Golfo de Alasca. *Gulf* Canada/USA
Alaska Peninsula 68 C3 *peninsula* Alaska, USA
Alaska Range 66 B2 *mountain range* Alaska, USA
Al-Asnam *see* Chlef
Al Awaynāt *see* Al 'Uwaynāt
Al 'Aynā 151 B7 Al Karak, W Jordan
Alazeya 147 G2 *river* NE Russian Federation
Al Bāb 150 B2 Ḥalab, N Syria
Albacete 125 E3 Castilla-La Mancha, C Spain
Al Baghdādī 152 B3 *var.* Khān al Baghdādī. SW Iraq
Al Bāha *see* Al Bāḥah
Al Bāḥah 153 B5 *var.* Al Bāha. Al Bāḥah, SW Saudi Arabia
Al Baḥr al Mayyit *see* Dead Sea
Alba Iulia 140 B4 *Ger.* Weissenburg, *Hung.* Gyulafehérvár; *prev.* Bălgrad, Karlsburg, Károly-Fehérvár. Alba, W Romania
Albania 133 C7 *off.* Republic of Albania, *Alb.* Republika e Shqipërisë, Shqipëria; *prev.* People's Socialist Republic of Albania. *Country* SE Europe
Albany 70 C3 *river* Ontario, S Canada
Albany 73 F3 *state capital* New York, NE USA
Albany 74 D3 Georgia, SE USA
Albany 78 B3 Oregon, NW USA
Albany 179 B7 Western Australia
Al Bāridah 150 C4 *var.* Bāridah. Ḥimṣ, C Syria
Al Baṣrah 152 C3 *Eng.* Basra; *hist.* Busra, Bussora. SE Iraq
Al Batrūn *see* Batroûn
Al Bayḍā' 103 G2 *var.* Beida. NE Libya
Albemarle Island *see* Isabela, Isla
Albemarle Sound 75 G1 *inlet* W Atlantic Ocean
Albergaria-a-Velha 124 B2 Aveiro, N Portugal
Albert 122 C3 Somme, N France
Alberta 69 E4 *province* SW Canada
Albert Edward Nyanza *see* Edward, Lake
Albert, Lake 105 B6 *var.* Albert Nyanza, Lac Mobutu Sese Seko. *Lake* Uganda/Congo (Zaire)
Albert Lea 77 F3 Minnesota, N USA
Albert Nyanza *see* Albert, Lake
Albi 123 C6 *anc.* Albiga. Tarn, S France
Ålborg 112 D3 *var.* Aalborg, Ålborg-Nørresundby; *anc.* Alburgum. Nordjylland, N Denmark
Ålborg-Nørresundby *see* Ålborg
Alborz, Reshteh-ye Kūhhā-ye 152 C2 *Eng.* Elburz Mountains. *Mountain range* N Iran
Albuquerque 80 D2 New Mexico, SW USA
Al Burayqah *see* Marsá al Burayqah
Alburgum *see* Ålborg
Albury 181 C7 New South Wales, SE Australia
Alcácer do Sal 124 B4 Setúbal, W Portugal
Alcalá de Henares 125 E3 *Ar.* Alkal'a; *anc.* Complutum. Madrid, C Spain
Alcamo 129 C7 Sicilia, Italy, C Mediterranean Sea
Alcañiz 125 F2 Aragón, NE Spain
Alcántara, Embalse de 124 C3 *reservoir* W Spain
Alcaudete 124 D4 Andalucía, S Spain
Alcázar *see* Ksar-el-Kebir
Alcoi *see* Alcoy
Alcoy 125 F4 *var.* Alcoi. País Valenciano, E Spain
Aldabra Group 111 G2 *island group* SW Seychelles
Aldan 147 F3 *river* NE Russian Federation
al Dar al Baida *see* Rabat
Alderney 122 A2 *island* Channel Islands
Aleg 106 C3 Brakna, SW Mauritania
Aleksandropol' *see* Gyumri
Aleksin 143 B5 Tul'skaya Oblast', W Russian Federation
Aleksinac 132 E4 Serbia, SE Yugoslavia
Alençon 122 B3 Orne, N France
Alenquer 95 E2 Pará, NE Brazil
Aleppo 144 *see* Ḥalab
Alert 69 F1 Ellesmere Island, Northwest Territories, N Canada
Alès 123 C6 *prev.* Alais. Gard, S France
Aleşd 140 B3 *Hung.* Élesd. Bihor, SW Romania
Alessandria 128 B2 *Fr.* Alexandrie. Piemonte, N Italy
Ålesund 117 A5 Møre og Romsdal, S Norway
Aleutian Basin 145 G3 *undersea feature* Bering Sea
Aleutian Islands 68 A3 *island group* Alaska, USA
Aleutian Range 66 A2 *mountain range* Alaska, USA
Aleutian Trench 145 H3 *undersea feature* S Bering Sea
Alexander Archipelago 68 D4 *island group* Alaska, USA
Alexander City 74 D2 Alabama, S USA
Alexander Island 186 A3 *island* Antarctica
Alexandra 183 B7 Otago, South Island, NZ
Alexándreia 136 B4 *var.* Alexándria. Kentrikí Makedonía, N Greece
Alexandria 104 B1 *Ar.* Al Iskandarīyah. N Egypt
Alexándria *see* Alexándreia
Alexandria 74 B3 Louisiana, S USA
Alexandria 77 F2 Minnesota, N USA
Alexandria 140 C5 Teleorman, S Romania
Alexandroúpoli 136 D3 *var.* Alexandroúpolis, *Turk.* Dedeagaç, Dedeagach. Anatolikí Makedonía kai Thráki, NE Greece
Alexandroúpolis *see* Alexandroúpoli

Al Fāshir see El Fasher
Alfatar 136 E1 Razgradska Oblast, NE Bulgaria
Alfeiós 137 B6 prev. Alfiós, anc. Alpheius, Alpheus. River S Greece
Alföld see Great Hungarian Plain
Alga 146 B4 Kaz. Algha. Aktyubinsk, NW Kazakhstan
Algarve 124 B4 cultural region S Portugal
Algeciras 124 C5 Andalucía, SW Spain
Algemesí 125 F3 País Valenciano, E Spain
Al-Genain see El Geneina
Alger 103 E1 var. Algiers, El Djazaïr, Al Jazair. Country capital (Algeria) N Algeria
Algeria 102 C3 off. Democratic and Popular Republic of Algeria. Country N Africa
Algerian Basin 112 C5 var. Balearic Plain undersea feature W Mediterranean Sea
Al Ghābah 153 E5 var. Ghaba. C Oman
Alghero 129 A5 Sardegna, Italy, C Mediterranean Sea
Al Ghurdaqah see Hurghada
Algiers see Alger
Al Golea see El Goléa
Algona 77 F3 Iowa, C USA
Al Ḩajār al Gharbī 153 D5 mountain range N Oman
Al Ḩasakah 150 D2 var. Al Hasijah, El Haseke, Fr. Hassetché. Al Ḩasakah, NE Syria
Al Hasijah see Al Ḩasakah
Al Ḩillah 152 B3 var. Hilla. C Iraq
Al Ḩisā 151 B7 Aţ Ţafīlah, W Jordan
Al Ḩudaydah 153 B6 Eng. Hodeida. W Yemen
Al Hufūf 152 C4 var. Hofuf. Ash Sharqīyah, NE Saudi Arabia
Aliákmonas 136 B4 prev. Aliákmon, anc. Haliacmon. River N Greece
Alíartos 137 C5 Stereá Ellás, C Greece
Alicante 125 F4 Cat. Alacant; Lat. Lucentum. País Valenciano, SE Spain
Alice 81 G5 Texas, SW USA
Alice Springs 180 A4 Northern Territory, C Australia
Aliki see Alykí
Alima 109 B6 river C Congo
Alindao 108 C4 Basse-Kotto, S Central African Republic
Aliquippa 72 D4 Pennsylvania, NE USA
Alistráti 136 C3 Kentrikí Makedonía, NE Greece
Alivéri 137 C5 var. Alivérion. Évvoia, C Greece
Alivérion see Alivéri
Al Jabal al Akhḑar 103 G2 mountain range NE Libya
Al Jabal ash Sharqī see Anti-Lebanon
Al Jafr 151 B7 Ma'ān, S Jordan
Al Jaghbūb 103 H3 NE Libya
Al Jahrā' 152 C4 var. Al Jahrah, Jahra. C Kuwait
Al Jahrah see Al Jahrā'
Al Jawf 152 B4 var. Jauf. Al Jawf, NW Saudi Arabia
Al Jazair see Alger
Al Jazīrah 150 E2 physical region Iraq/Syria
Al Jīzah see El Gîza
Al Junaynah see El Geneina
Al Karak 151 B7 var. El Kerak, Karak, Kerak; anc. Kir Moab, Kir of Moab. Al Karak, W Jordan
Al-Kasr al-Kebir see Ksar-el-Kebir
Al Khalīl see Hebron
Al Khārijah see El Khârga
Al Khufrah 103 H4 SE Libya
Al Khums 103 F2 var. Homs, Khoms, Khums. NW Libya
Alkmaar 118 C2 Noord-Holland, NW Netherlands
Al Kūt 152 C3 var. Kūt al 'Amārah, Kut al Imara. E Iraq
Al-Kuwait see Al Kuwayt
Al Kuwayt 152 C4 var. Al-Kuwait, Eng. Kuwait, Kuwait City; prev. Qurein. Country capital (Kuwait) E Kuwait
Al Lādhiqīyah 150 A3 Eng. Latakia, Fr. Lattaquié; anc. Laodicea, Laodicea ad Mare. Al Lādhiqīyah, W Syria
Allahābād 167 E3 Uttar Pradesh, N India
Allanmyo 168 B4 Magwe, C Myanmar
Allegheny Plateau 73 E3 mountain range New York/Pennsylvania, NE USA
Allentown 73 F4 Pennsylvania, NE USA
Alleppey 164 C3 var. Alappuzha; prev. Alleppi. Kerala, SW India
Alleppi see Alleppey
Alliance 76 D3 Nebraska, C USA
Al Līth 153 B5 Makkah, SW Saudi Arabia
Alma-Ata 144 see Almaty
Almada 124 B4 Setúbal, W Portugal
Al Madīnah 153 A5 Eng. Medina. Al Madīnah, W Saudi Arabia
Al Mafraq 151 B6 var. Mafraq. Al Mafraq, N Jordan
Al Mahdīyah see Mahdia
Al Mahrah 153 C6 mountain range E Yemen
Al Majma'ah 152 B4 Ar Riyāḑ, C Saudi Arabia
Al Mālikīyah 150 E1 Al Ḩasakah, NE Syria
Al Manāmah 152 C4 Eng. Manama. Country capital (Bahrain) N Bahrain
Al Manāşif 150 E3 mountain range E Syria
Almansa 125 F4 Castilla-La Mancha, C Spain
Al Marj 103 G2 var. Barka, It. Barce. NE Libya
Almaty 146 C5 var. Alma-Ata. Country capital (Kazakhstan) Almaty, SE Kazakhstan
Al Mawşil 152 B2 Eng. Mosul. N Iraq
Al Mayādīn 150 D3 var. Mayadin, Fr. Meyadine. Dayr az Zawr, E Syria
Al Mazra' see Al Mazra'ah
Al Mazra'ah 151 B6 var. Al Mazra', Mazra'a. Al Karak, W Jordan
Almelo 118 E3 Overijssel, E Netherlands
Almendra, Embalse de 124 C2 reservoir Castilla-León, NW Spain
Almendralejo 124 C4 Extremadura, W Spain
Almere 118 C3 var. Almere-stad. Flevoland, C Netherlands
Almere-stad see Almere
Almería 125 E5 Ar. Al-Mariyya; anc. Unci, Lat. Portus Magnus. Andalucía, S Spain
Al'met'yevsk 143 D5 Respublika Tatarstan, W Russian Federation
Al Mīnā' see El Mina
Al Minyā see El Minya
Almirante 85 E4 Bocas del Toro, NW Panama
Al Mudawwarah 151 B8 Ma'ān, SW Jordan
Al Mukallā 153 C6 var. Mukalla. SE Yemen
Al Obayyid see El Obeid
Alofi 177 F4 dependent territory capital (Niue) W Niue
Aloja 138 D3 Limbaži, N Latvia
Alónnisos 137 C5 island Vóreioi Sporádes, Greece, Aegean Sea
Álora 124 D5 Andalucía, S Spain
Alor, Kepulauan 171 E5 island group E Indonesia
Al Oued see El Oued
Alpen see Alps
Alpena 72 D2 Michigan, N USA
Alpes see Alps
Alpha Cordillera 188 B3 var. Alpha Ridge. Undersea feature Arctic Ocean
Alpha Ridge see Alpha Cordillera
Alphen see Alphen aan den Rijn
Alphen aan den Rijn 118 C3 var. Alphen. Zuid-Holland, C Netherlands
Alpi see Alps
Alpine 81 E4 Texas, SW USA
Alpi Transilvaniei see Carpaţii Meridionali
Alps 134 C1 Fr. Alpes, Ger. Alpen, It. Alpi. Mountain range C Europe
Al Qaḑārif see Gedaref
Al Qāmishlī 150 E1 var. Kamishli, Qamishly. Al Ḩasakah, NE Syria
Al Qaşrayn see Kasserine
Al Qayrawān see Kairouan
Al-Qsar see Ksar-el-Kebir
Al Qubayyāt see Qoubaïyât
Al Qunayţirah 151 B5 var. El Kuneitra, El Quneitra, Kuneitra, Qunaytra. Al Qunayţirah, SW Syria
Al Quşayr 150 B4 var. El Quseir, Quşayr, Fr. Kousseir. Ḩimş, W Syria
Al Quwayrah 151 B8 var. El Quweira. Ma'ān, SW Jordan
Alsace 122 E3 cultural region NE France
Alsdorf 126 A4 Nordrhein-Westfalen, W Germany
Alt see Olt
Alta 116 D2 Fin. Alattio. Finnmark, N Norway
Altai see Altai Mountains
Altai Mountains 158 C2 var. Altai, Chin. Altay Shan, Rus. Altay. Mountain range Asia/Europe
Altamaha River 75 E3 river Georgia, SE USA
Altamira 95 E2 Pará, NE Brazil
Altamura 129 E5 anc. Lupatia. Puglia, SE Italy
Altar, Desierto de 82 A1 var. Sonoran Desert. Desert Mexico/USA see also Sonoran Desert
Altay 158 C2 Chin. A-le-t'ai, Mong. Sharasume; prev. Ch'eng-hua, Chenghwa. Xinjiang Uygur Zizhiqu, NW China
Altay see Altai Mountains
Altay 158 D2 Govĭ-Altay, W Mongolia
Altay Shan see Altai Mountains
Altin Köprü 152 B3 var. Altun Kupri. N Iraq
Altiplano 93 F4 physical region W South America
Alton 72 B5 Illinois, N USA
Alton 72 B4 Missouri, C USA
Altoona 73 E4 Pennsylvania, NE USA
Alto Paraná see Paraná
Altun Kupri see Altin Köprü
Altun Shan 158 C3 var. Altyn Tagh. Mountain range NW China
Altus 81 F2 Oklahoma, C USA
Altyn Tagh see Altun Shan
Al Ubayyiḑ see El Obeid
Alūksne 138 D3 Ger. Marienburg. Alūksne, NE Latvia
Al 'Ulā 152 A4 Al Madīnah, NW Saudi Arabia
Al 'Umarī 151 C6 'Ammān, E Jordan
Alupka 141 F5 Respublika Krym, S Ukraine
Alushta 141 F5 Respublika Krym, S Ukraine
Al 'Uwaynāt 103 F4 var. Al Awaynāt. SW Libya
Alva 81 F1 Oklahoma, C USA
Alvarado 83 F4 Veracruz-Llave, E Mexico
Alvin 81 H4 Texas, SW USA
Al Wajh 152 A4 Tabūk, NW Saudi Arabia
Alwar 166 D3 Rājasthān, N India
Al Wari'ah 152 C4 Ash Sharqīyah, N Saudi Arabia
Alykí 136 C4 var. Aliki. Thásos, N Greece
Alytus 139 B5 Pol. Olita. Alytus, S Lithuania
Alzette 119 D8 river S Luxembourg
Amadeus, Lake 179 D5 seasonal lake Northern Territory, C Australia
Amadi 105 B5 Western Equatoria, SW Sudan
Amadjuak Lake 69 G3 lake Baffin Island, Northwest Territories, N Canada
Amakusa-nada 163 A7 gulf Kyūshū, SW Japan
Åmål 117 B6 Älvsborg, S Sweden
Amami-guntō 162 A3 island group SW Japan
Amami-Ō-shima 162 A3 island S Japan
Amantea 129 D6 Calabria, SW Italy
Amapá 95 E1 Amapá, NE Brazil
Amara see Al 'Amārah
Amarapura 168 B3 Mandalay, C Myanmar
Amarillo 81 E2 Texas, SW USA
Amay 119 C6 Liège, E Belgium
Amazon 95 E1 Sp. Amazonas. River Brazil/Peru
Amazon Basin 94 D2 basin N South America
Amazon, Mouths of the 95 F1 delta NE Brazil
Ambam 109 B5 Sud, S Cameroon
Ambanja 111 G2 Antsirañana, N Madagascar
Ambarchik 147 G2 Respublika Sakha (Yakutiya), NE Russian Federation
Ambato 92 B1 Tungurahua, C Ecuador
Ambérieu-en-Bugey 123 D5 Ain, E France
Amboasary 111 F4 Toliara, S Madagascar
Ambon 171 F4 prev. Amboina, Amboyna. Pulau Ambon, E Indonesia
Ambositra 111 G3 Fianarantsoa, SE Madagascar
Ambrim see Ambrym
Ambriz 110 A1 Bengo, NW Angola
Ambrym 176 D4 var. Ambrim. Island C Vanuatu
Amchitka Island 68 A2 island Aleutian Islands, Alaska, USA
Amdo 158 C5 Xizang Zizhiqu, W China
Ameland 118 D1 Fris. It Amelân. Island Waddeneilanden, N Netherlands
America-Antarctica Ridge 99 C7 undersea feature S Atlantic Ocean
American Falls Reservoir 78 E4 reservoir Idaho, NW USA
American Samoa 177 E4 US unincorporated territory W Polynesia
Amersfoort 118 D3 Utrecht, C Netherlands
Ames 77 F3 Iowa, C USA
Amfilochía 137 A5 var. Amfilokhía. Dytikí Ellás, C Greece
Amfilokhía see Amfilochía
Amga 147 F3 river NE Russian Federation
Amherst 71 F4 Nova Scotia, SE Canada
Amida see Diyarbakır
Amiens 122 C3 anc. Ambianum, Samarobriva. Somme, N France
Amíndaion see Amýntaio
Amindeo see Amýntaio
Amīndīvi Islands 164 A2 island group Lakshadweep, India, N Indian Ocean
Amirante Islands 111 G1 var. Amirantes Group. Island group C Seychelles
Amirantes Group see Amirante Islands
Amistad Reservoir 81 F4 var. Presa de la Amistad. Reservoir Mexico/USA
'Ammān 151 B6 var. Amman; anc. Philadelphia, Bibl. Rabbah Ammon, Rabbath Ammon. Country capital (Jordan) 'Ammān, NW Jordan
Amman 144 see 'Ammān
Ammassalik 114 D4 var. Angmagssalik. S Greenland
Ammóchostos 134 D5 var. Famagusta, Gazimağusa. E Cyprus
Āmol 152 D2 var. Amul. Māzandarān, N Iran
Amorgós 137 D6 island Kykládes, Greece, Aegean Sea
Amorgós 137 D6 Amorgós, Kykládes, Greece, Aegean Sea
Amos 70 D4 Québec, SE Canada
Amourj 106 D3 Hodh ech Chargui, SE Mauritania
Amoy see Xiamen
Ampato, Nevado 93 E4 mountain S Peru
Amposta 125 F2 Cataluña, NE Spain
Amrāvati 166 D4 prev. Amraoti. Mahārāshtra, C India
Amritsar 166 D2 Punjab, N India
Amstelveen 118 C3 Noord-Holland, C Netherlands
Amsterdam 118 C3 country capital (Netherlands) Noord-Holland, C Netherlands
Amsterdam Island 173 C6 island NE French Southern and Antarctic Territories
Am Timan 108 C3 Salamat, SE Chad
Amu Darya 154 D2 Rus. Amudar'ya, Taj. Dar"yoi Amu, Turkm. Amyderya, Uzb. Amudaryo; anc. Oxus. River C Asia
Amu-Dar'ya 155 E3 Lebapskiy Velayat, NE Turkmenistan
Amul see Āmol
Amund Ringnes Island 69 F2 island Northwest Territories, N Canada
Amundsen Basin see Fram Basin
Amundsen Gulf 69 E2 gulf Northwest Territories, N Canada
Amundsen Plain 186 A4 undersea feature S Pacific Ocean
Amundsen-Scott 186 B3 US research station Antarctica
Amundsen Sea 186 A4 sea S Pacific Ocean
Amuntai 170 D4 prev. Amoentai. Borneo, C Indonesia
Amur 147 G4 Chin. Heilong Jiang. River China/Russian Federation
Amvrosiyivka 141 H3 Rus. Amvrosiyevka. Donets'ka Oblast', SE Ukraine
Amýntaio 136 B4 var. Amindeo; prev. Amíndaion. Dytikí Makedonía, N Greece
Anabar 147 E2 river NE Russian Federation
An Abhainn Mhór see Blackwater
Anaco 91 E2 Anzoátegui, NE Venezuela
Anaconda 76 B2 Montana, NW USA
Anacortes 78 B1 Washington, NW USA
Anadolu Dağları see Doğu Karadeniz Dağları
Anadyr' 147 G1 river NE Russian Federation
Anadyr' 147 H1 Chukotskiy Avtonomnyy Okrug, NE Russian Federation
Anadyr, Gulf of 145 see Anadyrskiy Zaliv
Anadyrskiy Zaliv 147 H1 Eng. Gulf of Anadyr. Gulf NE Russian Federation
Anáfi 137 D7 anc. Anaphe. Island Kykládes, Greece, Aegean Sea
'Ānah see 'Annah
Anaheim 78 E2 California, W USA
Anaiza see 'Unayzah
Analalava 111 G2 Mahajanga, NW Madagascar
Anamur 148 C5 İçel, S Turkey
Anantapur 164 C2 Andhra Pradesh, S India
Anápolis 95 F3 Goiás, C Brazil
Anār 152 D3 Kermān, C Iran
Anatolia 148 C4 plateau C Turkey
Anatom 176 D5 var. Aneityum; prev. Kéamu. Island S Vanuatu
Añatuya 96 C3 Santiago del Estero, N Argentina
An Bhearú see Barrow
Anchorage 68 C3 Alaska, USA
Ancona 128 C3 Marche, C Italy
Ancud 97 B6 prev. San Carlos de Ancud. Los Lagos, S Chile
Åndalsnes 117 A5 Møre og Romsdal, S Norway
Andalucía 124 D4 cultural region S Spain
Andalusia 74 C3 Alabama, S USA
Andaman Islands 156 B4 island group India, NE Indian Ocean
Andaman Sea 156 C4 sea NE Indian Ocean
Andenne 119 C6 Namur, SE Belgium
Anderlues 119 B7 Hainaut, S Belgium
Anderson 72 C4 Indiana, N USA
Andes 96 B3 mountain range W South America
Andhra Pradesh 167 E5 state E India
Andijon 155 F2 Rus. Andizhan. Andijon Wiloyati, E Uzbekistan
Andikíthira see Antikýthira
Andipaxi see Antípaxoi
Andípsara see Antípsara
Ándissa see Ántissa
Andkhvoy 154 D3 Fāryāb, N Afghanistan
Andorra 123 A7 off. Principality of Andorra, Cat. Valls d'Andorra, Fr. Vallée d'Andorre. Country SW Europe
Andorra see Andorra la Vella
Andorra la Vella 123 A8 var. Andorra, Fr. Andorre la Vielle, Sp. Andorra la Vieja. Country capital (Andorra) C Andorra
Andorra la Vieja see Andorra la Vella
Andorre la Vielle see Andorra la Vella
Andover 121 D7 S England, UK
Andøya 116 C2 island C Norway
Andreanof Islands 68 A3 island group Aleutian Islands, Alaska, USA
Andrews 81 E3 Texas, SW USA
Andrew Tablemount 172 A4 var. Gora Andryu. Undersea feature W Indian Ocean
Andria 129 D5 Puglia, SE Italy
An Droichead Nua see Newbridge
Ándros 137 C6 island Kykládes, Greece, Aegean Sea
Ándros 137 D6 Ándros, Kykládes, Greece, Aegean Sea
Andros Island 86 B2 island NW Bahamas
Andros Town 86 C1 Andros Island, NW Bahamas
Aneityum see Anatom
Ānewetak see Enewetak Atoll
Angara 147 E4 river C Russian Federation
Angarsk 147 E4 Irkutskaya Oblast', S Russian Federation
Ånge 117 C5 Västernorrland, C Sweden
Ángel de la Guarda, Isla 82 B2 island NW Mexico
Angeles 171 E1 off. Angeles City. Luzon, N Philippines
Angel Falls see Ángel, Salto
Ángel, Salto 91 E3 Eng. Angel Falls. Waterfall E Venezuela
Ångermanälven 116 C4 river N Sweden
Angermünde 126 D3 Brandenburg, NE Germany
Angers 122 B4 anc. Juliomagus. Maine-et-Loire, NW France
Anglesey 121 C5 island NW Wales, UK
Anglet 123 A6 Pyrénées-Atlantiques, SW France
Angleton 81 H4 Texas, SW USA
Angmagssalik see Ammassalik
Ang Nam Ngum 168 C4 lake C Laos
Angola 110 B2 off. Republic of Angola; prev. People's Republic of Angola, Portuguese West Africa. Country SW Africa
Angola Basin 101 B5 undersea feature E Atlantic Ocean
Angostura, Presa de la 83 G5 reservoir SE Mexico
Angoulême 123 B5 anc. Iculisma. Charente, W France
Angoumois 123 B5 cultural region W France
Angren 155 F2 Toshkent Wiloyati, E Uzbekistan
Anguilla 87 G3 UK dependent territory E West Indies
Anguilla Cays 86 B2 islets SW Bahamas
Anhui 160 C5 var. Anhui Sheng, Anhwei, Wan. Admin. region province E China
Anhui Sheng see Anhui
Anhwei see Anhui
Anina 140 A4 Ger. Steierdorf, Hung. Stájerlakanina; prev. Ştaierdorf-Anina, Steierdorf-Anina, Steyerlak-Anina. Caraş-Severin, SW Romania
Anjou 122 B4 cultural region NW France
Anjouan 111 F2 var. Nzwani, Johanna Island. Island SE Comoros
Ankara 148 C3 prev. Angora, anc. Ancyra. Country capital (Turkey) Ankara, C Turkey
Ankeny 77 F3 Iowa, C USA
Anklam 126 D2 Mecklenburg-Vorpommern, NE Germany
Anykščiai 138 C4 Anykščiai, E Lithuania
An Longfort see Longford
An Mhuir Cheilteach see Celtic Sea
Annaba 103 E1 prev. Bône. NE Algeria
An Nafūd 152 B4 desert NW Saudi Arabia
'Annah 152 B3 var. 'Ānah. NW Iraq
An Najaf 152 B3 var. Najaf. S Iraq
Annamitique, Chaîne 168 D4 mountain range C Laos
Annapolis 73 F4 state capital Maryland, NE USA
Annapurna 167 E3 mountain C Nepal
An Nāqūrah see En Nâqoûra
Ann Arbor 72 C3 Michigan, N USA
An Nāşirīyah 152 C3 var. Nasiriya. SE Iraq
Annecy 123 D5 anc. Anneciacum. Haute-Savoie, E France
An Nīl al Azraq see Blue Nile
Anniston 74 D2 Alabama, S USA
Annotto Bay 86 B4 C Jamaica
An Ómaigh see Omagh
Anqing 160 D5 Anhui, E China
Anse La Raye 87 F1 NW Saint Lucia
Anshun 160 B6 Guizhou, S China
Ansongo 107 E3 Gao, E Mali
An Srath Bán see Strabane
Antakya 148 D4 anc. Antioch, Antiochia. Hatay, S Turkey
Antalaha 111 G2 Antsirañana, NE Madagascar
Antalya 148 B4 prev. Adalia, anc. Attaleia, Bibl. Attalia. Antalya, SW Turkey
Antalya, Gulf of see Antalya Körfezi
Antalya Körfezi 148 B4 var. Gulf of Adalia, Eng. Gulf of Antalya. Gulf SW Turkey
Antananarivo 111 G3 prev. Tananarive. Country capital (Madagascar) Antananarivo, C Madagascar
Antarctica 186 B3 continent
Antarctic Peninsula 186 A2 peninsula Antarctica
Antep see Gaziantep
Antequera 124 D5 anc. Anticaria, Antiquaria. Andalucía, S Spain
Antequera see Oaxaca
Antibes 123 D6 anc. Antipolis. Alpes-Maritimes, SE France
Anticosti, Île d' 71 F3 Eng. Anticosti Island. Island Québec, E Canada
Antigua 87 G3 island S Antigua and Barbuda, Leeward Islands
Antigua and Barbuda 87 G3 country E West Indies
Antikýthira 137 B7 var. Andikíthira. Island S Greece
Anti-Lebanon 150 B4 var. Jebel esh Sharqi, Ar. Al Jabal ash Sharqī, Fr. Anti-Liban. Mountain range Lebanon/Syria
Anti-Liban see Anti-Lebanon
Antípaxoi 137 A5 var. Andipaxi. Island Iónioi Nísoi, Greece, C Mediterranean Sea
Antipodes Islands 174 D5 island group S NZ
Antípsara 137 D5 var. Andípsara. Island E Greece
Ántissa 137 D5 var. Ándissa. Lésvos, E Greece
An tIúr see Newry
Antofagasta 96 B2 Antofagasta, N Chile
Antony 122 E2 Hauts-de-Seine, N France
Antserana see Antsirañana
An tSionainn see Shannon
Antsirañana 111 G2 var. Antserana; prev. Antsirane, Diégo-Suarez. Antsirañana, N Madagascar
Antsirane see Antsirañana
Antsohihy 111 G2 Mahajanga, NW Madagascar
An-tung see Dandong
Antwerp see Antwerpen
Antwerpen 119 C5 Eng. Antwerp, Fr. Anvers. Antwerpen, N Belgium
Anuradhapura 164 D3 North Central Province, C Sri Lanka
Anyang 160 C4 Henan, C China
A'nyêmaqên Shan 158 D4 mountain range C China
Anzio 129 C5 Lazio, C Italy
Aomori 162 D3 Aomori, Honshū, C Japan
Aóos see Vjosës, Lumi i
Aosta 128 A1 anc. Augusta Praetoria. Valle d'Aosta, NW Italy
Ao Thai see Thailand, Gulf of
Aoukâr 106 D3 var. Aouker. Plateau C Mauritania
Aouk, Bahr 108 C4 river Central African Republic/Chad
Aouker see Aoukâr
Aozou 108 C1 Borkou-Ennedi-Tibesti, N Chad
Apalachee Bay 74 D3 bay Florida, SE USA
Apalachicola River 74 D3 river Florida, SE USA
Apamama see Abemama
Apaporis, Río 90 C4 river Brazil/Colombia

Babuyan Channel 171 E1 channel N Philippines
Babuyan Island 171 E1 island N Philippines
Bacabal 95 F2 Maranhão, E Brazil
Bacău 140 C4 Hung. Bákó. Bacău, NE Romania
Băc Giang 168 D3 Ha Băc, N Vietnam
Bacheykava 139 D5 Rus. Bocheykovo. Vitsyebskaya Voblasts', N Belarus
Back 69 F3 river Northwest Territories, N Canada
Bačka Palanka 132 D3 prev. Palanka. Serbia, NW Yugoslavia
Bačka Topola 132 D3 Hung. Topolya; prev. Hung. Bácstopolya. Serbia, N Yugoslavia
Bac Liêu 169 D6 var. Vinh Loi. Minh Hai, S Vietnam
Bacolod 157 E4 off. Bacolod City. Negros, C Philippines
Bacolod City see Bacolod
Bácsszenttamás see Srbobran
Badajoz 124 C4 anc. Pax Augusta. Extremadura, W Spain
Baden-Baden 127 B6 anc. Aurelia Aquensis. Baden-Württemberg, SW Germany
Bad Freienwalde 126 D3 Brandenburg, NE Germany
Bad Hersfeld 126 B4 Hessen, C Germany
Bad Homburg see Bad Homburg vor der Höhe
Bad Homburg vor der Höhe 127 B5 var. Bad Homburg. Hessen, W Germany
Bá Dhún na nGall see Donegal Bay
Bad Ischl 127 D7 Oberösterreich, N Austria
Bad Krozingen 127 A6 Baden-Württemberg, SW Germany
Badlands 76 D2 physical region North Dakota, N USA
Badu Island 180 C1 island Queensland, NE Australia
Bad Vöslau 127 E6 Niederösterreich, NE Austria
Baetic Cordillera see Béticos, Sistemas
Baetic Mountains see Béticos, Sistemas
Bafatá 106 C4 C Guinea-Bissau
Baffin Bay 69 G2 bay Canada/Greenland
Baffin Island 69 G2 island Northwest Territories, NE Canada
Bafing 106 C3 headstream W Africa
Bafoussam 108 A4 Ouest, W Cameroon
Bafra 148 D2 Samsun, N Turkey
Bāft 152 D4 Kermān, S Iran
Bagaces 84 D4 Guanacaste, NW Costa Rica
Bagdad see Baghdād
Bagé 95 E5 Rio Grande do Sul, S Brazil
Baghdād 152 B3 var. Bagdad, Eng. Baghdad. Country capital (Iraq) C Iraq
Baghlān 155 E3 Baghlān, NE Afghanistan
Bago see Pegu
Bagoé 106 D4 river Ivory Coast/Mali
Bagrationovsk 138 A4 Ger. Preussisch Eylau. Kaliningradskaya Oblast', W Russian Federation
Bagrax Hu see Bosten Hu
Baguio 171 E1 off. Baguio City. Luzon, N Philippines
Bagzane, Monts 107 F3 mountain N Niger
Bahama Islands see Bahamas
Bahamas 86 C2 off. Commonwealth of the Bahamas. Country N West Indies
Bahamas 67 D6 var. Bahama Islands. Island group N West Indies
Bahāwalpur 166 C2 Punjab, E Pakistan
Bahía 95 F3 off. Estado da Bahia. State E Brazil
Bahía Blanca 97 C5 Buenos Aires, E Argentina
Bahía, Islas de la 84 C1 Eng. Bay Islands. Island group N Honduras
Bahir Dar 104 C4 var. Bahr Dar, Bahrdar Giyorgis. NW Ethiopia
Bahraich 167 E3 Uttar Pradesh, N India
Bahrain 152 C4 off. State of Bahrain, Dawlat al Bahrayn, Ar. Al Baḩrayn; prev. Bahrein, anc. Tylos or Tyros. Country SW Asia
Baḩr al Milḩ see Razāzah, Buḩayrat ar
Baḩrat Lūt see Dead Sea
Bahrat Tabariya see Tiberias, Lake
Bahr Dar see Bahir Dar
Bahrdar Giyorgis see Bahir Dar
Bahr el Azraq see Blue Nile
Bahr el Jebel see White Nile
Bahret Lut see Dead Sea
Bahr Tabariya, Sea of see Tiberias, Lake
Bahushewsk 139 E6 Rus. Bogushëvsk. Vitsyebskaya Voblasts', NE Belarus
Baia Mare 140 B3 Ger. Frauenbach, Hung. Nagybánya; prev. Neustadt. Maramureş, NW Romania
Baia Sprie 140 B3 Ger. Mittelstadt, Hung. Felsőbánya. Maramureş, NW Romania
Baïbokoum 108 B4 Logone-Oriental, SW Chad
Baidoa see Baydhabo
Baie-Comeau 71 E3 Québec, SE Canada
Baikal, Lake 184 see Baykal, Ozero
Baile Átha Luain see Athlone
Bailén 124 D4 Andalucía, S Spain
Baile na Mainistreach see Newtownabbey
Băileşti 140 B5 Dolj, SW Romania
Ba Illi 108 B3 Chari-Baguirmi, SW Chad
Bainbridge 74 D3 Georgia, SE USA
Bā'ir see Bāyir
Baireuth see Bayreuth
Bairiki 176 D2 country capital (Kiribati) Tarawa, NW Kiribati
Bairnsdale 181 C7 Victoria, SE Australia
Baishan 161 E3 prev. Hunjiang. Jilin, NE China
Baiyin 160 B4 Gansu, C China
Baja 131 C7 Bács-Kiskun, S Hungary
Baja California 80 A4 Eng. Lower California. Peninsula NW Mexico
Baja California 82 B2 state NW Mexico
Bajo Boquete see Boquete
Bajram Curri 133 D5 Kukës, N Albania
Bakala 108 C4 Ouaka, C Central African Republic
Bakan see Shimonoseki
Baker and Howland Islands 177 E2 US unincorporated territory W Polynesia
Baker Lake 69 F3 Northwest Territories, N Canada
Bakersfield 79 C7 California, W USA
Bakharden 154 C3 Turkm. Bäherden; prev. Bakherden. Akhalskiy Velayat, C Turkmenistan
Bakhchysaray 141 F5 Rus. Bakhchisaray. Respublika Krym, S Ukraine
Bakhmach 141 F1 Chernihivs'ka Oblast', N Ukraine
Bākhtarān 152 C3 prev. Kermānshāh, Qahremānshahr. Kermānshāhān, W Iran
Bakı 149 H2 Eng. Baku. Country capital (Azerbaijan) E Azerbaijan
Bakony 131 C7 Eng. Bakony Mountains, Ger. Bakonywald. Mountain range W Hungary
Baku 144 see Bakı
Balabac Island 161 C8 island W Philippines
Balabac Strait 170 D2 var. Selat Balabac. Strait Malaysia/Philippines
Ba'labakk see Baalbek
Balaguer 125 F2 Cataluña, NE Spain
Balakovo 143 C6 Saratovskaya Oblast', W Russian Federation
Bālā Morghāb 154 D4 Laghmān, NW Afghanistan
Balashov 143 B6 Saratovskaya Oblast', W Russian Federation
Balaton 131 C7 var. Lake Balaton, Ger. Plattensee. Lake W Hungary
Balaton, Lake see Balaton
Balbina, Represa 94 D1 reservoir NW Brazil
Balboa 85 G4 Panamá, C Panama
Balcarce 97 D5 Buenos Aires, E Argentina
Balclutha 183 B7 Otago, South Island, NZ
Baldy Mountain 76 C1 mountain Montana, NW USA
Bâle see Basel
Baleares, Islas 125 G3 Eng. Balearic Islands. Island group Spain, W Mediterranean Sea
Balearic Islands see Baleares, Islas
Balearic Plain see Algerian Basin
Baleine, Rivière à la 71 E2 river Québec, E Canada
Balen 119 C5 Antwerpen, N Belgium
Bāleshwar 167 F4 prev. Balasore. Orissa, E India
Bali 170 D5 island C Indonesia
Balıkesir 148 A3 Balıkesir, W Turkey
Balīkh, Nahr 150 C2 river N Syria
Balikpapan 170 D4 Borneo, C Indonesia
Balkan Mountains 136 C2 Bul./SCr. Stara Planina. Mountain range Bulgaria/Yugoslavia
Balkh 155 E3 anc. Bactra. Balkh, N Afghanistan
Balkhash 146 C5 Kaz. Balqash. Zhezkazgan, SE Kazakhstan
Balkhash, Lake 156 see Balkhash, Ozero
Balkhash, Ozero 146 C5 Eng. Lake Balkhash, Kaz. Balqash. Lake SE Kazakhstan
Balladonia 179 C6 Western Australia
Ballarat 181 C7 Victoria, SE Australia
Balleny Islands 186 B5 island group Antarctica
Ballinger 81 F3 Texas, SW USA
Balochistān see Baluchistān
Balş 140 B5 Olt, S Romania
Balsas 95 F2 Maranhão, E Brazil
Balsas, Río 83 E5 var. Río Mexcala. River S Mexico
Bal'shavik 139 D7 Rus. Bol'shevik. Homyel'skaya Voblasts', SE Belarus
Balta 140 D3 Odes'ka Oblast', SW Ukraine
Bălţi 140 D3 Rus. Bel'tsy. N Moldova
Baltic Sea 117 C7 Ger. Ostee, Rus. Baltiskoye More. Sea N Europe
Baltimore 73 F4 Maryland, NE USA
Baluchistān 166 B3 var. Balochistān, Beluchistan. Admin. region province SW Pakistan
Balvi 138 D4 Balvi, NE Latvia
Balykchy 155 G2 Kir. Ysyk-Köl; prev. Issyk-Kul', Rybach'ye. Issyk-Kul'skaya Oblast', NE Kyrgyzstan
Balzers 126 E2 S Liechtenstein
Bam 152 E4 Kermān, SE Iran
Bamako 106 D4 country capital (Mali) Capital District, SW Mali
Bambari 108 C4 Ouaka, C Central African Republic
Bamberg 127 C5 Bayern, SE Germany
Bamenda 108 A4 Nord-Ouest, W Cameroon
Banaba 176 D2 var. Ocean Island. Island Tungaru, W Kiribati
Bandaaceh 170 A3 var. Banda Atjeh; prev. Koetaradja, Kutaradja, Kutaraja. Sumatera, W Indonesia
Banda Atjeh see Bandaaceh
Bandama 106 D5 var. Bandama Fleuve. River S Ivory Coast
Bandama Fleuve see Bandama
Bandar 'Abbās see Bandar-e 'Abbās
Bandarbeyla 105 E5 var. Bender Beila, Bender Beyla. Bari, NE Somalia
Bandar-e 'Abbās 152 D4 var. Bandar 'Abbās; prev. Gombroon. Hormozgān, S Iran
Bandar-e Būshehr 152 C4 var. Būshehr, Eng. Bushire. Būshehr, S Iran
Bandar-e Khamīr 152 D4 Hormozgān, S Iran
Bandar-e Langeh 152 D4 var. Bandar-e Lengeh, Lingeh. Hormozgān, S Iran
Bandar-e Lengeh see Bandar-e Langeh
Bandar Kassim see Boosaaso
Bandarlampung 170 C4 prev. Tanjungkarang, Teloekbetoeng, Telukbetung. Sumatera, W Indonesia
Bandar Maharani see Muar
Bandar Masulipatnam see Machilīpatnam
Bandar Seri Begawan 170 D3 prev. Brunei Town. Country capital (Brunei) N Brunei
Bandar Sri Aman see Sri Aman
Banda Sea 171 F5 var. Laut Banda. Sea E Indonesia
Bandırma 148 A3 var. Penderma. Balıkesir, NW Turkey
Bandundu 109 C6 prev. Banningville. Bandundu, W Congo (Zaire)
Bandung 170 C5 prev. Bandoeng. Jawa, C Indonesia
Bangalore 164 C2 Karnātaka, S India
Bangassou 108 D4 Mbomou, SE Central African Republic
Banggai, Kepulauan 171 E4 island group C Indonesia
Banghāzī 103 G2 Eng. Bengazi, Benghazi, It. Bengasi. NE Libya
Bangka, Pulau 170 C4 island W Indonesia
Bangkok 156 see Krung Thep
Bangkok, Bight of see Krung Thep, Ao
Bangladesh 167 G3 off. People's Republic of Bangladesh; prev. East Pakistan. Country S Asia
Bangor 121 B5 Ir. Beannchar. E Northern Ireland, UK
Bangor 73 G2 Maine, NE USA
Bangor 121 C6 NW Wales, UK
Bangui 109 B5 country capital (Central African Republic) Ombella-Mpoko, SW Central African Republic
Bangweulu, Lake 105 B8 var. Lake Bengweulu. Lake N Zambia
Ban Hat Yai see Hat Yai
Ban Hin Heup 168 C4 Viangchan, C Laos
Ban Houayxay see Houayxay
Ban Houei Sai see Houayxay
Ban Hua Hin 169 C6 var. Hua Hin. Prachuap Khiri Khan, SW Thailand
Bani 106 D3 river S Mali
Banias see Bāniyās
Banī Suwayf see Beni Suef
Bāniyās 150 B3 var. Banias, Baniyas, Paneas. Tarţūs, W Syria
Baniyas see Bāniyās
Banja Luka 132 B3 NW Bosnia and Herzegovina
Banjarmasin 170 D4 prev. Bandjarmasin. Borneo, C Indonesia
Banjul 106 B3 prev. Bathurst. Country capital (Gambia) W Gambia
Banks Island 69 E2 island Banks Island, Northwest Territories, NW Canada
Banks Islands 176 D4 Fr. Îles Banks. Island group N Vanuatu
Banks Lake 78 B1 reservoir Washington, NW USA
Banks Peninsula 183 C6 peninsula South Island, NZ
Banks Strait 181 C8 strait SW Tasman Sea
Bānkura 167 F4 West Bengal, NE India
Ban Mak Khaeng see Udon Thani
Banmo see Bhamo
Bañolas see Banyoles
Ban Pak Phanang see Pak Phanang
Ban Sichon see Sichon
Banská Bystrica 131 C6 Ger. Neusohl, Hung. Besztercebánya. Stredné Slovensko, C Slovakia
Bantry Bay 121 A7 Ir. Bá Bheanntraí. Bay SW Ireland
Banya 136 E2 Burgaska Oblast, E Bulgaria
Banyak, Kepulauan 170 A3 prev. Kepulauan Banjak. Island group NW Indonesia
Banyo 108 B4 Adamaoua, NW Cameroon
Banyoles 125 G2 var. Bañolas. Cataluña, NE Spain
Banzare Seamounts 173 C7 undersea feature S Indian Ocean
Baoji 160 B4 var. Pao-chi, Paoki. Shaanxi, C China
Baoro 108 B4 Nana-Mambéré, W Central African Republic
Baoshan 160 A6 var. Pao-shan. Yunnan, SW China
Baotou 159 F3 var. Pao-t'ou, Paotow. Nei Mongol Zizhiqu, N China
Ba'qūbah 152 B3 var. Qubba. C Iraq
Baquerizo Moreno see Puerto Baquerizo Moreno
Bar 133 C5 It. Antivari. Montenegro, SW Yugoslavia
Baraawe 105 D6 It. Brava. Shabeellaha Hoose, S Somalia
Baraji, Hirfanli 148 C3 lake C Turkey
Bārāmati 166 C5 Mahārāshtra, W India
Baranavichy 139 B6 Pol. Baranowicze, Rus. Baranovichi. Brestskaya Voblasts', SW Belarus
Barbados 87 G1 country SE West Indies
Barbastro 125 F2 Aragón, NE Spain
Barbate de Franco 124 C5 Andalucía, S Spain
Barbuda 87 G3 island N Antigua and Barbuda
Barcaldine 180 C4 Queensland, E Australia
Barce see Al Marj
Barcelona 125 G2 anc. Barcino, Barcinona. Cataluña, E Spain
Barcelona 91 E2 Anzoátegui, NE Venezuela
Barcoo see Cooper Creek
Barcs 131 C7 Somogy, SW Hungary
Bardaï 108 C1 Borkou-Ennedi-Tibesti, N Chad
Bardejov 131 D5 Ger. Bartfeld, Hung. Bártfa. Východné Slovensko, NE Slovakia
Bardera see Baardheere
Bardere see Baardheere
Bareilly 167 E3 var. Bareli. Uttar Pradesh, N India
Bareli see Bareilly
Barendrecht 118 C4 Zuid-Holland, SW Netherlands
Barentin 122 C3 Seine-Maritime, N France
Barentsberg 115 G2 Spitsbergen, W Svalbard
Barentsøya 115 G2 island E Svalbard
Barents Sea 142 C2 Nor. Barents Havet, Rus. Barentsevo More. Sea Arctic Ocean
Barents Trough 113 E1 undersea feature SW Barents Sea
Bar Harbor 73 H2 Mount Desert Island, Maine, NE USA
Bari 129 E5 var. Bari delle Puglie; anc. Barium. Puglia, SE Italy
Bāridah see Al Bāridah
Bari delle Puglie see Bari
Barikot see Barīkowţ
Barīkowţ 155 F4 var. Barikot. Kunar, NE Afghanistan
Barillas 84 A2 var. Santa Cruz Barillas. Huehuetenango, NW Guatemala
Barinas 90 C2 Barinas, W Venezuela
Barisal 167 G4 Khulna, S Bangladesh
Barisan, Pegunungan 170 B4 mountain range Sumatera, W Indonesia
Barito, Sungai 170 D4 river Borneo, C Indonesia
Barium see Bari
Barka see Al Marj
Barkly Tableland 180 B3 plateau Northern Territory/Queensland, N Australia
Bârlad 140 D4 prev. Bîrlad. Vaslui, E Romania
Barlavento, Ilhas de 106 A2 var. Windward Islands. Island group N Cape Verde
Bar-le-Duc 122 D3 var. Bar-sur-Ornain. Meuse, NE France
Barlee, Lake 179 B6 lake Western Australia
Barlee Range 178 A4 mountain range Western Australia
Barletta 129 D5 anc. Barduli. Puglia, SE Italy
Barlinek 130 B3 Ger. Berlinchen. Gorzów, W Poland
Barmouth 121 C6 NW Wales, UK
Barnaul 146 D4 Altayskiy Kray, C Russian Federation
Barnet 121 A7 SE England, UK
Barnstaple 121 C7 SW England, UK
Baroghil Pass 155 F3 var. Kowtal-e Barowghīl. Pass Afghanistan/Pakistan
Baron'ki 139 E7 Rus. Boron'ki. Mahilyowskaya Voblasts', E Belarus
Barquisimeto 90 C2 Lara, NW Venezuela
Barra 120 B3 island NW Scotland, UK
Barra de Río Grande 85 E3 Región Autónoma Atlántico Sur, E Nicaragua
Barragem de Sobradinho see Sobradinho, Represa de
Barranca 92 C3 Lima, W Peru
Barrancabermeja 90 B2 Santander, N Colombia
Barranquilla 90 B1 Atlántico, N Colombia
Barreiro 124 B4 Setúbal, W Portugal
Barrier Range 181 C6 hill range New South Wales, SE Australia
Barrow 121 B6 Ir. An Bhearú. River SE Ireland
Barrow 68 D2 Alaska, USA
Barrow-in-Furness 121 C5 NW England, UK
Barrow Island 178 A4 island Western Australia
Barstow 79 C7 California, W USA
Bar-sur-Ornain see Bar-le-Duc
Bartang 155 F3 river SE Tajikistan
Bartica 91 F3 N Guyana
Bartın 148 C2 Zonguldak, N Turkey
Bartlesville 81 G1 Oklahoma, C USA
Bartoszyce 130 D2 Ger. Bartenstein. Olsztyn, N Poland
Baruun-Urt 159 F2 Sühbaatar, E Mongolia
Barú, Volcán 85 E5 var. Volcán de Chiriquí. Volcano W Panama
Barwon River 181 D5 river New South Wales, SE Australia
Barysaw 139 D6 Rus. Borisov. Minskaya Voblasts', NE Belarus
Basarabeasca 140 D4 Rus. Bessarabka. SE Moldova
Basel 127 A7 Eng. Basle, Fr. Bâle. Basel-Stadt, NW Switzerland
Basilan 171 E3 island SW Philippines
Basle see Basel
Basra 144 see Al Başrah
Bassano del Grappa 128 C2 Veneto, NE Italy
Bassein 168 A4 var. Pathein. Irrawaddy, SW Myanmar
Basse-Terre 87 G4 dependent territory capital (Guadeloupe) Basse Terre, SW Guadeloupe
Basse Terre 87 G4 island W Guadeloupe
Basseterre 87 G3 country capital (Saint Kitts and Nevis) Saint Kitts, Saint Kitts and Nevis
Bassikounou 106 D3 Hodh ech Chargui, SE Mauritania
Bass Strait 181 C7 strait SE Australia
Bassum 126 B3 Niedersachsen, NW Germany
Bastia 123 E7 Corse, France, C Mediterranean Sea
Bastogne 119 D7 Luxembourg, SE Belgium
Bastrop 74 B2 Louisiana, S USA
Bastyn' 139 B7 Rus. Bostyn'. Brestskaya Voblasts', SW Belarus
Basuo see Dongfang
Bata 109 A5 NW Equatorial Guinea
Batabanó, Golfo de 86 A2 gulf W Cuba
Batajnica 132 D3 Serbia, N Yugoslavia
Batangas 171 E2 off. Batangas City. Luzon, N Philippines
Bătdâmbâng 169 C5 prev. Battambang. Bătdâmbâng, NW Cambodia
Batéké, Plateaux 109 B6 plateau S Congo
Bath 121 D7 hist. Akermanceaster, anc. Aquae Calidae, Aquae Solis. SW England, UK
Bathinda 166 D2 Punjab, NW India
Bathsheba 87 G1 E Barbados
Bathurst 71 F4 New Brunswick, SE Canada
Bathurst 181 D6 New South Wales, SE Australia
Bathurst Island 178 D2 island Northern Territory, N Australia
Bathurst Island 69 F2 island Parry Islands, Northwest Territories, N Canada
Bāţin, Wādī al 152 C4 dry watercourse SW Asia
Batman 149 E4 var. Iluh. Batman, SE Turkey
Batna 103 E2 NE Algeria
Baton Rouge 74 B3 state capital Louisiana, S USA
Batroûn 150 A4 var. Al Batrūn. N Lebanon
Batticaloa 164 D3 Eastern Province, E Sri Lanka
Battipaglia 129 D5 Campania, S Italy
Bat'umi 149 F2 W Georgia
Batu Pahat 170 B3 prev. Bandar Penggaram. Johor, Peninsular Malaysia
Bauchi 107 G4 Bauchi, NE Nigeria
Bauer Basin 185 F3 undersea feature E Pacific Ocean
Bauska 138 C3 Ger. Bauske. Bauska, S Latvia
Bautzen 126 D4 Lus. Budyšin. Sachsen, E Germany
Bavarian Alps 127 C7 Ger. Bayrische Alpen. Mountain range Austria/Germany
Bavispe, Río 82 C2 river NW Mexico
Bawîti 104 B2 N Egypt
Bawku 107 E4 N Ghana
Bayamo 86 C3 Granma, E Cuba
Bayan Har Shan 158 D4 var. Bayan Khar. Mountain range C China
Bayanhongor 158 D2 Bayanhongor, C Mongolia
Bayan Khar see Bayan Har Shan
Bayano, Lago 85 G4 lake E Panama
Bay City 72 C3 Michigan, N USA
Bay City 81 G4 Texas, SW USA
Baydhabo 105 D6 var. Baydhowa, Isha Baydhabo, It. Baidoa. Bay, SW Somalia
Baydhowa see Baydhabo
Bayern 127 C6 cultural region SE Germany
Bayeux 122 B3 anc. Augustodurum. Calvados, N France
Bāyir 151 C7 var. Bā'ir. Ma'ān, S Jordan
Baykal, Ozero 147 E4 Eng. Lake Baikal. Lake S Russian Federation
Baymak 143 D6 Respublika Bashkortostan, W Russian Federation
Bayonne 123 A6 anc. Lapurdum. Pyrénées-Atlantiques, SW France
Bayramaly 154 D3 prev. Bayram-Ali. Maryyskiy Velayat, S Turkmenistan
Bayreuth 127 C5 var. Baireuth. Bayern, SE Germany
Bayrūt see Beyrouth
Baytown 81 H4 Texas, SW USA
Baza 125 E4 Andalucía, S Spain
Beagle Channel 97 C8 channel Argentina/Chile
Béal Feirste see Belfast
Beannchar see Bangor
Bear Lake 78 E4 lake Idaho/Utah, NW USA
Beas de Segura 125 E4 Andalucía, S Spain
Beata, Isla 87 E3 island SW Dominican Republic
Beatrice 77 F4 Nebraska, C USA
Beaufort Sea 68 D2 sea Arctic Ocean
Beaufort West 110 C5 Afr. Beaufort-Wes. Western Cape, SW South Africa
Beaumont 81 H3 Texas, SW USA
Beaune 122 D4 Côte d'Or, C France
Beauvais 122 C3 anc. Bellovacum, Caesaromagus. Oise, N France
Beaver Island 72 C2 island Michigan, N USA
Beaver Lake 81 H1 reservoir Arkansas, C USA
Beaver River 81 F1 river Oklahoma, C USA
Beāwar 166 C3 Rājasthān, N India
Bečej 132 D3 Ger. Altbetsche, Hung. Óbecse, Rácz-Becse; prev. Magyar-Becse, Stari Bečej. Serbia, N Yugoslavia
Béchar 102 D2 prev. Colomb-Béchar. W Algeria
Beckley 72 D5 West Virginia, NE USA
Bedford 121 D6 E England, UK
Bedum 118 E1 Groningen, NE Netherlands

INDEX

Coatzacoalcos 83 G4 var. Quetzalcoalco; prev. Puerto México. Veracruz-Llave, E Mexico
Cobán 84 B2 Alta Verapaz, C Guatemala
Cobar 181 C6 New South Wales, SE Australia
Cobija 93 E3 Pando, NW Bolivia
Coburg 127 C5 Bayern, SE Germany
Coca see Puerto Francisco de Orellana
Cochabamba 93 F4 hist. Oropeza. Cochabamba, C Bolivia
Cochin 164 C3 var. Kochi. Kerala, SW India
Cochinos, Bahía de 86 B2 Eng. Bay of Pigs. Bay SE Cuba
Cochrane 97 B7 Aisén, S Chile
Cochrane 70 C4 Ontario, S Canada
Cocibolca see Nicaragua, Lago de
Cockburn Town 87 E2 var. Grand Turk. dependent territory capital (Turks and Caicos Islands) Grand Turk Island, SE Turks and Caicos Islands
Cockpit Country, The 86 A4 physical region W Jamaica
Cocobeach 109 A5 Estuaire, NW Gabon
Coconino Plateau 80 B1 plain Arizona, SW USA
Coco, Río 85 E2 var. Río Wanki, Segoviao Wangkí. River Honduras / Nicaragua
Cocos Basin 156 C5 undersea feature E Indian Ocean
Cocos Island Ridge see Cocos Ridge
Cocos Islands 173 D5 island group E Indian Ocean
Cocos Ridge 67 C8 var. Cocos Island Ridge. Undersea feature E Pacific Ocean
Cod, Cape 73 G3 headland Massachusetts, NE USA
Codfish Island 183 A8 island SW NZ
Codlea 140 C4 Ger. Zeiden, Hung. Feketehalom. Braşov, C Romania
Cody 76 C2 Wyoming, C USA
Coeur d'Alene 78 C2 Idaho, NW USA
Coevorden 118 E2 Drenthe, NE Netherlands
Coffs Harbour 181 E6 New South Wales, SE Australia
Cognac 123 B5 anc. Compniacum. Charente, W France
Coiba, Isla de 85 E5 island SW Panama
Coihaique 97 B6 var. Coyhaique. Aisén, S Chile
Coimbatore 164 C3 Tamil Nādu, S India
Coimbra 124 B3 anc. Conimbria, Conimbriga. Coimbra, W Portugal
Coín 124 D5 Andalucía, S Spain
Coirib, Loch see Corrib, Lough
Colby 77 E4 Kansas, C USA
Colchester 121 E6 hist. Colneceaste, anc. Camulodunum. E England, UK
Col du Brenner see Brenner Pass
Coleman 81 F3 Texas, SW USA
Coleraine 120 B4 Ir. Cúil Raithin. N Northern Ireland, UK
Colesberg 110 C5 Northern Cape, C South Africa
Colima 82 D4 Colima, S Mexico
Coll 120 B3 island W Scotland, UK
College Station 81 G3 Texas, SW USA
Collie 179 A7 Western Australia
Colmar 122 E4 Ger. Kolmar. Haut-Rhin, NE France
Cöln see Köln
Cologne see Köln
Colombia 90 B3 off. Republic of Colombia. Country N South America
Colombian Basin 88 A1 undersea feature SW Caribbean Sea
Colombo 164 C4 country capital (Sri Lanka) Western Province, W Sri Lanka
Colón 85 G4 prev. Aspinwall. Colón, C Panama
Colonia Agrippina see Köln
Colón Ridge 67 B8 undersea feature E Pacific Ocean
Colorado 76 C4 off. State of Colorado; also known as Centennial State, Silver State. State C USA
Colorado City 81 F3 Texas, SW USA
Colorado Plateau 80 B1 plateau W USA
Colorado, Río 97 C5 river E Argentina
Colorado, Río see Colorado River
Colorado River 67 B5 var. Río Colorado. River Mexico / USA
Colorado River 81 G4 river Texas, SW USA
Colorado Springs 76 D5 Colorado, C USA
Columbia 78 B3 river Canada / USA
Columbia 75 E2 state capital South Carolina, SE USA
Columbia 73 E4 Maryland, NE USA
Columbia 77 G4 Missouri, C USA
Columbia 74 C1 Tennessee, S USA
Columbia Plateau 78 C3 plateau Idaho / Oregon, NW USA
Columbus 72 D4 state capital Ohio, N USA
Columbus 74 D2 Georgia, SE USA
Columbus 72 C4 Indiana, N USA
Columbus 74 C2 Mississippi, S USA
Columbus 77 F4 Nebraska, C USA
Colville Channel 182 D2 channel North Island, NZ
Colville River 68 D2 river Alaska, USA
Comacchio 128 C3 var. Commachio; anc. Comactium. Emilia-Romagna, N Italy
Comactium see Comacchio
Comalcalco 83 G4 Tabasco, SE Mexico
Coma Pedrosa, Pic de 123 A7 mountain NW Andorra
Comarapa 93 F4 Santa Cruz, C Bolivia
Comayagua 84 C2 Comayagua, W Honduras
Comer See see Como, Lago di
Comilla 167 G4 Ben. Kumillā. Chittagong, E Bangladesh
Comino 134 A5 Malt. Kemmuna. Island C Malta
Comitán 83 G5 var. Comitán de Domínguez. Chiapas, SE Mexico
Comitán de Domínguez see Comitán
Commachio see Comacchio
Commissioner's Point 74 A5 headland W Bermuda
Communism Peak see Kommunizm, Qullai
Como 128 B2 anc. Comum. Lombardia, N Italy
Comodoro Rivadavia 97 B6 Chubut, SE Argentina
Como, Lago di 128 B2 var. Lario, Eng. Lake Como, Ger. Comer See. Lake N Italy
Como, Lake see Como, Lago di
Comoros 111 F2 off. Federal Islamic Republic of the Comoros, Fr. République Fédérale Islamique des Comores. Country W Indian Ocean
Compiègne 122 C3 Oise, N France
Compostella see Santiago
Comrat 140 D4 Rus. Komrat. S Moldova
Conakry 106 C4 country capital (Guinea) Conakry, SW Guinea
Concarneau 122 A3 Finistère, NW France
Concepción 96 D2 var. Villa Concepción. Concepción, C Paraguay
Concepción see La Concepción
Concepción 97 B5 Bío Bío, C Chile
Concepción 93 G3 Santa Cruz, E Bolivia
Concepción de la Vega see La Vega
Conchos, Río 82 D2 river C Mexico
Conchos, Río 80 D4 river NW Mexico
Concord 73 G3 state capital New Hampshire, NE USA
Concordia 96 D4 Entre Ríos, E Argentina
Concordia 77 E4 Kansas, C USA
Côn Đao 169 E7 var. Con Son. Island S Vietnam
Condate see Cosne-Cours-sur-Loire
Condega 84 D3 Estelí, NW Nicaragua
Congo 109 D5 off. Republic of the Congo, Fr. Moyen-Congo; prev. Middle Congo. Country C Africa
Congo 109 C6 off. Republic of Zaire; prev. Belgian Congo, Congo (Kinshasa). Country C Africa
Congo 109 C6 var. Kongo, Fr. Zaire. River C Africa
Congo Basin 109 C6 drainage basin W Congo (Zaire)
Connacht see Connaught
Connaught 121 A5 var. Connacht, Ir. Chonnacht, Cúige. Cultural region W Ireland
Connecticut 73 F3 off. State of Connecticut; also known as Blue Law State, Constitution State, Land of Steady Habits, Nutmeg State. State NE USA
Connecticut 73 G3 river Canada / USA
Conroe 81 G3 Texas, SW USA
Consolación del Sur 86 A2 Pinar del Río, W Cuba
Con Son see Côn Đao
Constance see Konstanz
Constance, Lake 127 B7 Ger. Bodensee. Lake C Europe
Constanţa 140 D5 var. Küstendje, Eng. Constanza, Ger. Konstanza, Turk. Küstence. Constanţa, SE Romania
Constantia see Konstanz
Constantine 103 E2 var. Qacentina, Ar. Qoussantîna. NE Algeria
Constantinople see İstanbul
Constanz see Konstanz
Constanza see Constanţa
Coober Pedy 181 A5 South Australia
Cookeville 74 D1 Tennessee, S USA
Cook Islands 177 F4 territory in free association with NZ S Pacific Ocean
Cook, Mount 183 B6 prev. Aoraki, Aorangi. Mountain South Island, NZ
Cook Strait 183 D5 var. Raukawa. Strait NZ
Cooktown 180 D2 Queensland, NE Australia
Coolgardie 179 B6 Western Australia
Cooma 181 D7 New South Wales, SE Australia
Coon Rapids 77 F2 Minnesota, N USA
Cooper Creek 180 C4 var. Barcoo, Cooper's Creek. Seasonal river Queensland / South Australia
Cooper's Creek see Cooper Creek
Coos Bay 78 A3 Oregon, NW USA
Cootamundra 181 D6 New South Wales, SE Australia
Copacabana 93 E4 La Paz, W Bolivia
Copenhagen see København
Copiapó 96 B3 Atacama, N Chile
Copperas Cove 81 G3 Texas, SW USA
Coppermine 69 E3 var. Qurlurtuuq. Northwest Territories, NW Canada
Coquimbo 96 B3 Coquimbo, N Chile
Corabia 140 B5 Olt, S Romania
Coral Harbour 69 G3 Southampton Island, Northwest Territories, NE Canada
Coral Sea 174 B3 sea SW Pacific Ocean
Coral Sea Islands 176 B4 Australian external territory SW Pacific Ocean
Corantijn Rivier see Courantyne River
Corcaigh see Cork
Corcovado, Golfo 97 B6 gulf S Chile
Cordele 74 D3 Georgia, SE USA
Cordillera Ibérica see Ibérico, Sistema
Cordoba see Córdoba
Córdoba 124 D4 var. Cordoba, Eng. Cordova; anc. Corduba. Andalucía, SW Spain
Córdoba 96 C3 Córdoba, C Argentina
Córdoba 83 F4 Veracruz-Llave, E Mexico
Cordova see Córdoba
Cordova 68 C3 Alaska, USA
Corduba see Córdoba
Corentyne River see Courantyne River
Corfu see Kérkyra
Coria 124 C3 Extremadura, W Spain
Corinth see Kórinthos
Corinth 74 C1 Mississippi, S USA
Corinth, Gulf of see Korinthiakós Kólpos
Corinthiacus Sinus see Korinthiakós Kólpos
Corinto 84 C3 Chinandega, NW Nicaragua
Cork 121 A6 Ir. Corcaigh. S Ireland
Çorlu 148 A2 Tekirdağ, NW Turkey
Corner Brook 71 G3 Newfoundland, Newfoundland and Labrador, E Canada
Corn Islands see Maíz, Islas del
Cornwallis Island 69 F2 island Northwest Territories, N Canada
Coro 90 C1 prev. Santa Ana de Coro. Falcón, NW Venezuela
Corocoro 93 F4 La Paz, W Bolivia
Coromandel 182 D2 Waikato, North Island, NZ
Coromandel Coast 164 D2 coast E India
Coromandel Peninsula 182 D2 peninsula North Island, NZ
Coronado, Bahía de 84 D5 bay S Costa Rica
Coronel Dorrego 97 C5 Buenos Aires, E Argentina
Coronel Oviedo 96 D2 Caaguazú, SE Paraguay
Corozal 84 C1 Corozal, N Belize
Corpus Christi 81 G4 Texas, SW USA
Corrales 80 D2 New Mexico, SW USA
Corrib, Lough 121 A5 Ir. Loch Coirib. Lake W Ireland
Corrientes 96 D3 Corrientes, NE Argentina
Corriza see Korçë
Corse 123 E7 Eng. Corsica. Island France, C Mediterranean Sea
Corsica see Corse
Corsicana 81 G3 Texas, SW USA
Cortegana 124 C4 Andalucía, S Spain
Cortés 85 E5 var. Ciudad Cortés. Puntarenas, SE Costa Rica
Cortina d'Ampezzo 128 C1 Veneto, NE Italy
Coruche 124 B3 Santarém, C Portugal
Çoruh Nehri 149 E3 Geor. Chorokhi, Rus. Chorokh. River Georgia / Turkey
Çorum 148 D3 var. Chorum. Çorum, N Turkey
Corunna see A Coruña
Corvallis 78 B3 Oregon, NW USA
Corvo 124 A5 var. Ilha do Corvo. Island Azores, Portugal, NE Atlantic Ocean
Cosenza 129 D6 anc. Consentia. Calabria, SW Italy
Cosne-Cours-sur-Loire 122 C4 var. Cosne-sur-Loire; anc. Condate. Nièvre, C France
Cosne-sur-Loire see Cosne-Cours-sur-Loire
Costa Mesa 78 D2 California, W USA
Costa Rica 85 E4 off. Republic of Costa Rica. Country Central America
Cotagaita 93 F5 Potosí, S Bolivia
Côte d'Or 122 D4 cultural region C France
Cotonou 107 F5 var. Kotonu. S Benin
Cotrone see Crotone
Cotswold Hills 121 D6 var. Cotswolds. Hill range S England, UK
Cotswolds see Cotswold Hills
Cottbus 126 D4 prev. Kottbus. Brandenburg, E Germany
Council Bluffs 77 F4 Iowa, C USA
Courantyne River 91 G4 var. Corantijn Rivier, Corentyne River. River Guyana / Suriname
Courland Lagoon 138 A4 Ger. Kurisches Haff, Rus. Kurskiy Zaliv. Lagoon Lithuania / Russian Federation
Coutances 122 B3 anc. Constantia. Manche, N France
Couvin 119 C7 Namur, S Belgium
Coventry 121 D6 anc. Couentrey. C England, UK
Covilhã 124 C3 Castelo Branco, E Portugal
Cowan, Lake 179 B6 lake Western Australia
Coxen Hole see Roatán
Coxin Hole see Roatán
Coyhaique see Coihaique
Cozumel, Isla 83 H3 island SE Mexico
Cradock 110 C5 Eastern Cape, S South Africa
Craig 76 C4 Colorado, C USA
Craiova 140 B5 Dolj, SW Romania
Cranbrook 69 E5 British Columbia, SW Canada
Crane see The Crane
Crawley 121 E7 SE England, UK
Cremona 128 B2 Lombardia, N Italy
Cres 132 A3 It. Cherso; anc. Crexa. Island W Croatia
Crescent City 78 A4 California, W USA
Crescent Group 160 C7 island group C Paracel Islands
Creston 77 F4 Iowa, C USA
Crestview 74 D3 Florida, SE USA
Crete see Kríti
Créteil 122 E2 Val-de-Marne, N France
Crete, Sea of see Kritikó Pélagos
Creuse 122 B4 river C France
Crewe 121 D6 C England, UK
Crikvenica 132 A3 It. Cirquenizza; prev. Cirkvenica, Crjkvenica. Primorje-Gorski Kotar, NW Croatia
Crimea 113 F4 var. Krym, Eng. Crimea, Crimean Oblast; prev. Rus. Krymskaya ASSR, Krymskaya Oblast'. Admin. region province SE Ukraine
Crimean Oblast see Crimea
Cristóbal 85 G4 Colón, C Panama
Cristóbal Colón, Pico 90 B1 mountain N Colombia
Cristuru Secuiesc 140 C4 prev. Cristur, Cristuru Săcuiesc, Sitaş Cristuru, Ger. Kreutz, Hung. Székelykeresztúr, Szitás-Keresztúr. Harghita, C Romania
Crna Reka 133 D6 river S FYR Macedonia
Croatia 132 B3 off. Republic of Croatia, Ger. Kroatien, SCr. Hrvatska. Country SE Europe
Crocodile see Limpopo
Croia see Krujë
Croker Island 178 E2 island Northern Territory, N Australia
Cromwell 183 B7 Otago, South Island, NZ
Crooked Island 86 D2 island SE Bahamas
Crooked Island Passage 86 D2 channel SE Bahamas
Crookston 77 F1 Minnesota, N USA
Croton see Crotone
Crotona see Crotone
Crotone 129 E6 var. Cotrone; anc. Croton, Crotona. Calabria, SW Italy
Croydon 121 A8 SE England, UK
Crozet Basin 173 B6 undersea feature S Indian Ocean
Crozet Islands 173 B7 island group French Southern and Antarctic Territories
Crozet Plateau 173 B7 var. Crozet Plateaus. Undersea feature SW Indian Ocean
Crozet Plateaus see Crozet Plateau
Crystal Brook 181 B6 South Australia
Csorna 131 C6 Győr-Moson-Sopron, NW Hungary
Csurgó 131 C7 Somogy, SW Hungary
Cuando 110 C2 var. Kwando. River S Africa
Cuango 110 B1 var. Kwango. River Angola / Congo (Zaire) see also Kwango
Cuan na Gaillimhe see Galway Bay
Cuanza 110 B1 var. Kwanza. River C Angola
Cuauhtémoc 82 C2 Chihuahua, N Mexico
Cuautla 83 E4 Morelos, S Mexico
Cuba 86 B2 off. Republic of Cuba. Country W West Indies
Cubal 110 B2 Benguela, W Angola
Cubango 110 B2 var. Kavango, Kavengo, Kubango, Okavango, Okavanggo. River S Africa see also Okavango
Cubango 110 B2 var. Kuvango, Port. Vila Artur de Paiva, Vila da Ponte. Huíla, SW Angola
Cúcuta 90 C2 var. San José de Cúcuta. Norte de Santander, N Colombia
Cuddapah 164 C2 Andhra Pradesh, S India
Cuenca 125 E3 anc. Conca. Castilla-La Mancha, C Spain
Cuenca 92 B2 Azuay, S Ecuador
Cuernavaca 83 E4 Morelos, S Mexico
Cuiabá 95 E3 prev. Cuyabá. State capital Mato Grosso, SW Brazil
Cúige see Connaught
Cúige Laighean see Leinster
Cúige Mumhan see Munster
Cuijck 118 D4 Noord-Brabant, SE Netherlands
Cúil Raithin see Coleraine
Cuito 110 B2 var. Kwito. River SE Angola
Cukai 170 B3 var. Chukai, Kemaman. Terengganu, Peninsular Malaysia
Culiacán 82 C3 var. Culiacán Rosales, Culiacán-Rosales. Sinaloa, C Mexico
Culiacán-Rosales see Culiacán
Cullera 125 F3 País Valenciano, E Spain
Cullman 74 C2 Alabama, S USA
Culpepper Island see Darwin, Isla
Cumaná 91 E1 Sucre, NE Venezuela
Cumbal, Nevada de 90 A4 mountain SW Colombia
Cumberland 73 E4 Maryland, NE USA
Cumberland Plateau 74 D1 plateau E USA
Cumberland Sound 69 H3 inlet Baffin Island, Northwest Territories, NE Canada
Cumpas 82 B2 Sonora, NW Mexico
Cunene 101 C6 var. Kunene. River Angola / Namibia see also Kunene
Cunene 110 A3 province S Angola
Cuneo 128 A2 Fr. Coni. Piemonte, NW Italy
Cunnamulla 181 C5 Queensland, E Australia
Ćuprija 132 E4 Serbia, E Yugoslavia
Curaçao 87 E5 island Netherlands Antilles
Curicó 96 B4 Maule, C Chile
Curitiba 95 E4 prev. Curytiba. State capital Paraná, S Brazil
Curtea de Argeş 140 C4 var. Curtea-de-Arges. Argeş, S Romania
Curtea-de-Arges see Curtea de Argeş
Curtici 140 A4 Ger. Kurtitsch, Hung. Kürtös. Arad, W Romania
Curtis Island 180 E4 island Queensland, SE Australia
Cusco 93 E4 var. Cuzco. Cusco, C Peru
Cusset 123 C5 Allier, C France
Cutch, Gulf of see Kachchh, Gulf of
Cuttack 167 F4 Orissa, E India
Cuvier Plateau 173 E6 undersea feature E Indian Ocean
Cuxhaven 126 B2 Niedersachsen, NW Germany
Cuyuni, Río see Cuyuni River
Cuyuni River 91 F3 var. Río Cuyuni. River Guyana / Venezuela
Cuzco see Cusco
Cyclades see Kykládes
Cydonia see Chaniá
Cymru see Wales
Cyprus 134 C4 off. Republic of Cyprus, Gk. Kypros, Turk. Kıbrıs, Kıbrıs Cumhuriyeti. Country E Mediterranean Sea
Cythera see Kýthira
Cythnos see Kýthnos
Czech Republic 131 A5 Cz. Česká Republika. Country C Europe
Częstochowa 130 C4 Ger. Czenstochau, Tschenstochau, Rus. Chenstokhov. Częstochowa, S Poland
Człuchów 130 C3 Ger. Schlochau. Słupsk, NW Poland

D

Dabajuro 90 C1 Falcón, NW Venezuela
Dabeiba 90 B2 Antioquia, NW Colombia
Dąbrowa Tarnowska 131 D5 Tarnów, SE Poland
Dabryn' 139 C8 Rus. Dobryn'. Homyel'skaya Voblasts', SE Belarus
Dagana 106 B3 N Senegal
Dagda 138 D4 Krāslava, SE Latvia
Dagenham 121 B8 SE England, UK
Dağliq Qarabağ see Nagornyy Karabakh
Dagupan 171 E1 off. Dagupan City. Luzon, N Philippines
Da Hinggan Ling 159 G1 Eng. Great Khingan Range. Mountain range NE China
Dahm, Ramlat 153 B6 desert NW Yemen
Daimiel 124 D3 Castilla-La Mancha, C Spain
Daimoniá 137 B7 Pelopónnisos, S Greece
Dairen see Dalian
Dakar 106 B3 country capital (Senegal) W Senegal
Dakhla see Ad Dakhla
Dakoro 107 G3 Maradi, S Niger
Đakovica 133 D5 var. Djakovica, Alb. Gjakovë. Serbia, S Yugoslavia
Đakovo 132 C3 var. Djakovo, Hung. Diakovár. Osijek-Baranja, E Croatia
Dalai see Hulun Nur
Dalain Hob see Ejin Qi
Dalaman 148 A4 Muğla, SW Turkey
Dalandzadgad 159 E3 Ömnögovĭ, S Mongolia
Đa Lat 169 E6 Lâm Đông, S Vietnam
Dalby 181 D5 Queensland, E Australia
Dale City 73 E4 Virginia, NE USA
Dalhart 81 E1 Texas, SW USA
Dali 160 A6 var. Xiaguan. Yunnan, SW China
Dalian 160 D4 var. Dairen, Dalien, Lüda, Ta-lien, Rus. Dalny. Liaoning, NE China
Dalien see Dalian
Dallas 81 G2 Texas, SW USA
Dalmacija 132 B4 Eng. Dalmatia, Ger. Dalmatien, It. Dalmazia. Cultural region S Croatia
Dalny see Dalian
Dalton 74 D1 Georgia, SE USA
Daly Waters 180 A2 Northern Territory, N Australia
Damachava 139 A6 var. Damachova, Pol. Domaczewo, Rus. Domachëvo. Brestskaya Voblasts', SW Belarus
Damachova see Damachava
Damān 166 C4 Damān and Diu, W India
Damara 108 C4 Ombella-Mpoko, S Central African Republic
Damas see Dimashq
Damasco see Dimashq
Damascus 144 see Dimashq
Damāvand, Qolleh-ye 152 D3 mountain N Iran
Dammām see Ad Dammān
Damoûr 151 A5 var. Ad Dāmūr. W Lebanon
Dampier 178 A4 Western Australia
Dampier, Selat 171 F4 strait Irian Jaya, E Indonesia
Damqawt 153 D6 var. Damqut. E Yemen
Damqut see Damqawt
Damxung 158 C5 Xizang Zizhiqu, W China
Danakil Desert 104 D4 var. Afar Depression, Danakil Plain. Desert E Africa
Danakil Plain see Danakil Desert
Danané 106 D5 W Ivory Coast
Đă Năng 169 E5 prev. Tourane. Quang Nam-Đa Năng, C Vietnam
Danborg see Daneborg
Dandong 160 D3 var. Tan-tung; prev. An-tung. Liaoning, NE China
Daneborg 115 E3 var. Danborg. N Greenland
Dänew see Deynau
Dangerous Archipelago see Tuamotu, Îles
Danghara 155 E3 Rus. Dangara. SW Tajikistan
Danghe Nanshan 158 D3 mountain range W China
Dangla see Tanggula Shan
Dângrêk, Chuŏr Phnum 169 D5 var. Phanom Dang Raek, Phanom Dong Rak, Fr. Chaîne des Dangrek. Mountain range Cambodia / Thailand
Dangriga 84 C1 prev. Stann Creek. Stann Creek, E Belize
Danish West Indies see Virgin Islands (US)
Danlí 84 D2 El Paraíso, S Honduras
Danmarksstraedet see Denmark Strait
Dannenberg 126 C3 Niedersachsen, N Germany
Dannevirke 182 D4 Manawatu-Wanganui, North Island, NZ
Danube 113 E4 Bul. Dunav, Cz. Dunaj, Ger. Donau, Hung. Duna, Rom. Dunărea. River C Europe
Danville 73 E5 Virginia, NE USA
Dan Xian see Danxian
Danxian 160 C7 var. Dan Xian, Nada. Hainan, S China

Danziger Bucht see Danzig, Gulf of
Danzig, Gulf of 130 C2 var. Gulf of Gdańsk, Ger. Danziger Bucht, Pol. Zakota Gdańska, Rus. Gdan'skaya Bukhta. Gulf N Poland
Daqm see Duqm
Dar'ā 151 B5 var. Der'a, Fr. Déraa. Dar'ā, SW Syria
Darabani 140 C3 Botoşani, NW Romania
Daraut-Kurgan see Daroot-Korgon
Dardanelli see Çanakkale
Dar es Salaam 105 C7 Dar es Salaam, E Tanzania
Darfield 183 C6 Canterbury, South Island, NZ
Darfur 104 A4 var. Darfur Massif. Cultural region W Sudan
Darfur Massif see Darfur
Darhan 159 E2 Selenge, N Mongolia
Darien, Gulf of 90 A2 Sp. Golfo del Darién. Gulf S Caribbean Sea
Darién, Serranía del 85 H5 mountain range Colombia/Panama
Dario see Ciudad Darío
Darjeeling see Darjiling
Darjiling 167 F3 prev. Darjeeling. West Bengal, NE India
Darling River 181 C6 river New South Wales, SE Australia
Darlington 121 D5 N England, UK
Darmstadt 127 B5 Hessen, SW Germany
Darnah 103 G2 var. Dérna. NE Libya
Darnley, Cape 186 D2 headland Antarctica
Daroca 125 E2 Aragón, NE Spain
Daroot-Korgon 155 F3 var. Daraut-Kurgan. Oshskaya Oblast', SW Kyrgyzstan
Dartford 121 B8 SE England, UK
Dartmoor 121 C7 moorland SW England, UK
Dartmouth 71 F4 Nova Scotia, SE Canada
Darvaza 154 C2 Turkm. Derweze. Akhalskiy Velayat, C Turkmenistan
Darwin 178 D2 prev. Palmerston, Port Darwin. Territory capital Northern Territory, N Australia
Darwin, Isla 92 A4 var. Culpepper Island. Island W Ecuador
Daryācheh-ye Hāmūn see Şāberī, Hāmūn-e
Daryācheh-ye Sīstān see Şāberī, Hāmūn-e
Daryā-ye Morghāb see Murgab
Daryā-ye Pāmīr see Pamir
Daryoi Pomir see Pamir
Dashkawka 139 D6 Rus. Dashkovka. Mahilyowskaya Voblasts', E Belarus
Dashkhovuz 154 C2 Turkm. Dashhowuz; prev. Tashauz. Dashkhovuzskiy Velayat, N Turkmenistan
Datong 160 C3 var. Tatung, Ta-t'ung. Shanxi, C China
Daugavpils 138 D4 Ger. Dünaburg; prev. Rus. Dvinsk. Municipality Daugvapils, SE Latvia
Daung Kyun 169 B6 island S Myanmar
Dauphiné 123 D5 cultural region E France
Dāvangere 164 C2 Karnātaka, W India
Davao 171 F3 off. Davao City. Mindanao, S Philippines
Davao Gulf 171 F3 gulf Mindanao, S Philippines
Davenport 77 G3 Iowa, C USA
David 85 E5 Chiriquí, W Panama
Davie Ridge 173 A5 undersea feature W Indian Ocean
Davis 186 D3 Australian research station Antarctica
Davis Sea 186 D3 sea Antarctica
Davis Strait 114 B3 strait Baffin Bay/Labrador Sea
Dawei see Tavoy
Dax 123 B6 var. Ax; anc. Aquae Augustae, Aquae Tarbelicae. Landes, SW France
Dayr az Zawr 150 D3 var. Deir ez Zor. Dayr az Zawr, E Syria
Dayton 72 C4 Ohio, N USA
Daytona Beach 75 E4 Florida, SE USA
De Aar 110 C5 Northern Cape, C South Africa
Dead Sea 151 B6 var. Bahret Lut, Lacus Asphaltites, Ar. Al Baḥr al Mayyit, Baḥrat Lūt, Heb. Yam HaMelaḥ. Salt lake Israel/Jordan
Dealnu see Tana
Deán Funes 96 C3 Córdoba, C Argentina
Death Valley 79 C7 valley California, W USA
Debar 133 D6 Ger. Dibra, Turk. Debre. W FYR Macedonia
De Bildt see De Bilt
De Bilt 118 C3 var. De Bildt. Utrecht, C Netherlands
Debrecen 131 D6 Ger. Debreczin, Rom. Debreţin; prev. Debreczen. Hajdú-Bihar, E Hungary
Decatur 74 C1 Alabama, S USA
Decatur 72 B4 Illinois, N USA
Deccan 166 D5 Hind. Dakshin. Plateau C India
Děčín 130 B4 Ger. Tetschen. Severní Čechy, NW Czech Republic
Dedeagaç see Alexandroúpoli
Dedeagach see Alexandroúpoli
Dedemsvaart 118 E3 Overijssel, E Netherlands
Dee 120 C3 river NE Scotland, UK
Deering 68 C2 Alaska, USA
Deggendorf 127 D6 Bayern, SE Germany
Değirmenlik 134 C5 N Cyprus
Deh Bīd 152 D3 Fārs, C Iran
Dehli see Delhi
Deh Shū 154 D5 var. Deshu. Helmand, S Afghanistan
Deinze 119 B5 Oost-Vlaanderen, NW Belgium
Deir ez Zor see Dayr az Zawr
Deirgeirt, Loch see Derg, Lough
Dej 140 B3 Hung. Dés; prev. Deés. Cluj, NW Romania
Dékoa 108 C4 Kémo, C Central African Republic
De Land 75 E4 Florida, SE USA
Delano 79 C7 California, W USA
Delārām 154 D5 Farāh, SW Afghanistan
Delaware 73 F4 off. State of Delaware; also known as Blue Hen State, Diamond State, First State. State NE USA
Delaware 72 D4 Ohio, N USA
Delft 118 B4 Zuid-Holland, W Netherlands
Delfzijl 118 E1 Groningen, NE Netherlands
Delgo 104 B3 Northern, N Sudan
Delhi 166 D3 var. Dehli, Hind. Dilli; hist. Shahjahanabad. Delhi, N India
Delicias 82 D2 var. Ciudad Delicias. Chihuahua, N Mexico
Déli-Kárpátok see Carpaţii Meridionali
Delmenhorst 126 B3 Niedersachsen, NW Germany
Del Rio 81 F4 Texas, SW USA
Deltona 75 E4 Florida, SE USA
Demba 109 D6 Kasai Occidental, C Congo (Zaire)
Dembia 108 D4 Mbomou, SE Central African Republic
Demchok 156 var. Dêmqog. Disputed region China/India see also Dêmqog
Demchok 158 A4 var. Dêmqog. China/India see also Dêmqog
Demerara Plain 88 C2 undersea feature W Atlantic Ocean
Deming 80 C3 New Mexico, SW USA
Demmin 126 C2 Mecklenburg-Vorpommern, NE Germany
Demopolis 74 C2 Alabama, S USA
Dêmqog 155 var. Demchok. Disputed region China/India see also Demchok
Denali see McKinley, Mount
Dender 119 B6 Fr. Dendre. River W Belgium
Denekamp 118 E3 Overijssel, E Netherlands
Den Haag see 's-Gravenhage
Den Ham 118 E3 Overijssel, E Netherlands
Denham 179 A5 Western Australia
Den Helder 118 C2 Noord-Holland, NW Netherlands
Denia 125 F4 País Valenciano, E Spain
Deniliquin 181 C7 New South Wales, SE Australia
Denison 77 F3 Iowa, C USA
Denison 81 G2 Texas, SW USA
Denizli 148 B4 Denizli, SW Turkey
Denmark 117 A7 off. Kingdom of Denmark, Dan. Danmark; anc. Hafnia. Country N Europe
Denmark Strait 114 D4 var. Danmarksstraedet. Strait Greenland/Iceland
Dennery 87 F1 E Saint Lucia
Denow 155 E3 Rus. Denau. Surkhondaryo Wiloyati, S Uzbekistan
Denpasar 170 D5 prev. Paloe. Bali, C Indonesia
Denton 81 G2 Texas, SW USA
D'Entrecasteaux Islands 176 B3 island group SE PNG
Denver 76 D4 state capital Colorado, C USA
Der'a see Dar'ā
Déraa see Dar'ā
Dera Ghāzi Khān 166 C2 var. Dera Ghāzikhān. Punjab, C Pakistan
Dera Ghāzikhān see Dera Ghāzi Khān
Đeravica 133 D5 mountain S Yugoslavia
Derbent 143 B8 Respublika Dagestan, SW Russian Federation
Derby 121 D6 C England, UK
Dereli see Gónnoi
Derg, Lough 121 A6 Ir. Loch Deirgeirt. Lake W Ireland
Derhachi 141 G2 Rus. Dergachi. Kharkivs'ka Oblast', E Ukraine
De Ridder 74 A3 Louisiana, S USA
Dérna see Darnah
Derry see Londonderry
Derventa 132 B3 N Bosnia and Herzegovina
Deschutes River 78 B3 river Oregon, NW USA
Desē 104 C4 var. Desse, It. Dessie. N Ethiopia
Deseado, Río 97 B7 river S Argentina
Desertas, Ilhas 102 A2 island group Madeira, Portugal, NE Atlantic Ocean
Deshu see Deh Shū
Desierto de Altar see Sonoran Desert
Des Moines 77 F3 state capital Iowa, C USA
Desna 141 E2 river Russian Federation/Ukraine
Dessau 126 C4 Sachsen-Anhalt, E Germany
Desse see Desē
Dessie see Desē
Detroit 72 D3 Michigan, N USA
Detroit Lakes 77 F2 Minnesota, N USA
Deurne 119 D5 Noord-Brabant, SE Netherlands
Deva 140 B4 Ger. Diemrich, Hung. Déva. Hunedoara, W Romania
Đevđelija see Gevgelija
Deventer 118 D3 Overijssel, E Netherlands
Devils Lake 77 E1 North Dakota, N USA
Devoll see Devollit, Lumi i
Devollit, Lumi i 133 D6 var. Devoll. River SE Albania
Devon Island 69 F2 prev. North Devon Island. Island Parry Islands, Northwest Territories, NE Canada
Devonport 181 C8 Tasmania, SE Australia
Devrek 148 C2 Zonguldak, N Turkey
Dexter 77 H5 Missouri, C USA
Deynau 154 D3 var. Dyanev, Turkm. Dänew. Lebapskiy Velayat, NE Turkmenistan
Dezfūl 152 C3 var. Dizful. Khūzestān, SW Iran
Dezhou 160 D4 Shandong, E China
Dhaka 167 G4 prev. Dacca. Country capital (Bangladesh) Dhaka, C Bangladesh
Dhanbād 167 F4 Bihār, NE India
Dhekélia 134 C5 Eng. Dhekelia. Gk. Dekéleia. UK air base SE Cyprus
Dhidhimótikhon see Didymóteicho
Dhíkti Ori see Díkti
Dhodhekánisos see Dodekánisos
Dhomokós see Domokós
Dhráma see Dráma
Dhuusa Marreeb 105 E5 var. Dusa Marreb, It. Dusa Mareb. Galguduud, C Somalia
Diakovár see Đakovo
Diamantina, Chapada 95 F3 mountain range E Brazil
Diamantina Fracture Zone 173 E6 tectonic feature E Indian Ocean
Diarbekr see Diyarbakır
Dibrugarh 167 H3 Assam, NE India
Dickinson 76 D2 North Dakota, N USA
Didimotiho see Didymóteicho
Didymóteicho 136 D3 var. Dhidhimótikhon, Didimotiho. Anatolikí Makedonía kai Thráki, NE Greece
Diégo-Suarez see Antsiranana
Diekirch 119 D7 Diekirch, C Luxembourg
Điên Biên 168 D3 var. Bien Bien, Dien Bien Phu. Lai Châu, N Vietnam
Dien Bien Phu see Điên Biên
Diepenbeek 119 D6 Limburg, NE Belgium
Diepholz 126 B3 Niedersachsen, NW Germany
Dieppe 122 C2 Seine-Maritime, N France
Dieren 118 D4 Gelderland, E Netherlands
Differdange 119 D8 Luxembourg, SW Luxembourg
Digne 123 D6 var. Digne-les-Bains. Alpes-de-Haute-Provence, SE France
Digne-les-Bains see Digne
Digoin 122 C4 Saône-et-Loire, C France
Digul, Sungai 171 H5 prev. Digoel. River Irian Jaya, E Indonesia
Dihang see Brahmaputra
Dijon 122 D4 anc. Dibio. Côte d'Or, C France
Dikhil 104 D4 SW Djibouti
Dikson 146 D2 Taymyrskiy (Dolgano-Nenetskiy) Avtonomnyy Okrug, N Russian Federation
Díkti 137 D8 var. Dhíkti Ori. Mountain range Kríti, Greece, E Mediterranean Sea
Dili 171 F5 var. Dilli, Dilly. Timor, C Indonesia
Dilia 107 G3 var. Dillia. River SE Niger
Di Linh 169 E6 Lâm Đông, S Vietnam
Dilli see Delhi
Dilli see Dili
Dillia see Dilia
Dilling 104 B4 var. Ad Dalanj. Southern Kordofan, C Sudan
Dillon 76 B2 Montana, NW USA
Dilly see Dili
Dilolo 109 D7 Ngounié, S Gabon
Dimashq 151 B5 var. Ash Shām, Esh Sham, Eng. Damascus, Fr. Damas, It. Damasco. Country capital (Syria) Dimashq, SW Syria
Dimitrovgrad 136 D3 Khaskovska Oblast, S Bulgaria
Dimitrovgrad 143 C6 Ul'yanovskaya Oblast', W Russian Federation
Dimovo 136 B1 Oblast Montana, NW Bulgaria
Dinajpur 167 F3 Rajshahi, NW Bangladesh
Dinan 122 B3 Côtes d'Armor, NW France
Dinant 119 C7 Namur, S Belgium
Dinar 148 B4 Afyon, SW Turkey
Dinara see Dinaric Alps
Dinaric Alps 132 C4 var. Dinara. Mountain range Bosnia and Herzegovina/Croatia
Dindigul 164 C3 Tamil Nādu, SE India
Dingle Bay 121 A6 Ir. Bá an Daingin. Bay SW Ireland
Dinguiraye 106 C4 Haute-Guinée, N Guinea
Diourbel 106 B3 W Senegal
Dirē Dawa 105 D5 E Ethiopia
Dirk Hartog Island 179 A5 island Western Australia
Disappointment, Lake 178 C4 salt lake Western Australia
Dispur 167 G3 Assam, NE India
Divinópolis 95 F4 Minas Gerais, SE Brazil
Divo 106 D5 S Ivory Coast
Diyarbakır 149 E4 var. Diarbekr; anc. Amida. Dıyarbakır, SE Turkey
Dizful see Dezfūl
Djajapura see Jayapura
Djakovica see Đakovica
Djakovo see Đakovo
Djambala 109 B6 Plateaux, C Congo
Djambi see Jambi
Djanet 103 E4 prev. Fort Charlet. SE Algeria
Djéblé see Jablah
Djelfa 102 D2 var. El Djelfa. N Algeria
Djéma 108 D4 Haut-Mbomou, E Central African Republic
Djérablous see Jarābulus
Djerba see Jerba, Île de
Djérem 108 B4 river C Cameroon
Djevdjelija see Gevgelija
Djibouti 104 D4 off. Republic of Djibouti, var. Jibuti; prev. French Somaliland, French Territory of the Afars and Issas, Fr. Côte Française des Somalis, Territoire Français des Afars et des Issas. Country E Africa
Djibouti 104 D4 var. Jibuti. Country capital (Djibouti) E Djibouti
Djourab, Erg du 108 C2 dunes N Chad
Djúpivogur 115 E5 Austurland, SE Iceland
Dnieper 113 F4 Bel. Dnyapro, Rus. Dnepr, Ukr. Dnipro. River E Europe
Dnieper Lowland 141 E2 Bel. Prydnyaprowskaya Nizina, Ukr. Prydniprovs'ka Nyzovyna. Lowlands Belarus/Ukraine
Dniester 113 E4 Rom. Nistru, Rus. Dnestr, Ukr. Dnister; anc. Tyras. River Moldova/Ukraine
Dnipro see Dnieper
Dniprodzerzhyns'k 141 F3 Rus. Dneprodzerzhinsk; prev. Kamenskoye. Dnipropetrovs'ka Oblast', E Ukraine
Dniprodzerzhyns'ke Vodoskhovyshche 141 F3 Rus. Dneprodzerzhinskoye Vodokhranilishche. Reservoir C Ukraine
Dnipropetrovs'k 141 F3 Rus. Dnepropetrovsk; prev. Yekaterinoslav. Dnipropetrovs'ka Oblast', E Ukraine
Dniprorudne 141 F3 Rus. Dneprorudnoye. Zaporiz'ka Oblast', SE Ukraine
Doba 108 C4 Logone-Oriental, S Chad
Döbeln 126 D4 Sachsen, E Germany
Doberai, Jazirah 171 G4 Dut. Vogelkop. Peninsula Irian Jaya, E Indonesia
Doboj 132 C3 N Bosnia and Herzegovina
Dobre Miasto 130 D2 Ger. Guttstadt. Olsztyn, N Poland
Dobrich 136 E1 Rom. Bazargic; prev. Tolbukhin. Varnenska Oblast, NE Bulgaria
Dobrush 139 D7 Homyel'skaya Voblasts', SE Belarus
Dodecánese see Dodekánisos
Dodekánisos 137 D6 var. Nóties Sporádes, Eng. Dodecanese; prev. Dhodhekánisos. Island group SE Greece
Dodge City 77 E5 Kansas, C USA
Dodoma 101 D5 country capital (Tanzania) Dodoma, C Tanzania
Dodoma 105 C7 region C Tanzania
Dogana 128 E1 NE San Marino
Dōgo 163 B6 island Oki-shotō, SW Japan
Dogondoutchi 107 F3 Dosso, SW Niger
Doğubayazıt 149 F3 Ağrı, E Turkey
Doğu Karadeniz Dağları 149 E3 var. Anadolu Dağları. Mountain range NE Turkey
Doha 144 see Ad Dawḥah
Doire see Londonderry
Dokkum 118 D1 Friesland, N Netherlands
Dokuchayevs'k 141 G3 var. Dokuchayevsk. Donets'ka Oblast', SE Ukraine
Dokuchayevsk see Dokuchayevs'k
Doldrums Fracture Zone 98 C4 tectonic feature W Atlantic Ocean
Dôle 122 D4 Jura, E France
Dolisie 109 B6 prev. Loubomo. Le Niari, S Congo
Dolomites see Dolomitiche, Alpi
Dolomiti see Dolomitiche, Alpi
Dolomitiche, Alpi 128 C1 var. Dolomiti, Eng. Dolomites. Mountain range NE Italy
Dolores 96 D4 Buenos Aires, E Argentina
Dolores 84 B1 Petén, N Guatemala
Dolores 96 D4 Soriano, SW Uruguay
Dolores Hidalgo 83 E4 var. Ciudad de Dolores Hidalgo. Guanajuato, C Mexico
Dolyna 140 B2 Rus. Dolina. Ivano-Frankivs'ka Oblast', W Ukraine
Dolyns'ka 141 F3 Rus. Dolinskaya. Kirovohrads'ka Oblast', S Ukraine
Domachëvo see Damachava
Domaczewo see Damachava
Dombås 117 B5 Oppland, S Norway
Domel Island see Letsôk-aw Kyun
Domeyko 96 B3 Atacama, N Chile
Dominica 87 H4 off. Commonwealth of Dominica. Country E West Indies
Dominica Channel see Martinique Passage
Dominican Republic 87 E2 country C West Indies
Domokós 137 B5 var. Dhomokós. Stereá Ellás, C Greece
Don 143 B6 var. Duna, Tanais. River SW Russian Federation
Donau see Danube
Donauwörth 127 C6 Bayern, S Germany
Don Benito 124 C3 Extremadura, W Spain
Doncaster 121 D5 anc. Danum. N England, UK
Dondo 110 B1 Cuanza Norte, NW Angola
Donegal 121 B5 Ir. Dún na nGall. NW Ireland
Donegal Bay 121 A5 Ir. Bá Dhún na nGall. Bay NW Ireland
Donets 141 G2 river Russian Federation/Ukraine
Donets'k 141 G3 Rus. Donetsk; prev. Stalino. Donets'ka Oblast', E Ukraine
Dongfang 160 B7 var. Basuo. Hainan, S China
Dongguan 160 C6 Guangdong, S China
Đông Ha 168 E4 Quang Tri, C Vietnam
Đông Hơi 168 D4 Quang Binh, C Vietnam
Dongliao see Liaoyuan
Dongola 104 B3 var. Donqola, Dunqulah. Northern, N Sudan
Dongou 109 C5 La Likouala, NE Congo
Dongting Hu 160 C5 var. Tung-t'ing Hu. Lake S China
Donostia-San Sebastián 125 E1 País Vasco, N Spain
Donqola see Dongola
Doolow 105 D5 SE Ethiopia
Doornik see Tournai
Door Peninsula 72 C2 peninsula Wisconsin, N USA
Dooxo Nugaaleed 105 E5 var. Nogal Valley. Valley E Somalia
Dordogne 123 B5 cultural region SW France
Dordogne 123 B5 river W France
Dordrecht 118 C4 var. Dordt, Dort. Zuid-Holland, SW Netherlands
Dordt see Dordrecht
Dorohoi 140 C3 Botoşani, NE Romania
Dorotea 116 C4 Västerbotten, N Sweden
Dorre Island 179 A5 island Western Australia
Dort see Dordrecht
Dortmund 126 A4 Nordrhein-Westfalen, W Germany
Dos Hermanas 124 C4 Andalucía, S Spain
Dospad Dagh see Rhodope Mountains
Dospat 136 C3 Plovdivska Oblast, SW Bulgaria
Dothan 74 D3 Alabama, S USA
Dotnuva 138 B4 Kėdainiai, C Lithuania
Douai 122 C2 prev. Douay, anc. Duacum. Nord, N France
Douala 109 A5 var. Duala. Littoral, W Cameroon
Douglas 121 C5 dependent territory capital (Isle of Man) E Isle of Man
Douglas 80 C3 Arizona, SW USA
Douglas 76 D3 Wyoming, C USA
Douro 124 B2 Sp. Duero. River Portugal/Spain see also Duero
Dover 121 E7 Fr. Douvres; Lat. Dubris Portus. SE England, UK
Dover 73 F4 state capital Delaware, NE USA
Dover, Strait of 122 C2 var. Straits of Dover, Fr. Pas de Calais. Strait England, UK/France
Dover, Straits of see Dover, Strait of
Dovrefjell 117 B5 plateau S Norway
Downpatrick 121 B5 Ir. Dún Pádraig. SE Northern Ireland, UK
Dōzen 163 B6 island Oki-shotō, SW Japan
Drač see Durrës
Drachten 118 D2 Friesland, N Netherlands
Drăgăşani 140 B5 Vâlcea, SW Romania
Dragoman 136 B2 Sofiyska Oblast, W Bulgaria
Dra, Hamada du 102 C3 var. Hammada du Drâa, Haut Plateau du Dra. Plateau W Algeria
Drahichyn 139 B6 Pol. Drohiczyn Poleski, Rus. Drogichin. Brestskaya Voblasts', SW Belarus
Drakensberg 110 D5 mountain range Lesotho/South Africa
Drake Passage 89 B8 passage Atlantic Ocean/Pacific Ocean
Dralfa 136 D2 Razgradska Oblast, N Bulgaria
Dráma 136 C3 var. Dhráma. Anatolikí Makedonía kai Thráki, NE Greece
Drammen 117 B6 Buskerud, S Norway
Drau see Drava
Drava 132 C3 var. Drau, Eng. Drave, Hung. Dráva. River C Europe see also Drau
Dráva see Drava
Drave see Drava
Drawsko Pomorskie 130 B3 Ger. Dramburg. Koszalin, NW Poland
Drépano, Ákra 136 C4 var. Akra Dhrepanon. Headland N Greece
Dresden 126 D4 Sachsen, E Germany
Drin see Drinit, Lumi i
Drina 132 C3 river Bosnia and Herzegovina/Yugoslavia
Drinit, Lumi i 133 D5 var. Drin. River NW Albania
Drobeta-Turnu Severin 140 B5 prev. Turnu Severin. Mehedinţi, SW Romania
Drogheda 121 B5 Ir. Droichead Átha. NE Ireland
Drohobych 140 B2 Pol. Drohobycz, Rus. Drogobych. L'vivs'ka Oblast', NW Ukraine
Droichead Átha see Drogheda
Drôme 123 D5 cultural region SE France
Dronning Maud Land 186 B2 physical region Antarctica
Drummondville 71 E4 Québec, SE Canada
Druskininkai 139 B5 Pol. Druskienniki. Druskininkai, S Lithuania
Dryden 70 B3 Ontario, C Canada
Drysa 139 D5 Rus. Drissa. River N Belarus
Duala see Douala
Dubai 144 see Dubayy
Dubăsari 140 D3 Rus. Dubossary. NE Moldova
Dubawnt 69 F4 river Northwest Territories, NW Canada
Dubayy 152 D4 Eng. Dubai. Dubayy, NE UAE
Dubbo 181 D6 New South Wales, SE Australia
Dublin 121 B5 Ir. Baile Átha Cliath; anc. Eblana. Country capital (Ireland), E Ireland
Dublin 75 E2 Georgia, SE USA
Dubno 140 C2 Rivnens'ka Oblast', NW Ukraine
Dubrovnik 133 B5 It. Ragusa. Dubrovnik-Neretva, SE Croatia
Dubuque 77 G3 Iowa, C USA
Dudelange 119 D8 var. Forge du Sud, Ger. Dudelingen. Luxembourg, S Luxembourg
Dudelingen see Dudelange
Duero 124 D2 Port. Douro. River Portugal/Spain see also Douro

INDEX

Estelí 84 D3 Estelí, NW Nicaragua
Estella 125 E1 Navarra, N Spain
Estepona 124 D5 Andalucía, S Spain
Estevan 69 F5 Saskatchewan, S Canada
Estonia 138 D2 off. Republic of Estonia, Est. Eesti Vabariik, Ger. Estland, Latv. Igaunija; prev. Estonian SSR, Rus. Estonskaya SSR. Country NE Europe
Estrela, Serra da 124 C3 mountain range C Portugal
Estremoz 124 C4 Évora, S Portugal
Esztergom 131 C6 Ger. Gran; anc. Strigonium. Komárom-Esztergom, N Hungary
Étalle 119 D8 Luxembourg, SE Belgium
Etāwah 166 D3 Uttar Pradesh, N India
Ethiopia 105 C5 off. Federal Democratic Republic of Ethiopia; prev. Abyssinia, People's Democratic Republic of Ethiopia. Country E Africa
Ethiopian Highlands 105 C5 var. Ethiopian Plateau. Plateau N Ethiopia
Ethiopian Plateau see Ethiopian Highlands
Etna, Monte 129 C7 Eng. Mount Etna. Volcano Sicilia, Italy, C Mediterranean Sea
Etna, Mount see Etna, Monte
Etosha Pan 110 B3 salt lake N Namibia
Etoumbi 109 B5 Cuvette, NW Congo
Et Tafila see Aṭ Ṭafīlah
Ettelbrück 119 D8 Diekirch, C Luxembourg
'Eua 177 E5 prev. Middleburg Island. Island Tongatapu Group, SE Tonga
Euboea see Évvoia
Eucla 179 D6 Western Australia
Euclid 72 D3 Ohio, N USA
Eufaula Lake 81 G1 var. Eufaula Reservoir. Reservoir Oklahoma, C USA
Eufaula Reservoir see Eufaula Lake
Eugene 78 B3 Oregon, NW USA
Eupen 119 D6 Liège, E Belgium
Euphrates 144 B4 Ar. Al Furāt, Turk. Firat Nehri. River SW Asia
Eureka 79 A5 California, W USA
Eureka 76 A1 Montana, NW USA
Europa Point 125 H5 headland S Gibraltar
Europe 66 E1 continent
Eutin 126 C2 Schleswig-Holstein, N Germany
Euxine Sea see Black Sea
Evansdale 77 G3 Iowa, C USA
Evanston 72 B3 Illinois, N USA
Evanston 76 B4 Wyoming, C USA
Evansville 72 B5 Indiana, N USA
Eveleth 77 G1 Minnesota, N USA
Everard, Lake 181 A6 salt lake South Australia
Everest, Mount 158 B5 Chin. Qomolangma Feng, Nep. Sagarmatha. Mountain China/Nepal
Everett 78 B2 Washington, NW USA
Everglades, The 75 F5 wetland Florida, SE USA
Evje 117 A6 Aust-Agder, S Norway
Évora 124 B4 anc. Ebora, Lat. Liberalitas Julia. Évora, C Portugal
Évreux 122 C3 anc. Civitas Eburovicum. Eure, N France
Évros see Maritsa
Évry 122 E2 Essonne, N France
Évvoia 133 E8 Lat. Euboea. Island C Greece
Ewarton 86 B5 C Jamaica
Excelsior Springs 77 F4 Missouri, C USA
Exe 121 C7 river SW England, UK
Exeter 121 C7 anc. Isca Damnoniorum. SW England, UK
Exmoor 121 C7 moorland SW England, UK
Exmouth 121 C7 SW England, UK
Exmouth 178 A4 Western Australia
Exmouth Gulf 178 A4 gulf Western Australia
Exmouth Plateau 173 E5 undersea feature E Indian Ocean
Extremadura 124 C3 cultural and historical region W Spain
Exuma Cays 86 C1 islets C Bahamas
Exuma Sound 86 C1 sound C Bahamas
Eyre Mountains 183 A7 mountain range South Island, NZ
Eyre North, Lake 181 A5 salt lake South Australia
Eyre Peninsula 181 A6 peninsula South Australia
Eyre South, Lake 181 A5 salt lake South Australia

F

Faadhippolhu Atoll 164 B4 var. Fadiffolu, Lhaviyani Atoll. Atoll N Maldives
Fabens 80 D3 Texas, SW USA
Fada 108 C2 Borkou-Ennedi-Tibesti, E Chad
Fada-Ngourma 107 E4 E Burkina
Fadiffolu see Faadhippolhu Atoll
Faenza 128 C3 anc. Faventia. Emilia-Romagna, N Italy
Faeroe-Iceland Ridge 112 C1 undersea feature NW Norwegian Sea
Faeroe-Shetland Trough 112 C2 undersea feature NE Atlantic Ocean
Faeroes Islands 115 E5 Dan. Færøerne, Faer. Føroyar. Danish external territory N Atlantic Ocean
Faetano 128 E2 E San Marino
Făgăraş 140 C4 Ger. Fogarasch, Hung. Fogaras. Braşov, C Romania
Fagibina, Lake see Faguibine, Lac
Fagne 119 C7 hill range S Belgium
Faguibine, Lac 107 E3 var. Lake Fagibina. Lake NW Mali
Fahlun see Falun
Fahraj 152 E4 Kermān, SE Iran
Faial 124 A5 var. Ilha do Faial. Island Azores, Portugal, NE Atlantic Ocean
Fairbanks 68 D3 Alaska, USA
Fairfield 79 B6 California, W USA
Fair Isle 120 D2 island NE Scotland, UK
Fairlie 183 B6 Canterbury, South Island, NZ
Fairmont 77 F3 Minnesota, N USA
Faisalābād 166 C2 prev. Lyallpur. Punjab, NE Pakistan
Faizābād see Feyẕābād
Faizābād 167 E3 Uttar Pradesh, N India
Fakaofo Atoll 177 F3 island SE Tokelau
Falam 168 A3 Chin State, W Myanmar
Falconara Marittima 128 C3 Marche, C Italy
Falkland Islands 97 D7 var. Falklands, Islas Malvinas. UK dependent territory SW Atlantic Ocean
Falkland Plateau 89 D7 var. Argentine Rise. Undersea feature SW Atlantic Ocean
Falklands see Falkland Islands
Fallbrook 79 C8 California, W USA
Falmouth 121 C7 SW England, UK
Falmouth 86 A4 W Jamaica
Falster 117 B8 island SE Denmark
Fălticeni 140 C3 Hung. Falticsén. Suceava, NE Romania
Falun 117 C6 var. Fahlun. Kopparberg, C Sweden
Famagusta see Ammóchostos
Famagusta Bay see Kólpos Ammóchostos
Famenne 119 C7 physical region SE Belgium
Fang 168 C3 Chiang Mai, NW Thailand
Fano 128 C3 anc. Colonia Julia Fanestris, Fanum Fortunae. Marche, C Italy
Farafangana 111 G4 Fianarantsoa, SE Madagascar
Farāh 154 D4 var. Farah, Fararud. Farāh, W Afghanistan
Farāh Rūd 154 D4 river W Afghanistan
Faranah 106 C4 Haute-Guinée, S Guinea
Fararud see Farāh
Farasān, Jazā'ir 153 A6 island group SW Saudi Arabia
Farewell, Cape 182 C4 headland South Island, NZ
Farghona 155 F2 Rus. Fergana; prev. Novyy Margilan. Farghona Wiloyati, E Uzbekistan
Fargo 77 F2 North Dakota, N USA
Faribault 77 F2 Minnesota, N USA
Farīdābād 166 D3 Haryāna, N India
Farkhor 155 E3 Rus. Parkhar. SW Tajikistan
Farmington 77 G5 Missouri, C USA
Farmington 80 C1 New Mexico, SW USA
Faro 124 B5 Faro, S Portugal
Farquhar Group 111 G2 island group S Seychelles
Fastiv 141 E2 Rus. Fastov. Kyyivs'kaOblast', NW Ukraine
Fauske 116 C3 Nordland, C Norway
Faxaflói 114 D5 Eng. Faxa Bay. Bay W Iceland
Faya 108 C2 prev. Faya-Largeau, Largeau. Borkou-Ennedi-Tibesti, N Chad
Fayetteville 74 A1 Arkansas, C USA
Fayetteville 75 F1 North Carolina, SE USA
Fdérick see Fdérik
Fdérik 106 C2 var. Fdérick, Fr. Fort Gouraud. Tiris Zemmour, NW Mauritania
Fear, Cape 75 F2 headland Bald Head Island, North Carolina, SE USA
Fécamp 122 B3 Seine-Maritime, N France
Federation of the separate territories of see Malaysia
Fehérgyarmat 131 E6 Szabolcs-Szatmár-Bereg, E Hungary
Fehmarn 126 C2 island N Germany
Fehmarn Belt 126 C2 Ger. Fehmarnbelt. Strait Denmark/Germany
Feijó 94 C2 Acre, W Brazil
Feilding 182 D4 Manawatu-Wanganui, North Island, NZ
Feira see Feira de Santana
Feira de Santana 95 G3 var. Feira. Bahia, E Brazil
Felanitx 125 G3 anc. Canati, Felaniche. Mallorca, Spain, W Mediterranean Sea
Felidhu Atoll 164 B4 atoll C Maldives
Felipe Carrillo Puerto 83 H4 Quintana Roo, SE Mexico
Felixstowe 121 E6 E England, UK
Femunden 117 B5 lake S Norway
Fengcheng 160 D3 var. Feng-cheng, Fenghwangcheng. Liaoning, NE China
Feng-cheng see Fengcheng
Fenghwangcheng see Fengcheng
Fengtien see Liaoning
Fenoarivo 111 G3 Toamasina, E Madagascar
Fens, The 121 E6 wetland E England, UK
Feodosiya 141 F5 var. Kefe, It. Kaffa; anc. Theodosia. Respublika Krym, S Ukraine
Féres 136 D3 Anatolikí Makedonía kai Thráki, NE Greece
Fergus Falls 77 F2 Minnesota, N USA
Ferkessédougou 106 D4 N Ivory Coast
Fermo 128 C4 anc. Firmum Picenum. Marche, C Italy
Fernandina, Isla 92 A4 var. Narborough Island. Island Galapagos Islands, Ecuador, E Pacific Ocean
Fernando de Noronha 95 H2 island E Brazil
Fernando Po see Bioco, Isla de
Fernando Póo see Bioco, Isla de
Ferrara 128 C2 anc. Forum Alieni. Emilia-Romagna, N Italy
Ferreñafe 92 B3 Lambayeque, W Peru
Ferro see Hierro
Ferrol 124 B1 var. El Ferrol; prev. El Ferrol del Caudillo. Galicia, NW Spain
Ferwerd 118 D1 Fris. Ferwert. Friesland, N Netherlands
Fès 102 C2 Eng. Fez. N Morocco
Feteşti 140 D5 Ialomiţa, SE Romania
Fethiye 148 B4 Muğla, SW Turkey
Fetlar 120 D1 island NE Scotland, UK
Feyẕābād 155 F3 var. Faizabad, Faizābād, Feyzābād, Fyzabad. Badakhshān, NE Afghanistan
Fianarantsoa 111 F3 Fianarantsoa, C Madagascar
Fianga 108 B4 Mayo-Kébbi, SW Chad
Fier 133 C6 var. Fieri. Fier, SW Albania
Fieri see Fier
Figeac 123 C5 Lot, S France
Figig see Figuig
Figueira da Foz 124 B3 Coimbra, W Portugal
Figueres 125 G2 Cataluña, E Spain
Figuig 102 D2 var. Figig. E Morocco
Fiji 177 E5 off. Sovereign Democratic Republic of Fiji, Fij. Viti. Country SW Pacific Ocean
Filadelfia 84 D4 Guanacaste, W Costa Rica
Filiaşi 140 B5 Dolj, SW Romania
Filipstad 117 B6 Värmland, C Sweden
Finale Ligure 128 A3 Liguria, NW Italy
Finchley 121 A7 SE England, UK
Findlay 72 C4 Ohio, N USA
Finike 148 B4 Antalya, SW Turkey
Finland 116 D4 off. Republic of Finland, Fin. Suomen Tasavalta, Suomi. Country N Europe
Finland, Gulf of 117 D6 Est. Soome Laht, Fin. Suomenlahti, Ger. Finnischer Meerbusen, Rus. Finskiy Zaliv, Swe. Finska Viken. Gulf E Baltic Sea
Finnmarksvidda 116 D2 physical region N Norway
Finsterwalde 126 D4 Brandenburg, E Germany
Fiordland 183 A7 physical region South Island, NZ
Fiorina 128 E1 NE San Marino
Firenze 128 C3 Eng. Florence; anc. Florentia. Toscana, C Italy
Fischbacher Alpen 127 E7 mountain range E Austria
Fish 110 B4 var. Vis. River S Namibia
Fishguard 121 C6 Wel. Abergwaun. SW Wales, UK
Fisterra, Cabo 124 B1 headland NW Spain
Fitzroy Crossing 178 C3 Western Australia
Fitzroy River 178 C3 river Western Australia
Flagstaff 80 B2 Arizona, SW USA
Flanders 119 A6 Dut. Vlaanderen, Fr. Flandre. Cultural region Belgium/France
Flathead Lake 76 B1 lake Montana, NW USA
Flat Island 160 C8 island NE Spratly Islands
Flatts Village 74 B5 var. The Flatts Village. C Bermuda
Flensburg 126 B2 Schleswig-Holstein, N Germany
Flinders Island 181 C8 island Furneaux Group, Tasmania, SE Australia
Flinders Ranges 181 B6 mountain range South Australia
Flinders River 180 C3 river Queensland, NE Australia
Flin Flon 69 F5 Manitoba, C Canada
Flint 72 C3 Michigan, N USA
Flint Island 177 G4 island Line Islands, E Kiribati
Floreana, Isla see Santa María, Isla
Florence see Firenze
Florence 74 C1 Alabama, S USA
Florence 75 F2 South Carolina, SE USA
Florencia 90 B4 Caquetá, S Colombia
Florentia see Firenze
Flores 124 A5 island Azores, Portugal, NE Atlantic Ocean
Flores 171 E5 island Nusa Tenggara, C Indonesia
Flores 84 B1 Petén, N Guatemala
Flores Sea 170 D5 Ind. Laut Flores. Sea C Indonesia
Floriano 95 F2 Piauí, E Brazil
Florianópolis 95 F5 prev. Destêrro. State capital Santa Catarina, S Brazil
Florida 75 E4 off. State of Florida; also known as Peninsular State, Sunshine State. State SE USA
Florida 96 D4 Florida, S Uruguay
Florida Bay 75 E5 bay Florida, SE USA
Florida Keys 75 E5 island group Florida, SE USA
Florida, Straits of 86 B1 strait Atlantic Ocean/Gulf of Mexico
Flórina 136 B4 var. Phlórina. Dytikí Makedonía, N Greece
Florissant 77 G4 Missouri, C USA
Floúda, Ákra 137 D7 headland Astypálaia, Kykládes, Greece, Aegean Sea
Foča 132 C4 SE Bosnia and Herzegovina
Focşani 140 C4 Vrancea, E Romania
Foggia 129 D5 Puglia, SE Italy
Fogo 106 A3 island Ilhas de Sotavento, SW Cape Verde
Foix 123 B6 Ariège, S France
Folégandros 137 C7 island Kykládes, Greece, Aegean Sea
Foleyet 70 C4 Ontario, S Canada
Foligno 128 C4 Umbria, C Italy
Folkestone 121 E7 SE England, UK
Fond du Lac 72 B2 Wisconsin, N USA
Fongafale 177 E3 var. Funafuti. Country capital (Tuvalu) Funafuti Atoll, SE Tuvalu
Fonseca, Gulf of 84 C3 Sp. Golfo de Fonseca. Gulf Central America
Fontainebleau 122 C3 Seine-et-Marne, N France
Fontenay-le-Comte 122 B4 Vendée, NW France
Fontvieille 123 B8 SW Monaco
Fonyód 131 C7 Somogy, W Hungary
Foochow see Fuzhou
Forchheim 127 C5 Bayern, SE Germany
Forel, Mont 114 D4 mountain SE Greenland
Forfar 120 C3 E Scotland, UK
Forge du Sud see Dudelange
Forlì 128 C3 anc. Forum Livii. Emilia-Romagna, N Italy
Formentera 125 G4 anc. Ophiusa, Lat. Frumentum. Island Islas Baleares, Spain, W Mediterranean Sea
Formosa 96 D2 Formosa, NE Argentina
Formosa, Serra 95 E3 mountain range C Brazil
Formosa Strait see Taiwan Strait
Forrest City 74 B1 Arkansas, C USA
Fort Albany 70 C3 Ontario, C Canada
Fortaleza 95 G2 prev. Ceará. State capital Ceará, NE Brazil
Fortaleza 93 F2 Pando, N Bolivia
Fort-Bayard see Zhanjiang
Fort-Cappolani see Tidjikja
Fort Collins 76 D4 Colorado, C USA
Fort Davis 81 E3 Texas, SW USA
Fort-de-France 87 H4 prev. Fort-Royal. Dependent territory capital (Martinique) W Martinique
Fort Dodge 77 F3 Iowa, C USA
Fortescue River 178 A4 river Western Australia
Fort Frances 70 B4 Ontario, S Canada
Fort Good Hope 69 E3 var. Good Hope. Northwest Territories, NW Canada
Fort Gouraud see Fdérik
Forth 120 C4 river C Scotland, UK
Forth, Firth of 120 C4 estuary E Scotland, UK
Fort-Lamy see Ndjamena
Fort Lauderdale 75 F5 Florida, SE USA
Fort Liard 69 E4 var. Liard. Northwest Territories, W Canada
Fort Madison 77 G4 Iowa, C USA
Fort McMurray 69 E4 Alberta, C Canada
Fort McPherson 68 D3 var. McPherson. Northwest Territories, NW Canada
Fort Morgan 76 D4 Colorado, C USA
Fort Myers 75 E5 Florida, SE USA
Fort Nelson 69 E4 British Columbia, W Canada
Fort Peck Lake 76 C1 reservoir Montana, NW USA
Fort Pierce 75 F4 Florida, SE USA
Fort Providence 69 E4 var. Providence. Northwest Territories, W Canada
Fort St.John 69 E4 British Columbia, W Canada
Fort Scott 77 F5 Kansas, C USA
Fort Severn 70 C2 Ontario, C Canada
Fort-Shevchenko 146 A4 Mangistau, W Kazakhstan
Fort Simpson 69 E4 var. Simpson. Northwest Territories, W Canada
Fort Smith 69 E4 district capital Northwest Territories, W Canada
Fort Smith 74 B1 Arkansas, C USA
Fort Stockton 81 E3 Texas, SW USA
Fort-Trinquet see Bîr Mogreïn
Fort Vermilion 69 E4 Alberta, W Canada
Fort Walton Beach 74 C3 Florida, SE USA
Fort Wayne 72 C4 Indiana, N USA
Fort William 120 C3 N Scotland, UK
Fort Worth 81 G2 Texas, SW USA
Fort Yukon 68 D3 Alaska, USA
Fougamou 109 A6 Ngounié, C Gabon
Fougères 122 B3 Ille-et-Vilaine, NW France
Fou-hsin see Fuxin
Foulwind, Cape 183 B5 headland South Island, NZ
Foumban 108 A4 Ouest, NW Cameroon
Fou-shan see Fushun
Foveaux Strait 183 A8 strait S NZ
Foxe Basin 69 G3 sea Northwest Territories, N Canada
Fox Glacier 183 B6 West Coast, South Island, NZ
Fox Mine 69 F4 Manitoba, C Canada
Fraga 125 F2 Aragón, NE Spain
Fram Basin 188 C3 var. Amundsen Basin. Undersea feature Arctic Ocean
France 122 B4 off. French Republic, It./Sp. Francia; prev. Gaul, Gaule, Lat. Gallia. Country W Europe
Franceville 109 B6 var. Massoukou, Masuku. Haut-Ogooué, E Gabon
Francfort prev see Frankfurt am Main
Franche-Comté 122 D4 cultural region E France
Francis Case, Lake 77 E3 reservoir South Dakota, N USA
Francisco Escárcega 83 G4 Campeche, SE Mexico
Francistown 110 D3 North East, NE Botswana
Franconian Jura see Fränkische Alb
Frankenalb see Fränkische Alb
Frankenstein see Ząbkowice Śląskie
Frankenstein in Schlesien see Ząbkowice Śląskie
Frankfort 72 C5 state capital Kentucky, S USA
Frankfort on the Main see Frankfurt am Main
Frankfurt see Frankfurt am Main
Frankfurt am Main 127 B5 var. Frankfurt, Fr. Francfort; prev. Eng. Frankfort on the Main. Hessen, SW Germany
Frankfurt an der Oder 126 D3 Brandenburg, E Germany
Fränkische Alb 127 C6 var. Frankenalb, Eng. Franconian Jura. Mountain range S Germany
Franklin 74 C1 Tennessee, S USA
Franklin D.Roosevelt Lake 78 C1 reservoir Washington, NW USA
Frantsa-Iosifa, Zemlya 146 D1 Eng. Franz Josef Land. Island group N Russian Federation
Franz Josef Land 188 see Frantsa-Iosifa, Zemlya
Fraserburgh 120 D3 NE Scotland, UK
Fraser Island 180 E4 var. Great Sandy Island. Island Queensland, E Australia
Fredericksburg 73 E5 Virginia, NE USA
Fredericton 71 F4 New Brunswick, SE Canada
Frederikshåb see Paamiut
Fredrikstad 117 B6 Østfold, S Norway
Freeport 86 C1 Grand Bahama Island, N Bahamas
Freeport 81 H4 Texas, SW USA
Freetown 106 C4 country capital (Sierra Leone) W Sierra Leone
Freiburg see Freiburg im Breisgau
Freiburg im Breisgau 127 A6 var. Freiburg, Fr. Fribourg-en-Brisgau. Baden-Württemberg, SW Germany
Fremantle 179 A6 Western Australia
Fremont 77 F4 Nebraska, C USA
French Guiana 91 H3 var. Guiana, Guyane. French overseas department N South America
French Polynesia 175 F4 French overseas territory C Polynesia
French Southern and Antarctic Territories 173 B7 Fr. Terres Australes et Antarctiques Françaises. French overseas territory S Indian Ocean
Fresnillo 82 D3 var. Fresnillo de González Echeverría. Zacatecas, C Mexico
Fresnillo de González Echeverría see Fresnillo
Fresno 79 C6 California, W USA
Frías 96 C3 Santiago del Estero, N Argentina
Fribourg-en-Brisgau see Freiburg im Breisgau
Friedrichshafen 127 B7 Baden-Württemberg, S Germany
Frobisher Bay 114 B3 inlet Baffin Island, Northwest Territories, NE Canada
Frohavet 116 B4 sound C Norway
Frome, Lake 181 B6 salt lake South Australia
Frontera 83 G4 Tabasco, SE Mexico
Frontignan 123 C6 Hérault, S France
Frostviken see Kvarnbergsvattnet
Frøya 116 A4 island W Norway
Frunze see Bishkek
Frýdek-Místek 131 C5 Ger. Friedek-Mistek. Severní Morava, SE Czech Republic
Fu-chien see Fujian
Fu-chou see Fuzhou
Fuengirola 124 D5 Andalucía, S Spain
Fuerte Olimpo 96 D2 var. Olimpo. Alto Paraguay, NE Paraguay
Fuerte, Río 80 C5 river C Mexico
Fuerteventura 102 B3 island Islas Canarias, Spain, NE Atlantic Ocean
Fuhkien see Fujian
Fu-hsin see Fuxin
Fuji 163 D6 var. Huzi. Shizuoka, Honshū, S Japan
Fujian 160 D6 var. Fu-chien, Fuhkien, Fujian Sheng, Fukien, Min. Admin. region province SE China
Fujian Sheng see Fujian
Fuji-san 163 C6 var. Fujiyama, Eng. Mount Fuji. Mountain Honshū, SE Japan
Fujiyama see Fuji-san
Fukang 158 C2 Xinjiang Uygur Zizhiqu, W China
Fukien see Fujian
Fukui 163 C6 var. Hukui. Fukui, Honshū, SW Japan
Fukuoka 163 A7 var. Hukuoka; hist. Najima. Fukuoka, Kyūshū, SW Japan
Fukushima 162 D4 var. Hukusima. Fukushima, Honshū, C Japan
Fulda 127 B5 Hessen, C Germany
Funafuti see Fongafale
Funafuti Atoll 177 E3 atoll C Tuvalu
Funchal 102 A2 Madeira, Portugal, NE Atlantic Ocean
Fundy, Bay of 71 F5 bay Canada/USA
Furnes see Veurne
Fürth 127 C5 Bayern, S Germany
Furukawa 162 D4 var. Hurukawa. Miyagi, Honshū, C Japan
Fushun 160 D3 var. Fou-shan, Fu-shun. Liaoning, NE China
Fu-shun see Fushun
Fusin see Fuxin
Füssen 127 C7 Bayern, S Germany
Futog 132 D3 Serbia, NW Yugoslavia
Futuna, Île 177 E4 island S Wallis and Futuna
Fuxin 160 D3 var. Fou-hsin, Fu-hsin, Fusin. Liaoning, NE China

G

Grande Prairie 69 *E4* Alberta, W Canada
Grand Erg Occidental 102 *D3 desert* W Algeria
Grand Erg Oriental 103 *E3 desert* Algeria/Tunisia
Grande, Rio 67 *B6 var.* Río Bravo, *Sp.* Río Bravo del Norte, Bravo del Norte. *River* Mexico/USA
Grande, Rio 81 *F4 river* Texas, SW USA
Grande, Rio *see* Bravo, Río
Grande, Río 83 *E2 river* S Mexico
Grande Terre 87 *G3 island* E West Indies
Grand Falls 71 *G3* Newfoundland, Newfoundland and Labrador, SE Canada
Grand Forks 77 *E1* North Dakota, N USA
Grand Island 77 *E4* Nebraska, C USA
Grand Junction 76 *C4* Colorado, C USA
Grand Rapids 72 *C3* Michigan, N USA
Grand Rapids 77 *F1* Minnesota, N USA
Grand-Santi 91 *G3* W French Guiana
Gran Lago *see* Nicaragua, Lago de
Gran Malvina *see* West Falkland
Gran Paradiso 128 *A2 Fr.* Grand Paradis. *Mountain* NW Italy
Gran Santiago *see* Santiago
Grants 80 *C2* New Mexico, SW USA
Grants Pass 78 *B4* Oregon, NW USA
Granville 122 *B3* Manche, N France
Graulhet 123 *C6* Tarn, S France
Grave 118 *D4* Noord-Brabant, SE Netherlands
Grayling 68 *C2* Alaska, USA
Graz 127 *E7 prev.* Gratz. Steiermark, SE Austria
Great Abaco 86 *C1 var.* Abaco Island. *Island* N Bahamas
Great Alfold *see* Great Hungarian Plain
Great Ararat *see* Büyükağrı Dağı
Great Australian Bight 179 *D7 bight* S Australia
Great Barrier Island 182 *D2 island* N NZ
Great Barrier Reef 180 *D2 reef* Queensland, NE Australia
Great Basin 79 *C5 basin* W USA
Great Bear Lake 69 *E3 Fr.* Grand Lac de l'Ours. *Lake* Northwest Territories, NW Canada
Great Belt *see* Storebælt
Great Bend 77 *E5* Kansas, C USA
Great Bermuda *see* Bermuda
Great Britain *see* Britain
Great Comoro *see* Grande Comore
Great Dividing Range 180 *D4 mountain range* NE Australia
Greater Antarctica 186 *C3 var.* East Antarctica. *Physical region* Antarctica
Greater Antilles 86 *D3 island group* West Indies
Greater Caucasus 149 *G2 Az.* Bas Qafqaz Silsiläsi, *Geor.* Kavkasioni, *Rus.* Bol'shoy Kavkaz. *Mountain range* Asia/Europe
Greater Sunda Islands 156 *D5 var.* Sunda Islands. *Island group* Indonesia
Great Exhibition Bay 182 *C1 inlet* North Island, NZ
Great Exuma Island 86 *C2 island* C Bahamas
Great Falls 76 *B1* Montana, NW USA
Great Hungarian Plain 131 *C7 var.* Great Alfold, Plain of Hungary, *Hung.* Alföld. *Plain* SE Europe
Great Inagua 86 *D2 var.* Inagua Islands. *Island* S Bahamas
Great Indian Desert *see* Thar Desert
Great Karroo *see* Great Karoo
Great Lakes 67 *C5 lakes* Ontario, Canada/USA
Great Meteor Seamount *see* Great Meteor Tablemount
Great Meteor Tablemount 98 *B3 var.* Great Meteor Seamount. *Undersea feature* E Atlantic Ocean
Great Nicobar 165 *G3 island* Nicobar Islands, India, NE Indian Ocean
Great Plain of China 157 *E2 plain* E China
Great Plains 77 *E3 var.* High Plains. *Plains* Canada/USA
Great Rift Valley 105 *C5 var.* Rift Valley. *Depression* Asia/Africa
Great Ruaha 105 *C7 river* S Tanzania
Great Saint Bernard Pass 128 *A1 Fr.* Col du Grand-Saint-Bernard, *It.* Passo di Gran San Bernardo. *Pass* Italy/Switzerland
Great Salt Desert *see* Kavīr, Dasht-e
Great Salt Lake 76 *A3 salt lake* Utah, W USA
Great Salt Lake Desert 76 *A4 plain* Utah, W USA
Great Sand Sea 103 *H3 desert* Egypt/Libya
Great Sandy Desert 178 *C4 desert* Western Australia
Great Sandy Island *see* Fraser Island
Great Slave Lake 69 *E4 Fr.* Grand Lac des Esclaves. *Lake* Northwest Territories, NW Canada
Great Sound 74 *A5 bay* Bermuda, NW Atlantic Ocean
Great Victoria Desert 179 *C5 desert* South Australia/Western Australia
Great Wall of China 160 *C4 ancient monument* N China
Great Yarmouth 121 *E6 var.* Yarmouth. E England, UK
Gredos, Sierra de 124 *D3 mountain range* W Spain
Greece 137 *A5 off.* Hellenic Republic, *Gk.* Ellás; *anc.* Hellas. *Country* SE Europe
Greece 113 *E5* New York, NE USA
Greeley 76 *D4* Colorado, C USA
Green Bay 72 *B2 lake bay* Michigan/Wisconsin, N USA
Green Bay 72 *B2* Wisconsin, N USA
Greeneville 75 *E1* Tennessee, S USA
Greenland 114 *D3 Dan.* Grønland, *Inuit* Kalaallit Nunaat. *Danish external territory* NE North America
Greenland Sea 115 *F2 sea* Arctic Ocean
Green Mountains 73 *G2 mountain range* Vermont, NE USA
Greenock 120 *C4* W Scotland, UK
Green River 72 *C5 river* Kentucky, C USA
Green River 76 *B4 river* Utah, W USA
Green River 76 *B3* Wyoming, C USA
Greensboro 75 *F1* North Carolina, SE USA
Greenville 74 *B2* Mississippi, S USA
Greenville 75 *F1* North Carolina, SE USA
Greenville 75 *E1* South Carolina, SE USA
Greenville 81 *G2* Texas, SW USA
Greenwich 121 *B8* SE England, UK
Greenwood 74 *B2* Mississippi, S USA
Greenwood 75 *E2* South Carolina, SE USA
Gregory Range 180 *C3 mountain range* Queensland, E Australia
Greifswald 126 *D2* Mecklenburg-Vorpommern, NE Germany
Grenada 87 *G5 country* SE West Indies
Grenada 74 *C2* Mississippi, S USA
Grenadines, The 87 *H4 island group* Grenada/St Vincent and the Grenadines
Grenoble 123 *D5 anc.* Cularo, Gratianopolis. Isère, E France
Gresham 78 *B3* Oregon, NW USA
Grevená 136 *B4* Dytikí Makedonía, N Greece
Grevenmacher 119 *E8* Grevenmacher, E Luxembourg
Greymouth 183 *B5* West Coast, South Island, NZ
Grey Range 181 *C5 mountain range* New South Wales/Queensland, E Australia
Greytown *see* San Juan del Norte
Griffin 74 *D2* Georgia, SE USA
Grimari 108 *C4* Ouaka, C Central African Republic
Grimsby 121 *E5 prev.* Great Grimsby. E England, UK
Grobiņa 138 *B3 Ger.* Grobin. Liepāja, W Latvia
Groesbeek 118 *D4* Gelderland, SE Netherlands
Grójec 130 *D4* Radom, C Poland
Groningen 118 *E1* Groningen, NE Netherlands
Groote Eylandt 180 *B2 island* Northern Territory, N Australia
Grootfontein 110 *B3* Otjozondjupa, N Namibia
Groot Karasberge 110 *B4 mountain range* S Namibia
Groot Karoo *see* Great Karoo
Gros Islet 87 *F1* N Saint Lucia
Grosse Morava *see* Velika Morava
Grosseto 128 *B4* Toscana, C Italy
Grossglockner 127 *C7 mountain* W Austria
Groznyy 143 *B8* Chechenskaya Respublika, SW Russian Federation
Grudziądz 130 *C3 Ger.* Graudenz. Toruń, N Poland
Grums 117 *B6* Värmland, C Sweden
Gryazi 143 *B6* Lipetskaya Oblast', W Russian Federation
Gryfice 130 *B2 Ger.* Greifenberg, Greifenberg in Pommern. Szczecin, NW Poland
Guabito 85 *E4* Bocas del Toro, NW Panama
Guadalajara 125 *E3 Ar.* Wad Al-Hajarah; *anc.* Arriaca. Castilla-La Mancha, C Spain
Guadalajara 82 *D4* Jalisco, C Mexico
Guadalcanal 176 *C3 island* C Solomon Islands
Guadalquivir 124 *D4 river* W Spain
Guadalupe 82 *D3* Zacatecas, C Mexico
Guadalupe Peak 80 *D3 mountain* Texas, SW USA
Guadalupe River 81 *G4 river* SW USA
Guadarrama, Sierra de 125 *E2 mountain range* C Spain
Guadeloupe 87 *H3 French overseas department* E West Indies
Guadiana 124 *C4 river* Portugal/Spain
Guadix 125 *E4* Andalucía, S Spain
Guaimaca 84 *C2* Francisco Morazán, C Honduras
Guajira, Península de la 90 *B1 peninsula* N Colombia
Gualaco 84 *D2* Olancho, C Honduras
Gualán 84 *B2* Zacapa, C Guatemala
Gualdicciolo 128 *D1* NW San Marino
Gualeguaychú 96 *D4* Entre Ríos, E Argentina
Guam 176 *B1 US unincorporated territory* W Pacific Ocean
Guamúchil 82 *C3* Sinaloa, C Mexico
Guanabacoa 86 *B2* La Habana, W Cuba
Guanajuato 83 *E4* Guanajuato, C Mexico
Guanare 90 *C2* Portuguesa, N Venezuela
Guanare, Río 90 *D2 river* W Venezuela
Guangdong 160 *C6 var.* Guangdong Sheng, Kuang-tung, Kwangtung, Yue. Admin. region *province* S China
Guangdong Sheng *see* Guangdong
Guangxi *see* Guangxi Zhuangzu Zizhiqu
Guangxi Zhuangzu Zizhiqu 160 *C6 var.* Guangxi, Gui, Kuang-hsi, Kwangsi, *Eng.* Kwangsi Chuang Autonomous Region. Admin. region *autonomous region* S China
Guangyuan 160 *B5 var.* Kuang-yuan, Kwangyuan. Sichuan, C China
Guangzhou 160 *C6 var.* Kuang-chou, Kwangchow, *Eng.* Canton. Guangdong, S China
Guantánamo 86 *D3* Guantánamo, SE Cuba
Guaporé, Rio 94 *D3 var.* Río Iténez. *River* Bolivia/Brazil *see also* Iténez, Río
Guarda 124 *C3* Guarda, N Portugal
Guarumal 85 *F5* Veraguas, S Panama
Guasave 82 *C3* Sinaloa, C Mexico
Guatemala 84 *A2 off.* Republic of Guatemala. *Country* Central America
Guatemala Basin 67 *B7 undersea feature* E Pacific Ocean
Guatemala City *see* Ciudad de Guatemala
Guaviare 88 *B2 off.* Comisaría Guaviare. *Province* S Colombia
Guaviare, Río 90 *D3 river* E Colombia
Guayaquil 92 *A2 var.* Santiago de Guayaquil. Guayas, SW Ecuador
Guayaquil, Golfo de 92 *A2 var.* Gulf of Guayaquil. *Gulf* SW Ecuador
Guayaquil, Gulf of *see* Guayaquil, Golfo de
Guaymas 82 *B2* Sonora, NW Mexico
Gubadag 154 *C2 Turkm.* Tel'man; *prev.* Tel'mansk. Dashkhovuzskiy Velayat, N Turkmenistan
Guben 126 *D4 var.* Wilhelm-Pieck-Stadt. Brandenburg, E Germany
Gubkin 143 *B6* Belgorodskaya Oblast', W Russian Federation
Gudara *see* Ghūdara
Gudaut'a 149 *E1* NW Georgia
Guéret 122 *C4* Creuse, C France
Guernsey 121 *D8 UK dependent territory* NW Europe
Guerrero Negro 82 *A2* Baja California Sur, NW Mexico
Gui *see* Guangxi Zhuangzu Zizhiqu
Guiana *see* French Guiana
Guiana Highlands 94 *D1 var.* Macizo de las Guayanas. *Mountain range* N South America
Guidder *see* Guider
Guider 108 *B4 var.* Guidder. Nord, N Cameroon
Guidimouni 107 *G3* Zinder, S Niger
Guildford 121 *D7* SE England, UK
Guilin 160 *C6 var.* Kuei-lin, Kweilin. Guangxi Zhuangzu Zizhiqu, S China
Guimarães 124 *B2 var.* Guimaráes. Braga, N Portugal
Guinea 106 *C4 off.* Republic of Guinea, *var.* Guinée; *prev.* French Guinea, People's Revolutionary Republic of Guinea. *Country* W Africa
Guinea Basin 101 *A5 undersea feature* E Atlantic Ocean
Guinea-Bissau 106 *B4 off.* Republic of Guinea-Bissau, *Fr.* Guinée-Bissau, *Port.* Guiné-Bissau; *prev.* Portuguese Guinea. *Country* W Africa
Guinea, Gulf of 100 *B4 Fr.* Golfe de Guinée. *Gulf* E Atlantic Ocean
Güiria 91 *E1* Sucre, NE Venezuela
Guiyang 160 *B6 var.* Kuei-Yang, Kuei-yang, Kueyang, Kweiyang; *prev.* Kweichu. Guizhou, S China
Guizhou 160 *B6 var.* Guizhou Sheng, Kuei-chou, Kweichow, Qian. Admin. region *province* S China
Guizhou Sheng *see* Guizhou
Gujarāt 166 *C4 var.* Gujerat. Admin. region *state* W India
Gujerat *see* Gujarāt
Gujrānwāla 166 *D2* Punjab, NE Pakistan
Gujrāt 166 *D2* Punjab, E Pakistan
Gulbarga 164 *C1* Karnātaka, C India
Gulbene 138 *D3 Ger.* Alt-Schwanenburg. Gulbene, NE Latvia
Gulfport 74 *C3* Mississippi, S USA
Gulf, The 152 *C4 var.* Persian Gulf, *Ar.* Khalīj al 'Arabī, *Per.* Khalīj-e Fars. *Gulf* SE Asia
Guliston 155 *E2 Rus.* Gulistan. Sirdaryo Wiloyati, E Uzbekistan
Gulja *see* Yining
Gulkana 68 *D3* Alaska, USA
Gulu 105 *B6* N Uganda
Gulyantsi 136 *C1* Loveshka Oblast, NW Bulgaria
Guma *see* Pishan
Gümülcine *see* Komotiní
Gümüljina *see* Komotiní
Gümüşane *see* Gümüşhane
Gümüşhane 149 *E3 var.* Gümüşane, Gumushkhane. Gümüşhane, NE Turkey
Gumushkhane *see* Gümüşhane
Güney Doğu Toroslar 149 *E4 mountain range* SE Turkey
Gunnbjørn Fjeld 114 *D4 var.* Gunnbjörns Bjerge. *Mountain* C Greenland
Gunnbjörns Bjerge *see* Gunnbjørn Fjeld
Gunnedah 181 *D6* New South Wales, SE Australia
Gunnison 76 *C5* Colorado, C USA
Gurbantünggüt Shamo 158 *B2 desert* W China
Gurgan *see* Gorgān
Guri, Embalse de 91 *E2 reservoir* E Venezuela
Gurktaler Alpen 127 *D7 mountain range* S Austria
Gürün 148 *D3* Sivas, C Turkey
Gusau 107 *G4* Sokoto, N Nigeria
Gusev 138 *B4 Ger.* Gumbinnen. Kaliningradskaya Oblast', W Russian Federation
Gushgy 154 *D4 prev.* Kushka. Maryyskiy Velayat, S Turkmenistan
Gustavus 68 *D4* Alaska, USA
Güstrow 126 *C3* Mecklenburg-Vorpommern, NE Germany
Gütersloh 126 *B4* Nordrhein-Westfalen, W Germany
Guwāhāti 167 *G3 prev.* Gauhāti. Assam, NE India
Guyana 91 *F3 off.* Cooperative Republic of Guyana; *prev.* British Guiana. *Country* N South America
Guyane *see* French Guiana
Guymon 81 *E1* Oklahoma, C USA
Güzelyurt *see*Mórfou
Gvardeysk 138 *A4 Ger.* Tapaiu. Kaliningradskaya Oblast', W Russian Federation
Gwādar 166 *A3 var.* Gwadur. Baluchistān, SW Pakistan
Gwadur *see* Gwādar
Gwalior 166 *D3* Madhya Pradesh, C India
Gwanda 110 *D3* Matabeleland South, SW Zimbabwe
Gwy *see* Wye
Gyangzê 158 *C5* Xizang Zizhiqu, W China
Gyaring Co 158 *C5 lake* W China
Gympie 181 *E5* Queensland, E Australia
Gyomaendrőd 131 *D7* Békés, SE Hungary
Gyöngyös 131 *D6* Heves, NE Hungary
Győr 131 *C6 Ger.* Raab; *Lat.* Arrabona. Győr-Moson-Sopron, NW Hungary
Gýtheio 137 *B6 var.* Githio; *prev.* Yíthion. Pelopónnisos, S Greece
Gyumri 149 *F2 var.* Giumri, *Rus.* Kumayri; *prev.* Aleksandropol', Leninakan. W Armenia
Gyzylarbat 154 *C2 prev.* Kizyl-Arvat. Balkanskiy Velayat, W Turkmenistan

H

Haabai *see* Ha'apai Group
Haacht 119 *C6* Vlaams Brabant, C Belgium
Haaksbergen 118 *E3* Overijssel, E Netherlands
Ha'apai Group 177 *F4 var.* Haabai. *Island group* C Tonga
Haapsalu 138 *D2 Ger.* Hapsal. Läänemaa, W Estonia
Haarlem 118 *C3 prev.* Harlem. Noord-Holland, W Netherlands
Haast 183 *B6* West Coast, South Island, NZ
Hachijō-jima 163 *D6 var.* Hatizyô Zima. *Island* Izu-shotō, SE Japan
Hachinohe 162 *D3* Aomori, Honshū, C Japan
Hadama *see* Nazrēt
Haddummati Atoll *see* Hadhdhunmathi Atoll
Hadejia 107 *G3 river* N Nigeria
Hadejia 107 *G4* Jigawa, N Nigeria
Hadera 151 *A6* Haifa, C Israel
Hadhdhunmathi Atoll 164 *A5 var.* Haddummati Atoll, Laamu Atoll. *Atoll* S Maldives
Ha Đông 168 *D3 var.* Hadong. Ha Tây, N Vietnam
Hadong *see* Ha Đông
Ḥaḍramawt 153 *C6 Eng.* Hadhramaut. *Mountain range* S Yemen
Haerbin *see* Harbin
Haerhpin *see* Harbin
Hafren *see* Severn
Hagerstown 73 *E4* Maryland, NE USA
Ha Giang 168 *D3* Ha Giang, N Vietnam
Hagondange 122 *D3* Moselle, NE France
Haguenau 122 *E3* Bas-Rhin, NE France
Haicheng 160 *D3* Liaoning, NE China
Haidarabad *see* Hyderābād
Haifa *see* Ḥefa
Haifong *see* Hai Phong
Haikou 160 *C7 var.* Hai-k'ou, Hoihow, *Fr.* Hoï-Hao. Hainan, S China
Hai-k'ou *see* Haikou
Ḥā'il 152 *B4 off.* Minṭaqah Ḥā'il. *Province* N Saudi Arabia
Hai-la-erh *see* Hailar
Hailar 159 *F1 var.* Hai-la-erh; *prev.* Hulun. Nei Mongol Zizhiqu, N China
Hailuoto 116 *D4 Swe.* Karlö. *Island* W Finland
Hainan 160 *B7 var.* Hainan Sheng, Qiong. Admin. region *province* S China
Hainan Dao 160 *C7 island* S China
Hainan Sheng *see* Hainan
Haines 68 *D4* Alaska, USA
Hainichen 126 *D4* Sachsen, E Germany
Hai Phong 168 *D3 var.* Haifong, Haiphong. N Vietnam
Haiphong *see* Hai Phong
Haiti 86 *D3 off.* Republic of Haiti. *Country* C West Indies
Haiya 104 *C3* Red Sea, NE Sudan
Hajdúhadház 131 *D6* Hajdú-Bihar, E Hungary
Hajîne *see* Abū Ḥardān
Hakodate 162 *D3* Hokkaidō, NE Japan
Ḥalab 150 *B2 Eng.* Aleppo, *Fr.* Alep; *anc.* Beroea. Ḥalab, NW Syria
Ḥalānīyāt, Juzur al 153 *D6 var.* Jazā'ir Bin Ghalfān, *Eng.* Kuria Muria Islands. *Island group* S Oman
Halberstadt 126 *C4* Sachsen-Anhalt, C Germany
Halden 117 *B6 prev.* Fredrikshald. Østfold, S Norway
Halfmoon Bay 183 *A8 var.* Oban. Stewart Island, Southland, NZ
Halifax 71 *F4* Nova Scotia, SE Canada
Halkida *see* Chalkída
Halle 119 *B6 Fr.* Hal. Vlaams Brabant, C Belgium
Halle 126 *C4 var.* Halle an der Saale. Sachsen-Anhalt, C Germany
Halle an der Saale *see* Halle
Halle-Neustadt 126 *C4* Sachsen-Anhalt, C Germany
Halley 186 *B2 UK research station* Antarctica
Hall Islands 174 *B2 island group* C Micronesia
Halls Creek 178 *C3* Western Australia
Halmahera, Pulau 171 *F3 prev.* Djailolo, Gilolo, Jailolo. *Island* E Indonesia
Halmahera Sea 171 *F4 Ind.* Laut Halmahera. *Sea* E Indonesia
Halmstad 117 *B7* Halland, S Sweden
Hama *see* Ḥamāh
Hamada 163 *B6* Shimane, Honshū, SW Japan
Hamadān 152 *C3 anc.* Ecbatana. Hamadān, W Iran
Ḥamāh 150 *B3 var.* Hama; *anc.* Epiphania, *Bibl.* Hamath. Ḥamāh, W Syria
Hamamatsu 163 *D6 var.* Hamamatu. Shizuoka, Honshū, S Japan
Hamamatu *see* Hamamatsu
Hamar 117 *B5 prev.* Storhammer. Hedmark, S Norway
Hamath *see* Ḥamāh
Hamburg 126 *B3* Hamburg, N Germany
Ḥamḍ, Wādī al 152 *A4 dry watercourse* W Saudi Arabia
Hämeenlinna 117 *D5 Swe.* Tavastehus. Häme, SW Finland
Hamersley Range 178 *A4 mountain range* Western Australia
Hamhŭng 161 *E3* C North Korea
Hami 158 *C3 var.* Ha-mi, *Uigh.* Kumul, Qomul. Xinjiang Uygur Zizhiqu, NW China
Ha-mi *see* Hami
Hamilton 74 *C2* Alabama, S USA
Hamilton 70 *D5* Ontario, S Canada
Hamilton 120 *C4* S Scotland, UK
Hamilton 182 *D3* Waikato, North Island, NZ
Ḥamīm, Wādī al 103 *G2 river* NE Libya
Hamīs Musait *see* Khamīs Mushayt
Hamiton 74 *A5 dependent territory capital* (Bermuda) C Bermuda
Hamm 126 *B4 var.* Hamm in Westfalen. Nordrhein-Westfalen, W Germany
Hammada du Drâa *see* Dra, Hamada du
Hammamet, Golfe de 134 *D3 Ar.* Khalīj al Ḥammāmāt. *Gulf* NE Tunisia
Ḥammār, Hawr al 152 *C3 lake* SE Iraq
Hamm in Westfalen *see* Hamm
Hampden 183 *B7* Otago, South Island, NZ
Hampstead 121 *A7* SE England, UK
Hamrun 134 *B5* C Malta
Hâncești *see* Hîncești
Handan 160 *C4 var.* Han-tan. Hebei, E China
Haneda 162 *A2 international airport* (Tōkyō) Tōkyō, Honshū, S Japan
HaNegev 151 *A7 Eng.* Negev. *Desert* S Israel
Hanford 79 *C6* California, W USA
Hangayn Nuruu 158 *D2 mountain range* C Mongolia
Hang-chou *see* Hangzhou
Hangchow *see* Hangzhou
Hangö *see* Hanko
Hangzhou 160 *D5 var.* Hang-chou, Hangchow. Zhejiang, SE China
Hania *see* Chaniá
Hanka, Lake *see* Khanka, Lake
Hanko 117 *D6 Swe.* Hangö. Uusimaa, SW Finland
Han-k'ou *see* Wuhan
Hankow *see* Wuhan
Hanmer Springs 183 *C5* Canterbury, South Island, NZ
Hannibal 77 *G4* Missouri, C USA
Hannover 126 *B3 Eng.* Hanover. Niedersachsen, NW Germany
Hanöbukten 117 *B7 bay* S Sweden
Ha Nôi 168 *D3 Eng.* Hanoi, *Fr.* Ha noï. *Country capital* (Vietnam) N Vietnam
Hanoi 156 *see* Ha Nôi
Han Shui 159 *E4 river* C China
Han-tan *see* Handan
Hantsavichy 139 *B6 Pol.* Hancewicze, *Rus.* Gantsevichi. Brestskaya Voblasts', SW Belarus
Hanyang *see* Wuhan
Hanzhong 160 *B5* Shaanxi, C China
Hāora 167 *F4 prev.* Howrah. West Bengal, NE India
Haparanda 116 *D4* Norrbotten, N Sweden
Haradok 139 *E5 Rus.* Gorodok. Vitsyebskaya Voblasts', N Belarus
Haradzyets 139 *B6 Rus.* Gorodets. Brestskaya Voblasts', SW Belarus
Haramachi 162 *D4* Fukushima, Honshū, E Japan
Harany 139 *D5 Rus.* Gorany. Vitsyebskaya Voblasts', N Belarus
Harare 110 *D3 prev.* Salisbury. *Country capital* (Zimbabwe) Mashonaland East, NE Zimbabwe
Harbavichy 139 *E6 Rus.* Gorbovichi. Mahilyowskaya Voblasts', E Belarus
Harbel 106 *C5* W Liberia
Harbin 161 *E2 var.* Haerbin, Ha-erh-pin, Kharbin; *prev.* Haerhpin, Pingkiang, Pinkiang. Heilongjiang, NE China
Hardangerfjorden 117 *A6 fjord* S Norway
Hardangervidda 117 *A6 plateau* S Norway
Hardenberg 118 *E3* Overijssel, E Netherlands

INDEX

Hypanis see Kuban'
Hyrcania see Gorgān
Hyvinkää 117 D5 Swe. Hyvinge. Uusimaa, S Finland

I

Ialomiţa 140 C5 river SE Romania
Iaşi 140 D3 Ger. Jassy. Iaşi, NE Romania
Ibadan 107 F5 Oyo, SW Nigeria
Ibagué 90 B3 Tolima, C Colombia
Ibar 132 D4 Alb. Ibër. River C Yugoslavia
Ibarra 92 B1 var. San Miguel de Ibarra. Imbabura, N Ecuador
Iberian Mountains see Ibérico, Sistema
Iberian Peninsula 112 B4 physical region Portugal/Spain
Iberian Plain 112 B4 undersea feature E Atlantic Ocean
Ibérico, Sistema 125 E2 var. Cordillera Ibérica, Eng. Iberian Mountains. Mountain range NE Spain
Ibiza see Eivissa
Ibo see Sassandra
Ica 92 D4 Ica, SW Peru
Içá see Putumayo, Río
Icaria see Ikaría
Içá, Rio 94 C2 var. Río Putumayo. River NW South America see also Putumayo, Río
Iceland 115 E4 off. Republic of Iceland, Dan. Island, Icel. Ísland. Country N Atlantic Ocean
Iceland Basin 112 B1 undersea feature N Atlantic Ocean
Icelandic Plateau see Iceland Plateau
Iceland Plateau 188 B5 var. Icelandic Plateau. Undersea feature S Greenland Sea
Iconium see Konya
Idabel 81 H2 Oklahoma, C USA
Idaho 78 D3 off. State of Idaho; also known as Gem of the Mountains, Gem State. State NW USA
Idaho Falls 78 E3 Idaho, NW USA
Idensalmi see Iisalmi
Idfu 104 B2 var. Edfu. SE Egypt
Ídhra see Ýdra
Idi Amin, Lac see Edward, Lake
Idîni 106 B2 Trarza, W Mauritania
Idlib 150 B3 Idlib, NW Syria
Idre 117 B5 Kopparberg, C Sweden
Iecava 138 C3 Bauska, S Latvia
Ieper 119 A6 Fr. Ypres. West-Vlaanderen, W Belgium
Ierápetra 137 D8 Kríti, Greece, E Mediterranean Sea
Ierisós see Ierissós
Ierissós 136 C4 var. Ierisós. Kentrikí Makedonía, N Greece
Iferouâne 107 G2 Agadez, N Niger
Ifôghas, Adrar des 107 E2 var. Adrar des Iforas. Mountain range NE Mali
Igarka 146 D3 Krasnoyarskiy Kray, N Russian Federation
Iglesias 129 A5 Sardegna, Italy, C Mediterranean Sea
Igloolik 69 G2 Northwest Territories, N Canada
Igoumenítsa 136 A4 Ípeiros, W Greece
Iguaçu, Rio 95 E4 Sp. Río Iguazú. River Argentina/Brazil see also Iguazú, Río
Iguaçu, Salto do 95 E4 Sp. Cataratas del Iguazú; prev. Victoria Falls. Waterfall Argentina/Brazil see also Iguazú, Cataratas del
Iguala 83 E4 var. Iguala de la Independencia. Guerrero, S Mexico
Iguala de la Independencia see Iguala
Iguîdi, 'Erg 102 C3 var. Erg Iguid. Desert Algeria/Mauritania
Ihavandiffulu Atoll see Ihavandippolhu Atoll
Ihavandippolhu Atoll 164 A3 var. Ihavandiffulu Atoll. Atoll N Maldives
Ihosy 111 F4 Fianarantsoa, S Madagascar
Iisalmi 116 E4 var. Idensalmi. Kuopio, C Finland
IJssel 118 D3 var. Yssel. River Netherlands/Germany
IJsselmeer 118 C2 prev. Zuider Zee. Lake N Netherlands
IJsselmuiden 118 D3 Overijssel, E Netherlands
Ijzer 119 A6 river W Belgium
Ikaría 137 D6 var. Kariot, Nicaria, Nikaria; anc. Icaria. Island Dodekánisos, Greece, Aegean Sea
Ikela 109 D6 Equateur, C Congo (Zaire)
Iki 163 A7 island SW Japan
Ilagan 171 E1 Luzon, N Philippines
Ilave 93 E4 Puno, S Peru
Iława 130 D3 Ger. Deutsch-Eylau. Olsztyn, N Poland
Ilebo 109 C6 prev. Port-Francqui. Kasai Occidental, W Congo (Zaire)
Île-de-France 122 C3 cultural region N France
Îles de la Société see Société, Archipel de la
Îles Tubuai see Australes, Îles
Ilfracombe 121 C7 SW England, UK
Ilha Caviana see Caviana de Fora, Ilha
Ilha de Madeira see Madeira
Ilha do Corvo see Corvo
Ilha do Faial see Faial
Ilha do Pico see Pico
Ilha do Porto Santo see Porto Santo
Ilha Graciosa see Graciosa
Ilhas dos Açores see Azores
Ilha Terceira see Terceira
Ílhavo 124 B2 Aveiro, N Portugal
Ili 144 C3 Kaz. Ile, Rus. Reka Ili. River China/Kazakhstan
Iliamna Lake 68 C3 lake Alaska, USA
Ilici see Elche
Iligan 171 E2 off. Iligan City. Mindanao, S Philippines
Illapel 96 B4 Coquimbo, C Chile
Illichivs'k 141 E4 Rus. Il'ichevsk. Odes'ka Oblast', SW Ukraine
Illicis see Elche
Illinois 72 A4 off. State of Illinois; also known as Prairie State, Sucker State. State C USA
Illinois River 72 B4 river Illinois, N USA
Ilo 93 E4 Moquegua, SW Peru
Iloilo 171 E2 off. Iloilo City. Panay Island, C Philippines
Ilorin 107 F4 Kwara, W Nigeria
Îlots de Bass see Marotiri
Ilovlya 143 B6 Volgogradskaya Oblast', SW Russian Federation
İluh see Batman
Il'yaly 154 C2 var. Yylanly. Dashkhovuzskiy Velayat, N Turkmenistan
Imatra 117 E5 Kymi, SE Finland
Imbros see Gökçeada
İmişli 149 H3 Rus. Imishli. C Azerbaijan
Imola 128 C3 Emilia-Romagna, N Italy
Imperatriz 95 F2 Maranhão, NE Brazil
Imperia 128 A3 Liguria, NW Italy
Impfondo 109 C5 La Likouala, NE Congo
Imphāl 167 H3 Manipur, NE India
Imroz Adası see Gökçeada
Inagua Islands see Great Inagua
Inagua Islands see Little Inagua
Inarijärvi 116 D2 Lapp. Aanaarjävri, Swe. Enareträsk. Lake N Finland
Inawashiro-ko 163 D5 var. Inawasiro Ko. Lake Honshū, C Japan
Inawasiro Ko see Inawashiro-ko
İncesu 148 D3 Kayseri, C Turkey
Inch'ŏn 161 E4 off. Inch'ŏn-gwangyŏksi, Jap. Jinsen; prev. Chemulpo. NW South Korea
Incudine, Monte 123 E7 mountain Corse, France, C Mediterranean Sea
Indefatigable Island see Santa Cruz, Isla
Independence 77 F4 Missouri, C USA
Independence Fjord 115 E1 fjord N Greenland
Independence Mountains 78 C4 mountain range Nevada, W USA
India 156 B3 off. Republic of India, var. Indian Union, Union of India, Hind. Bhārat. Country S Asia
Indiana 72 B4 off. State of Indiana; also known as The Hoosier State. State N USA
Indianapolis 72 C4 state capital Indiana, N USA
Indian Church 84 C1 Orange Walk, N Belize
Indian Desert see Thar Desert
Indianola 77 F4 Iowa, C USA
Indigirka 147 F2 river NE Russian Federation
Indija 132 D3 Hung. India; prev. Indjija. Serbia, N Yugoslavia
Indomed Fracture Zone 173 B6 tectonic feature SW Indian Ocean
Indonesia 170 B4 off. Republic of Indonesia, Ind. Republik Indonesia; prev. Dutch East Indies, Netherlands East Indies, United States of Indonesia. Country SE Asia
Indore 166 D4 Madhya Pradesh, C India
Indus 166 C2 Chin. Yindu He; prev. Yin-tu Ho. River S Asia
Indus Cone see Indus Fan
Indus Fan 144 C5 var. Indus Cone. Undersea feature N Arabian Sea
Indus, Mouths of the 166 B4 delta S Pakistan
İnebolu 148 C2 Kastamonu, N Turkey
Ineu 140 A4 Hung. Borosjenő; prev. Inău. Arad, W Romania
Infiernillo, Presa del 83 E4 reservoir S Mexico
Inglewood 78 D2 California, W USA
Ingolstadt 127 C6 Bayern, S Germany
Inhambane 111 E4 Inhambane, SE Mozambique
Inhulets' 141 F3 Rus. Ingulets. Dnipropetrovs'ka Oblast', E Ukraine
I-ning see Yining
Inis see Ennis
Inis Ceithleann see Enniskillen
Inn 127 C6 river C Europe
Innaanganeq 114 C1 var. Kap York. Headland NW Greenland
Inner Hebrides 120 B4 island group W Scotland, UK
Inner Islands 111 H1 var. Central Group. Island group NE Seychelles
Inner Mongolia 159 F3 var. Nei Mongol, Eng. Inner Mongolia, Inner Mongolian Autonomous Region; prev. Nei Monggol Zizhiqu. Admin. region autonomous region N China
Inner Mongolian Autonomous Region see Inner Mongolia
Innisfail 180 D3 Queensland, NE Australia
Inniskilling see Enniskillen
Innsbruch see Innsbruck
Innsbruck 127 C7 var. Innsbruch. Tirol, W Austria
Inoucdjouac see Inukjuak
Inowrocław 130 C3 Ger. Hohensalza; prev. Inowrazlaw. Bydgoszcz, C Poland
I-n-Salah 102 D3 var. In Salah. C Algeria
In Salah see I-n-Salah
Insula see Lille
Inta 142 E3 Respublika Komi, NW Russian Federation
International Falls 77 F1 Minnesota, N USA
Inukjuak 70 D2 var. Inoucdjouac; prev. Port Harrison. Québec, NE Canada
Inuuvik see Inuvik
Inuvik 68 D3 var. Inuuvik. District capital Northwest Territories, NW Canada
Invercargill 183 A7 Southland, South Island, NZ
Inverness 120 C3 N Scotland, UK
Investigator Ridge 173 D5 undersea feature E Indian Ocean
Investigator Strait 181 B7 strait South Australia
Inyangani 110 D3 mountain NE Zimbabwe
Ioánnina 136 A4 var. Janina, Yannina. Ípeiros, W Greece
Iola 77 F5 Kansas, C USA
Ionia Basin see Ionian Basin
Ionian Basin 112 D5 var. Ionia Basin. Undersea feature Ionian Sea, C Mediterranean Sea
Ionian Islands see Iónioi Nísoi
Ionian Sea 135 E3 Gk. Iónio Pélagos, It. Mar Ionio. Sea C Mediterranean Sea
Iónioi Nísoi 137 A5 Eng. Ionian Islands. Island group W Greece
Íos 137 D6 var. Nio. Island Kykládes, Greece, Aegean Sea
Íos 137 D6 Íos, Kykládes, Greece, Aegean Sea
Iowa 77 F3 off. State of Iowa; also known as The Hawkeye State. State C USA
Iowa City 77 G3 Iowa, C USA
Iowa Falls 77 G3 Iowa, C USA
Ipel' 131 C6 var. Ipoly, Ger. Eipel. River Hungary/Slovakia
Ipiales 90 A4 Nariño, SW Colombia
Ipoh 170 B3 Perak, Peninsular Malaysia
Ipoly 131 C6 var. Ipel', Ger. Eipel. River Hungary/Slovakia
Ippy 108 C4 Ouaka, C Central African Republic
Ipswich 121 E6 hist. Gipeswic. E England, UK
Ipswich 181 E5 Queensland, E Australia
Iqaluit 69 H3 prev. Frobisher Bay. District capital Baffin Island, Northwest Territories, NE Canada
Iquique 96 B1 Tarapacá, N Chile
Iquitos 92 C1 Loreto, N Peru
Irákleio 137 D7 var. Herakleion, Eng. Candia; prev. Iráklion. Kríti, Greece, E Mediterranean Sea
Iráklion see Irákleio
Iran 152 C3 off. Islamic Republic of Iran; prev. Persia. Country SW Asia
Iranian Plateau 152 D3 var. Plateau of Iran. plateau N Iran
Iran, Plateau of see Iranian Plateau
Irapuato 83 E4 Guanajuato, C Mexico
Iraq 152 B3 off. Republic of Iraq, Ar. 'Irāq. Country SW Asia
Irbid 151 B5 Irbid, N Jordan
Irbīl see Arbīl
Ireland 112 C3 Lat. Hibernia. Island Ireland/UK
Ireland, Republic of 121 A5 off. Republic of Ireland, var. Ireland, Ir. Éire. Country NW Europe
Irian Barat see Irian Jaya
Irian Jaya 171 H4 var. Irian Barat, West Irian, West New Guinea; prev. Dutch New Guinea, Netherlands New Guinea. Admin. region province E Indonesia
Iringa 105 C7 Iringa, C Tanzania
Iriomote-jima 162 A4 island Sakishima-shotō, SW Japan
Iriona 84 D2 Colón, NE Honduras
Irish Sea 121 C5 Ir. Muir Éireann. Sea C British Isles
Irkutsk 147 E4 Irkutskaya Oblast', S Russian Federation
Irminger Basin see Reykjanes Basin
Iroise 122 A3 sea NW France
Iron Mountain 72 B2 Michigan, N USA
Ironwood 72 B1 Michigan, N USA
Irrawaddy 168 B2 var. Ayeyarwady. River W Myanmar
Irrawaddy, Mouths of the 169 A5 delta SW Myanmar
Irtish see Irtysh
Irtysh 146 C4 var. Irtish, Kaz. Ertis. River C Asia
Irún 125 E1 País Vasco, N Spain
Isabela, Isla 92 A4 var. Albemarle Island. Island Galapagos Islands, Ecuador, E Pacific Ocean
Isaccea 140 D4 Tulcea, E Romania
Isachsen 69 F1 Ellef Ringnes Island, Northwest Territories, N Canada
Ísafjördhur 115 E4 Vestfirdhir, NW Iceland
Isbarta see Isparta
Ise 163 C6 Mie, Honshū, SW Japan
Isère 123 D5 river E France
Isernia 129 D5 var. Æsernia. Molise, C Italy
Ise-wan 163 C6 bay S Japan
Isha Baydhabo see Baydhabo
Ishigaki-jima 162 A4 var. Isigaki Zima. Island Sakishima-shotō, SW Japan
Ishikari-wan 162 C2 bay Hokkaidō, NE Japan
Ishim 146 C4 Kaz. Esil. River Kazakhstan/Russian Federation
Ishim 146 C4 Tyumenskaya Oblast', C Russian Federation
Ishinomaki 162 D4 var. Isinomaki. Miyagi, Honshū, C Japan
Ishkoshim 155 F3 Rus. Ishkashim. S Tajikistan
Isigaki Zima see Ishigaki-jima
Isinomaki see Ishinomaki
Isiro 109 E5 Haut-Zaïre, NE Congo (Zaire)
Iskăr see Iskŭr
İskenderun 148 D4 Eng. Alexandretta. Hatay, S Turkey
İskenderun Körfezi 150 A2 Eng. Gulf of Alexandretta. Gulf S Turkey
Iskŭr 136 C2 var. Iskăr. River NW Bulgaria
Iskŭr, Yazovir 136 B2 prev. Yazovir Stalin. Reservoir W Bulgaria
Isla Cristina 124 C4 Andalucía, S Spain
Islāmābād 166 C1 country capital (Pakistan) Federal Capital Territory Islāmābād, NE Pakistan
I-n-Sâkâne, 'Erg 107 E2 desert N Mali
Islas de los Galápagos see Galapagos Islands
Islas Malvinas see Falkland Islands
Islay 120 B4 island SW Scotland, UK
Isle 123 B5 river W France
Isle of Man 121 B5 UK crown dependency NW Europe
Ismailia see Ismâ'ilîya
Ismâ'ilîya 104 B1 var. Ismailia. N Egypt
Ismid see İzmit
Isna 104 B2 var. Esna. SE Egypt
Isoka 110 D1 Northern, NE Zambia
Isola Grossa see Dugi Otok
Isola Lunga see Dugi Otok
Isole Lipari see Eolie, Isole
Isparta 148 B4 var. Isbarta. Isparta, SW Turkey
İspir 149 E3 Erzurum, NE Turkey
Israel 151 A7 off. State of Israel, var. Medinat Israel, Heb. Yisrael, Yisra'el. Country SW Asia
Issiq Köl see Issyk-Kul', Ozero
Issoire 123 C5 Puy-de-Dôme, C France
Issyk-Kul', Ozero 155 G2 var. Issiq Köl, Kir. Ysyk-Köl. Lake E Kyrgyzstan
İstanbul 148 B2 Bul. Tsarigrad, Eng. Istanbul; prev. Constantinople, anc. Byzantium. İstanbul, NW Turkey
İstanbul Boğazı 148 B2 var. Bosporus Thracius, Eng. Bosphorus, Bosporus, Turk. Karadeniz Boğazı. Strait NW Turkey
Istra 132 A3 Eng. Istria, Ger. Istrien. Cultural region NW Croatia
Istra 128 D2 Eng. Istria. Peninsula NW Croatia
Itabuna 95 G3 Bahia, E Brazil
Itagüí 90 B3 Antioquia, W Colombia
Itaipú, Represa de 95 E4 reservoir Brazil/Paraguay
Itaituba 95 E2 Pará, NE Brazil
Italy 128 C3 off. The Italian Republic, It. Italia, Republica Italiana. Country S Europe
Italy 112 D4 Texas, SW USA
Iténez, Río see Guaporé, Rio
Ithaca 73 E3 New York, NE USA
Itoigawa 163 C5 Niigata, Honshū, C Japan
Itseqqortoormiit see Ittoqqortoormiit
Ittoqqortoormiit 115 E3 var. Itseqqortoormiit, Dan. Scoresbysund, Eng. Scoresby Sound. C Greenland
Iturup, Ostrov 162 E1 island Kuril'skiye Ostrova, SE Russian Federation
Itzehoe 126 B2 Schleswig-Holstein, N Germany
Ivalo 116 D2 Lapp. Avveel, Avvil. Lappi, N Finland
Ivanava 139 B7 Pol. Janów, Janów Poleski, Rus. Ivanovo. Brestskaya Voblasts', SW Belarus
Ivanhoe 181 C6 New South Wales, SE Australia
Ivano-Frankivs'k 140 C2 Ger. Stanislau, Pol. Stanisławów, Rus. Ivano-Frankovsk; prev. Stanislav. Ivano-Frankivs'ka Oblast', W Ukraine
Ivanovo 143 B5 Ivanovskaya Oblast', W Russian Federation
Ivatsevichy 139 B6 Pol. Iwacewicze, Rus. Ivantsevichi, Ivatsevichi. Brestskaya Voblasts', SW Belarus
Ivigtut see Ivittuut
Ivittuut 114 B4 var. Ivigtut. S Greenland
Iviza see Eivissa
Ivory Coast 106 D4 off. Republic of the Ivory Coast, Fr. Côte d'Ivoire, République de la Côte d'Ivoire. Country W Africa
Ivujivik 70 D1 Québec, NE Canada
Iwaki 163 D5 Fukushima, Honshū, N Japan
Iwakuni 163 B7 Yamaguchi, Honshū, SW Japan
Iwanai 162 C2 Hokkaidō, NE Japan
Iwate 162 D3 Iwate, Honshū, N Japan
Ixtapa 83 E5 Guerrero, S Mexico
Ixtepec 83 F5 Oaxaca, SE Mexico
Iyo-nada 163 B7 sea S Japan
Izabal, Lago de 84 B2 prev. Golfo Dulce. Lake E Guatemala
Īzad Khvāst 152 D3 Fārs, C Iran
Izegem 119 A6 prev. Iseghem. West-Vlaanderen, W Belgium
Izhevsk 143 D5 prev. Ustinov. Udmurtskaya Respublika, NW Russian Federation
Izmayil 140 D4 Rus. Izmail. Odes'ka Oblast', SW Ukraine
İzmir 148 A3 prev. Smyrna. İzmir, W Turkey
İzmit 148 B2 var. Ismid; anc. Astacus. Kocaeli, NW Turkey
İznik Gölü 148 B3 lake NW Turkey
Izu-hantō 163 D6 peninsula Honshū, S Japan
Izu Shichito see Izu-shotō
Izu-shotō 163 D6 var. Izu Shichito. Island group S Japan
Izvor 136 B2 Sofiyska Oblast, W Bulgaria
Izyaslav 140 C2 Khmel'nyts'ka Oblast', W Ukraine
Izyum 141 G2 Kharkivs'ka Oblast', E Ukraine

J

Jabal ash Shifā 152 A4 desert NW Saudi Arabia
Jabalpur 167 E4 prev. Jubbulpore. Madhya Pradesh, C India
Jabbūl, Sabkhat al 150 B2 salt flat NW Syria
Jablah 150 A3 var. Jeble, Fr. Djéblé. Al Lādhiqīyah, W Syria
Jaca 125 F1 Aragón, NE Spain
Jacaltenango 84 A2 Huehuetenango, W Guatemala
Jackson 74 B2 state capital Mississippi, S USA
Jackson 77 H5 Missouri, C USA
Jackson 74 C1 Tennessee, S USA
Jackson Head 183 A6 headland South Island, NZ
Jacksonville 75 E3 Florida, SE USA
Jacksonville 72 B4 Illinois, N USA
Jacksonville 75 F1 North Carolina, SE USA
Jacksonville 81 G3 Texas, SW USA
Jacmel 86 D3 var. Jaquemel. S Haiti
Jacobābād 166 B3 Sind, SE Pakistan
Jaén 124 D4 Andalucía, SW Spain
Jaén 92 B2 Cajamarca, N Peru
Jaffna 164 D3 Northern Province, N Sri Lanka
Jagannath see Puri
Jagdalpur 167 E5 Madhya Pradesh, C India
Jagdaqi 159 G1 Nei Mongol Zizhiqu, N China
Jagodina 132 D4 prev. Svetozarevo. Serbia, C Yugoslavia
Jahra see Al Jahrā'
Jaipur 166 D3 prev. Jeypore. Rājasthān, N India
Jaisalmer 166 C3 Rājasthān, NW India
Jajce 132 B3 W Bosnia and Herzegovina
Jakarta 170 C5 prev. Djakarta, Dut. Batavia. Country capital (Indonesia) Jawa, C Indonesia
Jakobstad 116 D4 Fin. Pietarsaari. Vaasa, W Finland
Jalālābād 155 F4 var. Jalalabad, Jelalabad. Nangarhār, E Afghanistan
Jalandhar 166 D2 prev. Jullundur. Punjab, N India
Jalapa see Xalapa
Jalapa 84 D3 Nueva Segovia, NW Nicaragua
Jalapa Enríquez see Xalapa
Jalpa 82 D4 Zacatecas, C Mexico
Jālū 103 G3 var. Jūlā. NE Libya
Jaluit Atoll 176 D2 var. Jālwōj. Atoll Ralik Chain, S Marshall Islands
Jālwōj see Jaluit Atoll
Jamaame 105 D6 It. Giamame; prev. Margherita. Jubbada Hoose, S Somalia
Jamaica 86 A4 country W West Indies
Jamaica 88 A1 island W West Indies
Jamaica Channel 86 D3 channel Haiti/Jamaica
Jamālpur 167 F3 Bihār, NE India
Jambi 170 B4 var. Telanaipura; prev. Djambi. Sumatera, W Indonesia
James Bay 70 C3 bay Ontario/Québec, E Canada
James River 77 E2 river North Dakota/South Dakota, N USA
James River 73 E5 river Virginia, NE USA
Jamestown 73 E3 New York, NE USA
Jamestown 77 E2 North Dakota, N USA
Jammu 166 D2 prev. Jummoo. Jammu and Kashmir, NW India
Jammu and Kashmīr 166 D1 disputed region India/Pakistan
Jāmnagar 166 C4 prev. Navanagar. Gujarāt, W India
Jamshedpur 167 F4 Bihār, NE India
Jamuna see Brahmaputra
Janaúba 95 F3 Minas Gerais, SE Brazil
Janesville 72 B3 Wisconsin, N USA
Janīn see Jenīn
Janina see Ioánnina
Jan Mayen 115 F4 Norwegian dependency N Atlantic Ocean
Jánoshalma 131 C7 SCr. Jankovac. Bács-Kiskun, S Hungary
Japan 162 C4 var. Nippon, Jap. Nihon. Country E Asia
Japan, Sea of 162 A4 var. East Sea, Rus. Yapanskoye More. Sea NW Pacific Ocean
Japan Trench 157 F1 undersea feature NW Pacific Ocean
Japiim 94 C2 var. Máncio Lima. Acre, W Brazil
Japurá, Rio 94 C2 var. Río Caquetá, Yapurá. River Brazil/Colombia see also Caquetá, Río
Jaqué 85 G5 Darién, SE Panama
Jaquemel see Jacmel
Jarablos see Jarābulus
Jarābulus 150 C2 var. Jarablos, Jerablus, Fr. Djérablous. Ḩalab, N Syria
Jardines de la Reina, Archipiélago de los 86 B2 island group C Cuba
Jarocin 130 C4 Kalisz, C Poland
Jarosław 131 E5 Ger. Jaroslau, Rus. Yaroslav. Przemyśl, SE Poland
Jarqŭrghon 155 E3 Rus. Dzharkurgan. Surkhondaryo Wiloyati, S Uzbekistan
Jarvis Island 177 G2 US unincorporated territory C Pacific Ocean
Jasło 131 D5 Krosno, SE Poland
Jastrzębie-Zdrój 131 C5 Katowice, S Poland
Jataí 95 E3 Goiás, C Brazil
Játiva see Xàtiva
Jauf see Al Jawf
Jaunpiebalga 138 D3 Gulbene, NE Latvia
Jaunpur 167 E3 Uttar Pradesh, N India
Java 184 A3 prev. Djawa. Island C Indonesia
Javalambre 125 E3 mountain E Spain
Javari, Rio 94 C2 var. Yavarí. River Brazil/Peru
Java Sea 170 D4 Ind. Laut Jawa. Sea W Indonesia

Kárpathos *137 E7* Kárpathos, SE Greece
Karpaty *see* Carpathian Mountains
Karpenísi *137 B5 prev.* Karpenísion. Stereá Ellás, C Greece
Kars *149 F2 var.* Qars. Kars, NE Turkey
Kārsava *138 D4 Ger.* Karsau; *prev.* Rus. Korsovka. Ludza, E Latvia
Karskiye Vorota, Proliv *142 E2 Eng.* Kara Strait. *Strait* N Russian Federation
Karskoye More *146 D2 Eng.* Kara Sea. *Sea* Arctic Ocean
Karyés *136 C4 var.* Karies. Ágion Óros, N Greece
Kárystos *137 C6 var.* Káristos. Évvoia, C Greece
Kasai *109 C6 var.* Cassai, Kassai. *River* Angola/Congo (Zaire)
Kasaji *109 D7* Shaba, S Congo (Zaire)
Kasama *110 D1* Northern, N Zambia
Kāsaragod *164 B2* Kerala, SW India
Kāshān *152 C3* Eşfahān, C Iran
Kashi *158 A3 Chin.* Kaxgar, K'o-shih, *Uigh.* Kashgar. Xinjiang Uygur Zizhiqu, NW China
Kasongo *109 D6* Maniema, E Congo (Zaire)
Kasongo-Lunda *109 C7* Bandundu, SW Congo (Zaire)
Kásos *137 D7 island* S Greece
Kaspiysk *143 B8* Respublika Dagestan, SW Russian Federation
Kassai *see* Kasai
Kassala *104 C4* Kassala, E Sudan
Kassel *126 B4 prev.* Cassel. Hessen, C Germany
Kasserine *103 E2 var.* Al Qaşrayn. W Tunisia
Kastamonu *148 C2 var.* Castamoni, Kastamuni. Kastamonu, N Turkey
Kastamuni *see* Kastamonu
Kastaneá *136 B4* Kentrikí Makedonía, N Greece
Kastélli *137 C7* Kríti, Greece, E Mediterranean Sea
Kastoría *136 B4* Dytikí Makedonía, N Greece
Kástro *137 C6* Sífnos, Kykládes, Greece, Aegean Sea
Kastsyukovichy *139 E7 Rus.* Kostyukovichi. Mahilyowskaya Voblasts', E Belarus
Kastsyukowka *139 D7 Rus.* Kostyukovka. Homyel'skaya Voblasts', SE Belarus
Kasulu *105 B7* Kigoma, W Tanzania
Kasumiga-ura *163 D5 lake* Honshū, S Japan
Katahdin, Mount *73 G1 mountain* Maine, NE USA
Katalla *68 C3* Alaska, USA
Katana *see* Qaţanā
Katanning *179 B7* Western Australia
Katawaz *see* Zarghūn Shahr
Katchall Island *165 F3 island* Nicobar Islands, India, NE Indian Ocean
Kateríni *136 B4* Kentrikí Makedonía, N Greece
Katha *168 B2* Sagaing, N Myanmar
Katherine *180 A2* Northern Territory, N Australia
Kathmandu *156 C3 prev.* Kantipur. *Country capital* (Nepal) Central, C Nepal
Katikati *182 D3* Bay of Plenty, North Island, NZ
Katima Mulilo *110 C3* Caprivi, NE Namibia
Katiola *106 D4* C Ivory Coast
Káto Achaïa *137 B5 var.* Kato Ahaia, Káto Akhaía. Dytikí Ellás, S Greece
Kato Ahaia *see* Káto Achaïa
Káto Akhaía *see* Káto Achaïa
Katoúna *137 A5* Dytikí Ellás, C Greece
Katowice *131 C5 Ger.* Kattowitz. Katowice, S Poland
Katsina *107 G3* Katsina, N Nigeria
Kattaqŭrghon *155 E2 Rus.* Kattakurgan. Samarqand Wiloyati, C Uzbekistan
Kattavía *137 E7* Ródos, Dodekánisos, Greece, Aegean Sea
Kattegat *117 B7 Dan.* Kattegatt. *Strait* N Europe
Kauai *79 A7 Haw.* Kaua'i. *Island* Hawaiian Islands, Hawaii, USA, C Pacific Ocean
Kaufbeuren *127 C6* Bayern, S Germany
Kaunas *138 B4 Ger.* Kauen, *Pol.* Kowno; *prev.* Rus. Kovno. Kaunas, C Lithuania
Kavadarci *133 E6 Turk.* Kavadar. C FYR Macedonia
Kavajë *133 C6 It.* Cavaia, Kavaja. Tiranë, W Albania
Kavála *136 C3 prev.* Kavālla. Anatolikí Makedonía kai Thráki, NE Greece
Kāvali *164 D2* Andhra Pradesh, E India
Kavango *see* Cubango
Kavaratti Island *164 A3 island* Lakshadweep, India, N Indian Ocean
Kavarna *136 E2* Varnenska Oblast, NE Bulgaria
Kavengo *see* Cubango
Kavīr, Dasht-e *152 D3 var.* Great Salt Desert. *Salt pan* N Iran
Kavīr-e Lūt *see* Lūt, Dasht-e
Kawagoe *163 D5* Saitama, Honshū, S Japan
Kawasaki *162 A2* Kanagawa, Honshū, S Japan
Kawerau *182 E3* Bay of Plenty, North Island, NZ
Kaya *107 E3* C Burkina
Kayan *168 B4* Yangon, SW Myanmar
Kayan, Sungai *170 D3 prev.* Kajan. *River* Borneo, C Indonesia
Kayes *106 C3* Kayes, W Mali
Kayseri *148 D3 var.* Kaisaria; *anc.* Caesarea Mazaca, Mazaca. Kayseri, C Turkey
Kazach'ye *147 F2* Respublika Sakha (Yakutiya), NE Russian Federation
Kazakhskiy Melkosopochnik *146 C4 Eng.* Kazakh Uplands, Kirghiz Steppe, *Kaz.* Saryarqa. *Uplands* C Kazakhstan
Kazakhstan *146 B4 off.* Republic of Kazakhstan, *var.* Kazakstan, *Kaz.* Qazaqstan, Qazaqstan Respublikasy; *prev.* Kazakh Soviet Socialist Republic, *Rus.* Kazakhskaya SSR. *Country* C Asia
Kazakh Uplands *144 see* Kazakhskiy Melkosopochnik
Kazan' *143 C5* Respublika Tatarstan, W Russian Federation
Kazanlŭk *136 D2 prev.* Kazanlik. Khaskovska Oblast, C Bulgaria
Kazbegi *see* Kazbek
Kazbek *149 F1 var.* Kazbegi, *Geor.* Mqinvartsveri. *Mountain* N Georgia
Kāzerūn *152 D4* Fārs, S Iran
Kazvin *see* Qazvīn
Kéa *137 C6 prev.* Kéos, *anc.* Ceos. *Island* Kykládes, Greece, Aegean Sea
Kéa *137 C6* Kéa, Kykládes, Greece, Aegean Sea
Kea, Mauna *79 B8 mountain* Hawaii, USA, C Pacific Ocean
Kéamu *see* Anatom
Kearney *77 E4* Nebraska, C USA
Keban Barajı *149 E3 reservoir* C Turkey
Kebkabiya *104 A4* Northern Darfur, W Sudan
Kebnekaise *116 C3 mountain* N Sweden
Kecskemét *131 D7* Bács-Kiskun, C Hungary
Kediri *170 D5* Jawa, C Indonesia
Keelung *see* Chilung
Keetmanshoop *110 B4* Karas, S Namibia
Kefallinía *137 A5 var.* Kefallonía. *Island* Iónioi Nísoi, Greece, C Mediterranean Sea
Kefallonía *see* Kefallinía
Kefe *see* Feodosiya
Kehl *127 A6* Baden-Württemberg, SW Germany
Keila *138 D2 Ger.* Kegel. Harjumaa, NW Estonia
Keïta *107 F3* Tahoua, C Niger
Keitele *116 D4 lake* C Finland
Keith *181 B7* South Australia
Kĕk-Art *155 G2 prev.* Alaykel', Alay-Kuu. Oshskaya Oblast', SW Kyrgyzstan
Kékes *131 C6 mountain* N Hungary
Kelamayi *see* Karamay
Kelang *see* Klang
Kelat *see* Kalāt
Kelifskiy Uzboy *154 D3 salt marsh* E Turkmenistan
Kelkit Çayı *149 E3 river* N Turkey
Kelmė *138 B4* Kelmė, C Lithuania
Kélo *108 B4* Tandjilé, SW Chad
Kelowna *69 E5* British Columbia, SW Canada
Kelso *78 B2* Washington, NW USA
Keluang *170 B3 var.* Kluang. Johor, Peninsular Malaysia
Kem' *142 B3* Respublika Kareliya, NW Russian Federation
Kemah *149 E3* Erzincan, E Turkey
Kemaman *see* Cukai
Kemerovo *146 D4 prev.* Shcheglovsk. Kemerovskaya Oblast', C Russian Federation
Kemi *116 D4* Lappi, NW Finland
Kemijärvi *116 D3 Swe.* Kemiträsk. Lappi, N Finland
Kemijoki *116 D3 river* NW Finland
Kemin *155 G2 prev.* Bystrovka. Chuyskaya Oblast', N Kyrgyzstan
Kempele *116 D4* Oulu, C Finland
Kempten *127 B7* Bayern, S Germany
Kendal *121 D5* NW England, UK
Kendari *171 E4* Sulawesi, C Indonesia
Kenedy *81 G4* Texas, SW USA
Kenema *106 C4* SE Sierra Leone
Këneurgench *154 C2 Turkm.* Köneürgench; *prev.* Kunya-Urgench. Dashkhovuzskiy Velayat, N Turkmenistan
Kenge *109 C6* Bandundu, SW Congo (Zaire)
Keng Tung *168 C3 var.* Kentung. Shan State, E Myanmar
Kénitra *102 C2 prev.* Port-Lyautey. NW Morocco
Kennett *77 H5* Missouri, C USA
Kennewick *78 C2* Washington, NW USA
Kenora *70 A3* Ontario, S Canada
Kenosha *72 B3* Wisconsin, N USA
Kentau *146 B5* Yuzhnyy Kazakhstan, S Kazakhstan
Kentucky *72 C5 off.* Commonwealth of Kentucky; also known as The Bluegrass State. *State* C USA
Kentucky Lake *72 B5 reservoir* Kentucky/Tennessee, S USA
Kentung *see* Keng Tung
Kenya *105 C6 off.* Republic of Kenya. *Country* E Africa
Keokuk *77 G4* Iowa, C USA
Kępno *130 C4* Kalisz, C Poland
Keppel Island *see* Niuatoputapu
Kepulauan Sangihe *see* Sangir, Kepulauan
Kerak *see* Al Karak
Kerala *164 C2 state* S India
Kerasunt *see* Giresun
Keratea *see* Keratéa
Keratéa *137 C6 var.* Keratea. Attikí, C Greece
Kerbala *see* Karbalā'
Kerbela *see* Karbalā'
Kerch *141 G5 Rus.* Kerch'. Respublika Krym, SE Ukraine
Kerchens'ka Protska *see* Kerch Strait
Kerchenskiy Proliv *see* Kerch Strait
Kerch Strait *141 G4 var.* Bosporus Cimmerius, Enikale Strait, *Rus.* Kerchenskiy Proliv, *Ukr.* Kerchens'ka Protska. *Strait* Black Sea/Sea of Azov
Kerguelen *173 C7 island* C French Southern and Antarctic Territories
Kerguelen Plateau *173 C7 undersea feature* S Indian Ocean
Kerí *137 A6* Zákynthos, Iónioi Nísoi, Greece, C Mediterranean Sea
Kerikeri *182 D2* Northland, North Island, NZ
Kerkenah, Îles de *134 D4 var.* Kerkenna Islands, *Ar.* Juzur Qarqannah. *Island group* E Tunisia
Kerkenna Islands *see* Kerkenah, Îles de
Kerki *154 D3* Lebapskiy Velayat, E Turkmenistan
Kérkira *see* Kérkyra
Kerkrade *119 D6* Limburg, SE Netherlands
Kerkuk *see* Kirkūk
Kérkyra *136 A4 var.* Kérkira, *Eng.* Corfu. *Island* Iónioi Nísoi, Greece, C Mediterranean Sea
Kermadec Islands *184 C4 island group* NZ, SW Pacific Ocean
Kermadec Trench *175 E4 undersea feature* SW Pacific Ocean
Kermān *152 D3 var.* Kirman; *anc.* Carmana. Kermān, C Iran
Kerrville *81 F4* Texas, SW USA
Kerulen *159 E2 Chin.* Herlen He, *Mong.* Herlen Gol. *River* China/Mongolia
Kerýneia *134 C5 var.* Girne, Kyrenia. N Cyprus
Kesennuma *162 D4* Miyagi, Honshū, C Japan
Keszthely *131 C7* Zala, SW Hungary
Ketchikan *68 D4* Revillagigedo Island, Alaska, USA
Kettering *121 D6* C England, UK
Kettering *72 C4* Ohio, N USA
Keuruu *117 D5* Keski-Suomi, C Finland
Keweenaw Peninsula *72 B1 peninsula* Michigan, N USA
Key Largo *75 F5* Key Largo, Florida, SE USA
Key West *75 E5* Florida Keys, Florida, SE USA
Khabarovsk *147 G4* Khabarovskiy Kray, SE Russian Federation
Khairpur *166 B3* Sind, SE Pakistan
Khalīj al 'Aqabah *see* Aqaba, Gulf of
Khalīj al 'Arabī *see* Gulf, The
Khalīj-e Fars *see* Gulf, The
Khalkidikí *see* Chalkidikí
Khalkís *see* Chalkída
Khambhāt, Gulf of *166 C4 Eng.* Gulf of Cambay. *Gulf* W India
Khamīs Mushayt *153 B6 var.* Hamīs Musait. 'Asīr, SW Saudi Arabia
Khānābād *155 E3* Kunduz, NE Afghanistan
Khān al Baghdādī *see* Al Baghdādī
Khandwa *166 D4* Madhya Pradesh, C India
Khanh *see* Soc Trăng
Khaniá *see* Chaniá
Khanka, Lake *161 E2 var.* Hsing-k'ai Hu, Lake Hanka, *Chin.* Xingkai Hu, *Rus.* Ozero Khanka. *Lake* China/Russian Federation
Khanthabouli *168 D4 prev.* Savannakhét. Savannakhét, S Laos
Khanty-Mansiysk *146 C3 prev.* Ostyako-Voguls'k. Khanty-Mansiyskiy Avtonomnyy Okrug, C Russian Federation
Khān Yūnis *151 A7 var.* Khān Yūnus. S Gaza Strip
Khān Yūnus *see* Khān Yūnis
Khanzi *see* Ghanzi
Kharagpur *167 F4* West Bengal, NE India
Kharbin *see* Harbin
Kharkiv *141 G2 Rus.* Khar'kov. Kharkivs'ka Oblast', NE Ukraine
Kharmanli *136 D3* Khaskovska Oblast, S Bulgaria
Khartoum *104 B4 var.* El Khartûm, Khartum. *Country capital* (Sudan) Khartoum, C Sudan
Khartum *see* Khartoum
Khasavyurt *143 B8* Respublika Dagestan, SW Russian Federation
Khāsh, Dasht-e *154 D5 Eng.* Khash Desert. *Desert* SW Afghanistan
Khashim Al Qirba *see* Khashm el Girba
Khashm al Qirbah *see* Khashm el Girba
Khashm el Girba *104 C4 var.* Khashim Al Qirba, Khashm al Qirbah. Kassala, E Sudan
Khaskovo *136 D3* Khaskovska Oblast, S Bulgaria
Khaydarkan *155 F2 var.* Khaydarken. Oshskaya Oblast', SW Kyrgyzstan
Khaydarken *see* Khaydarkan
Khelat *see* Kalāt
Kherson *141 E4* Khersons'ka Oblast', S Ukraine
Kheta *147 E2 river* N Russian Federation
Khíos *see* Chíos
Khiwa *154 D2 Rus.* Khiva. Khorazm Wiloyati, W Uzbekistan
Khmel'nyts'kyy *140 C2 Rus.* Khmel'nitskiy; *prev.* Proskurov. Khmel'nyts'ka Oblast', W Ukraine
Khodasy *139 E6 Rus.* Khodosy. Mahilyowskaya Voblasts', E Belarus
Khodoriv *140 C2 Pol.* Chodorów, *Rus.* Khodorov. L'vivs'ka Oblast', NW Ukraine
Khodzhent *see* Khŭjand
Khoi *see* Khvoy
Khojend *see* Khŭjand
Khokand *see* Qŭqon
Kholm *155 E3 var.* Tashqurghan, *Pash.* Khulm. Balkh, N Afghanistan
Khoms *see* Al Khums
Khong Sedone *see* Muang Khôngxédôn
Khon Kaen *168 D4 var.* Muang Khon Kaen. Khon Kaen, E Thailand
Khor *147 G4* Khabarovskiy Kray, SE Russian Federation
Khorat *see* Nakhon Ratchasima
Khorugh *155 F3 Rus.* Khorog. S Tajikistan
Khotan *see* Hotan
Khouribga *102 B2* C Morocco
Khovd *see* Hovd
Khowst *155 F4* Paktīā, E Afghanistan
Khoy *see* Khvoy
Khoyniki *139 D8 Rus.* Khoyniki. Homyel'skaya Voblasts', SE Belarus
Khrebet Kolymskiy *see* Kolyma Range
Khrebet Kopetdag *see* Koppeh Dāgh
Khrebet Lomonsova *see* Lomonosov Ridge
Khudzhand *see* Khŭjand
Khŭjand *155 E2 var.* Khodzhent, Khojend, *Rus.* Khudzhand; *prev.* Leninabad, *Taj.* Leninobod. N Tajikistan
Khulm *see* Kholm
Khulna *167 G4* Khulna, SW Bangladesh
Khums *see* Al Khums
Khust *140 B3 Cz.* Chust, Husté, *Hung.* Huszt. Zakarpats'ka Oblast', W Ukraine
Khvoy *152 C2 var.* Khoi, Khoy. Āzarbāyjān-e Bākhtarī, NW Iran
Khyber Pass *166 C1 var.* Kowtal-e Khaybar. *Pass* Afghanistan/Pakistan
Kiangmai *see* Chiang Mai
Kiang-ning *see* Nanjing
Kiangsi *see* Jiangxi
Kiangsu *see* Jiangsu
Kiáto *137 B6 prev.* Kiáton. Pelopónnisos, S Greece
Kiayi *see* Chiai
Kibangou *109 B6* Le Niari, SW Congo
Kibombo *109 D6* Maniema, E Congo (Zaire)
Kičevo *133 D6* SW FYR Macedonia
Kidderminster *121 D6* C England, UK
Kiel *126 B2* Schleswig-Holstein, N Germany
Kielce *130 D4 Rus.* Keltsy. Kielce, SE Poland
Kieler Bucht *126 B2 bay* N Germany
Kiev *see* Kyyiv
Kiffa *106 C3* Assaba, S Mauritania
Kigali *105 B6 country capital* (Rwanda) C Rwanda
Kigoma *105 B7* Kigoma, W Tanzania
Kihnu *138 C2 var.* Kihnu Saar, *Ger.* Kühnö. *Island* SW Estonia
Kihnu Saar *see* Kihnu
Kii-suidō *163 C7 strait* S Japan
Kikinda *132 D3 Ger.* Grosskikinda, *Hung.* Nagykikinda; *prev.* Velika Kikinda. Serbia, N Yugoslavia
Kikládhes *see* Kykládes
Kikwit *109 C6* Bandundu, W Congo (Zaire)
Kilien Mountains *see* Qilian Shan
Kilimane *see* Quelimane
Kilimanjaro *105 C7 var.* Uhuru Peak. *Mountain* NE Tanzania
Kilimanjaro *101 E5 region* E Tanzania
Kilingi-Nõmme *138 D3 Ger.* Kurkund. Pärnumaa, SW Estonia
Kilis *148 D4* Gaziantep, S Turkey
Kiliya *140 D4 Rom.* Chilia-Nouă. Odes'ka Oblast', SW Ukraine
Kilkenny *121 B6 Ir.* Cill Chainnigh. S Ireland
Kilkís *136 B3* Kentrikí Makedonía, N Greece
Killarney *121 A6 Ir.* Cill Airne. SW Ireland
Killeen *81 G3* Texas, SW USA
Kilmain *see* Quelimane
Kilmarnock *120 C4* W Scotland, UK
Kilwa *see* Kilwa Kivinje
Kilwa Kivinje *105 C7 var.* Kilwa. Lindi, SE Tanzania
Kimberley *110 C4* Northern Cape, C South Africa
Kimberley Plateau *178 C3 plateau* Western Australia
Kimch'aek *161 E3 prev.* Sŏngjin. E North Korea
Kinabalu, Gunung *170 D3 mountain* East Malaysia
Kindersley *69 F5* Saskatchewan, S Canada
Kindia *106 C4* Guinée-Maritime, SW Guinea
Kindley Field *74 A4 air base* E Bermuda
Kindu *109 D6 prev.* Kindu-Port-Empain. Maniema, C Congo (Zaire)
Kineshma *143 C5* Ivanovskaya Oblast', W Russian Federation
King Island *181 B8 island* Tasmania, SE Australia
Kingman *80 A1* Arizona, SW USA
Kingman Reef *177 E2 US territory* C Pacific Ocean
Kingsford Smith *180 E2 international airport* (Sydney) New South Wales, SE Australia
King's Lynn *121 E6 var.* Bishop's Lynn, Kings Lynn, Lynn, Lynn Regis. E England, UK
King Sound *178 B3 sound* Western Australia
Kingsport *75 E1* Tennessee, S USA
Kingston *86 B5 country capital* (Jamaica) E Jamaica
Kingston *73 F3* New York, NE USA
Kingston *70 D5* Ontario, SE Canada
Kingston upon Hull *121 D5 var.* Hull. E England, UK
Kingston upon Thames *121 A8* SE England, UK
Kingstown *87 H4 country capital* (Saint Vincent and the Grenadines) Saint Vincent, Saint Vincent and the Grenadines
Kingsville *81 G5* Texas, SW USA
King William Island *69 F3 island* Northwest Territories, N Canada Arctic Ocean
Kinrooi *119 D5* Limburg, NE Belgium
Kinshasa *109 B6 prev.* Léopoldville. *Country capital* (Congo (Zaire)) Kinshasa, W Congo (Zaire)
Kintyre *120 B4 peninsula* W Scotland, UK
Kinyeti *105 B5 mountain* S Sudan
Kiparissía *see* Kyparissía
Kipili *105 B7* Rukwa, W Tanzania
Kipushi *109 D8* Shaba, SE Congo (Zaire)
Kirdzhali *see* Kŭrdzhali
Kirghiz Range *155 F2 Rus.* Kirgizskiy Khrebet; *prev.* Alexander Range. *Mountain range* Kazakhstan/Kyrgyzstan
Kirghiz Steppe *144 see* Kazakhskiy Melkosopochnik
Kiriath-Arba *see* Hebron
Kiribati *177 F2 off.* Republic of Kiribati. *Country* C Pacific Ocean
Kırıkhan *148 D4* Hatay, S Turkey
Kırıkkale *148 C3* Kırıkkale, C Turkey
Kirin *see* Jilin
Kirinyaga *105 C6 prev.* Mount Kenya. *Volcano* C Kenya
Kirishi *142 B4 var.* Kirisi. Leningradskaya Oblast', NW Russian Federation
Kirisi *see* Kirishi
Kiritimati *177 G2 prev.* Christmas Island. *Atoll* Line Islands, E Kiribati
Kirkenes *116 E2 var.* Kirkkoniemi. Finnmark, N Norway
Kirkkoniemi *see* Kirkenes
Kirkland Lake *70 D4* Ontario, S Canada
Kırklareli *148 A2 prev.* Kirk-Kilissa. Kırklareli, NW Turkey
Kirkpatrick, Mount *186 B3 mountain* Antarctica
Kirksville *77 G4* Missouri, C USA
Kirkūk *152 B3 var.* Karkūk, Kerkuk. N Iraq
Kirkwall *120 C2* NE Scotland, UK
Kirkwood *77 G4* Missouri, C USA
Kirman *see* Kermān
Kir Moab *see* Al Karak
Kirov *143 C5 prev.* Vyatka. Kirovskaya Oblast', NW Russian Federation
Kirovo-Chepetsk *143 D5* Kirovskaya Oblast', NW Russian Federation
Kirovohrad *141 E3 Rus.* Kirovograd; *prev.* Kirovo, Yelizavetgrad, Zinov'yevsk. Kirovohrads'ka Oblast', C Ukraine
Kīrthar Range *166 B3 mountain range* S Pakistan
Kirun' *see* Chilung
Kiruna *116 C3* Norrbotten, N Sweden
Kisangani *109 D5 prev.* Stanleyville. Haut-Zaïre, NE Congo (Zaire)
Kislovodsk *143 B7* Stavropol'skiy Kray, SW Russian Federation
Kismaayo *105 D6 var.* Chisimayu, Kismayu, *It.* Chisimaio. Jubbada Hoose, S Somalia
Kismayu *see* Kismaayo
Kissidougou *106 C4* Guinée-Forestière, S Guinea
Kissimmee, Lake *75 E4 lake* Florida, SE USA
Kisumu *105 C6 prev.* Port Florence. Nyanza, W Kenya
Kisvárda *131 E6 Ger.* Kleinwardein. Szabolcs-Szatmár-Bereg, E Hungary
Kita *106 D3* Kayes, W Mali
Kitakyūshū *163 A7 var.* Kitakyûsyû. Fukuoka, Kyūshū, SW Japan
Kitakyûsyû *see* Kitakyūshū
Kitami *162 D2* Hokkaidō, NE Japan
Kitchener *70 C5* Ontario, S Canada
Kíthira *see* Kýthira
Kíthnos *see* Kýthnos
Kitimat *68 D4* British Columbia, SW Canada
Kitinen *116 D3 river* N Finland
Kitob *155 E3 Rus.* Kitab. Qashqadaryo Wiloyati, S Uzbekistan
Kitwe *110 D2 var.* Kitwe-Nkana. Copperbelt, C Zambia
Kitwe-Nkana *see* Kitwe
Kitzbühler Alpen *127 C7 mountain range* W Austria
Kivalina *68 C2* Alaska, USA
Kivalo *116 D3 ridge* C Finland
Kivertsi *140 C1 Pol.* Kiwerce, *Rus.* Kivertsy. Volyns'ka Oblast', NW Ukraine
Kivu, Lake *109 E6 Fr.* Lac Kivu. *Lake* Rwanda/Congo (Zaire)
Kızıl Irmak *148 C3 river* C Turkey
Kizil Kum *see* Kyzyl Kum
Kladno *131 A5* Střední Čechy, NW Czech Republic
Klagenfurt *127 D7 Slvn:* Celovec. Kärnten, S Austria
Klaipėda *138 B3 Ger.* Memel. Klaipėda, NW Lithuania
Klamath Falls *78 B4* Oregon, NW USA
Klamath Mountains *78 A4 mountain range* California/Oregon, W USA
Klang *170 B3 var.* Kelang; *prev.* Port Swettenham. Selangor, Peninsular Malaysia
Klarälven *117 B6 river* Norway/Sweden
Klatovy *131 A5 Ger.* Klattau. Západní Čechy, SW Czech Republic
Klazienaveen *118 E2* Drenthe, NE Netherlands
Klein Karas *110 B4* Karas, S Namibia
Kleisoúra *137 A5* Ípeiros, W Greece
Klerksdorp *110 D4* North-West, N South Africa

L

INDEX

Lyepyel' *139 D5 Rus.* Lepel'. Vitsyebskaya Voblasts', N Belarus
Lyme Bay *121 C7 bay* S England, UK
Lynchburg *73 E5* Virginia, NE USA
Lynn Regis *see* King's Lynn
Lyon *123 D5 Eng.* Lyons; *anc.* Lugdunum. Rhône, E France
Lyozna *139 E6 Rus.* Liozno. Vitsyebskaya Voblasts', NE Belarus
Lypovets' *140 D2 Rus.* Lipovets. Vinnyts'ka Oblast', C Ukraine
Lysychans'k *141 H3 Rus.* Lisichansk. Luhans'ka Oblast', E Ukraine
Lyttelton *183 C6* Canterbury, South Island, NZ
Lyubotyn *141 G2 Rus.* Lyubotin. Kharkivs'ka Oblast', E Ukraine
Lyulyakovo *136 E2 prev.* Keremitlik. Burgaska Oblast, E Bulgaria
Lyusina *139 B6 Rus.* Lyusino. Brestskaya Voblasts', SW Belarus

M

Ma'ān *151 B7* Ma'ān, SW Jordan
Maardu *138 D2 Ger.* Maart. Harjumaa, NW Estonia
Ma'aret-en-Nu'man *see* Ma'arrat an Nu'mān
Ma'arrat an Nu'mān *150 B3 var.* Ma'aret-en-Nu'man, *Fr.* Maarret enn Naamâne. Idlib, NW Syria
Maarret enn Naamâne *see* Ma'arrat an Nu'mān
Maaseik *119 D5 prev.* Maeseyck. Limburg, NE Belgium
Maastricht *119 D6 var.* Maestricht; *anc.* Traietum ad Mosam, Traiectum Tungorum. Limburg, SE Netherlands
Macao *160 C6 Chin.* Aomen, *Port.* Macau. *Portugese special territory* E Asia
Macapá *95 E1 state capital* Amapá, N Brazil
Macassar *see* Ujungpandang
MacCluer Gulf *see* Berau, Teluk
Macdonnell Ranges *178 D4 mountain range* Northern Territory, C Australia
Macedonia, FYR *133 D6 off.* the Former Yugoslav Republic of Macedonia, *var.* Macedonia, *Mac.* Makedonija, *abbrev.* FYR Macedonia, FYROM. *Country* SE Europe
Maceió *95 G3 state capital* Alagoas, E Brazil
Machachi *92 B1* Pichincha, C Ecuador
Machala *92 B2* El Oro, SW Ecuador
Machanga *111 E3* Sofala, E Mozambique
Machilīpatnam *164 D1 var.* Bandar Masulipatnam. Andhra Pradesh, E India
Machiques *90 C2* Zulia, NW Venezuela
Macías Nguema Biyogo *see* Bioco, Isla de
Măcin *140 D5* Tulcea, SE Romania
Macizo de las Guayanas *see* Guiana Highlands
Mackay *180 D4* Queensland, NE Australia
Mackay, Lake *178 C4 salt lake* Northern Territory/Western Australia
Mackenzie *69 E3 river* Northwest Territories, NW Canada
Mackenzie Bay *186 D3 bay* Antarctica
Mackenzie Mountains *68 D3 mountain range* Northwest Territories, NW Canada
Macleod, Lake *178 A4 lake* Western Australia
Macomb *72 A4* Illinois, N USA
Macomer *129 A5* Sardegna, Italy, C Mediterranean Sea
Macon *74 D2* Georgia, SE USA
Macon *77 G4* Missouri, C USA
Mâcon *123 D5 anc.* Matisco, Matisco Ædourum. Saône-et-Loire, C France
Macquarie Ridge *186 C5 undersea feature* SW Pacific Ocean
Macuspana *83 G4* Tabasco, SE Mexico
Ma'dabā *151 B6 var.* Mādabā, Madeba; *anc.* Medeba. 'Ammān, NW Jordan
Madagascar *111 F3 off.* Democratic Republic of Madagascar, *Malg.* Madagasikara; *prev.* Malagasy Republic. *Country* W Indian Ocean
Madagascar *111 F3 island* W Indian Ocean
Madagascar Basin *101 E7 undersea feature* W Indian Ocean
Madagascar Plateau *101 E7 var.* Madagascar Ridge, Madagascar Rise, *Rus.* Madagaskarskiy Khrebet. *Undersea feature* W Indian Ocean
Madagascar Ridge *see* Madagascar Plateau
Madagascar Rise *see* Madagascar Plateau
Madagaskarskiy Khrebet *see* Madagascar Plateau
Madang *176 B3* Madang, N PNG
Madanīyīn *see* Médenine
Made *118 C4* Noord-Brabant, S Netherlands
Madeba *see* Ma'dabā
Madeira *102 A2 var.* Ilha de Madeira. *Island* Portugal, NE Atlantic Ocean
Madeira *102 A2 var.* Madeira, *Port.* Arquipélago da Madeira. *Island group* Portugal, NE Atlantic Ocean
Madeira Plain *98 C3 undersea feature* E Atlantic Ocean
Madeira, Rio *94 D2 Sp.* Río Madera. *River* Bolivia/Brazil *see also* Madera, Río
Madeleine, Îles de la *71 F4 Eng.* Magdalen Islands. *Island group* Québec, E Canada
Madera *79 B6* California, W USA
Madhya Pradesh *167 E4 prev.* Central Provinces and Berar. *Admin. region state* C India
Madīnat ath Thawrah *150 C2 var.* Ath Thawrah. Ar Raqqah, N Syria Asia
Madison *72 B3 state capital* Wisconsin, N USA
Madison *77 F3* South Dakota, N USA
Madiun *170 D5 prev.* Madioen. Jawa, C Indonesia
Madona *138 D4 Ger.* Modohn. Madona, E Latvia
Madras *see* Tamil Nādu
Madras *164 D2 var.* Chennai. Tamil Nādu, S India
Madre de Dios *88 B4 off.* Departamento de Madre de Dios. *Department* E Peru
Madre de Dios, Río *93 E3 river* Bolivia/Peru
Madre del Sur, Sierra *83 E5 mountain range* S Mexico
Madre, Laguna *83 F3 lagoon* NE Mexico
Madre, Laguna *81 G5 lake* Texas, SW USA
Madre Occidental, Sierra *82 C3 var.* Western Sierra Madre. *Mountain range* C Mexico
Madre Oriental, Sierra *83 E3 var.* Eastern Sierra Madre. *Mountain range* C Mexico
Madrid *124 D3 country capital* (Spain) Madrid, C Spain
Madurai *164 C3 prev.* Madura, Mathurai. Tamil Nādu, S India
Madura, Pulau *170 D5 prev.* Madoera. *Island* C Indonesia
Maebashi *163 D5 var.* Maebasi, Mayebashi. Gunma, Honshū, S Japan
Maebasi *see* Maebashi
Mae Nam Khong *see* Mekong
Mae Nam Nan *168 C4 river* NW Thailand
Mae Nam Yom *168 C4 river* W Thailand
Maestricht *see* Maastricht
Maewo *176 D4 prev.* Aurora. *Island* C Vanuatu
Mafia *105 D7 island* E Tanzania
Mafraq *see* Al Mafraq
Magadan *147 G3* Magadanskaya Oblast', E Russian Federation
Magangué *90 B2* Bolívar, N Colombia
Magdalena *88 A2 off.* Departamento del Magdalena. *Province* N Colombia
Magdalena *93 F3* Beni, N Bolivia
Magdalena *82 B1* Sonora, NW Mexico
Magdalena, Isla *82 B3 island* W Mexico
Magdalena, Río *90 B2 river* C Colombia
Magdeburg *126 C4* Sachsen-Anhalt, C Germany
Magelang *170 C5* Jawa, C Indonesia
Magellan, Strait of *97 B8 Sp.* Estrecho de Magallanes. *Strait* Argentina/Chile
Magerøy *see* Magerøya
Magerøya *116 D1 var.* Magerøy. *Island* N Norway
Maggiore, Lake *128 B1 It.* Lago Maggiore. *Lake* Italy/Switzerland
Maglaj *132 C3* N Bosnia and Herzegovina
Maglie *129 E6* Puglia, SE Italy
Magna *76 B4* Utah, W USA
Magnesia *see* Manisa
Magnitogorsk *146 B4* Chelyabinskaya Oblast', C Russian Federation
Magta' Lahjar *106 C3 var.* Magta Lahjar, Magta' Lahjar, Magta Lahjar. Brakna, SW Mauritania
Magway *see* Magwe
Magwe *168 A3 var.* Magway. Magwe, W Myanmar
Mahajanga *111 F2 var.* Majunga. Mahajanga, NW Madagascar
Mahakam, Sungai *170 D4 var.* Koetai, Kutai. *River* Borneo, C Indonesia
Mahalapye *110 D3 var.* Mahalatswe. Central, SE Botswana
Mahalatswe *see* Mahalapye
Mahān *152 D3* Kermān, E Iran
Mahanādi *167 F4 river* E India
Mahārāshtra *166 D5 state* W India
Mahbés *see* El Mahbas
Mahbūbnagar *166 D5* Andhra Pradesh, C India
Mahdia *103 F2 var.* Al Mahdīyah, Mehdia. NE Tunisia
Mahé *111 H1 island* Inner Islands, NE Seychelles
Mahia Peninsula *182 E4 peninsula* North Island, NZ
Mahilyow *139 D6 Rus.* Mogilëv. Mahilyowskaya Voblasts', E Belarus
Mahmūd-e 'Erāqī *see* Maḩmūd-e Rāqī
Maḩmūd-e Rāqī *155 E4 var.* Mahmūd-e 'Erāqī. Kāpīsā, NE Afghanistan
Mahón *125 H3 Cat.* Maó, *Eng.* Port Mahon; *anc.* Portus Magonis. Menorca, Spain, W Mediterranean Sea
Maicao *90 C1* La Guajira, N Colombia
Mai Ceu *see* Maych'ew
Mai Chio *see* Maych'ew
Maidstone *121 E7* SE England, UK
Maiduguri *107 H4* Borno, NE Nigeria
Maimāna *see* Meymaneh
Main *127 B5 river* C Germany
Mai-Ndombe, Lac *109 C6 prev.* Lac Léopold II. *Lake* W Congo (Zaire)
Maine *73 G2 off.* State of Maine; also known as Lumber State, Pine Tree State. *State* NE USA
Maine *122 B3 cultural region* NW France
Maine, Gulf of *73 H2 gulf* NE USA
Main Island *see* Bermuda
Mainland *120 C2 island* Orkney, N Scotland, UK
Mainland *120 D1 island* Shetland, NE Scotland, UK
Mainz *127 B5 Fr.* Mayence. Rheinland-Pfalz, SW Germany
Maio *106 A3 var.* Mayo. *Island* Ilhas de Sotavento, SE Cape Verde
Maisur *see* Karnātaka
Maisur *see* Mysore
Maizhokunggar *158 C5* Xizang Zizhiqu, W China
Maíz, Islas del *85 E3 var.* Corn Islands. *Island group* SE Nicaragua
Mājro *see* Majuro Atoll
Majunga *see* Mahajanga
Majuro Atoll *176 D2 var.* Mājro. *Atoll* Ratak Chain, SE Marshall Islands
Makale *see* Mek'elē
Makarov Basin *188 B3 undersea feature* Arctic Ocean
Makarska *132 B4 It.* Macarsca. Split-Dalmacija, SE Croatia
Makasar *see* Ujungpandang
Makassar *see* Ujungpandang
Makassar Strait *170 D4 Ind.* Selat Makasar. *Strait* C Indonesia
Makay *111 F3 var.* Massif du Makay. *Mountain range* SW Madagascar
Makeni *106 C4* C Sierra Leone
Makhachkala *146 A4 prev.* Petrovsk-Port. Respublika Dagestan, SW Russian Federation
Makin *176 D2 prev.* Pitt Island. *Atoll* Tungaru, W Kiribati
Makira *see* San Cristobal
Makiyivka *141 G3 Rus.* Makeyevka; *prev.* Dmitriyevsk. Donets'ka Oblast', E Ukraine
Makkah *153 A5 Eng.* Mecca. Makkah, W Saudi Arabia
Makkovik *71 F2* Newfoundland and Labrador, NE Canada
Makó *131 D7 Rom.* Macău. Csongrád, SE Hungary
Makoua *109 B5* Cuvette, C Congo
Makran Coast *152 E4 coastal region* SE Iran
Makrany *139 A6 Rus.* Mokrany. Brestskaya Voblasts', SW Belarus
Mākū *152 B2* Āžarbāyjān-e Bākhtarī, NW Iran
Makurdi *107 G4* Benue, C Nigeria
Mala *see* Malaita
Malabār Coast *164 B3 coast* SW India
Malabo *109 A5 prev.* Santa Isabel. *Country capital* (Equatorial Guinea) Isla de Bioco, NW Equatorial Guinea
Malacca *see* Melaka
Malacca, Strait of *170 B3 Ind.* Selat Malaka. *Strait* Indonesia/Malaysia
Malacky *131 C6 Hung.* Malacka. Západné Slovensko, W Slovakia
Maladzyechna *139 C5 Pol.* Molodeczno, *Rus.* Molodechno. Minskaya Voblasts', C Belarus
Málaga *124 D5 anc.* Malaca. Andalucía, S Spain
Malagarasi River *105 B7 river* W Tanzania
Malaita *176 C3 var.* Mala. *Island* N Solomon Islands
Malakal *105 B5* Upper Nile, S Sudan
Malakula *see* Malekula
Malang *170 D5* Jawa, C Indonesia
Malange *see* Malanje
Malanje *110 B1 var.* Malange. Malanje, NW Angola
Mälaren *117 C6 lake* C Sweden
Malatya *149 E4 anc.* Melitene. Malatya, SE Turkey
Mala Vyska *141 E3 Rus.* Malaya Viska. Kirovohrads'ka Oblast', S Ukraine
Malawi *111 E1 off.* Republic of Malaŵi; *prev.* Nyasaland, Nyasaland Protectorate. *Country* S Africa
Malawi, Lake *see* Nyasa, Lake
Malay Peninsula *156 D4 peninsula* Malaysia/Thailand
Malaysia *170 B3 var.* Federation of Malaysia; *prev.* the separate territories of Federation of Malaya, Sarawak and Sabah (North Borneo) and Singapore. *Country* SE Asia
Malaysia, Federation of *see* Malaysia
Malbork *130 C2 Ger.* Marienburg, Marienburg in Westpreussen. Elbląg, N Poland
Malchin *126 C3* Mecklenburg-Vorpommern, N Germany
Malden *77 H5* Missouri, C USA
Malden Island *177 G3 prev.* Independence Island. *Atoll* E Kiribati
Maldives *164 A4 off.* Maldivian Divehi, Republic of Maldives. *Country* N Indian Ocean
Male' *164 B4* Male' Atoll, C Maldives
Male' Atoll *164 B4 var.* Kaafu Atoll. *Atoll* C Maldives
Malekula *176 D4 var.* Malakula; *prev.* Mallicolo. *Island* W Vanuatu
Malesína *137 C5* Stereá Ellás, E Greece
Malheur Lake *78 C3 lake* Oregon, NW USA
Mali *107 E3 off.* Republic of Mali, *Fr.* République du Mali; *prev.* French Sudan, Sudanese Republic. *Country* W Africa
Malik, Wadi al *see* Milk, Wadi el
Mali Kyun *169 B5 var.* Tavoy Island. *Island* Mergui Archipelago, S Myanmar
Malindi *105 D7* Coast, SE Kenya
Malko Tŭrnovo *136 E3* Burgaska Oblast, SE Bulgaria
Mallaig *120 B3* N Scotland, UK
Mallawi *104 B2* C Egypt
Mallicolo *see* Malekula
Mallorca *125 G3 Eng.* Majorca; *anc.* Baleares Major. *Island* Islas Baleares, Spain, W Mediterranean Sea
Malmberget *116 C3* Norrbotten, N Sweden
Malmédy *119 D6* Liège, E Belgium
Malmö *117 B7* Malmöhus, S Sweden
Maļoeļap *see* Maloelap Atoll
Maloelap Atoll *176 D1 var.* Maļoeļap. *Atoll* E Marshall Islands
Małopolska *130 D4 plateau* S Poland
Malozemel'skaya Tundra *142 D3 physical region* NW Russian Federation
Malta *129 C8 off.* Republic of Malta. *Country* C Mediterranean Sea
Malta *129 C8 island* Malta, C Mediterranean Sea
Malta *76 C1* Montana, NW USA
Malta *138 D4* Rēzekne, SE Latvia
Malta Channel *129 C8 It.* Canale di Malta. *Strait* Italy/Malta
Maluku *171 F4 Dut.* Molukken, *Eng.* Moluccas; *prev.* Spice Islands. *Island group* E Indonesia
Malung *117 B6* Kopparberg, C Sweden
Malyn *140 D2 Rus.* Malin. Zhytomyrs'ka Oblast', N Ukraine
Mamberamo, Sungai *171 H4 river* Irian Jaya, E Indonesia
Mambij *see* Manbij
Mamonovo *138 A4 Ger.* Heiligenbeil. Kaliningradskaya Oblast', W Russian Federation
Mamoré, Rio *93 F3 river* Bolivia/Brazil
Mamou *106 C4* Moyenne-Guinée, W Guinea
Mamoudzou *111 F2 dependent territory capital* (Mayotte) C Mayotte
Mamuno *110 C3* Ghanzi, W Botswana
Manacor *125 G3* Mallorca, Spain, W Mediterranean Sea
Manado *171 F3 prev.* Menado. Sulawesi, C Indonesia
Managua *84 D3 country capital* (Nicaragua) Managua, W Nicaragua
Managua, Lago de *84 C3 var.* Xolotlán. *Lake* W Nicaragua
Manakara *111 G4* Fianarantsoa, SE Madagascar
Manama *144 see* Al Manāmah
Mananjary *111 G3* Fianarantsoa, SE Madagascar
Manapouri, Lake *183 A7 lake* South Island, NZ
Manar *see* Mannar
Manas, Gora *155 E2 mountain* Kyrgyzstan/Uzbekistan
Manaus *94 D2 prev.* Manáos. *State capital* Amazonas, NW Brazil
Manavgat *148 B4* Antalya, SW Turkey
Manbij *150 C2 var.* Mambij, *Fr.* Membidj. Ḩalab, N Syria
Manchester *121 D5 Lat.* Mancunium. NW England, UK
Manchester *73 G3* New Hampshire, NE USA
Man-chou-li *see* Manzhouli
Manchuria *157 E1 cultural region* NE China
Máncio Lima *see* Japiim
Mand *see* Mand, Rūd-e
Mandalay *168 B3* Mandalay, C Myanmar
Mandan *77 E2* North Dakota, N USA
Mandeville *86 B5* C Jamaica
Mándra *137 C6* Attikí, C Greece
Mand, Rūd-e *152 D4 var.* Mand. *River* S Iran
Mandurah *179 A6* Western Australia
Manduria *129 E5* Puglia, SE Italy
Mandya *164 C2* Karnātaka, C India
Manfredonia *129 D5* Puglia, SE Italy
Mangai *109 C6* Bandundu, W Congo (Zaire)
Mangaia *177 G5 island group* S Cook Islands
Mangalia *140 D5 anc.* Callatis. Constanța, SE Romania
Mangalmé *108 C3* Guéra, SE Chad
Mangalore *164 B2* Karnātaka, W India
Mangaung *see* Bloemfontein
Mango *see* Sansanné-Mango
Mangoky *111 F3 river* W Madagascar
Manhattan *77 F4* Kansas, C USA
Manicouagan, Réservoir *70 D3 lake* Québec, E Canada
Manihiki *177 G4 atoll* N Cook Islands
Manihiki Plateau *175 E3 undersea feature* C Pacific Ocean
Maniitsoq *114 C3 var.* Manîtsoq, *Dan.* Sukkertoppen. S Greenland
Manila *171 E1 off.* City of Manila. *Country capital* (Philippines) Luzon, N Philippines
Manisa *148 A3 var.* Manissa; *prev.* Saruhan, *anc.* Magnesia. Manisa, W Turkey
Manissa *see* Manisa
Manitoba *69 F5 province* S Canada
Manitoba, Lake *69 F5 lake* Manitoba, S Canada
Manitoulin Island *70 C4 island* Ontario, S Canada
Manîtsoq *see* Maniitsoq
Manizales *90 B3* Caldas, W Colombia
Manjimup *179 A7* Western Australia
Mankato *77 F3* Minnesota, N USA
Manlleu *125 G2* Cataluña, NE Spain
Manly *180 E1* New South Wales, SE Australia
Manmād *166 C5* Mahārāshtra, W India
Mannar *164 C3 var.* Manar. Northern Province, NW Sri Lanka
Mannar, Gulf of *164 C3 gulf* India/Sri Lanka
Mannheim *127 B5* Baden-Württemberg, SW Germany
Manono *109 E7* Shabo, SE Congo (Zaire)
Manosque *123 D6* Alpes-de-Haute-Provence, SE France
Manra *177 F3 prev.* Sydney Island. *Atoll* Phoenix Islands, C Kiribati
Mansa *110 D2 prev.* Fort Rosebery. Luapula, N Zambia
Mansel Island *69 G3 island* Northwest Territories, NE Canada
Mansfield *72 D4* Ohio, N USA
Manta *92 A2* Manabí, W Ecuador
Manteca *79 B6* California, W USA
Mantova *128 B2 Eng.* Mantua, *Fr.* Mantoue. Lombardia, NW Italy
Manuae *177 G4 island* S Cook Islands
Manukau *see* Manurewa
Manurewa *182 D3 var.* Manukau. Auckland, North Island, NZ
Manzanares *125 E3* Castilla-La Mancha, C Spain
Manzanillo *82 D4* Colima, SW Mexico
Manzanillo *86 C3* Granma, E Cuba
Manzhouli *159 F1 var.* Man-chou-li. Nei Mongol Zizhiqu, N China
Mao *108 B3* Kanem, W Chad
Maoke, Pegunungan *171 H4 Dut.* Sneeuw-gebergte, *Eng.* Snow Mountains. *Mountain range* Irian Jaya, E Indonesia
Maoming *160 C6* Guangdong, S China
Mapmaker Seamounts *157 H2 undersea feature* N Pacific Ocean
Maputo *110 D4 prev.* Lourenço Marques. *Country capital* (Mozambique) Maputo, S Mozambique
Marabá *95 F2* Pará, NE Brazil
Maracaibo *90 C1* Zulia, NW Venezuela
Maracaibo, Lago de *90 C2 var.* Lake Maracaibo. *Inlet* NW Venezuela
Maracaibo, Lake *see* Maracaibo, Lago de
Maracay *90 D2* Aragua, N Venezuela
Marada *see* Marādah
Marādah *103 G3 var.* Marada. N Libya
Maradi *107 G3* Maradi, S Niger
Maragha *see* Marāgheh
Marāgheh *152 C2 var.* Maragha. Āžarbāyjān-e Khāvarī, NW Iran
Marajó, Baía de *95 F1 bay* N Brazil
Marajó, Ilha de *95 E1 island* N Brazil
Marakesh *see* Marrakech
Maramba *see* Livingstone
Maranhão *95 F2 off.* Estado do Maranhão. *State* E Brazil
Marañón, Río *92 B2 river* N Peru
Maraş *see* Kahramanmaraş
Marash *see* Kahramanmaraş
Marathon *70 C4* Ontario, S Canada
Marathónas *137 C5 prev.* Marathón. Attikí, C Greece
Marbella *124 D5* Andalucía, S Spain
Marble Bar *178 B4* Western Australia
Marburg an der Lahn *126 B4 hist.* Marburg. Hessen, W Germany
March *see* Morava
Marche *123 C5 cultural region* C France
Marche *128 C3 cultural region* E Italy
Marche-en-Famenne *119 C7* Luxembourg, SE Belgium
Marchena, Isla *92 B4 var.* Bindloe Island. *Island* Galapagos Islands, Ecuador, E Pacific Ocean
Mar Chiquita, Laguna *96 C3 lake* C Argentina
Marcounda *see* Markounda
Mardān *166 C1* North-West Frontier Province, N Pakistan
Mar del Plata *97 D5* Buenos Aires, E Argentina
Mardin *149 E4* Mardin, SE Turkey
Maré *176 D5 island* Îles Loyauté, E New Caledonia
Marea Neagră *see* Black Sea
Mare Creticum *see* Kritikó Pélagos
Mareeba *180 D3* Queensland, NE Australia
Margarita, Isla de *91 E1 island* N Venezuela
Margate *121 E7 prev.* Mergate. SE England, UK
Marghita *140 B3 Hung.* Margitta. Bihor, NW Romania
Marhanets' *141 F3 Rus.* Marganets. Dnipropetrovs'ka Oblast', E Ukraine
María Cleofas, Isla *82 C4 island* C Mexico
Maria Island *181 C8 island* Tasmania, SE Australia
María Madre, Isla *82 C4 island* C Mexico
María Magdalena, Isla *82 C4 island* C Mexico
Mariana Trench *157 G4 undersea feature* W Pacific Ocean
Mariánské Lázně *131 A5 Ger.* Marienbad. Západní Čechy, W Czech Republic
Marías, Islas *82 C4 island group* C Mexico
Maribor *127 E7 Ger.* Marburg. NE Slovenia
Marica *see* Maritsa
Maridi *105 B5* Western Equatoria, SW Sudan
Marie Byrd Land *186 A3 physical region* Antarctica
Marie-Galante *87 G4 var.* Ceyre to the Caribs. *Island* SE Guadeloupe
Mariental *110 B4* Hardap, SW Namibia
Mariestad *117 B6* Skaraborg, S Sweden
Marietta *74 D2* Georgia, SE USA
Marijampolė *138 B4 prev.* Kapsukas. Marijampolė, S Lithuania
Marília *95 E4* São Paulo, S Brazil
Marín *124 B1* Galicia, NW Spain
Mar"ina Horka *139 C6 Rus.* Mar'ina Gorka. Minskaya Voblasts', C Belarus
Maringá *95 E4* Paraná, S Brazil
Marion *77 G3* Iowa, C USA
Marion *72 D4* Ohio, N USA

Mil'kovo *147 H3* Kamchatskaya Oblast', E Russian Federation
Milk River *76 C1 river* Montana, NW USA
Milk River *69 E5* Alberta, SW Canada
Milk, Wadi el *104 B4 var.* Wadi al Malik. *River* C Sudan
Milledgeville *75 E2* Georgia, SE USA
Mille Lacs Lake *77 F2 lake* Minnesota, N USA
Millerovo *143 B6* Rostovskaya Oblast', SW Russian Federation
Mílos *137 C7 island* Kykládes, Greece, Aegean Sea
Mílos *137 C6* Mílos, Kykládes, Greece, Aegean Sea
Milton *183 B7* Otago, South Island, NZ
Milton Keynes *121 D6* SE England, UK
Milwaukee *72 B3* Wisconsin, N USA
Min *see* Fujian
Mīnā' Qābūs *172 B3* NE Oman
Minas Gerais *95 F3 off.* Estado de Minas Gerais. *State* E Brazil
Minatitlán *83 F4* Veracruz-Llave, E Mexico
Minbu *168 A3* Magwe, W Myanmar
Minch, The *120 B3 var.* North Minch. *Strait* NW Scotland, UK
Mindanao *171 F2 island* S Philippines
Mindanao Sea *see* Bohol Sea
Mindelheim *127 C6* Bayern, S Germany
Mindello *see* Mindelo
Mindelo *106 A2 var.* Mindello; *prev.* Porto Grande. São Vicente, N Cape Verde
Minden *126 B4 anc.* Minthun. Nordrhein-Westfalen, NW Germany
Mindoro *171 E2 island* N Philippines
Mindoro Strait *171 E2 strait* W Philippines
Mineral Wells *81 F2* Texas, SW USA
Mingäçevir *149 G2 Rus.* Mingechaur, Mingechevir. C Azerbaijan
Mingāora *166 C1 var.* Mingora, Mongora. North-West Frontier Province, N Pakistan
Mingora *see* Mingāora
Minho *124 B2 former province* N Portugal
Minho *see* Miño
Minicoy Island *164 B3 island* SW India
Minius *see* Miño
Minna *107 G4* Niger, C Nigeria
Minneapolis *77 F2* Minnesota, N USA
Minnesota *77 F2 off.* State of Minnesota; also known as Gopher State, New England of the West, North Star State. *State* N USA
Miño *124 B2 var.* Mino, Minius, *Port.* Minho. *River* Portugal/Spain *see also* Minho
Mino *see* Miño
Minot *77 E1* North Dakota, N USA
Minsk *139 C6 country capital* (Belarus) Minskaya Voblasts', C Belarus
Minskaya Wzvyshsha *139 C6 mountain range* C Belarus
Minto, Lac *70 D2 lake* Québec, C Canada
Minya *see* El Minya
Miraflores *82 C3* Baja California Sur, W Mexico
Miranda de Ebro *125 E1* La Rioja, N Spain
Miri *170 D3* Sarawak, East Malaysia
Mirim Lagoon *95 E5 var.* Lake Mirim, *Sp.* Laguna Merín. *Lagoon* Brazil/Uruguay
Mirim, Lake *see* Mirim Lagoon
Mírina *see* Mýrina
Mīrjāveh *152 E4* Sīstān va Balūchestān, SE Iran
Mirny *186 C3 Russian research station* Antarctica
Mirnyy *147 F3* Respublika Sakha (Yakutiya), NE Russian Federation
Mīrpur Khās *166 B3* Sind, SE Pakistan
Mirtóo Pélagos *137 C6 Eng.* Mirtoan Sea; *anc.* Myrtoum Mare. *Sea* S Greece
Miskito Coast *see* Mosquito Coast
Miskitos, Cayos *85 E2 island group* NE Nicaragua
Miskolc *131 D6* Borsod-Abaúj-Zemplén, NE Hungary
Misool, Pulau *171 F4 island* Maluku, E Indonesia
Mişrātah *103 F2 var.* Misurata. NW Libya
Mission *81 G5* Texas, SW USA
Mississippi *74 B2 off.* State of Mississippi; also known as Bayou State, Magnolia State. *State* SE USA
Mississippi Delta *74 B4 delta* Louisiana, S USA
Mississippi River *67 C6 river* C USA
Missoula *76 B1* Montana, NW USA
Missouri *77 F5 off.* State of Missouri; also known as Bullion State, Show Me State. *State* C USA
Missouri River *77 E3 river* C USA
Mistassini, Lac *70 D3 lake* Québec, SE Canada
Mistelbach an der Zaya *127 E6* Niederösterreich, NE Austria
Misti, Volcán *93 E4 mountain* S Peru
Misurata *see* Mişrātah
Mitchell *181 D5* Queensland, E Australia
Mitchell *77 E3* South Dakota, N USA
Mitchell, Mount *75 E1 mountain* North Carolina, SE USA
Mitchell River *180 C2 river* Queensland, NE Australia
Mi Tho *see* My Tho
Mitilíni *see* Mytilíni
Mito *163 D5* Ibaraki, Honshū, S Japan
Mits'iwa *see* Massawa
Mitú *90 C4* Vaupés, SE Colombia
Mitumba, Monts *109 E7 var.* Chaîne des Mitumba, Mitumba Range. *Mountain range* E Congo (Zaire)
Mitumba Range *see* Mitumba, Monts
Miyako *162 D4* Iwate, Honshū, C Japan
Miyako-jima *163 D6 island* Sakishima-shotō, SW Japan
Miyakonojō *163 B8 var.* Miyakonzyô. Miyazaki, Kyūshū, SW Japan
Miyakonzyô *see* Miyakonojō
Miyāneh *see* Mīāneh
Miyazaki *163 B8* Miyazaki, Kyūshū, SW Japan
Mizil *140 C5* Prahova, SE Romania
Miziya *136 C1* Oblast Montana, NW Bulgaria
Mizpé Ramon *151 A7* Southern, S Israel
Mjøsa *117 B6 var.* Mjøsen. *Lake* S Norway
Mjøsen *see* Mjøsa
Mladenovac *132 D4* Serbia, C Yugoslavia
Mława *130 D3* Ciechanów, C Poland
Mljet *133 B5 It.* Meleda; *anc.* Melita. *Island* S Croatia
Mmabatho *110 C4* North-West, N South Africa
Moab *76 B5* Utah, W USA
Moab, Kir of *see* Al Karak
Moa Island *180 C1 island* Queensland, NE Australia
Moanda *109 B6 var.* Mouanda. Haut-Ogooué, SE Gabon
Moba *109 E7* Shaba, E Congo (Zaire)
Mobay *see* Montego Bay
Mobaye *109 C5* Basse-Kotto, S Central African Republic
Moberly *77 G4* Missouri, C USA
Mobile *74 C3* Alabama, S USA
Mobutu Sese Seko, Lac *see* Albert, Lake
Mochudi *110 C4* Kgatleng, SE Botswana
Mocímboa da Praia *111 F2 var.* Vila de Mocímboa da Praia. Cabo Delgado, N Mozambique
Môco *110 B2 var.* Morro de Môco. *Mountain* W Angola
Mocoa *90 A4* Putumayo, SW Colombia
Mocuba *111 E3* Zambézia, NE Mozambique
Modena *128 B3 anc.* Mutina. Emilia-Romagna, N Italy
Modesto *79 B6* California, W USA
Modica *129 C7 anc.* Motyca. Sicilia, Italy, C Mediterranean Sea
Modriča *132 C3* N Bosnia and Herzegovina
Moe *181 C7* Victoria, SE Australia
Moero, Lac *see* Mweru, Lake
Mogadishu *see* Muqdisho
Mogilno *130 C3* Bydgoszcz, C Poland
Mohammedia *102 C2 prev.* Fédala. NW Morocco
Mohave, Lake *79 D7 reservoir* Arizona/Nevada, W USA
Mohawk River *73 F3 river* New York, NE USA
Mohéli *111 F2 var.* Mwali, Mohilla, Mohila, *Fr.* Moili. *Island* S Comoros
Mohila *see* Mohéli
Mohilla *see* Mohéli
Mohns Ridge *115 F3 undersea feature* Greenland Sea/Norwegian Sea
Moho *93 E4* Puno, SW Peru
Mohoro *105 C7* Pwani, E Tanzania
Mohyliv-Podil's'kyy *140 D3 Rus.* Mogilev-Podol'skiy. Vinnyts'ka Oblast', C Ukraine
Moi *117 A6* Rogaland, S Norway
Moili *see* Mohéli
Mo i Rana *116 C3* Nordland, C Norway
Mõisaküla *138 D3 Ger.* Moiseküll. Viljandimaa, S Estonia
Moissac *123 B6* Tarn-et-Garonne, S France
Mojácar *125 E5* Andalucía, S Spain
Mojave Desert *79 D7 plain* California, W USA
Moktama *see* Martaban
Mol *119 C5 prev.* Moll. Antwerpen, N Belgium
Molde *117 A5* Møre og Romsdal, S Norway
Moldo-Too, Khrebet *155 G2 prev.* Khrebet Moldotau. *Mountain range* C Kyrgyzstan
Moldova *140 D3 off.* Republic of Moldova, *var.* Moldavia; *prev.* Moldovan SSR, *Rus.* Moldavskaya SSR. *Country* SE Europe
Moldova Nouă *140 A4 Ger.* Neumoldowa, *Hung.* Újmoldova. Caraş-Severin, SW Romania
Moldoveanul *see* Vârful Moldoveanu
Molfetta *129 E5* Puglia, SE Italy
Mollendo *93 E4* Arequipa, SW Peru
Mölndal *117 B7* Göteborg och Bohus, S Sweden
Molochans'k *141 G4 Rus.* Molochansk. Zaporiz'ka Oblast', SE Ukraine
Molodezhnaya *186 C2 Russian research station* Antarctica
Molokai *79 B8 Haw.* Moloka'i. *Island* Hawaii, USA, C Pacific Ocean
Molokai Fracture Zone *185 E2 tectonic feature* NE Pacific Ocean
Molopo *110 C4 seasonal river* Botswana/South Africa
Mólos *137 B5* Stereá Ellás, C Greece
Moluccas *157 see* Maluku
Molucca Sea *171 F4 Ind.* Laut Maluku. *Sea* E Indonesia
Mombasa *105 D7 international airport* Coast, SE Kenya
Mombasa *105 D7* Coast, SE Kenya
Mombetsu *see* Monbetsu
Momchilgrad *136 D3 prev.* Mastanli. Khaskovska Oblast, S Bulgaria
Møn *117 B8 prev.* Möen. *Island* SE Denmark
Monaco *123 E6 off.* Principality of Monaco. *Country* W Europe
Monaco *123 C7 var.* Monaco-Ville; *anc.* Monoecus. *Country capital* (Monaco) S Monaco
Monaco, Port de *123 C8 bay* S Monaco
Monaco-Ville *see* Monaco
Monahans *81 E3* Texas, SW USA
Mona, Isla *87 E3 island* W Puerto Rico
Mona Passage *87 E3 Sp.* Canal de la Mona. *Channel* Dominican Republic/Puerto Rico
Monbetsu *162 D2 var.* Mombetsu, Monbetu. Hokkaidō, NE Japan
Monbetu *see* Monbetsu
Moncalieri *128 A2* Piemonte, NW Italy
Monchegorsk *142 C2* Murmanskaya Oblast', NW Russian Federation
Monclova *82 D2* Coahuila de Zaragoza, NE Mexico
Moncton *71 F4* New Brunswick, SE Canada
Mondovì *128 A2* Piemonte, NW Italy
Monfalcone *128 D2* Friuli-Venezia Giulia, NE Italy
Monforte *124 C1* Galicia, NW Spain
Mongo *108 C3* Guéra, C Chad
Mongolia *158 C2 Mong.* Mongol Uls. *Country* E Asia
Mongolia, Plateau of *156 D1 plateau* E Mongolia
Mongora *see* Mingāora
Mongu *110 C2* Western, W Zambia
Monkchester *see* Newcastle upon Tyne
Monkey Bay *111 E2* Southern, SE Malawi
Monkey River *see* Monkey River Town
Monkey River Town *84 C2 var.* Monkey River. Toledo, SE Belize
Monoecus *see* Monaco
Mono Lake *79 C6 lake* California, W USA
Monóvar *125 F4* País Valenciano, E Spain
Monroe *74 B2* Louisiana, S USA
Monrovia *106 C5 country capital* (Liberia) W Liberia
Mons *119 B6 Dut.* Bergen. Hainaut, S Belgium
Monselice *128 C2* Veneto, NE Italy
Montagnes Rocheuses *see* Rocky Mountains
Montana *76 B1 off.* State of Montana; also known as Mountain State, Treasure State. *State* NW USA
Montana *136 C2 prev.* Ferdinand, Mikhaylovgrad. Oblast Montana, NW Bulgaria
Montargis *122 C4* Loiret, C France
Montauban *123 B6* Tarn-et-Garonne, S France
Montbéliard *122 D4* Doubs, E France
Mont Cenis, Col du *123 D5 pass* E France
Mont-de-Marsan *123 B6* Landes, SW France
Monteagudo *93 G4* Chuquisaca, S Bolivia
Monte-Carlo *123 C8* NE Monaco
Monte Caseros *96 D3* Corrientes, NE Argentina
Monte Cristi *86 D3 var.* San Fernando de Monte Cristi. NW Dominican Republic
Montegiardino *128 E2* SE San Marino
Montego Bay *86 A4 var.* Mobay. W Jamaica
Montélimar *123 D5 anc.* Acunum Acusio, Montilium Adhemari. Drôme, E France
Montemorelos *83 E3* Nuevo León, NE Mexico
Montenegro *133 C5 Serb.* Crna Gora. Admin. region *republic* SW Yugoslavia
Monte Patria *96 B3* Coquimbo, N Chile
Monterey *see* Monterrey
Monterey *79 B6* California, W USA
Monterey Bay *79 A6 bay* California, W USA
Montería *90 B2* Córdoba, NW Colombia
Montero *93 G4* Santa Cruz, C Bolivia
Monterrey *83 E3 var.* Monterey. Nuevo León, NE Mexico
Montes Claros *95 F3* Minas Gerais, SE Brazil
Montevideo *96 D4 country capital* (Uruguay) Montevideo, S Uruguay
Montevideo *77 F2* Minnesota, N USA
Montgenèvre, Col de *123 D5 pass* France/Italy
Montgomery *74 D2 state capital* Alabama, S USA
Monthey *127 A7* Valais, SW Switzerland
Montluçon *122 C4* Allier, C France
Montoro *124 D4* Andalucía, S Spain
Montpelier *73 G2 state capital* Vermont, NE USA
Montpellier *123 C6* Hérault, S France
Montréal *71 E4 Eng.* Montreal. Québec, SE Canada
Montrose *76 C5* Colorado, C USA
Montrose *120 D3* E Scotland, UK
Montserrat *87 G3 var.* Emerald Isle. *UK dependent territory* E West Indies
Monywa *168 B3* Sagaing, C Myanmar
Monza *128 B2* Lombardia, N Italy
Monze *110 D2* Southern, S Zambia
Monzón *125 F2* Aragón, NE Spain
Moonie *181 D5* Queensland, E Australia
Moora *179 A6* Western Australia
Moore *81 G1* Oklahoma, C USA
Moore, Lake *179 B6 lake* Western Australia
Moorhead *77 F2* Minnesota, N USA
Moose *70 C3 river* Ontario, S Canada
Moosehead Lake *73 G1 lake* Maine, NE USA
Moosonee *70 C3* Ontario, SE Canada
Mopti *107 E3* Mopti, C Mali
Moquegua *93 E4* Moquegua, SE Peru
Mora *117 C5* Kopparberg, C Sweden
Morales *84 C2* Izabal, E Guatemala
Morant Bay *86 B5* E Jamaica
Moratalla *125 E4* Murcia, SE Spain
Morava *131 C5 var.* March. *River* C Europe *see also* March
Morava *see* Velika Morava
Moravia *131 B5* Iowa, C USA
Moray Firth *120 C3 inlet* N Scotland, UK
Morea *see* Pelopónnisos
Moreau River *76 D2 river* South Dakota, N USA
Moree *181 D5* New South Wales, SE Australia
Morelia *83 E4* Michoacán de Ocampo, S Mexico
Morena, Sierra *124 C4 mountain range* S Spain
Moreni *140 C5* Dâmboviţa, S Romania
Mórfou *134 C5* W Cyprus
Morgan City *74 B3* Louisiana, S USA
Morghāb, Daryā-ye *154 D4 var.* Murgap Deryasy, *Rus.* Murgab. *River* Afghanistan/Turkmenistan
Morioka *162 D4* Iwate, Honshū, C Japan
Morlaix *122 A3* Finistère, NW France
Mornington Abyssal Plain *99 A7 undersea feature* SE Pacific Ocean
Mornington Island *180 B2 island* Wellesley Islands, Queensland, N Australia
Morocco *102 B3 off.* Kingdom of Morocco, *Ar.* Al Mamlakah. *Country* N Africa
Morocco *see* Marrakech
Morogoro *105 C7* Morogoro, E Tanzania
Moro Gulf *171 E3 gulf* S Philippines
Morón *86 C2* Ciego de Ávila, C Cuba
Mörön *158 D2* Hövsgöl, N Mongolia
Morondava *111 F3* Toliara, W Madagascar
Moroni *111 F2 country capital* (Comoros) Grande Comore, NW Comoros
Morotai, Pulau *171 F3 island* Maluku, E Indonesia
Morotiri *see* Marotiri
Morrinsville *182 D3* Waikato, North Island, NZ
Morris *77 F2* Minnesota, N USA
Morris Jesup, Kap *115 E1 headland* N Greenland
Morro de Môco *see* Môco
Morvan *122 D4 physical region* C France
Moscow *144 see* Moskva
Moscow *78 C2* Idaho, NW USA
Mosel *127 A5 Fr.* Moselle. *River* W Europe *see also* Moselle
Moselle *119 E8 Ger.* Mosel. *River* W Europe *see also* Mosel
Moselle *122 D3 department* NE France
Mosgiel *183 B7* Otago, South Island, NZ
Moshi *105 C7* Kilimanjaro, NE Tanzania
Mosjøen *116 B4* Nordland, C Norway
Moskva *143 B5 Eng.* Moscow. *Country capital* (Russian Federation) Gorod Moskva, W Russian Federation
Moskva *155 E3 Rus.* Moskovskiy; *prev.* Chubek. SW Tajikistan
Mosonmagyaróvár *131 C6 Ger.* Wieselburg-Ungarisch-Altenburg; *prev.* Moson and Magyaróvár, *Ger.* Wieselburg and Ungarisch-Altenburg. Győr-Moson-Sopron, NW Hungary
Mosquito Coast *85 E3 var.* Miskito Coast. *Coastal region* E Nicaragua
Mosquitos, Golfo de los *85 F4 Eng.* Mosquito Gulf. *Gulf* N Panama
Moss *117 B6* Østfold, S Norway
Mosselbaai *110 C5 var.* Mosselbai, *Eng.* Mossel Bay. Western Cape, SW South Africa
Mossendjo *109 B6* Le Niari, SW Congo
Mossoró *95 G2* Rio Grande do Norte, NE Brazil
Most *130 A4 Ger.* Brüx. Severní Čechy, NW Czech Republic
Mosta *134 B5 var.* Musta. C Malta
Mostaganem *102 D2 var.* Mestghanem. NW Algeria
Mostar *132 C4* S Bosnia and Herzegovina
Mosul *144 see* Al Mawşil
Mota del Cuervo *125 E3* Castilla-La Mancha, C Spain
Motagua, Río *84 B2 river* Guatemala/Honduras
Motril *124 D5* Andalucía, S Spain
Motru *140 B4* Gorj, SW Romania
Motueka *183 C5* Tasman, South Island, NZ
Motul *83 H3 var.* Motul de Felipe Carrillo Puerto. Yucatán, SE Mexico
Motul de Felipe Carrillo Puerto *see* Motul
Mouanda *see* Moanda
Mouhoun *see* Black Volta
Mouila *109 A6* Ngounié, C Gabon
Mould Bay *69 E2* Prince Patrick Island, Northwest Territories, N Canada
Moulins *122 C4* Allier, C France
Moulmein *168 B4 var.* Maulmain, Mawlamyine. Mon State, S Myanmar
Moundou *108 B4* Logone-Occidental, SW Chad
Moŭng Roessei *169 D5* Bătdâmbâng, W Cambodia
Moun Hou *see* Black Volta
Mountain Home *74 B1* Arkansas, C USA
Mount Ara *see* Büyükağrı Dağı
Mount Cook *183 B6* Canterbury, South Island, NZ
Mount Desert Island *73 H2 island* Maine, NE USA
Mount Fuji *see* Fuji-san
Mount Gambier *181 B7* South Australia
Mount Isa *180 B3* Queensland, C Australia
Mount Magnet *179 B5* Western Australia
Mount Pleasant *77 G4* Iowa, C USA
Mount Pleasant *72 C3* Michigan, N USA
Mount Vernon *72 B5* Illinois, N USA
Mount Vernon *78 B1* Washington, NW USA
Mourdi, Dépression du *108 C2 desert lowland* Chad/Sudan
Mouscron *119 A6 Dut.* Moeskroen. Hainaut, W Belgium
Mouse River *see* Souris River
Moussoro *108 B3* Kanem, W Chad
Moyen Atlas *102 C2 Eng.* Middle Atlas. *Mountain range* N Morocco
Moyobamba *92 B2* San Martín, NW Peru
Moyu *158 B3 var.* Karakax. Xinjiang Uygur Zizhiqu, NW China
Moyynkum, Peski *155 F1 Kaz.* Moyynqum. *Desert* S Kazakhstan
Mozambique *111 E3 off.* Republic of Mozambique; *prev.* People's Republic of Mozambique, Portuguese East Africa. *Country* S Africa
Mozambique Basin *see* Natal Basin
Mozambique Channel *111 E3 Fr.* Canal de Mozambique, *Mal.* Lakandranon' i Mozambika. *Strait* W Indian Ocean
Mozambique Plateau *101 D7 var.* Mozambique Rise. *Undersea feature* SW Indian Ocean
Mozambique Rise *see* Mozambique Plateau
Mpama *109 B6 river* C Congo
Mpika *110 D2* Northern, NE Zambia
Mqinvartsveri *see* Kazbek
Mrągowo *130 D2 Ger.* Sensburg. Olsztyn, NE Poland
Mtwara *105 D8* Mtwara, SE Tanzania
Mualo *see* Messalo, Rio
Muang Chiang Rai *see* Chiang Rai
Muang Kalasin *see* Kalasin
Muang Không *169 D5* Champasak, S Laos
Muang Khôngxédôn *169 D5 var.* Khong Sedone. Salavan, S Laos
Muang Khon Kaen *see* Khon Kaen
Muang Lampang *see* Lampang
Muang Loei *see* Loei
Muang Lom Sak *see* Lom Sak
Muang Nakhon Sawan *see* Nakhon Sawan
Muang Namo *168 C3* Oudômxai, N Laos
Muang Nan *see* Nan
Muang Phalan *168 D4 var.* Muang Phalane. Savannakhét, S Laos
Muang Phalane *see* Muang Phalan
Muang Phayao *see* Phayao
Muang Phitsanulok *see* Phitsanulok
Muang Phrae *see* Phrae
Muang Roi Et *see* Roi Et
Muang Sakon Nakhon *see* Sakon Nakhon
Muang Samut Prakan *see* Samut Prakan
Muang Sing *168 C3* Louang Namtha, N Laos
Muang Ubon *see* Ubon Ratchathani
Muar *170 B3 var.* Bandar Maharani. Johor, Peninsular Malaysia
Mucojo *111 F2* Cabo Delgado, N Mozambique
Mudanjiang *161 E3 var.* Mu-tan-chiang. Heilongjiang, NE China
Mudon *169 B5* Mon State, S Myanmar
Muenchen *see* Munich
Muenster *see* Münster
Mufulira *110 D2* Copperbelt, C Zambia
Mughla *see* Muğla
Muğla *148 A4 var.* Mughla. Muğla, SW Turkey
Mūḩ, Sabkhat al *150 C3 lake* C Syria
Muir Éireann *see* Irish Sea
Muisne *92 A1* Esmeraldas, NW Ecuador
Mukacheve *140 B3 Hung.* Munkács, *Rus.* Mukachevo. Zakarpats'ka Oblast', W Ukraine
Mukalla *see* Al Mukallā
Mula *125 E4* Murcia, SE Spain
Mulaku Atoll *164 B4 var.* Meemu Atoll. *Atoll* C Maldives
Muleshoe *81 E2* Texas, SW USA
Mulhacén *125 E5 var.* Cerro de Mulhacén. *Mountain* S Spain
Mulhouse *122 E4 Ger.* Mülhausen. Haut-Rhin, NE France
Muller, Pegunungan *170 D4 Dut.* Müller-gerbergte. *Mountain range* Borneo, C Indonesia
Müllheim *127 A6* Baden-Württemberg, SW Germany
Mull, Isle of *120 B4 island* W Scotland, UK
Mulongo *109 D7* Shaba, SE Congo (Zaire)
Multān *166 C2* Punjab, E Pakistan
Mumbai *see* Bombay
Munamägi *see* Suur Munamägi

N

New Brunswick 71 E4 *Fr.* Nouveau-Brunswick. *Province* SE Canada
New Caledonia 176 D4 *var.* Kanaky, *Fr.* Nouvelle-Calédonie. *French overseas territory* SW Pacific Ocean
New Caledonia 176 C5 *island* SW Pacific Ocean
New Caledonia Basin 174 C4 *undersea feature* W Pacific Ocean
Newcastle *see* Newcastle upon Tyne
Newcastle 181 D6 New South Wales, SE Australia
Newcastle upon Tyne 120 D4 *var.* Newcastle; *hist.* Monkchester, *Lat.* Pons Aelii. NE England, UK
New Delhi 166 D3 *country capital* (India) Delhi, N India
Newfoundland 71 G3 *Fr.* Terre-Neuve. *Island* Newfoundland and Labrador, SW Canada
Newfoundland and Labrador 71 F2 *Fr.* Terre Neuve. *Province* E Canada
Newfoundland Basin 98 B3 *undersea feature* NW Atlantic Ocean
New Georgia Islands 176 C3 *island group* NW Solomon Islands
New Glasgow 71 F4 Nova Scotia, SE Canada
New Goa *see* Panaji
New Guinea 176 A3 *Dut.* Nieuw Guinea, *Ind.* Irian. *Island* Indonesia/PNG
New Hampshire 73 F2 *off.* State of New Hampshire; also known as The Granite State. *State* NE USA
New Haven 73 G3 Connecticut, NE USA
New Iberia 74 B3 Louisiana, S USA
New Ireland 176 C3 *island* NE PNG
New Jersey 73 F4 *off.* State of New Jersey; also known as The Garden State. *State* NE USA
Newman 178 B4 Western Australia
Newmarket 121 E6 E England, UK
New Mexico 80 C2 *off.* State of New Mexico; also known as Land of Enchantment, Sunshine State. *State* SW USA
New Orleans 74 B3 Louisiana, S USA
New Plymouth 182 C4 Taranaki, North Island, NZ
Newport 72 C4 Kentucky, S USA
Newport 121 D7 S England, UK
Newport 121 C7 SE Wales, UK
Newport 73 G2 Vermont, NE USA
Newport News 73 F5 Virginia, NE USA
New Providence 86 C1 *island* N Bahamas
Newquay 121 C7 SW England, UK
Newry 121 B5 *Ir.* An tIúr. SE Northern Ireland, UK
New Sarum *see* Salisbury
New Siberian Islands 145 *see* Novosibirskiye Ostrova
New South Wales 181 C6 *state* SE Australia
Newton 77 G3 Iowa, C USA
Newtownabbey 121 B5 *Ir.* Baile na Mainistreach. E Northern Ireland, UK
New Ulm 77 F2 Minnesota, N USA
New York 73 F4 New York, NE USA
New York 73 F3 *state* NE USA
New Zealand 182 A4 *abbrev.* NZ. *Country* SW Pacific Ocean
Neyveli 164 C2 Tamil Nādu, SE India
Ngangzê Co 158 B5 *lake* W China
Ngaoundéré 108 B4 *var.* N'Gaoundéré. Adamaoua, N Cameroon
N'Giva 110 B3 *var.* Ondjiva, *Port.* Vila Pereira de Eça. Cunene, S Angola
Ngo 109 B6 Plateaux, SE Congo
Ngoko 109 B5 *river* Cameroon/Congo
Ngourti 107 H3 Diffa, E Niger
Nguigmi 107 H3 *var.* N'Guigmi. Diffa, SE Niger
Nguru 107 G3 Yobe, NE Nigeria
Nha Trang 169 E6 Khanh Hoa, S Vietnam
Niagara Falls 72 D3 *waterfall* Canada/USA
Niagara Falls 73 E3 New York, NE USA
Niagara Falls 70 D5 Ontario, S Canada
Niamey 107 F3 *country capital* (Niger) Niamey, SW Niger
Niangay, Lac 107 E3 *lake* E Mali
Nia-Nia 109 E5 Haut-Zaïre, NE Congo (Zaire)
Nias, Pulau 170 A3 *island* W Indonesia
Nicaragua 84 D3 *off.* Republic of Nicaragua. *Country* Central America
Nicaragua, Lago de 84 D4 *var.* Cocibolca, Gran Lago, *Eng.* Lake Nicaragua. *Lake* S Nicaragua
Nicaragua, Lake *see* Nicaragua, Lago de
Nicaria *see* Ikaría
Nice 123 D6 *It.* Nizza; *anc.* Nicaea. Alpes-Maritimes, SE France
Nicephorium *see* Ar Raqqah
Nicholas II Land *see* Severnaya Zemlya
Nicholls Town 86 C1 Andros Island, NW Bahamas
Nicobar Islands 156 B4 *island group* India, E Indian Ocean
Nicosia 134 C5 *Gk.* Lefkosía, *Turk.* Lefkoşa. *Country capital* (Cyprus) C Cyprus
Nicoya 84 D4 Guanacaste, W Costa Rica
Nicoya, Golfo de 84 D5 *gulf* W Costa Rica
Nicoya, Península de 84 D4 *peninsula* NW Costa Rica
Nidzica 130 D3 *Ger.* Niedenburg. Olsztyn, N Poland
Niedere Tauern 131 A6 *mountain range* C Austria
Nieuw Amsterdam 91 G3 Commewijne, NE Suriname
Nieuw-Bergen 118 D4 Limburg, SE Netherlands
Nieuwegein 118 C4 Utrecht, C Netherlands
Nieuw Nickerie 91 G3 Nickerie, NW Suriname
Niğde 148 C4 Niğde, C Turkey
Niger 107 F3 *off.* Republic of Niger. *Country* W Africa
Niger 107 F4 *river* W Africa
Nigeria 107 F4 *off.* Federal Republic of Nigeria. *Country* W Africa
Niger, Mouths of the 107 F5 *delta* S Nigeria
Nihon *see* Japan
Niigata 163 D5 Niigata, Honshū, C Japan
Niihama 163 B7 Ehime, Shikoku, SW Japan
Niihau 79 A7 *island* Hawaii, USA, C Pacific Ocean
Nii-jima 163 D6 *island* E Japan
Nijkerk 118 D3 Gelderland, C Netherlands
Nijlen 119 C5 Antwerpen, N Belgium
Nijmegen 118 D4 *Ger.* Nimwegen; *anc.* Noviomagus. Gelderland, SE Netherlands
Nikaria *see* Ikaría
Nikel' 142 C2 Murmanskaya Oblast', NW Russian Federation
Nikiniki 171 E5 Timor, S Indonesia
Nikopol' 141 F3 Dnipropetrovs'ka Oblast', SE Ukraine
Nikšić 133 C5 Montenegro, SW Yugoslavia
Nikumaroro 177 E3 *prev.* Gardner Island, Kemins Island. *Atoll* Phoenix Islands, C Kiribati
Nikunau 177 E3 *var.* Nukunau; *prev.* Byron Island. *Atoll* Tungaru, W Kiribati
Nile 100 D3 *Ar.* Nahr an Nīl. *River* N Africa
Nile 104 B2 *former province* NW Uganda
Nile Delta 104 B1 *delta* N Egypt
Nîmes 123 C6 *anc.* Nemausus, Nismes. Gard, S France
Nine Degree Channel 164 B3 *channel* India/Maldives
Ninetyeast Ridge 173 D5 *undersea feature* E Indian Ocean
Ninety Mile Beach 182 C1 *beach* North Island, NZ
Ningbo 160 D5 *var.* Ning-po, Yin-hsien; *prev.* Ninghsien. Zhejiang, SE China
Ninghsien *see* Ningbo
Ning-po *see* Ningbo
Ningxia 160 B4 *off.* Ningxia Huizu Zizhiqu, *var.* Ning-hsia, Ningsia, *Eng.* Ningsia Hui, Ningsia Hui Autonomous Region. Admin. region *autonomous region* N China
Ningxia Huizu Zizhiqu *see* Ningxia
Nio *see* Íos
Niobrara River 77 E3 *river* Nebraska/Wyoming, C USA
Nioro 106 D3 *var.* Nioro du Sahel. Kayes, W Mali
Nioro du Sahel *see* Nioro
Niort 122 B4 Deux-Sèvres, W France
Nipigon 70 B4 Ontario, S Canada
Nipigon, Lake 70 B3 *lake* Ontario, S Canada
Nippon *see* Japan
Niš 133 E5 *Eng.* Nish, *Ger.* Nisch; *anc.* Naissus. Serbia, SE Yugoslavia
Nişab 152 B4 Al Ḥudūd ash Shamālīyah, N Saudi Arabia
Nisibin *see* Nusaybin
Nisiros *see* Nísyros
Nisko 130 E4 Tarnobrzeg, SE Poland
Nísyros 137 E7 *var.* Nisiros. *Island* Dodekánisos, Greece, Aegean Sea
Nitra 131 C6 *Ger.* Neutra, *Hung.* Nyitra. *River* W Slovakia
Nitra 131 C6 *Ger.* Neutra, *Hung.* Nyitra. Západné Slovensko, SW Slovakia
Niuatobutabu *see* Niuatoputapu
Niuatoputapu 177 E4 *var.* Niuatobutabu; *prev.* Keppel Island. *Island* N Tonga
Niue 177 F4 *self-governing territory in free association with NZ* S Pacific Ocean
Niulakita 177 E3 *var.* Nurakita. *Atoll* S Tuvalu
Niutao 177 E3 *atoll* NW Tuvalu
Nivernais 122 C4 *cultural region* C France
Nizāmābād 166 D5 Andhra Pradesh, C India
Nizhnekamsk 143 C5 Respublika Tatarstan, W Russian Federation
Nizhnevartovsk 146 D3 Khanty-Mansiyskiy Avtonomnyy Okrug, C Russian Federation
Nizhniy Novgorod 143 C5 *prev.* Gor'kiy. Nizhegorodskaya Oblast', W Russian Federation
Nizhniy Odes 142 D4 Respublika Komi, NW Russian Federation
Nizhnyaya Tunguska 147 E3 *Eng.* Lower Tunguska. *River* N Russian Federation
Nizhyn 141 E1 *Rus.* Nezhin. Chernihivs'ka Oblast', NE Ukraine
Njazidja *see* Grande Comore
Njombe 105 C8 Iringa, S Tanzania
Nkayi 109 B6 *prev.* Jacob. La Bouenza, S Congo
Nkongsamba 108 A4 *var.* N'Kongsamba. Littoral, W Cameroon
Nmai Hka 168 B2 *var.* Me Hka. *River* N Myanmar
Nobeoka 163 B7 Miyazaki, Kyūshū, SW Japan
Noboribetsu 162 D3 *var.* Noboribetu. Hokkaidō, NE Japan
Noboribetu *see* Noboribetsu
Nogales 80 B3 Arizona, SW USA
Nogales 82 B1 Sonora, NW Mexico
Nogal Valley *see* Dooxo Nugaaleed
Nokia 117 D5 Häme, SW Finland
Nokou 108 B3 Kanem, W Chad
Nola 109 B5 Sangha-Mbaéré, SW Central African Republic
Nolinsk 143 C5 Kirovskaya Oblast', NW Russian Federation
Nongkaya *see* Nong Khai
Nong Khai 168 C4 *var.* Mi Chai, Nongkaya. Nong Khai, E Thailand
Nonouti 176 D2 *prev.* Sydenham Island. *Atoll* Tungaru, W Kiribati
Noord-Beveland 118 B4 *var.* North Beveland. *Island* SW Netherlands
Noordwijk aan Zee 118 C3 Zuid-Holland, W Netherlands
Nora 117 C6 Örebro, C Sweden
Norak 155 E3 *Rus.* Nurek. W Tajikistan
Nord 115 F1 N Greenland
Nordaustlandet 115 G1 *island* NE Svalbard
Norden 126 A3 Niedersachsen, NW Germany
Norderstedt 126 B3 Schleswig-Holstein, N Germany
Nordfriesische Inseln *see* North Frisian Islands
Nordhausen 126 C4 Thüringen, C Germany
Nordhorn 126 A3 Niedersachsen, NW Germany
Nordkapp 116 D1 *Eng.* North Cape. *Headland* N Norway
Norfolk 77 E3 Nebraska, C USA
Norfolk 73 F5 Virginia, NE USA
Norfolk Island 174 D4 *Australian external territory* SW Pacific Ocean
Norfolk Ridge 174 D4 *undersea feature* W Pacific Ocean
Norias 81 G5 Texas, SW USA
Noril'sk 146 D3 Taymyrskiy (Dolgano-Nenetskiy) Avtonomnyy Okrug, N Russian Federation
Norman 81 G1 Oklahoma, C USA
Normandie 122 B3 *Eng.* Normandy. *Cultural region* N France
Normandy *see* Normandie
Normanton 180 C3 Queensland, NE Australia
Norrköping 117 C6 Östergötland, S Sweden
Norrtälje 117 C6 Stockholm, C Sweden
Norseman 179 B6 Western Australia
North Albanian Alps 133 C5 *Alb.* Bjeshkët e Namuna, *SCr.* Prokletije. *Mountain range* Albania/Yugoslavia
Northallerton 121 D5 N England, UK
Northam 179 A6 Western Australia
North America 66 *continent*
Northampton 121 D6 C England, UK
North Andaman 165 F2 *island* Andaman Islands, India, NE Indian Ocean
North Australian Basin 173 E5 *Fr.* Bassin Nord de l' Australie. *Undersea feature* E Indian Ocean
North Bay 70 D4 Ontario, S Canada
North Beveland *see* Noord-Beveland
North Cape 98 D1 *headland* New Ireland, NE PNG
North Cape 182 C1 *headland* North Island, NZ
North Cape 188 *see* Nordkapp
North Carolina 75 E1 *off.* State of North Carolina; also known as Old North State, Tar Heel State, Turpentine State. *State* SE USA
North Channel 72 D2 *lake channel* Canada/USA
North Charleston 75 F2 South Carolina, SE USA
North Dakota 76 D2 *off.* State of North Dakota; also known as Flickertail State, Peace Garden State, Sioux State. *State* N USA
Northeim 126 B4 Niedersachsen, C Germany
Northern Cook Islands 177 F4 *island group* N Cook Islands
Northern Cyprus, Turkish Republic of 134 D5 *disputed region* N Cyprus
Northern Dvina *see* Severnaya Dvina
Northern Ireland 120 B4 *var.* The Six Counties. *Political division* UK
Northern Mariana Islands 174 B1 *US commonwealth territory* W Pacific Ocean
Northern Sporades *see* Vóreioi Sporádes
Northern Territory 176 A5 *territory* N Australia
North European Plain 113 E3 *plain* N Europe
Northfield 77 F2 Minnesota, N USA
North Fiji Basin 174 D3 *undersea feature* N Coral Sea
North Frisian Islands 126 B2 *var.* Nordfriesische Inseln. *Island group* N Germany
North Huvadhu Atoll 164 B5 *var.* Gaafu Alifu Atoll. *Atoll* S Maldives
North Island 182 B2 *island* N NZ
North Korea 161 E3 *off.* Democratic People's Republic of Korea, *Kor.* Chosŏn-minjujuŭi-inmin-kanghwaguk. *Country* E Asia
North Little Rock 74 B1 Arkansas, C USA
North Minch *see* Minch, The
North Mole 125 G4 *harbour wall* NW Gibraltar
North Platte 77 E4 Nebraska, C USA
North Platte River 76 D4 *river* C USA
North Pole 188 B3 *pole* Arctic Ocean
North Saskatchewan 69 F5 *river* Alberta/Saskatchewan, S Canada
North Sea 112 C3 *Dan.* Nordsøen, *Dut.* Noordzee, *Fr.* Mer du Nord, *Ger.* Nordsee, *Nor.* Nordsjøen; *prev.* German Ocean, *Lat.* Mare Germanicum. *Sea* NW Europe
North Siberian Lowland 144 *see* Severo-Sibirskaya Nizmennost'
North Siberian Plain *see* Severo-Sibirskaya Nizmennost'
North Taranaki Bight 182 C3 *gulf* North Island, NZ
North Uist 120 B3 *island* NW Scotland, UK
Northwest Atlantic Mid-Ocean Canyon 66 E4 *undersea feature* N Atlantic Ocean
North West Highlands 120 C3 *mountain range* N Scotland, UK
Northwest Pacific Basin 145 G4 *undersea feature* NW Pacific Ocean
Northwest Providence Channel 86 C1 *channel* N Bahamas
Northwest Territories 69 E3 *Fr.* Territoires du Nord-Ouest. *Territory* NW Canada
Northwind Plain 188 B2 *undersea feature* Arctic Ocean
Norton Sound 68 C2 *inlet* Alaska, USA
Norway 117 A5 *off.* Kingdom of Norway, *Nor.* Norge. *Country* N Europe
Norwegian Basin 115 F4 *undersea feature* NW Norwegian Sea
Norwegian Sea 115 F4 *Nor.* Norske Havet. *Sea* NE Atlantic Ocean
Norwich 121 E6 E England, UK
Noshiro 162 D4 *var.* Nosiro; *prev.* Noshirominato. Akita, Honshū, C Japan
Noshirominato *see* Noshiro
Nosiro *see* Noshiro
Nosivka 141 E1 *Rus.* Nosovka. Chernihivs'ka Oblast', NE Ukraine
Noşratābād 152 E3 Sīstān va Balūchestān, E Iran
Nossob 110 C4 *river* E Namibia
Noteć 130 C3 *Ger.* Netze. *River* NW Poland
Nóties Sporádes *see* Dodekánisos
Nottingham 121 D6 C England, UK
Nouâdhibou 106 B2 *prev.* Port-Étienne. Dakhlet Nouâdhibou, W Mauritania
Nouakchott 106 B2 *country capital* (Mauritania) Nouakchott District, SW Mauritania
Nouméa 176 C5 *dependent territory capital* (New Caledonia) Province Sud, S New Caledonia
Nouvelle-Calédonie *see* New Caledonia
Nova Gorica 127 D8 W Slovenia
Nova Gradiška 132 C3 *Ger.* Neugradisk, *Hung.* Újgradiska. Brod-Posavina, NE Croatia
Nova Iguaçu 95 F4 Rio de Janeiro, SE Brazil
Novara 128 B2 *anc.* Novaria. Piemonte, NW Italy
Nova Scotia 71 F4 *Fr.* Nouvelle Écosse. *Province* SE Canada
Nova Scotia 67 E5 *physical region* SE Canada
Novaya Sibir', Ostrov 147 F1 *island* Novosibirskiye Ostrova, NE Russian Federation
Novaya Zemlya 142 D1 *island group* N Russian Federation
Novaya Zemlya Trench *see* East Novaya Zemlya Trench
Novgorod 142 B4 Novgorodskaya Oblast', W Russian Federation
Novi Iskŭr 136 C2 Grad Sofiya, W Bulgaria
Novi Pazar 133 D5 *Turk.* Yenipazar. Serbia, S Yugoslavia
Novi Sad 132 D3 *Ger.* Neusatz, *Hung.* Újvidék. Serbia, N Yugoslavia
Novoazovs'k 141 G4 *Rus.* Novoazovsk. Donets'ka Oblast', E Ukraine
Novocheboksarsk 143 C5 Chuvashskaya Respublika, W Russian Federation
Novocherkassk 143 B7 Rostovskaya Oblast', SW Russian Federation
Novodvinsk 142 C3 Arkhangel'skaya Oblast', NW Russian Federation
Novohrad-Volyns'kyy 140 D2 *Rus.* Novograd-Volynskiy. Zhytomyrs'ka Oblast', N Ukraine
Novokazalinsk 146 B4 *Kaz.* Zhangaqazaly. Kzyl-Orda, SW Kazakhstan
Novokuznetsk 146 D4 *prev.* Stalinsk. Kemerovskaya Oblast', S Russian Federation
Novolazarevskaya 186 C2 *Russian research station* Antarctica
Novo Mesto 127 E8 *Ger.* Rudolfswert; prev. *Ger.* Neustadtl. SE Slovenia
Novomoskovs'k 141 F3 *Rus.* Novomoskovsk. Dnipropetrovs'ka Oblast', E Ukraine
Novomoskovsk 143 B5 Tul'skaya Oblast', W Russian Federation
Novorossiysk 143 A7 Krasnodarskiy Kray, SW Russian Federation
Novoshakhtinsk 143 B6 Rostovskaya Oblast', SW Russian Federation
Novosibirsk 146 D4 Novosibirskaya Oblast', C Russian Federation
Novosibirskiye Ostrova 147 F1 *Eng.* New Siberian Islands. *Island group* N Russian Federation
Novotroitsk 143 D6 Orenburgskaya Oblast', W Russian Federation
Novotroyits'ke 141 F4 *Rus.* Novotroitskoye. Khersons'ka Oblast', S Ukraine
Novovolyns'k 140 C1 *Rus.* Novovolynsk. Volyns'ka Oblast', NW Ukraine
Novy Dvor 139 B6 *Rus.* Novyy Dvor. Hrodzyenskaya Voblasts', W Belarus
Novyy Buh 141 E3 *Rus.* Novyy Bug. Mykolayivs'ka Oblast', S Ukraine
Novyy Uzen' 146 A4 *Kaz.* Zhangaözen. Mangistau, W Kazakhstan
Nowogard 130 B2 *var.* Nowógard, *Ger.* Naugard. Szczecin, NW Poland
Nowógard *see* Nowogard
Nowy Dwór Mazowiecki 130 D3 Warszawa, C Poland
Nowy Sącz 131 D5 *Ger.* Neu Sandec. Nowy Sącz, S Poland
Nowy Tomyśl 130 B3 *var.* Nowy Tomysl. Poznań, W Poland
Noyon 122 C3 Oise, N France
Nsanje 111 E3 Southern, S Malawi
Nsawam 107 E5 SE Ghana
Ntomba, Lac 109 C6 *var.* Lac Tumba. *Lake* NW Congo (Zaire)
Nubian Desert 104 B3 *desert* NE Sudan
Nueva Gerona 86 B2 Isla de la Juventud, S Cuba
Nueva Rosita 82 D2 Coahuila de Zaragoza, NE Mexico
Nuevitas 86 C2 Camagüey, E Cuba
Nuevo, Bajo 85 G1 *island* NW Colombia
Nuevo Casas Grandes 82 C1 Chihuahua, N Mexico
Nuevo, Golfo 97 C6 *gulf* S Argentina
Nuevo Laredo 83 E2 Tamaulipas, NE Mexico
Nui Atoll 177 E3 *atoll* W Tuvalu
Nûk *see* Nuuk
Nuku'alofa 177 E5 *country capital* (Tonga) Tongatapu, S Tonga
Nukufetau Atoll 177 E3 *atoll* C Tuvalu
Nukulaelae Atoll 177 E3 *var.* Nukulailai. *Atoll* E Tuvalu
Nukulailai *see* Nukulaelae Atoll
Nukunau *see* Nikunau
Nukunonu Atoll 177 E3 *island* C Tokelau
Nukus 154 C2 Qoraqalpoghiston Respublikasi, W Uzbekistan
Nullarbor Plain 179 C6 *plateau* South Australia/Western Australia
Nunap Isua *see* Uummannarsuaq
Nuneaton 121 D6 C England, UK
Nunivak Island 68 B2 *island* Alaska, USA
Nunspeet 118 D3 Gelderland, E Netherlands
Nuoro 129 A5 Sardegna, Italy, C Mediterranean Sea
Nuquí 90 A3 Chocó, W Colombia
Nurakita *see* Niulakita
Nuremberg *see* Nürnberg
Nurmes 116 E4 Pohjois-Karjala, E Finland
Nürnberg 127 C5 *Eng.* Nuremberg. Bayern, S Germany
Nurota 155 E2 *Rus.* Nurata. Nawoiy Wiloyati, C Uzbekistan
Nusa Tenggara 171 E5 *Eng.* Lesser Sunda Islands. *Island group* C Indonesia
Nusaybin 149 F4 *var.* Nisibin. Manisa, SE Turkey
Nuuk 114 C4 *var.* Nûk, *Dan.* Godthaab, Godthåb. *Dependent territory capital* (Greenland) SW Greenland
Nyagan' 146 C3 Khanty-Mansiyskiy Avtonomnyy Okrug, N Russian Federation
Nyainqêntanglha Shan 158 C5 *mountain range* W China
Nyala 104 A4 Southern Darfur, W Sudan
Nyamapanda 110 D3 Mashonaland East, NE Zimbabwe
Nyamtumbo 105 C8 Ruvuma, S Tanzania
Nyandoma 142 C4 Arkhangel'skaya Oblast', NW Russian Federation
Nyantakara 105 B7 Kagera, NW Tanzania
Nyasa, Lake 111 E2 *var.* Lake Malawi; *prev.* Lago Nyassa. *Lake* E Africa
Nyasvizh 139 C6 *Pol.* Nieśwież, *Rus.* Nesvizh. Minskaya Voblasts', C Belarus
Nyaunglebin 168 B4 Pegu, SW Myanmar
Nyeri 105 C6 Central, C Kenya
Nyima 158 C5 Xizang Zizhiqu, W China
Nyíregyháza 131 D6 Szabolcs-Szatmár-Bereg, NE Hungary
Nykøbing 117 B8 Storstrøm, SE Denmark
Nyköping 117 C6 Södermanland, S Sweden
Nylstroom 110 D4 Northern, NE South Africa
Nyngan 181 D6 New South Wales, SE Australia
Nyurba 147 F3 Respublika Sakha (Yakutiya), NE Russian Federation
Nyzhn'ohirs'kyy 141 F4 *Rus.* Nizhnegorskiy. Respublika Krym, S Ukraine
Nzega 105 C7 Tabora, C Tanzania
Nzérékoré 106 D4 Guinée-Forestière, SE Guinea
Nzwani *see* Anjouan

O

Oahu 79 A7 *Haw.* O'ahu. *Island* Hawaii, USA, C Pacific Ocean
Oak Harbor 78 B1 Washington, NW USA
Oakland 79 B6 California, W USA
Oamaru 183 B7 Otago, South Island, NZ
Oaxaca 83 F5 *var.* Oaxaca de Juárez; *prev.* Antequera. Oaxaca, SE Mexico
Oaxaca de Juárez *see* Oaxaca
Ob' 144 C2 *river* C Russian Federation
Obal' 139 D5 *Rus.* Obol'. Vitsyebskaya Voblasts', N Belarus
Oban *see* Halfmoon Bay
Oban 120 C4 W Scotland, UK
Obando *see* Puerto Inírida
Obeliai 138 C4 Rokiškis, NE Lithuania
Oberhollabrunn *see* Tulln
Ob, Gulf of 144 *see* Obskaya Guba
Obihiro 162 D2 Hokkaidō, NE Japan

P

País Vasco 125 E1 *cultural region* N Spain
Paita 92 B3 Piura, NW Peru
Pakanbaru *see* Pekanbaru
Pakaraima Mountains 91 E3 *var.* Serra Pacaraim, Sierra Pacaraima. *Mountain range* N South America
Pakistan 166 A2 *off.* Islamic Republic of Pakistan, *var.* Islami Jamhuriya e Pakistan. *Country* S Asia
Paknam *see* Samut Prakan
Pakokku 168 A3 Magwe, C Myanmar
Pak Phanang 169 C7 *var.* Ban Pak Phanang. Nakhon Si Thammarat, SW Thailand
Pakruojis 138 C4 Pakruojis, N Lithuania
Paks 131 C7 Tolna, S Hungary
Paksé *see* Pakxé
Pakxé 169 D5 *var.* Paksé. Champasak, S Laos
Palafrugell 125 G2 Cataluña, NE Spain
Palagruža 133 B5 *It.* Pelagosa. *Island* SW Croatia
Palaiá Epídavros 137 C6 Pelopónnisos, S Greece
Palaiseau 122 D2 Essonne, N France
Palamós 125 G2 Cataluña, NE Spain
Palamuse 138 E2 *Ger.* Sankt-Bartholomäi. Jõgevamaa, E Estonia
Pālanpur 166 C4 Gujarāt, W India
Palapye 110 D3 Central, SE Botswana
Palau 176 A2 *var.* Belau. *Country* W Pacific Ocean
Palawan 171 E2 *island* W Philippines
Palawan Passage 170 D2 *passage* W Philippines
Paldiski 138 D2 *prev.* Baltiski, *Eng.* Baltic Port, *Ger.* Baltischport. Harjumaa, NW Estonia
Palembang 170 B4 Sumatera, W Indonesia
Palencia 124 D2 *anc.* Palantia, Pallantia. Castilla-León, NW Spain
Palermo 129 C7 *Fr.* Palerme; *anc.* Panhormus, Panormus. Sicilia, Italy, C Mediterranean Sea
Pāli 166 C3 Rājasthān, N India
Palikir 176 C2 *country capital* (Micronesia) Pohnpei, E Micronesia
Palimé *see* Kpalimé
Palioúri, Ákra 136 C4 *var.* Akra Kanestron. *Headland* N Greece
Palk Strait 164 C3 *strait* India/Sri Lanka
Palliser, Cape 183 D5 *headland* North Island, NZ
Palma 125 G3 *var.* Palma de Mallorca. Mallorca, Spain, W Mediterranean Sea
Palma del Río 124 D4 Andalucía, S Spain
Palma de Mallorca *see* Palma
Palmar Sur 85 E5 Puntarenas, SE Costa Rica
Palma Soriano 86 C3 Santiago de Cuba, E Cuba
Palm Beach 180 E1 New South Wales, SE Australia
Palmer 186 A2 *US research station* Antarctica
Palmer Land 186 A3 *physical region* Antarctica
Palmerston 177 F4 *island* S Cook Islands
Palmerston North 182 D4 Manawatu-Wanganui, North Island, NZ
Palmi 129 D7 Calabria, SW Italy
Palmira 90 B3 Valle del Cauca, W Colombia
Palm Springs 79 D7 California, W USA
Palmyra *see* Tudmur
Palmyra Atoll 177 G2 *US privately owned unincorporated territory* C Pacific Ocean
Palo Alto 79 B6 California, W USA
Palu 171 E4 *prev.* Paloe. Sulawesi, C Indonesia
Pamiers 123 B6 Ariège, S France
Pamir 155 *var.* Daryā-ye Pāmīr, *Taj.* Dar"yoi Pomir. *River* Afghanistan/Tajikistan *see also* Pāmīr, Daryā-ye
Pamirs 155 F3 *Pash.* Daryā-ye Pāmīr, *Rus.* Pamir. *Mountain range* C Asia
Pâmiut *see* Paamiut
Pamlico Sound 75 G1 *sound* North Carolina, SE USA
Pampa 81 E1 Texas, SW USA
Pampas 96 C4 *plain* C Argentina
Pamplona 125 E1 *Basq.* Iruñea; *prev.* Pampeluna, *anc.* Pompaelo. Navarra, N Spain
Pamplona 90 C2 Norte de Santander, N Colombia
Panaji 164 B1 *var.* Pangim, Panjim, New Goa. Goa, W India
Panama 85 G5 *off.* Republic of Panama. *Country* Central America
Panamá 85 G4 *var.* Ciudad de Panamá, *Eng.* Panama City. *Country capital* (Panama) Panamá, C Panama
Panama Basin 67 C8 *undersea feature* E Pacific Ocean
Panama Canal 85 F4 *canal* E Panama
Panama City *see* Panamá
Panama City 74 D3 Florida, SE USA
Panamá, Golfo de 85 G5 *var.* Gulf of Panama. *Gulf* S Panama
Panama, Gulf of *see* Panamá, Golfo de
Panamá, Isthmus of *see* Panamá, Istmo de
Panamá, Istmo de 85 G4 *Eng.* Isthmus of Panama; *prev.* Isthmus of Darien. *Isthmus* E Panama
Panay Island 171 E2 *island* C Philippines
Pančevo 132 D3 *Ger.* Pantschowa, *Hung.* Pancsova. Serbia, N Yugoslavia
Paneas *see* Bāniyās
Panevėžys 138 C4 Panevėžys, C Lithuania
Pangim *see* Panaji
Pangkalpinang 170 C4 Pulau Bangka, W Indonesia
Pang-Nga *see* Phang-Nga
Panjim *see* Panaji
Pánormos 137 C7 Kríti, Greece, E Mediterranean Sea
Pantanal 95 E3 *var.* Pantanalmato-Grossense. *Swamp* SW Brazil
Pantanalmato-Grossense *see* Pantanal
Pantelleria, Isola di 129 B7 *island* SW Italy
Pánuco 83 E3 Veracruz-Llave, E Mexico
Pao-chi *see* Baoji
Paoki *see* Baoji
Paola 134 B5 E Malta
Pao-shan *see* Baoshan
Pao-t'ou *see* Baotou
Paotow *see* Baotou
Papagayo, Golfo de 84 C4 *gulf* NW Costa Rica
Papakura 182 D3 Auckland, North Island, NZ
Papantla 83 F4 *var.* Papantla de Olarte. Veracruz-Llave, E Mexico
Papantla de Olarte *see* Papantla
Papeete 177 H4 *dependent territory capital* (French Polynesia) Tahiti, W French Polynesia
Paphos *see* Páfos
Papilė 138 B3 Akmenė, NW Lithuania
Papillion 77 F4 Nebraska, C USA
Papua, Gulf of 176 B3 *gulf* S PNG
Papua New Guinea 176 B3 *off.* Independent State of Papua New Guinea; *prev.* Territory of Papua and New Guinea, *abbrev.* PNG. *Country* NW Melanesia
Papuk 132 C3 *mountain range* NE Croatia
Pará 95 E2 *off.* Estado do Pará. *State* NE Brazil
Pará *see* Belém
Paracel Islands 157 E3 *disputed territory* SE Asia
Paraćin 132 D4 Serbia, C Yugoslavia
Paragua, Río 91 E3 *river* SE Venezuela
Paraguay 96 D2 *var.* Río Paraguay. *River* C South America
Paraguay 96 C2 *country* C South America
Paraguay, Río *see* Paraguay
Paraíba 95 G2 *off.* Estado da Paraíba; *prev.* Parahiba, Parahyba. *State* E Brazil
Parakou 107 F4 C Benin
Paramaribo 91 G3 *country capital* (Suriname) Paramaribo, N Suriname
Paramushir, Ostrov 147 H3 *island* SE Russian Federation
Paraná 95 E5 *off.* Estado do Paraná. *State* S Brazil
Paraná 89 C5 *var.* Alto Paraná. *River* C South America
Paraná 95 E4 Entre Ríos, E Argentina
Paranéstio 136 C3 Anatolikí Makedonía kai Thráki, NE Greece
Paraparaumu 183 D5 Wellington, North Island, NZ
Parchim 126 C3 Mecklenburg-Vorpommern, N Germany
Parczew 130 E4 Biała Podlaska, E Poland
Pardubice 131 B5 *Ger.* Pardubitz. Východní Čechy, C Czech Republic
Parechcha 139 B5 *Rus.* Porech'ye. Hrodzyenskaya Voblasts', NE Belarus
Parecis, Chapada dos 94 D3 *var.* Serra dos Parecis. *Mountain range* W Brazil
Parepare 171 E4 Sulawesi, C Indonesia
Párga 137 A5 Ípeiros, W Greece
Paria, Gulf of 91 E1 *var.* Golfo de Paria. *Gulf* Trinidad and Tobago/Venezuela
Parika 91 F2 NE Guyana
Paris 122 D1 *anc.* Lutetia, Lutetia Parisiorum, Parisii. *Country capital* (France) Paris, N France
Paris 81 G2 Texas, SW USA
Parkersburg 72 D4 West Virginia, NE USA
Parkes 181 D6 New South Wales, SE Australia
Parma 128 B2 Emilia-Romagna, N Italy
Parnahyba *see* Parnaíba
Parnaíba 95 F2 *var.* Parnahyba. Piauí, E Brazil
Pärnu 138 D2 *Ger.* Pernau, *Latv.* Pērnava; *prev.* Rus. Pernov. Pärnumaa, SW Estonia
Pärnu 138 D2 *var.* Parnu Jõgi, *Ger.* Pernau. *River* SW Estonia
Pärnu-Jaagupi 138 D2 *Ger.* Sankt-Jakobi. Pärnumaa, SW Estonia
Parnu Jõgi *see* Pärnu
Pärnu Laht 138 D2 *Ger.* Pernauer Bucht. *Bay* SW Estonia
Páros 137 C6 *island* Kykládes, Greece, Aegean Sea
Páros 137 D6 Páros, Kykládes, Greece, Aegean Sea
Parral *see* Hidalgo del Parral
Parral 96 B4 Maule, C Chile
Parramatta 180 D1 New South Wales, SE Australia
Parras 82 D3 *var.* Parras de la Fuente. Coahuila de Zaragoza, NE Mexico
Parras de la Fuente *see* Parras
Parsons 77 F5 Kansas, C USA
Pasadena 79 C7 California, W USA
Pasadena 81 H4 Texas, SW USA
Paşcani 140 C3 *Hung.* Páskán. Iaşi, NE Romania
Pasco 78 C2 Washington, NW USA
Pas de Calais *see* Dover, Strait of
Pasewalk 126 D3 Mecklenburg-Vorpommern, NE Germany
Pasinler 149 F3 Erzurum, NE Turkey
Pasłęk 130 D2 *Ger.* Preußisch Holland. Elbląg, N Poland
Pasni 166 A3 Baluchistān, SW Pakistan
Paso de Indios 97 B6 Chubut, S Argentina
Passau 127 D6 Bayern, SE Germany
Passo del Brennero *see* Brenner Pass
Passo Fundo 95 E5 Rio Grande do Sul, S Brazil
Pastavy 139 C5 *Pol.* Postawy, *Rus.* Postavy. Vitsyebskaya Voblasts', NW Belarus
Pastaza, Río 92 B2 *river* Ecuador/Peru
Pasto 90 A4 Nariño, SW Colombia
Pasvalys 138 C4 Pasvalys, N Lithuania
Patagonia 89 B7 *physical region* Argentina/Chile
Patalung *see* Phatthalung
Patani *see* Pattani
Patavium *see* Padova
Patea 182 D4 Taranaki, North Island, NZ
Paterson 73 F3 New Jersey, NE USA
Pathein *see* Bassein
Pátmos 137 D6 *island* Dodekánisos, Greece, Aegean Sea
Patna 167 F3 *var.* Azimabad. Bihār, N India
Patnos 149 F3 Ağrı, E Turkey
Patos, Lagoa dos 95 E5 *lagoon* S Brazil
Pátra 137 B5 *Eng.* Patras; *prev.* Pátrai. Dytikí Ellás, S Greece
Pattani 169 C7 *var.* Patani. Pattani, SW Thailand
Pattaya 169 C5 Chon Buri, S Thailand
Patuca, Río 84 D2 *river* E Honduras
Pau 123 B6 Pyrénées-Atlantiques, SW France
Paulatuk 69 E3 Northwest Territories, NW Canada
Paungde 168 B4 Pegu, C Myanmar
Pavia 128 B2 *anc.* Ticinum. Lombardia, N Italy
Pāvilosta 138 B3 Liepāja, W Latvia
Pavlikeni 136 D2 Loveshka Oblast, N Bulgaria
Pavlodar 146 C4 Pavlodar, NE Kazakhstan
Pavlohrad 141 G3 *Rus.* Pavlograd. Dnipropetrovs'ka Oblast', E Ukraine
Pawn 168 B3 *river* C Myanmar
Paxoí 137 A5 *island* Iónioi Nísoi, Greece, C Mediterranean Sea
Payo Obispo *see* Chetumal
Paysandú 96 D4 Paysandú, W Uruguay
Pazar 149 E2 Rize, NE Turkey
Pazardzhik 136 C3 *prev.* Tatar Pazardzhik. Plovdivska Oblast, SW Bulgaria
Pearl River 74 B3 *river* Louisiana/Mississippi, S USA
Pearsall 81 F4 Texas, SW USA
Peć 133 D5 *Alb.* Pejë, *Turk.* Ipek. Serbia, S Yugoslavia
Pechora 142 D3 *river* NW Russian Federation
Pechora 142 D3 Respublika Komi, NW Russian Federation
Pechorskoye More 142 D2 *Eng.* Pechora Sea. *Sea* NW Russian Federation
Pecos 81 E3 Texas, SW USA
Pecos River 81 E3 *river* New Mexico/Texas, SW USA
Pécs 131 C7 *Ger.* Fünfkirchen; *Lat.* Sopianae. Baranya, SW Hungary
Pedra Lume 106 A3 Sal, NE Cape Verde
Pedro Cays 86 C3 *island group* S Jamaica
Pedro Juan Caballero 96 D2 Amambay, E Paraguay
Peer 119 D5 Limburg, NE Belgium
Pegasus Bay 183 C6 *bay* South Island, NZ
Pegu 168 B4 *var.* Bago. Pegu, SW Myanmar
Pehuajó 96 C4 Buenos Aires, E Argentina
Pei-ching *see* Beijing
Peine 126 B3 Niedersachsen, C Germany
Pei-p'ing *see* Beijing
Peipus, Lake 138 E3 *Est.* Peipsi Järv, *Ger.* Peipus-See, *Rus.* Chudskoye Ozero. *Lake* Estonia/Russian Federation
Peiraías 137 C6 *prev.* Piraiévs, *Eng.* Piraeus. Attikí, C Greece
Pèk 168 D4 *var.* Xieng Khouang; *prev.* Xiangkhoang. Xiangkhoang, N Laos
Pekalongan 170 C4 Jawa, C Indonesia
Pekanbaru 170 B3 *var.* Pakanbaru. Sumatera, W Indonesia
Pekin 72 B4 Illinois, N USA
Peking *see* Beijing
Pelagie, Isole 129 B8 *island group* SW Italy
Pelly Bay 69 G3 Northwest Territories, N Canada
Peloponnese *see* Pelopónnisos
Peloponnesus *see* Pelopónnisos
Pelopónnisos 137 B6 *var.* Morea, *Eng.* Peloponnese; *anc.* Peloponnesus. *Peninsula* S Greece
Pematangsiantar 170 B3 Sumatera, W Indonesia
Pemba 111 F2 *prev.* Port Amelia, Porto Amélia. Cabo Delgado, NE Mozambique
Pemba 105 D7 *island* E Tanzania
Pembroke 70 D4 Ontario, SE Canada
Penang *see* George Town
Penang *see* Pinang, Pulau
Penas, Golfo de 97 A7 *gulf* S Chile
Penderma *see* Bandırma
Pendleton 78 C3 Oregon, NW USA
Pend Oreille, Lake 78 D2 *lake* Idaho, NW USA
Peneius *see* Pineiós
Peng-pu *see* Bengbu
Peniche 124 B3 Leiria, W Portugal
Péninsule de la Gaspésie *see* Gaspé, Péninsule de
Pennine Alps 127 A8 *Fr.* Alpes Pennines, *It.* Alpi Pennine; *Lat.* Alpes Penninae. *Mountain range* Italy/Switzerland
Pennine Chain *see* Pennines
Pennines 121 D5 *var.* Pennine Chain. *Mountain range* N England, UK
Pennsylvania 72 D3 *off.* Commonwealth of Pennsylvania; also known as The Keystone State. *State* NE USA
Penobscot River 73 G2 *river* Maine, NE USA
Penong 181 A6 South Australia
Penonomé 85 F5 Coclé, C Panama
Penrhyn 177 G3 *atoll* N Cook Islands
Penrhyn Basin 175 F3 *undersea feature* C Pacific Ocean
Penrith 180 D1 New South Wales, SE Australia
Penrith 121 D5 NW England, UK
Pensacola 74 C3 Florida, SE USA
Pentecost 176 D4 *Fr.* Pentecôte. *Island* C Vanuatu
Penza 143 C6 Penzenskaya Oblast', W Russian Federation
Penzance 121 C7 SW England, UK
Peoria 72 B4 Illinois, N USA
Perchtoldsdorf 127 E6 Niederösterreich, NE Austria
Percival Lakes 178 C4 *lakes* Western Australia
Perdido, Monte 125 F1 *mountain* NE Spain
Perece Vela Basin *see* West Mariana Basin
Pereira 90 B3 Risaralda, W Colombia
Pergamino 96 C4 Buenos Aires, E Argentina
Périgueux 123 C5 *anc.* Vesuna. Dordogne, SW France
Perito Moreno 97 B6 Santa Cruz, S Argentina
Perlas, Archipiélago de las 85 G5 *Eng.* Pearl Islands. *Island group* SE Panama
Perlas, Laguna de 85 E3 *Eng.* Pearl Lagoon. *Lagoon* E Nicaragua
Perleberg 126 C3 Brandenburg, N Germany
Perm' 146 C3 *prev.* Molotov. Permskaya Oblast', NW Russian Federation
Pernambuco 95 G2 *off.* Estado de Pernambuco. *State* E Brazil
Pernambuco Abyssal Plain *see* Pernambuco Plain
Pernambuco Plain 99 C5 *var.* Pernambuco Abyssal Plain. *Undersea feature* E Atlantic Ocean
Pernau *see* Pärnu
Pernik 136 B2 *prev.* Dimitrovo. Sofiyska Oblast, W Bulgaria
Perote 83 F4 Veracruz-Llave, E Mexico
Perovsk *see* Kzyl-Orda
Perpignan 123 C6 Pyrénées-Orientales, S France
Perryton 81 F1 Texas, SW USA
Perryville 77 H5 Missouri, C USA
Persian Gulf *see* Gulf, The
Perth 179 A6 *state capital* Western Australia
Perth 120 C4 C Scotland, UK
Perth Basin 173 E6 *undersea feature* SE Indian Ocean
Peru 92 C3 *off.* Republic of Peru. *Country* W South America
Peru *see* Beru
Peru Basin 99 A5 *undersea feature* E Pacific Ocean
Peru-Chile Trench 88 A4 *undersea feature* E Pacific Ocean
Perugia 128 C4 *Fr.* Pérouse; *anc.* Perusia. Umbria, C Italy
Péruwelz 119 B6 Hainaut, SW Belgium
Pervomays'k 141 E3 *prev.* Ol'viopol'. Mykolayivs'ka Oblast', S Ukraine
Pervyy Kuril'skiy Proliv 147 H3 *strait* E Russian Federation
Pesaro 128 C3 *anc.* Pisaurum. Marche, C Italy
Pescara 128 D4 *anc.* Aternum, Ostia Aterni. Abruzzi, C Italy
Peshāwar 166 C1 North-West Frontier Province, N Pakistan
Peshkopi 133 C6 *var.* Peshkopia, Peshkopija. Dibër, NE Albania
Peshkopia *see* Peshkopi
Peshkopija *see* Peshkopi
Peski Karakumy *see* Garagumy
Pessac 123 B5 Gironde, SW France
Petach-Tikva *see* Petah Tiqwa
Petah Tiqva *see* Petah Tiqwa
Petah Tiqwa 151 A6 *var.* Petach-Tikva, Petah Tiqva. Tel Aviv, C Israel
Pétange 119 D8 Luxembourg, SW Luxembourg
Petchaburi *see* Phetchaburi
Peterborough 121 E6 *prev.* Medeshamstede. E England, UK
Peterborough 70 D5 Ontario, SE Canada
Peterborough 181 B6 South Australia
Peterhead 120 D3 NE Scotland, UK
Peter I Island 186 A3 *Norwegian dependency* Antarctica
Petermann Bjerg 115 E3 *mountain* C Greenland
Petersburg 73 E5 Virginia, NE USA
Peters Mine 91 F3 *var.* Peter's Mine. N Guyana
Peto 83 H4 Yucatán, SE Mexico
Petoskey 72 C2 Michigan, N USA
Petra *see* Wādī Mūsā
Petrich 136 C3 Sofiyska Oblast, SW Bulgaria
Petrinja 132 B3 Sisak-Moslavina, C Croatia
Petrodvorets 142 A4 *Fin.* Pietarhovi. Leningradskaya Oblast', NW Russian Federation
Petrograd *see* Sankt-Peterburg
Petropavlovsk 146 C4 *Kaz.* Petropavl. Severnyy Kazakhstan, N Kazakhstan
Petropavlovsk-Kamchatskiy 147 H3 Kamchatskaya Oblast', E Russian Federation
Petroşani 140 B4 *var.* Petroşeni, *Ger.* Petroschen, *Hung.* Petrozsény. Hunedoara, W Romania
Petroschen *see* Petroşani
Petroşeni *see* Petroşani
Petrozavodsk 146 B2 *Fin.* Petroskoi. Respublika Kareliya, NW Russian Federation
Petrozsény *see* Petroşani
Pevek 147 G1 Chukotskiy Avtonomnyy Okrug, NE Russian Federation
Pezinok 131 C6 *Ger.* Bösing, *Hung.* Bazin. Západné Slovensko, SW Slovakia
Pforzheim 127 B6 Baden-Württemberg, SW Germany
Pfungstadt 127 B5 Hessen, W Germany
Phangan, Ko 169 C6 *island* SW Thailand
Phang-Nga 169 B7 *var.* Pang-Nga, Phangnga. Phangnga, SW Thailand
Phangnga *see* Phang-Nga
Phanom Dang Raek *see* Dângrêk, Chuŏr Phnum
Phanom Dong Rak *see* Dângrêk, Chuŏr Phnum
Phan Rang *see* Phan Rang-Thap Cham
Phan Rang-Thap Cham 169 E6 *var.* Phanrang, Phan Rang, Phan Rang Thap Cham. Ninh Thuân, S Vietnam
Phan Thiêt 169 E6 Binh Thuân, S Vietnam
Pharnacia *see* Giresun
Phatthalung 169 C7 *var.* Padalung, Patalung. Phatthalung, SW Thailand
Phayao 168 C4 *var.* Muang Phayao. Phayao, NW Thailand
Phenix City 74 D2 Alabama, S USA
Phet Buri *see* Phetchaburi
Phetchaburi 169 C5 *var.* Bejraburi, Petchaburi, Phet Buri. Phetchaburi, SW Thailand
Philadelphia *see* 'Ammān
Philadelphia 73 F4 Pennsylvania, NE USA
Philippine Basin 157 F3 *undersea feature* W Pacific Ocean
Philippines 171 E1 *off.* Republic of the Philippines. *Country* SE Asia
Philippines 171 E1 *island group* W Pacific Ocean
Philippine Sea 157 F3 *sea* W Pacific Ocean
Philippine Trench 174 A1 *undersea feature* W Philippine Sea
Phitsanulok 168 C4 *var.* Bisnulok, Muang Phitsanulok, Pitsanulok. Phitsanulok, C Thailand
Phlórina *see* Flórina
Phnom Penh *see* Phnum Penh
Phnum Penh 169 D6 *var.* Phnom Penh. *Country capital* (Cambodia) Phnum Penh, S Cambodia
Phoenix 80 B2 *state capital* Arizona, SW USA
Phoenix Islands 177 E3 *island group* C Kiribati
Phôngsali 168 C3 *var.* Phong Saly. Phôngsali, N Laos
Phong Saly *see* Phôngsali
Phrae 168 C4 *var.* Muang Phrae, Prae. Phrae, NW Thailand
Phra Nakhon Si Ayutthaya *see* Ayutthaya
Phra Thong, Ko 169 B6 *island* SW Thailand
Phuket 169 B7 *var.* Bhuket, Puket, *Mal.* Ujung Salang; *prev.* Junkseylon, Salang. Phuket, SW Thailand
Phuket, Ko 169 B7 *island* SW Thailand
Phumĭ Kâmpóng Trâbêk 169 D5 Kâmpóng Chhnăng, N Cambodia
Phumĭ Sâmraông 169 D5 Poŭthĭsăt, NW Cambodia
Phu Vinh *see* Tra Vinh
Piacenza 128 B2 *Fr.* Paisance; *anc.* Placentia. Emilia-Romagna, N Italy
Piatra-Neamţ 140 C4 *Hung.* Karácsonkő. Neamţ, NE Romania
Piauí 95 F2 *off.* Estado do Piauí; *prev.* Piauhy. *State* E Brazil
Picardie 122 C3 *Eng.* Picardy. *Cultural region* N France
Pichilemu 96 B4 Libertador, C Chile
Pico 124 A5 *var.* Ilha do Pico. *Island* Azores, Portugal, NE Atlantic Ocean
Picos 95 F2 Piauí, E Brazil
Picton 183 C5 Marlborough, South Island, NZ
Piedras Negras 83 E2 *var.* Ciudad Porfirio Díaz. Coahuila de Zaragoza, NE Mexico
Pielinen 116 E4 *var.* Pielisjärvi. *Lake* E Finland
Pielisjärvi *see* Pielinen
Piemonte 128 A2 *Eng.* Piedmont. *Cultural region* NW Italy

S

Saint George 181 *D5* Queensland, E Australia
Saint George 76 *A5* Utah, W USA
St.George's 87 *G5 country capital* (Grenada) SW Grenada
St-Georges 91 *H3* E French Guiana
St-Georges 71 *E4* Québec, SE Canada
St George's Channel 121 *B6 channel* Ireland / Wales, UK
St George's Island 74 *B4 island* E Bermuda
Saint Helena 101 *B6 UK dependent territory* C Atlantic Ocean
St.Helena Bay 110 *B5 bay* SW South Africa
St Helier 121 *D8 dependent territory capital* (Jersey) S Jersey, Channel Islands
Saint Ignace 72 *C2* Michigan, N USA
St-Jean, Lac 71 *E4 lake* Québec, SE Canada
Saint Joe River 78 *D2 river* Idaho, NW USA
Saint John 73 *H1 river* Canada / USA
St.John 71 *F4* New Brunswick, SE Canada
St John's 87 *G3 country capital* (Antigua and Barbuda) Antigua, Antigua and Barbuda
St.John's 71 *H3* Newfoundland, Newfoundland and Labrador, E Canada
Saint Joseph 77 *F4* Missouri, C USA
St Julian's 134 *B5* N Malta
St Kilda 120 *A3 island* NW Scotland, UK
Saint Kitts and Nevis 87 *F3 off.* Federation of Saint Christopher and Nevis, *var.* Saint Christopher-Nevis. *Country* E West Indies
St-Laurent-du-Maroni 91 *H3 var.* St-Laurent. NW French Guiana
St.Lawrence 71 *E4 Fr.* Fleuve St-Laurent. *River* Canada / USA
St.Lawrence, Gulf of 71 *F3 gulf* NW Atlantic Ocean
Saint Lawrence Island 68 *B2 island* Alaska, USA
St-Lô 122 *B3 anc.* Briovera, Laudus. Manche, N France
St-Louis 122 *E4* Haut-Rhin, NE France
Saint Louis 77 *G4* Missouri, C USA
Saint Louis 106 *B3* NW Senegal
Saint Lucia 87 *E1 country* SE West Indies
Saint Lucia Channel 87 *H4 channel* Martinique / Saint Lucia
St-Malo 122 *B3* Ille-et-Vilaine, NW France
St-Malo, Golfe de 122 *A3 gulf* NW France
St Matthew's Island *see* Zadetkyi Kyun
St.Matthias Group 176 *B3 island group* NE PNG
St-Maur-des-Fossés 122 *E2* Val-de-Marne, N France
St.Moritz 127 *B7 Ger.* Sankt Moritz, *Rmsch.* San Murezzan. Graubünden, SE Switzerland
St-Nazaire 122 *A4* Loire-Atlantique, NW France
St-Omer 122 *C2* Pas-de-Calais, N France
Saint Paul 77 *F2 state capital* Minnesota, N USA
St-Paul, Île 173 *C6 var.* St.Paul Island. *Island* NE French Southern and Antarctic Territories
St Peter Port 121 *D8 dependent territory capital* (Guernsey) C Guernsey, Channel Islands
Saint Petersburg *see* Sankt-Peterburg
Saint Petersburg 75 *E4* Florida, SE USA
St-Pierre and Miquelon 67 *E5 Fr.* Îles St-Pierre et Miquelon. *French territorial collectivity* NE North America
St-Quentin 122 *C3* Aisne, N France
Saint Vincent 87 *G4 island* N Saint Vincent and the Grenadines
Saint Vincent and the Grenadines 67 *D7 country* SE West Indies
Saint Vincent Passage 87 *H4 passage* Saint Lucia / Saint Vincent and the Grenadines
Saipan 174 *B1 island country capital* (Northern Mariana Islands) S Northern Mariana Islands
Sajama, Nevado 93 *F4 mountain* W Bolivia
Sajószentpéter 131 *D6* Borsod-Abaúj-Zemplén, NE Hungary
Sakākah 152 *B4* Al Jawf, NW Saudi Arabia
Sakakawea, Lake 76 *D1 reservoir* North Dakota, N USA
Sakata 162 *D4* Yamagata, Honshū, C Japan
Sakhalin 157 *see* Sakhalin, Ostrov
Sakhalin, Ostrov 147 *G4 var.* Sakhalin. *Island* SE Russian Federation
Sakhon Nakhon *see* Sakon Nakhon
Şäki 149 *G2 Rus.* Sheki; *prev.* Nukha. NW Azerbaijan
Sakishima-shotō 162 *A3 var.* Sakisima Syotô. *Island group* SW Japan
Sakisima Syotô *see* Sakishima-shotō
Sakiz *see* Saqqez
Sakiz-Adasi *see* Chíos
Sakon Nakhon 168 *D4 var.* Muang Sakon Nakhon, Sakhon Nakhon. Sakon Nakhon, E Thailand
Saky 141 *F5 Rus.* Saki. Respublika Krym, S Ukraine
Sal 106 *A3 island* Ilhas de Barlavento, NE Cape Verde
Sala 117 *C6* Västmanland, C Sweden
Salacgrīva 138 *C3 Est.* Salatsi. Limbaži, N Latvia
Sala Consilina 129 *D5* Campania, S Italy
Salado, Río 96 *C3 river* C Argentina
Salado, Río 94 *D5 river* E Argentina
Şalālah 153 *D6* SW Oman
Salamá 84 *B2* Baja Verapaz, C Guatemala
Salamanca 124 *D2 anc.* Helmantica, Salmantica. Castilla-León, NW Spain
Salamanca 96 *B4* Coquimbo, C Chile
Salamīyah 150 *B3 var.* As Salamīyah. Ḩamāh, W Syria
Salang *see* Phuket
Salantai 138 *B3* Kretinga, NW Lithuania
Salavan 169 *D5 var.* Saravan, Saravane. Salavan, S Laos
Salavat 143 *D6* Respublika Bashkortostan, W Russian Federation
Sala y Gomez 185 *F4 island* Chile, E Pacific Ocean
Sala y Gomez Fracture Zone *see* Sala y Gomez Ridge
Sala y Gomez Ridge 185 *G4 var.* Sala y Gomez Fracture Zone. *Tectonic feature* SE Pacific Ocean
Šalčininkai 139 *C5* Šalčininkai, SE Lithuania
Saldus 138 *B3 Ger.* Frauenburg. Saldus, W Latvia
Sale 181 *C7* Victoria, SE Australia
Salé 102 *C2* NW Morocco
Salekhard 146 *D3 prev.* Obdorsk. Yamalo-Nenetskiy Avtonomnyy Okrug, N Russian Federation
Salem 78 *B3 state capital* Oregon, NW USA
Salem 164 *C2* Tamil Nādu, SE India
Salerno 129 *D5 anc.* Salernum. Campania, S Italy
Salerno, Golfo di 129 *C5 Eng.* Gulf of Salerno. *Gulf* S Italy
Salihorsk 139 *C7 Rus.* Soligorsk. Minskaya Voblasts', S Belarus
Salima 111 *E2* Central, C Malawi
Salina 77 *E5* Kansas, C USA
Salina Cruz 83 *F5* Oaxaca, SE Mexico
Salinas 79 *B6* California, W USA
Salinas 92 *A2* Guayas, W Ecuador
Salisbury 121 *D7 var.* New Sarum. S England, UK
Sallyana *see* Salyan
Salmon River 78 *D3 river* Idaho, NW USA
Salmon River Mountains 78 *D3 mountain range* Idaho, NW USA
Salo 117 *D6* Turku-Pori, SW Finland
Salon-de-Provence 123 *D6* Bouches-du-Rhône, SE France
Salonta 140 *A3 Hung.* Nagyszalonta. Bihor, W Romania
Sal'sk 143 *B7* Rostovskaya Oblast', SW Russian Federation
Salt *see* As Salt
Salta 96 *C2* Salta, NW Argentina
Saltash 121 *C7* SW England, UK
Saltillo 83 *E3* Coahuila de Zaragoza, NE Mexico
Salt Lake City 76 *B4 state capital* Utah, W USA
Salto 96 *D4* Salto, N Uruguay
Salton Sea 79 *D8 lake* California, W USA
Salvador 95 *G3 prev.* São Salvador. Bahia, E Brazil
Salween 156 *C2 Bur.* Thanlwin, *Chin.* Nu Chiang, Nu Jiang. *River* SE Asia
Salyan 167 *E3 var.* Sallyana. Mid Western, W Nepal
Salzburg 127 *D6 anc.* Juvavum. Salzburg, N Austria
Salzgitter 126 *C4 prev.* Watenstedt-Salzgitter. Niedersachsen, C Germany
Salzwedel 126 *C3* Sachsen-Anhalt, N Germany
Samakhixai 169 *E5 var.* Attapu, Attopeu. Attapu, S Laos
Samalayuca 82 *C1* Chihuahua, N Mexico
Samar 171 *F2 island* C Philippines
Samara 146 *B3 prev.* Kuybyshev. Samarskaya Oblast', W Russian Federation
Samarang *see* Semarang
Samarinda 170 *D4* Borneo, C Indonesia
Samarqand 155 *E2 Rus.* Samarkand. Samarqand Wiloyati, C Uzbekistan
Samawa *see* As Samāwah
Sambalpur 167 *F4* Orissa, E India
Sambava 111 *G2* Antsiraṅana, NE Madagascar
Sambir 140 *B2 Rus.* Sambor. L'vivs'ka Oblast', NW Ukraine
Sambre 122 *D2 river* Belgium / France
Samfya 110 *D2* Luapula, N Zambia
Saminatal 126 *E2 valley* Austria / Liechtenstein
Samnān *see* Semnān
Sam Neua *see* Xam Nua
Samoa 177 *E4 off.* Independent State of Western Samoa, *var.* Sāmoa-i-Sisifo. *Country* W Polynesia
Samoa Basin 175 *E3 undersea feature* W Pacific Ocean
Samobor 132 *A2* Grad Zagreb, N Croatia
Sámos 137 *E6 prev.* Limín Vathéos. Sámos, Dodekánisos, Greece, Aegean Sea
Sámos 137 *D6 island* Dodekánisos, Greece, Aegean Sea
Samosch *see* Someş
Samothráki 136 *C4 anc.* Samothrace. *Island* NE Greece
Samothráki 136 *D4* Samothráki, NE Greece
Sampit 170 *C4* Borneo, C Indonesia
Samsun 148 *D2 anc.* Amisus. Samsun, N Turkey
Samtredia 149 *F2* W Georgia
Samui, Ko 169 *C6 island* SW Thailand
Samut Prakan 169 *C5 var.* Muang Samut Prakan, Paknam. Samut Prakan, C Thailand
San 131 *E5 river* SE Poland
San 106 *D3* Ségou, C Mali
Şan'ā' 153 *B6 Eng.* Sana. *Country capital* (Yemen) W Yemen
Sana 132 *B3 river* NW Bosnia and Herzegovina
Sana 144 *see* Şan'ā'
Sanae 186 *B2 South African research station* Antarctica
Sanaga 109 *B5 river* C Cameroon
San Ambrosio, Isla 89 *A5 Eng.* San Ambrosio Island. *Island* W Chile
Sanandaj 152 *C3 prev.* Sinneh. Kordestān, W Iran
San Andrés, Isla de 85 *F3 island* NW Colombia
San Andrés Tuxtla 83 *F4 var.* Tuxtla. Veracruz-Llave, E Mexico
San Angelo 81 *F3* Texas, SW USA
San Antonio 81 *F4* Texas, SW USA
San Antonio 84 *B2* Toledo, S Belize
San Antonio 96 *B4* Valparaíso, C Chile
San Antonio Oeste 97 *C5* Río Negro, E Argentina
San Antonio River 81 *G4 river* Texas, SW USA
Sanāw 153 *C6 var.* Sanaw. NE Yemen
San Benedicto, Isla 82 *B4 island* W Mexico
San Benito 84 *B1* Petén, N Guatemala
San Benito 81 *G5* Texas, SW USA
San Bernardino 79 *C7* California, W USA
San Blas 82 *C3* Sinaloa, C Mexico
San Blas, Cape 74 *D3 headland* Florida, SE USA
San Blas, Cordillera de 85 *G4 mountain range* NE Panama
San Carlos *see* Quesada
San Carlos 80 *B2* Arizona, SW USA
San Carlos 84 *D4* Río San Juan, S Nicaragua
San Carlos de Bariloche 97 *B5* Río Negro, SW Argentina
San Carlos del Zulia 90 *C2* Zulia, W Venezuela
San Clemente Island 79 *B8 island* Channel Islands, California, W USA
San Cristobal 176 *C4 var.* Makira. *Island* SE Solomon Islands
San Cristóbal *see* San Cristóbal de Las Casas
San Cristóbal 90 *C2* Táchira, W Venezuela
San Cristóbal de Las Casas 83 *G5 var.* San Cristóbal. Chiapas, SE Mexico
San Cristóbal, Isla 92 *B4 var.* Chatham Island. *Island* Galapagos Islands, Ecuador, E Pacific Ocean
Sancti Spíritus 86 *B2* Sancti Spíritus, C Cuba
Sandakan 170 *D3* Sabah, East Malaysia
Sandanski 136 *C3 prev.* Sveti Vrach. Sofiyska Oblast, SW Bulgaria
Sanday 120 *D2 island* NE Scotland, UK
Sanders 80 *C2* Arizona, SW USA
Sand Hills 76 *D3 mountain range* Nebraska, C USA
San Diego 79 *C8* California, W USA
Sandnes 117 *A6* Rogaland, S Norway
Sandomierz 130 *D4 Rus.* Sandomir. Tarnobrzeg, SE Poland
Sandoway 168 *A4* Arakan State, W Myanmar
Sandpoint 78 *C1* Idaho, NW USA
Sand Springs 81 *G1* Oklahoma, C USA
Sandusky 72 *D3* Ohio, N USA
Sandvika 117 *A6* Akershus, S Norway
Sandviken 117 *C6* Gävleborg, C Sweden
Sandy Bay 125 *H5 bay* E Gibraltar
Sandy City 76 *B4* Utah, W USA
Sandy Lake 70 *B3 lake* Ontario, C Canada
San Esteban 84 *D2* Olancho, C Honduras
San Felipe 90 *D1* Yaracuy, NW Venezuela
San Felipe de Puerto Plata *see* Puerto Plata
San Félix, Isla 89 *A5 Eng.* San Felix Island. *Island* W Chile
San Fernando 124 *C5 prev.* Isla de León. Andalucía, S Spain
San Fernando 90 *D2 var.* San Fernando de Apure. Apure, C Venezuela
San Fernando 78 *D1* California, W USA
San Fernando 87 *H5* Trinidad, Trinidad and Tobago
San Fernando de Apure *see* San Fernando
San Fernando del Valle de Catamarca 96 *C3 var.* Catamarca. Catamarca, NW Argentina
San Fernando de Monte Cristi *see* Monte Cristi
San Francisco 79 *B6* California, W USA
San Francisco del Oro 82 *C2* Chihuahua, N Mexico
San Francisco de Macorís 87 *E3* C Dominican Republic
San Gabriel 92 *B1* Carchi, N Ecuador
San Gabriel Mountains 78 *E1 mountain range* California, W USA
Sangir, Kepulauan 171 *F3 var.* Kepulauan Sangihe. *Island group* N Indonesia
Sāngli 164 *B1* Mahārāshtra, W India
Sangmélima 109 *B5* Sud, S Cameroon
Sangre de Cristo Mountains 80 *D1 mountain range* Colorado / New Mexico, C USA
San Ignacio 84 *B1 prev.* Cayo, El Cayo. Cayo, W Belize
San Ignacio 82 *B2* Baja California Sur, W Mexico
San Ignacio 93 *F3* Beni, N Bolivia
San Joaquin Valley 79 *B7 valley* California, W USA
San Jorge, Golfo 97 *C6 var.* Gulf of San Jorge. *Gulf* S Argentina
San Jorge, Gulf of *see* San Jorge, Golfo
San José *see* San José del Guaviare
San Jose 79 *B6* California, W USA
San José 84 *B3 var.* Puerto San José. Escuintla, S Guatemala
San José 93 *G3 var.* San José de Chiquitos. Santa Cruz, E Bolivia
San José 85 *E4 country capital* (Costa Rica) San José, C Costa Rica
San José de Chiquitos *see* San José
San José de Cúcuta *see* Cúcuta
San José del Guaviare 90 *C4 var.* San José. Guaviare, S Colombia
San Juan 87 *F3 dependent territory capital* (Puerto Rico) NE Puerto Rico
San Juan *see* San Juan de los Morros
San Juan 96 *B4* San Juan, W Argentina
San Juan Bautista 96 *D3* Misiones, S Paraguay
San Juan Bautista Tuxtepec *see* Tuxtepec
San Juan de Alicante 125 *F4* País Valenciano, E Spain
San Juan del Norte 85 *E4 var.* Greytown. Río San Juan, SE Nicaragua
San Juan de los Morros 90 *D2 var.* San Juan. Guárico, N Venezuela
San Juanito, Isla 82 *C4 island* C Mexico
San Juan Mountains 80 *D1 mountain range* Colorado, C USA
San Juan River 80 *C1 river* Colorado / Utah, W USA
San Julián *see* Puerto San Julián
Sankt Gallen 127 *B7 var.* St.Gallen, *Eng.* Saint Gall, *Fr.* St-Gall. Sankt Gallen, NE Switzerland
Sankt-Peterburg 142 *B4 prev.* Leningrad, Petrograd, *Eng.* Saint Petersburg, *Fin.* Pietari. Leningradskaya Oblast', NW Russian Federation
Sankt Pölten 127 *E6* Niederösterreich, N Austria
Sankuru 109 *D6 river* C Congo (Zaire)
Şanlıurfa 149 *E4 prev.* Sanli Urfa, Urfa, *anc.* Edessa. Şanlıurfa, S Turkey
San Lorenzo 92 *A1* Esmeraldas, N Ecuador
San Lorenzo 93 *G5* Tarija, S Bolivia
San Lorenzo, Isla 92 *C4 island* W Peru
Sanlúcar de Barrameda 124 *C5* Andalucía, S Spain
San Luis 82 *A1 var.* San Luis Río Colorado. Sonora, NW Mexico
San Luis 84 *B2* Petén, NE Guatemala
San Luis 96 *C4* San Luis, C Argentina
San Luis Obispo 79 *B7* California, W USA
San Luis Potosí 83 *E3* San Luis Potosí, C Mexico
San Luis Río Colorado *see* San Luis
San Marcos 84 *A2* San Marcos, W Guatemala
San Marcos 81 *G4* Texas, SW USA
San Marino 128 *D1 off.* Republic of San Marino. *Country* S Europe
San Marino 128 *E1 country capital* (San Marino) C San Marino
San Martín 186 *A2 Argentinian research station* Antarctica
San Mateo 91 *E2* Anzoátegui, NE Venezuela
San Matías 93 *H3* Santa Cruz, E Bolivia
San Matías, Golfo 97 *C5 var.* Gulf of San Matías. *Gulf* E Argentina
San Matías, Gulf of *see* San Matías, Golfo
Sanmenxia 160 *C4 var.* Shan Xian. Henan, C China
Sânmiclăuş Mare *see* Sânnicolau Mare
San Miguel 82 *D2* Coahuila de Zaragoza, N Mexico
San Miguel 84 *C3* San Miguel, SE El Salvador
San Miguel de Ibarra *see* Ibarra
San Miguel de Tucumán 96 *C3 var.* Tucumán. Tucumán, N Argentina
San Miguelito 85 *G4* Panamá, C Panama
San Miguel, Río 93 *G3 river* E Bolivia
Sannār *see* Sennar
Sânnicolaul-Mare *see* Sânnicolau Mare
Sânnicolau Mare 140 *A4 var.* Sânnicolaul-Mare, *Hung.* Nagyszentmiklós; *prev.* Sânmiclăuş Mare, Sînnicolau Mare. Timiş, W Romania
Sanok 131 *E5* Krosno, SE Poland
San Pablo 93 *F5* Potosí, S Bolivia
San Pedro 82 *D3 var.* San Pedro de las Colonias. Coahuila de Zaragoza, NE Mexico
San Pedro 84 *C1* Corozal, NE Belize
San-Pédro 106 *D5* S Ivory Coast
San Pedro de la Cueva 82 *C2* Sonora, NW Mexico
San Pedro de las Colonias *see* San Pedro
San Pedro de Lloc 92 *B3* La Libertad, NW Peru
San Pedro Mártir, Sierra 82 *A1 mountain range* NW Mexico
San Pedro Sula 84 *C2* Cortés, NW Honduras
San Rafael 96 *B4* Mendoza, W Argentina
San Rafael Mountains 79 *C7 mountain range* California, W USA
San Ramón de la Nueva Orán 96 *C2* Salta, N Argentina
San Remo 128 *A3* Liguria, NW Italy
San Salvador 84 *B3 country capital* (El Salvador) San Salvador, SW El Salvador
San Salvador de Jujuy 96 *C2 var.* Jujuy. Jujuy, N Argentina
San Salvador, Isla 92 *A4 prev.* Watlings Island. *Island* E Bahamas
Sansanné-Mango 107 *E4 var.* Mango. N Togo
Sansepolcro 128 *C3* Toscana, C Italy
San Severo 129 *D5* Puglia, SE Italy
Santa Ana 93 *F3* Beni, N Bolivia
Santa Ana 78 *D2* California, W USA
Santa Ana 84 *B3* Santa Ana, NW El Salvador
Santa Ana Mountains 78 *E2 mountain range* California, W USA
Santa Barbara 79 *C7* California, W USA
Santa Barbara 82 *C2* Chihuahua, N Mexico
Santa Catalina Island 79 *B8 island* Channel Islands, California, W USA
Santa Catarina 95 *E5 off.* Estado de Santa Catarina. *State* S Brazil
Santa Clara 86 *B2* Villa Clara, C Cuba
Santa Clarita 78 *D1* California, W USA
Santa Comba 124 *B1* Galicia, NW Spain
Santa Cruz 93 *G4 var.* Santa Cruz de la Sierra. Santa Cruz, C Bolivia
Santa Cruz 79 *B6* California, W USA
Santa Cruz 108 *E2* São Tomé, C Sao Tome and Principe
Santa Cruz Barillas *see* Barillas
Santa Cruz de la Sierra *see* Santa Cruz
Santa Cruz del Quiché 84 *B2* Quiché, W Guatemala
Santa Cruz de Tenerife 102 *A3* Tenerife, Islas Canarias, Spain, NE Atlantic Ocean
Santa Cruz, Isla 92 *B4 var.* Indefatigable Island, Isla Chávez. *Island* Galapagos Islands, Ecuador, E Pacific Ocean
Santa Cruz Islands 176 *D3 island group* E Solomon Islands
Santa Cruz, Río 97 *B7 river* S Argentina
Santa Elena 84 *B1* Cayo, W Belize
Santa Fe 80 *D1 state capital* New Mexico, SW USA
Santa Fe 96 *C4* Santa Fe, C Argentina
Santa Genoveva 82 *B3 mountain* W Mexico
Santa Isabel 176 *C3 var.* Bughotu. *Island* N Solomon Islands
Santa Lucia Range 79 *B7 mountain range* California, W USA
Santa Margarita, Isla 82 *B3 island* W Mexico
Santa Maria 124 *A5 island* Azores, Portugal, NE Atlantic Ocean
Santa Maria 79 *B7* California, W USA
Santa Maria 95 *E5* Rio Grande do Sul, S Brazil
Santa María, Isla 92 *A4 var.* Isla Floreana, Charles Island. *Island* Galapagos Islands, Ecuador, E Pacific Ocean
Santa Marta 90 *B1* Magdalena, N Colombia
Santa Monica 78 *D1* California, W USA
Santana 108 *E2* São Tomé, S Sao Tome and Principe
Santander 124 *D1* Cantabria, N Spain
Santanilla, Islas 85 *E1 Eng.* Swan Islands. *Island* NE Honduras
Santarém 124 *B3 anc.* Scalabis. Santarém, W Portugal
Santarém 95 *E2* Pará, N Brazil
Santa Rosa *see* Santa Rosa de Copán
Santa Rosa 79 *B6* California, W USA
Santa Rosa 96 *C4* La Pampa, C Argentina
Santa Rosa de Copán 84 *C2 var.* Santa Rosa. Copán, W Honduras
Santa Rosa Island 79 *B8 island* California, W USA
Sant Carles de la Rápida *see* Sant Carles de la Ràpita
Sant Carles de la Ràpita 125 *F3 var.* Sant Carles de la Rápida. Cataluña, NE Spain
Santiago 96 *B4 var.* Gran Santiago. *Country capital* (Chile) Santiago, C Chile
Santiago 124 *B1 var.* Santiago de Compostela, *Eng.* Compostella; *anc.* Campus Stellae. Galicia, NW Spain
Santiago 87 *E3 var.* Santiago de los Caballeros. N Dominican Republic
Santiago 106 *A3 var.* São Tiago. *Island* Ilhas de Sotavento, S Cape Verde
Santiago *see* Santiago de Cuba
Santiago 85 *F5* Veraguas, S Panama

Sheridan 76 C2 Wyoming, C USA
Sherman 81 G2 Texas, SW USA
's-Hertogenbosch 118 C4 *Fr.* Bois-le-Duc, *Ger.* Herzogenbusch. Noord-Brabant, S Netherlands
Shetland Islands 120 D1 *island group* NE Scotland, UK
Shibarghān *see* Sheberghān
Shiberghān *see* Sheberghān
Shibetsu 162 D2 *var.* Sibetu. Hokkaidō, NE Japan
Shibh Jazīrat Sīnā' *see* Sinai
Shibushi-wan 163 B8 *bay* SW Japan
Shigatse *see* Xigazê
Shih-chia-chuang *see* Shijiazhuang
Shihezi 158 C2 Xinjiang Uygur Zizhiqu, NW China
Shihmen *see* Shijiazhuang
Shijiazhuang 160 C4 *var.* Shih-chia-chuang; *prev.* Shihmen. Hebei, E China
Shikārpur 166 B3 Sind, S Pakistan
Shikoku 163 C7 *var.* Sikoku. *Island* SW Japan
Shikoku Basin 157 F2 *var.* Sikoku Basin. *Undersea feature* N Philippine Sea
Shikotan, Ostrov 162 E2 *Jap.* Shikotan-tō. *Island* NE Russian Federation
Shilabo 105 D5 SE Ethiopia
Shiliguri 167 F3 *prev.* Siliguri. West Bengal, NE India
Shilka 147 F4 *river* S Russian Federation
Shimbir Berris *see* Shimbiris
Shimbiris 104 E4 *var.* Shimbir Berris. *Mountain* N Somalia
Shimoga 164 C2 Karnātaka, W India
Shimonoseki 163 A7 *var.* Simonoseki; *hist.* Akamagaseki, Bakan. Yamaguchi, Honshū, SW Japan
Shinano-gawa 163 C5 *var.* Sinano Gawa. *River* Honshū, C Japan
Shīndand 154 D4 Farāh, W Afghanistan
Shingū 163 C6 *var.* Singû. Wakayama, Honshū, SW Japan
Shinjō 162 D4 *var.* Sinzyô. Yamagata, Honshū, C Japan
Shinyanga 105 C7 Shinyanga, NW Tanzania
Shiprock 80 C1 New Mexico, SW USA
Shirāz 152 D4 *var.* Shīrāz. Fārs, S Iran
Shivpuri 166 D3 Madhya Pradesh, C India
Shizugawa 162 D4 Miyagi, Honshū, NE Japan
Shizuoka 163 D6 *var.* Sizuoka. Shizuoka, Honshū, S Japan
Shklow 139 D6 *Rus.* Shklov. Mahilyowskaya Voblasts', E Belarus
Shkodër 133 C5 *var.* Shkodra, *It.* Scutari, *SCr.* Skadar. Shkodër, NW Albania
Shkodra *see* Shkodër
Shkubinit, Lumi i 133 C6 *var.* Shkumbî, Shkumbin. *River* C Albania
Shkumbî *see* Shkubinit, Lumi i
Shkumbin *see* Shkubinit, Lumi i
Sholāpur *see* Solāpur
Shostka 141 F1 Sums'ka Oblast', NE Ukraine
Show Low 80 B2 Arizona, SW USA
Shpola 141 E3 Cherkas'ka Oblast', N Ukraine
Shreveport 74 A2 Louisiana, S USA
Shrewsbury 121 D6 *hist.* Scrobesbyrig'. W England, UK
Shu 146 C5 *Kaz.* Shū. Zhambyl, SE Kazakhstan
Shuang-liao *see* Liaoyuan
Shumagin Islands 68 B3 *island group* Alaska, USA
Shumen 136 D2 Varnenska Oblast, NE Bulgaria
Shumilina 139 E5 *Rus.* Shumilino. Vitsyebskaya Voblasts', NE Belarus
Shuqrah 153 B7 *var.* Shaqrā. SW Yemen
Shwebo 168 B3 Sagaing, C Myanmar
Shyichy 139 C7 *Rus.* Shiichi. Homyel'skaya Voblasts', SE Belarus
Shymkent 146 B5 *prev.* Chimkent. Yuzhnyy Kazakhstan, S Kazakhstan
Shyshchytsy 139 C6 *Rus.* Shishchitsy. Minskaya Voblasts', C Belarus
Si *see* Syr Darya
Siam, Gulf of *see* Thailand, Gulf of
Sian *see* Xi'an
Siang *see* Brahmaputra
Siangtan *see* Xiangtan
Šiauliai 138 B4 *Ger.* Schaulen. Šiauliai, N Lithuania
Sibay 143 D6 Respublika Bashkortostan, W Russian Federation
Šibenik 132 B4 *It.* Sebenico. Šibenik, S Croatia
Siberia 144 *see* Sibir'
Siberut, Pulau 170 A4 *prev.* Siberoet. *Island* Kepulauan Mentawai, W Indonesia
Sibetu *see* Shibetsu
Sibi 166 B2 Baluchistān, SW Pakistan
Sibir' 147 E3 *var.* Siberia. *Physical region* NE Russian Federation
Sibiti 109 B6 La Lékoumou, S Congo
Sibiu 140 B4 *Ger.* Hermannstadt, *Hung.* Nagyszeben. Sibiu, C Romania
Sibolga 170 B3 Sumatera, W Indonesia
Sibu 170 D3 Sarawak, East Malaysia
Sibut 108 C4 *prev.* Fort-Sibut. Kémo, S Central African Republic
Sibuyan Sea 171 E2 *sea* C Philippines
Sichon 169 C6 *var.* Ban Sichon, Si Chon. Nakhon Si Thammarat, SW Thailand
Sichuan 160 B5 *var.* Chuan, Sichuan Sheng, Ssu-ch'uan, Szechuan, Szechwan. Admin. region *province* C China
Sichuan Pendi 160 B5 *depression* C China
Sichuan Sheng *see* Sichuan
Sicilia 129 C7 *Eng.* Sicily; *anc.* Trinacria. *Island* Italy, C Mediterranean Sea
Sicilian Channel *see* Sicily, Strait of
Sicily *see* Sicilia
Sicily, Strait of 129 B7 *var.* Sicilian Channel. *Strait* C Mediterranean Sea
Sicuani 93 E4 Cusco, S Peru
Sidári 136 A4 Kérkyra, Iónioi Nísoi, Greece, C Mediterranean Sea
Sidas 170 C4 Borneo, C Indonesia
Siderno 129 D7 Calabria, SW Italy
Sîdi Barrâni 104 A1 NW Egypt
Sidi Bel Abbès 102 D2 *var.* Sidi bel Abbès, Sidi-Bel-Abbès. NW Algeria
Sidirókastro 136 C3 *prev.* Sidhirókastron. Kentrikí Makedonía, NE Greece
Sidley, Mount 186 B4 *mountain* Antarctica
Sidney 76 D1 Montana, NW USA
Sidney 76 D4 Nebraska, C USA
Sidney 72 C4 Ohio, N USA
Sidon *see* Saïda
Sidra *see* Surt
Siedlce 130 E3 *Ger.* Sedlez, *Rus.* Sesdlets. Siedlce, E Poland
Siegen 126 B4 Nordrhein-Westfalen, W Germany
Siemiatycze 130 E3 Białystok, E Poland
Siena 128 B3 *Fr.* Sienne; *anc.* Saena Julia. Toscana, C Italy
Sieradz 130 C4 Sieradz, C Poland
Sierpc 130 D3 Płock, C Poland
Sierra de Soconusco *see* Sierra Madre
Sierra Leone 106 C4 *off.* Republic of Sierra Leone. *Country* W Africa
Sierra Leone Basin 98 C4 *undersea feature* E Atlantic Ocean
Sierra Leone Ridge *see* Sierra Leone Rise
Sierra Leone Rise 98 C4 *var.* Sierra Leone Ridge, Sierra Leone Schwelle. *Undersea feature* E Atlantic Ocean
Sierra Leone Schwelle *see* Sierra Leone Rise
Sierra Madre 84 B2 *var.* Sierra de Soconusco. *Mountain range* Guatemala/Mexico
Sierra Madre *see* Madre Occidental, Sierra
Sierra Nevada 79 C6 *mountain range* W USA
Sierra Pacaraima *see* Pakaraima Mountains
Sierra Vieja 80 D3 *mountain range* Texas, SW USA
Sierra Vista 80 B3 Arizona, SW USA
Sífnos 137 C6 *anc.* Siphnos. *Island* Kykládes, Greece, Aegean Sea
Sigli 170 A3 Sumatera, W Indonesia
Siglufjördhur 115 E4 Nordhurland Vestra, N Iceland
Signal Peak 80 A2 *mountain* Arizona, SW USA
Signan *see* Xi'an
Signy 186 A2 *UK research station* South Orkney Islands, Antarctica
Siguatepeque 84 C2 Comayagua, W Honduras
Siguiri 106 D4 Haute-Guinée, NE Guinea
Siilinjärvi 116 E4 Kuopio, C Finland
Siirt 149 F4 *var.* Sert; *anc.* Tigranocerta. Siirt, SE Turkey
Sikandarabad *see* Secunderābād
Sikasso 106 D4 Sikasso, S Mali
Sikeston 77 H5 Missouri, C USA
Sikhote-Alin', Khrebet 147 G4 *mountain range* SE Russian Federation
Siking *see* Xi'an
Siklós 131 C7 Baranya, SW Hungary
Sikoku *see* Shikoku
Sikoku Basin *see* Shikoku Basin
Šilalė 138 B4 Šilalė, W Lithuania
Silchar 167 G3 Assam, NE India
Silesia 130 B4 Montana, NW USA
Silifke 148 C4 *anc.* Seleucia. İçel, S Turkey
Siling Co 158 C5 *lake* W China
Silinhot *see* Xilinhot
Silistra 136 E1 *var.* Silistria; *anc.* Durostorum. Razgradska Oblast, NE Bulgaria
Silistria *see* Silistra
Sillamäe 138 E2 *Ger.* Sillamäggi. Ida-Virumaa, NE Estonia
Šilutė 138 B4 *Ger.* Heydekrug. Šilutė, W Lithuania
Silvan 149 E4 Dıyarbakır, SE Turkey
Silverek 149 E4 Şanlıurfa, SE Turkey
Simanggang *see* Sri Aman
Simanichy 139 C7 *Rus.* Simonichi. Homyel'skaya Voblasts', SE Belarus
Simav 148 B3 Kütahya, W Turkey
Simav Çayı 148 A3 *river* NW Turkey
Simeto 129 C7 *river* Sicilia, Italy, C Mediterranean Sea
Simeulue, Pulau 170 A3 *island* NW Indonesia
Simferopol' 141 F5 Respublika Krym, S Ukraine
Simitli 136 C3 Sofiyska Oblast, SW Bulgaria
Şimleu Silvaniei 140 B3 *Hung.* Szilágsomlyó; *prev.* Şimlăul Silvaniei, Şimleul Silvaniei. Sălaj, NW Romania
Simonoseki *see* Shimonoseki
Simpelveld 119 D6 Limburg, SE Netherlands
Simplon Pass 127 B8 *pass* S Switzerland
Simpson *see* Fort Simpson
Simpson Desert 180 B4 *desert* Northern Territory/South Australia
Sīnā' *see* Sinai
Sinai 104 C2 *var.* Sinai Peninsula, *Ar.* Shibh Jazīrat Sīnā', Sīnā'. *Physical region* NE Egypt
Sinaia 140 C4 Prahova, SE Romania
Sinai Peninsula *see* Sinai
Sinano Gawa *see* Shinano-gawa
Sincelejo 90 B2 Sucre, NW Colombia
Sind 166 B3 *var.* Sindh. Admin. region *province* SE Pakistan
Sindelfingen 127 B6 Baden-Württemberg, SW Germany
Sindh *see* Sind
Sindi 138 D2 *Ger.* Zintenhof. Pärnumaa, SW Estonia
Sines 124 B4 Setúbal, S Portugal
Singan *see* Xi'an
Singapore 170 A1 *off.* Republic of Singapore. *Country* SE Asia
Singapore 170 B3 *country capital* (Singapore) S Singapore
Singen 127 B6 Baden-Württemberg, S Germany
Singida 105 C7 Singida, C Tanzania
Singkang 171 E4 Sulawesi, C Indonesia
Singkawang 170 C3 Borneo, C Indonesia
Singora *see* Songkhla
Singû *see* Shingū
Sining *see* Xining
Siniscola 129 A5 Sardegna, Italy, C Mediterranean Sea
Sinj 132 B4 Split-Dalmacija, SE Croatia
Sinkiang *see* Xinjiang Uygur Zizhiqu
Sinkiang Uighur Autonomous Region *see* Xinjiang Uygur Zizhiqu
Sinnamarie *see* Sinnamary
Sinnamary 91 H3 *var.* Sinnamarie. N French Guiana
Sînnicolau Mare *see* Sânnicolau Mare
Sinoie, Lacul 140 D5 *prev.* Lacul Sinoe. *Lagoon* SE Romania
Sinop 148 D2 *anc.* Sinope. Sinop, N Turkey
Sinsheim 127 B6 Baden-Württemberg, SW Germany
Sint Maarten 87 G3 *Eng.* Saint Martin. *Island* N Netherlands Antilles
Sint-Michielsgestel 118 C4 Noord-Brabant, S Netherlands
Sint-Niklaas 119 B5 *Fr.* Saint-Nicolas. Oost-Vlaanderen, N Belgium
Sint-Pieters-Leeuw 119 B6 Vlaams Brabant, C Belgium
Sintra 124 B3 *prev.* Cintra. Lisboa, W Portugal
Sinujiif 105 E5 Nugaal, NE Somalia
Sinus Aelaniticus *see* Aqaba, Gulf of
Sinyang *see* Xinyang
Sinzyô *see* Shinjō
Sion 127 A7 *Ger.* Sitten; *anc.* Sedunum. Valais, SW Switzerland
Sioux City 77 F3 Iowa, C USA
Sioux Falls 77 F3 South Dakota, N USA
Siping 160 D3 *var.* Ssu-p'ing, Szeping; *prev.* Ssu-p'ing-chieh. Jilin, NE China
Siple, Mount 186 A4 *mountain* Siple Island, Antarctica
Siquirres 85 E4 Limón, E Costa Rica
Siracusa 129 D7 *Eng.* Syracuse. Sicilia, Italy, C Mediterranean Sea
Sir Darya *see* Syr Darya
Sir Edward Pellew Group 180 B2 *island group* Northern Territory, NE Australia
Siret 140 C3 *var.* Siretul, *Ger.* Sereth, *Rus.* Seret, *Ukr.* Siret. *River* Romania/Ukraine
Siret *see* Siret
Siretul *see* Siret
Sirikit Reservoir 168 C4 *lake* N Thailand
Sīrjān 152 D4 *prev.* Sa'īdābād. Kermān, S Iran
Sirna *see* Sýrna
Şırnak 149 F4 Şırnak, SE Turkey
Síros *see* Sýros
Sirte *see* Surt
Sirte, Gulf of *see* Surt, Khalīj
Sisak 132 B3 *var.* Siscia, *Ger.* Sissek, *Hung.* Sziszek; *anc.* Segestica. Sisak-Moslavina, C Croatia
Siscia *see* Sisak
Sisimiut 114 C3 *var.* Holsteinborg, Holsteinsborg, Holstenborg, Holstensborg. S Greenland
Sissek *see* Sisak
Sistema Penibético *see* Béticos, Sistemas
Siteía 137 D8 *var.* Sitía. Kríti, Greece, E Mediterranean Sea
Sitges 125 G2 Cataluña, NE Spain
Sitía *see* Siteía
Sittang 168 B4 *var.* Sittoung. *River* S Myanmar
Sittard 119 D5 Limburg, SE Netherlands
Sittoung *see* Sittang
Sittwe 168 A3 *var.* Akyab. Arakan State, W Myanmar
Siuna 84 D3 Región Autónoma Atlántico Norte, NE Nicaragua
Siut *see* Asyût
Sivas 148 D3 *anc.* Sebastia, Sebaste. Sivas, C Turkey
Sivers'kyy Donets' 141 G2 *Rus.* Severskiy Donets. *River* Russian Federation/Ukraine *see also* Severskiy Donets
Siwa 104 A2 *var.* Sīwah. NW Egypt
Sīwah *see* Siwa
Six-Fours-les-Plages 123 D6 Var, SE France
Siyäzän 149 H2 *Rus.* Siazan'. NE Azerbaijan
Sizuoka *see* Shizuoka
Sjar *see* Sääre
Sjælland 117 B8 *Eng.* Zealand, *Ger.* Seeland. *Island* E Denmark
Sjenica 133 D5 *Turk.* Seniça. Serbia, SW Yugoslavia
Skadar *see* Shkodër
Skagerak *see* Skagerrak
Skagerrak 117 A6 *var.* Skagerak. *Channel* N Europe
Skagit River 78 B1 *river* Washington, NW USA
Skalka 116 C3 *lake* N Sweden
Skaudvilė 138 B4 Tauragė, SW Lithuania
Skegness 121 E6 E England, UK
Skellefteå 116 D4 Västerbotten, N Sweden
Skellefteälven 116 C4 *river* N Sweden
Ski 117 B6 Akershus, S Norway
Skíathos 137 C5 Skíathos, Vóreioi Sporádes, Greece, Aegean Sea
Skidal' 139 B5 *Rus.* Skidel'. Hrodzyenskaya Voblasts', W Belarus
Skiftet 138 C1 *Fin.* Kihti. *Strait* Gulf of Bothnia/Gulf of Finland
Skíros *see* Skýros
Skópelos 137 C5 Skópelos, Vóreioi Sporádes, Greece, Aegean Sea
Skopje 133 D6 *var.* Üsküb, *Turk.* Üsküp; *prev.* Skoplje, *anc.* Scupi. *Country capital* (FYR Macedonia) N FYR Macedonia
Skoplje *see* Skopje
Skovorodino 147 F4 Amurskaya Oblast', SE Russian Federation
Skuodas 138 B3 *Ger.* Schoden, *Pol.* Szkudy. Skuodas, NW Lithuania
Skye, Isle of 120 B3 *island* NW Scotland, UK
Skýros 137 C5 *var.* Skíros. Skýros, Vóreioi Sporádes, Greece, Aegean Sea
Skýros 137 C5 *var.* Skíros; *anc.* Scyros. *Island* Vóreioi Sporádes, Greece, Aegean Sea
Slagelse 117 B7 Vestsjælland, E Denmark
Slatina 140 B5 Olt, S Romania
Slavonska Požega 132 C3 *prev.* Požega, *Ger.* Poschega, *Hung.* Pozsega. Požega-Slavonija, NE Croatia
Slavonski Brod 132 C3 *Ger.* Brod, *Hung.* Bród; *prev.* Brod, Brod na Savi. Brod-Posavina, NE Croatia
Slavuta 140 C2 Khmel'nyts'ka Oblast', NW Ukraine
Slawharad 139 E7 *Rus.* Slavgorod. Mahilyowskaya Voblasts', E Belarus
Sławno 130 C2 Słupsk, NW Poland
Sléibhte Chill Mhantáin *see* Wicklow Mountains
Slēmānī *see* As Sulaymānīyah
Sliema 134 B5 N Malta
Sligeach *see* Sligo
Sligo 121 A5 *Ir.* Sligeach. NW Ireland
Sliven 136 D2 *var.* Slivno. Burgaska Oblast, E Bulgaria
Slivnitsa 136 B2 Sofiyska Oblast, W Bulgaria
Slivno *see* Sliven
Slobozia 140 C5 Ialomiţa, SE Romania
Slonim 139 B6 *Pol.* Słonim, *Rus.* Slonim. Hrodzyenskaya Voblasts', W Belarus
Slovakia 131 C6 *off.* Slovenská Republika, *Ger.* Slowakei, *Hung.* Szlovákia, *Slvk.* Slovensko. *Country* C Europe
Slovenia 127 D8 *off.* Republic of Slovenia, *Ger.* Slowenien, *Slvn.* Slovenija. *Country* SE Europe
Slovenské Rudohorie 131 D6 *Eng.* Slovak Ore Mountains, *Ger.* Slowakisches Erzgebirge, Ungarisches Erzgebirge. *Mountain range* C Slovakia
Slov''yans'k 141 G3 *Rus.* Slavyansk. Donets'ka Oblast', E Ukraine
Słubice 130 B3 *Ger.* Frankfurt. Gorzów, W Poland
Sluch 140 D1 *river* NW Ukraine
Słupsk 130 C2 *Ger.* Stolp. Słupsk, NW Poland
Slutsk 139 C6 *Rus.* Slutsk. Minskaya Voblasts', S Belarus
Smallwood Reservoir 71 F2 *lake* Newfoundland and Labrador, S Canada
Smara 102 B3 *var.* Es Semara. N Western Sahara
Smarhon' 139 C5 *Pol.* Smorgonie, *Rus.* Smorgon'. Hrodzyenskaya Voblasts', W Belarus
Smederevo 132 D4 *Ger.* Semendria. Serbia, N Yugoslavia
Smederevska Palanka 132 D4 Serbia, C Yugoslavia
Smila 141 E2 *Rus.* Smela. Cherkas'ka Oblast', C Ukraine
Smiltene 138 D3 *Ger.* Smilten. Valka, N Latvia
Smøla 116 A4 *island* W Norway
Smolensk 143 A5 Smolenskaya Oblast', W Russian Federation
Snake 66 B4 *river* Yukon Territory, NW Canada
Snake River 78 C3 *river* NW USA
Snake River Plain 78 D4 *plain* Idaho, NW USA
Sneek 118 D2 Friesland, N Netherlands
Sněžka 130 B4 *Ger.* Schneekoppe. *Mountain* N Czech Republic
Śniardwy, Jezioro 130 D3 *Ger.* Spirdingsee. *Lake* NE Poland
Snina 131 E5 *Hung.* Szinna. Východné Slovensko, E Slovakia
Snowdonia 121 C6 *mountain range* NW Wales, UK
Snyder 81 F3 Texas, SW USA
Sobradinho, Represa de 95 F2 *var.* Barragem de Sobradinho. *Reservoir* E Brazil
Sochi 143 A7 Krasnodarskiy Kray, SW Russian Federation
Société, Archipel de la 177 G4 *var.* Archipel de Tahiti, Îles de la Société, *Eng.* Society Islands. *Island group* W French Polynesia
Society Islands 175 *see* Société, Archipel de la
Socorro 80 D2 New Mexico, SW USA
Socorro, Isla 82 B5 *island* W Mexico
Socotra 144 *see* Suquṭrā
Soc Trăng 169 D6 *var.* Khanh. Soc Trăng, S Vietnam
Socuéllamos 125 E3 Castilla-La Mancha, C Spain
Sodankylä 116 D3 Lappi, N Finland
Sodari *see* Sodiri
Söderhamn 117 C5 Gävleborg, C Sweden
Södertälje 117 C6 Stockholm, C Sweden
Sodiri 104 B4 *var.* Sawdirī, Sodari. Northern Kordofan, C Sudan
Sofia *see* Sofiya
Sofiya 136 C2 *var.* Sophia, *Eng.* Sofia; *Lat.* Serdica. *Country capital* (Bulgaria) Grad Sofiya, W Bulgaria
Sogamoso 90 B3 Boyacá, C Colombia
Sognefjorden 117 A5 *fjord* NE North Sea
Sohâg 104 B2 *var.* Sawhāj, Suliag. C Egypt
Sohar *see* Ṣuḥār
Sohm Plain 98 B3 *undersea feature* NW Atlantic Ocean
Sohrau *see* Żory
Sokal' 140 C2 *Rus.* Sokal. L'vivs'ka Oblast', NW Ukraine
Söke 148 A4 Aydın, SW Turkey
Sokhumi 149 E1 *Rus.* Sukhumi. NW Georgia
Sokodé 107 F4 C Togo
Sokol 142 C4 Vologodskaya Oblast', NW Russian Federation
Sokółka 130 E3 Białystok, NE Poland
Sokolov 131 A5 *Ger.* Falkenau an der Eger; *prev.* Falknov nad Ohří. Západní Čechy, W Czech Republic
Sokone 106 B3 W Senegal
Sokoto 107 F4 *river* NW Nigeria
Sokoto 107 F3 Sokoto, NW Nigeria
Sokotra *see* Suquṭrā
Solāpur 156 B3 *var.* Sholāpur. Mahārāshtra, W India
Solca 140 C3 *Ger.* Solka. Suceava, N Romania
Sol, Costa del 124 D5 *coastal region* S Spain
Soldeu 123 B7 NE Andorra
Solec Kujawski 130 C3 Bydgoszcz, W Poland
Soledad *see* East Falkland
Soledad 90 B1 Anzoátegui, NE Venezuela
Solikamsk 146 C3 Permskaya Oblast', NW Russian Federation
Sol'-Iletsk 143 D6 Orenburgskaya Oblast', W Russian Federation
Solingen 126 A4 Nordrhein-Westfalen, W Germany
Sollentuna 117 C6 Stockholm, C Sweden
Solok 170 B4 Sumatera, W Indonesia
Solomon Islands 176 C3 *prev.* British Solomon Islands Protectorate. *Country* W Pacific Ocean
Solomon Islands 176 C3 *island group* PNG/Solomon Islands
Solomon Sea 176 B3 *sea* W Pacific Ocean
Soltau 126 B3 Niedersachsen, NW Germany
Sol'tsy 142 A4 Novgorodskaya Oblast', W Russian Federation
Solwezi 110 D2 North Western, NW Zambia
Sōma 162 D4 Fukushima, Honshū, C Japan
Somalia 105 D5 *off.* Somali Democratic Republic, *Som.* Jamuuriyada Demuqraadiga Soomaaliyeed, Soomaaliya; *prev.* Italian Somaliland, Somaliland Protectorate. *Country* E Africa
Somali Basin 101 E5 *undersea feature* W Indian Ocean
Sombor 132 C3 *Hung.* Zombor. Serbia, NW Yugoslavia
Someren 119 D5 Noord-Brabant, SE Netherlands
Somerset 74 A5 *var.* Somerset Village. W Bermuda
Somerset 72 C5 Kentucky, S USA
Somerset Island 69 F2 *island* Queen Elizabeth Islands, Northwest Territories, NW Canada
Somerset Island 74 A5 *island* W Bermuda
Somerset Village *see* Somerset
Somers Islands *see* Bermuda
Somerton 80 A2 Arizona, SW USA
Someş 140 B3 *var.* Somesch, Someşul, Szamos, *Ger.* Samosch. *River* Hungary/Romania
Somesch *see* Someş
Someşul *see* Someş
Somme 122 C2 *river* N France
Somotillo 84 C3 Chinandega, NW Nicaragua
Somoto 84 D3 Madriz, NW Nicaragua
Songea 105 C8 Ruvuma, S Tanzania
Sông Hông Hà *see* Red River
Songkhla 169 C7 *var.* Songkla, *Mal.* Singora. Songkhla, SW Thailand
Songkla *see* Songkhla

Świebodzice 130 B4 Ger. Freiburg in Schlesien, Swiebodzice. Wałbrzych, SW Poland
Świebodzin 130 B3 Ger. Schwiebus. Zielona Góra, W Poland
Świecie 130 C3 Ger. Schwertberg. Bydgoszcz, N Poland
Swindon 121 D7 S England, UK
Świnoujście 130 B2 Ger. Swinemünde. Szczecin, NW Poland
Switzerland 127 A7 off. Swiss Confederation, Fr. La Suisse, Ger. Schweiz, It. Svizzera; anc. Helvetia. Country C Europe
Sycaminum see Ḩefa
Sydney 180 D1 state capital New South Wales, SE Australia
Sydney 71 G4 Cape Breton Island, Nova Scotia, SE Canada
Syedpur see Saidpur
Syemyezhava 139 C6 Rus. Semezhevo. Minskaya Voblasts', C Belarus
Syene see Aswân
Syeverodonets'k 141 H3 Rus. Severodonetsk. Luhans'ka Oblast', E Ukraine
Syktyvkar 142 D4 prev. Ust'-Sysol'sk. Respublika Komi, NW Russian Federation
Sylhet 167 G3 Chittagong, NE Bangladesh
Synel'nykove 141 G3 Dnipropetrovs'ka Oblast', E Ukraine
Syowa 186 C2 Japanese research station Antarctica
Syracuse 73 E3 New York, NE USA
Syrdariya see Syr Darya
Syr Darya 146 B4 var. Sai Hun, Sir Darya, Syrdarya, Kaz. Syrdariya, Rus. Syrdar'ya, Uzb. Sirdaryo; anc. Jaxartes. River C Asia
Syria 150 B3 off. Syrian Arab Republic, var. Siria, Syrie, Ar. Al-Jumhūrīyah al-'Arabīyah as-Sūrīyah, Sūrīya. Country SW Asia
Syrian Desert 151 D5 Ar. Al Hamad, Bādiyat ash Shām. Desert SW Asia
Sýrna 137 E7 var. Sirna. Island Kykládes, Greece, Aegean Sea
Sýros 137 C6 var. Síros. Island Kykládes, Greece, Aegean Sea
Syvash, Zatoka 141 F4 Rus. Zaliv Syvash. Inlet S Ukraine
Syzran' 143 C6 Samarskaya Oblast', W Russian Federation
Szamos see Someş
Szamotuły 130 B3 Poznań, W Poland
Szczecin 130 B3 Eng./Ger. Stettin. Szczecin, NW Poland
Szczecinek 130 B2 Ger. Neustettin. Koszalin, NW Poland
Szczeciński, Zalew 130 A2 var. Stettiner Haff, Ger. Oderhaff. Bay Germany/Poland
Szczytno 130 D3 Ger. Ortelsburg. Olsztyn, NE Poland
Szechuan see Sichuan
Szechwan see Sichuan
Szeged 131 D7 Ger. Szegedin, Rom. Seghedin. Csongrád, SE Hungary
Székesfehérvár 131 C6 Ger. Stuhlweissenberg; anc. Alba Regia. Fejér, W Hungary
Szekszárd 131 C7 Tolna, S Hungary
Szenttamás see Srbobran
Szeping see Siping
Sziszek see Sisak
Szolnok 131 D6 Jász-Nagykun-Szolnok, C Hungary
Szombathely 131 B6 Ger. Steinamanger; anc. Sabaria, Savaria. Vas, W Hungary
Szprotawa 130 B4 Ger. Sprottau. Zielona Góra, W Poland

T

Table Rock Lake 81 G1 reservoir Arkansas/Missouri, C USA
Tábor 131 B5 Jižní Čechy, SW Czech Republic
Tabora 105 B7 Tabora, W Tanzania
Tabrīz 152 C2 var. Tebriz; anc. Tauris. Āzarbāyjān-e Khāvarī, NW Iran
Tabuaeran 177 G2 prev. Fanning Island. Atoll Line Islands, E Kiribati
Tabūk 152 A4 Tabūk, NW Saudi Arabia
Täby 117 C6 Stockholm, C Sweden
Tachov 131 A5 Ger. Tachau. Západní Čechy, W Czech Republic
Tacloban 171 F2 off. Tacloban City. Leyte, C Philippines
Tacna 93 E4 Tacna, SE Peru
Tacoma 78 B2 Washington, NW USA
Tacuarembó 96 D4 prev. San Fructuoso. Tacuarembó, C Uruguay
Tademaït, Plateau du 102 D3 plateau C Algeria
Tadmor see Tudmur
Tadmur see Tudmur
Tādpatri 164 C2 Andhra Pradesh, E India
Taegu 161 E4 off. Taegu-gwangyŏksi, var. Daegu, Jap. Taikyū. SE South Korea
Taejŏn 161 E4 off. Taejŏn-gwangyŏksi, Jap. Taiden. C South Korea
Tafassâsset, Ténéré du 107 G2 desert N Niger
Tafila see Aṭ Ṭafīlah
Taganrog 143 A7 Rostovskaya Oblast', SW Russian Federation
Taganrog, Gulf of 141 G4 Rus. Taganrogskiy Zaliv, Ukr. Tahanroz'ka Zatoka. Gulf Russian Federation/Ukraine
Taguatinga 95 F3 Tocantins, C Brazil
Tagus 124 C3 Port. Rio Tejo, Sp. Río Tajo. River Portugal/Spain
Tagus Plain 112 A4 undersea feature E Atlantic Ocean
Tahat 103 E4 mountain SE Algeria
Tahiti 177 H4 island Îles du Vent, W French Polynesia
Tahlequah 81 G1 Oklahoma, C USA
Tahoe, Lake 79 B5 lake California/Nevada, W USA
Tahoua 107 F3 Tahoua, W Niger
T'aichung 160 D6 Jap. Taichū; prev. Taiwan. C Taiwan
Taieri 183 B7 river South Island, NZ
Taihape 182 D4 Manawatu-Wanganui, North Island, NZ
Tailem Bend 181 B7 South Australia
T'ainan 160 D6 Jap. Tainan; prev. Dainan. S Taiwan
T'aipei 160 D6 Jap. Taihoku; prev. Daihoku. Country capital (Taiwan) N Taiwan
Taiping 170 B3 Perak, Peninsular Malaysia
Taiwan 160 D6 off. Republic of China, var. Formosa, Formo'sa. Country E Asia
T'aiwan Haihsia see Taiwan Strait
Taiwan Haixia see Taiwan Strait
Taiwan Strait 160 D6 var. Formosa Strait, Chin. T'aiwan Haihsia, Taiwan Haixia. Strait China/Taiwan
Taiyuan 160 C4 prev. T'ai-yuan, T'ai-yüan, Yangku. Shanxi, C China
Ta'izz 153 B7 SW Yemen
Tajikistan 155 E3 off. Republic of Tajikistan, Rus. Tadzhikistan, Taj. Jumhurii Tojikiston; prev. Tajik S.S.R. Country C Asia
Tak 168 C4 var. Rahaeng. Tak, W Thailand
Takao see Kaohsiung
Takaoka 163 C5 Toyama, Honshū, SW Japan
Takapuna 182 D2 Auckland, North Island, NZ
Takhiatosh 154 C2 Rus. Takhiatash. Qoraqalpoghiston Respublikasi, W Uzbekistan
Takhtakŭpir 154 D1 Rus. Takhtakupyr. Qoraqalpoghiston Respublikasi, NW Uzbekistan
Takikawa 162 D2 Hokkaidō, NE Japan
Takla Makan Desert 156 see Taklimakan Shamo
Taklimakan Shamo 158 B3 Eng. Takla Makan Desert. Desert NW China
Takow see Kaohsiung
Takutea 177 G4 island S Cook Islands
Talachyn 139 D6 Rus. Tolochin. Vitsyebskaya Voblasts', NE Belarus
Talamanca, Cordillera de 85 E5 mountain range S Costa Rica
Talara 92 B2 Piura, NW Peru
Talas 155 F2 Talasskaya Oblast', NW Kyrgyzstan
Talaud, Kepulauan 171 F3 island group E Indonesia
Talavera de la Reina 124 D3 anc. Caesarobriga, Talabriga. Castilla-La Mancha, C Spain
Talca 96 B4 Maule, C Chile
Talcahuano 97 B5 Bío Bío, C Chile
Taldykorgan 146 C5 Kaz. Taldyqorghan; prev. Taldy-Kurgan. Taldykorgan, SE Kazakhstan
Ta-lien see Dalian
Taliq-an see Tāloqān
Tal'ka 139 C6 Rus. Tal'ka. Minskaya Voblasts', C Belarus
Tallahassee 74 D3 prev. Muskogean. State capital Florida, SE USA
Tall al Abyaḑ see At Tall al Abyaḑ
Tallinn 138 D2 Ger. Reval, Rus. Tallin; prev. Revel. Country capital (Estonia) Harjumaa, NW Estonia
Tall Kalakh 150 B4 var. Tell Kalakh. Ḩimş, C Syria
Tallulah 74 B2 Louisiana, S USA
Talnakh 146 D3 Taymyrskiy (Dolgano-Nenetskiy) Avtonomnyy Okrug, N Russian Federation
Tal'ne 141 E3 Rus. Tal'noye. Cherkas'ka Oblast', C Ukraine
Taloga 81 F1 Oklahoma, C USA
Tāloqān 155 E3 var. Taliq-an. Takhār, NE Afghanistan
Talsi 138 C3 Ger. Talsen. Talsi, NW Latvia
Taltal 96 B2 Antofagasta, N Chile
Talvik 116 D2 Finnmark, N Norway
Tamabo, Banjaran 170 D3 mountain range East Malaysia
Tamale 107 E4 C Ghana
Tamana 177 E3 prev. Rotcher Island. Atoll Tungaru, W Kiribati
Tamanrasset 103 E4 var. Tamenghest. S Algeria
Tamar 121 C7 river SW England, UK
Tamar see Tudmur
Tamatave see Toamasina
Tamazunchale 83 E4 San Luis Potosí, C Mexico
Tambacounda 106 C3 SE Senegal
Tambov 143 B6 Tambovskaya Oblast', W Russian Federation
Tambura 105 B5 Western Equatoria, SW Sudan
Tamchaket see Tâmchekkeţ
Tâmchekkeţ 106 C3 var. Tamchaket. Hodh el Gharbi, S Mauritania
Tamenghest see Tamanrasset
Tamiahua, Laguna de 83 F4 lagoon E Mexico
Tamil Nādu 164 C3 prev. Madras. State SE India
Tam Ky 169 E5 Quang Nam-Đa Năng, C Vietnam
Tampa 75 E4 Florida, SE USA
Tampa Bay 75 E4 bay Florida, SE USA
Tampere 117 D5 Swe. Tammerfors. Häme, SW Finland
Tampico 83 E3 Tamaulipas, C Mexico
Tamworth 181 D6 New South Wales, SE Australia
Tana 116 D2 var. Tenojoki, Fin. Teno, Lapp. Dealnu. River Finland/Norway see also Teno
Tana 116 D2 Finnmark, N Norway
Tanabe 163 C7 Wakayama, Honshū, SW Japan
T'ana Hāyk' 104 C4 Eng. Lake Tana. Lake NW Ethiopia
Tanais see Don
Tanami Desert 178 D3 desert Northern Territory, N Australia
Ţăndărei 140 D5 Ialomiţa, SE Romania
Tandil 97 D5 Buenos Aires, E Argentina
Tanega-shima 163 B8 island Nansei-shotō, SW Japan
Tane Range 168 B4 Bur. Tanen Taunggyi. Mountain range W Thailand
Tanezrouft 102 D4 desert Algeria/Mali
Ţanf, Jabal aţ 150 D4 mountain SE Syria
Tanga 101 E5 Tanga, E Tanzania
Tanga 105 C7 region E Tanzania
Tanganyika, Lake 105 B7 lake E Africa
Tangeh-ye Hormoz see Hormuz, Strait of
Tanger 102 C2 var. Tangiers, Tangier, Fr./Ger. Tangerk, Sp. Tánger; anc. Tingis. NW Morocco
Tangerk see Tanger
Tanggula Shan 158 C4 var. Dangla, Tangla Range. Mountain range W China
Tangier see Tanger
Tangiers see Tanger
Tangla Range see Tanggula Shan
Tangra Yumco 158 B5 var. Tangro Tso. Lake W China
Tangro Tso see Tangra Yumco
Tangshan 160 D3 var. T'ang-shan. Hebei, E China
T'ang-shan see Tangshan
Tanimbar, Kepulauan 171 F5 island group Maluku, E Indonesia
Tanna 176 D4 island S Vanuatu
Tan-Tan 102 B3 SW Morocco
Tan-tung see Dandong
Tanzania 105 C7 off. United Republic of Tanzania, Swa. Jamhuri ya Muungano wa Tanzania; prev. German East Africa, Tanganyika and Zanzibar. Country E Africa
Taoudenit see Taoudenni
Taoudenni 107 E2 var. Taoudenit. Tombouctou, N Mali
Tapa 138 E2 Ger. Taps. Lääne-Virumaa, NE Estonia
Tapachula 83 G5 Chiapas, SE Mexico
Tapajós, Rio 95 E2 var. Tapajóz. River NW Brazil
Tapajóz see Tapajós, Rio
Ţarābulus 103 F2 var. Ţarābulus al Gharb, Eng. Tripoli. Country capital (Libya) NW Libya
Ţarābulus see Tripoli
Ţarābulus al Gharb see Ţarābulus
Ţarābulus ash Shām see Tripoli
Taraclia 140 D4 Rus. Tarakilya. S Moldova
Taranaki, Mount 182 C4 var. Egmont. Mountain North Island, NZ
Tarancón 125 E3 Castilla-La Mancha, C Spain
Taranto 129 E5 var. Tarentum. Puglia, SE Italy
Taranto, Golfo di 129 E6 Eng. Gulf of Taranto. Gulf S Italy
Tarapoto 92 C2 San Martín, N Peru
Tarare 123 D5 Rhône, E France
Tarascon 123 D6 Bouches-du-Rhône, SE France
Tarawa 176 D2 atoll Tungaru, W Kiribati
Tarazona 125 E2 Aragón, NE Spain
Tarbes 123 B6 anc. Bigorra. Hautes-Pyrénées, S France
Tarcoola 181 A6 South Australia
Taree 181 D6 New South Wales, SE Australia
Tarentum see Taranto
Târgovişte 140 C5 prev. Tirgovişte. Dâmboviţa, S Romania
Târgu Jiu 140 B4 prev. Tîrgu Jiu. Gorj, W Romania
Târgul-Neamţ see Târgu-Neamţ
Târgu Mureş 140 B4 prev. Oşorhei, Tîrgu Mures, Ger. Neumarkt, Hung. Marosvásárhely. Mureş, C Romania
Târgu-Neamţ 140 C3 var. Târgul-Neamţ; prev. Tîrgu-Neamţ. Neamţ, NE Romania
Târgu Ocna 140 C4 Hung. Aknavásár; prev. Tîrgu Ocna. Bacău, E Romania
Târgu Secuiesc 140 C4 Ger. Neumarkt, Szekler Neumarkt, Hung. Kezdivásárhely; prev. Chezdi-Oşorheiu, Târgul-Săcuiesc, Tîrgu Secuiesc. Covasna, E Romania
Tarija 93 G5 Tarija, S Bolivia
Tarīm 153 C6 C Yemen
Tarim Basin 156 C2 basin NW China
Tarim He 158 B3 river NW China
Tarma 92 C3 Junín, C Peru
Tarn 123 C6 cultural region S France
Tarn 123 C6 river S France
Tarnobrzeg 130 D4 Tarnobrzeg, SE Poland
Tarnów 131 D5 Tarnów, SE Poland
Tarragona 125 G2 anc. Tarraco. Cataluña, E Spain
Tàrrega 125 F2 var. Tarrega. Cataluña, NE Spain
Tarsus 148 C4 İçel, S Turkey
Tartu 138 D3 Ger. Dorpat; prev. Rus. Yurev, Yur'yev. Tartumaa, SE Estonia
Ţarţūs 150 A3 Fr. Tartouss; anc. Tortosa. Tarţūs, W Syria
Ta Ru Tao, Ko 169 B7 island S Thailand
Tarvisio 128 D2 Friuli-Venezia Giulia, NE Italy
Tashi Chho Dzong see Thimphu
Tashkent 144 see Toshkent
Tash-Kumyr 155 F2 Kir. Tash-Kömür. Dzhalal-Abadskaya Oblast', W Kyrgyzstan
Tashqurghan see Kholm
Tasikmalaya 170 C5 prev. Tasikmalaja. Jawa, C Indonesia
Tasman Basin 174 C5 var. East Australian Basin. Undersea feature S Tasman Sea
Tasman Bay 183 C5 inlet South Island, NZ
Tasmania 181 B8 prev. Van Diemen's Land. State SE Australia
Tasmania 184 B4 island SE Australia
Tasman Plateau 174 C5 var. South Tasmania Plateau. Undersea feature SW Tasman Sea
Tasman Sea 174 C5 sea SW Pacific Ocean
Tassili-n-Ajjer 103 E4 plateau E Algeria
Tatabánya 131 C6 Komárom-Esztergom, NW Hungary
Tathlīth 153 B5 'Asīr, S Saudi Arabia
Tatra Mountains 131 D5 Ger. Tatra, Hung. Tátra, Pol./Slvk. Tatry. Mountain range Poland/Slovakia
Ta-t'ung see Datong
Tatvan 149 F3 Bitlis, SE Turkey
Ta'ū 177 F4 var. Tau. Island Manua Islands, E American Samoa
Tau see Ta'ū
Taukum, Peski 155 G1 desert SE Kazakhstan
Taumarunui 182 D4 Manawatu-Wanganui, North Island, NZ
Taungdwingyi 168 B3 Magwe, C Myanmar
Taunggyi 168 B3 Shan State, C Myanmar
Taunton 121 C7 SW England, UK
Taupo 182 D3 Waikato, North Island, NZ
Taupo, Lake 182 D3 lake North Island, NZ
Tauragė 138 B4 Ger. Tauroggen. Tauragė, SW Lithuania
Tauranga 182 D3 Bay of Plenty, North Island, NZ
Tauris see Tabrīz
Tavas 148 B4 Denizli, SW Turkey
Tavira 124 C5 Faro, S Portugal
Tavoy 169 B5 var. Dawei. Tenasserim, S Myanmar
Tavoy Island see Mali Kyun
Tawakoni, Lake 81 G2 reservoir Texas, SW USA
Tawau 170 D3 Sabah, East Malaysia
Ţawkar see Tokar
Tawzar see Tozeur
Taxco 83 E4 var. Taxco de Alarcón. Guerrero, S Mexico
Taxco de Alarcón see Taxco
Tay 120 C3 river C Scotland, UK
Taylor 81 G3 Texas, SW USA
Taymā' 152 A4 Tabūk, NW Saudi Arabia
Taymyr, Ozero 147 E2 lake N Russian Federation
Taymyr, Poluostrov 147 E2 peninsula N Russian Federation
Taz 146 D3 river N Russian Federation
T'bilisi 149 G2 Eng. Tiflis. Country capital (Georgia) SE Georgia
T'bilisi 144 B4 international airport S Georgia
Tchien see Zwedru
Tchongking see Chongqing
Tczew 130 C2 Ger. Dirschau. Gdańsk, N Poland
Te Anau 183 A7 Southland, South Island, NZ
Te Anau, Lake 183 A7 lake South Island, NZ
Teapa 83 G4 Tabasco, SE Mexico
Teate see Chieti
Tebingtinggi 170 B3 Sumatera, N Indonesia
Tebriz see Tabrīz
Techirghiol 140 D5 Constanţa, SE Romania
Tecomán 82 D4 Colima, SW Mexico
Tecpan 83 E5 var. Tecpan de Galeana. Guerrero, S Mexico
Tecpan de Galeana see Tecpan
Tecuci 140 C4 Galaţi, E Romania
Tedzhen 154 C3 Turkm. Tejen. Akhalskiy Velayat, S Turkmenistan
Tedzhen see Harīrūd
Tees 121 D5 river N England, UK
Tefé 94 D2 Amazonas, N Brazil
Tegal 170 C4 Jawa, C Indonesia
Tegelen 119 D5 Limburg, SE Netherlands
Tegucigalpa 84 C3 country capital (Honduras) Francisco Morazán, SW Honduras
Teheran see Tehrān
Tehrān 152 C3 var. Teheran. Country capital (Iran) Tehrān, N Iran
Tehuacán 83 F4 Puebla, S Mexico
Tehuantepec 83 F5 var. Santo Domingo Tehuantepec. Oaxaca, SE Mexico
Tehuantepec, Golfo de 83 F5 var. Gulf of Tehuantepec. Gulf S Mexico
Tehuantepec, Gulf of see Tehuantepec, Golfo de
Tehuantepec, Isthmus of see Tehuantepec, Istmo de
Tehuantepec, Istmo de 83 F5 var. Isthmus of Tehuantepec. Isthmus SE Mexico
Tejen see Harīrūd
Te Kao 182 C1 Northland, North Island, NZ
Tekax 83 H4 var. Tekax de Álvaro Obregón. Yucatán, SE Mexico
Tekax de Álvaro Obregón see Tekax
Tekeli 146 C5 Taldykorgan, SE Kazakhstan
Tekirdağ 148 A2 It. Rodosto; anc. Bisanthe, Raidestos, Rhaedestus. Tekirdağ, NW Turkey
Te Kuiti 182 D3 Waikato, North Island, NZ
Tela 84 C2 Atlántida, NW Honduras
Telanaipura see Jambi
Tel Aviv-Jaffa see Tel Aviv-Yafo
Tel Aviv-Yafo 151 A6 var. Tel Aviv-Jaffa. Tel Aviv, C Israel
Teles Pirés see São Manuel, Rio
Telish 136 C2 prev. Azizie. Loveshka Oblast, NW Bulgaria
Tell Abiad see At Tall al Abyaḑ
Tell Abyad see At Tall al Abyaḑ
Tell Kalakh see Tall Kalakh
Tell Shedadi see Ash Shadādah
Telšiai 138 B3 Ger. Telschen. Telšiai, NW Lithuania
Temerin 132 D3 Serbia, N Yugoslavia
Temirtau 146 C4 prev. Samarkandski, Samarkandskoye. Karaganda, C Kazakhstan
Tempio Pausania 129 A5 Sardegna, Italy, C Mediterranean Sea
Temple 81 G3 Texas, SW USA
Temuco 97 B5 Araucanía, C Chile
Temuka 183 B6 Canterbury, South Island, NZ
Tenasserim 169 B6 Tenasserim, S Myanmar
Ténenkou 106 D3 Mopti, C Mali
Ténéré 107 G3 physical region C Niger
Tenerife 102 A3 island Islas Canarias, Spain, NE Atlantic Ocean
Tengger Shamo 159 E3 desert N China
Tengréla 106 D4 var. Tingréla. N Ivory Coast
Tenkodogo 107 E4 S Burkina
Tennant Creek 180 A3 Northern Territory, C Australia
Tennessee 74 C1 off. State of Tennessee; also known as The Volunteer State. State SE USA
Tennessee River 74 C1 river S USA
Teno see Tana
Tenojoki see Tana
Tepelena see Tepelenë
Tepelenë 133 C7 var. Tepelena, It. Tepeleni. Gjirokastër, S Albania
Tepeleni see Tepelenë
Tepic 82 D4 Nayarit, C Mexico
Teplice 130 A4 Ger. Teplitz; prev. Teplice-Šanov, Teplitz-Schönau. Severní Čechy, NW Czech Republic
Tequila 82 D4 Jalisco, SW Mexico
Teraina 177 G2 prev. Washington Island. Atoll Line Islands, E Kiribati
Teramo 128 C4 anc. Interamna. Abruzzi, C Italy
Tercan 149 E3 Erzincan, NE Turkey
Terceira 124 A5 var. Ilha Terceira. Island Azores, Portugal, NE Atlantic Ocean
Teresina 95 F2 var. Therezina. State capital Piauí, NE Brazil
Termia see Kýthnos
Términos, Laguna de 83 G4 lagoon SE Mexico
Termiz 155 E3 Rus. Termez. Surkhondaryo Wiloyati, S Uzbekistan
Termoli 128 D4 Molise, C Italy
Terneuzen 119 B5 var. Neuzen. Zeeland, SW Netherlands
Terni 128 C4 anc. Interamna Nahars. Umbria, C Italy
Ternopil' 140 C2 Pol. Tarnopol, Rus. Ternopol'. Ternopil's'ka Oblast', W Ukraine
Terracina 129 C5 Lazio, C Italy
Terrassa 125 G2 Cast. Tarrasa. Cataluña, E Spain
Terre Adélie 186 C4 disputed region SE Antarctica
Terre Haute 72 B4 Indiana, N USA
Territoire du Yukon see Yukon Territory
Terschelling 118 C1 Fris. Skylge. Island Waddeneilanden, N Netherlands
Teruel 125 F3 anc. Turba. Aragón, E Spain
Tervel 136 E1 prev. Kurtbunar, Rom. Curtbunar. Varnenska Oblast, NE Bulgaria
Tervueren see Tervuren
Tervuren 119 C6 var. Tervueren. Vlaams Brabant, C Belgium
Teseney 104 C4 var. Tessenei. W Eritrea
Tessalit 107 E2 Kidal, NE Mali
Tessaoua 107 G3 Maradi, S Niger
Tessenderlo 119 C5 Limburg, NE Belgium
Tessenei see Teseney
Testigos, Islas los 91 E1 island group N Venezuela
Tete 111 E2 Tete, NW Mozambique
Teterow 126 C3 Mecklenburg-Vorpommern, NE Germany
Tétouan 102 C2 var. Tetouan, Tetuán. N Morocco
Tetovo 133 D5 Alb. Tetova, Tetovë, Turk. Kalkandelen. NW FYR Macedonia
Tetuán see Tétouan
Tevere 128 C4 Eng. Tiber. River C Italy
Teverya 151 B5 var. Tiberias. Northern, N Israel
Te Waewae Bay 183 A7 bay South Island, NZ
Texarkana 74 A2 Arkansas, C USA
Texarkana 81 H2 Texas, SW USA
Texas 81 F3 off. State of Texas; also known as The Lone Star State. State S USA

Trzebnica 130 C4 Ger. Trebnitz. Wrocław, SW Poland
Tsalka 149 F2 S Georgia
Tsamkong see Zhanjiang
Tsangpo see Brahmaputra
Tsarevo 136 E2 prev. Michurin. Burgaska Oblast, SE Bulgaria
Tsaritsyn see Volgograd
Tsetserleg 158 D2 Arhangay, C Mongolia
Tshela 109 B6 Bas-Zaïre, W Congo (Zaire)
Tshikapa 109 C7 Kasai Occidental, SW Congo (Zaire)
Tshuapa 109 D6 river C Congo (Zaire)
Tshwane see Pretoria
Tsinan see Jinan
Tsing Hai see Qinghai Hu
Tsingtao see Qingdao
Tsingtau see Qingdao
Tsinkiang see Quanzhou
Tsintao see Qingdao
Tsitsihar see Qiqihar
Tsu 163 C6 var. Tu. Mie, Honshū, SW Japan
Tsugaru-kaikyō 162 C3 strait N Japan
Tsumeb 110 B3 Otjikoto, N Namibia
Tsuruga 163 C6 var. Turuga. Fukui, Honshū, SW Japan
Tsuruoka 162 D4 var. Turuoka. Yamagata, Honshū, C Japan
Tsushima 163 A7 var. Tsushima-tō, Tusima. Island group SW Japan
Tsushima-tō see Tsushima
Tsyerakhovka 139 D8 Rus. Terekhovka. Homyel'skaya Voblasts', SE Belarus
Tsyurupyns'k 141 E4 Rus. Tsyurupinsk. Khersons'ka Oblast', S Ukraine
Tu see Tsu
Tuamotu Fracture Zone 175 H3 tectonic feature E Pacific Ocean
Tuamotu, Îles 177 H4 var. Archipel des Tuamotu, Dangerous Archipelago, Tuamotu Islands. Island group N French Polynesia
Tuamotu Islands 175 see Tuamotu, Îles
Tuapi 85 E2 Región Autónoma Atlántico Norte, NE Nicaragua
Tuapse 143 A7 Krasnodarskiy Kray, SW Russian Federation
Tuba City 80 B1 Arizona, SW USA
Tubbergen 118 E3 Overijssel, E Netherlands
Tubize 119 B6 Dut. Tubeke. Walloon Brabant, C Belgium
Tubmanburg 106 C5 NW Liberia
Ţubruq 103 H2 Eng. Tobruk, It. Tobruch. NE Libya
Tubuai Islands see Australes, Îles
Tucker's Town 74 B5 E Bermuda
Tucson 80 B3 Arizona, SW USA
Tucumán see San Miguel de Tucumán
Tucumcari 81 E2 New Mexico, SW USA
Tucupita 91 E2 Delta Amacuro, NE Venezuela
Tucuruí, Represa de 95 F2 reservoir NE Brazil
Tudela 125 E2 Basq. Tutera; anc. Tutela. Navarra, N Spain
Tudmur 150 C3 var. Tadmur, Tamar, Gk. Palmyra; Bibl. Tadmor. Ḥimş, C Syria
Tuguegarao 171 E1 Luzon, N Philippines
Tuktoyaktuk 69 E3 Northwest Territories, NW Canada
Tukums 138 C3 Ger. Tuckum. Tukums, W Latvia
Tula 143 B5 Tul'skaya Oblast', W Russian Federation
Tulancingo 83 E4 Hidalgo, C Mexico
Tulare Lake Bed 79 C7 salt flat California, W USA
Tulcán 92 B1 Carchi, N Ecuador
Tulcea 140 D5 Tulcea, E Romania
Tul'chyn 140 D3 Rus. Tul'chin. Vinnyts'ka Oblast', C Ukraine
Tuléar see Toliara
Tulia 81 E2 Texas, SW USA
Tulle 123 C5 anc. Tutela. Corrèze, C France
Tulln 127 E6 var. Oberhollabrunn. Niederösterreich, NE Austria
Tully 180 D3 Queensland, NE Australia
Tulsa 81 G1 Oklahoma, C USA
Tuluá 90 B3 Valle del Cauca, W Colombia
Tulun 147 E4 Irkutskaya Oblast', S Russian Federation
Tumaco 90 A4 Nariño, SW Colombia
Tumba, Lac see Ntomba, Lac
Tumbes 92 A2 Tumbes, NW Peru
Tumkūr 164 C2 Karnātaka, W India
Tumuc Humac Mountains 95 E1 var. Serra Tumucumaque. Mountain range N South America
Tunduru 105 C8 Ruvuma, S Tanzania
Tundzha 136 D3 Turk. Tunca Nehri. River Bulgaria/Turkey see also Tunca Nehri
Tungabhadra Reservoir 164 C2 lake S India
Tungaru 177 E2 prev. Gilbert Islands. Island group W Kiribati
T'ung-shan see Xuzhou
Tungsten 68 D4 Northwest Territories, W Canada
Tung-t'ing Hu see Dongting Hu
Tunis 103 E1 var. Tūnis. Country capital (Tunisia) NE Tunisia
Tūnis see Tunis
Tunis, Golfe de 134 D3 Ar. Khalīj Tūnis. Gulf NE Tunisia
Tunisia 103 F2 off. Republic of Tunisia, Ar. Al Jumhūrīyah at Tūnisīyah, Fr. République Tunisienne. Country N Africa
Tunja 90 B3 Boyacá, C Colombia
Tuong Buong see T,ơng Đ,ơng
Tupelo 74 C2 Mississippi, S USA
Tupiza 93 G5 Potosí, S Bolivia
Turabah 153 B5 Makkah, W Saudi Arabia
Turangi 182 D4 Waikato, North Island, NZ
Turan Lowland 154 C2 var. Turan Plain, Kaz. Turan Oypaty, Rus. Turanskaya Nizmennost', Turk. Turan Pesligi, Uzb. Turon Pasttekisligi. Plain C Asia
Turan Oypaty see Turan Lowland
Turan Pesligi see Turan Lowland
Turan Plain see Turan Lowland
Turanskaya Nizmennost' see Turan Lowland
Ţurayf 152 A3 Al Ḥudūd ash Shamālīyah, NW Saudi Arabia
Turbat 166 A3 Baluchistān, SW Pakistan
Turda 140 B4 Ger. Thorenburg, Hung. Torda. Cluj, NW Romania
Turfan see Turpan
Turin see Torino
Turkana, Lake see Rudolf, Lake
Turkestan 146 B5 Kaz. Türkistan. Yuzhnyy Kazakhstan, S Kazakhstan
Turkey 148 B3 off. Republic of Turkey, Turk. Türkiye Cumhuriyeti. Country SW Asia
Turkmenbashi 154 B2 prev. Krasnovodsk. Balkanskiy Velayat, W Turkmenistan
Turkmenistan 154 B2 off. Turkmenistan; prev. Turkmenskaya Soviet Socialist Republic. Country C Asia
Turkmenskiy Zaliv 154 B2 Turkm. Türkmen Aylagy. Lake gulf W Turkmenistan
Turks and Caicos Islands 87 E2 UK dependent territory N West Indies
Turlock 79 B6 California, W USA
Turnagain, Cape 182 D4 headland North Island, NZ
Turnhout 119 C5 Antwerpen, N Belgium
Turnov 130 B4 Ger. Turnau. Východní Čechy, N Czech Republic
Turnu Măgurele 140 B5 var. Turnu-Măgurele. Teleorman, S Romania
Turon Pasttekisligi see Turan Lowland
Turpan 158 C3 var. Turfan. Xinjiang Uygur Zizhiqu, NW China
Turpan Pendi 158 C3 Eng. Turpan Depression. Depression NW China
Tŭrtkŭl 154 D2 Rus. Turtkul'; prev. Petroaleksandrovsk. Qoraqalpoghiston Respublikasi, W Uzbekistan
Turuga see Tsuruga
Turuoka see Tsuruoka
Tuscaloosa 74 C2 Alabama, S USA
Tusima see Tsushima
Tuticorin 164 C3 Tamil Nādu, SE India
Tutrakan 136 D1 Razgradska Oblast, NE Bulgaria
Tutuila 177 F4 island W American Samoa
Tuvalu 177 E3 prev. Ellice Islands. Country SW Pacific Ocean
Ţuwayq, Jabal 153 C5 mountain range C Saudi Arabia
Tuxpán 83 F4 var. Tuxpán de Rodríguez Cano. Veracruz-Llave, E Mexico
Tuxpan 82 D4 Jalisco, C Mexico
Tuxpan 82 D4 Nayarit, C Mexico
Tuxpán de Rodríguez Cano see Tuxpán
Tuxtepec 83 F4 var. San Juan Bautista Tuxtepec. Oaxaca, S Mexico
Tuxtla 83 G5 var. Tuxtla Gutiérrez. Chiapas, SE Mexico
Tuxtla see San Andrés Tuxtla
Tuxtla Gutiérrez see Tuxtla
Tuy Hoa 169 E5 Phu Yên, S Vietnam
Tuz Gölü 148 C3 lake C Turkey
Tuzla 132 C3 NE Bosnia and Herzegovina
Tver' 142 B4 prev. Kalinin. Tverskaya Oblast', W Russian Federation
Twin Falls 78 D4 Idaho, NW USA
Tychy 131 D5 Ger. Tichau. Katowice, S Poland
Tyler 81 G3 Texas, SW USA
Tympáki 137 C8 var. Timbaki; prev. Timbákion. Kríti, Greece, E Mediterranean Sea
Tynda 147 F4 Amurskaya Oblast', SE Russian Federation
Tyne 120 D4 river N England, UK
Tyôsi see Chôshi
Tyre see Soûr
Týrnavos 136 B4 var. Tírnavos. Thessalía, C Greece
Tyrrhenian Sea 129 B6 It. Mare Tirreno. Sea N Mediterranean Sea
Tyumen' 146 C3 Tyumenskaya Oblast', C Russian Federation
Tyup 155 G2 Kir. Tüp. Issyk-Kul'skaya Oblast', NE Kyrgyzstan
Tywyn 121 C6 W Wales, UK
Tzekung see Zigong
T,ơng Đ,ơng 168 D4 var. Tuong Buong. Nghê An, N Vietnam

U

Uanle Uen see Wanlaweyn
Uaupés, Rio see Vaupés, Río
Ubangi 109 C5 Fr. Oubangui. River C Africa
Ubangi-Shari see Central African Republic
Ube 163 B7 Yamaguchi, Honshū, SW Japan
Ubeda 125 E4 Andalucía, S Spain
Uberaba 95 F4 Minas Gerais, SE Brazil
Uberlândia 95 F4 Minas Gerais, SE Brazil
Ubol Rajadhani see Ubon Ratchathani
Ubol Ratchathani see Ubon Ratchathani
Ubon Ratchathani 169 D5 var. Muang Ubon, Ubol Rajadhani, Ubol Ratchathani, Udon Ratchathani. Ubon Ratchathani, E Thailand
Ubrique 124 D5 Andalucía, S Spain
Ucayali, Río 92 D3 river C Peru
Uchiura-wan 162 D3 bay NW Pacific Ocean
Uchquduq 154 D2 Rus. Uchkuduk. Nawoiy Wiloyati, N Uzbekistan
Uchtagan, Peski 154 C2 Turkm. Uchtagan Gumy. Desert NW Turkmenistan
Udaipur 166 C3 prev. Oodeypore. Rājasthān, N India
Uddevalla 117 B6 Göteborg och Bohus, S Sweden
Udine 128 D2 anc. Utina. Friuli-Venezia Giulia, NE Italy
Udintsev Fracture Zone 186 A5 tectonic feature S Pacific Ocean
Udipi see Udupi
Udon Ratchathani see Ubon Ratchathani
Udon Thani 168 C4 var. Ban Mak Khaeng, Udorndhani. Udon Thani, N Thailand
Udorndhani see Udon Thani
Udupi 164 B2 var. Udipi. Karnātaka, SW India
Uele 109 D5 var. Welle. River NE Congo (Zaire)
Uelzen 126 C3 Niedersachsen, N Germany
Ufa 143 D6 Respublika Bashkortostan, W Russian Federation
Ugāle 138 C2 Ventspils, NW Latvia
Uganda 105 B6 off. Republic of Uganda. Country E Africa
Uglovka 142 B4 var. Okulovka. Novgorodskaya Oblast', W Russian Federation
Uhuru Peak see Kilimanjaro
Uíge 110 B1 Port. Carmona, Vila Marechal Carmona. Uíge, NW Angola
Uinta Mountains 76 B4 mountain range Utah, W USA
Uitenhage 110 C5 Eastern Cape, S South Africa
Uithoorn 118 C3 Noord-Holland, C Netherlands
Ujelang Atoll 176 C1 var. Wujlān. Atoll Ralik Chain, W Marshall Islands
Ujungpandang 171 E4 var. Macassar, Makassar; prev. Makasar. Sulawesi, C Indonesia
Ujung Salang see Phuket
Ukhta 146 C3 Respublika Komi, NW Russian Federation
Ukiah 79 B5 California, W USA
Ukmergė 138 C4 Pol. Wiłkomierz. Ukmergė, C Lithuania
Ukraine 140 C2 off. Ukraine, Rus. Ukraina, Ukr. Ukrayina; prev. Ukrainian Soviet Socialist Republic, Ukrainskaya S.S.R. Country SE Europe
Ulaanbaatar 159 E2 Eng. Ulan Bator. Country capital (Mongolia) Töv, C Mongolia
Ulaangom 158 C2 Uvs, NW Mongolia
Ulan Bator 156 see Ulaanbaatar
Ulanhad see Chifeng
Ulan-Ude 147 E4 prev. Verkhneudinsk. Respublika Buryatiya, S Russian Federation
Ulft 118 E4 Gelderland, E Netherlands
Ullapool 120 C3 N Scotland, UK
Ulm 127 B6 Baden-Württemberg, S Germany
Ulsan 161 E4 Jap. Urusan. SE South Korea
Ulster 121 B5 cultural region N Ireland
Ulungur Hu 158 B2 lake NW China
Uluru 179 D5 var. Ayers Rock. Rocky outcrop Northern Territory, C Australia
Ulyanivka 141 E3 Rus. Ul'yanovka. Kirovohrads'ka Oblast', C Ukraine
Ul'yanovsk 143 C5 prev. Simbirsk. Ul'yanovskaya Oblast', W Russian Federation
Uman' 141 E3 Rus. Uman. Cherkas'ka Oblast', C Ukraine
Umán 83 H3 Yucatán, SE Mexico
Umanak see Uummannaq
Umanaq see Uummannaq
Umbro-Marchigiano, Appennino 128 C3 Eng. Umbrian-Machigian Mountains. Mountain range C Italy
Umeå 116 C4 Västerbotten, N Sweden
Umeälven 116 C4 river N Sweden
Umiat 68 D2 Alaska, USA
Umm Buru 104 A4 Western Darfur, W Sudan
Umm Durmān see Omdurman
Umm Ruwaba 104 C4 var. Umm Ruwābah, Um Ruwāba. Northern Kordofan, C Sudan
Umm Ruwābah see Umm Ruwaba
Umnak Island 68 A3 island Aleutian Islands, Alaska, USA
Um Ruwāba see Umm Ruwaba
Umtali see Mutare
Umtata 110 D5 Eastern Cape, SE South Africa
Una 132 B3 river Bosnia and Herzegovina/Croatia
Unac 132 B3 river W Bosnia and Herzegovina
Unalaska Island 68 A3 island Aleutian Islands, Alaska, USA
'Unayzah 152 B4 var. Anaiza. Al Qaşīm, C Saudi Arabia
Uncía 93 F4 Potosí, C Bolivia
Uncompahgre Peak 76 B5 mountain Colorado, C USA
Ungava Bay 71 E1 bay Québec, E Canada
Ungava, Péninsule d' 70 D1 peninsula Québec, SE Canada
Ungheni 140 D3 Rus. Ungeny. W Moldova
Unimak Island 68 B3 island Aleutian Islands, Alaska, USA
Union 75 E1 South Carolina, SE USA
Union City 74 Tennessee, S USA
United Arab Emirates 153 C5 Ar. Al Imārāt al 'Arabīyah al Muttaḥidah, abbrev. UAE; prev. Trucial States. Country SW Asia
United Kingdom 121 B5 off. UK of Great Britain and Northern Ireland, abbrev. UK. Country NW Europe
United States of America 67 B5 off. United States of America, var. America, The States, abbrev. U.S., USA. Country
Unst 120 D1 island NE Scotland, UK
Ünye 148 D2 Ordu, W Turkey
Upala 84 D4 Alajuela, NW Costa Rica
Upata 91 E2 Bolívar, E Venezuela
Upemba, Lac 109 D7 lake SE Congo (Zaire)
Upernavik 114 C2 var. Upernivik. C Greenland
Upernivik see Upernavik
Upington 110 C4 Northern Cape, W South Africa
Upolu 177 F4 island SE Samoa
Upper Klamath Lake 78 A4 lake Oregon, NW USA
Upper Lough Erne 121 A5 lake SW Northern Ireland, UK
Upper Red Lake 77 F1 lake Minnesota, N USA
Uppsala 117 C6 Uppsala, C Sweden
Ural 144 B3 Kaz. Zayyq. River Kazakhstan/Russian Federation
Ural Mountains 144 see Ural'skiye Gory
Ural'sk 146 B3 Kaz. Oral. Zapadnyy Kazakhstan, NW Kazakhstan
Ural'skiye Gory 146 C3 var. Ural'skiy Khrebet, Eng. Ural Mountains. Mountain range Kazakhstan/Russian Federation
Ural'skiy Khrebet see Ural'skiye Gory
Uraricoera 94 D1 Roraima, N Brazil
Urbandale 77 F3 Iowa, C USA
Uren' 143 C5 Nizhegorodskaya Oblast', W Russian Federation
Urganch 154 D2 Rus. Urgench; prev. Novo-Urgench. Khorazm Wiloyati, W Uzbekistan
Urgut 155 E3 Samarqand Wiloyati, C Uzbekistan
Uroševac 133 D5 Alb. Ferizaj. Serbia, S Yugoslavia
Ŭroteppa 155 E2 Rus. Ura-Tyube. NW Tajikistan
Uruapan 83 E4 var. Uruapan del Progreso. Michoacán de Ocampo, SW Mexico
Uruapan del Progreso see Uruapan
Uruguai, Rio see Uruguay
Uruguay 96 D4 off. Oriental Republic of Uruguay; prev. La Banda Oriental. Country E South America
Uruguay 96 D3 var. Rio Uruguai, Río Uruguay. River E South America
Uruguay, Río see Uruguay
Urumchi see Ürümqi
Urumqi see Ürümqi
Ürümqi 158 C3 var. Tihwa, Urumchi, Urumqi, Urumtsi, Wu-lu-k'o-mu-shi, Wu-lu-mu-ch'i; prev. Ti-hua. Autonomous region capital Xinjiang Uygur Zizhiqu, NW China
Urumtsi see Ürümqi
Urup, Ostrov 147 H4 island Kuril'skiye Ostrova, SE Russian Federation
Urziceni 140 C5 Ialomiţa, SE Romania
Usa 142 E3 river NW Russian Federation
Uşak 148 B3 prev. Ushak. Uşak, W Turkey
Ushuaia 97 B8 Tierra del Fuego, S Argentina
Usinsk 142 E3 Respublika Komi, NW Russian Federation
Üsküb see Skopje
Üsküp see Skopje
Usmas Ezers 138 B3 lake NW Latvia
Usol'ye-Sibirskoye 147 E4 Irkutskaya Oblast', C Russian Federation
Ussel 123 C5 Corrèze, C France
Ussuriysk 147 G5 prev. Nikol'sk, Nikol'sk-Ussuriyskiy, Voroshilov. Primorskiy Kray, SE Russian Federation
Ustica, Isola d' 129 B6 island S Italy
Ust'-Ilimsk 147 E4 Irkutskaya Oblast', C Russian Federation
Ústí nad Labem 130 A4 Ger. Aussig. Severní Čechy, N Czech Republic
Ustka 130 C2 Ger. Stolpmünde. Słupsk, NW Poland
Ust'-Kamchatsk 147 H2 Kamchatskaya Oblast', E Russian Federation
Ust'-Kamenogorsk 146 D5 Kaz. Öskemen. Vostochnyy Kazakhstan, E Kazakhstan
Ust'-Kut 147 E4 Irkutskaya Oblast', C Russian Federation
Ust'-Olenëk 147 E3 Respublika Sakha (Yakutiya), NE Russian Federation
Ust Urt see Ustyurt Plateau
Ustyurt Plateau 154 B1 var. Ust Urt, Uzb. Ustyurt Platosi. Plateau Kazakhstan/Uzbekistan
Ustyurt Platosi see Ustyurt Plateau
Usulután 84 C3 Usulután, SE El Salvador
Usumacinta, Río 84 B1 river Guatemala/Mexico
Utah 80 A1 off. State of Utah; also known as Beehive State, Mormon State. State W USA
Utah Lake 76 B4 lake Utah, W USA
Utena 138 C4 Utena, E Lithuania
Utica 73 F3 New York, NE USA
Utrecht 118 C4 Lat. Trajectum ad Rhenum. Utrecht, C Netherlands
Utsunomiya 163 D5 var. Utunomiya. Tochigi, Honshū, S Japan
Uttar Pradesh 167 E3 prev. United Provinces, United Provinces of Agra and Oudh. State N India
Utunomiya see Utsunomiya
Uulu 138 D2 Pärnumaa, SW Estonia
Uummannaq 114 C3 var. Umanak, Umanaq. C Greenland
Uummannarsuaq 114 B5 var. Nunap Isua, Dan. Kap Farvel, Eng. Cape Farewell. Headland S Greenland
Uvalde 81 F4 Texas, SW USA
Uvaravichy 139 D7 Rus. Uvarovichi. Homyel'skaya Voblasts', SE Belarus
Uvea, Île 177 E4 island N Wallis and Futuna
Uvs Nuur 158 C1 var. Ozero Ubsu-Nur. Lake Mongolia/Russian Federation
'Uwaynāt, Jabal al 104 A3 var. Jebel Uweinat. Mountain Libya/Sudan
Uyo 107 G5 Akwa Ibom, S Nigeria
Uyuni 93 F5 Potosí, W Bolivia
Uzbekistan 154 D2 off. Republic of Uzbekistan. Country C Asia
Uzhhorod 140 B2 Rus. Uzhgorod; prev. Ungvár. Zakarpats'ka Oblast', W Ukraine
Užice 132 D4 prev. Titovo Užice. Serbia, W Yugoslavia

V

Vaal 110 D4 river C South Africa
Vaals 119 D6 Limburg, SE Netherlands
Vaasa 117 D5 Swe. Vasa; prev. Nikolainkaupunki. Vaasa, W Finland
Vaassen 118 D3 Gelderland, E Netherlands
Vác 131 C6 Ger. Waitzen. Pest, N Hungary
Vadodara 166 C4 prev. Baroda. Gujarāt, W India
Vaduz 126 E2 country capital (Liechtenstein) W Liechtenstein
Váh 131 C5 Ger. Waag, Hung. Vág. River W Slovakia
Väinameri 138 C2 prev. Muhu Väin, Ger. Moon-Sund. Sea E Baltic Sea
Valachia see Wallachia
Valday 142 B4 Novgorodskaya Oblast', W Russian Federation
Valdecañas, Embalse de 124 D3 reservoir W Spain
Valdepeñas 125 E4 Castilla-La Mancha, C Spain
Valdés, Península 97 C6 peninsula SE Argentina
Valdez 68 C3 Alaska, USA
Valdia see Weldiya
Valdivia 97 B5 Los Lagos, C Chile
Val-d'Or 70 D4 Québec, SE Canada
Valdosta 75 E3 Georgia, SE USA
Valence 123 D5 anc. Valentia, Valentia Julia, Ventia. Drôme, E France
Valencia 78 D1 California, W USA
Valencia 90 D1 Carabobo, N Venezuela
Valencia 125 F3 País Valenciano, E Spain
Valencia, Golfo de 125 F3 var. Gulf of Valencia. Gulf E Spain
Valencia, Gulf of see Valencia, Golfo de
Valenciennes 122 D2 Nord, N France
Valera 90 C2 Trujillo, NW Venezuela
Valga 138 D3 Ger. Walk, Latv. Valka. Valgamaa, S Estonia
Valira 123 A8 river Andorra/Spain
Valjevo 132 C4 Serbia, W Yugoslavia
Valjok 116 D2 Finnmark, N Norway
Valka 138 D3 Ger. Walk. Valka, N Latvia
Valkenswaard 119 D5 Noord-Brabant, S Netherlands
Valladolid 124 D2 Castilla-León, NW Spain
Valladolid 83 H3 Yucatán, SE Mexico
Vall d'Uxó 125 F3 País Valenciano, E Spain
Valle de La Pascua 90 D2 Guárico, N Venezuela
Valledupar 90 B1 Cesar, N Colombia
Vallejo 79 B6 California, W USA
Vallenar 96 B3 Atacama, N Chile
Valletta 129 C8 prev. Valetta. Country capital (Malta) E Malta
Valley City 77 E2 North Dakota, N USA
Valls 125 G2 Cataluña, NE Spain
Valmiera 138 D3 Est. Volmari, Ger. Wolmar. Valmiera, N Latvia
Valozhyn 139 C5 Pol. Wołożyn, Rus. Volozhin. Minskaya Voblasts', C Belarus
Valparaiso 72 C3 Indiana, N USA
Valparaíso 96 B4 Valparaíso, C Chile
Valverde del Camino 124 C4 Andalucía, S Spain
Van 149 F3 Van, E Turkey
Vanadzor 149 F2 prev. Kirovakan. N Armenia
Vancouver 68 D5 British Columbia, SW Canada

W

Z

MAP FINDER

NORTH & WEST ASIA *144-145*

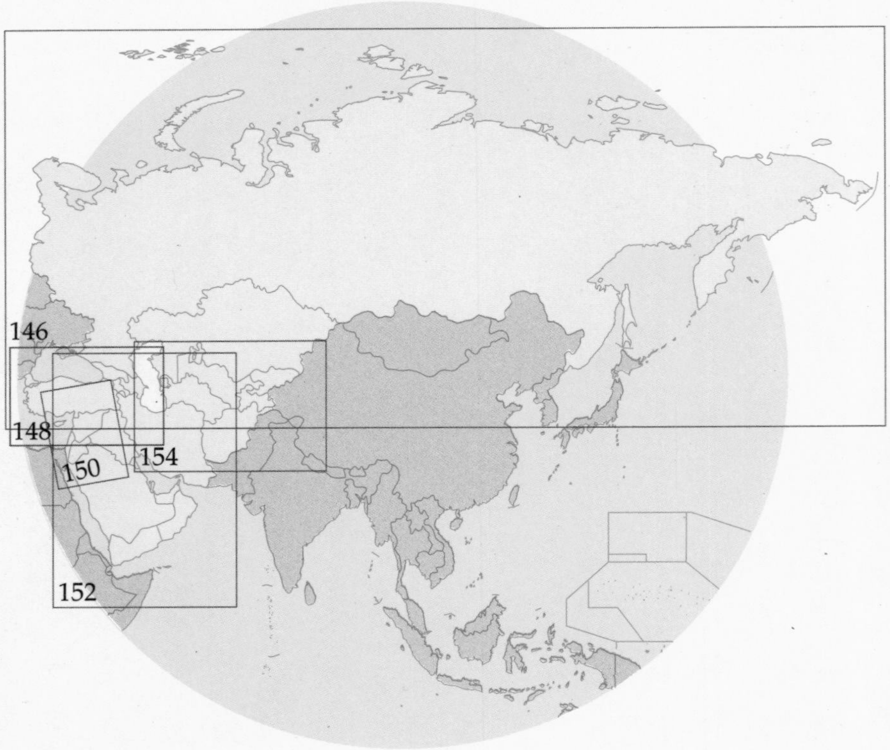

SOUTH & EAST ASIA *156-157*

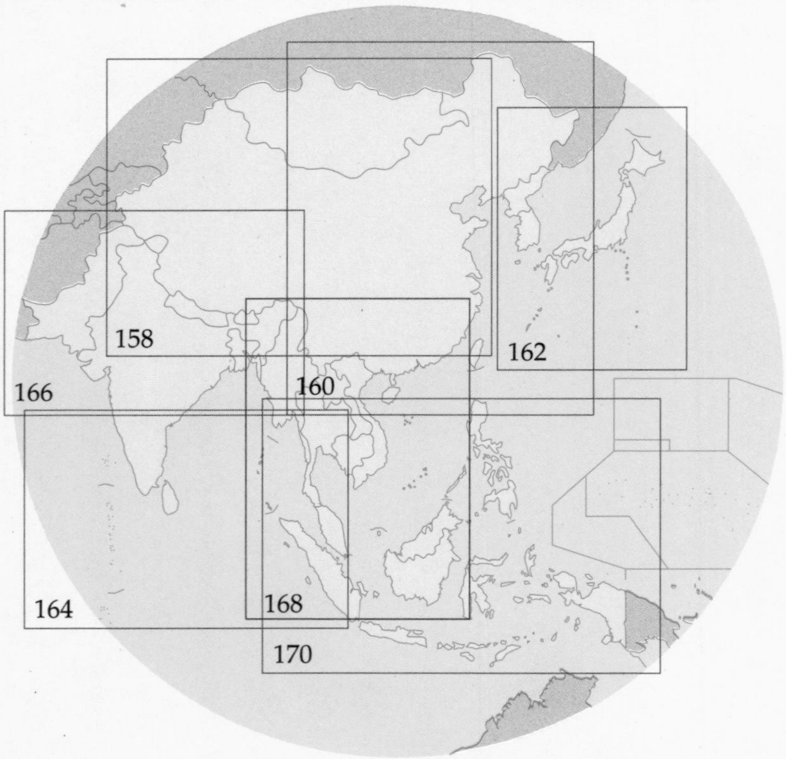